Fodor's 04

IRELAND

Where to Stay and Eat
for All Budgets

Must-See Sights
and Local Secrets

Ratings You Can Trust

Fodor's Travel Publications   New York, Toronto, London, Sydney, Auckland
www.fodors.com

FODOR'S IRELAND 2004

Editors: Lisa Dunford; Deborah Kaufman; Laura M. Kidder, senior editor

Editorial Production: Ira-Neil Dittersdorf
Editorial Contributors: John Babb, Muriel Bolger, Naomi Coleman, Alannah Hopkin, Anto Howard, Anneliese Paull
Maps: David Lindroth, *cartographer;* Rebecca Baer and Bob Blake, *map editors*
Design: Fabrizio La Rocca, *creative director;* Guido Caroti, *art director;* Melanie Marin, *senior picture editor*
Production/Manufacturing: Robert B. Shields
Cover Photo (Dingle Peninsula): Nik Wheeler

COPYRIGHT

ISBN 1–4000–1272–4

ISSN 0071–6464

SPECIAL SALES

Fodor's Travel Publications are available at special discounts for bulk purchases for sales promotions or premiums. Special editions, including personalized covers, excerpts of existing guides, and corporate imprints, can be created in large quantities for special needs. For more information, contact your local bookseller or write to Special Markets, Fodor's Travel Publications, 1745 Broadway, New York, New York 10019. Inquiries from Canada should be directed to your local Canadian bookseller or sent to Random House of Canada, Ltd., Marketing Department, 2775 Matheson Boulevard East, Mississauga, Ontario L4W 4P7. Inquiries from the United Kingdom should be sent to Fodor's Travel Publications, 20 Vauxhall Bridge Road, London SW1V 2SA, England.

AN IMPORTANT TIP & AN INVITATION

Although all prices, opening times, and other details in this book are based on information supplied to us at press time, changes occur all the time in the travel world, and Fodor's cannot accept responsibility for facts that become outdated or for inadvertent errors or omissions. So **always confirm information when it matters,** especially if you're making a detour to visit a specific place. Your experiences—positive and negative—matter to us. If we have missed or misstated something, **please write to us.** We follow up on all suggestions. Contact the Ireland editors at editors@fodors.com or c/o Fodor's at 1745 Broadway, New York, New York 10019.

PRINTED IN THE UNITED STATES OF AMERICA

10 9 8 7 6 5 4 3 2 1

DESTINATION IRELAND

All the talk in Ireland these days is of change: an affluence previously unknown in the nation's history has led to a boom in the creation of luxury hotels, innovative restaurants, first-class golf courses, and stylish nightclubs. But beneath all the excitement and hurly-burly of newness, something essential and magical endures. This quintessence of Irishness is hard to define, but it has something to do with the myriad shades of green coloring a landscape that can shift suddenly from fertile plain to rugged coastal mountains. It's evident in the unique character and history of each of the 32 counties—and in the fierce loyalty each receives from its sons and daughters. It's visible in the pace at which people live their lives, even in the middle of unprecedented prosperity, always taking time to laugh, sip a pint, and extend a warm welcome to a stranger. The ability to linger is still cherished here, right alongside the art of storytelling and the courtesy of sharing in a round at the pub. Have a fabulous trip!

Karen Cure, Editorial Director

CONTENTS

ABOUT THIS BOOK

There's no doubt that the best source for travel advice is a like-minded friend who's just been where you're headed. But with or without that friend, you'll have a better trip with a Fodor's guide in hand. Once you've learned to find your way around its pages, you'll be in great shape to find your way around your destination.

SELECTION

Our goal is to cover the best properties, sights, and activities in their category, as well as the most interesting communities to visit. We make a point of including local food-lovers' hot spots as well as neighborhood options, and we avoid all that's touristy unless it's really worth your time. You can go on the assumption that everything you read about in this book is recommended wholeheartedly by our writers and editors. Flip to On the Road with Fodor's to learn more about who they are. It goes without saying that no property mentioned in the book has paid to be included.

RATINGS

Orange stars ★ denote sights and properties that our editors and writers consider the very best in the area covered by the entire book. These, the best of the best, are listed in the Fodor's Choice section in the front of the book. Black stars ★ highlight the sights and properties we deem Highly Recommended, the don't-miss sights within any region. Fodor's Choice and Highly Recommended options in each region are usually listed on the title page of the chapter covering that region. Use the index to find complete descriptions. In cities, sights pinpointed with numbered map bullets ❶ in the margins tend to be more important than those without bullets.

SPECIAL SPOTS

Watch for Off the Beaten Path sights. Some are out of the way, some are quirky, and all are worth your while. If the munchies hit while you're exploring, look for Need a Break? suggestions.

TIME IT RIGHT

Wondering when to go? Check On the Calendar up front and chapters' Timing sections for weather and crowd overviews and best days and times to visit.

SEE IT ALL

Use Fodor's exclusive Great Itineraries as a model for your trip. (For a good overview of the entire destination, follow those that begin the book, or mix regional itineraries from several chapters.) In cities, Good Walks guide you to important sights in each neighborhood; ▶ indicates the starting points of walks and itineraries in the text and on the map.

BUDGET WELL

Hotel and restaurant price categories from ¢ to $$$$ are defined in the opening pages of each chapter—expect to find a balanced selection for every budget. For attractions, we always give standard adult admission fees; reductions are usually available for children, students, and senior citizens. Look in Discounts & Deals in Smart Travel Tips for information on destination-wide ticket schemes. Want to pay with plastic? AE, DC, MC, V following restaurant and hotel listings indicate whether American Express, Diners Club, MasterCard, or Visa are accepted.

BASIC INFO

Smart Travel Tips lists travel essentials for the entire area covered by the book; city- and region-specific basics end each chapter. To find the best way to get around, see individual modes of travel ("By Car," "By Train"). We assume you'll check Web sites or call for particulars.

ON THE MAPS	Maps throughout the book show you what's where and help you find your way around. Black and orange numbered bullets **❶** **❶** in the text correlate to bullets on maps.
BACKGROUND	In general, we give background information within the chapters in the course of explaining sights as well as in Close-Up boxes and in Understanding Ireland at the end of the book. To get in the mood, review the suggestions in Books & Movies.
FIND IT FAST	Within the book, chapters are arranged in a roughly east-to-west direction starting with Dublin. Chapters are divided into small regions, within which towns are covered in logical geographical order; attractive routes and interesting places between towns are flagged as En Route. Heads at the top of each page help you find what you need within a chapter.
DON'T FORGET	Restaurants are open for lunch and dinner daily unless we state otherwise; we mention dress only when there's a specific requirement and reservations only when they're essential or not accepted— it's always best to book ahead. Hotels have private baths, phone, TVs, and air-conditioning and operate on the European Plan (a.k.a. EP, meaning without meals), unless otherwise indicated (all-inclusive with meals and beverages included; BP, breakfast plan with full breakfast; CP, Continental plan with Continental breakfast; FAP, full American plan, with all meals; MAP, modified American plan with breakfast and dinner). We always list facilities but not whether you'll be charged extra to use them, so when pricing accommodations, find out what's included.
SYMBOLS	

Many Listings

- ★ Fodor's Choice
- ★ Highly recommended
- ⊠ Physical address
- ✛ Directions
- ⌂ Mailing address
- ☎ Telephone
- 🖷 Fax
- ⊕ On the Web
- ✉ E-mail
- 🖾 Admission fee
- ☉ Open/closed times
- ⚑ Start of walk/itinerary
- Ⓜ Metro stations
- ▭ Credit cards

Outdoors

- 🏌 Golf
- ⛺ Camping

Hotels & Restaurants

- ▦ Hotel
- ⇌ Number of rooms
- ⚲ Facilities
- ¡◎¡ Meal plans
- ✕ Restaurant
- ⟋ Reservations
- 🏛 Dress code
- ↘ Smoking
- ⚏ BYOB
- ✕▦ Hotel with restaurant that warrants a visit

Other

- ☕ Family-friendly
- 🚩 Contact information
- ⇨ See also
- ⊠ Branch address
- ☞ Take note

Time Zones

Numbers below vertical bands relate each zone to Greenwich Mean Time (0 hrs.). Local times frequently differ from these general indications, as indicated by light-face numbers on map.

ON THE ROAD WITH FODOR'S

A trip takes you out of yourself. Concerns of life at home completely disappear, driven away by more immediate thoughts—about, say, what marvels will beguile the next day, or where you'll have dinner. That's where Fodor's comes in. We make sure that you know all your options, so that you don't miss something that's around the next bend just because you didn't know it was there. Because the best memories of your trip might well have nothing to do with what you came to Ireland to see, we guide you to sights large and small all over the region. You might set out to explore Georgian Dublin and shop on Grafton Street, but back at home you find yourself unable to forget the rugged coast, the languid days of golfing or fly-fishing, and the out-of-the-way pubs you discovered. With Fodor's at your side, serendipitous discoveries are never far away.

Our success in showing you every corner of the Emerald Isle is a credit to our extraordinary writers. Although there's no substitute for travel advice from a good friend who knows your style, our contributors are the next best thing—the kind of people you would poll for travel advice if you knew them.

John Babb honed his journalistic skills at the Canadian Broadcasting Corporation in Toronto before he moved to Warsaw, Poland, where he spent two years working as a business journalist. He has been laying low in Dublin for the last few years, studying Irish culture.

Freelance editor and journalist Muriel Bolger is a travel writer and regular contributor to *Abroad Travel Magazine, Food & Wine Magazine,* and other publications in Ireland. She updated the Southeast and Irish Greens chapters. Her interests are numerous and varied and when not pursuing these or traveling she edits *Irish Interiors* and *Irish Exteriors* magazines.

Naomi Coleman is a freelance writer with a keen interest in the arts—particularly music—and travel. She's also a regular contributor to television and radio programs in Ireland and the United Kingdom. She updated Dublin's dining section as well as the Southeast and Irish Greens chapters.

A full-time freelance writer who lives near the sea in County Cork, Alannah Hopkin, our veteran contributor, has worked on the guide since 1985. This year she covered the Midlands, the southwest, and the west. Alannah has published a book on the cult of St. Patrick, a book-length guide to County Cork, two novels, and several short stories. She writes on travel and the arts for the London *Sunday Times* and contributes regularly to the *Irish Examiner* and the *Irish Times.*

Anto Howard, who worked on the Dublin and Dublin Environs chapters, is a Northside Dublin native who studied at Trinity College before acquiring his U.S. green card. He lived in New York, where he worked as a travel writer, editor, and playwright, before returning to Ireland. Anto (short for Anthony) is also the author of *Fodor's Escape to Ireland.*

1 Dublin

Dublin is an intimate capital that's a graceful mix of elegant Georgian buildings, wrought-iron canals and bridges, an army of booksellers, and 800-odd pubs. Ireland chooses to exempt artists from taxes, designating them national resources of sorts, and filmmakers, painters, and writers are part of the local scenery, along with the "rale Dubs," or "jackeens"—the breezy natives. Here, on both sides of the River Liffey, are sights that nearly encompass the city's entire history—let's not forget that Dublin has been, in sequence, a Celtic settlement, a Norse encampment, and the citadel-seat of the British colonizers.

Although Dublin can be sophisticated, it hasn't lost such simple pleasures as waking to the tinkling of glass bottles with round silver caps, delivered to the stoop by a milkman; afternoon tea at Bewley's with scones slathered with Kerry Gold butter; waitresses in black dresses and starched aprons; or breakfast "the likes of which you'll never see again," your landlady will promise. Added to these ageless pleasures is Dublin's amazing economic and cultural renaissance. The city is in the throes of its most dramatic transformation since the Georgian era. Both the old Dublin and the new are colossally entertaining.

2 Dublin Environs

The counties surrounding Dublin constitute the Pale, the area most strongly influenced by English rule. Ancestral homes of the dwindling members of the Anglo-Irish ascendancy dot the landscape, and lords and baronets down on their luck have turned hoteliers and welcome guests with adaptable grace. The Wicklow Mountains are tantalizingly close to the capital's southern edge. Wicklow's evocative monastic settlement at Glendalough; the scenic wooded valley is also home to abbeys, castles, great houses, and gardens. Several Neolithic ruins are to the north in the Boyne Valley, where layers of history penetrate down into earlier, unknowable ages.

3 The Midlands

These small, watery counties are portrayed as places to get *through* on the way to somewhere more interesting. Closer exploration of these unsung plains, however, reveals historic towns, abbey ruins, grand houses, and a gamut of outdoor activities—including some of Europe's finest fishing. County Tipperary's rolling green flatlands and Galtee Mountains are known for champion greyhounds and the stud farms that have turned out winners for generations. The Midlands are home to such sights as Strokestown House, Birr Castle Gardens, Emo Court and Gardens, and the monastic ruins of Clonmacnoise. You'll also find you're welcomed here without anyone haranguing you to buy sweaters or shamrock table linen.

4 The Southeast

In the low-lying southeast, rich pastureland extends to a coastline of estuarial mudflats; low cliffs that fringe deep bays; and long, sandy beaches. County Wexford was named by the Vikings after the consort of their one-eyed god Odin; it still bears the stamp of those fearless, seagoing settlers in its steep pathways and fine seafood. Wexford isn't far from Kilkenny, a fine medieval city known for its artisans, and Waterford City, where the eponymous crystal is made at the confluence of three great rivers—the Nore, the Barrow, and the Suir. There's some very fertile farmland in Tipperary's Golden Vale. The Rock of Cashel, seat of the Kings of Munster for 700 years (where St. Patrick said his first mass in Ireland) is here, along with Cahir Castle, one of the few places to resist Cromwell's hordes.

⑤ The Southwest

Cork lends its name to Ireland's second-largest city, a port town that's full of canals and bridges and has a bustling mercantile center. It was once home to writers Sean O'Faolain and Frank O'Connor and is today a city of sport. Its team is always in the championship finals of hurling, that fast and furious ancient game that makes soccer look like kick-the-can. The city is also one of the few places where they still play the 2,000-year-old game of bowls at which the Irish giant Cuchulainn used to excel. If your taste runs to less athletic entertainment, head for the exquisite seaside village of Kinsale.

Travelers have been thrilling to County Kerry's natural beauty for centuries—whether they've gazed down from the heights of Killarney or out at the Blasket Islands. Seabirds reel and wild donkeys graze among hedges awash in crimson velvet flowers; fields explode with deep yellow gorse, may-blossom, and honeysuckle against a dark-blue sky. To the north of Kerry, County Limerick is famed as horse country.

⑥ The West

The landscape in the counties of Clare, Galway, and Mayo varies from the barren limestone Burren to the majestic Cliffs of Moher to the looming Twelve Bens. Galway is Ireland's fastest growing city and a buzzing university town. It's also the departure point for the Aran Islands, celebrated by playwright J. M. Synge in *Riders to the Sea*. Just to the west are the wild shores and the mountains of Connemara, loved by painters, writers, and seekers of silence. It's a Gaeltacht (Irish-speaking area), and it's known for its ponies—descendants of the Andalusian horses that swam ashore from the Spanish fleet and bred with Celtic stock descended from the Ice Age horses. To the north, quiet scenery of County Mayo has always appealed to discerning travelers.

⑦ The Northwest

County Donegal, in the far northwest, is ruggedly beautiful, with a rocky coast, turbulent surf, forlorn mountains, and windswept plateaus. It's full of legends about giants and witches, not to mention fairies known as *pishogues*. Irish is widely spoken here, and the music is famous; traditional groups, such as Clannad and De Dannaan, named after the prehistoric followers of the goddess Dana, are local heroes. When Enya, daughter of local musicians, hit the top of the charts in Europe and the United States with her Irish–New Age instrumentals, the roof flew off a pub in Gweedore, where spontaneous sessions for the music-loving community are regular happenings.

⑧ Northern Ireland

In 1921 the ancient provinces of Munster, Leinster, and Connaught—plus three of Ulster province's nine counties—became the Irish Republic. Ulster's other six counties remained the part of Britain known as Northern Ireland. As a song goes: "One of Ireland's four green fields is still in strangers' hands." The region is know for the beauty of the Antrim coast from Carncastle to Bushmills; the Giant's Causeway, a glorious geologic accident; the rich farm- and lake lands of Fermanagh; and the austere Mourne Mountains. People are as friendly and witty here as they are in the republic.

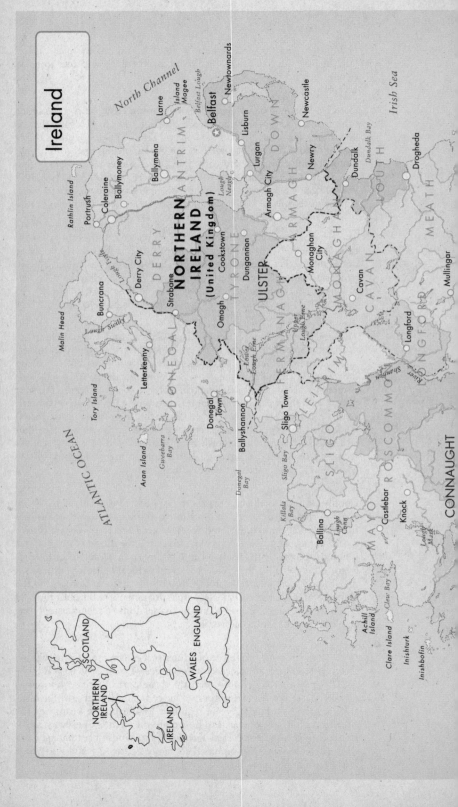

Ireland

North Channel

Rathlin Island

Malin Head

Tory Island

ATLANTIC OCEAN

Aran Island

Gweebarra Bay

Lough Swilly

Island Magee

Larne

Belfast Lough

Belfast

Newtownards

Newcastle

Irish Sea

ANTRIM

Ballymena

Lisburn

DOWN

Newcastle

Ballymoney

Coleraine

Portrush

Lough Neagh

Lurgan

Armagh City

Newry

Dundalk

Dundalk Bay

Drogheda

DERRY

NORTHERN IRELAND
(United Kingdom)

Derry City

Strabane

Cookstown

Dungannon

TYRONE

ARMAGH

Monaghan City

MEATH

Buncrana

Letterkenny

Omagh

ULSTER

FERMANAGH

MONAGHAN

Cavan

CAVAN

Mullingar

DONEGAL

Upper Lough Erne

Lower Lough Erne

Longford

LONGFORD

Donegal Town

Ballyshannon

Sligo Town

LEITRIM

River Shannon

Donegal Bay

Sligo Bay

SLIGO

ROSCOMMON

CONNAUGHT

Killala Bay

Ballina

Lough Conn

Castlebar

Knock

MAYO

Lough Mask

Achill Island

Clare Island

Clew Bay

Inishturk

Inishbofin

SCOTLAND

NORTHERN IRELAND

IRELAND

WALES

ENGLAND

Republic of Ireland

40 miles
60 km

St. George's Channel

DUBLIN
Dublin
Dun Laoghaire
Bray
Wicklow Town
Arklow
Gorey
Wexford Town

WICKLOW
Naas
KILDARE
LEINSTER
CARLOW
WEXFORD
Athy
Kilkenny City
Carrick-on-Suir
Waterford City

WESTMEATH
REPUBLIC OF IRELAND
Athlone
Ballinasloe
Portlaoise
LAOIS
OFFALY
Rosecrea
Birr
KILKENNY
Clonmel
Dungarvon
Youghal

CONNAUGHT
Galway City
Lough Corrib
Galway Bay
GALWAY
Nenagh
Thurles
TIPPERARY
Cashel
Tipperary Town
WATERFORD
Fermoy
Midleton
Cobh
Cork City
Kinsale

Ennis
CLARE
Limerick City
LIMERICK
Newcastle West
MUNSTER
Mallow
CORK
Bandon
Clonakilty
Skibbereen

Kilrush
Listowel
Tralee
KERRY
Killarney

Mouth of the Shannon
Aran Islands
Dingle Peninsula
Dingle Bay
Iveragh Peninsula
Kenmare Bay
Bantry Bay
Mizen Head
Blasket Islands
Skellig Rocks

ICELAND
Reykjavík

NORTHERN IRELAND
SCOTLAND
Edinburgh
Belfast
IRELAND
Irish Sea
Dublin
UNITED KINGDOM
WALES
ENGLAND
Cardiff
London
The Hague

NORWAY
Bergen
North Sea
Skagerrak
DENMARK
Hamburg
NETHERLANDS
Amsterdam
Rotterdam
GERMAN
Brussels
Bonn
BELGIUM
Frankfurt
Paris
LUXEMBOURG
Zürich
Munich
Bern
SWITZERLAND
LIECHTENSTEIN
Lyon
Milan
Venice
Lju

ATLANTIC OCEAN

English Channel

Bay of Biscay

PORTUGAL
Madrid
ANDORRA
Lisbon
SPAIN
Seville
Granada
Gibraltar

Nice
Monte Carlo
MONACO
Marseille
Florence
Corsica
Barcelona
Sardinia
Balearic Islands
Mediterranean Sea
Tyrrhenian S

MOROCCO
ALGERIA
TUNISIA

0   400 miles
0   600 km

Europe

FINLAND

Gulf
of
Bothnia

Oslo

SWEDEN

Helsinki

Gulf of Finland

St. Petersburg

Stockholm

Tallinn

ESTONIA

Göteborg

Riga

LATVIA

Moscow

Kattegat

Copenhagen

LITHUANIA

Kaunas

Baltic Sea

RUSSIA

Vilnius

Minsk

RUSSIA

Kaliningrad

Berlin

POLAND

BELARUS

NY

Warsaw

Kraków

Prague

CZECH

REPUBLIC

UKRAINE

Kiev

SLOVAKIA

Vienna

Bratislava

Salzburg

Budapest

MOLDOVA

AUSTRIA

HUNGARY

Chișinău

SLOVENIA

ROMANIA

Ljubljana

Zagreb

CROATIA

Novi Sad

Bucharest

BOSNIA AND

HERZEGOVINA

Belgrade

Adriatic Sea

Sarajevo

SERBIA

Black Sea

Rome

MONTENEGRO

YUGOSLAVIA

KOSOVO

BULGARIA

ITALY

Podgorica

Pristina

Sofia

Naples

Skopje

MACEDONIA

Istanbul

Tirane

Ankara

ALBANIA

TURKEY

Sea

GREECE

Aegean
Sea

Ionian
Sea

Sicily

Athens

MALTA

Crete

CYPRUS

Mediterranean Sea

The East & the South

5 to 8 days

Dublin's literary charm and Georgian riches, rugged County Wicklow, and the historic Meath plains are all just a few hours' drive apart. In the south you'll find fishing towns and bustling markets, coastal panoramas, and stunning mountain-and-lake scenery.

DUBLIN

1 to 3 days. James Joyce's Dublin holds treasures for all sorts. Literary types: explore Trinity College, Beckett's stomping grounds, and its legendary *Book of Kells*. Visit key Joyce sights, the Dublin Writers Museum, and indulge in the *Dublin Literary Pub Crawl*. Joyce fanatics: arrive a week before Bloomsday (June 16) for Bloomstime celebrations. Literary or not, spend some time strolling around the city center and take in the elegant Georgian architecture around St. Stephen's Green, the austere Dublin Castle, and the national treasures in the museums around Merrion Square and pedestrian Grafton Street. Check out Temple Bar, Dublin's hip zone,

and by all means join locals in this city-of-1,000-pubs for a foamy pint in the late afternoon. Pay your respects by taking a tour of the ever-popular Guinness Brewery and Storehouse. Night options: catch a show at W. B. Yeats's old stomping grounds, the Abbey Theatre; see some Victorian music hall at the Olympia Theatre; or listen to traditional or alternative music at any number of pubs or other venues. Spend as much time as you can muster in pubs—the real center of Dublin activity. Last-call arrives early, even here, so if you're still revved, go to Lesson Street and hit the nightclubs. For a dose of unmitigated Irish enthusiasm, join the roaring crowds at Croke Park and see some traditional Gaelic football and hurling.

BOYNE VALLEY & COUNTY WICKLOW

2 days. Rent a car or join an organized tour and head out to the Boyne Valley, a short trip north of the capital. Spend the morning walking among the Iron Age ruins of the rolling Hill of Tara. After a picnic lunch on top of the hill,

drive through ancient Kells and then to Newgrange, one of Europe's most spectacular prehistoric tombs. One thousand years older than Stonehenge, the great white-quartz structure merits two or three hours. Spend the rest of your day driving through the low hills and valleys of County Meath and to the Georgian village of Slane. Dominating the town are elegant Slane Castle and 500-foot Slane Hill. Back track to Kells or continue on to Drogheda and spend the night. The following day, drive through the County Wicklow mountains. You might want to stop in one of the small, quiet towns along the Wicklow Way, a hiking trail, and go for a short hike. Drive on to stately Powerscourt House, whose grounds are perhaps the finest in the country. On the way to Glendalough and the medieval monastery of the hermit St. Kevin, stop for a bite in Roundwood, Ireland's highest village.

WEST CORK & KERRY

2 days. Head southwest to Cork City, perfect for half a day of walking. Drive directly south to Kinsale, an old fishing town turned resort, with many good restaurants. A slow 3- or 4-hour drive along the coast and up through the small towns of West Cork takes you through the kind of landscape that inspired Ireland's nickname, the Emerald Isle. Spend the night in the market town of Skibbereen. Next morning, cross into County Kerry and head straight for Killarney, right at the center of a scattering of azure lakes and heather-clad mountains. It's a good base

for exploring your pick of three great Atlantic-pounded peninsulas: the Beara Peninsula, the Ring of Kerry, and the Dingle Peninsula. All offer stunning ocean views, hilly landscapes, and welcoming towns with good B&Bs. The 5-hour drive back to Dublin takes you through Limerick City and the lakes of the Midlands.

Irish Manors & Castles
5 to 7 days

If you have an interest in architecture, interior design, and history (including the sinister and macabre kind), consider a tour of Ireland's manors and castles. You might even decide to splurge and stay at one of the grand country-house hotels along the way. It's best to go between June and September, when the most houses are open.

DUBLIN & ENVIRONS

2 to 3 days. Right in the center of Dublin are historic Dublin Castle and the elegant, 18th-century Royal Hospital Kilmainham. Walk along the inner-city stretch of the River Liffey for excellent views of two of architect James Gandon's Georgian masterpieces, the Custom House and the Four Courts. South of the river, Georgian domestic town architecture is at its best on Merrion Square and Fitzwilliam Street. On Day 2 go west of Dublin to Castletown House, one of Ireland's most magnificent Georgian structures, in Celbridge, County Kildare; it serves as the headquarters of the Irish Georgian Society. From here head south into County Wicklow to visit Russborough House near Blessington.

THE ROAD TO CORK

1 day. Leave early from Dublin, heading southwest to Cork. On the way, stop in Portarlington to visit the Emo Court and Gardens, another James Gandon design and one of the finest large country houses near Dublin open to the public. You'll pass the Rock of Cashel on your way to Cahir Castle. Continue to Cork City. If you have time, stop at the coastal bulwark Charles Fort, about half an hour south of the city. Spend the night in Cork.

AROUND KILLARNEY

2 to 3 days. From Cork City, a short detour off the main road to Killarney leads to ruined 15th-century Blarney Castle, where you can kiss the famed Blarney Stone. Nearby Blarney House was built in 1784 in Scottish baronial style. In Killarney National Park, Muckross House, a mid-Victorian manor, is worth seeing for its grounds full of flowers and outstanding rock garden. After a night in Killarney, head north to the Shannon estuary, on whose shore looms Glin Castle, ancestral home of the great Anglo-Norman Fitzgeralds. Stop for tea or dinner at Adare Manor. Stay overnight in or near Limerick City or Ennis.

MAP KEY

Irish Manors & Castles

The East & the South

The West & the North

6 to 7 days

"To hell or to Connaught" was the choice given the native population by Cromwell, and indeed the harsh, barren landscape of parts of the west and north might appear cursed to the eye of an uprooted farmer. But there's an appeal in the very wildness of counties Clare, Galway, Mayo, Sligo, and Donegal—their stunning, steep coastlines hammered and shaped for aeons by the Atlantic. Here, in isolated communities, you'll hear locals speaking Irish as they go about their business. The arrival of peace has really opened the lush pastures of long-suffering Northern Ireland to travelers.

GALWAY & CLARE

2 days. A 3-hour drive west from Dublin leads straight to the 710-foot Cliffs of Moher, perhaps the single most impressive sight in Ireland. Using the waterside village of Ballyvaughan as your base, spend a day exploring the lunar landscape of the harsh, limestone Burren. In spring it becomes a mighty rock garden of exotic colors. The next morning head north out of Ballyvaughan toward Galway City. On the way you'll pass 2-million-year-old Ailwee Cave and picture-perfect Kinvara. Galway City, spectacularly overlooking Galway Bay, is rapidly growing, vibrant, and packed with culture and history. If time allows, drive west to Ros an Mhil (Rossaveal) and take a boat to the fabled Aran Islands. Spend the night in Galway City.

NORTH & WEST TO DONEGAL

2 days. Northwest of Galway City is tiny Clifden, with some of the country's best Atlantic views. From here, head east through one of the most beautiful stretches of road in Connemara—through Kylemore Valley, home of Kylemore Abbey, a huge Gothic Revival castle. After seeing the castle and its grounds, head north through tiny Leenane (the setting of the hit Broadway play, *The Beauty Queen of Leenane*) and on to the most attractive town in County Mayo, Westport. It's the perfect spot to spend the night: the 18th-century planned town is on an inlet of Clew Bay, and some of the west coast's finest beaches are nearby. Your drive north leads right through the heart of Yeats Country in Sligo. Just north of cozy Sligo Town is the stark outline of a great hill, Ben Bulben, in whose shadow poet Yeats wanted to be buried. South of town, follow the signposted Yeats Trail around woody, gorgeously scenic Lough Gill. Continuing north, you pass Yeats's simple grave in unassuming Drumcliff, a 3000 BC tomb in Creevykeel, and small Donegal Town. Head north through Letterkenny on the tight, meandering roads, into the windswept mountains and along the jagged coastline of northern Donegal. A trip on a fishing boat to one of the many islands off the coast is a must, as is a slow drive along the coast from the Gweedore Headland, covered with heather and gorse, to the former plantation village of Dunfanaghy (Dun Fionnachaid), heart of Donegal's Gaelic-speaking Gaeltacht region and a friendly place to spend the night.

NORTHERN IRELAND

2 days. Begin exploring the province in historic, divided Derry City (called Londonderry by Unionists), Northern Ireland's second city. A few hours is sufficient to take in the views from the old city walls and the fascinating murals of the Catholic Bogside district. Continue on to two of the region's main attractions, the 13th-century Norman fortress of Dunluce Castle and the Giant's Causeway, shaped from volcanic rock some 60 million years ago. Heading south, sticking to coastal roads for the best scenery, you'll soon pass through the Glens of Antrim, whose green hills roll down into the sea. Tucked away in the Glens are a number of small, unpretentious towns with great hotels. Early in the morning, head straight to Northern Ireland's capital, Belfast. The old port city, gray and often wet, is a fascinating place recovering from years of strife. A morning of driving through its streets will have to suffice before you head west through the rustic, pretty countryside to Lough Neagh, the largest lake in the British Isles. It's time to head back to Dublin, but if you're ahead of schedule, take the longer route that passes though the glorious Mountains of Mourne and around icy-blue Carlingford Lough.

MAP KEY

The West & the North

°C		°F
100		212
40		105
37		98.6
30		90
25		80
20		70
15		60
10		50
5		40
0		32
–5		20
–10		
–15		10
–20		0

In summer the weather is pleasant, the days are long (daylight lasts until after 10 in late June and July), and the countryside is green. But there are crowds in popular holiday spots, and prices for accommodations are at their peak. As British and Irish school vacations overlap from late-June to mid-September, vacationers descend on popular coastal resorts in the south, west, and east. Unless you're determined to enjoy the short (July and August) swimming season, it's to visit Ireland outside peak travel months.

Fall and spring are good times to travel (late September can be dry and warm, although the weather can be unpredictable). Seasonal hotels and restaurants close from early or mid-November until mid-March or Easter. During this off-season, prices are lower than in summer, but your selection is limited, and many minor attractions close. St. Patrick's Week gives a focal point to a spring visit, but some Americans may find the saint's-day celebrations a little less enthusiastic than the ones back home. Dublin, however, has a weekend-long series of activities, including a parade and the Lord Mayor's Ball. If you're planning an Easter visit, don't forget that most theaters close from Thursday to Sunday of Holy Week (the week preceding Easter), and all bars and restaurants, except those serving hotel residents, close on Good Friday.

Many hotels arrange Christmas packages with entertainment and outdoor activities abound. Mid-November to mid-February is either too cold or too wet for all but the keenest golfers, although some of the coastal links courses are playable. There are open fires in almost all hotels and bars, and, with extra time on their hands, people take an added interest in visitors.

Climate

🗓 Forecasts **Irish Meteorological Service** ⊕ www.meteireann.ie **Marine Call** ☎ 0891/505365 for marine forecasts. **Weathercall** ☎ 0891/500427 for Northern Ireland forecasts. **Weather Channel Connection** ☎ 900/932–8437, 95¢ a minute from a Touch-Tone phone ⊕ www.weather.com.

DUBLIN

Jan.	47F	8C	May	59F	15C	Sept.	63F	17C
	34	1		43	6		49	9
Feb.	47F	8C	June	65F	18C	Oct.	58F	14C
	36	2		49	9		43	6
Mar.	50F	10C	July	68F	20C	Nov.	50F	10C
	38	3		52	11		40	4
Apr.	56F	13C	Aug.	67F	20C	Dec.	47F	8C
	40	4		52	11		38	3

BELFAST

Jan.	43F	6C	May	59F	15C	Sept.	61F	16C
	36	2		43	6		49	9
Feb.	45F	7C	June	65F	18C	Oct.	56F	13C
	36	2		49	9		45	7
Mar.	49F	9C	July	65F	18C	Nov.	49F	9C
	38	3		52	11		40	4
Apr.	54F	12C	Aug.	65F	18C	Dec.	45F	7C
	50	4		52	11		38	3

ON THE CALENDAR

Hundreds of festivals and events are held annually in Ireland. Here are some of the better known and better attended. If you plan to visit during one of them, book well in advance.

WINTER

December

The yearling, foal, and breeding stock sale at Goff's Bloodstock Sales, Kill, County Kildare, shows how the rich buy and sell their prized horses. On December 26, St. Stephen's Day, the traditional Wren Boys in blackface and fancy dress wander the streets of some towns asking for money and singing (these days much of the money goes to charity); by far the most extravagant celebration takes place on Sandymount Green in Dublin.

SPRING

March

The Adare Jazz Festival in County Limerick fills the town's pubs with great jazz. The annual Arklow Music Festival includes orchestra, choir, solo singing, and drama competitions. Castleward Opera performs at Belfast's Grand Opera House. For three weeks on either side of St. Patrick's Day, the Celtic Spring Festival brings theatrical and rock music performances, and an Irish-language festival to Derry. Ireland's major St. Patrick's event is the Dublin Festival and Parade, which includes a fireworks show and guest bands from the United States.

For 10 days, the Dublin Film Festival presents films from Ireland and around the world, plus other events for cineastes. Dublin's Feis Ceoil is a festival of traditional Irish music. At Killarney's Bands of every stripe and size march in step and blow their horns in the annual Limerick International Band Festival, which immediately follows the city's St. Patrick's Day celebrations.

April

The Antiques and Collectibles Fair brings dealers from all parts of Ireland to Dublin. With Easter arrives one of the biggest events of the racing calendar, the 2-day Fairyhouse Easter Racing Festival, about 19 km (12 mi) north of Dublin.

May

Twenty-one days of concerts, competitions (including a marathon), and exhibitions take place during the Belfast Civic Festival; festivities kick off with the Lord Mayor's Show, a parade. Heritage properties and private gardens open to the public during the County Wicklow Garden Festival. The Fleadh Nua, the annual festival of traditional Irish music, song, and dance, takes place in Ennis, County Clare.

The Galway Early Music Festival fills the Galway City with the sounds of pre-Baroque Irish and European music. Sixty-plus traditional music sessions take place over the first weekend in May at Kinvara's Cuckoo Fleadh. The Murphy's International Mussel Fair in Bantry, County Cork, celebrates the peak of the harvest season for this delicacy. Theater, literary readings, and plenty of music fill the calendar of the Sligo Arts Festival, which continues into early June.

SUMMER	
June	Pick up some decorating tips while you're swooning over Schubert at the AIB Music Festival in Great Irish Homes, which puts on classical-music concerts in some of Ireland's finest country houses. Devoted Joyceans celebrate the fictional wanderings of *Ulysses*'s Leopold and Molly Bloom and Stephen Daedalus on June 16 (the day the novel was set, in 1904) in Dublin with Bloomsday; readings, dramatizations, and pilgrimages take place around the city. The Budweiser Irish Derby at the Curragh Racecourse, County Kildare, is the biggest race event of the year. Carlow celebrates the arts in its annual Éigse Carlow Arts Festival.
	Ballycastle puts on its own lively 3-day music and dance folk festival, the Fleadh Amhrán agus Rince. Cartoonists congregate in the Wicklow village of Rathdrum for the annual Guinness International Cartoon Festival. Listowel Writers' Week, one of Ireland's leading literary festivals, brings writers, poets, and lovers of literature together in this County Kerry town. The Weavers' Fair and Vintage Weekend comes to Ardara in County Donegal; the fair has as much to do with music, dance, and having fun as it does with selling homespun.
July	On July 12 Belfast and other towns throughout the north commemorate the 1690 Battle of the Boyne. The Coalisland International Music Festival attracts folk bands from all over Europe to County Tyrone. On the last Sunday in July, thousands of pilgrims climb the rocky slopes of Croagh Patrick (2,500 feet) in County Mayo to honor St. Patrick. The Eagle Wing Festival at Groomsport in County Down celebrates 300 years of links with America; it has music, line dancing, lectures, and American food.
	Galway is jam-packed for the 2-week Galway Arts Festival, which includes theater, film, music of all kinds, art exhibits, and a parade. Bachelors from throughout the country strut their stuff in Mullingar for the Guinness International Bachelor Festival. The Murphy's Irish Open Golf Championship is held one of Ireland's premier links courses. The streets and pubs of Dublin's Temple Bar district resound day and night to jazz and blues during the Temple Bar Blues Festival.
Late July–early Aug.	Across the whole of County Derry the country's best musicians take part in the Festival of Popular Irish Music. The Galway Races start the day after Galway's Arts Festival ends for a week of revelry. Would-be beauty queens come to County Donegal from as far away as Australia and New Zealand to compete in the Mary of Dungloe International Festival.
August	Aeronautical enthusiasts should check out the Abbeyshrule Fly-in Festival and Air Show in County Longford. The Ballyshannon Folk and Traditional Music Festival in County Donegal is one of the best of the season. On the third Thursday, the Connemara Pony Show brings Ireland's finest yearlings and stallions to Clifden, County Galway. Kinvara, County Galway, hosts the Cruinniú na mBád (Festival of the Gathering of the Boats), in which brown-sailed Galway hookers laden with turf race across Galway Bay.

The highlight of the traditional music calendar is the Fleadh Cheoil na hEireann (pronounced flah kee'yo na erin). The International Story-telling Festival, a long weekend of simple entertainment for kids, takes place on Cape Clear Island, off the southwest coast near Baltimore. The Kerrygold Dublin Horse Show attracts a fashionable set to watch the best in Irish bloodstock. The Kilkenny Arts Week is a marvelous assemblage of classical music, art exhibits, and theater. If you're in the neighborhood of Ballycastle, County Antrim, don't miss Ireland's oldest fair, Oul' Lammas Fair, held every year since 1606 on the last Monday and Tuesday in August.

The 3-day Puck Fair in Killorglin, County Kerry, retains vestiges of old pre-Christian fertility rites, like the garlanding with flowers of a large billy goat to signify his being crowned king. The world-famous Rose of Tralee International Festival selects a "Rose of Tralee" from an international lineup of young women of Irish descent and packs this County Kerry town in the process. The competition coincides with the Tralee Races. Everyone's got the beat at the Waterford Spraoi, an international rhythm festival.

FALL

September

The Appalachian and Bluegrass Music Festival traces the roots of Appalachian music back to Ireland at the Ulster American Folk Park in Omagh, County Tyrone. Indulge in the "food of the gods" at the start of the oyster season at the Galway International Oyster Festival. The hugely popular Hurling and Gaelic Football Finals are played in Croke Park Stadium in Dublin.

Troupes from all over Europe compete at Waterford's Theatre Royal during the annual International Festival of Light Opera. Single people of all ages from throughout Ireland and beyond flock to County Clare for the Lisdoonvarna Matchmaking Festival in the hopes of finding a spouse—or at least a date. Opera Northern Ireland kicks off its autumn season in the Grand Opera House in Belfast.

October

At the Cork Film Festival new feature-length films and documentaries from Ireland and abroad share the bill with short films. The festival usually takes place during the second week of October. The Cork Jazz Festival draws jazz lovers late in October. Runners fill the streets of Dublin in the Dublin City Marathon. The Dublin Theatre Festival puts on 10 visiting international productions, 10 Irish plays (most of them new), a children's festival, and a fringe of 60-plus plays. Kinsale opens its best restaurants for the International Gourmet Festival. The Wexford Opera Festival brings in international stars to perform three rarely heard operas in a tiny Georgian theater.

November

The Belfast Festival at Queen's University is the city's preeminent arts festival, with hundreds of musical, film, theater, and ballet performances. The Irish Rugby Football season gets under way in Dublin with games between Ireland and nations *not* in the Six Nations group (Scotland, Wales, England, France, Italy, and Ireland). The 3-day Millstreet Indoor International Horse Show brings equestrian enthusiasts to this County Cork town.

Cuisine Irlandaise

Ireland is in the throes of a food revolution. Many of the nation's chefs are young and widely traveled; they've absorbed the best influences of Europe, North America, and the Pacific Rim, and are producing a Pan-European, postmodern cuisine. This new Irish cuisine—sometimes referred to as *cuisine Irlandaise*—has moved beyond the heavy roast beef and Yorkshire pudding styles of the old Anglo-Irish country houses. Chefs are taking simple, traditional dishes—Clonakilty black pudding, Clare nettle soup, Galway oysters, Cong wild salmon—and sprucing them up with more exotic, complicated preparations. The result: smart, unusual combinations of the best local, often organic, ingredients.

Regional cooking is a strength of Irish cuisine, and some of the best restaurants are tucked away in small fishing villages or remote locations. Hotel dining rooms vary in quality, but the best country-house hotels offer some of Europe's finest dining. Diehard traditionalists will still find many examples of old Celtic cooking in bars serving lunches of Irish stew, boiled bacon and cabbage, or steamed mussels. The national drink, Guinness, is a pitch-black, malted stout—one of the great beers of the world. With raw oysters and Tabasco, it is a blissful marriage of opposites.

Fishing

Ireland is well known as a game-angling resort: wild Atlantic salmon, wild brown trout, and sea trout abound in the rivers, lakes, and estuaries; and offshore is the deep-sea challenge. Coarse fishing (for all fish that are not trout or salmon) is also an option.

In the Midlands, the River Shannon and its system of lakes attract anglers from around the world. Beam, rudd, tench, roach, perch, and hybrids are the main varieties; pike roam select waters. Monaghan, Cavan, Boyle, and the small lakes to the east and west of Lough Derg are the best coarse fishing areas, and you can find brown-trout lakes and rivers around Birr, Banagher, Mullingar, and Roscommon. For pike, you'll find the most fruitful areas around Cavan, Clones, Cootehill, Castleblaney, Kingscourt, Carrick-on-Shannon, Boyle, Belturbet, and Butlersbridge.

The southwest has of sea-angling facilities, a wealth of salmon and trout rivers, and terrific surroundings—be it the black-slate cliffs of the coast or the vegetation of Killarney and the Ring of Kerry. You can shore fish along the coast from Cobh in the east to Foynes in the west. Although the whole region has great lake and river fishing, most anglers head for Waterville or Killarney. Coarse anglers will find pike at Macroom and coarse-angling facilities at Mallow and Fermoy. Game fishing for wild Atlantic salmon, wild brown trout, and sea trout is one of the main attractions of the west.

In the northwest there's so much space and so much water that it can feel as if you have the whole place to yourself. The best area for brown trout angling is around Bundoran, including Lough Melvin. In western County Donegal, you'll have good opportunities for catching sea trout. Plenty of salmon and brown trout live in the rivers of southern County Donegal and northern County Sligo. You'll find more brown trout in the loughs near Dunfanaghy in northern County Donegal, near Bundoran on the border of Donegal and

Sligo counties, and in the border area of Sligo and Leitrim counties. Pike and coarse anglers can cast their lines in the abundant County Leitrim lakes.

With a 606-km (466-mi) coastline, part on the Atlantic and part on the Irish Sea, as well as major lakes and an abundance of unpolluted rivers, the north is a great place for anglers. Set your rod for salmon on the Bann, Bush, and Foyle rivers and for brown trout in their tributaries. There are bigger lake trout in Loughs Neagh, Melvin, and Erne, although pike and other coarse (white) fish abound in the Erne. Turbot and plaice are taken off the north coast, where sea bass may be caught from the shore.

Gaelic Games

Gaelic football and hurling are played in most parts of the republic. Gaelic football is an extremely fast and rough form of football (closer to rugby than American football) that involves two teams of 15 that kick and run around a field with a round, soccerlike ball. The rules are complicated, but the skill and speed of the players make it exciting and impressive to watch, even if you don't quite understand what's going on. Hurling, considered by many to be the world's fastest field game, also involves two teams of 15 that use a 3-foot wooden stick with a broad base to catch and hurl a leather-covered ball toward goalposts; a typical game produces several injuries.

Gaelic games are organized by the Gaelic Athletic Association (GAA) and you can watch them free of charge at local GAA fields and sports centers around the republic. Interprovincial games and All-Ireland finals are played in July and August at the GAA stadiums in Cork and Dublin. Croke Park in Dublin is usually where the annual All-Ireland finals are held. Tickets for these matches can be hard to obtain, but the events are televised.

Golf

There are more than 360 golf courses in Ireland—including Northern Ireland—from world-famous championship links courses to scenic 9-holers. About 50 of these courses have opened in the last two years. Choose between the challenging links of the Atlantic coast, the more subtle layouts on the eastern seaboard, and the mature parklands of the inland courses.

Some of the best parkland courses are in the southeast, and there's also a championship links course at Rosslare. Mount Juliet, near Kilkenny, has been publicly acclaimed by Nick Faldo as one of Europe's best. Although the parkland courses of the Midlands may lack the spectacular challenge of the country's more famous scenic and coastal greens, they have a quiet charm all their own. Many of the southwest's 18-hole courses are world-famous, championship clubs amid wonderful scenery.

Hiking

Wicklow's gentle, rolling hills are a terrific place to begin an Irish walking vacation. Devoted hikers come from all over the world to traverse the 137-km (85-mi) Wicklow Way, the first long-distance trail to open in Ireland and one of the best. The route begins in Marlay Park, just a few miles south of Dublin. It follows rough sheep tracks, forest firebreaks, and old bog roads, and much of it is above 1,600 feet.

Two trails cross the southeast, with its wooded hills, rich farmland, and rivers. The South Leinster Way begins in the County Carlow town of Kildavin and makes its way southwest over Mt. Leinster and the River Barrow, terminating in Carrick-on-Suir. The Munster Way leads through the Vee Gap in the Knockmealdown Mountains and on to Clogheen. The many forest park trails (at Killykeen, Lough Key, and Dun a Ri) and narrow country roads are great for touring the Midlands on foot. The impressive Slieve Bloom Way, to the east of Birr, runs through the Slieve Bloom Mountains on a 50-km (30-mi) circular route—it has deep glens, rock formations, waterfalls, and great mountain views.

The far southwest around Killarney and Dingle is classic hiking country, with a true feeling of wilderness—even though you're never more than 3 or 4 km (2 or 3 mi) from civilization. Two signposted, long-distance trails wind through the region: the 214-km (134-mi) Kerry Way begins in Killarney and loops around the Ring of Kerry, and the 153-km (95-mi) Dingle Way loops from Tralee around the Dingle Peninsula. Both routes consist of paths and "green (unsurfaced) roads," with some stretches linked by surfaced roads. The 209-km (130-mi) Beara Way is mainly an off-road walk around West Cork's rugged Beara Peninsula.

The 168-km (104-mi) Blackwater Way follows the lower slopes of the Knockmealdown Mountains to the rich farms and woodlands of the Blackwater Valley. Sheep's Head Way encircles the Sheep's Head Peninsula and has glorious views of Bantry Bay along its 88-km (55-mi) route. There are other trails in Killarney National Park; Gougane Barra, northeast of Ballylickey off R584 in County Cork; Farran, off N22 about 16 km (10 mi) west of Cork City in County Cork; the Ballyhoura Mountains on the Cork-Limerick border, off N20 at Ballyhea about 16 km (10 mi) north of Buttevant; and Currachase Forest Park, east of Askeaton off N69 in County Limerick.

The Burren Way runs from Lahinch Promenade to Ballyvaughan on the shores of Galway Bay, a distance of 35 km (22 mi). It takes you through the heart of the Burren's limestone landscape, with ever-changing views of the Aran Islands and the bay. The Western Way's County Galway section extends from Oughterard on Lough Corrib through the mountains of Connemara to Leenane on Killary Harbour, a distance of 50 km (30 mi). The 177-km (110-mi) County Mayo section, known as the Western Way (Mayo) and the Foxford Way, continues past Killary Harbour to Westport on Clew Bay, inland to Newport and across the boglands to the Ox Mountains east of Ballina. The Newport Bangor Trail runs for 48 km (30 mi) through the Nephin Mountain range in northwest Mayo. A 387-km (240-mi) route through Irish-speaking Connemara stretches along the shores of Galway Bay from Spiddle to Carraroe, Carna, Letterfrack, and Clonbur, on the northern shore of Lough Corrib.

In the northwest's mountain districts (such as the Blue Stacks, near Donegal Town) you can get in some satisfyingly rough walks with dramatic views. Long-distance footpaths are scattered across County Donegal, in County Leitrim, and around Lough Gill in County Sligo. Good shorter trails are also accessible within Glenveagh National Park. Northern Ireland is also magnificent walking country. Ask at tourist offices for details of their local walking and cycling trails, 14 of which spring off the Ulster Way, an 896-km (560-mi) trek for serious hikers that runs around the six counties and links up with marked trails on the other side of the border.

Irish Wares

Few visitors leave Ireland without purchasing a tweed hat or a hand-knit Aran sweater, a linen tablecloth or a piece of Waterford crystal. In Dublin look for antiques, books, and *au courant* European and Irish fashions. Cork City offers less variety but quite a few surprises, and Galway has its share of galleries, bookstores, and offbeat boutiques. Most crafts shops sell a mix of goods from all over the country. Keep an eye open for signs indicating "craft workshops," where independent craftspeople sell directly from their studios.

The best of the north's traditional products, many made according to time-honored methods, include exquisite linen and superior handmade woolen garments. Handmade lacework also remains a handicraft from the countrywomen of some Northern Ireland districts. Traditional music CDs and the unadorned blackthorn walking stick are two good choices at the other end of the price scale.

Literature

Ireland has produced a large number of renowned authors for a country of its size. Four Nobel Prize winners—George Bernard Shaw, William Butler Yeats, Samuel Beckett, and Seamus Heaney—head a list that includes the likes of Oscar Wilde, Sean O'Casey, Sean O'Faolain, Brian Friel, and Edna O'Brien. Indeed, the country's literary heritage is evident everywhere you go. In Dublin you'll find James Joyce's Liffey; Dean Swift's cathedral; Trinity College, alma mater of the 18th-century Anglo-Irish writers; and the Abbey Theatre, a potent symbol of Ireland's great playwrights. Yeats opens up the country of Sligo; the Aran Islands were the inspiration of J. M. Synge; there's Frank O'Connor's Cork; Castletownshend, home of Somerville and Ross; Oliver Goldsmith's Lissoy; and Frank McCourt's Limerick.

Irish writing developed its distinctive traits largely because of the country's physical isolation. Not even Julius Caesar wanted to conquer Ireland, and centuries later, it remained uninfluenced by the cultural excitement of the Renaissance. In the end, it produced a literature that conquered distant shores, partly through its grand dramatic tradition. In any event, sit a while in Dublin's Davy Byrne's pub, order a glass of Burgundy and a Gorgonzola sandwich (as Joyce's Leopold Bloom once did), and spend an hour studying a map of Ireland. The beguiling names on it—Ballyvourney, Labasheeda, Toorenamblath, Clonmacnoise—may fire your poetic imagination, too.

Music

This is the land of *ceol agus craic*, which, loosely translated, means "music and merriment." Wherever you go you'll hear a musical air to accompany the scenery, and every town buzzes with its own blend of styles and sounds. The traditional music scene, far from becoming fossilized as a tourist fixture, has evolved with each generation, remaining lively and contemporary while still embracing the craft and skill of its past exponents.

Young traditional musicians are also unafraid to experiment with the music of other cultures, and it's not unusual to discover exciting mixtures of trad, folk, African rhythms, jazz improvisations, and even Appalachian mountain music. The deep-rooted musical tastes of the Irish are reflected in the live music scene in pubs, clubs, and theaters; a check of local event guides will turn up a wealth of live entertainment from rock to folk to traditional, and it's often possible to go into a small local venue and find a world-class artist in performance, whose talents are unsung outside a small circle of knowledgeable friends and fans.

The Pub

Just how important is an Irish pub? Irish Pub, a Dublin-based company, has shipped more than 1,000 of its five styles of "ready-to-pour" pubs—Victorian Dublin, Gaelic, Irish Brewery Pub, Irish Pub Shop, and Irish Country Cottage—to more than 35 countries around the world, at about $300,000 a pop. Back on their home turf, pubs are pillars of Irish social life—places to chat, listen, learn, and gossip about everything from horse racing to philosophy. Many pubs now serve food at lunchtime; many but not quite all also serve tea and coffee during daylight hours. A word about music in pubs: If it's in the main bar of a pub, you'll seldom have to pay a cover charge. If, however, you're really enjoying the *craic*, as it's called, it is good form to buy a pint for the performers. To dance in a fully amplified band in a room adjacent to the bar you may have to pay a cover.

The Races

Greyhound racing has roots deep in the Celtic psyche, and Irish dogs are considered to be among the best in the world. Races are held at night, and a bar and restaurant are usually within the stadium. Dublin is home to two dog racing tracks: Harolds Cross and Shelbourne Park.

There's a horse race—with some of the planet's finest thoroughbreds—somewhere in Ireland almost every day of the year. The flat season runs from March to November; steeplechases are held throughout the year. Several courses—there are some 28 in all—are within easy reach of Dublin. The Curragh Racecourse, in Dublin's environs, hosts the Irish Derby and other international horse races. Fairyhouse in County Meath is the site of the Irish Grand National. Some of the best meetings are held in the summer at smaller courses: Killarney in mid-July, Galway in late July–early August, Tramore in mid-August, Tralee in late August, and Listowel in late September. There are two horse racing tracks in Northern Ireland—the one at Downpatrick is particularly atmospheric.

FODOR'S CHOICE

The sights, restaurants, hotels, and other travel experiences on these pages are our editors' top picks—our Fodor's Choices. They're the best of their type in the area covered by the book—not to be missed and always worth your time. In the destination chapters that follow, you will find all the details.

LODGING

$$$$ **Ardtara House**, Upperlands, Northern Ireland. A gorgeously furnished 19th-century country house in a village with a working mill that's the last reminder of a once-thriving linen industry.

$$$$ **Kildare Hotel and Country Club**, Straffan, Co. Kildare. A most indulgent place with an Arnold Palmer–designed golf course, clay target shooting, and game fishing, among other things.

$$$$ **Merrion**, Dublin. Four Georgian town houses, loads of marble, meandering gardens, and a spa.

$$$$ **Mount Juliet**, Thomastown, Co. Kilkenny. *Another* Georgian mansion on hundreds of acres? Yup. This one has a Jack Nicklaus–designed golf course and the usual estate sports: riding, archery, angling, and shooting.

$$$$ **Park Hotel**, Kenmare, Co. Kerry. The views from this stone château are of the Caha Mountains and terraced lawns that sweep down to the bay.

$$$$ **St. Ernan's House**, Donegal Town. Imagine a handsome 19th-century country house on its own wooded, tidal island, and the term *unwind* takes on new meaning.

$$$–$$$$ **Castle Leslie**, Glaslough, Co. Monaghan. Hard to say which is more beautiful: the 1870 Gothic and Italianate structure or the reflection of it in the nearby lake. It's no wonder Paul McCartney and Heather Mills got married here.

$$$–$$$$ **Longueville House**, Mallow, Co. Cork. Come for the tranquility and the Irish-French dishes made with produce from the family farm, garden, and river.

$$–$$$$ **Ballynahinch Castle**, Recess, Co. Galway. A river's-edge hotel in rugged Connemara that's long been favored by statesmen and stars, for its Persian rugs, leather chesterfields, and wooded acres.

$$$ **Dunbrody House**, New Ross, Co. Wexford. An antiques-filled Georgian manor with pastoral views and a Continental restaurant.

$$$ **Moy House**, Lahinch, Co. Clare. A cliff-top, 18th-century, Italianate manse with views of gardens or the sea. It seems worlds away from the here and the now.

$$–$$$ **Ash-Rowan Guest House**, Belfast, Northern Ireland. In the former home of Thomas Andrews, designer of the *Titanic*, you can sit in the lounge and devour one of the many books scattered around the house.

$$-$$$	**Barberstown Castle**, Straffan, Co. Kildare. What's a castle without a keep? The one here dates from the 13th century. Turf fires, period reproductions, and theme restaurants shed light on this structure's 750-odd years.
$$-$$$	**La Stampa**, Dublin. Who said that velvet bedspreads from Paris wouldn't work in an Asian scheme? Certainly not the designers who dressed this boutique hotel.

BUDGET LODGING

$$	**Delphi Lodge**, Leenane, Co. Mayo. A lakeside Georgian sporting lodge surrounded by wildly beautiful mountain scenery.
$-$$	**Ariel Guest House**, Dublin. A Waterford-crystal chandelier is just one of the charms of this Victorian redbrick in leafy Ballsbridge. The friendly owner is another.
$-$$	**Crookedwood House**, Mullingar, Co. Westmeath. Rooms in this 200-year-old rectory are spacious and reasonably priced. Save your money to splurge on dinner in the restaurant; look for updated takes—and German twists—on salmon, pheasant, venison, pork.
$	**Hotel St. George**, Dublin. Georgian details fill this house at the top of O'Connell Street, an enviable location.
¢-$	**Ballymakeigh House**, Youghal, Co. Cork. It's a creeper-clad farmhouse amid lush dairy country—a true embodiment of the Ireland most people imagine.
¢-$	**Norman Villa**, Galway City. A tasteful Victorian town house characterized by a location that offers the best of all urban worlds.
¢	**Green Gate**, Ardvally, Co. Donegal. Its four rooms are in a thatched cottage overlooking Ardara, the Atlantic, and other spectacular Donegal scenes.

RESTAURANTS

$$$$	**Ballymaloe House**, Shanagarry, Co. Cork. It's an elegant inn whose restaurant continues to revolutionize and refine Irish cooking and whose cooking school consistently turns out Ireland's top chefs.
$$$$	**Cromleach Lodge**, Castlebaldwin, Co. Sligo. Outstanding views *and* food. Expect quirky dishes with multidimensional flavors.
$$$$	**Patrick Guilbaud**, Dublin. Flawless food, impeccable service. Don't even think about skipping this place or the specialty duck à l'orange. As for the plate of five chocolate desserts—life is short.
$$$$	**Rathsallagh House**, Dunlavin, Co. Wicklow. Think enthusiastic country-house cooking with an internationalist edge—produce from organic gardens, game in season, seafood specialties.
$$$$	**Shanks**, Bangor, Northern Ireland. Robbie Millar has a diver *hand-pick* scallops from the sea. The dishes here blend Asian spicing with European techniques and local ingredients; the results are piquant and exciting.

$$$–$$$$	**The Vintage,** Kinsale, Co. Cork. It's worth a jaunt to this seaside town just for the whole lobster in a mustard-whiskey sauce that's served here.
$$$–$$$$	**Wineport Lodge,** Athlone, Co. Westmeath. The energetic, imaginative menu of this informal lakeside restaurant changes every eight weeks; braised lamb shank and roast venison are among the seasonal fare.
$$$	**Halo,** Dublin. The chef is French so your seared, cured salmon is both artful and delicious. The designer is Irish, and the space—soaring ceiling, dark woods, warm task lighting—is moody and mysterious yet inviting.
$$–$$$	**Casino House,** Killbrittain, Co. Cork. Farmhouse turned restaurant where Irish country cooking has an elegant edge and flavors full of verve.
$$–$$$	**Deane's,** Belfast, Northern Ireland. Eclectic, Thai-influenced Michael Deane concocts innovative east–west dishes. Subtle spicing adds spirit-enhancing gusto to the meal.
$$–$$$	**Erriseask House,** Ballyconneely, Co. Galway. Think seasonal, market-fresh produce, meats, and seafood. And think contemporary, too.
$$–$$$	**Wine Vault,** Waterford City. An Elizabethan town house with a beguiling 350-label wine cellar and an intriguing Irish menu.

BUDGET RESTAURANTS

$–$$	**Corncrake Restaurant,** Carndonagh, Co. Donegal. When local flavors mix with Continental cuisine the result is the kind of great flair you find here.
$–$$	**Jaipur,** Dublin. A contemporary dining room with both classical and cutting-edge Indian food.
$–$$	**O'Gradys Restaurant & Guesthouse,** Waterford City. The modest exterior hints at the low-key, family-friendly interior but gives few clues of how sophisticated the seafood dishes can be.
¢	**Busyfeet & Coco Café,** Dublin. A quirky eatery where the salads and sandwiches are organic and healthful. Lots of veggies, lots of hummus.
¢	**Poppies Country Cooking,** Enniskerry, Co. Wicklow. The cozy setting, hearty entrées, and rhubarb crumble entice people back time and again for breakfast, lunch, or tea.

CHURCHES & MONASTERIES

	Clonmacnoise, Co. Offaly. This isolated monastery at the confluence of two rivers was famous throughout Europe as a center for learning. It's also a royal burial ground.
	Glendalough, Co. Wicklow. A monastery founded by a hermit in the 6th century, attacked by Vikings in the 9th and 10th centuries, and plundered by English soldiers in the 12th century—your typical Irish ruins.

Jerpoint Abbey, Co. Kilkenney. Cistercian church, tomb, and cloisters from the 12th century; the facade's decorative figures—human and otherwise—are beloved.

Kylemore Abbey, Kylemore Valley. It's hard to believe that this graystone Gothic-Revival pile was built as a residence in the 1860s rather than as the home for Benedictine nuns that it is today.

Rock of Cashel, Co. Tipperary. A cluster of ruins—cathedral, chapel, round tower—crowning a circular, mist-shrouded rock that rises from a plain.

St. Patrick's Cathedral, Dublin. The national cathedral of the Church of Ireland is old, massy, wrapped in legend, and draped with history.

GOLF

Ballybunion Golf Club, Co. Kerry. On the Old Course, one of the country's classics, each and every hole is a pleasure.

The K Club, Co. Kildare. You'd have to be a non-golfer *and* a hermit not to have heard of this course, one of the country's most prestigious and demanding.

Mount Juliet Golf Course, Co. Kilkenney. A championship parkland course with a little something for every golfer.

Portmarnock Golf Club, Co. Dublin. One of the nation's "Big Four" golf clubs (along with Ballybunion, Royal County Down, and Royal Portrush), Portmarnock is a links course near Dublin.

Royal County Down, Northern Ireland. A lunar landscape makes this course as beautiful as it is difficult.

Royal Portrush, Co. Antrim, Northern Ireland. Portrush has hosted the British Open and is favored by Ireland's most renowned golfers.

HISTORIC SIGHTS

Newgrange, Co. Meath. It's older than Stonehenge and built with 250,000 tons of stones. Come in the morning during winter solstice, when 20 minutes of light illuminate the interior.

Trinity College, Dublin. The university founded by Queen Elizabeth provided the greats—Beckett, Wilde, Stoker—with 40 acres of stomping grounds. It's also home to the masterfully illuminated *Book of Kells.*

MUSEUMS

Chester Beatty Library, Dublin. Who knew that Ireland was home to one of the world's largest collections of Islamic and Far Eastern manuscripts and art?

Museum of Country Life, Turlough, Co. Mayo. The objects on display transport you back to a time when water came from wells and clothes were made by hand—often by the light of a winter's fire fueled by turf cut straight out of a bog.

National Gallery of Ireland, Dublin. Dutch masters, French Impressionists, and great Irish painters, too—all in a manageable collection.

Ulster Folk and Transport Museum, Belfast, Northern Ireland. On one side of the road is a living museum with a reconstructed buildings and docents dressed in character. On the other side of the road is a collection of vehicles made in the region.

Waterford Treasures, Waterford City. A thousand years of history unfolds with an artful blend of audiovisuals and artifacts.

NATURE

Giant's Causeway, Co. Antrim, Northern Ireland. There are equal measures of legend and science surrounding this rock formation—a cluster of 37,000-odd volcanic basalt pillars.

Glenveagh National Park. It's County Donegal at its wildest and most dramatic: 24,000 acres of mountain, moorland, lakes, and woods.

Killary Harbour, Kylemore Valley. The dark, deep waters of this narrow fjord—which runs between County Mayo's Mweelrea Mountains and County Galway's Dorruagh Mountains—are as haunting as the reflections in them.

PUBS

Crown Liquor Saloon, Belfast, Northern Ireland. This ornate, snug-filled pub is so true to its Victorian roots that it's still lit by gas lamps.

Grogans, Dublin. A William Street hangout packed with creative types.

Monk's Pub, Ballyvaughan, Co. Clare. A waterfront watering hole where the bar food is almost as good as the Irish tunes and the folk music.

Stag's Head, Dublin. An old gathering place where students and theater folk mix.

Tiġ Neaċhtain (Naughton's Pub), Galway City. Grab a spot in a snug and spend an evening listening to traditional music at this popular pub in the heart of the old town.

PURE IRELAND

Aghadoe, near Killarney. Even Queen Victoria was overwhelmed by the views from this town. At dusk the island-studded Lower Lake glows under an expansive sky.

Ballyhack, Co. Waterford. Thatched cottages and an imposing 16th-century castle are highlights of a village surrounded by green hills.

Blasket Islands, off Dingle Peninsula, Co. Kerry. Slea Head's cliffs, above a beautiful and treacherous coastline, are a marvelous place from which to view these rugged, uninhabited islands.

Georgian Squares on a Sunday, Dublin. Tranquil, evergreen Merrion Square is full of great architecture and sculpture. The 27-acre St. Stephen's Green has flower gardens and expansive lawns.

Kenny's Bookshop, Galway City. Five floors of secondhand and antiquarian prints, maps, and books—many covering Ireland—as well as painting and sculpture by Irish artists.

Kilmore Quay, Co. Wexford. A timeless town of whitewashed houses, fishermen, and the sea.

STATELY HOMES

Castletown House, Co. Kildare. Andrea Palladio would probably have approved of this large splendid house. The interior is filled with 18th-centruy furniture and details.

Strokestown Park House, Co. Rosscommon. Some wings date from the 17th century, others from the 18th and 19th centuries. The furnishings are all original; intriguing structural details and curiosities abound.

SMART TRAVEL TIPS

Finding out about your destination before you leave home means you won't squander time organizing everyday minutiae once you've arrived. You'll be more street-wise when you hit the ground as well, better prepared to explore the aspects of Ireland that drew you here in the first place. The organizations in this section can provide information to supplement this guide; contact them for up-to-the-minute details, and consult the A to Z sections that end each chapter for facts on the various topics as they relate to the country's many regions. Happy landings!

ADDRESSES

We have tried to provide full addresses for hotels, restaurants, and sights, though many of Ireland's villages and towns are so tiny they barely have street names, much less house numbers. If in doubt, ask for directions. Outside of Dublin and Northern Ireland, postal codes aren't really used; what's more important here is the county, so be sure to include it when addressing an envelope.

AIR TRAVEL

From North America and the United Kingdom, Aer Lingus, the national flag carrier, has the most direct flights to Ireland. There are no direct flights from Australia or New Zealand. Regular service is available from most major airports in Ireland to many U.K. cities, including Leeds, Manchester, and Glasgow.

Flying into Ireland involves few hassles, although an increase in traffic in the last decade has caused a slight increase in flight delays and time spent waiting for baggage to clear customs. Flights within Ireland tend to be filled with business travelers. The lack of competition on internal routes coupled with the country's relatively small size make train and car travel more affordable and pleasurable options.

BOOKING

When you book, **look for nonstop flights** and **remember that "direct" flights stop at least once.** Try to avoid connecting flights, which require a change of plane. Two airlines may operate a connecting flight jointly, so ask whether your airline operates every segment of the trip; you may find that the carrier you prefer flies you only part of the way. To find more booking tips and to check prices and make on-line flight reservations, log on to www.fodors.com.

CARRIERS

Aer Lingus operates regularly scheduled flights to Shannon and Dublin from New York's JFK, Boston's Logan, Chicago's O'Hare, and LAX. Delta has a daily departure from Atlanta that flies first to Shannon and on to Dublin. Continental flies daily direct to Dublin and Shannon, departing from Newark Liberty International Airport in New Jersey. With the exception of special offers, the prices of the four airlines tend to be similar.

London to Dublin is one of the world's busiest international air routes. Aer Lingus, British Airways, and British Midland all have several daily flights. Ryanair—famous for its cheap, no-frills service—offers several daily flights from London Gatwick, Luton, and Stanstead airports. With such healthy competition, bargains abound. British Airways, British Midlands, and low-cost airline Easyjet offer regularly scheduled flights to Belfast from London Heathrow Airport.

Aer Lingus provides service within Ireland to Dublin, Cork, Galway, Kerry, and Shannon. Aer Arann Express flies from Dublin to Cork, Derry, Donegal, Galway, Knock, and Sligo. EuroCeltic offers a daily flight weekdays from Dublin to Donegal, Sligo, and Waterford, and British Airways has daily service between Dublin and Derry.

🛪 Airlines Aer Arann Express ☎ 1890/462-726 in the Republic of Ireland; 0800/587-2324 in the U.K.; 3531/814-1058 in the U.S., Canada, Australia, and New Zealand ⊕ www.aerarannexpress.com. **Aer Lingus** ☎ 800/474-7424 in the U.S. and Canada; 0845/084-4444 in the U.K.; 02/9244-2123 in Australia; 09/308-3351 in New Zealand ⊕ www. aerlingus.com. **British Airways** ☎ 800/147-9297 in the U.S. and Canada; 0845/773-3377 in the U.K.; 02/ 8904-8800 in Australia; 0800/274-8477 in New Zealand ⊕ www.britishairways.com. **British Midlands** ☎ 0870/607-0555 in the U.K. ⊕ www.flybmi. com. **Continental** ☎ 800/231-0856 in the U.S. ⊕ www.continental.com. **Delta** ☎ 800/241-4141 in the U.S. and Canada ⊕ www.delta.com. **EuroCeltic Airways** ☎ 0818/300-100 in Ireland; 08700/400-100 in the U.K. ⊕ www.euroceltic.com. **Ryanair** ☎ 0871/246-0000 in the U.K. ⊕ www.ryanair.com.

CHECK-IN & BOARDING

Checking in and boarding an outbound plane tends to be civilized. Security is professional but not overbearing, and airport staffers are usually helpful and patient. In the busy summer season lines can get long, and you should play it safe and arrive a couple hours before your flight.

Always **find out your carrier's policy.** Plan to arrive at the airport about two hours before your scheduled departure time for domestic flights and 2½ to 3 hours before international flights. You may need to arrive earlier if you're flying from one of the busier airports or during peak air-traffic times. To avoid delays at airport-security checkpoints, try not to wear any metal. Jewelry, belt and other buckles, steel-toe shoes, barrettes, and underwire bras are among the items that can set off detectors.

Assuming that not everyone with a ticket will show up, airlines routinely overbook planes. When everyone does, airlines ask for volunteers to give up their seats. In return, these volunteers usually get a several-hundred-dollar flight voucher, which can be used toward the purchase of another ticket, and are rebooked on the next flight out. If there are not enough volunteers, the airline must choose who will be denied boarding. The first to get bumped are passengers who checked in late and those flying on discounted tickets, so **get to the gate and check in as early as possible,** especially during peak periods. Always **bring a government-issued photo ID to the airport;** even when it's not required, a passport is best.

CUTTING COSTS

It's smart to **call a number of airlines and check the Internet;** when you are quoted a good price, **book it on the spot**—the same fare may not be available the next day, or even the next hour. Always **check different routings** and look into using alternate airports. Also, price off-peak flights, which may be significantly less expensive than others. Travel agents, especially low-fare specialists (⇨ Discounts and Deals), are helpful.

Consolidators are another good source. They buy tickets for scheduled flights at reduced rates from the airlines, then sell them at prices that beat the best fare available directly from the airlines. Sometimes you can even get your money back if you need to return the ticket. Carefully read the fine print detailing penalties for changes and cancellations, purchase the ticket with a credit card, and **confirm your consolidator reservation with the airline.**

Many airlines, singly or in collaboration, offer discount air passes that allow foreigners to travel economically in a particular country or region. These visitor passes usually must be reserved and purchased before you leave home. Information about passes often can be found on most airlines' international Web pages, which tend to be aimed at travelers from outside the carrier's home country. Also, try typing the name of the pass into a search engine, or search for "pass" within the Web site.

Charter carriers, such as Sceptre Charters, offer flights to Dublin and Shannon from various U.S. cities. Air Canada Vacations and Regent Holidays fly from Canada. Note that in certain seasons, usually fall and winter, their charter deals include mandatory hotel and car-rental packages.

🛈 Charters **Air Canada Vacations** ☎ 888/247-2262 ⊕ www.aircanadavacations.com. **Regent Holidays** ☎ 800/387-4860 in Canada. **Sceptre Charters** ☎ 800/221-0924 ⊕ www.sceptreireland.com.

🛈 Consolidators **AirlineConsolidator.com** ☎ 888/468-5385 ⊕ www.airlineconsolidator.com; for international tickets. **Best Fares** ☎ 800/576-8255 or 800/576-1600 ⊕ www.bestfares.com; $59.90 annual membership. **Cheap Tickets** ☎ 800/377-1000 or 888/922-8849 ⊕ www.cheaptickets.com. **Expedia** ☎ 800/397-3342 or 404/728-8787 ⊕ www.expedia.com. **Hotwire** ☎ 866/468-9473 or 920/330-9418 ⊕ www.hotwire.com. **Now Voyager Travel** ✉ 45 W. 21st St., 5th fl., New York, NY 10010 ☎ 212/459-1616 🖷 212/243-2711 ⊕ www.nowvoyagertravel.com. **Onetravel.com** ⊕ www.onetravel.com. **Orbitz** ☎ 888/656-4546 ⊕ www.orbitz.com. **Priceline.com** ⊕ www.priceline.com. **Travelocity** ☎ 888/709-5983; 877/282-2925 in Canada; 0870/111-7060 in the U.K. ⊕ www.travelocity.com.

🛈 Discount Passes **Boomerang Pass**, Qantas, ☎ 800/227-4500; 0845/774-7767 in the U.K.; 131-313 in Australia; 0800/808-767 in New Zealand ⊕ www.qantas.com. **FlightPass**, EuropebyAir ☎ 888/387-2479 ⊕ www.europebyair.com.

ENJOYING THE FLIGHT

State your seat preference when purchasing your ticket, and then repeat it when you confirm and when you check in. For more legroom, you can request one of the few emergency-aisle seats at check-in, if you are capable of lifting at least 50

pounds—a Federal Aviation Administration requirement of passengers in these seats. Seats behind a bulkhead also offer more legroom, but they don't have underseat storage. Don't sit in the row in front of the emergency aisle or in front of a bulkhead, where seats may not recline.

Ask the airline whether a snack or meal is served on the flight. If you have dietary concerns, **request special meals when booking.** These can be vegetarian, low-cholesterol, or kosher, for example. It's a good idea to pack some healthful snacks and a small (plastic) bottle of water in your carry-on bag. On long flights, try to maintain a normal routine, to help fight jet lag. At night, **get some sleep.** By day, **eat light meals, drink water** (not alcohol), and **move around the cabin** to stretch your legs. For additional jet-lag tips consult *Fodor's FYI: Travel Fit & Healthy* (available at bookstores everywhere).

FLYING TIMES

Flying time to Ireland is 6½ hours from New York, 7½ hours from Chicago, 10 hours from Los Angeles, 1 hour from London, and 27 hours from Sydney.

HOW TO COMPLAIN

If your baggage goes astray or your flight goes awry, complain right away. Most carriers require that you **file a claim immediately.** The Aviation Consumer Protection Division of the Department of Transportation publishes *Fly-Rights,* which discusses airlines and consumer issues and is available on-line. You can also find articles and information on mytravelrights.com, the Web site of the nonprofit Consumer Travel Rights Center.

🛈 Airline Complaints **Aviation Consumer Protection Division** ✉ U.S. Department of Transportation, C-75, Room 4107, 400 7th St. SW, Washington, DC 20590 ☎ 202/366-2220 ⊕ www.dot.gov/airconsumer. **Federal Aviation Administration Consumer Hotline** ✉ for inquiries: FAA, 800 Independence Ave. SW, Washington, DC 20591 ☎ 800/322-7873 ⊕ www.faa.gov.

RECONFIRMING

Check the status of your flight before you leave for the airport. You can do this on your carrier's Web site, by linking to a flight-status checker (many Web booking services offer these), or by calling your carrier or travel agent. Always confirm international flights at least 72 hours ahead of the scheduled departure time.

AIRPORTS

The major gateways to Ireland are Dublin Airport (DUB) on the east coast, 10 km (6 mi) north of the city center, and Shannon Airport (SNN) on the west coast, 25 km (16 mi) west of Limerick. Two airports serve Belfast: Belfast International Airport (BFS) at Aldergrove, 24 km (15 mi) from the city, handles local and U.K. flights, as well as all other international traffic; Belfast City Airport (BHD), 6½ km (4 mi) from the city, handles local and United Kingdom flights only. In addition, the City of Derry Airport (LDY) receives flights from Dublin, Manchester, Birmingham, and Glasgow in the United Kingdom.

🛪 Airport Information **Belfast City Airport** ☎ 028/9045-7745 🌐 www.belfastcityairport.com. **Belfast International Airport at Aldergrove** ☎ 028/9448-4848 🌐 www.belfastairport.com. **City of Derry Airport** ☎ 028/7181-0784 🌐 www. cityofderryairport.com. **Dublin Airport** ☎ 01/814-1111 🌐 www.aer-rianta.ie. **Shannon Airport** ☎ 061/712-000 🌐 www.shannonairport.com.

DUTY-FREE SHOPPING

Duty-free shopping isn't available for people traveling between European Union (EU) countries, and you can no longer buy duty-free goods aboard many international Aer Lingus flights. If you like to shop and you're on one of these flights, stock up on goods at the airport before boarding. For duty-free allowances when entering Ireland from a non-EU country, *see* Customs & Duties.

BOAT & FERRY TRAVEL

The ferry is a convenient way to get to and from Ireland from elsewhere in Europe, particularly the United Kingdom. There are six main ferry ports to Ireland. Four in the republic at Dublin Port, Dun Laoghaire, Rosslare, and Cork and two in Northern Ireland at Belfast and Larne. The cost of your trip can vary substantially, so spend time with a travel agent and compare prices carefully. Bear in mind, too, that flying can be cheaper, so look into all types of transportation before booking.

Irish Ferries operates the *Ulyssess,* the world's largest car ferry, on its Dublin to Holyhead, Wales, route (3 hrs, 15 mins); there's also a swift service (1 hr, 50 mins) between these two ports. There are several trips daily. The company also runs between Rosslare and Pembroke, Wales (3 hrs, 45 mins), and has service to France. Stena Line sails several times a day between Dublin and Holyhead (3 hrs, 15 mins) and has swift service to Dun Laoghaire (1 hr, 40 mins). The company also runs a fast craft (1 hr, 45 mins) and a superferry (3 hrs, 15 mins) between Belfast and Stranraer, Scotland, as well as a fast craft (1 hr, 40 mins) and a superferry (3 hrs, 30 mins) between Rosslare and Fishguard, Wales. There are several trips daily on both routes.

There's SeaCat service between Dublin and Liverpool (3 hrs, 45 mins); between Dublin and Belfast and the Isle of Man (2 hrs, 45 mins); and between Belfast and Troon, Scotland (2 hrs, 30 mins), and Heysham in northwestern England (3 hrs, 55 mins). Norse Merchant offers a Dublin and Belfast to Liverpool service (8 hrs). P&O Irish Sea vessels run between Larne and several U.K. destinations, including Troon, Scotland (4 hrs), a couple times a day. The company also sails from Dublin to Liverpool daily (7 hrs, 30 mins) or Mostyn (6 hrs) in England three times a week. Passengers with cars can also sail between Dublin (18 hrs) or Rosslare (20 hrs) and Cherbourg, France, three times a week. Swansea Cork Ferries travels between Swansea and Cork from mid-March to early November. The crossing takes 10 hours, but easy access by road to both ports makes this longer sea route a good choice for motorists.

A 10-minute car ferry crosses the River Suir between Ballyhack in County Wexford and Passage East (near Arthurstown) in County Waterford, introducing you to two pretty fishing villages. The ferry operates continuously during daylight hours and costs €4.45 per car, €1 for foot passengers. A boat from Tarbert in County Kerry leaves every hour on the half hour for Killimer in County Clare; return ferries leave Killimer every hour on the hour. The 30-minute journey across the Shannon Estuary costs €8.90 per car, €2.55 for foot passengers. The scenic Cork Harbor crossing allows those traveling from West Cork or Kinsale to Cobh and the east coast to bypass the city center. The five-minute car

ferry runs from Glenbrook (near Ringask-
iddy) in the west to Carrigaloe (near
Cobh) in the east and operates continuously from 7:15 AM to 12:45 AM daily. It
costs €3.80 per car, €0.75 for foot passengers.

There are regular services to the Aran Is-
lands from Galway City, Rossaveal in
County Galway, and Doolin in County
Clare. Ferries also sail to Inishbofin off the
Galway coast and Arranmore off the
Donegal coast, and to Bere, Sherkin, and
Cape Clear islands off the coast of County
Cork. The islands are all small enough to
explore on foot, so the ferries are for foot
passengers and bicycles only. Other islands—the Blaskets and the Skelligs in
Kerry, Rathlin, and Tory off the Donegal
coast—can be reached by private arrangements with local boatmen. Full details on
ferries to the islands are available in a pub-
lication from the Irish Tourist Board (ITB,
also known as Bord Fáilte).

FARES & SCHEDULES

You can get schedules and purchase tickets, with a credit card if you like, directly
from the ferry lines. You can also pick
them up at Dublin tourism offices and
from any major travel agent in Ireland or
the United Kingdom. Payment must be
made in the currency of the country of the
port of departure.

🚢 Boat & Ferry Information **Irish Ferries**
☎ 1890/313131 in Ireland; 08705/171717 in the U.K.;
0143/944694 in France ⊕ www.irishferries.ie. **Norse
Merchant** ☎ 01/819-2999 in Ireland; 0870/600-
4321 in the U.K. ⊕ www.norsemerchant.com. **P&O
Irish Sea** ☎ 1800/409049 in Ireland; 0870/2424777
in the U.K.; 0803/013013 in France ⊕ www.
poirishsea.com **SeaCat** ☎ 01/836-4019 in Ireland;
08705/523523 in Northern Ireland; 0151/236-2061 in
the U.K.; 0129/231-9103 in Scotland; 01624/645695 in
the Isle of Man ⊕ www.seacat.co.uk. **Stena Line**
☎ 01/204-7777 in Ireland; 028/9074-7747 in Northern Ireland; 08705/707070 in the U.K. ⊕ www.
stenaline.co.uk. **Swansea Cork Ferries** ☎ 021/427-
1166 in Ireland; 01792/456116 in the U.K. ⊕ www.
swansea-cork.ie.

BUSINESS HOURS

Business hours are 9–5, sometimes later in
the larger towns. In smaller towns, stores
often close from 1 to 2 for lunch. If a holiday falls on a weekend, most businesses
are closed on Monday as well.

BANKS & OFFICES

Banks are open 10–4 weekdays. In small
towns they may close from 12:30 to 1:30.
They remain open until 5 one afternoon
per week; the day of week varies, although
it's usually Thursday. Post offices are open
weekdays 9–5 and Saturday 9–1; some of
the smaller country offices close for lunch.

In Northern Ireland bank hours are weekdays 9:30–4:30. Post offices are open
weekdays 9–5:30, Saturday 9–1. Some
close for an hour at lunch.

GAS STATIONS

There are some 24-hour gas stations along
the highways; otherwise, hours vary from
morning rush hour to late evenings.

MUSEUMS & SIGHTS

Museums and sights are generally open
Tuesday–Saturday 10–5 and Sunday 2–5.

PHARMACIES

Most pharmacies are open Monday–Saturday 9–5:30 or 6. Larger towns and cities
often have 24-hour establishments.

SHOPS

Most shops are open Monday–Saturday
9–5:30 or 6. Once a week—normally
Wednesday, Thursday, or Saturday—they
close at 1 PM. These times do *not* apply to
Dublin, where stores generally stay open
later, and they can vary from region to region, so it's best to check locally. Larger
malls usually stay open late once a week—
generally until 9 on Thursday or Friday.

Shops in Belfast are open weekdays
9–5:30, with a late closing on Thursday,
usually at 9. Elsewhere in Northern Ireland, shops close for the afternoon once a
week, usually Wednesday or Thursday;
check locally. In addition, most smaller
shops close for an hour or so at lunch.

BUS TRAVEL

In the Republic of Ireland, long-distance
bus services are operated by Bus Éireann,
which also provides local services in Cork,
Galway, Limerick, and Waterford. There's
really only one class, and prices are similar
for all seats. Note, though, that outside of
the peak season, services are limited; some
routes (e.g., Killarney–Dingle) disappear
altogether. There's often only one trip a
day on the express routes, and one a week

to some of the more remote villages. To ensure that your proposed bus journey is feasible, buy a copy of Bus Éireann's timetable—€1.30 from any bus terminal—or check on-line. Many of the destination indicators are in Irish, so make sure you get on the right bus.

Numerous bus companies run between Britain and the Irish Republic, but be ready for long hours on the road and possible delays. All use either the Holyhead–Dublin or Fishguard/Pembroke–Rosslare ferry routes. National Express, a consortium of companies, has Supabus (as its vehicles are known) services from all major British cities to more than 90 Irish destinations. Slattery's, an Irish company, has services from London, Manchester, Liverpool, Oxford, Birmingham, Leeds, and North Wales to more than 100 Irish destinations.

In Northern Ireland, all buses are operated by the state-owned Ulsterbus. Service is generally good, with particularly useful links to those towns not served by train. Ulsterbus also offers tours. Buses to Belfast run from London and from Birmingham, making the Stranraer–Port of Belfast crossing. Contact National Express.

RESERVATIONS & PAYING

Check with the bus office to see if reservations are accepted for your route; if not, show up early to get a seat. Note: prepaid tickets don't apply to a particular bus time, just a route, so if one vehicle is full you can try another. You can buy tickets at the main tourist offices, at the bus station, or on the bus (though it's cash only for the latter option).

You can save money by buying a multiday pass, some of which can be combined with the rail service. There are also some cost-cutting passes that will give access to travel in both Northern Ireland and the Republic of Ireland. A Freedom of Northern Ireland ticket costs £42 for seven days' unlimited bus and rail travel—a really good deal when you consider that a one-day ticket costs £12. In the republic, passes include the Irish Explorer Rail and Bus Pass, the Irish Rambler Card, the Irish Rover Card, and the Emerald Card. Contact Bus Éireann or Ulsterbus for details.
🚌 Bus Information **Bus Éireann** ☎ 01/836-6111 in the Republic of Ireland ⊕ www.buseireann.ie. **National Express** ☎ 08705/808-080 in the U.K.

⊕ www.nationalexpress.co.uk. **Slattery's** ☎ 020/7482-1604 in the U.K. **Ulsterbus** ☎ 028/9033-3000 in Northern Ireland ⊕ www.ulsterbus.co.uk.

CAMERAS & PHOTOGRAPHY

Nature has blessed Ireland with spectacular landscapes. In addition to cliffs, hills, and beaches, sunsets along the north and west coast can be particularly dramatic because of the variable cloud cover and the clarity of light. Take a step outside at dusk during your visit wherever you may be and see if you can catch a sunset. The *Kodak Guide to Shooting Great Travel Pictures* (available at bookstores everywhere) is loaded with tips.
📷 Photo Help **Kodak Information Center** ☎ 800/242-2424 ⊕ www.kodak.com.

EQUIPMENT PRECAUTIONS

Don't pack film and equipment in checked luggage, where it is much more susceptible to damage. X-ray machines used to view checked luggage are extremely powerful and therefore are likely to ruin your film. Try to **ask for hand inspection of film,** which becomes clouded after repeated exposure to airport X-ray machines, and **keep videotapes and computer disks away from metal detectors.** Always **keep film, tape, and computer disks out of the sun.** Carry an extra supply of batteries, and **be prepared to turn on your camera, camcorder, or laptop** to prove to airport security personnel that the device is real.

FILM & DEVELOPING

Major brands of film are available throughout Ireland, although 24-hour developing is found only in cities. Advantix film and developing are available in larger centers. A roll of 36-exposure color film will cost between €6 and €8.

VIDEOS

Videotape is widely available. The local tape standard is PAL, and a standard 180-minute cassette costs around €5.

CAR RENTAL

If you're renting a car in the Irish Republic and intend to visit Northern Ireland (or vice versa), make this clear when you get your car, and check that the rental insurance applies when you cross the border.

Renting a car in Ireland is far more expensive than organizing a rental before you leave home. Rates in Dublin for an economy car with a manual transmission and unlimited mileage cost run from €35 a day and €175 a week to €60 a day and €305 a week, depending on the season. This includes the republic's 12½% tax on car rentals. Rates in Belfast begin at £30 a day and £160 a week and go up to around £35 a day and £200 a week, *not* including the 17½% tax on car rentals in the north.

Both manual and automatic transmissions are readily available, though automatics will cost extra. Typical economy car models include Toyota Corolla, Ford Mondeo, and Nissan Micra. Minivans, luxury cars (Mercedes or Alfa Romeos), and four-wheel-drive vehicles (say, a Jeep Cherokee) are also options, but the daily rates are high. Argus Rent A Car and Dan Dooley have convenient locations at Dublin, Shannon, Belfast, and Belfast City airports as well as at ferry ports.

F Major Agencies **Alamo** ☎ 800/522-9696 ⊕ www.alamo.com. **Avis** ☎ 800/331-1084; 800/879-2847 in Canada; 0870/606-0100 in the U.K.; 02/9353-9000 in Australia; 09/526-2847 in New Zealand ⊕ www.avis.com. **Budget** ☎ 800/527-0700; 0870/156-5656 in the U.K. ⊕ www.budget.com. **Dollar** ☎ 800/800-6000; 0124/622-0111 in the U.K., where it's affiliated with Sixt; 02/9223-1444 in Australia ⊕ www.dollar.com. **Hertz** ☎ 800/654-3001; 800/263-0600 in Canada; 0870/844-8844 in the U.K.; 02/9669-2444 in Australia; 09/256-8690 in New Zealand ⊕ www.hertz.com. **National Car Rental** ☎ 800/227-7368; 0870/600-6666 in the U.K. ⊕ www.nationalcar.com.

CUTTING COSTS

For a good deal, **book through a travel agent who will shop around.** Also, **price local car-rental companies**—whose prices may be lower still, although their service and maintenance may not be as good as those of major rental agencies—and **research rates on the Internet.** Remember to ask about required deposits, cancellation penalties, and drop-off charges if you're planning to pick up the car in one city and leave it in another. If you're traveling during a holiday period, also make sure that a confirmed reservation guarantees you a car.

Do **look into wholesalers,** companies that don't own fleets but rent in bulk from those that do and often offer better rates than traditional car-rental operations. Prices are best during off-peak periods. Rentals booked through wholesalers often must be paid for before you leave home.
F Local Agencies **Argus** ☎ 01/490-4444 in Dublin; 048/9442-3444 in Belfast ⊕ www.argus-rentacar.com. **Dan Dooley** ☎ 800/331-9301 in the U.S.; 0800/282189 in the U.K.; 062/53103 in Ireland ⊕ www.dan-dooley.ie.
F Wholesalers **Auto Europe** ☎ 207/842-2000 or 800/223-5555 ⊕ www.autoeurope.com. **Destination Europe Resources** (DER) ✉ 9501 W. Devon Ave., Rosemont, IL 60018 ☎ 800/782-2424 ⊕ www.der.com. **Europe by Car** ☎ 212/581-3040 or 800/223-1516 ⊕ www.europebycar.com. **Kemwel** ☎ 800/678-0678 ⊕ www.kemwel.com.

INSURANCE

When driving a rented car you're generally responsible for any damage to or loss of the vehicle. Collision policies that car-rental companies sell for European rentals typically do not cover stolen vehicles. Before you rent—and purchase collision or theft coverage—see what coverage you already have under the terms of your personal auto-insurance policy and credit cards. Note that some rental agencies require that you present a letter from your credit card company (discussing its insurance coverage for cardholders) when you pick up your car. Also, there may be limits on the number of days a rental agency will allow your credit card policy to cover you for. Ask lots of questions before booking.

REQUIREMENTS & RESTRICTIONS

In Ireland your own driver's license is acceptable. An International Driver's Permit, which is recognized universally, is a good idea; it's available from the American or Canadian Automobile Association and, in the United Kingdom, from the Automobile Association or Royal Automobile Club.

Most rental companies require you to be over 23 to rent a car in Ireland (a few will rent to those over 21) and to have had a license for more than a year. Some companies refuse to rent to visitors over 70. Children under 12 years of age aren't allowed to ride in the front seat unless in a properly fitted child seat.

SURCHARGES

Before you pick up a car in one city and leave it in another, **ask about drop-off charges or one-way service fees,** which can be substantial. Note, too, that some rental agencies charge extra if you return the car before the time specified in your contract. To avoid a hefty refueling fee, **fill the tank just before you turn in the car,** but be aware that gas stations near the rental outlet may overcharge. It's almost never a deal to buy the tank of gas that's in the car when you rent it; the understanding is that you'll return it empty, but some fuel usually remains.

Drivers between the ages of 21 and 25 and 70 and 75 will probably be subject to an insurance surcharge—if they're allowed to drive a rental car at all. An additional driver will add about €5 a day to your car rental, and a child seat costs about €19 for the rental and will require 24-hour advance notice.

CAR TRAVEL

Roads in the Irish Republic are generally good, though four-lane highways, or motorways, are the exception rather than the rule. In addition, many roads twist and wind their way up and down hills and through towns, which can slow you down. On small, rural roads **watch out for cattle and sheep**; they may be just around the next bend. Reckless drivers are also a problem in the countryside so remain cautious and alert.

Road signs in the republic are generally in both Irish (Gaelic) and English; in the northwest and Connemara, most are in Irish only, so get a good road map. On the new green signposts distances are in kilometers; on the old white signposts they're in miles. Knowing the name of the next town on your itinerary is more important than knowing the route number: neither the small local signposts nor the local people refer to roads by official numbers. Traffic signs are the same as in the rest of Europe, and roadway markings are standard.

There are no border checkpoints between the republic and Northern Ireland, where the road network is excellent and, outside Belfast, uncrowded. Road signs and traffic regulations conform to the British system.

All ferries on both principal routes to the Irish Republic take cars. Fishguard and Pembroke are relatively easy to reach by road. The car trip to Holyhead, on the other hand, is sometimes difficult: delays

on the A55 North Wales coastal road aren't unusual. Car ferries to Belfast leave from the Scottish port of Stranraer and the English city of Liverpool; those to Larne leave from Stranraer and Cairnryan. Speed limits are generally 95 to 100 kph (roughly 60 to 70 mph) on the motorways, 90 kph (50 mph) on other roads, and 50 kph (30 mph) in towns.

EMERGENCY SERVICES

Membership in a breakdown service is a good idea if you're using your own car in Ireland. The Automobile Association of Ireland is a sister organization of its English counterpart and is highly recommended.
Automobile Association of Ireland ☎ 01/617-9999 ⊕ www.aaireland.ie.

GASOLINE

You'll find gas stations along most roads. Self-service is the norm in larger establishments. Major credit cards and traveler's checks are usually accepted. Prices are near the lower end for Europe with unleaded gas priced around €0.85 a liter, or more than double the gasoline costs in the United States. Prices vary significantly from station to station, so it's worth driving around the block.

ROAD CONDITIONS

Most roads are paved and make for easy travel. Roads are classified as *M, N,* or *R*: those designated with an *M* for "motorway" are double-lane divided highways with paved shoulders; *N*, or national, routes are generally undivided highways with shoulders; and *R*, or regional, roads tend to be very narrow and twisty.

Watch for traffic at rush hours in Dublin, Cork, Limerick, Belfast, and Galway. Rush hour in Dublin starts at about 7 AM until 9:30 AM and 5 PM to 7 PM; special events such as football or soccer games will also tie up traffic in and around the city.

In Dublin especially, there are plenty of pedestrians, and jaywalking is common, so be careful—particularly at intersections. In winter, fog and black ice can be a problem; reduce speeds when traveling over bridges or in shaded areas where ice is likely to accumulate.

ROAD MAPS

Road maps can be found at most gas stations and bookstores.

RULES OF THE ROAD

The Irish, like the British, **drive on the left-hand side of the road.** Safety belts must be worn by the driver and all passengers, and children under 12 must travel in the back unless riding in a car seat. It's compulsory for motorcyclists and their passengers to wear helmets.

Drunk-driving laws are strict. The legal limit is 80 mg of alcohol per 100 ml of blood. Ireland has a Breathalyzer test, which the police can administer anytime. If you refuse to take it, the odds are you'll be prosecuted anyway. As always, the best advice is **don't drink if you plan to drive.**

Note that a continuous white line down the center of the road prohibits passing. Barred markings on the road and flashing yellow beacons indicate a crossing, where pedestrians have right of way. At a junction of two roads of equal importance, the driver to the right has right of way.

Despite the relatively light traffic, parking in towns can be a problem. Signs with the letter *P* indicate that parking is permitted; a stroke through the *P* warns you to stay away or you'll be liable for a fine of €19.05–€63.50; however, if you get towed, the fine is €190.45. In Dublin and Cork, parking lots are your best bet, but check the rate first in Dublin; they can vary wildly.

In Northern Ireland there are plenty of parking lots in the towns (usually free except in Belfast), and you should use them. In Belfast, you can't park your car in some parts of the city center, more because of congestion than security problems.

CHILDREN IN IRELAND

Involve your youngsters as you outline your trip. When packing, include things to keep them busy en route. On sightseeing days try to schedule activities of special interest to your children. Although most attractions and bus and rail journeys offer a rate of half price or less for children, **look for "family tickets,"** which may be cheaper and usually cover two adults and up to four children. If you're renting a car, don't forget to **arrange for a car seat** when you reserve. For general advice about traveling with children, consult *Fodor's FYI: Travel with Your Baby* (available in bookstores everywhere).

FLYING

If your children are 2 or older, **ask about children's airfares.** As a rule, infants under 2 not occupying a seat fly at greatly reduced fares or even for free. But if you want to guarantee a seat for an infant, you have to pay full fare. Consider flying during off-peak days and times; most airlines will grant an infant a seat without a ticket if there are available seats. When booking, **confirm carry-on allowances** if you're traveling with infants. In general, for babies charged 10% to 50% of the adult fare you are allowed one carry-on bag and a collapsible stroller; if the flight is full, the stroller may have to be checked or you may be limited to less.

Experts agree that it's a good idea to use safety seats aloft for children weighing less than 40 pounds. Airlines set their own policies: if you use a safety seat, U.S. carriers usually require that the child be ticketed, even if he or she is young enough to ride free, because the seats must be strapped into regular seats. And even if you pay the full adult fare for the seat, it may be worth it, especially on longer trips. Do **check your airline's policy about using safety seats during takeoff and landing.** Safety seats are not allowed everywhere in the plane, so get your seat assignments as early as possible.

When reserving, **request children's meals or a freestanding bassinet** (not available at all airlines) if you need them. But note that bulkhead seats, where you must sit to use the bassinet, may lack an overhead bin or storage space on the floor.

FOOD

Most of the food will feel familiar to children, from the traditional bacon-and-eggs breakfast to fish-and-chips. Pubs are your best bet if you want to be guaranteed children will recognize what they're eating. In the larger centers fast-food chains such as McDonald's, KFC, and Pizza Hut are common.

Hotel and pub restaurants often have children's menus and high chairs. Unlike in Great Britain, Irish licensing laws allow children under 14 into pubs—although they may not consume alcohol on the premises until they're 18, and they're expected to leave by anywhere from 5:30 to 7 PM, depending on how busy the pub gets.

WHERE TO STAY

Most hotels in Ireland allow children under a certain age to stay in their parents' room at no extra charge, but others charge for them as extra adults; be sure to **find out the cutoff age for children's discounts.** Family-friendly hotels at all levels will offer cots, cribs, and baby-sitting services, though for an additional charge. Only more expensive hotels are likely to have swimming pools.

SIGHTS & ATTRACTIONS

Places that are especially appealing to children are indicated by a rubber-duckie icon (🦆) in the margin. There are plenty of attractions in Dublin to amuse children, including castles, museums, and zoos. Keep an eye on the weather; if you happen upon a good day, children can amuse themselves for hours at one of the many beaches.

A sampling of theater productions for children can be found at local playhouses around the country. Listings of upcoming events are published in the *Irish Times* (€1.40) "The Ticket" supplement each Wednesday.

🔳 Local Information *Irish Times* ⊕ www.ireland. com.

SUPPLIES & EQUIPMENT

Familiar brands of items and supplies for babies and children are available in every town and village; check the supermarket or family grocery store. A 400-g (14.29-oz) box of powdered baby formula will cost around €5.10 and 600 ml of pre-mixed formula is about €7.60. Disposable diapers will cost between €5.10 and €6.35 for a package of 26.

TRANSPORTATION

Children under 16 years of age ride the train for half price and infants ride for free. Car seats are permitted, though bassinets aren't available for infants. Buses operate under the same system.

Car seats are readily available at car-rental firms, but most do require 24 hours' advance notice. Children under 12 years of age can't ride in the front seat unless in a car seat.

COMPUTERS ON THE ROAD

If you're traveling with a laptop, carry a spare battery and adapter. Most laptops will work at both 120V and 220V, but you will need an adapter so the plug will fit in the socket. In the countryside, a surge protector is a good idea as well.

CONSUMER PROTECTION

Whether you're shopping for gifts or purchasing travel services, **pay with a major credit card** whenever possible, so you can cancel payment or get reimbursed if there's a problem (and you can provide documentation). If you're doing business with a particular company for the first time, **contact your local Better Business Bureau and the attorney general's offices** in your state and (for U.S. businesses) the company's home state as well. Have any complaints been filed? Finally, if you're buying a package or tour, always **consider travel insurance** that includes default coverage (⇨ Insurance).

🔳 BBBs **Council of Better Business Bureaus** ✉ 4200 Wilson Blvd., Suite 800, Arlington, VA 22203 ☎ 703/276-0100 ⊕ www.bbb.org.

CRUISE TRAVEL

Cruise travel in Ireland consists of sailing the inland waterways. The Shannon River system provides a great alternative to traveling overland to see the interior of the country. In some cases bicycles can be rented so you can drop anchor and explore.

🔳 Cruise Lines **Ireland Line Cruisers** ✉ Killaloe ☎ 061/375011. **Leisure Afloat Ltd.** ✉ Shellumsrath House, Kilkenny ☎ 056/64395 ⊕ www. leisureafloat.com. **Riversdale Barge Holidays** ✉ Ballinamore ☎ 078/44122. **Shannon Castle Line** ✉ Williamstown Harbor, Whitegate ☎ 061/927042. **Silver Line Cruisers** ✉ The Marina, Banagher ☎ 0509/51112 ⊕ www.silverlinecruisers.com. **Waveline Cruisers** ✉ Quigley's Marina, Killinure Point, Glassan ☎ 0902/85711 ⊕ www.waveline.ie.

CUSTOMS & DUTIES

When shopping abroad, **keep receipts** for all purchases. Upon reentering the country, **be ready to show customs officials what you've bought.** Pack purchases together in an easily accessible place. If you think a duty is incorrect, appeal the assessment. If you object to the way your clearance was handled, note the inspector's badge number. In either case, first ask to see a supervisor. If the problem isn't resolved, write to the appropriate authorities, beginning with the port director at your point of entry.

IN IRELAND

Duty-free allowances have been abolished for those traveling between countries in the EU. For goods purchased outside the EU, you may import duty-free: (1) 200 cigarettes or 100 cigarillos or 50 cigars or 250 grams of smoking tobacco; (2) 2 liters of wine, and either 1 liter of alcoholic drink over 22% volume or 2 liters of alcoholic drink under 22% volume (sparkling or fortified wine included); (3) 50 grams (60 mls) of perfume and ¼ liter of toilet water; and (4) other goods (including beer) to a value of €180.30 per person (€92.70 per person for travelers under 15 years of age).

Goods that cannot be freely imported to the Irish Republic include firearms, ammunition, explosives, illegal drugs, indecent or obscene books and pictures, oral smokeless tobacco products, meat and meat products, poultry and poultry products, plants and plant products (including shrubs, vegetables, fruit, bulbs, and seeds), and hay or straw even used as packing. Domestic cats and dogs from outside the United Kingdom and live animals from outside Northern Ireland must be quarantined for six months.

No animals or pets of any kind may be brought into Northern Ireland without a 6-month quarantine. Other items that may not be imported include fresh meats, plants and vegetables, controlled drugs, and firearms and ammunition. ⓕ **Customs and Excise** ✉ Irish Life Building, 2nd floor, Middle Abbey St., Dublin 1 ☎ 01/878-8811 ⊕ www.revenue.ie. **HM Customs and Excise** ✉ Portcullis House, 21 Cowbridge Rd. E, Cardiff CF11 9SS ☎ 0845/010-9000 or 0208/929-0152; 0208/929-6731 or 0208/910-3602 complaints ⊕ www.hmce.gov.uk.

IN AUSTRALIA

Australian residents who are 18 or older may bring home A$400 worth of souvenirs and gifts (including jewelry), 250 cigarettes or 250 grams of cigars or other tobacco products, and 1,125 ml of alcohol (including wine, beer, and spirits). Residents under 18 may bring back A$200 worth of goods. Members of the same family traveling together may pool their allowances. Prohibited items include meat products. Seeds, plants, and fruits need to be declared upon arrival. ⓕ **Australian Customs Service** ⊕ Regional Director, Box 8, Sydney, NSW 2001 ☎ 02/9213-2000 or 1300/363263; 02/9364-7222 or 1800/803-006 quarantine-inquiry line ⊕ www.customs.gov.au.

IN CANADA

Canadian residents who have been out of Canada for at least seven days may bring in C$750 worth of goods duty-free. If you've been away fewer than seven days but more than 48 hours, the duty-free allowance drops to C$200. If your trip lasts 24 to 48 hours, the allowance is C$50. You may not pool allowances with family members. Goods claimed under the C$750 exemption may follow you by mail; those claimed under the lesser exemptions must accompany you. Alcohol and tobacco products may be included in the seven-day and 48-hour exemptions but not in the 24-hour exemption. If you meet the age requirements of the province or territory through which you reenter Canada, you may bring in, duty-free, 1.5 liters of wine or 1.14 liters (40 imperial ounces) of liquor or 24 12-ounce cans or bottles of beer or ale. Also, if you meet the local age requirement for tobacco products, you may bring in, duty-free, 200 cigarettes and 50 cigars. Check ahead of time with the Canada Customs and Revenue Agency or the Department of Agriculture for policies regarding meat products, seeds, plants, and fruits.

You may send an unlimited number of gifts (only one gift per recipient, however) worth up to C$60 each duty-free to Canada. Label the package UNSOLICITED GIFT—VALUE UNDER $60. Alcohol and tobacco are excluded. ⓕ **Canada Customs and Revenue Agency** ✉ 2265 St. Laurent Blvd., Ottawa, Ontario K1G 4K3 ☎ 800/461-9999, 204/983-3500, or 506/636-5064 ⊕ www.ccra.gc.ca.

IN NEW ZEALAND

All homeward-bound residents may bring back NZ$700 worth of souvenirs and gifts; passengers may not pool their allowances, and children can claim only the concession on goods intended for their own use. For those 17 or older, the duty-free allowance also includes 4.5 liters of wine or beer; one 1,125-ml bottle of spirits; and either 200 cigarettes, 250 grams of tobacco, 50 cigars, *or* a combination of the three up to 250 grams. Meat products, seeds, plants, and fruits must be declared upon arrival to the Agricultural Services Department.

New Zealand Customs ✉ Head office: The Customhouse, 17–21 Whitmore St., Box 2218, Wellington ☎ 09/300–5399 or 0800/428–786 ⊕ www.customs.govt.nz.

IN THE U.K.

If you are a U.K. resident and your journey was wholly within the EU, you probably won't have to pass through customs when you return to the United Kingdom. If you plan to bring back large quantities of alcohol or tobacco, check EU limits beforehand. In most cases, if you bring back more than 200 cigars, 3,200 cigarettes, 10 liters of spirits, 110 liters of beer, and/or 90 liters of wine, you have to declare the goods upon return.

HM Customs and Excise ✉ Portcullis House, 21 Cowbridge Rd. E, Cardiff CF11 9SS ☎ 0845/010–9000 or 0208/929–0152; 0208/929–6731 or 0208/910–3602 complaints ⊕ www.hmce.gov.uk.

IN THE U.S.

U.S. residents who have been out of the country for at least 48 hours may bring home, for personal use, $800 worth of foreign goods duty-free, as long as they haven't used the $800 allowance or any part of it in the past 30 days. This exemption may include 1 liter of alcohol (for travelers 21 and older), 200 cigarettes, and 100 non-Cuban cigars. Family members from the same household who are traveling together may pool their $800 personal exemptions. For fewer than 48 hours, the duty-free allowance drops to $200, which may include 50 cigarettes, 10 non-Cuban cigars, and 150 ml of alcohol (or 150 ml of perfume containing alcohol). The $200 allowance cannot be combined with other individuals' exemptions, and if you exceed it, the full value of all the goods will be taxed. Antiques, which the U.S. Bureau of Customs and Border Protection defines as objects more than 100 years old, enter duty-free, as do original works of art done entirely by hand, including paintings, drawings, and sculptures. This doesn't apply to folk art or handicrafts, which are in general dutiable.

You may also send packages home duty-free, with a limit of one parcel per ad-dressee per day (except alcohol or tobacco products or perfume worth more than $5). You can mail up to $200 worth of goods for personal use; label the package PERSONAL USE and attach a list of its contents and their retail value. If the package contains your used personal belongings, mark it AMERICAN GOODS RETURNED to avoid paying duties. You may send up to $100 worth of goods as a gift; mark the package UNSOLICITED GIFT. Mailed items do not affect your duty-free allowance on your return.

To avoid paying duty on foreign-made high-ticket items you already own and will take on your trip, register them with Customs before you leave the country. Consider filing a Certificate of Registration for laptops, cameras, watches, and other digital devices identified with serial numbers or other permanent markings; you can keep the certificate for other trips. Otherwise, bring a sales receipt or insurance form to show that you owned the item before you left the United States.

U.S. Bureau of Customs and Border Protection ✉ for inquiries and equipment registration, 1300 Pennsylvania Ave. NW, Washington, DC 20229 ☎ 877/287–8667 or 202/354–1000 ⊕ www.customs.gov ✉ for complaints, Customer Satisfaction Unit, 1300 Pennsylvania Ave. NW, Room 5.5D, Washington, DC 20229.

DISABILITIES & ACCESSIBILITY

Ireland has only recently begun to provide facilities such as ramps and accessible toilets for people with disabilities. Public transportation also lags behind. Visitors with disabilities will often find, however, that the helpfulness of the Irish makes up for the lack of amenities.

Local Resources Disability Action ✉ 2 Annadale Ave., Belfast ☎ 028/9029–7880 ⊕ www.disabilityaction.org. **Irish Wheelchair Association** ✉ Aras Cuchulainn, Blackheath Dr., Clontarf, Dublin 3 ☎ 01/818–6400 ⊕ www.iwa.ie. **National Disability Resource Center** ✉ 44 N. Great George's St., Dublin ☎ 01/874–7503.

WHERE TO STAY

In Dublin, the Conrad Dublin International has some of the best amenities for people using wheelchairs, including a ramped entrance, access to all floors, and bedrooms with adapted bathrooms. Jurys Christchurch Inn is also fully accessible to people using wheelchairs. Up north, the Belfast Hilton is the best bet.

RESERVATIONS

When discussing accessibility with an operator or reservations agent, **ask hard questions.** Are there any stairs, inside *or* out? Are there grab bars next to the toilet *and* in the shower/tub? How wide is the doorway to the room? To the bathroom? For the most extensive facilities meeting the latest legal specifications, **opt for newer accommodations.** If you reserve through a toll-free number, consider also calling the hotel's local number to confirm the information from the central reservations office. Get confirmation in writing when you can.

TRANSPORTATION

Dublin airport is accessible for people using wheelchairs. Assistance will be needed at other airports. The trains of the suburban rail system in Dublin (DART) have wheelchair access, but not all stations do. The national rail system cars don't permit wheelchairs to move through the aisles, so accommodation is made in the vestibule area of the carriage, which is spacious and air-conditioned, though isolated. Few buses are equipped for wheelchairs, but several taxi companies operate wheelchair-accessible cars. Hand-controlled cars are no longer available for rent in Ireland due to the high cost of insurance.

🖪 Complaints **Aviation Consumer Protection Division** (⇨ Air Travel) for airline-related problems. **Departmental Office of Civil Rights** ⊠ for general inquiries, U.S. Department of Transportation, S-30, 400 7th St. SW, Room 10215, Washington, DC 20590 ☎ 202/366-4648 ⊕ www.dot.gov/ost/docr/index. htm. **Disability Rights Section** ⊠ NYAV, U.S. Department of Justice, Civil Rights Division, 950 Pennsylvania Ave. NW, Washington, DC 20530 ☎ ADA information line 202/514-0301; 800/514-0301; 202/514-0383 TTY; 800/514-0383 TTY ⊕ www.ada.gov. **U.S. Department of Transportation Hotline** ☎ for disability-related air-travel problems, 800/778-4838 or 800/455-9880 TTY.

TRAVEL AGENCIES

In the United States, the Americans with Disabilities Act requires that travel firms serve the needs of all travelers. Some agencies specialize in working with people with disabilities.

🖪 Travelers with Mobility Problems **Access Adventures/B. Roberts Travel** ⊠ 206 Chestnut Ridge Rd., Scottsville, NY 14624 ☎ 585/889-9096 ⊕ www.brobertstravel.com, run by a former physical-rehabilitation counselor. **CareVacations** ⊠ No. 5, 5110-50 Ave., Leduc, Alberta, Canada, T9E 6V4 ☎ 780/986-6404 or 877/478-7827 ⊕ www. carevacations.com, for group tours and cruise vacations. **Flying Wheels Travel** ⊠ 143 W. Bridge St., Box 382, Owatonna, MN 55060 ☎ 507/451-5005 ⊕ www.flyingwheelstravel.com.

DISCOUNTS & DEALS

Be sure to take advantage of the Heritage Service Heritage Card, which gives you access to 65 Heritage sites for €19.05 (the family pass is €45.70). Cards are sold in Ireland at all Heritage Service sites.

Be a smart shopper and **compare all your options** before making decisions. A plane ticket bought with a promotional coupon from travel clubs, coupon books, and direct-mail offers or purchased on the Internet may not be cheaper than the least expensive fare from a discount ticket agency. And always keep in mind that what you get is just as important as what you save.

DISCOUNT RESERVATIONS

To save money, **look into discount reservations services** with Web sites and toll-free numbers, which use their buying power to get a better price on hotels, airline tickets (⇨ Air Travel), even car rentals. When booking a room, always **call the hotel's local toll-free number** (if one is available) rather than the central reservations number—you'll often get a better price. Always ask about special packages or corporate rates.

When shopping for the best deal on hotels and car rentals, **look for guaranteed exchange rates,** which protect you against a falling dollar. With your rate locked in, you won't pay more, even if the price goes up in the local currency.

🖪 Airline Tickets **Air 4 Less** ☎ 800/AIR4LESS; low-fare specialist.

🖪 Hotel Rooms **Accommodations Express** ☎ 800/444-7666 or 800/277-1064 ⊕ www. accommodationsexpress.com. **Hotels.com** ☎ 800/ 246-8357 or 214/369-1246 ⊕ www.hotels.com. **Steigenberger Reservation Service** ☎ 800/223-5652 ⊕ www.srs-worldhotels.com. **Travel Interlink** ☎ 800/888-5898 ⊕ www.travelinterlink. com. **Turbotrip.com** ☎ 800/473-7829 ⊕ www. turbotrip.com.

PACKAGE DEALS

Don't confuse packages and guided tours. When you buy a package, you travel on your own, just as though you had planned the trip yourself. Fly/drive packages, which combine airfare and car rental, are often a good deal. In cities, ask the local visitor's bureau about hotel packages that include tickets to major museum exhibits or other special events. If you **buy a rail/drive pass,** you may save on train tickets and car rentals. All Eurailpass holders get a discount on Eurostar fares through the Channel Tunnel and often receive reduced rates for buses, hotels, ferries, and car rentals.

EATING & DRINKING

It wasn't so long ago that people shared jokes about Ireland's stodgy, overcooked, slightly gray food. But in the last decade there have been changes in all aspects of Irish life, including food and drink. The country is going through a culinary renaissance, and Dublin chefs are leading the charge. They're putting nouvelle spins on Irish favorites. And, spurred on by a wave of new immigration, ethnic eateries of all types have sprung up in most major towns and cities.

The restaurants we list are the cream of the crop in each price category. They're indicated in the text by ✕. Establishments denoted by ✕🖾 stand out equally for their restaurants and their rooms.

CATEGORY	COST*
$$$$	over €29
$$$	€22–€29
$$	€15–€22
$	€8–€15
¢	under €8

In Republic of Ireland: all prices are person for a main course at dinner and are given in euros.

CATEGORY	COST*
$$$$	over £22
$$$	£18–£22
$$	£13–£18
$	£7–£13
¢	under £7

In Northern Ireland: all prices are person for a main course at dinner and are given in pounds sterling.

MEALS & SPECIALTIES

A postmodern renaissance in Irish cuisine has lead to a pursuit for authenticity.

Many of the finer restaurants in Dublin, Cork, and Galway now offer a couple of dishes that are variations on a traditional theme. *Coddle,* a boiled stew of bacon, sausage, and smoked meats, is an old Dublin favorite.

A typical Irish breakfast includes fried eggs, bacon, black and white puddings, sausage, and a pot of tea. Lunch might feature a hearty sandwich; dinners usually include meat and two vegetables. Some of the best food is found at family bed-and-breakfasts and in inexpensive cafés.

Irish smoked salmon—usually served on brown soda bread with plenty of butter—is among the finest in the world, and many a wondrous dish has been created around the humble cockle and mussel, abundant in the clear Atlantic waters. Galway and the west are rapidly becoming famous for their oyster beds.

Of course there's the omnipresent potato, too. The Irish have many words for the humble spud, and they've invented plenty of ways to serve it up. The best of these is "boxty," a traditional pancake of once- and twice-cooked potatoes: it makes the perfect bed for a beef-and-Guinness stew, or the equally hearty lamb casserole.

MEALTIMES

Unless otherwise noted, the restaurants listed in this guide are open daily for lunch and dinner.

Breakfast is served from 7 to 10, lunch runs from 1 to 2:30, and dinners are usually mid-evening occasions.

Pubs are generally open Monday and Tuesday 10:30 AM–11:30 PM and Thursday–Saturday 10:30 AM–12:30 AM. The famous Holy Hour, which required city pubs to close from 2:30 to 3:30, was abolished in 1988, and afternoon opening is now at the discretion of the owner or manager; few bother to close. On Sunday, pubs are open 12:30 PM–12:30 AM or later on certain Sundays. All pubs close on Christmas Day and Good Friday, but hotel bars are open for guests.

Pubs in Northern Ireland are open 11:30 AM–11 PM Monday–Saturday and 12:30 PM–2:30 PM and 7 PM–10 PM on Sunday. Sunday opening is at the owner's or manager's discretion.

PAYING

Traveler's checks and credit cards are widely accepted, although it's cash-only at smaller pubs and takeout restaurants.

RESERVATIONS & DRESS

Reservations are always a good idea; we mention them only when they're essential or not accepted. Book as far ahead as you can, and reconfirm as soon as you arrive. (Large parties should always call ahead to check the reservations policy.) We mention dress only when men are required to wear a jacket or a jacket and tie.

WINE, BEER & SPIRITS

All types of alcoholic beverages are available in Ireland. Beer and wine are sold in shops and supermarkets, and you can get drinks "to go" at some bars, although at inflated prices. Stout (Guinness, Murphy's, Beamish) is the Irish beer; whiskey comes in many brands, the most notable being Bushmills and Jameson, and is smoother and more blended than Scotch.

ELECTRICITY

The current in Ireland is 220 volts, 50 cycles alternating current (AC); wall outlets take plugs with three prongs. To use electric-powered equipment purchased in the U.S. or Canada, **bring a converter and adapter.** If your appliances are dual-voltage, you'll need only an adapter. Don't use 110-volt outlets marked FOR SHAVERS ONLY for high-wattage appliances such as blow-dryers. Most laptops operate equally well on 110 and 220 volts and so require only an adapter.

EMBASSIES & CONSULATES

🔳 Australia ✉ Fitzwilton House, Wilton Terr., Dublin 2 ☎ 01/676-1517.
🔳 Canada ✉ 65 St. Stephen's Green, Dublin 2 ☎ 01/478-1988 ✉ 35 The Hill, Groomsport Co. Down BT19 6JS ☎ 028/9127-2060.
🔳 New Zealand ✉ New Balance House, 118A Lisburn Rd., Glenavy, Co. Antrim BT29 4NY ☎ 028/9264-8098.
🔳 United Kingdom ✉ 29 Merrion Rd., Dublin 4 ☎ 01/205-3700.
🔳 United States ✉ 42 Elgin Rd., Ballsbridge, Dublin 4 ☎ 01/668-7122 ✉ Queen's House, 14 Queen St., Golden Mile, Belfast BT1 6EQ ☎ 028/9032-8239.

EMERGENCIES

The only emergency number you have to know in Ireland is 999. Wherever you are, this number will connect you with local police (the Garda), ambulance, and fire services. All three services are very professional, and you can expect a prompt response to your call. An Garda Síochána, Ireland's national police force (often just referred to as the Garda) has an official Web site with contact information for local stations.
🔳 Ambulance, fire, police ☎ 999 An Garda Síochána ⊕ www.garda.ie.

ETIQUETTE & BEHAVIOR

The Irish are a casual, comfortable lot who aren't too particular about points of etiquette. Handshakes are more common than hugs, although public displays of affection—in moderation—are often seen. Two things to note, though, are the great respect of the younger Irish for their elders and the great respect of all churchgoers for the sermon (hence, no talking during the service).

GAY & LESBIAN TRAVEL

In 1993 the Republic of Ireland began to replace virulently homophobic laws (inherited from British rule and enforced up to the 1970s) with some of the most gay-progressive statutes in the EU. Homosexual acts have been decriminalized, and hate crimes and discrimination in the workplace and public accommodation are now illegal.

This enlightened legal environment, however, doesn't readily translate into the same public lesbian and gay presence you find in U.S. and other European cities. Outside the republic's major cities—Dublin, Cork, and Galway—signs of gay life can be difficult to find, and even in these cities you're likely to find them only in small pockets: a pub here, a café there. If you do encounter any difficulties as a gay traveler, it's likely to be with lodging establishments. Proprietors at even some of the most upscale places may resist letting a room with one bed to same-sex couples; at other establishments, no one may so much as raise an eyebrow. Test the waters in advance: be explicit about what you want when you make your reservation.

🖪 Gay- & Lesbian-Friendly Travel Agencies **Different Roads Travel** ⊠ 8383 Wilshire Blvd., Suite 520, Beverly Hills, CA 90211 ☎ 323/651-5557 or 800/429-8747 (Ext. 14 for both). **Kennedy Travel** ⊠ 130 W. 42nd St., Suite 401, New York, NY 10036 ☎ 212/840-8659 or 800/237-7433 ⊟ 212/730-2269 ⊕ www.kennedytravel.com. **Now, Voyager** ⊠ 4406 18th St., San Francisco, CA 94114 ☎ 415/626-1169 or 800/255-6951 ⊕ www.nowvoyager.com. **Skylink Travel and Tour** ⊠ 1455 N. Dutton Ave., Suite A, Santa Rosa, CA 95401 ☎ 707/546-9888 or 800/225-5759 ⊟ 707/636-0951; serving lesbian travelers.

CORK

Ireland's second-largest city has the country's only lesbian and gay community center and a decade-old gay bar. The Cork Film Festival, held in October, incorporates the Irish Lesbian and Gay Film Festival.

The Lesbian and Gay Line operates Wednesday 7 PM–9 PM and Saturday 3 PM–5 PM; it functions as a lesbian hot line Thursday 8 PM–10 PM. Loafers is Cork's main gay bar. The Other Place, a lesbian and gay community center, houses a bookstore and café and hosts Friday- and Saturday-night dances.

🖪 Cork Contacts **Cork Lesbian Line** ☎ 021/425-4710. **Gay Information Cork** ☎ 021/427-1087. **Loafers** ⊠ 26 Douglas St. ☎ 021/311612. **The Other Place** ⊠ 8 S. Main St. ☎ 021/278470.

DUBLIN

By far, Dublin has more accessible lesbian and gay life than any other city in Ireland. Consult the *Gay Community News,* Ireland's free monthly lesbian and gay newspaper, and *In Dublin* for current information about what's going on in the community. The Gay Switchboard Dublin operates Sunday–Friday 8 PM–10 PM and Saturday 3:30 PM–6 PM. The George is the city's main gay bar, with a mainly male crowd, while Out on the Liffey draws both men and women.

🖪 Dublin Contacts *Gay Community News* (GCN) ☎ 01/671-9076 or 01/671-0939 ⊕ www.gcn.ie. **Gay Switchboard Dublin** ☎ 01/872-1055. **The George** ⊠ 89 S. Great George's St. ☎ 01/478-2983. *In Dublin* ⊠ 3-7 Camden Pl. ☎ 01/478-4322.

GALWAY

A young populace, a progressive university, and a few outstanding theater companies help make Ireland's bohemian left-coast city one of the country's most gay-friendly places. Zulu's Bar is Galway's first specifically gay bar. The Attic has gay nights on Friday and Sunday.

🖪 Galway Contacts **The Attic @ Liquid** ⊠ Salthill ☎ 091/522715. **Galway Gay Helpline** ☎ 091/566134 operates Tuesday and Thursday 8 PM–10 PM. **Galway Lesbian Helpline** ☎ 091/564611 operates Wednesday 8 PM–10 PM. **Zulu's Bar** ⊠ Raven's Terr. ☎ 091/581204.

GUIDEBOOKS

Plan well and you won't be sorry. Guidebooks are excellent tools—and you can take them with you. You may want to check out color-photo-illustrated *Fodor's Exploring Ireland,* which is thorough on culture and history, and *Fodor's Escape to Ireland,* which highlights unique experiences. Pocket-size *Citypack Dublin* includes a foldout map. All are available at on-line retailers and bookstores everywhere.

HEALTH

Ireland is a very safe country for travel, with virtually no risk of health problems from food, drink, or insects. The weather, however, is another story; be sure to dress for the cold and rain or you may find yourself plagued by a constant chill.

HOLIDAYS

Irish national holidays in 2004 are as follows: January 1 (New Year's Day); March 17 (St. Patrick's Day); April 9 (Good Friday); April 12 (Easter Monday); May 3 (May Day); June 7 and August 2 (summer bank holidays); October 25 (autumn bank holiday); and December 25–26 (Christmas and St. Stephen's Day). If you plan to visit at Easter, remember that theaters and cinemas are closed for the last three days of the preceding week.

In Northern Ireland the following are holidays: March 17 (St. Patrick's Day); May 3 (May Day); May 31 (spring bank holiday); July 12 (Battle of the Boyne); and August 30 (summer bank holiday) and December 25–26 (Christmas and Boxing Day).

INSURANCE

The most useful travel-insurance plan is a comprehensive policy that includes coverage for trip cancellation and interruption, default, trip delay, and medical expenses (with a waiver for preexisting conditions).

Without insurance you'll lose all or most of your money if you cancel your trip, regardless of the reason. Default insurance covers you if your tour operator, airline, or cruise line goes out of business. Trip-delay covers expenses that arise because of bad weather or mechanical delays. Study the fine print when comparing policies.

If you're traveling internationally, a key component of travel insurance is coverage for medical bills incurred if you get sick on the road. Such expenses aren't generally covered by Medicare or private policies. U.K. residents can buy a travel-insurance policy valid for most vacations taken during the year in which it's purchased (but check preexisting-condition coverage). British and Australian citizens need extra medical coverage when traveling overseas.

Always **buy travel policies directly from the insurance company**; if you buy them from a cruise line, airline, or tour operator that goes out of business you probably won't be covered for the agency or operator's default, a major risk. Before making any purchase, **review your existing health and home-owner's policies** to find what they cover away from home.

Travel Insurers In the U.S.: **Access America** ✉ 6600 W. Broad St., Richmond, VA 23230 ☎ 800/284-8300 ⊕ www.accessamerica.com. **Travel Guard International** ✉ 1145 Clark St., Stevens Point, WI 54481 ☎ 715/345-0505 or 800/826-1300 ⊕ www.travelguard.com.

In the U.K.: **Association of British Insurers** ✉ 51 Gresham St., London EC2V 7HQ ☎ 020/7600-3333 ⊕ www.abi.org.uk. In Canada: **RBC Insurance** ✉ 6880 Financial Dr., Mississauga, Ontario L5N 7Y5 ☎ 800/565-3129 ⊕ www.rbcinsurance.com. In Australia: **Insurance Council of Australia** ✉ Insurance Enquiries and Complaints, Level 3, 56 Pitt St., Sydney, NSW 2000 ☎ 1300/363683 or 02/9251-4456 ⊕ www.iecltd.com.au. In New Zealand: **Insurance Council of New Zealand** ✉ Level 7, 111-115 Customhouse Quay, Box 474, Wellington ☎ 04/472-5230 ⊕ www.icnz.org.nz.

LANGUAGE

Irish (also known as Gaelic)—a Celtic language related to Scots Gaelic, Breton, and Welsh—is the official national language. Though English is technically the second language of the country, it is, in fact, the everyday tongue of 95% of the population. Nowadays just about all Irish speakers are fluent in English.

Irish-speaking communities are found mainly in sparsely populated rural areas along the western seaboard, on some but not all islands, and in pockets in West Cork and County Waterford. Irish-speaking areas are known as Gaeltacht (pronounced *gale*-taukt). Although most road signs in Ireland are given in both English and Irish, within Gaeltacht areas the signs are often in Irish only. A good touring map will give both Irish and English names to places within the Gaeltacht. You really need only know two Irish words: *fir* (men) and *mná* (women)—useful vocabulary for a trip to a public toilet.

LODGING

You should try to sample from Ireland's vast range of accommodations. In Dublin and other cities, boutique hotels combine luxury with contemporary (and often truly Irish) design. Manors and castles offer a unique combination of luxury and history. Less impressive, but equally charming, are the provincial inns and country hotels with simple but adequate facilities. You'll meet a wide cross section of Irish people by hopping from one B&B to the next, or you can keep to yourself for a week or two in a thatched cottage. ITB-approved guest houses and B&Bs display a green shamrock outside and are usually considered more reputable than those without. Hotels and other accommodations in Northern Ireland are similar to those in the Republic of Ireland.

The ITB has a grading system and publishes a list of "approved" hotels, guest houses, B&Bs, farmhouses, hostels, and campgrounds. For each accommodation, the list gives a maximum charge that can't be exceeded without special authorization. Prices must be displayed in every room; if the hotel oversteps its limit, don't hesitate to complain to the hotel manager and/or the ITB.

The lodgings we list are the cream of the crop in each price category. We always list the facilities that are available, but we don't specify whether they cost extra; when pricing accommodations, always ask what's included and what costs extra. Lodgings are assigned price categories based on the range from their least-expensive standard double room at high season (excluding holidays) to the most expensive. Lodgings marked ✕⊡ are lodgings whose restaurants warrant a special trip.

Assume that hotels operate on the European Plan (EP, with no meals) unless we specify that they use the Breakfast Plan (BP, with a full breakfast), the Continental Plan (CP, with a Continental breakfast), the Full American Plan (FAP, all meals), or the Modified American Plan (MAP, with breakfast and dinner).

CATEGORY	COST*
$$$$	over €230
$$$	€180–€230
$$	€130–€180
$	€80–€130
¢	under €80

Republic of Ireland: All prices are in euros and are for two people in a double room, including VAT and a service charge (often applied in larger hotels).

CATEGORY	COST*
$$$$	over £160
$$$	£115–£160
$$	£80–£115
$	£50–£80
¢	under £50

All prices are in pounds sterling and are for two people in a double room, including VAT and a service charge (often applied in larger hotels).

APARTMENT RENTALS

If you want a home base that's roomy enough for a family and comes with cooking facilities, **consider a furnished rental.** These can save you money, especially if you're traveling with a group. Home-exchange directories sometimes list rentals as well as exchanges.

International Agents At Home Abroad ⊠ 405 E. 56th St., Suite 6H, New York, NY 10022 ☎ 212/421-9165 ⊕ www.athomeabroadinc.com. **Hideaways International** ⊠ 767 Islington St., Portsmouth, NH 03801 ☎ 603/430-4433 or 800/843-4433 ⊕ www.hideaways.com, membership $145. **Hometours International** ⊠ 1108 Scottie La., Knoxville, TN 37919 ☎ 865/690-8484 or 866/367-4668 ⊕ http://thor.he.net/~hometour/. **Interhome** ⊠ 1990 N.E. 163rd St., Suite 110, North Miami Beach, FL 33162 ☎ 305/940-2299 or 800/882-6864 ⊕ www.interhome.us. **Villas and Apartments Abroad** ⊠ 370 Lexington Ave., Suite 1401, New York, NY 10017 ☎ 212/897-5045 or 800/433-3020 🖷 212/897-5039 ⊕ www.ideal-villas.com. **Villas International** ⊠ 4340 Redwood Hwy., Suite D309, San Rafael, CA 94903 ☎ 415/499-9490 or 800/221-2260 ⊕ www.villasintl.com.

B&BS

B&Bs are classified by the ITB as either town homes, country homes, or farmhouses. Many town and country B&Bs now have at least one bedroom with a bathroom, but don't expect this as a matter of course. B&Bs often charge an extra €0.60–€1.30 for a bath or shower. If this is in the family bathroom, you should ask about using it.

The Irish farms that offer rooms by the week with partial or full board are more likely to be modern bungalows or undistinguished two-story houses than creeper-clad Georgian mansions. Room and part board—breakfast and an evening meal—start at €267 per week.

Many travelers don't bother booking a B&B in advance. They are so plentiful in rural areas that it's often more fun to leave the decision open, allowing yourself a choice of final destinations for the night.

Reservations Services Bed & Breakfast Association of Northern Ireland ☎ 28/7082-3823. **Irish Farm Holidays** ⊠ 2 Michael St., Limerick ☎ 61/400700 ⊕ www.irishfarmholidays.com. **Northern Ireland Farm and Country Holidays Association** ⊠ 63 Somerton Rd., Belfast ☎ 28/8284-1325 ⊕ www.nischa.com. **Town & Country Homes Association** ⊠ Belleek Rd., Ballyshannon, Co. Donegal ☎ 71/982-2222 ⊕ www.townandcountry.ie.

CAMPING

An abundance of coastal campsites compensates for the shortage of inland ones. Rates start at about €5 per tent, €8 per caravan (RV) overnight.

COTTAGES

Vacation cottages, which are usually in clusters, are rented by the week. Although often built in the traditional style, they have central heating and all the other modern conveniences. It's essential to reserve in advance.

Reservations Services Irish Cottage Holiday Homes Association ⊠ Bracken Court, Bracken Rd., Sandyford, Dublin 8 ☎ 01/205-2777 ⊕ www.irishcottageholidays.com. **Northern Ireland Self-Catering Holidays Association** ⊠ 63 Somerton Rd., Belfast BT15 4DD ☎ 28/9077-6174 ⊕ www.nischa.com.

GUEST HOUSES, CASTLES & MANORS

To qualify as a guest house, establishments must have at least five bedrooms, though in cities they often have more. Some guest houses are above a bar or restaurant; others are part of a home. As a rule, they're cheaper (some include an optional evening meal) and offer fewer amenities than hotels. But often that's where the differences end. Most have high standards of cleanliness and hospitality. Some even have a bathroom, a TV, and a direct-dial phone in each room.

An organization known as Premier Guesthouses is a good place to begin your search. For information on stays at manor houses and castles, contact Ireland's Blue Book of Country Houses & Restaurants or Hidden Ireland, to organizations whose members include some very distinctive properties.

Reservations Services Hidden Ireland ⌂ Box 31, Westport, Co. Mayo ☎ 98/66650 in Westport; 01/662-7166 in Dublin ⊕ www.hiddenireland.com. **Ireland's Blue Book** ⊠ 8 Mount Street Crescent, Dublin 2 ☎ 01/676-9914 ⊕ www.irelandsbluebook.com. **Premier Guesthouses** ⊠ Bracken Court, Bracken Rd., Sandyford, Dublin 8 ☎ 01/205-2826 ⊕ www.premierguesthouses.com.

HOME EXCHANGES

If you'd like to exchange your home for someone else's, **join a home-exchange organization,** which will send you its updated listings of available exchanges for a year and will include your own listing in at least one of them. It's up to you to make specific arrangements.

Exchange Clubs HomeLink International ⌂ Box 47747, Tampa, FL 33647 ☎ 813/975-9825 or 800/638-3841 ⊕ www.homelink.org; $110 yearly for a listing, on-line access, and catalog; $40 without catalog. **Intervac U.S.** ⊠ 30 Corte San Fernando, Tiburon, CA 94920 ☎ 800/756-4663 ⊕ www.intervacus.com; $105 yearly for a listing, on-line access, and a catalog; $50 without catalog.

HOSTELS

No matter what your age, you can **save on lodging costs by staying at hostels.** Membership in any HI national hostel association, open to travelers of all ages, allows you to stay in HI-affiliated hostels at member rates; one-year membership is about $28 for adults (C$35 for a two-year minimum membership in Canada, £13.50 in the U.K., A$52 in Australia, and NZ$40 in New Zealand); hostels charge about $10–$30 per night. Members have priority if the hostel is full; they're also eligible for discounts around the world, even on rail

and bus travel in some countries. In Dublin, hostels cater mostly to students. Hostels are plentiful outside the capital though often you can find B&B's for a comparable price.

International Organizations Hostelling International–USA ⊠ 8401 Colesville Rd., Suite 600, Silver Spring, MD 20910 ☎ 301/495-1240 ⊟ 301/495-6697 ⊕ www.hiayh.org. **Hostelling International–Canada** ⊠ 205 Catherine St., Suite 400, Ottawa, Ontario K2P 1C3 ☎ 613/237-7884 or 800/663-5777 ⊟ 613/237-7868 ⊕ www.hihostels.ca. **YHA England and Wales** ⊠ Trevelyan House, Dimple Rd., Matlock, Derbyshire DE4 3YH, U.K. ☎ 0870/870-8808, 0870/770-8868, or 0162/959-2700 ⊟ 0870/770-6127 ⊕ www.yha.org.uk. **YHA Australia** ⊠ 422 Kent St., Sydney, NSW 2001 ☎ 02/9261-1111 ⊟ 02/9261-1969 ⊕ www.yha.com.au. **YHA New Zealand** ⊠ Level 4, Torrens House, 195 Hereford St., Box 436, Christchurch ☎ 03/379-9970 or 0800/278-299 ⊟ 03/365-4476 ⊕ www.yha.org.nz.

Irish Organizations Independent Holiday Hostels ⊠ 57 Lower Gardiner St., Northside Dublin 1 ☎ 01/836-4700 ⊕ www.hostels-ireland.com. **Irish Youth Hostel Association (An Óige)** ⊠ 67 Mountjoy St., Dublin 7 ☎ 01/830-4555 ⊕ www.irelandyha.org. **Northern Ireland Hostelling International** ☎ 28/9032-4733 ⊕ www.hini.org.uk.

HOTELS

Standard features in most hotels include private bath, air-conditioning, two twin beds (you can usually ask for a king-size instead), TV (often with VCR), free parking, and no-smoking rooms. There's usually no extra charge for these services. All hotels listed have private bath unless otherwise noted.

Information & Bookings Ireland Hotels Federation ⊠ 13 Northbrook Rd., Dublin 6 ☎ 01/497-6459 ⊕ www.irelandhotels.com. **ITB** ⊕ www.tourismireland.com/info-accomodation. **Northern Ireland Hotels Federation** ⊠ Midland Building, Whitla St., Belfast BT15 1JP ☎ 28/9035-1110 ⊕ www.nihf.co.uk.

Toll-Free Numbers Best Western ☎ 800/528-1234 ⊕ www.bestwestern.com. **Choice** ☎ 800/424-6423 ⊕ www.choicehotels.com. **Clarion** ☎ 800/424-6423 ⊕ www.choicehotels.com. **Comfort Inn** ☎ 800/424-6423 ⊕ www.choicehotels.com. **Four Seasons** ☎ 800/332-3442 ⊕ www.fourseasons.com. **Hilton** ☎ 800/445-8667 ⊕ www.hilton.com. **Holiday Inn** ☎ 800/465-4329 ⊕ www.sixcontinentshotels.com. **Howard Johnson** ☎ 800/446-4656 ⊕ www.hojo.com. **Marriott** ☎ 800/228-9290 ⊕ www.marriott.com. **Le Meridien** ☎ 800/543-4300 ⊕ www.lemeridien-hotels.com. **Quality Inn** ☎ 800/424-6423 ⊕ www.choicehotels.com.

Radisson ☎ 800/333-3333 ⊕ www.radisson.com.
Westin Hotels & Resorts ☎ 800/228-3000
⊕ www.starwood.com/westin.

MAIL & SHIPPING

Letters take a week to 10 days to reach the
United States and Canada, 3 to 5 days to
reach the United Kingdom.

POSTAL RATES

Airmail rates to the United States and
Canada from the Irish Republic are €0.60
for letters and postcards. Mail to all European countries goes by air automatically,
so airmail stickers or envelopes are not required. Rates are €0.40 for letters and
postcards.

Rates from Northern Ireland are 43p for
letters and 37p for postcards (not over 10
grams). To the rest of the United Kingdom
and the Irish Republic, rates are 26p for
first-class letters and 20p for second class.

RECEIVING MAIL

Mail can be held for collection at any post
office free of charge for up to three
months. It should be addressed to the recipient "c/o Poste Restante." In Dublin,
use the General Post Office. The Irish
postal service, known as An Post, has a
Web site with a branch locator and loads
of other postal information.
An Post ⊕ www.anpost.ie. General Post Office
✉ O'Connell St., Dublin 1 ☎ 01/705-8833.

MEDIA

NEWSPAPERS & MAGAZINES

In Ireland, there are three national daily
broadsheet newspapers, the *Irish Times*
and the *Irish Independent*—both Dublin
based—and the *Irish Examiner,* which is
published in Cork. The *Irish Times* is the
most authoritative and esteemed of the
three; the *Irish Independent* is the most
popular; and the *Irish Examiner* is widely
read in the southern counties. The British
Daily Star and the *Sun* also have Irish
editions.

The *Evening Herald* is the only nationwide
evening newspaper. The *Evening Echo* is
published by the Examiner group and sold
in the Cork region. There are five Irish
Sunday newspapers: the very popular and
opinion-focused *Sunday Independent*; the
more intellectual *Sunday Tribune*; the

business-oriented *Sunday Business Post*;
the popular tabloid, *Sunday World*; and
Ireland on Sunday. Regional weekly newspapers are published in almost every
county. In Northern Ireland, the main
dailies are the *Belfast Telegraph* and the
Belfast Newsletter. The British broadsheet
and tabloid dailies and Sunday newspapers
are widely available throughout Ireland.

RADIO & TELEVISION

Radio Telefis Éireann (RTÉ) is Ireland's
national television and radio network.
There are two television channels—RTÉ 1,
which concentrates on news and documentaries, and Network 2, which carries more
feature films and light entertainment
shows. TV3 is a private channel with a lot
of American and British soaps and situa-
tion comedies. TG4 is an Irish-language
channel (with English subtitles). The
British television channels (BBC 1, BBC 2,
UTV, Channel 4) and many satellite channels—including SkyNews, SkyMovies,
SkySports, CNN, MTV, and TV5 Europe—are also widely available.

There are two 24-hour national radio stations in Ireland—Radio 1 (mainly talk
shows) and the popular music-dominated
station, 2FM. FM3 is a classical music station that is broadcast in the early mornings and evenings on the same wavelength
as the daytime Irish-language radio station, Raidio Na Gaeltachta. There are
more than 25 local commercial radio stations whose broadcasting standards vary
from county to county. All the BBC radio
channels are also available.

MONEY MATTERS

A modest hotel in Dublin costs about
€130 a night for two; this figure can be
reduced to under €90 by staying in a reg-
istered guest house or inn, and reduced to
less than €45 by staying in a suburban
B&B. Lunch, consisting of a good one-
dish plate of bar food at a pub, costs
around €8; a sandwich at the same pub,
about €3. In Dublin's better restaurants,
dinner will run around €25–€40 per person, excluding drinks and tip.

Theater and entertainment in most places
are inexpensive—about €18 for a good
seat, and double that for a big-name, pop-
music concert. For the price of a few
drinks and (in Dublin and Killarney) a
small entrance fee of about €2, you can

spend a memorable evening at a *seisun* (pronounced *say-shoon*) in a music pub. Entrance to most public galleries is free, but stately homes and similar attractions charge anywhere from €4 to a whopping €8 per person.

Just about everything is more expensive in Dublin, so add at least 10% to these sample prices: cup of coffee, €1; pint of beer, €3; soda, €1.20; and 2-km (1-mi) taxi ride, €5.10. Travelers from the United Kingdom will find value when visiting Ireland. Due to the exchange rate, Canadians, Australians, New Zealanders, and—to a lesser extent, Americans—will find Ireland a little pricey when they convert costs to their home currency.

Hotels and meals in Northern Ireland are less expensive than in the United Kingdom and the Republic of Ireland. Also, the lower level of taxation makes dutiable goods such as gasoline, alcoholic drinks, and tobacco cheaper.

Prices throughout this guide are given for adults. Substantially reduced fees are almost always available for children, students, and senior citizens. For information on taxes, *see* Taxes.

ATMS

ATMs are found in all major towns. Most major banks are connected to CIRRUS or PLUS systems; there is a four-digit maximum for your PIN.

CREDIT CARDS

Throughout this guide, the following abbreviations are used: AE, American Express; DC, Diners Club; MC, MasterCard; and V, Visa. Note that when using your credit card, **check that the merchant is putting the transaction through in euros or pounds sterling.** If he or she puts it through in the currency of your home country—a transaction called a dynamic currency conversion—the exchange rate might be less favorable and the service charges higher than if you allow the credit card company to do the conversion for you.

Reporting Lost Cards **American Express** ☎ 0353/1205-5111. **Diners Club** ☎ 0353/661-1800. **MasterCard** ☎ 1800/557378. **Visa** ☎ 1800/558002.

CURRENCY

The Irish Republic is a member of the European Monetary Union (EMU). Euro notes come in denominations of €500, €200, €100, €50, €20, €10, and €5. The euro is divided into 100 cents, and coins are available as €2 and €1 and 50, 20, 10, 5, 2, and 1 cents.

The unit of currency in Northern Ireland is the pound sterling (£), divided into 100 pence (p). The bills (called notes) are 50, 20, 10, and 5 pounds. Coins are £2, £1, 50p, 20p, 10p, 5p, 2p, and 1p.

CURRENCY EXCHANGE

At this writing, one euro is equal to US$1.12, CAN$1.55, U.K.77p, AUS$1.71, and NZ$1.92. One pound sterling is equal to €1.42, US$1.59, CAN$2.21, AUS$2.43, and NZ$2.73. Rates fluctuate regularly, though, particularly for the euro, so monitor them closely.

For the most favorable rates, **change money through banks.** Although ATM transaction fees may be higher abroad than at home, ATM rates are excellent because they're based on wholesale rates offered only by major banks. You won't do as well at exchange booths in airports or rail and bus stations, in hotels, in restaurants, or in stores. To avoid lines at airport exchange booths, **get a bit of local currency before you leave home.**

Exchange Services **International Currency Express** ✉ 427 N. Camden Dr., Suite F, Beverly Hills, CA 90210 ☎ 888/278-6628 orders ⊕ www.foreignmoney.com. **Thomas Cook International Money Services** ☎ 800/287-7362 orders and retail locations ⊕ www.us.thomascook.com.

TRAVELER'S CHECKS

Do you need traveler's checks? It depends on where you're headed. If you're going to rural areas and small towns, go with cash; traveler's checks are best used in cities. Lost or stolen checks can usually be replaced within 24 hours. To ensure a speedy refund, buy your own traveler's checks—don't let someone else pay for them: irregularities like this can cause delays. The person who bought the checks should make the call to request a refund.

SPORTS & THE OUTDOORS

BICYCLING

Ireland is a cyclist's paradise. The scenery is phenomenal, the roads are flat—with some gently rising hills—and uncrowded, repair and support services are good, and the distance from one village to the next is rarely more than 16 km (10 mi). Most ferries will transport bikes for free. If there's room, Irish buses and Irish Rail will transport them for a small fee. All that said, foul weather and rough roads in remote areas are all too common, so rain gear and spare parts are musts.

Most bike-rental shops offer 18- to 24-gear mountain bikes with index gears and rear carriers for about €15 per day or €65 per week. A refundable deposit of about €65 is often required. For a fee of €16 or so, you can rent a bike at one location and drop it off at another. Book well in advance between May and September, as demand is high and availability is limited. Raleigh Ireland has dealers all over the country who do repairs and rentals.

If you enjoy bird life and sea vistas, try planning a coastal route, perhaps in the southeast. Between Arklow and Wexford it's predominantly flat with expanses of sandy beaches. The Hook Peninsula between Wexford and Waterford has a network of small quiet roads, many of them leading to tranquil fishing villages. If you travel from Waterford to Dungarvan via Dunmore East and Tramore you'll see a variety of scenery combining cliff-top rides with stretches of beachfront.

In the Midlands, level terrain means a less strenuous ride. The twisting roads are generally in good condition, and there are pleasant picnic spots in the many state-owned forests just off the main roads. Bord Fáilte recommends two long tours: one in the Athlone-Mullingar-Roscommon area and another in the Cavan-Monaghan-Mullingar region. Avoid the major trunk roads that bisect the region.

The scenery is truly spectacular in the southwest around Glengarriff, Killarney, and Dingle. The length of the hills—rather than their steepness—is the challenge here, but without the hills there wouldn't be such great views. A less-strenuous option is the coast of West Cork between Kinsale and Glengarriff. The Beara Peninsula is popular for its varied coastal scenery and relative lack of vehicles. Traffic can be a problem in July and August on the Ring of Kerry, where there's a lack of alternative routes to the one main circuit.

Most airlines accommodate bikes as luggage, provided they're dismantled and boxed; check with individual airlines about packing requirements. Some airlines sell bike boxes, which are often free at bike shops, for about $15 (bike bags can be considerably more expensive). International travelers often can substitute a bike for a piece of checked luggage at no charge; otherwise, the cost is about $100. U.S. and Canadian airlines charge $40–$80 each way.

⚐ Bike Maps Discovery Series ⊠ Ordnance Survey, Phoenix Park, Dublin 8 ☎ 01/820-6439 or 01/820-6443.

⚐ Bike Tours & Rentals Irish Cycling Safaris ⊠ Belfield Bike Shop, Belfield House, University College, Dublin 4 ☎ 01/260-0749 ⊕ www.cyclingsafaris.com. **Raleigh Ireland** ⊠ Raleigh House, Kylemore Rd., Dublin ☎ 01/626-1333.

BOATING

In the west, you can still see Galway hookers—solid, heavy, broad-beamed sailing boats with distinctive, gaff-rigged, brownish-red sails—on the waters of Galway Bay. Enthusiasts maintain a small fleet and hold frequent races in July and August.

Because of the demands of Irish insurance laws, boat charter is still in its infancy in the Republic of Ireland, with only one company in business for bareboat charter. For the same reason, dinghy rentals are not widespread, and you will need to demonstrate your competence. Sailboats, on the other hand, are relatively easy to rent. Wet suits (also rentable) are essential for sailboarding except on the hottest days in July and August. Rental of sailboarding equipment, including wet suits, starts at about €13 an hour. Sailing dinghies, as well as sailboards, can be rented by the hour (from about €8) or by the day (from about €26). Dinghy- and sailboard-rental contacts are listed under the towns that provide them.

The average cost of a six-berth yacht between 28 and 35 feet ranges from €152 per person per week (low season) to €254 (high season). Contact Sail Ireland Charters for bareboat charters. For details of residential dinghy sailing courses contact Glenans Irish Sailing Club. The club offers one- and two-week courses in sailing and board-sailing at its two centers. One is based on an otherwise uninhabited island in Clew Bay near Westport. The other is in Baltimore in West Cork.

In Northern Ireland Ulster Cruising School offers yacht rentals from £285 per person per week (low season) to £345 (high season). Contact Sailing Holidays in Ireland for information on both the republic and Northern Ireland.

🖪 **Glenans Irish Sailing Club** ⊠ 28 Merrion Sq., Dublin 2 ☎ 01/661-1481 ⊕ www.glenans-ireland. com. **Sailing Holidays in Ireland** ⊕ www. sailingireland.com. **Sail Ireland Charters** ⊠ Trident Hotel, Kinsale, Co. Cork ☎ 021/477-2927 ⊕ www. sailireland.com. **Ulster Cruising School** ⊠ Carrickfergus Marina, The Marina 3 Quayside, Carrickfergus, Co. Antrim ☎ 028/9336-6668 ⊕ www. ulstercruising.com.

FISHING

Salmon and sea trout restrictions limit your catch to one of either variety per day between January and May. The best period for sea trout is from June to late September. Permits are necessary for salmon and sea-trout fishing on privately owned waters or club waters. Besides the permit for the use of a certain stretch of water, those who wish to fish for salmon and sea trout by rod and line must also have a state license. In the Irish Republic, these licenses (€31.75 annually, or €12.70 for 21 days) are available in some tackle shops or from the Central Fisheries Board. No license is required for brown trout, rainbow trout, or coarse fish, including pike. Note that you must purchase share certificates if you intend to do coarse fishing or angling for brown trout in County Donegal; the rates are €3.80 for one day, €6.35 for 21 days, or €15.25 for a season. Contact the Northwestern Regional Fisheries Board for more information.

Northern Ireland's system of pricing and administrating fishing licenses and permits can seem anachronistic, unnecessarily complex, and bewildering. No license is needed for sea fishing. To catch freshwater fish, whether coarse or game, you need a rod license from the Fisheries Conservancy Board. You will need a license from the Foyle Fisheries Commission if you are fishing in the Derry area. Depending on the area, you may need a local permit. The good news is that all fishing licenses and Department of Agriculture and Fisheries permits are available from the Northern Irish Tourist Board (NITB) Information Centre. A number of tourist information offices and tackle shops around the province stock fishing licenses and permits.

A license costs approximately £10 for eight days. You must also obtain a permit from the owner of the waters in which you plan to fish. Most of the waters in Northern Ireland are owned by the Department of Agriculture, which charges about £15 for a 15-day permit, £3.50 for a 3-day one. If you plan to fish outside the jurisdiction of the Department of Agriculture, you must obtain a permit from one of the local clubs.

🖪 **Central Fisheries Board** ⊠ Balngowan House, Mobhi Boreen, Glasnevin, Dublin 9 ☎ 01/837-9206 ⊕ www.cfb.ie. **Department of Agriculture** ⊠ Fisheries Division, Dundonald House, Upper Newtownards Rd., Belfast BT4 3SB ☎ 028/9052-4999 ⊕ www.dardni.gov.uk. **Fisheries Conservancy Board** ⊠ FCB, 1 Mahon Rd., Portadown, BT62 3EE ☎ 028/3833-4666 ⊕ www.fcbni.org. **Foyle Fisheries Commission** ⊠ 22 Victoria Rd., Derry BT47 2AB ☎ 028/7134-2100. **Northern Regional Fisheries Board** ⊠ Ballyshannon, Co. Donegal ☎ 072/51435. **Northwestern Regional Fisheries Board** ⊠ Ballina, Co. Mayo ☎ 096/22623. **Southern Regional Fisheries Board** ⊠ Anglesea St., Clonmel, Co. Tipperary ☎ 052/80055. **South Western Regional Fisheries Board** ⊠ 1 Nevilles Terr., Macroom, Co. Cork ☎ 026/41221.

FOOTBALL & HURLING

Soccer (football) has increased in popularity over the last two decades with the dramatic successes of the Republic of Ireland team; most of the major towns and cities have a semiprofessional club in the National League that runs from August to May every year. For a truly Irish sports experience you should try to attend one of two Gaelic games, either football or hurling; the first is played with a soccer-type ball that is kicked out of the hands, and the second with a wooden stick and a hard ball very much like a baseball. The speed and skill on display in both games can be breathtaking. An intercounty championship takes place from May through September.

🖪 **Football Association of Ireland** ⊠ 80 Merrion Sq., Dublin 2 ☎ 01/676-6864 ⊕ www.fai.ie. **Gaelic Athletic Association** ⊠ Croke Park, Dublin 4 ☎ 01/836-3222 ⊕ www.gaa.ie.

GOLF

What makes Irish golf so great—and increasingly popular—is quite simply the natural architecture. The wild, wonderful coastline seems to be made for links golf. Most famous of these, of course, is the celebrated Ballybunion. Fortunately, links courses can be played year-round—an asset in a rainy country like Ireland. Pack plenty of sweaters and rain gear, and make sure you're in good shape: electric cars are only available at the most expensive courses. Golf clubs and bags can be rented almost anywhere. With the exception of the ancient Royal Belfast, all golf clubs in Ireland are happy to have visitors (and charge well for the privilege), and several tour operators have made golf excursions an art, so it's really easy to have the trip of a lifetime.

Golf Information **Golfing Union of Ireland** ⊠ 81 Eglington Rd., Donnybrook, Dublin 1 ☎ 01/269-4111 ⊕ www.gui.ie.

Golf Tour Operators **Absolute Golf & Travel** ☎ 877/545-4653 ⊕ www.absolutely-golf.com. **Atlantic Golf Company** ☎ 800/542-6224 ⊕ www.atlanticgolf.com. **Destination Golf** ⊠ 416 West 13th St., Suite 313, New York, NY 10014 ☎ 800/441-9329 ⊕ www.destinations-golf.com. **Golf International, Inc.** ⊠ 14 E. 38th St., New York, NY 10016 ☎ 212/986-9176 or 800/833-1389 ⊕ www.golfinternational.com. **Irish Links Tours & Travel, Inc.** ⊠ 400 Main St., Suite 202, Stamford, CT 06901 ☎ 203/363-0970 or 800/824-6538 ⊕ www.irish-links.com. **Jerry Quinlan's Celtic Golf** ⊠ 1129 Rte. 9 S, Cape May, NJ 08210 ☎ 609/465-0600 or 800/535-6148 ⊕ www.jqcelticgolf.com. **Owenoak International Golf Travel** ⊠ 40 Richards Ave., Norwalk, CT 06854 ☎ 203/854-9000 or 800/426-4498 ⊕ www.owenoak.com.

HIKING

Hikers from all over the world spend weeks on the almost 30 major and countless minor trails covering the country. As with biking, the relatively flat landscape, stunning scenery, and nearness of towns to each other make hiking a relatively carefree activity. A tent is always a good idea, but you can certainly plan any walk so that you reach civilization every night. Pack for wind and rain, as there will always be some. A good ordinance survey map is also useful.

The ITB provides free information sheets on long-distance paths, set up throughout the country over the last few years with the consent of local landowners. You can also get route information from the Contact Field Officer, Long Distance Walking Routes Committee. Routes are indicated by trail markers and signposts. Most are between 30 and 60 km (18 and 37 mi) in length, with the exception of the Wicklow

Way, the first to be opened and still one of the best. It's a 137-km (85-mi) trail that begins in the Dublin suburbs before winding its way through the Wicklow mountains. Much of the route lies above 1,600 feet and follows rough sheep tracks, forest firebreaks, and old bog roads. Whether you're a novice or veteran hiker, Wicklow's gentle hills are a terrific place to begin an Irish walking vacation. Other popular hiking options include the Kerry Way, which starts and ends in Killarney, and the Donegal Walk across the center of wild rugged County Donegal.

In Northern Ireland, there is the challenge of the 790-km (491-mi) Ulster Way, a footpath that travels through spectacular coastal scenery. You can also try Waymarked Ways Northern Ireland, a network of eight walking routes—six more are being developed. (The 14 walks add up to about 600 km/373 mi.) The Countryside Access and Activity Network for Northern Ireland (CAAN) distributes the brochure free; you can also get it from the Northern Ireland Tourist Board Information Centre. Each route has a specific map guide to accompany it, and is available individually at tourist information centers (50p). The complete set of eight guides are available from CAAN for £5.50. Tougher walks in the hills are outlined in the informative handbook in the Irish Walks series, No. 4, *The North East,* by Richard Rogers, published by Gill & Macmillan, which is available in book and sporting goods stores in Northern Ireland; it gives precise details of 45 hill walks, complete with descriptions of the wildflowers you'll see along the way. For hikes in the Mountains of Mourne, you can obtain maps and details of suggested routes from the Mourne Countryside Centre. Walking Cycling Ireland members organize walking and cycling tours. Cross Country International and Destinations Ireland offer a wide range of walking trips.

CAAN ⊠ House of Sport, Upper Malone Rd., Belfast, Co. Antrim ☎ 028/9038-3848 ⊕ www.countrysiderecreation.com. **Cross Country International** ☎ 800/828-8768 ⊕ www.walkingvacations.com. **Destinations Ireland** ⊠ 416 W. 13th St., Suite 313, New York, NY 10014 ☎ 800/832-1848 ⊕ www.destinations-ireland.com. **Field Officer, Long Distance Walking Routes Committee** ⊠ Irish Sports Council, 21 Fitzwilliam Sq., Dublin 2 ☎ 01/676-3837. **Walking Cycling Ireland** ⊕ www.kerna.ie/wci.

HORSEBACK RIDING

You're never more than a few miles from a riding center, and the variety of riding possibilities is one of Ireland's major attractions. Short gallops or weeklong guided trips are available. Terrains include beaches, mountain tracks, forests, and flat farmland ideal for cantering. Dublin's environs have excellent horseback riding. Stables on the city's outskirts give immediate access to suitable riding areas. In the city itself, Phoenix Park has superb, quiet riding conditions away from the busy main road that bisects the park. About 20 riding stables in the greater Dublin area have horses for hire by the hour or the day, for novices and experienced riders. A few also operate as equestrian centers and give lessons. Prices vary a great deal, but expect to pay around €19 an hour.

If you have any equestrian skills at all, you will probably want to ride some of the fine horses bred in the southeast. Inland, the terrain is mainly arable farmland, although the long, sandy beaches of the coast are regularly used as gallops. Most establishments have riding for about €50 an hour—booking is generally essential—and many stables offer hunting packages to the more experienced rider; rates are available on request.

Sitting on the back of a horse or pony is a great way to travel into places that are out of bounds to motorists. Woodland, beaches, and rough country become accessible on guided rides, some suitable for complete beginners. There are some 35 riding and trekking centers in Northern Ireland, and several of them offer accommodations.

Ask the Association of Irish Riding Establishments for information on recognized establishments that offer full riding vacations—including lodging. You can also contact the New York–based tour operation Destinations Ireland about its equestrian packages in the republic. For details on approved centers in Northern Ireland, contact the British Horse Society.

⛃ **Association of Irish Riding Establishments** ✉ Mespil Hall, Kill, Co. Kildare ☎ 045/877208 ⊕ www.horseireland.com. **British Horse Society** ✉ Stoneleigh Deer Park, Kenilworth, Warwickshire ☎ 08701/202-244 ⊕ www.bhs.org.uk. **Destinations Ireland** ✉ 416 W. 13th St., Suite 313, New York, NY 10014 ☎ 800/832-1848 ⊕ www. destinations-ireland.com.

SURFING

Expect great surfing along the Atlantic shores of counties Donegal and Sligo. Head to Strandhill, Rossnowlagh, and Bundoran on the Sligo and south County Donegal coasts or to Marble Strand and Rosapenna in north County Donegal. These areas have excellent surfing conditions, although even at the height of summer only the most brave will venture in without a wet suit. Take note that in Ireland a surf shop can rent surfing equipment to individuals taking lessons. Establishments recommended by the European Surf Federation and Irish Surfing Association have approved, qualified instructors, and are insured to give surfing instruction.

⛃ **Irish Surfing Association** ✉ Tigh-na-Mara, Rossnowlagh, Co. Donegal ☎ 096/49020.

PACKING

In Ireland you can experience all four seasons in a day. There can be damp chilly stretches even in July and August, the warmest months of the year. Layers are the best way to go. Pack several long- and short-sleeve T-shirts (in winter, some should be thermal or silk shirts), a sweatshirt, a lightweight sweater, a heavyweight sweater, and a hooded, waterproof windbreaker that's large enough to go over several layers if necessary. A portable umbrella is absolutely essential, and the smaller and lighter it is, the better as you'll want it with you every second. And you should bring at least two pairs of walking shoes; footwear can get soaked in minutes and then take hours to dry.

The Irish are generally informal about clothes. In the more expensive hotels and restaurants people dress formally for dinner, and a jacket and tie may be required in bars after 7 PM, but very few places operate a strict dress policy. Younger travelers should note that old or tattered blue jeans and running shoes are forbidden in certain bars and dance clubs.

If you're used to packing things or stowing dirty clothes in plastic shopping or drawstring bags, bring your own. About the only place you'll find them here is in the closets of better hotel rooms (for on-site dry cleaning and laundry). All Irish stores use only paper bags, and these often get soggy as soon as you step outside. Also, although salesclerks are good about wrapping crystal and pottery for travel, you can never be too careful with such items; bring along some bubblewrap of your own.

In your carry-on luggage, **pack an extra pair of eyeglasses or contact lenses and enough of any medication** you take to last a few days longer than the entire trip. You may also ask your doctor to write a spare prescription using the drug's generic name, as brand names may vary from country to country. In luggage to be checked, **never pack prescription drugs, valuables, or undeveloped film.** And don't forget to carry with you the addresses of offices that handle refunds of lost traveler's checks. Check *Fodor's How to Pack* (available at on-line retailers and bookstores everywhere) for more tips.

To avoid customs and security delays, carry medications in their original packaging. Don't pack any sharp objects in your carry-on luggage, including knives of any size or material, scissors, and corkscrews, or anything else that might arouse suspicion.

To avoid having your checked luggage chosen for hand inspection, don't cram bags full. The U.S. Transportation Security Administration suggests packing shoes on top and placing personal items you don't want touched in clear plastic bags.

CHECKING LUGGAGE

You're allowed to carry aboard one bag and one personal article, such as a purse or a laptop computer. Make sure what you carry on fits under your seat or in the overhead bin. Get to the gate early, so you can board as soon as possible, before the overhead bins fill up.

Baggage allowances vary by carrier, destination, and ticket class. On international flights, you're usually allowed to check two bags weighing up to 70 pounds (32 kilograms) each, although a few airlines allow checked bags of up to 88 pounds (40 kilograms) in first class. Some international carriers don't allow more than 66 pounds (30 kilograms) per bag in business class and 44 pounds (20 kilograms) in economy. On domestic flights, the limit is usually 50 to 70 pounds (23 to 32 kilograms) per bag. In general, carry-on bags shouldn't exceed 40 pounds (18 kilograms). Most airlines won't accept bags that weigh more than 100 pounds (45

kilograms) on domestic or international flights. Check baggage restrictions with your carrier before you pack.

Airline liability for baggage is limited to $2,500 per person on flights within the United States. On international flights it amounts to $9.07 per pound or $20 per kilogram for checked baggage (roughly $640 per 70-pound bag), with a maximum of $634.90 per piece, and $400 per passenger for unchecked baggage. You can buy additional coverage at check-in for about $10 per $1,000 of coverage, but it often excludes a rather extensive list of items, shown on your airline ticket.

Before departure, **itemize your bags' contents** and their worth, and label the bags with your name, address, and phone number. (If you use your home address, cover it so potential thieves can't see it readily.) Include a label inside each bag and **pack a copy of your itinerary.** At check-in, **make sure each bag is correctly tagged** with the destination airport's three-letter code. Because some checked bags will be opened for hand inspection, the U.S. Transportation Security Administration recommends that you leave luggage unlocked or use the plastic locks offered at check-in. TSA screeners place an inspection notice inside searched bags, which are re-sealed with a special lock.

If your bag has been searched and contents are missing or damaged, file a claim with the TSA Consumer Response Center as soon as possible. If your bags arrive damaged or fail to arrive at all, file a written report with the airline before leaving the airport.

PASSPORTS & VISAS

When traveling internationally, **carry your passport** even if you don't need one (it's always the best form of ID) and **make two photocopies of the data page** (one for someone at home and another for you, carried separately from your passport). If you lose your passport, promptly call the nearest embassy or consulate and the local police.

U.S. passport applications for children under age 14 require consent from both parents or legal guardians; both parents must appear together to sign the application. If only one parent appears, he or she must submit a written statement from the other parent authorizing passport issuance for the child. A parent with sole authority must present evidence of it when applying; acceptable documentation includes the child's certified birth certificate listing only the applying parent, a court order specifically permitting this parent's travel with the child, or a death certificate for the non-applying parent. Application forms and instructions are available on the Web site of the U.S. State Department's Bureau of Consular Affairs (⊕ www.travel.state.gov).

ENTERING IRELAND

All U.S., Canadian, Australian, and New Zealand citizens, even infants, need a valid passport to enter Ireland for stays of up to 90 days. Citizens of the United Kingdom, when traveling on flights departing from Great Britain, do not need a passport to enter Ireland. Passport requirements for Northern Ireland are the same as for the republic.

PASSPORT OFFICES

The best time to apply for a passport or to renew is in fall and winter. Before any trip, check your passport's expiration date, and, if necessary, renew it as soon as possible.

◪ Australian Citizens **Passports Australia** ☎ 131-232 ⊕ www.passports.gov.au. ◪ Canadian Citizens **Passport Office** ✉ to mail in applications: 200 Promenade du Portage, Hull, Québec J8X 4B7 ☎ 819/994-3500; 800/567-6868; 866/255-7655 TTY ⊕ www.ppt.gc.ca. ◪ New Zealand Citizens **New Zealand Passports Office** ☎ 0800/22-5050 or 04/474-8100 ⊕ www. passports.govt.nz. ◪ U.K. Citizens **U.K. Passport Service** ☎ 0870/ 521-0410 ⊕ www.passport.gov.uk. ◪ U.S. Citizens **National Passport Information Center** ☎ 900/225-5674 or 900/225-7778 TTY (calls are 55¢ per minute for automated service or $1.50 per minute for operator service); 888/362-8668 or 888/498-3648 TTY (calls are $5.50 each) ⊕ www. travel.state.gov.

SAFETY

The theft of car radios, mobile phones, cameras, video recorders, and other items of value from cars is common in Dublin and other major cities and towns. Never leave any valuable items on car seats or in the foot space between the back and front seats or in the glove compartments. In fact, never leave anything whatsoever in sight in your car—even if you're leaving it for only a short time. You should also

think twice about leaving valuables in your car while visiting tourist attractions anywhere in the country.

Don't wear a money belt or a waist pack, both of which peg you as a tourist. Distribute your cash and any valuables (including your credit cards and passport) between a deep front pocket, an inside jacket or vest pocket, and a hidden money pouch. Do not reach for the money pouch once you're in public.

WOMEN IN IRELAND

If you carry a purse, choose one with a zipper and a thick strap that you can drape across your body; adjust the length so that the purse sits in front of you at or above hip level. (Don't wear a money belt or a waist pack.) Store only enough money in the purse to cover casual spending. Distribute the rest of your cash and any valuables between deep front pockets, inside jacket or vest pockets, and a concealed money pouch.

SENIOR-CITIZEN TRAVEL

To qualify for age-related discounts, **mention your senior-citizen status up front** when booking hotel reservations (not when checking out) and before you're seated in restaurants (not when paying the bill). Be sure to have identification on hand. When renting a car, ask about promotional car-rental discounts, which can be cheaper than senior-citizen rates.

◪ Educational Programs **Elderhostel** ✉ 11 Ave. de Lafayette, Boston, MA 02111-1746 ☎ 877/426-8056; 978/323-4141 international callers; 877/426-2167 TTY ⊕ www.elderhostel.org. **Interhostel** ✉ University of New Hampshire, 6 Garrison Ave., Durham, NH 03824 ☎ 603/862-1147 or 800/733-9753 ⊕ www.learn.unh.edu.

SHOPPING

Once a destination rich only in tales of leprechauns and fairies, Ireland has experienced an economic revival that has created a wealth of new shopping opportunities. From the souvenir shop selling the local woolen goods, linens, and crystal to internationally known retailers, the country has something for everyone's taste.

KEY DESTINATIONS

On a weekend, trying to navigate Grafton Street, Dublin's pedestrian shopping promenade, is not unlike being caught in rush-hour traffic. This is the heart of shopping in the country. Upscale department stores filled with designer labels can be found on the main strip, and fine boutiques await discovery just off the beaten path, making Dublin a great shopping destination.

Other major cities, such as Belfast, Cork, and Galway, will also have a wide variety of stores, including a few large department stores. The west is the place for those chunky Aran sweaters and hand-knitted knitwear of all types. Donegal is famous for its tweed, of course, and for crystal you can choose between world-famous Waterford and slightly less expensive Cavan. Northern Ireland, especially Belfast, has a long tradition of producing fine Irish linens.

SMART SOUVENIRS

Top-quality antiques shops are concentrated around Dublin's Francis Street area, but it's still possible to pick up modestly priced pieces of 18th- and 19th-century silver, 19th-century pewter, and antique period furniture elsewhere—try Cork City, Castlecomer, Kilkenny, Galway City, and Limerick.

Irish lead crystal is justifiably world famous. The best known of all, Waterford glass, is on sale all over Ireland in department stores and crafts shops. The demand is so great that substantial export orders can take weeks or even months to fill. Check out the lesser-known crystals—Cork, Dublin, Kinsale, Tipperary, Tyrone, and Galway crystal—and the less formal, uncut glass from Jerpoint and Stoneyford. Locally made Parian china is a thin, fine, and pale product of very high quality and workmanship. Elaborate flower motifs and a basket-weave design are two distinctive features of this china, which has been a specialty of Belleek, on the Donegal-Fermanagh border, for more than 100 years.

Dublin and Cork City are the best spots for antique jewelry, but don't despair if the prices are beyond your resources. Beautiful reproductions of such Celtic treasures as the Tara brooch are on sale for a fraction of the antique price. Other good buys include Claddagh friendship rings (Galway City is a particularly good place to shop for these) and beautiful pieces by modern silversmiths.

Made of plain, undyed wool, Aran sweaters are durable, soft, and often weatherproof and can be astonishingly warm. Not so long ago, these pullovers were worn by every County Donegal fisherman, usually made to a design belonging exclusively to his own family. Today there's a greater variety in patterns, but most of the sweaters still have that unmistakable Aran look.

Aran sweaters were developed by the women of the Aran Isles to provide a working garment that was warm, comfortable, and weatherproof. The religious symbols and folk motifs woven into distinctive patterns once enabled local people to identify one another's families and localities. Even today, no two Arans are alike: if you want to buy a hand-knit, take your time and wait till you find one that really strikes your fancy. Cheaper and less durable Arans are referred to as "hand-loomed," which is another way of saying "machine-made." Other types of sweaters include classic, blue, fisherman's rib sweaters; homespun, hand-dyed hand-knits; picture sweaters; and sophisticated mohair garments.

A pure linen blouse, like an Aran sweater, can last forever. Designs are classic, so they won't become dated. Linen handkerchiefs for men make useful gifts. Damask tablecloths and crocheted-linen place mats make ideal wedding gifts. Most Irish linen is made in Northern Ireland.

The best selection of traditional tweeds is still found in the specialist tweed shops of Counties Galway and Donegal. Weavers can also be found at work in Kerry, Dublin, Wicklow, Cork, and elsewhere in Connemara. Tweeds vary a good deal in type, from rugged-looking garments to clothes with jewel-like colors that have been popularized by Avoca Handweavers.

Irish whiskey has an altogether different taste from Scotch whisky, and a different spelling, too. Well-known brands include Powers, Paddy, Jameson, and Bushmills. There are also two excellent Irish liqueurs: Irish Mist, which contains whiskey and honey, and Bailey's Irish Cream, a concoction of whiskey and cream, sometimes drunk on ice as an aperitif.

Smoked salmon can vary greatly in taste and quality. Make sure it's wild salmon, not farmed; and if the label tells you what sort of wood it was smoked over, opt for oak chips. A cheaper but also delicious alternative is smoked trout. Or go for whole farmhouse cheeses like St. Killian's—a Camembert-like pasteurized cheese. More exotic and more expensive are the handmade farmhouse cheeses, each from an individual herd of cows. Milleens, Durrus, and Gubbeen are all excellent, though strong when ripe. A milder alternative is the Gouda-like Coolea cheese, found in most duty-free shops.

On the Aran Islands, sally rods are woven into attractive baskets (once used for potatoes or turf), and colorful woven belts, known as *críoses,* are hand-plaited from strands of wool. Handwoven woolen or mohair shawls or rugs provide an affordable touch of luxury. Musical instruments, traditionally made furniture, handmade beeswax candles, and dried flower arrangements are among Ireland's many other handicrafts.

STUDENTS IN IRELAND

To save money, **look into deals available through student-oriented travel agencies.** To qualify you'll need a bona fide student ID card. Members of international student groups are also eligible.

IDs & Services STA Travel ✉ 10 Downing St., New York, NY 10014 ☎ 212/627-3111; 800/777-0112 24-hr service center ☎ 212/627-3387 ⊕ www.sta. com. **Travel Cuts** ✉ 187 College St., Toronto, Ontario M5T 1P7, Canada ☎ 800/592-2887 in the U.S.; 416/979-2406; 866/246-9762 in Canada ☎ 416/979-8167 ⊕ www.travelcuts.com.

TAXES

VALUE-ADDED TAX

When leaving the Irish Republic, U.S. and Canadian visitors get a refund of the value-added tax (VAT), which currently accounts for a hefty 20% of the purchase price of many goods and 13.5% of those that fall outside the luxury category. Apart from clothing, most items of interest to visitors, right down to ordinary toilet soap, are rated at 21%. VAT is not refundable, however, on accommodation, car rental, meals, or any other form of personal services received on vacation.

Many crafts outlets and department stores operate a system called Cashback, which enables U.S. and Canadian visitors to collect VAT rebates in the currency of their choice at Dublin or Shannon Airport on departure. Some stores give you the rebate at the register; with others you claim your refund after you've returned home. Refunds forms must be picked up at the time of purchase, and they must be stamped by customs before you leave for home. If a store gives you a refund at the register, you'll also be given papers to have stamped by customs; you'll then put the papers in an envelope (also provided by the store) and mail it before you leave. Most major stores deduct VAT at the time of sale if goods are to be shipped overseas; however, there's a shipping charge.

When leaving Northern Ireland, U.S. and Canadian visitors can also get a refund of the 17.5% VAT by the over-the-counter and the direct-export methods. Most larger stores provide these services upon request and will handle the paperwork. For the over-the-counter method, you must spend more than £75 in one store. Ask the store for Form VAT 407 (you must have identification—passports are best), to be given to customs when you leave the country. The refund will be forwarded to you in about eight weeks (minus a small service charge) either in the form of a sterling check or as a credit to your charge card. The direct-export method, where the goods are shipped directly to your home, is more cumbersome. VAT Form 407/1/93 must be certified by customs, police, or a notary public when you get home and then sent back to the store, which will refund your money.

A refund service can save you some hassle, for a fee. Global Refund is a Europe-wide service with 190,000 affiliated stores and more than 700 refund counters—at every major airport and border crossing. Its refund form is called a Tax Free Check. The service issues refunds in the form of cash, check, or credit-card adjustment, minus a processing fee. If you don't have time to wait at the refund counter, you can mail in the form instead.

V.A.T. Refunds Global Refund ✉ 99 Main St., Suite 307, Nyack, NY 10960 ☎ 800/566-9828 ⊕ www.globalrefund.com.

TELEPHONES

Ireland's telephone system is up to the standards of the United Kingdom and the United States. Direct-dialing is common;

local phone numbers have five to eight digits. You can make international calls from most phones, and some cell phones also work here, depending on the carrier.

Do not make calls from your hotel room unless it's absolutely necessary. Practically all hotels add 200% to 300% to the cost.

AREA & COUNTRY CODES

The country code for Ireland is 353; for Northern Ireland, which is part of the United Kingdom telephone system, 44. The local area code for Northern Ireland is 028. However, when dialing Northern Ireland from the republic you can simply dial 048 without using the U.K. country code. When dialing an Irish number from abroad, drop the initial 0 from the local area code. The country code is 1 for the United States and Canada, 61 for Australia, 64 for New Zealand, and 44 for the United Kingdom.

DIRECTORY & OPERATOR ASSISTANCE

If the operator has to connect your call, it will cost at least one-third more than direct dial.

▶ Directory Information **Republic of Ireland** ☎ 11811 for directory inquiries in the Republic and Northern Ireland; 11818 for U.K. and international numbers; 114 for operator assistance with international calls; 10 for operator assistance for calls in Ireland, Northern Ireland, and the U.K. **Northern Ireland and the U.K.** ☎ 192 for directory inquiries in Northern Ireland and the U.K.; 153 for international directory inquiries, which includes the Republic; 155 for the international operator; 100 for operator assistance for calls in the U.K. and Northern Ireland.

INTERNATIONAL CALLS

The international prefix from Ireland is 00. For calls to Great Britain (except Northern Ireland), dial 0044 before the exchange code, and drop the initial zero of the local code. For the United States and Canada dial 001, for Australia 0061, and for New Zealand 0064.

LOCAL CALLS

To make a local call just dial the number direct. Public phones take either coins (€0.25 for a call) or cards, but not both. At coin phones just pick up the receiver and deposit the money before you dial the number. At card phones pick up the re-

ceiver, wait until the display tells you to insert the card, then dial. In the Republic, €0.25 will buy you a three-minute local call; around €1 is needed for a three-minute long-distance call within the republic. In Northern Ireland, a local call costs 10p.

LONG-DISTANCE CALLS

To make a long-distance call, just dial the area code, then the number. The local code for Northern Ireland is 028, unless you're dialing from the republic, in which case you dial 048 or 4428, followed by the eight-digit number.

LONG-DISTANCE SERVICES

AT&T, MCI, and Sprint access codes make calling long-distance convenient, but you may find the local access number blocked in many hotel rooms. First ask the hotel operator to connect you. If the hotel operator balks, ask for an international operator, or dial the international operator yourself. One way to improve your odds of getting connected to your long-distance carrier is to travel with more than one company's calling card (a hotel may block Sprint, for example, but not MCI). If all else fails, call from a pay phone.

▶ Access Codes **AT&T Direct** ☎ 1800/550000 from the Republic of Ireland; 0500/890011 from Northern Ireland. **MCI WorldPhone** ☎ 1800/551001 from the Republic of Ireland, 0800/890222 from Northern Ireland using BT; 0500/890222 using C&W. **Sprint International Access** ☎ 1800/552001 from the Republic of Ireland; 0800/890877 from Northern Ireland using BT; 0500/890877 using C&W.

PHONE CARDS

"Callcards" are sold in post offices and newsagents. These come in denominations of 10, 20, and 50 units and range in price from about €2.55 for 10 calls to €20.30 for 100 calls.

PUBLIC PHONES

Public pay phones can be found in street booths and in restaurants, hotels, bars, and shops, some of which display a sign saying YOU CAN PHONE FROM HERE. There are at least three models of pay phones; read the instructions or ask for assistance.

TIME

Dublin is 5 hours ahead of New York and 8 hours ahead of Los Angeles and Vancouver. It's 9 hours behind Auckland, and 10 hours behind Sydney and Melbourne.

TIPPING

In some hotels and restaurants a service charge of around 10%—rising to 15% in plush spots—is added to the bill. If in doubt, ask whether service is included. In places where it is included, tipping isn't necessary unless you have received particularly good service. If there's no service charge, add a minimum of 10% to the total.

Tip taxi drivers about 10% of the fare displayed by the meter. Hackney cabs, who make the trip for a prearranged sum, don't expect tips. There are few porters and plenty of baggage trolleys at airports, so tipping is usually not an issue; if you use a porter, €1 is the minimum. Tip hotel porters at least €1 per suitcase. Hairdressers normally expect about 10% of the total spent. You don't tip in pubs, but for waiter service in a bar, a hotel lounge, or a Dublin lounge bar, leave about €1. It's not customary to tip for concierge service.

TOURS & PACKAGES

Because everything is prearranged on a prepackaged tour or independent vacation, you spend less time planning—and often get it all at a good price.

BOOKING WITH AN AGENT

Travel agents are excellent resources. But it's a good idea to collect brochures from several agencies, as some agents' suggestions may be influenced by relationships with tour and package firms that reward them for volume sales. If you have a special interest, **find an agent with expertise in that area**; the American Society of Travel Agents (ASTA; ⇨ Travel Agencies) has a database of specialists worldwide. You can log on to the group's Web site to find an ASTA travel agent in your neighborhood.

Make sure your travel agent knows the accommodations and other services of the place being recommended. Ask about the hotel's location, room size, beds, and whether it has a pool, room service, or programs for children, if you care about these. Has your agent been there or sent others whom you can contact? Do some homework on your own: local tourism boards can provide information about lesser-known and small-niche operators, some of which may sell only direct.

BUYER BEWARE

Each year consumers are stranded or lose their money when tour operators—even large ones with excellent reputations—go out of business. So **check out the operator.** Ask several travel agents about its reputation, and try to **book with a company that has a consumer-protection program.** (Look for information in the company's brochure.) In the United States, members of the National Tour Association and the United States Tour Operators Association are required to set aside funds to cover payments and travel arrangements in the event that the company defaults. It's also a good idea to choose a company that participates in the American Society of Travel Agents' Tour Operator Program; ASTA will act as mediator in any disputes between you and your tour operator.

Remember that the more your package or tour includes, the better you can predict the ultimate cost of your vacation. Make sure you know exactly what is covered, and **beware of hidden costs.** Are taxes, tips, and transfers included? Entertainment and excursions? These can add up.

🔳 Tour-Operator Recommendations **American Society of Travel Agents** (⇨ Travel Agencies). **National Tour Association (NTA)** ✉ 546 E. Main St., Lexington, KY 40508 ☎ 859/226-4444 or 800/682-8886 🖷 859/226-4404 ⊕ www.ntaonline.com. **United States Tour Operators Association (USTOA)** ✉ 275 Madison Ave., Suite 2014, New York, NY 10016 ☎ 212/599-6599 ⊕ www.ustoa.com.

TRAIN TRAVEL

The republic's Irish Rail trains are generally reliable, reasonably priced, and comfortable. You can easily reach all the principal towns from Dublin, though services between provincial cities are roundabout. To get to Cork City from Wexford, for example, you have to go via Limerick Junction. It's often quicker, though perhaps less comfortable, to take a bus. Most mainline trains have one standard class. Round-trip tickets are usually cheapest.

Northern Ireland Railways has three main rail routes, all operating out of Belfast's Central Station. These are north to Derry, via Ballymena and Coleraine; east to Bangor along the shores of Belfast Lough; and south to Dublin and the Irish Republic. Note that Eurailpasses aren't valid in Northern Ireland.

CUTTING COSTS

To save money, **look into rail passes.** But be aware that if you don't plan to cover many miles, you may come out ahead by buying individual tickets.

Ireland (excluding Northern Ireland) is one of 17 countries in which you can **use Eurailpasses,** which provide unlimited first-class rail travel, in all of the participating countries, for the duration of the pass. If you plan to rack up the miles, get a standard pass. These are available for 15 days ($572), 21 days ($740), one month ($918), two months ($1,298), and three months ($1,606). If your plans call for only limited train travel, **look into a Europass,** which costs less money than a Eurailpass. Unlike with Eurailpasses, you get a limited number of travel days, in a limited number of countries, during a specified time period. For example, a two-month pass ($360) allows 5 days of rail travel but costs $200 less than the least expensive Eurailpass; 15 days of travel in two months costs $710. Keep in mind that the Europass is good only in France, Germany, Italy, Spain, and Switzerland, and the number of countries you can visit is further limited by the type of pass you buy. For example, the basic two-month pass allows you to visit only three of the five participating countries.

In addition to standard Eurailpasses, **ask about special rail-pass plans.** Among these are the Eurail Youthpass (for those under age 26), the Eurail Saverpass (which gives a discount for two or more people traveling together), a Eurail Flexipass (which allows a certain number of travel days within a set period), the Euraildrive Pass and the Europass Drive (which combines travel by train and rental car). Whichever pass you choose, you must **purchase your pass before you leave** for Europe.

The Irish Explorer Rail & Bus Pass covers all the state-run and federal railways and bus lines throughout the republic. It does not apply to the north or to transportation within the cities. An 8-day ticket for use on buses *and* trains during a 15-day period is €127. The Emerald Isle Card offers unlimited bus and train travel anywhere in Ireland and Northern Ireland, valid within cities as well. An 8-day pass gives you eight days of travel over a 15-day period; it costs roughly €150. A pass for 15 days of travel over a 30-day period costs about €255. Irish Rail International provides details on both passes.

In Northern Ireland, Rail Runabout tickets, entitling you to seven days' unlimited travel on scheduled rail services April–October, are available from main Northern Ireland Railway stations. They cost £35 for adults, £18 for children under 16 and senior citizens. Interrail tickets are also valid in Northern Ireland. ▣ Information & Passes **CIE Tours International** ☐ 100 Hanover Ave., Box 501, Cedar Knolls, NJ 07927 ☎ 800/243-8687 ⊕ www.cietours.com. **DER Travel Services** ✉ 9501 W. Devon Ave., Rosemont, IL 60018 ☎ 888/337-7350 ⊕ www.dertravel.com. **Rail Europe** ✉ 44 S Broadway, No. 11, White Plains, NY 10601 ☎ 800/438-7245 ⊕ www.raileurope.com ✉ 2087 Dundas E, Suite 105, Mississauga, Ontario L4X 2V7 ☎ 800/361-7245.

▣ Train Information **Irish Rail** (Iarnrod Éireann) ☎ 01/836-6222 ⊕ www.irishrail.ie, the rail division of CIE. **Northern Ireland Railways** ☎ 028/9089-9411 ⊕ www.translink.co.uk.

RESERVATIONS

Many travelers assume that rail passes guarantee them seats on the trains they wish to ride. Not so. You need to **book seats ahead even if you are using a rail pass;** seat reservations are required on some European trains, particularly high-speed trains, and are a good idea on trains that may be crowded—particularly in summer on popular routes. You will also need a reservation if you purchase sleeping accommodations.

TRAVEL AGENCIES

A good travel agent puts your needs first. Look for an agency that has been in business at least five years, emphasizes customer service, and has someone on staff who specializes in your destination. In addition, **make sure the agency belongs to a professional trade organization.** The American Society of Travel Agents (ASTA)—the largest and most influential in the field with more than 20,000 members in some 140 countries—maintains a strict code of ethics and will step in to help mediate any agent–client disputes involving ASTA members if necessary. ASTA (whose motto is "Without a travel agent, you're on your own") also maintains a Web site that includes a directory of agents. (If a travel agency is also acting as your tour operator, *see* Buyer Beware *in* Tours and Packages.)

🚹 Local Agent Referrals **American Society of Travel Agents** (ASTA) ✉ 1101 King St., Suite 200, Alexandria, VA 22314 ☎ 703/739-2782; 800/965-2782 24-hr hot line ⊕ www.astanet.com. **Association of British Travel Agents** ✉ 68-71 Newman St., London W1T 3AH ☎ 020/7637-2444 ⊕ www.abta.com. **Association of Canadian Travel Agencies** ✉ 130 Albert St., Suite 1705, Ottawa, Ontario K1P 5G4 ☎ 613/237-3657 ⊕ www.acta.ca. **Australian Federation of Travel Agents** ✉ Level 3, 309 Pitt St., Sydney, NSW 2000 ☎ 02/9264-3299 ⊕ www.afta.com.au. **Travel Agents' Association of New Zealand** ✉ Level 5, Tourism and Travel House, 79 Boulcott St., Box 1888, Wellington 6001 ☎ 04/499-0104 ⊕ www.taanz.org.nz.

VISITOR INFORMATION

Learn more about foreign destinations by checking government-issued travel advisories and country information. For a broader picture, consider information from more than one country. For information on travel in the Irish Republic, contact the **Irish Tourist Board** (ITB or Bord Fáilte; ⊕ www.ireland.travel.ie or www.tourismireland.com), known as Bord Fáilte (pronounced board *fal*-cha). Information on travel in the north is available from the **Northern Ireland Tourist Board** (NITB; ⊕ www.discovernorthernireland.com).

🚹 ITB **Ireland** ✉ Baggot St. Bridge, Dublin 2 ☎ 01/602-4000, 669/792083, or 1850/230330 [within Ireland]. **U.K.** ✉ Ireland House, 150 New Bond St., London W1Y 0AQ ☎ 020/7493-3201. **U.S.** ✉ 345 Park Ave., New York, NY 10154 ☎ 212/418-0800 or 800/223-6470 ⊕ www.shamrock.org.
🚹 NITB **Northern Ireland** ✉ 59 North St., Belfast BT1 1NB ☎ 028/9023-1221. **Canada** ✉ 2 Bloor St. W, Suite 1501, Toronto, Ontario M4W 3E2 ☎ 416/925-6368. **U.K.** ✉ 24 Haymarket, London SW1 4DG ☎ 020/7766-9920; 08701/555-250 info line. **U.S.** ✉ 551 5th Ave., Suite 701, New York, NY 10176 ☎ 212/922-0101 or 800/326-0036.
🚹 Government Advisories **U.S. Department of State** ✉ Overseas Citizens Services Office, Room 4811, 2201 C St. NW, Washington, DC 20520 ☎ 202/647-5225 interactive hot line; 888/407-4747 ⊕ www.travel.state.gov; enclose a cover letter with your request and a business-size SASE. **Consular Affairs Bureau of Canada** ☎ 800/267-6788 or 613/944-6788 ⊕ www.voyage.gc.ca. **U.K. Foreign and Commonwealth Office** ✉ Travel Advice Unit, Consular Division, Old Admiralty Building, London SW1A 2PA ☎ 020/7008-0232 or 020/7008-0233 ⊕ www.fco.gov.uk/travel. **Australian Department of Foreign Affairs and Trade** ☎ 02/6261-1299 Consular Travel Advice Faxback Service ⊕ www.dfat.gov.au. **New Zealand Ministry of Foreign Affairs and Trade** ☎ 04/439-8000 ⊕ www.mft.govt.nz.

WEB SITES

Do check out the World Wide Web when planning your trip. You'll find everything from weather forecasts to virtual tours of famous cities. Be sure to **visit Fodors.com** (⊕ www.fodors.com), a complete travel-planning site. You can research prices and book plane tickets, hotel rooms, rental cars, vacation packages, and more. In addition, you can post your pressing questions in the Travel Talk section. Other planning tools include a currency converter and weather reports, and there are loads of links to travel resources.

For lots of entertaining bits—Irish and otherwise—visit ⊕ www.irishabroad.com. Its sister site, www.irishsights.com, has links to Irish sites of all types. Some of the most popular sites are the Doras Directory (www.doras.ie) and Heritage Ireland (www.heritageireland.ie). In addition, many of the leading newspapers of Ireland (⇨ Media) have their own Web sites, which can be gold mines of timely information.

Officially designated Heritage Towns are featured on www.heritagetowns.com. For information on arts events of all kinds, try www.art.ie, which is affiliated with and has links to the arts councils of both the Irish Republic and Northern Ireland. For more information on counties in the west of Ireland, try www.trueireland.com. Portion's of the Bord Fáilte's eloquent magazine, *Ireland of the Welcomes*, are available on-line (www.irelandofthewelcomes.com).

DUBLIN

1

FODOR'S CHOICE

Ariel Guest House, *Ballsbridge*

Busyfeet & Coco Café, *Southside*

Chester Beatty Library, *Dublin West*

Georgian Squares on a Sunday, *Southside*

Grogans, *Southside pub*

Halo, *Northside restaurant*

Hotel Saint George, *Northside*

Jaipur, *Southside restaurant*

La Stampa, *Southside hotel*

Merrion, *Southside hotel*

National Gallery of Ireland, *Southside*

Patrick Guilbaud, *Southside restaurant*

St. Patrick's Cathedral, *Dublin West*

Stag's Head, *Southside pub*

Trinity College, *Southside*

HIGHLY RECOMMENDED

Christ Church Cathedral, *Dublin West*

Dublin City Gallery, The Hugh Lane, *Northside*

Dublin Writers Museum, *Northside*

Guinness Brewery and Storehouse, *Dublin West*

Malahide Castle, *North County Dublin*

National Museum, *Southside*

Olympia Theatre, *Temple Bar*

Royal Hospital Kilmainham, *Dublin West*

Many other great hotels and restaurants enliven this area. For other favorites, look for the black stars as you read this chapter.

By Anto
Howard

IN HIS INIMITABLE, irresistible way, James Joyce immortalized Dublin in his *Ulysses, Dubliners,* and *A Portrait of the Artist as a Young Man,* filling his works with the people he knew, with their own words, and with not a few of his own. As it turns out, he became one of Dublin's most famous exiles. Disappointed with the city's provincial outlook and small-town manners, he departed in 1902, at the age of 20 (his famed peers Sean O'Casey and Samuel Beckett soon followed). If, however, Joyce were to return to his genteel hometown today and take an extended, quasi-Homeric odyssey through the city (as he does so famously in *Ulysses*), would he even recognize Dublin as his "Dear Dirty Dumpling, foostherfather of fingalls and dotthergills"?

What would he make of Temple Bar—the city's erstwhile down-at-the-heels neighborhood now crammed with restaurants and stylish hotels in its reborn state as Dublin's "Left Bank"? Or the old market area of Smithfield, whose makeover has seen it "Cinderelled" into an impressive plaza and summer venue for big-name concerts? Or of the new Irishness, where every aspect of Celtic culture is red-hot: from Martin McDonagh's Broadway hit *The Beauty Queen of Leenane,* to *Riverdance,* the old Irish mass-jig gone global? Plus, the returned Joyce would be stirred by the songs of U2, fired up by the films of Neil Jordan, and moved by the poems of Nobel laureate Seamus Heaney. In short, Irish is in. As for Ireland's capital, elegant shops and hotels, galleries, art-house cinemas, coffeehouses, and a stunning variety of restaurants are springing up on almost every street in Dublin, transforming the genteel city that once suffocated Joyce into a place almost as cosmopolitan as the Paris to which he fled.

Forget the Vikings and the English. Fast-forward to the new Dublin, where the army of invaders landing at the intersection of O'Connell Street and Temple Lane are London lads on a wild bachelor night, Europeans in search of a chic weekend getaway, African and Asian immigrants seeking employment, and representatives from the United States of the "FBI"—or foreign-born Irish. Thanks to "the Celtic Tiger"—the nickname given to the roaring Irish economy—this most intimate capital city in Western Europe has become a boomtown.

Dublin's popularity has provoked a goodly number of its citizens to protest that the rapid transformation of their heretofore tranquil city has changed its spirit and character. With the recent slowdown in the Irish economic miracle, these skeptics await the outcome of "Dublin: The Sequel"—can the "new Dublin" get beyond the rage stage and recover its rate of phenomenal growth or will it, like London, have to suffer recession and crisis to rediscover its soul?

Happily, enough of the old Dublin remains to enchant. After all, it's the fundamentals—the Georgian elegance of Merrion Square, the Norman drama of Christ Church Cathedral, a foamy pint at an atmospheric pub—that still gratify. Fittingly, some of the more recent developments hark back to the earliest. Two multimedia shows in the downtown area testify that Norsemen were responsible for the city's original boom (various neighborhood names, such as Howth, Leixlip, and Dalkey, echo their historic presence). In ancient days, more than 1,500 years ago, Dublin had been little more than a crossroads—albeit a critical one—of four of the main thoroughfares that traversed the country. Then, it had two names: Baile Atha Cliath, meaning City of the Hurdles, which was bestowed by Celtic traders in the 2nd century AD and which you can still see on buses and billboards throughout the city; and Dubhlinn, or "dark pool," named for a body of water (the murkiness of the water was caused by peat) believed to have been where Dublin Castle now stands.

It will take you about a week to cover almost all of the Dublin Exploring suggestions listed in this chapter, including the side trips. But in three or even two days, you can see many city-center sights and probably come away with a greater familiarity of the city than you could establish in a similar length of time in any of Europe's other capitals.

If you have 1 day

Touring the largest city in Ireland in the space of a day sounds like an impossible goal, but if you're determined you can do it in the span of a single sunrise-to-sunset day. Think Dublin 101. South of the Liffey are graceful squares and fashionable terraces from Dublin's elegant Georgian heyday; interspersed with some of the city's leading sights, this area is perfect for an introductory tour of the city. You might begin at O'Connell Bridge—as Dublin has no central focal point, most natives have, traditionally, regarded it as the city's Piccadilly Circus or Times Square. Then head south down Westmoreland Street on your way to view one of Dublin's most spectacular buildings, James Gandon's 18th-century Parliament House, now the Bank of Ireland building. To fuel up for the walk ahead, first stop at Bewley's Oriental Café at 12 Westmoreland Street, an institution that has been supplying Dubliners with coffee and buns since 1842. After you drink in the grand colonnade of the Bank of Ireland building, cross the road to the genteel elegant campus of Trinity College—the oldest seat of Irish learning. Your first stop should be the Old Library, to see the staggering Long Room and Ireland's greatest art treasure, the *Book of Kells*, one of the world's most famous—and most beautiful—illuminated manuscripts.

Leave the campus and take a stroll along Grafton Street, Dublin's ritziest shopping street and—"Who will buy my beautiful roses?"—open-air flower market. Appropriately enough, one of the city's favorite relaxation spots, the lovely little park of St. Stephen's Green, is nearby. Head over to the northeast corner of the park to find ground zero for the city's cultural institutions. Here, surrounding the four points of Leinster House (built by the earl of Kildare, Ireland's first patron of Palladianism), are the National Museum, replete with artifacts and exhibits dating from prehistoric times; the National Gallery of Ireland (don't miss the Irish collection and the Caravaggio *Taking of Christ*); the National Library; and the Natural History Museum. Depending on your interests, pick one to explore, and then make a quick detour westward to Merrion Square—among Dublin's most famous Georgian landmarks.

For a lovely lunch, head back to St. Stephen's Green and the Victorian Le Méridien Shelbourne—the lobby salons glow with Waterford chandeliers and blazing fireplaces. From St. Stephen's Green walk west for 10 minutes to pay your respects to St. Paddy—St. Patrick's Cathedral. If, instead, the Dublin of artists and poets is more your speed, hop a double-decker bus and head north of the Liffey to the Dublin Writers Museum. End the day with a performance at the nearby Gate Theatre, another Georgian eye-knocker, or spend the evening exploring the cobbled streets, many cafés, and shops of Dublin's bohemian quarter, the compact Temple Bar area, back on the south bank of the Liffey. Because you couldn't fit in a stop at the Guinness

Brewery and Storehouse, top the evening off with a pint at the Stag's Head pub just across Dame Street.

If you have
3 days The above tour is the grand curtain-raiser for this itinerary. Dedicate your second day to the areas north and west of the city center. In the morning, cross the Liffey via O'Connell Bridge and walk up O'Connell Street, the city's widest thoroughfare, stopping to visit the General Post Office—the besieged headquarters of the 1916 rebels—on your way to the Dublin Writers Museum (if you didn't have a chance to visit on your first day) and the Dublin City Gallery, The Hugh Lane. Be sure to join the thousands of Dubliners strolling down Henry, Moore, and Mary streets, the Northside's pedestrian shopping area. In the afternoon, head back to the Liffey for a quayside walk by Dublin's most imposing structure, the Custom House; then head west to the Guinness Brewery and Storehouse. Hop a bus or catch a cab back into the city for a blow-out dinner at the glamorous Tea Room in Temple Bar's Clarence hotel. Spend the evening on a literary pub crawl to see where the likes of Beckett and Behan held court, perhaps joining a special guided tour. On the third day tour the northern outskirts of Dublin from Glasnevin Cemetery and the National Botanic Gardens across to the sublime Marino Casino in Marino and the quaint fishing village of Howth. Back in the city, have tea at Bewley's and catch a musical performance at the Olympia Theatre or a play at the Abbey Theatre.

If you have
5 days Follow the two itineraries above and then head west to start your fourth day at Dublin's dawn—a living history of Dublin can be seen at medieval Dublinia, across the street from ancient Christ Church Cathedral, whose underground crypt is Dublin's oldest structure. Head north, jumping across the Liffey to the Four Courts, James Gandon's Georgian masterpiece and the home of the Irish judiciary. Recross the river to the Southside and go west again to visit the Royal Hospital Kilmainham—which houses the Irish Museum of Modern Art—and Kilmainham Gaol, where the leaders of the Easter Uprising were executed following their capture. Return via Dublin Castle, residence of British power in Ireland for nearly 800 years, and now the home of the Chester Beatty Library, containing Chinese and Turkish exhibits. On your fifth and final day explore the southern outskirts of the city, accessible by DART train, including the suburban areas of Dalkey and Sandycove (where you can visit the James Joyce Martello Tower), and the busy ferry port of Dun Laoghaire. Before returning to the city center, take a stroll along the 5-km (3-mi) beach of Sandymount Strand—that is, if Irish skies are smiling.

In 837, Norsemen from Scandinavia carried out the first invasion of Dublin, only to be followed by other waves of warriors staking their claim to the city—from the 12th-century Anglo-Normans to Oliver Cromwell in 1651. Not until the 18th century did Dublin reach a period of glory, when a golden age of enlightened patronage by wealthy nobles turned the city into one of Europe's most prepossessing capitals. Streets and squares, such as Merrion and Fitzwilliam squares, were constructed with neoclassic dignity and Palladian grace. If Dublin today is still redolent in parts of the elegance of the 18th century, it is due to the eminently refined Georgian style of art and architecture, which flowered in the city between 1714 and 1820 during the English reigns of the three Georges. To satisfy the taste for luxury of the often-titled, unusually wealthy members of society, lemon-color chintz borders, gilded Derbyshire pier tables, and Adamesque wood paneling were installed in the salons of town houses. The arts also flourished: Handel, the German-born English composer, wrote much of his great oratorio *Messiah* here, where it was first performed in 1742. But the aura of "the glorious eighteenth" was short-lived; in 1800, the Act of Union brought Ireland and Britain together in a common United Kingdom, and political power moved from Dublin to London. Dublin quickly lost its cultural and social sparkle as many members of the nobility moved to the new power center, turning Ireland practically overnight into "the Cinderella of all nations," in historian Maurice Craig's words.

The 19th century proved to be a time of political turmoil and agitation, although Daniel O'Connell, the first Catholic lord mayor of Dublin (his statue dominates O'Connell Street), won early success with the introduction of Catholic Emancipation in 1829. During the late 1840s, Dublin escaped the worst effects of the famine, caused by potato blight, that ravaged much of southern and western Ireland. As an emerging Victorian middle class introduced an element of genteel snobbery to the city, Dublin began a rapid outward expansion to the enclaves of Ballsbridge, Rathgar, and Rathmines on the Southside, and Clontarf and Drumcondra on the Northside.

The city entered a period of cultural ferment in the first decade of the 20th century—an era that had its political apotheosis in the Easter Uprising of 1916. A war aimed at winning independence from Britain began in County Tipperary in 1919 and lasted for three years. During the Civil War, which followed the establishment of the Irish Free State in December 1921, two architectural gems, the Four Courts and the Custom House, came under fire and were severely damaged. The capital had to be rebuilt during the 1920s. After the Civil War ended, Dublin entered a new era of political and cultural conservatism, which continued until the late 1970s. Amazingly, the major turning point in Dublin's fortunes occurred in 1972, when Ireland, emerging from 40 years of isolationism, joined the European Economic Community (EEC). In the 1980s, while the economy remained in the grasp of recession, Dublin and Ireland once again turned to the cultural sphere to announce themselves to the rest of the world. Irish musicians stormed the American and British barricades of rock and roll. Bob Geldof and the Boomtown Rats ("I Don't Like Mondays") and Chris de Burgh were among the most prominent of the musicians who found audiences well beyond their native shores, but it was U2 that climbed to the topmost heights of rock-and-roll stardom, forging a permanent place in international popular culture for Irish musicians. Sinéad O'Connor, the Cranberries, and the Corrs have since followed, and more are on the fast track.

If the 1980s saw the ascent of Irish rock stars, the 1990s and the first years of the 21st century were truly the boom years—a decade of broadly improved economic fortunes, major capital investment, declining unemployment, and reversing patterns of immigration—all set in motion to a great extent by Ireland's participation in the EEC (now the European Union, or EU). When Ireland overwhelmingly approved the new EU treaty in 1992, it was one of the poorest European nations; it qualified for EU grants of all kinds. Since then, money has, quite simply, *poured* into Ireland—nowhere more so than in Dublin. The International Financial Services Centre, gleaming behind the two-centuries-old Custom House, is one of the most overt signs of the success the city has had in attracting leading multinational corporations, particularly those in telecommunications, software, and service industries. In 2000 the government announced that Ireland was the world's biggest exporter of software. In the spring of 1998, the Irish overwhelmingly voted in favor of membership in the single European currency; since January 2002, Ireland's main currency has been the euro, and the pound has been withdrawn from circulation. The recent downturn in the global economy has slowed the Celtic Tiger to a crawling pace, and economists argue over the future prospects for a country so dependent on exports.

Today, roughly half of the Irish Republic's population of 3.6 million people lives in Dublin and its suburbs. This is a city of young people—astonishingly so. Students from all over Ireland attend Trinity College and the city's dozen other universities and colleges. On weekends, their counterparts from Paris, London, and Rome fly in, swelling the city's youthful contingent, crowding its pubs and clubs to overflowing. After graduating, more and more young people are sticking around rather than emigrating to New York or London, filling new jobs set up by multinational corporations and contributing to the hubbub that's evident everywhere.

All this development has not been without growing pains; with London-like house prices, increased crime, and major traffic problems, Dubliners are at last suffering the woes so familiar to city dwellers around the world. An influx of immigrants has caused resentment among some of the otherwise famously hospitable Irish. "Me darlin' Dublin's dead and gone" goes the old traditional ballad, but the rebirth, at times difficult and a little messy, has been a spectacular success.

EXPLORING DUBLIN

In Dublin's fair city—"where the girls are so pretty" went the centuries-old ditty. Today, parts of the city—particularly the vast, uniform housing projects of the northern suburbs—may not be fair or pretty. But even if you're not conscious of it while you're in the city center, Dublin is in a beautiful setting: it loops around the edge of Dublin Bay and on a plain at the edge of the gorgeous, green Dublin and Wicklow mountains, rising softly just to the south. From the famous Four Courts building in the heart of town, the sight of the city, the bay, and the mountains may take your breath away.

From north to south, Dublin stretches 16 km (10 mi). From its center, immediately adjacent to the port area and the River Liffey, the city spreads westward for an additional 10 km (6 mi); in total, it covers 28,000 acres. But its heart is far more compact than these numbers indicate. As in Paris, London, Florence, and so many other cities throughout the world, a river runs right through Dublin. The River Liffey divides the capital into the "Northside" and the "Southside," as everyone calls the two principal center-city areas, and almost all the major sights in the area are well within less than an hour's walk of one another.

Coverage is organized into eight sections exploring the main neighborhoods of Dublin city, plus two excursions into County Dublin—the first to the southern suburbs, the latter to the northern. The first section—North of the Liffey—covers numerous major cultural sights, including the James Joyce Centre, Gate Theatre, Dublin Writers Museum, and Dublin City Gallery, The Hugh Lane. The next two sections—City Center and Dublin's Georgian Heart—focus on many of the Southside's major sights: Trinity College, St. Stephen's Green, Merrion Square, and Grafton Street. The fourth section—Temple Bar—takes you through this revived neighborhood, which is still the hottest, hippest zone in the capital. The Grand Canal and Ballsbridge, the fifth section, covers noteworthy sights along the canal, beginning in the northeast part of the city and ending in the southwest. It also covers the genteel suburb of Ballsbridge. The next section—Dublin West—picks up across Dame Street from Temple Bar and continues west to the Guinness Brewery and Storehouse, the city's most popular attraction. It also includes the rapidly developing Smithfield district, which locals are already hailing as the future "Temple Bar of the Northside." The seventh section—The Liberties—takes you on a brief stroll through working-class Dublin, a historic but often overlooked part of the city. Finally, the Phoenix Park and Environs section covers the most western fringe of the Northside and the great public park itself.

If you're visiting Dublin for more than two or three days, you'll probably want to explore farther afield. There's plenty to see and do a short distance from the city center—in the suburbs of both north and south County Dublin. These destinations are covered in the Side Trips section.

Because of its compact size and traffic congestion (brought on in the last few years by an astronomical increase in the number of vehicles), *pedestrian* traffic—especially on the city center's busiest streets during rush hour—is astonishing. Watch where you stop to consult your map or you're liable to be swept away by the ceaseless flow of the bustling crowds.

North of the Liffey

If you stand on O'Connell Bridge or the pedestrian-only Ha'penny span, you'll get excellent views up and down the River Liffey, in Gaelic known as the *abha na life,* which James Joyce transcribed phonetically as Anna Livia in *Finnegan's Wake.* Here, framed with embankments just like those along Paris's Seine, the river nears the end of its 128-km (80-mi) journey from the Wicklow Mountains into the Irish Sea. And near the bridges, you begin a pilgrimage into James Joyce country—north of the Liffey, in the center of town—and the captivating sights of Dublin's Northside, a mix of densely thronged shopping streets and refurbished genteel homes.

The Northside *absolutely* warrants a walk, for three reasons: major cultural institutions (the Gate Theatre, the James Joyce Centre, the Dublin Writers Museum, and the Dublin City Gallery, The Hugh Lane), sights of historical significance with ties to Irish Republicanism, and vibrant busy streets.

During the 18th century, most of the upper echelons of Dublin society lived in the Georgian houses in the Northside—around Mountjoy Square—and shopped along Capel Street, which was lined with stores selling fine furniture and silver. But Southside development—Merrion Square in 1764, the Georgian Leinster House in 1745, and Fitzwilliam Square in 1825—permanently changed the Northside's fortunes. The city's fashionable social center crossed the Liffey, and although some of the Northside's illustrious inhabitants stuck it out, this area gradually became more run-down. The Northside's fortunes have changed, however. Once-derelict swaths of houses, especially on and near the Liffey, have been rehabilitated, and large shopping centers have opened on Mary and Jervis streets. A huge shopping mall and entertainment complex is planned for O'Connell Street, right where the defunct Cartlon Cinema stands. Most impressive of all is the Spire, O'Connell Street's new 395-foot-high stainless-steel monument. Precisely because the exciting redevelopment that transformed Temple Bar is still in its early stages here—*because* it's a place on the cusp of transition—the Northside is an intriguing part of town.

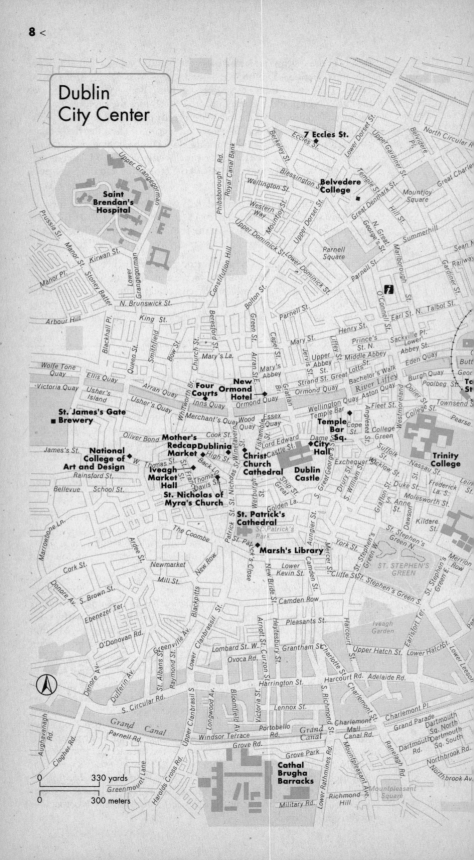

Dublin City Center

7 Eccles St.

Belvedere College

Saint Brendan's Hospital

St. James's Gate Brewery

National College of Art and Design

Mother's Redcap Market

Iveagh Market Hall

St. Nicholas of Myra's Church

Four Courts

New Ormond Hotel

Dublinia

Christ Church Cathedral

Dublin Castle

Temple Bar Sq.

City Hall

Trinity College

St. Patrick's Cathedral

Marsh's Library

St. Patrick's Park

ST. STEPHEN'S GREEN

Iveagh Garden

Cathal Brugha Barracks

0   330 yards

0   300 meters

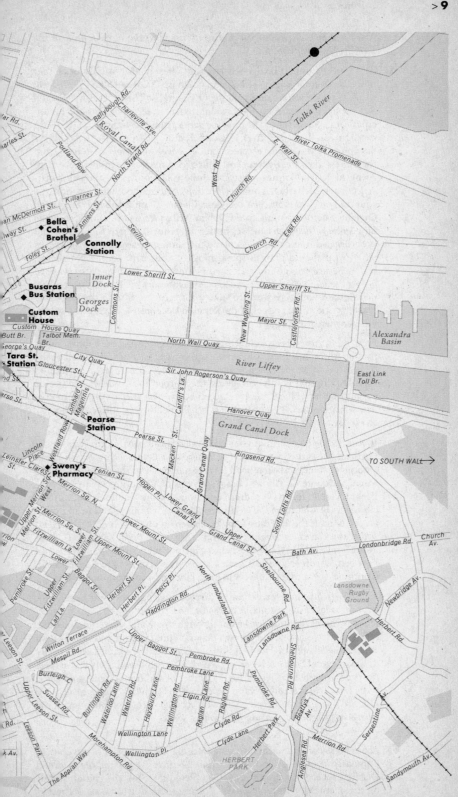

Numbers in the text correspond to numbers in the margin and on the Dublin Northside map.

a good
walk

Begin at O'Connell Bridge—if you look closely at it you'll notice that it is wider than it is long—and head north up **O'Connell Street** ❶ ▶. Stop to admire the monument to Daniel O'Connell, "The Liberator," erected as a tribute to the great orator's achievement in securing Catholic Emancipation in 1829 (note the obvious scars from the fighting of 1916 on the figures). Towering over O'Connell and everyone else in Dublin is **the Spire** ❷, the newly erected stainless-steel monument. Across from the Spire stands the **General Post Office** ❸, a major site in the Easter Uprising of 1916. Continuing north, follow O'Connell to the southeastern corner of Parnell Square. Heading counterclockwise around the square, you'll pass in turn the **Gate Theatre** ❹ and **Abbey Presbyterian Church** ❺ before coming to the **Dublin Writers Museum** ❻ and the **Dublin City Gallery, The Hugh Lane** ❼, both on the north side of the square and both housed in glorious neoclassic mansions; these are the two places where you should plan to spend most of your time on the Northside. Either before you go in or after you come out, you might also want to visit the solemn yet serene **Garden of Remembrance** ❽. Before leaving Parnell Square you may want to take a moment to admire the elaborate plasterwork in the chapel of the **Rotunda Hospital** ❾, toward the southwest corner of the square.

From here, you have two choices: to continue exploring the cultural sights that lie to the northeast of Parnell Square and east of O'Connell Street or to head to Moore, Henry, and Mary streets for a flavor of middle-class Dublin that you won't get on the spiffier Southside. If you decide to shop with the locals, leave Parnell Square via the southwestern corner. Moore Street is your first left off Parnell Street and leads directly to Henry Street.

If you decide to continue your cultural explorations, jump two blocks northeast of Parnell Square to the **James Joyce Centre** ❿, on North Great George's Street, and then head farther northeast to the once glamorous **Mountjoy Square** ⑪. About 1 km (½ mi) east of Mountjoy Square is Croke Park, a Gaelic football stadium and home of the Gaelic Athletic Association's **GAA Museum** ⑫. Return to Mountjoy Square and head north, stopping in at the **St. Francis Xavier Church** ⑬ on Gardiner Street. Head south on Gardiner Street to Summerhill, turn right, and walk west along Summerhill. Make a left onto Marlborough Street (parallel to and between Gardiner and O'Connell streets) to visit the **Pro-Cathedral** ⑭. Continue down to the quays and jog a block east to the **Custom House** ⑮.

TIMING The Northside has fewer major attractions than the Southside and, overall, is less picturesque. As a result, you're unlikely to want to stroll leisurely here. If you zipped right through this walk, you could be done in less than two hours. But the two major cultural institutions—the Dublin Writers Museum and the Dublin City Gallery, The Hugh Lane—easily deserve several hours each, so it's worth doing this walk only if you have the time to devote to them. Also, a number of additional sights connected with James Joyce and *Ulysses*—covered in "A Walk Through Joyce's Dublin"—are in the vicinity, so if you're a devoted Joycean, consult the CloseUp box before setting out on this walk.

What to See

❺ **Abbey Presbyterian Church.** A soaring spire marks the exterior of this church, popularly known as Findlater's Church—after Alex Findlater, a noted Dublin grocer who endowed it. Completed in 1864, the church stands on the northeast corner of Parnell Square; the inside has a stark Presby-

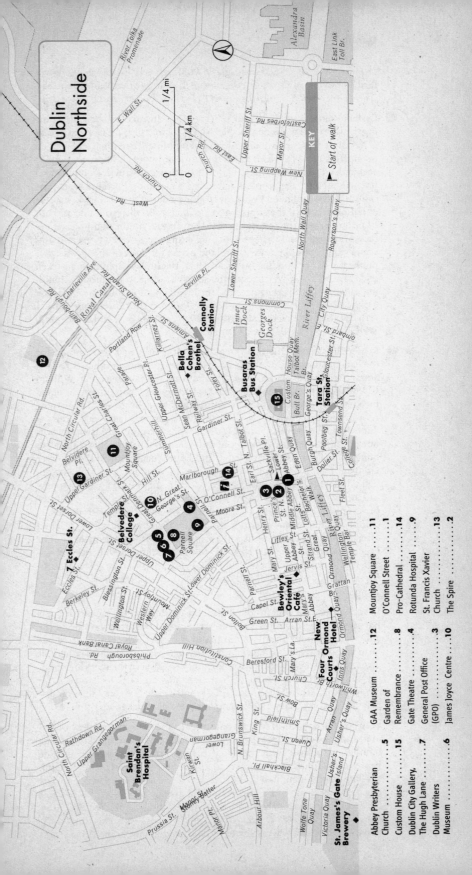

Dublin Northside

KEY

▲ Start of walk

St. James's Gate Brewery ◆

Abbey Presbyterian Church 5	GAA Museum 12
Custom House 15	Garden of Remembrance 8
Dublin City Gallery, The Hugh Lane 7	Gate Theatre 4
Dublin Writers Museum 6	General Post Office (GPO) 3
	James Joyce Centre ...10

Mountjoy Square 11	
O'Connell Street 1	
Pro-Cathedral 14	
Rotunda Hospital 9	
St. Francis Xavier Church 13	
The Spire 2	

terian mood, despite stained-glass windows and ornate pews. For a bird's-eye view of the area, take the small staircase that leads to the balcony. ⊠ *Parnell Sq., Northside* ☏ *01/837–8600* ☏ *Free* ⊙ *Hrs vary.*

⑮ Custom House. Seen at its best reflected in the waters of the Liffey during the short interval when the high tide is on the turn, the Custom House is the city's most spectacular Georgian building. Extending 375 feet on the north side of the river, this is the work of James Gandon, an English architect who arrived in Ireland in 1781, when construction commenced (it continued for 10 years). Crafted from gleaming Portland stone, the central portico is linked by arcades to the pavilions at either end. A statue of Commerce tops the copper dome, which is on the puny side and out of proportion to the rest of the building; statues on the main facade are based on allegorical themes. Note the exquisitely carved lions and unicorns supporting the arms of Ireland at the far ends of the facade. Republicans set the building on fire in 1921, but it was completely restored and now houses government offices. A visitor center traces the building's history and significance, and the life of Gandon. ⊠ *Custom House Quay, Northside* ☏ *01/878–7660* ⊕ *www.visitdublin.com* ☏ *€1* ⊙ *Mid-Mar.–Oct., weekdays 10–12:30, weekends 2–5; Nov.–mid-Mar., Wed.–Fri. 10–12:30, Sun. 2–5.*

★ ❼ Dublin City Gallery, The Hugh Lane. Built originally as a town house for the earl of Charlemont in 1762, this residence was so grand its Parnell Square street was nicknamed "Palace Row" in its honor. Sir William Chambers, who also built the Marino Casino for Charlemont, designed the structure in the best Palladian manner. Its delicate and rigidly correct facade, extended by two demilune arcades, was fashioned from the "new" white Ardmulcan stone (now seasoned to gray). Charlemont was one of the cultural locomotives of 18th-century Dublin—his walls were hung with Titians and Hogarths, and he frequently dined with Oliver Goldsmith and Sir Joshua Reynolds—so he would undoubtedly be delighted that his home is now a gallery, named after Hugh Lane, a nephew of Lady Gregory (Yeats's aristocratic patron). Lane collected both Impressionist paintings and 19th-century Irish and Anglo-Irish works. A complicated agreement with the National Gallery in London (reached after heated diplomatic dispute) stipulates that a portion of the 39 French paintings amassed by Lane shuttle back and forth between London and here. You can see Pissarro's *Printemps,* Manet's *Eva Gonzales,* Morisot's *Jour d'Été,* and, the jewel of the collection, Renoir's *Les Parapluies.*

In something of a snub to the British art establishment, the late Francis Bacon's partner donated the entire contents of the artist's studio to the gallery. The studio of Britain's arguably premier 20th-century artist has been reconstructed in all its gaudy glory in a permanent display here. It gives you, however, a unique opportunity to observe the working methods of the artist responsible for such masterpieces as *Study After Velázquez 1950* and the tragic splash-and-crash *Triptych.* Also on display are Bacon's diary, books, and anything else picked up off his floor.

Between the collection of Irish paintings in the National Gallery of Ireland and the superlative works on display here, you can quickly become familiar with Irish 20th-century art. Irish artists represented include Roderic O'Conor, well known for his views of the west of Ireland; William Leech, including his *Girl with a Tinsel Scarf* (ca. 1912) and *The Cigarette*; and the most famous of the group, Jack B. Yeats (W. B.'s brother). The museum has a dozen of his paintings, including *Ball Alley* (ca. 1927) and *There Is No Night* (1949). There's also strikingly displayed stained-glass work by early-20th-century Irish master artisans

A PLAYWRIGHT ON EVERY CORNER

DUBLIN PACKS MORE LITERARY PUNCH *per square foot than practically any other spot on the planet—largely because of the ferment that took hold at the end of the 19th century, when two main cultural movements emerged. In 1893, Douglas Hyde, a Protestant and later the first president of Ireland, founded the Gaelic League (Conradh na Gaelige), with a goal of preserving the Irish language and Gaelic traditions. The poet W. B. Yeats also played a pivotal role in the Irish literary renaissance. With funding from his patron Annie Horniman, Yeats and Lady Gregory founded the Abbey Theatre in 1903 (it opened in 1904), to develop and produce a decidedly Irish repertoire. With this new venue, and the growing prominence of such playwrights as Sean O'Casey and J. M. Synge, Irish literature thrived. The Dublin Writers Museum gives a terrific introduction to this story and to the more than two dozen major writers Ireland subsequently produced. To go further back in literary history, head for Trinity College, where you can see a few pages of the legendary 9th-century Book of Kells and stroll through the hallowed campus where Samuel Beckett studied and where a theater now bears his name. If you're an Oscar Wilde fan, you may want to pay homage to him at 1 Merrion Square, where his parents once lived. The CloseUp box "A Walk Through Joyce's Dublin" guides you through some key sites connected with Joyce and his novel. And if you want to stock up on anecdotes about the relationship between the pint and the pen, check out the Dublin Literary Pub Crawl, a guide available in Dublin bookstores, or take a guided tour of literary pubs.*

Harry Clarke and Evie Hone. ⊠ *Parnell Sq. N, Northside* ☎ *01/874–1903* ⊕ *www.hughlane.ie* ⊠ *Gallery free; Bacon Studio €7, free Tues. 9:30–5)* ⊙ *Tues.–Thurs. 9:30–6, Fri. and Sat. 9:30–5, Sun. 11–5.*

★ ⑥ **Dublin Writers Museum.** "If you would know Ireland—body and soul—you must read its poems and stories," wrote Yeats in 1891. Further investigation into the Irish way with words can be found here at this unique museum, in a magnificently restored 18th-century town house on the north side of Parnell Square. The mansion, once the home of John Jameson, of the Irish whiskey family, centers on an enormous drawing room, gorgeously decorated with paintings, Adamesque plasterwork, and a deep Edwardian lincrusta frieze. Rare manuscripts, diaries, posters, letters, limited and first editions, photographs, and other mementos commemorate the lives and works of the nation's greatest writers—and there are *many* of them, so leave plenty of time—including Joyce, Shaw, J. M. Synge, Lady Gregory, Yeats, Beckett, and many others. On display are an 1804 edition of Swift's *Gulliver's Travels,* an 1899 first edition of Bram Stoker's *Dracula,* and an 1899 edition of Wilde's *Ballad of Reading Gaol.* There's even a special "Teller of Tales" exhibit showcasing Behan, O'Flaherty, and O'Faoláin. Readings are periodically held. The bookshop and café make this an ideal place to spend a rainy afternoon. If you lose track of time and stay until the closing hour, you might want to dine at Chapter One, a highly regarded restaurant in the basement, which would have had Joyce ecstasizing about its currant-sprinkled scones. ⊠ *18 Parnell Sq. N, Northside* ☎ *01/872–2077* ⊕ *www. visitdublin.com* ⊠ *€6* ⊙ *June–Aug., weekdays 10–6, Sat. 10–5, Sun. 11–5; Sept.–May, Mon.–Sat. 10–5, Sun. 11–5.*

⑫ **GAA Museum.** In the bowels of Croke Park, the main stadium and headquarters of the GAA (Gaelic Athletics Association), this museum gives you a great introduction to native Irish sport. The four Gaelic games (football, hurling, camogie, and handball) are explained in detail, and if you're brave enough you can have a go yourself. High-tech displays take you through the history and highlights of the games. *National Awakening* is a really smart, interesting short film reflecting the key impact of the GAA on the emergence of the Irish Nation and the forging of a new Irish identity. The exhilarating *A Day in September* captures the thrill and passion of All Ireland finals day—the annual denouement of the intercounty hurling and Gaelic football—every bit as important to the locals as the Super Bowl is to sports fans in the United States. Tours of the stadium, the fourth largest in Europe, are available. ⊠ *New Stand, Croke Park, North County Dublin* ☎ *01/855–8176* ⊕ *www.gaa. ie* ⊡ *Museum €5, museum and stadium tour €8* ⊙ *Mon.–Sat. 9:30–5, Sun. noon–5.*

❽ Garden of Remembrance. Opened in 1966, 50 years after the Easter Uprising of 1916, the garden in Parnell Square commemorates those who died fighting for Ireland's freedom. At the garden's entrance is a large plaza; steps lead down to the fountain area, graced with a sculpture by contemporary Irish artist Oisín Kelly, based on the mythological Children of Lír, who were turned into swans. The garden serves as an oasis of tranquillity in the middle of the busy city. ⊠ *Parnell Sq., Northside* ⊡ *Free* ⊙ *Daily 9–5.*

❹ Gate Theatre. The Gate has been one of Dublin's most important theaters since its founding in 1929 by Micháel MacLiammóir and Hilton Edwards, who also founded Galway City's An Taibhdhearc as the national Irish-language theater. The Gate stages many innovative productions by Irish playwrights as well as foreign playwrights—and plenty of foreign actors have performed here, including Orson Welles (his first paid performance) and James Mason (early in his career). Shows here begin as soon as you walk into the auditorium—a Georgian masterwork designed by Richard Johnston in 1784 as an assembly room for the Rotunda Hospital complex. ⊠ *Cavendish Row, Northside* ☎ *01/874–4045* ⊙ *Shows Mon.–Sat.*

❸ General Post Office. Known as the GPO, this is one of the great civic buildings of Dublin's Georgian era, but it's famous because of the role it played in the Easter Uprising. The building, with its impressive neoclassical facade, was designed by Francis Johnston and built by the British between 1814 and 1818 as a center of communications. This gave it great strategic importance—and was one of the reasons why it was chosen by the insurgent forces in 1916 as a headquarters. Here, on Easter Monday, 1916, the Republican forces, about 2,000 in number and under the guidance of Pádrig Pearse and James Connolly, stormed the building and issued the Proclamation of the Irish Republic. After a week of shelling, the GPO lay in ruins; 13 rebels were ultimately executed, including Connolly, who was dying of gangrene from a leg shattered in the fighting and had to be propped up in a chair before the firing squad. Most of the original building was destroyed, though the facade survived—you can still see the scars of bullets on its pillars. Rebuilt and subsequently reopened in 1929, it became a working post office with an attractive two-story main concourse. A bronze sculpture depicting the dying Cuchulainn, a leader of the Red Branch Knights in Celtic mythology, sits in the front window. The 1916 Proclamation and the names of its signatories are inscribed on the green marble plinth. ⊠ *O'Connell St., Northside* ☎ *01/872–8888* ⊕ *www.anpost.ie* ⊡ *Free* ⊙ *Mon.–Sat. 8–8, Sun. 10:30–6.*

need a
break?
For a real Irish pub lunch, stop in at **John M. Keating** (✉ 14 Mary St., Northside ☎ 01/873–1567), at the corner of Mary and Jervis streets; head upstairs, where you can sit at a low table and chat with locals. At the Jervis Street branch of Dublin's famous **Bewley's Oriental Café** (✉ Jervis Shopping Centre, Jervis and Mary Sts., Northside ☎ 01/677–6761) the coffee is almost as good as the people-watching.

⑩ **James Joyce Centre.** Everyone in Ireland has at least *heard* of James Joyce (1882–1941)—especially since a copy of his censored and suppressed *Ulysses* was one of the top status symbols of the early 20th century. Joyce is of course now acknowledged as one of the greatest modern authors, and his *Dubliners, Finnegan's Wake,* and *A Portrait of the Artist as a Young Man* can even be read as quirky "travel guides" to Dublin. Open to the general public, this restored 18th-century Georgian town house, once the dancing academy of Professor Denis J. Maginni (which many will recognize from *Ulysses*), is a center for Joycean studies and events related to the author. It has an extensive library and archives, exhibition rooms, a bookstore, and a café. The collection includes letters from Beckett, Joyce's guitar and cane, and a celebrated edition of *Ulysses* illustrated by Matisse. The center is the main organizer of "Bloomstime," which marks the week leading up to June 16's Bloomsday celebrations. (Bloomsday, June 16, is the single day *Ulysses* chronicles, as Leopold Bloom winds his way around Dublin in 1904.) ✉ *35 N. Great George's St., Northside* ☎ *01/878–8547* ⊕ *www.jamesjoyce.ie* ▢ €*4.50* ◷ *Mon.–Sat., 9:30–5, Sun. 12:30–5.*

⑪ **Mountjoy Square.** Built over the course of the two decades leading up to 1818, this Northside square was once surrounded by elegant terraced houses. Today only the northern side remains intact. The houses on the once derelict southern side have been converted into apartments. Irishman Brian Boru, who led his soldiers to victory against the Vikings in the Battle of Clontarf in 1014, was said to have pitched camp before the confrontation on the site of Mountjoy Square. Playwright Sean O'-Casey once lived here at No. 35 and used the square as a setting for *The Shadow of a Gunman.*

▶ ❶ **O'Connell Street.** Dublin's most famous thoroughfare, which is 150 feet wide, was previously known as Sackville Street, but its name was changed in 1924, two years after the founding of the Irish Free State. After the devastation of the 1916 Easter Uprising, the Northside street had to be almost entirely reconstructed, a task that took until the end of the 1920s. At one time the main attraction of the street, Nelson's Pillar, a Doric column towering over the city center and a marvelous vantage point, was blown up in 1966, the 50th anniversary of the Easter Uprising. The Spire was built in its place in early 2003, and today this gigantic, stainless-steel monument dominates the street. The large monument at the south end of the street is dedicated to Daniel O'Connell (1775–1847), "The Liberator," and was erected in 1854 as a tribute to the orator's achievement in securing Catholic Emancipation in 1829. Seated winged figures represent the four Victories—Courage, Eloquence, Fidelity, and Patriotism—all exemplified by O'Connell. Ireland's four ancient provinces—Munster, Leinster, Ulster, and Connacht—are identified by their respective coats of arms. Look closely and you'll notice that O'Connell is wearing a glove on one hand, as he did for much of his adult life, a self-imposed penance for shooting a man in a duel. Alongside O'Connell is another noted statue, a modern rendition of Joyce's Anna Livia, seen as a lady set within a waterfall and now nicknamed by locals the "floozy in the Jacuzzi." O'Connell Bridge, the main

CloseUp

A WALK THROUGH JOYCE'S DUBLIN

J AMES JOYCE'S GENIUS for fashioning high art out of his day-to-day life brought him literary immortality and makes him, even today and possibly for all time, the world's most famous Dubliner. He set all of his major works—Dubliners, A Portrait of the Artist as a Young Man, Ulysses, and Finnegan's Wake—in the city where he was born and spent the first 22 years of his life, and although he spent the next 36 years in self-imposed exile, he never wrote about anywhere else. Joyce knew and remembered Dublin in such detail that he claimed that if the city were destroyed, it could be rebuilt in its entirety from his written works.

Joyceans flock to Dublin annually on June 16 to commemorate Bloomsday, the day in 1904 on which Leopold Bloom wanders through the city in Ulysses. Why this day? It had been an important one for Joyce—when he and his wife-to-be, Nora Barnacle, had their first date. Today Bloomsday has evolved into "Bloomstime," with events taking place in the days leading up to the 16th, then all day and well into the night. Even if you don't make it to Dublin on Bloomsday, you can still roam its streets, sniffing out Bloom's—and Joyce's—haunts.

Begin in the heart of the Northside, on **Prince's Street,** next to the GPO, where the office of the old and popular Freeman's Journal newspaper (published 1763–1924) was located before it was destroyed during the 1916 Easter Uprising. Bloom was a newspaper advertisement canvasser for the Journal. Leopold and Molly Bloom's fictional home stood at **7 Eccles Street,** north of Parnell Square. Between 1893 and 1898, Joyce studied at **Belvedere College** (🕿 01/874–3974) under the Jesuits; it's housed in a splendid 18th-century mansion on Great Denmark Street. The **James Joyce Centre** (🕿 01/878–8547 ⊕ www.jamesjoyce. ie), a few steps away from Belvedere College on North Great George's Street, is the hub of Bloomsday celebrations. The site of **Bella Cohen's Brothel** (✉ 82 Railway St., Northside) is in an area that in Joyce's day contained many such houses of ill repute. On the western edge of the Northside, the **New Ormond Hotel** (✉ Upper Ormond Quay, Northside 🕿 01/872–1811) was an afternoon rendezvous spot for Bloom.

Across the Liffey, walk up Grafton Street to Davy Byrne's Pub and then proceed via Molesworth Street to the **National Library**—where Bloom has a near meeting with Blazes Boylan, his wife's lover, and looks for a copy of an advertisement. No establishment mentioned by Joyce has changed less since his time than **Sweny's Pharmacy** (✉ Lincoln Pl., Southside), at the back of Trinity College, which still has its black-and-white exterior and an interior crammed with potions and vials.

Several key Joyce sights lie outside the city center. On February 2, 1882, Joyce was born in the genteel southern suburb of Rathgar, at **41 Brighton Square,** where he spent the first two years of his life. (Bus 15A and Bus 15B make the 5-km [3-mi] journey.) Other sights with Joyce connections are **Sandymount Strand,** the **James Joyce Martello Tower,** and **One Martello Terrace** in Bray.

bridge spanning the Liffey (wider than it is long), marks the street's southern end.

need a break? **Conway's** (✉ Parnell St. near Upper O'Connell St., Northside ☎ 01/873–2687), founded in 1745, is reputed to be Dublin's second-oldest pub. It's unpretentious and has great pub-grub. One of Dublin's oldest hotels, dating to 1817, the **Gresham** (✉ Upper O'Connell St., Northside ☎ 01/874–6881) is a pleasant, old-fashioned spot for a morning coffee or afternoon tea.

🟤 **Pro-Cathedral.** Dublin's principal Catholic cathedral (also known as St. Mary's) is a great place to hear the best Irish male voices—a Palestrina choir, in which the great Irish tenor John McCormack began his career, sings in Latin here every Sunday at 11. The cathedral, built between 1816 and 1825, has a classical church design—on a suitably epic scale. The church's facade, with a six-Doric-pillared portico, is based on the Temple of Theseus in Athens; the interior is modeled after the Grecian-Doric style of St-Philippe du Roule in Paris. But the building was never granted full cathedral status, nor has the identity of its architect ever been discovered; the only clue is in the church ledger, which lists a "Mr. P." as the builder. ✉ *Marlborough St., Northside* ☎ *01/874–5441* ⊕ *www.procathedral.ie* ✉ *Free* ☉ *Daily 8–6.*

🟤 **Rotunda Hospital.** The Rotunda, founded in 1745 as the first maternity hospital in Ireland and Britain, was designed on a grand scale by architect Richard Castle (1690–1751), with a three-story tower and a copper cupola. It's now most worth a visit for its chapel, with elaborate plasterwork executed by Bartholomew Cramillion between 1757 and 1758, appropriately honoring motherhood. The Gate Theatre, in a lavish Georgian assembly room, is on the O'Connell Street side of this large complex. ✉ *Parnell St., Northside* ☎ *01/873–0700.*

🟤 **St. Francis Xavier Church.** One of the city's finest churches in the classical style, the Jesuit St. Francis Xavier's was begun in 1829, the year of Catholic Emancipation, and was completed three years later. The building is designed in the shape of a Latin cross, with a distinctive Ionic portico and an unusual coffered ceiling. The striking, faux-marble high altarpiece, decorated with lapis lazuli, came from Italy. The church appears in James Joyce's story "Grace." ✉ *Upper Gardiner St., Northside* ☎ *01/836–3411* ✉ *Free* ☉ *Daily 7 AM–8:30 PM.*

🟤 **The Spire.** Although it has been christened the "Stiletto in the Ghetto" by some local wags, most people agree that this needlelike monument is the most exciting thing to happen to Dublin's skyline in decades. The Spire, also known as the Monument of Light, was originally planned as part of the city's millennium celebrations. But Ian Ritchie's spectacular 395-foot-high monument wasn't erected until the beginning of 2003. Seven times taller than the nearby General Post Office, the stainless-steel structure rises from the spot where Nelson's Pillar once stood. Approximately 10 feet in diameter at its base, the softly lighted monument narrows to only 1 foot at its apex—the upper part of the Spire sways gently when the wind blows. The monument's creators envisioned it serving as a beacon for the whole of the city, and it will certainly be the first thing you see as you drive into Dublin from the airport. ✉ *O'Connell St., Northside.*

City Center

Dublin's center of gravity had traditionally been O'Connell Bridge, a diplomatic landmark in that it avoided locating the center to the north or south of the river—as strong local loyalties still prevailed among "Northsiders" and "Southsiders," and neither group would ever accept that the city's center lay on the other's side of the river. The economic boom, however, has seen diplomacy fall by the wayside—Dublin's heart now beats loudest southward across the Liffey, due in part to a large-scale refurbishment and pedestrianization of Grafton Street, which made this already upscale shopping address *the* street to shop, stop, and be seen. At the foot of Grafton Street is the city's most famous and recognizable landmark, Trinity College; at the top of it is Dublin's most popular strolling retreat, St. Stephen's Green, a 27-acre landscaped park with flowers, lakes, bridges, and Dubliners enjoying a time-out.

Numbers in the text correspond to numbers in the margin and on the Dublin Southside map.

a good walk

Start at **Trinity College** ⑯ ⌐, exploring the quadrangle as you head to the Old Library to see the *Book of Kells*. If you want to see modern art, visit the collection housed in the Douglas Hyde Gallery, just inside the Nassau Street entrance to the college. When you come back out the front gate, you can either stop in at the **Bank of Ireland** ⑰, a neoclassic masterpiece that was once the seat of the Irish Parliament, or make an immediate left and head south along **Grafton Street** ⑱, the pedestrian spine of the Southside. The **Dublin Tourism** ⑲ office, in a medieval former church, is just off Grafton Street, on the corner of Suffolk Street. If Grafton Street's shops whet your appetite for more browsing and shopping, turn right down Wicklow Street, then left onto South William Street to **Powerscourt Townhouse Centre** ⑳, where a faux-Georgian atrium (very dubiously set within one of Dublin's greatest 18th-century mansions) houses high-end shops and pleasant cafés. The **Dublin Civic Museum** ㉑ is next door to Powerscourt, across the alley on its south flank. If you're doing well on time and want to explore the shopping streets farther east, jog via the alley one block west to Drury Street, from which you can access the Victorian **George's Street Arcade** ㉒. Head back to Grafton Street, where Bewley's Oriental Café, a Dublin institution, is a good place for a break. Grafton Street ends at the northwest corner of **St. Stephen's Green** ㉓, Dublin's most popular public garden, which absolutely requires a stroll-through. The Georgian **Newman House** ㉔ is on the south side of the green. Amble back across the green, exiting onto the northeast corner, at which stands the grand **Le Méridien Shelbourne** ㉕, a wonderful place for afternoon tea or a quick pint at one of its two pubs. The **Huguenot Cemetery** ㉖ is just down the street from the hotel, on the same side. If you want to see more art, head for the **RHA Gallagher Gallery** ㉗.

TIMING Dublin's city center is so compact you could race through this walk in an hour, but in order to gain full advantage of what is on offer, set aside at least half a day—if you can—to explore the treasures of Trinity College (which can easily take up at least an hour or more) and amble up and around Grafton Street to St. Stephen's Green.

What to See

⑰ **Bank of Ireland.** Across the street from the west facade of Trinity College stands one of Dublin's most striking buildings, now the Bank of Ireland but formerly the original home of Irish Parliament. Sir Edward Lovett Pearce designed the central section in 1729; three other architects would ultimately be involved in the building's construction. A pedimented portico fronted by six massive Corinthian columns dominates the grand facade, which follows the curve of Westmoreland Street as it meets College Green, once a Viking meeting place and burial ground. Two years after Parliament was abolished in 1801 under the Act of Union, which brought Ireland under the direct rule of Britain, the building was bought for €50,790 by the Bank of Ireland. Inside, stucco rosettes adorn the coffered ceiling in the pastel-hue, colonnaded, clerestoried main banking hall, at one time the Court of Requests, where citizens' petitions were heard. Just down the hall is the original House of Lords, with an oak-panel nave, a 1,233-piece Waterford glass chandelier, and tapestries depicting the Battle of the Boyne and the Siege of Derry; ask a guard to show you in. Visitors are welcome during normal banking hours; the Dublin historian and author Éamonn Mac Thomáis conducts brief guided tours every Tuesday at 10:30, 11:30, and 1:45. Accessed via Foster Place South, the small alley on the bank's east flank, the Bank of Ireland Arts Centre frequently exhibits contemporary Irish art and has a permanent exhibition devoted to the bank's "Journey Through 200 Years." ⊠ *2 College Green, Southside* ☎ *01/677–6801 for bank, 01/671–1488 for Arts Centre* ⊕ *www.visitdublin.com* ⊠ *Bank free, Arts Centre €1* ☉ *Bank Mon.–Wed. and Fri. 10–4, Thurs. 10–5; Arts Centre Tues.–Fri. 10–4, Sat. 2–5, Sun. 10–1.*

㉑ Dublin Civic Museum. Built between 1765 and 1771 as an exhibition hall for the Society of Artists, this building later was used as the City Assembly House, precursor of City Hall. The museum's esoteric collection includes Stone Age flints, Viking coins, old maps and prints of the city, and the sculpted head of British admiral Horatio Nelson, which used to top Nelson's Pillar, beside the General Post Office on O'Connell Street; the column was toppled by an explosion in 1966 on the 50th anniversary of the Easter Uprising. The museum also holds temporary exhibitions relating to the city. ⊠ *58 S. William St., Southside* ☎ *01/ 679–4260* ⊕ *www.dublincity.ie* ⊠ *Free* ☉ *Tues.–Sat. 10–6, Sun. 11–2.*

㉙ Dublin Tourism. Churches are not just for prayers, as this deconsecrated medieval church proves. Resurrected as a visitor center, St. Andrew's, fallen into ruin after years of neglect, now houses Dublin Tourism, a private organization that provides the most complete information on Dublin's sights, restaurants, and hotels; you can even rent a car here. The office offers reservations facilities for all Dublin hotels, as well as guided tours, a plethora of brochures, and a gift shop. A pleasant café upstairs serves sandwiches and drinks. ⊠ *St. Andrew's Church, Suffolk St., Southside* ☎ *01/605–7700, 1850/230330 (in Ireland)* ⊕ *www. visitdublin.com* ☉ *July–Sept., Mon.–Sat. 8:30–6, Sun. 11–5:30; Oct.–June, daily 9–6.*

㉒ George's Street Arcade. This Victorian covered market fills the block between Drury Street to the west and South Great George's Street to the east. Two dozen or so stalls sell books, prints, clothing (mostly secondhand), exotic foodstuffs, and trinkets. ⊠ *S. Great George's St., Southside* ☉ *Mon.–Sat. 9–6.*

> **need a break?** With its mahogany bar, mirrors, and plasterwork ceilings, **Long Hall Pub** (⊠ 51 S. Great George's St., Southside ☎ 01/475–1590) is one of Dublin's most ornate traditional taverns. It's a good place to take a break with a sandwich and a pint of Guinness.

㉘ Grafton Street. It's no more than 200 yards long and about 20 feet wide, but brick-lined Grafton Street, open only to pedestrians, can make a claim to be the most humming street in the city, if not in all of Ireland. It's one of Dublin's vital spines: the most direct route between the front door of Trinity College and St. Stephen's Green, and the city's premier shopping street, with Dublin's most distinguished department store, Brown Thomas, as well as tried and trusted Marks & Spencer. Both on Grafton Street itself and in the smaller alleyways that radiate off it, there are dozens

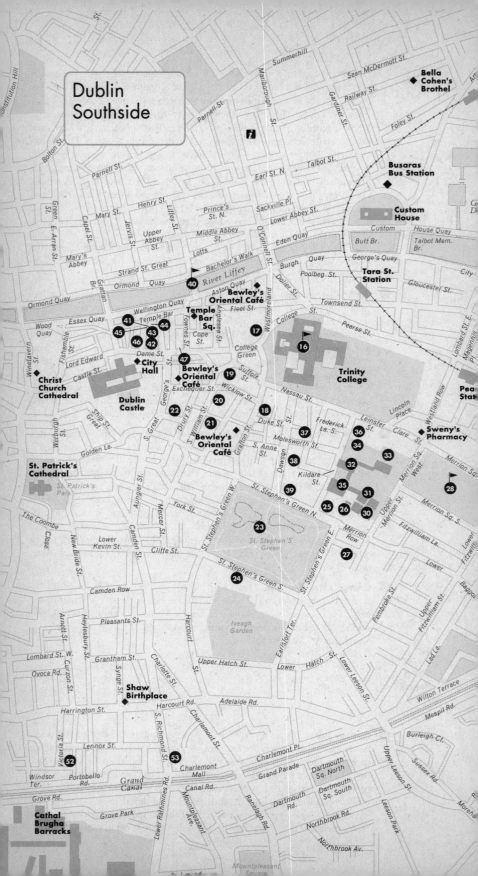

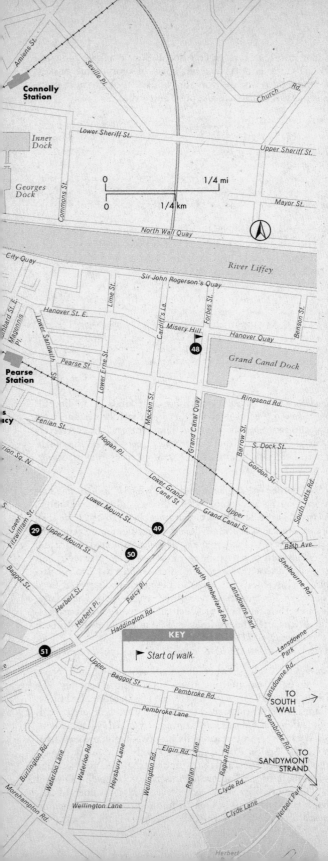

of independent stores, a dozen or so colorful flower sellers, and some of the Southside's most popular watering holes. In summertime, buskers from all over the country and the world line both sides of the street, pouring out the sounds of drum, whistle, pipe, and string.

need a break? The granddaddy of the capital's cafés, **Bewley's Oriental Café** has been serving coffee and buns to Dubliners since it was founded by Quakers in 1842, and now has four locations. Bewley's trademark stained-glass windows were designed by Harry Clarke (1889–1931), Ireland's most distinguished early-20th-century artist in this medium. All the branches are fine places in which to observe Dubliners of all ages and occupations. The aroma of coffee is irresistible, and the dark interiors—marble-top tables, bentwood chairs, and mahogany trim—evoke a more leisurely Dublin. The food is overpriced and not particularly good, but people-watching here over a cup of coffee or tea is a quintessential Dublin experience. (If you're interested in a more modern cup of coffee, check out the Metro Café, nearby at 43 South William Street—it's one of Dublin's best haunts for the caffeine-addicted and its staff is devoid of the devil-may-care, pseudo-existential inefficiency that seems to plague so many other Dublin cafés.) The Grafton Street branch of Bewley's stays open until 1 AM Sunday through Thursday and 4 AM Friday through Saturday; the Westmoreland Street branch closes daily at 9 PM. ⊠ *78 Grafton St., Southside* ☎ *01/677–6761 for all locations* ⊠ *12 Westmoreland St., Southside.*

㉖ Huguenot Cemetery. One of the last such burial grounds in Dublin, this cemetery was used in the late 17th century by French Protestants who had fled persecution in their native land. The cemetery gates are rarely open, but you can view the grounds from the street—it's on the northeast corner across from the square. ⊠ *27 St. Stephen's Green N, Southside.*

㉕ Le Méridien Shelbourne. The ebullient, redbrick, white-wood-trimmed facade of the Shelbourne has commanded "the best address in Dublin" from the north side of St. Stephen's Green since 1865. In 1921 the Irish Free State's constitution was drafted here in a first-floor suite. The most financially painless way to soak up the hotel's old-fashioned luxury and genteel excitement is to step past the entrance—note the statues of Nubian princesses and attendant slaves—for afternoon tea (€17.15 per person, including sandwiches and cakes) in the green-wallpapered Lord Mayor's Lounge or for a drink in one of its two bars, the Shelbourne Bar and the Horseshoe Bar, both of which are thronged with businesspeople and politicos after the workday ends. Famed novelist Elizabeth Bowen wrote her novel *The Hotel* about this very place. ⊠ *27 St. Stephen's Green, Southside* ☎ *01/676–6471* ⊕ *www.shelbourne.ie.*

㉔ Newman House. One of the greatest glories of Georgian Dublin, Newman House is actually two imposing town houses joined together. The earlier of the two, No. 85 St. Stephen's Green (1738), originally known as Clanwilliam House, was designed by Richard Castle, favored architect of Dublin's rich and famous, and features a winged Palladian window on the Wicklow granite facade. It has two landmarks of Irish Georgian style: the Apollo Room, decorated with stuccowork depicting the sun god and his muses; and the magnificent Saloon, "the supreme example of Dublin Baroque," according to scholars Jacqueline O'Brien and Desmond Guinness. The Saloon is crowned with an exuberant ceiling aswirl with cupids and gods, created by the Brothers Lafranchini, the finest *stuccadores* (plasterworkers) of 18th-century Dublin. Next door at No. 86 (1765), the staircase, on pastel-color walls, is one of the city's most beautiful rococo examples—with floral swags and musical instruments picked out in cake-frosting white. Catholic University (described by James Joyce in *A Portrait of the Artist as a Young Man*) was established in this building in 1850, with Cardinal John Henry Newman as its first rector. To explore the houses you must join a guided tour. At the back of Newman House lie Iveagh Gardens, a delightful hideaway with statues and sunken gardens that remains one of Dublin's best-kept secrets (you can enter via Earlsfort Terrace and Harcourt Street). ✉ *85–86 St. Stephen's Green, Southside* ☎ *01/475–7255* ⊕ *www. visitdublin.com* 🖾 *House and garden €4* ☯ *Tours June–Aug., Tues.–Fri. at noon, 2, 3, and 4; Sat. at 2, 3, and 4; Sun. at 11, noon, and 1.*

⓴ Powerscourt Townhouse Centre. Lucky man, this Viscount Powerscourt. In the mid-18th century, not only did he build Ireland's most spectacular country house, in Enniskerry, County Wicklow (which bears the family name), but he also decided to rival that structure's grandeur with one of Dublin's largest stone mansions. Staffed with 22 servants and built of granite from the viscount's own quarry in the Wicklow Hills, Powerscourt House was a major statement in the Palladian style designed by Robert Mack in 1771—a massive, Baroque-style edifice that towers over the little street it sits on (note the top story, framed by massive volutes, which was once intended as an observatory). The interior decoration runs from rococo salons by James McCullagh to Adamesque plasterwork by Michael Stapleton to—surprise!—an imaginative shopping atrium, installed in and around the covered courtyard. The stores here include high-quality Irish crafts shops and numerous food stalls. The mall exit leads to the Carmelite Church of St. Teresa's and Johnson's Court. Beside the church, a pedestrian lane leads onto Grafton Street. ✉ *59 S. William St., Southside* ☎ *01/679–4144* ☯ *Mon.–Wed. and Fri. 10–6, Thurs. 10–8, Sat. 9–6, Sun. noon–6 (limited shops open Sun.).*

㉗ RHA Gallagher Gallery. The Royal Hibernian Academy, an old Dublin institution, is housed in a well-lighted building, one of the largest exhibition spaces in the city. The gallery holds adventurous exhibitions of the best in contemporary art, both from Ireland and abroad. ✉ *15 Ely Pl., off St. Stephen's Green, Southside* ☎ *01/661–2558* ⊕ *www. royalhibernianacademy.com* 🖾 *Free* ☯ *Mon.–Wed., Fri., and Sat. 11–5, Thurs. 11–8, Sun. 2–5.*

㉓ St. Stephen's Green. Dubliners call it simply Stephen's Green, and green it is (year-round)—a verdant, 27-acre Southside square that was an open common used for the public punishment of criminals until 1664. After a long period of decline, it became a private park in 1814—the first time in its history that it was closed to the general public. Its fortunes changed again in 1880, when Sir Arthur Guinness, later Lord Ardiluan (a member of the Guinness brewery family), paid for it to be laid out anew. Flower gardens, formal lawns, a Victorian bandstand, and an ornamental lake with lots of waterfowl are all within the park's borders, connected by paths guaranteeing that strolling here or just passing through will offer up unexpected delights (like palm trees). Among the park's many statues are a memorial to Yeats and another to Joyce by Henry Moore, and the *Three Fates*, a dramatic group of bronze female figures watching over human destiny. In the 18th century the walk on the north side of the green was referred to as the Beaux Walk because most of Dublin's gentlemen's clubs were in town houses here. Today it is dominated by Le Méridien Shelbourne. On the south side is the alluring Georgian-gorgeous Newman House. 🖾 *Free* ☯ *Daily sunrise–sunset.*

▶ **⑯**   **Trinity College.** Founded in 1592 by Queen Elizabeth I to "civilize" (Her
Fodor'sChoice   Majesty's word) Dublin, Trinity is Ireland's oldest and most famous col-
★   lege. The memorably atmospheric campus is a must; here you can track
the shadows of some of the more noted alumni, such as Jonathan Swift
(1667–1745), Oscar Wilde (1854–1900), Bram Stoker (1847–1912), and
Samuel Beckett (1906–89). Trinity College, Dublin (familiarly known
as TCD), was founded on the site of the confiscated Priory of All Hal-
lows. For centuries Trinity was the preserve of the Protestant church.
A free education was offered to Catholics—provided that they accepted
the Protestant faith. As a legacy of this condition, until 1966 Catholics
who wished to study at Trinity had to obtain a dispensation from their
bishop or face excommunication. Today more than 70% of Trinity's students are Catholics, an indication of how far away those days seem to
today's generation.

Trinity's grounds cover 40 acres. Most of its buildings were constructed
in the 18th and early 19th centuries. The extensive **West Front,** with a
classical pedimented portico in the Corinthian style, faces College Green
and is directly across from the Bank of Ireland; it was built between 1755
and 1759, and is possibly the work of Theodore Jacobsen, architect of
London's Foundling Hospital. The design is repeated on the interior, so
the view is the same both from outside the gates and from the quadrangle inside. On the lawn in front of the inner facade stand statues of
orator Edmund Burke (1729–97) and dramatist Oliver Goldsmith
(1730–74), two other alumni. Like the West Front, **Parliament Square**
(commonly known as Front Square), the cobblestone quadrangle that
lies just beyond this first patch of lawn, also dates from the 18th century. On the right side of the square is Sir William Chambers's theater,
or Examination Hall, dating from the mid-1780s, which contains the
college's most splendid Adamesque interior, designed by Michael Stapleton. The hall houses an impressive organ retrieved from an 18th-cen-
tury Spanish ship and a gilded oak chandelier from the old House of
Commons; concerts are sometimes held here. The chapel, which stands
on the left of the quadrangle, has stucco ceilings and fine woodwork.
Both the theater and the chapel were designed by Scotsman William Chambers in the late 18th century. The looming campanile, or bell tower, is
the symbolic heart of the college; erected in 1853, it dominates the center of the square. To the left of the campanile is the Graduates Memorial Building, or GMB. Built in 1892, the slightly Gothic building now
contains both the Philosophical and Historical Societies, Trinity's ancient and fiercely competitive debating groups. At the back of the square
stands old redbrick Rubrics, looking rather ordinary and out of place
among the gray granite and cobblestones. Rubrics, now used as rooms
for students and faculty, dates from 1690, making it the oldest building still standing.

The **Old Library** houses Ireland's largest collection of books and
manuscripts; its principal treasure is the *Book of Kells,* generally considered to be the most striking manuscript ever produced in the Anglo-
Saxon world and one of the greatest masterpieces of early Christian art.
The book, which dates to the 9th century, is a splendidly illuminated
version of the Gospels. It was once thought to be lost—the Vikings looted
the book in 1007 for its jeweled cover but ultimately left the manuscript
behind. In the 12th century, Guardius Cambensis declared that the
book was made by an angel's hand in answer to a prayer of St. Bridget;
in the 20th century, scholars decided instead that the book originated
on the island of Iona in Scotland, where followers of St. Colomba lived
until the island came under siege in the early to mid-9th century. They
fled to Kells, County Meath, taking the book with them. The 680-page

work was rebound in four volumes in 1953, two of which are usually displayed at a time, so you typically see no more than four original pages. (Some wags have taken to calling it the "Page of Kells.") However, such is the incredible workmanship of the *Book of Kells* that one folio contains the equivalent of many other manuscripts. On some pages, it has been determined that within a quarter inch, no fewer than 158 interlacements of a ribbon pattern of white lines on a black background can be discerned—little wonder some historians feel this book contains all the designs to be found in Celtic art. Note, too, the extraordinary colors, some of which were derived from shellfish, beetles' wings, and crushed pearls. The most famous page shows the "XPI" monogram (symbol of Christ), but if this page is not on display, you can still see a replica of it, and many of the other lavishly illustrated pages, in the adjacent exhibition—dedicated to the history, artistry, and conservation of the book—through which you must pass to see the originals.

Because of the fame and beauty of the *Book of Kells,* it is all too easy to overlook the other treasures in the library. They include the *Book of Armagh,* a 9th-century copy of the New Testament that also contains St. Patrick's Confession, and the legendary *Book of Durrow,* a 7th-century Gospel book from County Offaly. You may have to wait in line to enter the library; it's less busy early in the day.

The main library room, also known as the Long Room, is one of Dublin's most staggering sights. At 213 feet long and 42 feet wide, it contains in its 21 alcoves approximately 200,000 of the 3 million volumes in Trinity's collection. Originally the room had a flat plaster ceiling, but in 1859–60 the need for more shelving resulted in a decision to raise the level of the roof and add the barrel-vaulted ceiling and the gallery bookcases. Since the 1801 Copyright Act, the college has received a copy of every book published in Britain and Ireland, and a great number of these publications must be stored in other parts of the campus and beyond. Of note are the carved Royal Arms of Queen Elizabeth I above the library entrance—the only surviving relic of the original college buildings—and, lining the Long Room, a grand series of marble busts, of which the most famous is Roubiliac's depiction of Jonathan Swift. The Trinity College Library Shop sells books, clothing, jewelry, and postcards. ⊠ *Front Sq., Southside* ☎ *01/608–2308* ⊕ *www.tcd.ie* ⊠ *€7.50* ☉ *June–Sept., Mon.–Sat. 9:30–5, Sun. 9:30–4:30; Oct.–May, Mon.–Sat. 9:30–5, Sun. noon–4:30.*

Trinity College's stark, modern Arts and Social Sciences Building, with an entrance on Nassau Street, houses the **Douglas Hyde Gallery of Modern Art,** which concentrates on contemporary art exhibitions and has its own bookstore. Also in the building, down some steps from the gallery, is a snack bar with coffee, tea, sandwiches, and students willing to talk about life in the old college. ⊠ *Nassau St., Southside* ☎ *01/608–1116* ⊠ *Free* ☉ *Mon.–Wed. and Fri. 11–6, Thurs. 11–7, Sat. 11–4:45.*

The **New Berkeley Library,** the main student library at Trinity, was built in 1967 and named after the philosopher and alumnus George Berkeley. The small open space in front of the library contains a spherical brass sculpture designed by Arnaldo Pomodoro. A very modern, sleek extension dominates the Nassau Street side of campus. The library is not open to the general public. ⊠ *Nassau St., Southside* ☎ *01/677–2941* ⊕ *www. tcd.ie* ☉ *Grounds daily 8 AM–10 PM.*

In the Thomas Davis Theatre in the arts building, the **"Dublin Experience,"** a 45-minute audiovisual presentation, explains the history of the city over the last 1,000 years. ✉ *Nassau St., Southside* ☎ *01/608–1688* 🖂 *€5* ◷ *Late-May–Oct., daily 10–5; shows every hr on the hr.*

Dublin's Georgian Heart

If there's one travel poster that signifies "Dublin" more than any other, it's the one that depicts 50 or so Georgian doorways—door after colorful door, all graced with lovely fanlights upheld by columns. A building boom began in Dublin in the early 18th century as the Protestant ascendancy constructed town houses for themselves and civic structures for their city in the style that came to be known as Georgian, for the four successive British Georges who ruled from 1714 through 1830. The Georgian architectural rage owed much to architects like James Gandon and Richard Castle. They and others were influenced by Andrea Palladio (1508–80), whose *Four Books of Architecture* were published in the 1720s in London and helped to precipitate the revival of his style, which swept through England and its colonies. Never again would Dublin be so "smart," so filled with decorum and style, nor its visitors' book so full of aristocratic names. Dublin's Southside is a veritable shop window of the Georgian style, though there are many other period sights to be found in the Northside (for instance, the august interiors of the Dublin Writers Museum and Belvedere College, or James Gandon's great civic structures, the Custom House and the Four Courts, found quayside).

Numbers in the text correspond to numbers in the margin and on the Dublin Southside map.

a good walk

When Dublin was transformed into a Georgian metropolis, people came from all over to admire the new pillared and corniced city. Today, walking through Fitzwilliam Square or Merrion Street Upper, you can still admire vistas of calm Georgian splendor. Begin your Palladian promenade at the northeast corner of St. Stephen's Green—here, in front of the men's clubs, was the Beaux Walk, a favorite 18th-century gathering place for fashionable Dubliners. Chances are you won't bump into a duke on his way to a Handel concert or an earl on his way to a rout, ball, and supper, but then, you won't have to dodge pigs either, which used to dot the cityscape back then. Walk north on Merrion Street to **Merrion Square** ㉘ ▸—one of Dublin's most attractive squares. The east side of Merrion Square and its continuation, Fitzwilliam Street, form what is known as "the Georgian mile," which, unlike some Irish miles, actually measures less than a kilometer. On a clear day the Dublin Mountains are visible in the distance and the prospect has almost (thanks to the ugly, modern office block of the Electricity Supply Board) been preserved to give an impression of the spacious feel of 18th-century Dublin. Walk down the south side of the square to **Number Twenty-Nine** ㉙. Cut back through the square to visit the refurbished **Government Buildings** ㉚, the **Natural History Museum** ㉛, **Leinster House** ㉜, and/or the **National Gallery of Ireland** ㉝. The last leg of this walk is up Kildare Street to the **National Library** ㉞, passing the back of Leinster House to the **National Museum** ㉟. Stop in at the **Heraldic Museum** ㊱ if you're eager to find your family crest. A short walk west along Molesworth Street takes you to Dawson Street (the site of the annual and popular August Antiques Fair). **St. Ann's Church** ㊲, the **Royal Irish Academy** ㊳, and **Mansion House** ㊴ are all on the left side as you walk down toward St. Stephen's Green. If you're interested in George Bernard Shaw you may want to take a 15-minute walk from the Green to the Shaw Birthplace. From the bottom of Dawson Street, make a right and then a left around the green until you arrive at Harcourt Street. After a short walk south, make a right onto Harrington Street and a right again onto Synge Street and Shaw's house.

TIMING Dublin is so compact you could race through this walk in two hours, if you don't linger anywhere or set foot in one of the museums. But the treasures at the National Gallery and the National Museum, and the green tranquillity of Merrion Square may slow you down. Many of Dublin's finest sights along the way and dozens of the city's most historic pubs may also entice you. So if you don't get too distracted, do this walk over the course of a half-day.

What to See

30 Government Buildings. The swan song of British architecture in the capital, this enormous complex, a landmark of "Edwardian Baroque," was the last neoclassical edifice to be erected by the British government. It was designed by Sir Aston Webb, who did many of the similarly grand buildings in London's Piccadilly Circus, as the College of Science in the early 1900s. Following a major restoration, these buildings became the offices of the Department of the *taoiseach* (the prime minister, pronounced *tea*-shuck) and the *tánaiste* (the deputy prime minister, pronounced tawn-*ish*-ta). Fine examples of contemporary Irish furniture and carpets populate the offices. A stained-glass window, known as "My Four Green Fields," was originally made by Evie Hone for the 1939 World Trade Fair in New York. It depicts the four ancient provinces of Ireland: Munster, Ulster, Leinster, and Connacht. The government offices are accessible only via 45-minute guided tours given on Saturday, though they are dramatically illuminated every night. ⊠ *Upper Merrion St., Southside* ☎ *01/662–4888* 🎟 *Free; pick up tickets from National Gallery on day of tour* ⊙ *Tours Sat. 10:30–3:30.*

36 Heraldic Museum. Looking for something original for your wall? If you're a Fitzgibbon from Limerick, a Cullen from Waterford, or a McSweeney from Cork, chances are your family designed, begged, borrowed, or stole a coat of arms somewhere in its history. The Heraldic Museum has hundreds of family-crest flags, coins, stamps, and silver, all highlighting the uses and development of heraldry in Ireland. ⊠ *2 Kildare St., Southside* ☎ *01/661–4877* 🎟 *Free* ⊙ *Mon.–Wed. 10–8:30, Thurs. and Fri. 10–4:30, Sat. 10–12:30; guided tours by appointment.*

32 Leinster House. Commissioned by the Duke of Leinster and built in 1745, this residence—Dublin's Versailles—almost single-handedly ignited the Georgian style that dominated Dublin for 100 years. It was not only the largest private home in the city but Richard Castle's first structure in Ireland (Castle, a follower of Palladio, designed some of the country's most important Palladian country houses). Inside, the grand salons were ornamented with coffered ceilings, Rembrandts, and Van Dycks, fitting settings for the parties often given by the duke's wife (and celebrated beauty), Lady Emily Lennox. The building has two facades: the one facing Merrion Square is designed in the style of a country house; the other, on Kildare Street, resembles that of a town house. This latter façade—if you ignore the ground-floor level—was a major inspiration for Irishman James Hoban's designs for the White House in Washington, D.C. Built in hard Ardbracan limestone, the house's exterior makes a cold impression, and, in fact, the duke's heirs pronounced the house "melancholy" and fled. Today, the house is the seat of Dáil Éireann (the House of Representatives, pronounced dawl *e*-rin) and Seanad Éireann (the Senate, pronounced shanad *e*-rin), which together constitute the Irish Parliament. When the Dáil is not in session, tours can be arranged weekdays; when the Dáil is in session, tours are available only on Monday and Friday. The Dáil visitors' gallery is included in the tour, although

THE AGE OF ELEGANCE

EXTRAORDINARY DUBLIN!" *sigh art lovers and connoisseurs of the 18th century. It was during the "gorgeous eighteenth" that this* duckling of a city was transformed into a preening swan, largely by the Georgian style of art and architecture that flowered between 1714 and 1820 during the reigns of the three English Georges. Today Dublin remains in good part a sublimely Georgian city, thanks to enduring grace notes: the commodious and uniformly laid out streets, the genteel town squares, the redbrick mansions accented with demilune fan windows. The great 18th-century showpieces are **Merrion, Fitzwilliam, Mountjoy,** and **Parnell squares. Merrion Square East,** the longest Georgian street in town, reveals scenes of decorum, elegance, polish, and charm, all woven into a "tapestry of rosy brick and white enamel," to quote the 18th-century connoisseur Horace Walpole. Setting off the facades are fan-lighted doors (often lacquered in black, green, yellow, or red) and the celebrated "patent reveal" window trims—thin plaster linings painted white to catch the light. These demilune fanlights—as iconic of the city as clock towers are of Zurich—are often in neoclassical Adamesque style.

Many exteriors appear severely plain, but don't be fooled: these town houses can be compared to bonbons whose sheaths of hard chocolate conceal deliciously creamy centers. Just behind their stately front doors are entry rooms and stairways

aswirl with tinted rococo plasterwork, often the work of stuccadores, or plasterworkers from Italy (including the talented Lafranchini brothers). The magnificent **Newman House,** one of the very finest of Georgian houses, is open to the public. **Belvedere College** (✉ 6 Great Denmark St., Northside ☎ 01/874–3974) is open by appointment only.

The Palladian style—as the Georgian style was then called—began to reign supreme in domestic architecture in 1745, when the Croesus-rich earl of Kildare returned from an Italian grand tour and built a gigantic Palladian palace called **Leinster House** in the seedy section of town. "Where I go, fashion will follow," he declared, and indeed it did. By then, the Anglo-Irish elite had given the city London airs by building the **Parliament House** (now the Bank of Ireland), the **Royal Exchange** (now City Hall), the **Custom House,** and the **Four Courts** in the new style. But this phase of high fashion came to an end with the Act of Union: according to historian Maurice Craig, "On the last stroke of midnight, December 31, 1800, the gaily caparisoned horses turned into mice, the coaches into pumpkins, the silks and brocades into rags, and Ireland was once again the Cinderella among the nations." It was nearly 150 years before the spotlight shone once again on 18th-century Dublin, thanks to the conservation efforts of the **Irish Georgian Society** (✉ 74 Merrion Sq., Southside ☎ 01/676–7053 ⊕ www.irishgeorgiansociety.org).

---

it can be accessed on days when the Dáil is in session and tours are not available. To arrange a visit, contact the public relations office. ✉ *Kildare St., Southside* ☎ *01/618–3000 for public-relations office* ⊕ *www. irlgov.ie* ✉ *Free.*

39 **Mansion House.** The mayor of Dublin resides at the Mansion House, which dates from 1710. It was built for Joshua Dawson, who later sold the property to the government on condition that "one loaf of double refined sugar of six pounds weight" be delivered to him every Christmas. In 1919 the Declaration of Irish Independence was adopted here. The house is not open to the public. ✉ *Dawson St., Southside.*

► **28** **Merrion Square.** Created between 1762 and 1764, this tranquil square a few blocks to the east of St. Stephen's Green is lined on three sides by some of Dublin's best-preserved Georgian town houses, many of which have brightly painted front doors crowned by intricate fanlights. Leinster House, the Natural History Museum, and the National Gallery line the west side of the square. It's on the other sides, however, that the Georgian terrace streetscape comes into its own—the finest houses are on the north border. Even when the flower gardens here are not in bloom, the vibrant, mostly evergreen grounds, dotted with sculpture and threaded with meandering paths, are worth a stroll. Several distinguished Dubliners have lived on the square, including Oscar Wilde's parents, Sir William and "Speranza" Wilde (No. 1); Irish national leader Daniel O'Connell (No. 58); and authors W. B. Yeats (Nos. 52 and 82) and Sheridan LeFanu (No. 70). As you walk past the houses, read the plaques on the house facades, which identify the former inhabitants. Until 50 years ago, the square was a fashionable residential area, but today most of the houses are offices. At the south end of Merrion Square, on Upper Mount Street, stands the Church of Ireland St. Stephen's Church. Known locally as the "pepper canister" church because of its cupola, the structure was inspired in part by Wren's churches in London. ⊠ *Southside* ☉ *Daily sunrise–sunset.*

㉝ **National Gallery of Ireland.** Caravaggio's *The Taking of Christ* (1602), Reynolds's *First Earl of Bellamont* (1773), Vermeer's *Lady Writing a Letter with Her Maid* (ca. 1670) . . . you get the picture. The National Gallery of Ireland—the first in a series of major civic buildings on the west side of Merrion Square—is one of Europe's finest smaller art museums, with more than 3,000 works. Unlike Europe's largest art museums, which are almost guaranteed to induce Stendhal's syndrome, the National Gallery can be thoroughly covered in a morning or afternoon without inducing exhaustion. An 1854 Act of Parliament provided for the establishment of the museum, which was helped along by William Dargan (1799–1867), who was responsible for building much of Ireland's railway network in the 19th century (he is honored by a statue on the front lawn). The 1864 building was designed by Francis Fowke, who was also responsible for London's Victoria & Albert Museum.

Fodor'sChoice
★

A highlight of the museum is the major collection of paintings by Irish artists from the 17th through 20th centuries, including works by Roderic O'Conor (1860–1940), Sir William Orpen (1878–1931), William Leech (1881–1968), and Jack B. Yeats (1871–1957), the brother of W. B. Yeats and by far the best-known Irish painter of the 20th century. Yeats painted portraits and landscapes in an abstract expressionist style not unlike that of the later Bay Area Figurative painters of the 1950s and 1960s. His *The Liffey Swim* (1923) is particularly worth seeing for its Dublin subject matter (the annual swim is still held, usually on the first weekend in September).

The collection also claims exceptional paintings from the 17th-century French, Dutch, Italian, and Spanish schools. Among the highlights are those mentioned above (the spectacular Caravaggio made headlines around the world when it was found hanging undiscovered in a Jesuit house not far from the museum) and Rembrandt's *Rest on the Flight into Egypt* (1647), Poussin's *The Holy Family* (1649) and *Lamentation over the Dead Christ* (ca. 1655–60), and, somewhat later than these, Goya's *Portrait of Doña Antonia Zárate* (circa 1810). Don't miss the portrait of the *First Earl of Bellamont* (1773) by Reynolds; the earl was among the first to introduce the Georgian fashion to Ireland, and this portrait stunningly flaunts the extraordinary style of the man himself. The French Impressionists are represented with paintings by Monet, Sisley, and Pissarro. The British collection and the Irish National Portrait collection are displayed in the northern wing of the gallery, while the

Millennium Wing, a standout of postmodern architecture in Dublin, houses part of the permanent collection and also stages major international traveling exhibits. The amply stocked gift shop is a good place to pick up books on Irish artists. Free guided tours are available on Saturday at 3 and on Sunday at 2, 3, and 4. ⊠ *Merrion Sq. W, Southside* ☎ *01/661–5133* ⊕ *www.nationalgallery.ie* ✉ *Free; special exhibits €10* ⊘ *Mon.–Wed., Fri., and Sat. 9:30–5:30, Thurs. 9:30–8:30, Sun. noon–5:30.*

need a break?

Fitzer's (⊠ Merrion Sq. W, Southside· ☎ 01/661–4496), the National Gallery's self-service restaurant, is a find—one of the city's best spots for an inexpensive, top-rate lunch. The 16 to 20 daily menu items are prepared with an up-to-date take on European cuisine. It's open Monday–Saturday 10–5:30 (lunch is served noon–2:30) and Sunday 2–5.

❸❹ National Library. Ireland is one of the few countries in the world where one can happily admit to being a writer. And few countries as geographically diminutive as Ireland have garnered as many recipients of the Nobel Prize for Literature. Along with works by W. B. Yeats (1923), George Bernard Shaw (1925), Samuel Beckett (1969), and Seamus Heaney (1995), the National Library contains first editions of every major Irish writer, including books by Jonathan Swift, Oliver Goldsmith, and James Joyce (who used the library as the scene of the great literary debate in *Ulysses*). In addition, almost every book ever published in Ireland is kept here, along with an unequaled selection of old maps and an extensive collection of Irish newspapers and magazines—more than 5 million items in all. The main Reading Room opened in 1890 to house the collections of the Royal Dublin Society. Beneath its dramatic domed ceiling, countless authors have researched and written their books over the years. The library also has a free genealogical consultancy service that can advise you on how to trace your Irish ancestors. ⊠ *Kildare St., Southside* ☎ *01/661–8811* ⊕ *www.nli.ie* ✉ *Free* ⊘ *Mon.–Wed. 10–9, Thurs. and Fri. 10–5, Sat. 10–1.*

★ ❸❺ National Museum. Ireland's National Museum, on the other side of Leinster House from the National Library, houses a fabled collection of Irish artifacts dating from 7000 BC to the present. Organized around a grand rotunda, the museum is elaborately decorated, with mosaic floors, marble columns, balustrades, and fancy ironwork. It has the largest collection of Celtic antiquities in the world, including gold jewelry, carved stones, bronze tools, and weapons. The Treasury collection, including some of the museum's most renowned pieces, is open on a permanent basis. Among the priceless relics on display are the 8th-century Ardagh Chalice, a two-handle silver cup with gold filigree ornamentation; the bronze-coated, iron St. Patrick's Bell, the oldest surviving example (5th–8th centuries) of Irish metalwork; the 8th-century Tara Brooch, an intricately decorated piece made of white bronze, amber, and glass; and the 12th-century bejeweled oak Cross of Cong, covered with silver and bronze panels. The Road to Independence Room is devoted to the 1916 Easter Uprising and the War of Independence (1919–21); displays here include uniforms, weapons, banners, and a piece of the flag that flew over the General Post Office during Easter Week, 1916. Upstairs, Viking Age Ireland is a permanent exhibit on the Norsemen, featuring a full-size Viking skeleton, swords, leather works recovered in Dublin and surrounding areas, and a replica of a small Viking boat. In contrast to the ebullient late-Victorian architecture of the main museum building, the design of the National Museum Annexe is purely functional; it hosts

ANCESTOR-HUNTING

THE LATE PRESIDENT KENNEDY *and former President Reagan are only two among many thousands of Americans who have been drawn to Ireland in an attempt to track down their ancestors. So popular has this become that Ireland today has numerous facilities for those in search of their past. However, before you begin some genealogical Sherlock Holmesing, you'll need some detailed information. The memories of elderly relatives about the place from which they or their forebears emigrated, for example, is often a useful starting point. The county name is helpful, but the name of their village or town is even better. It can lead quickly to parish registers, often going back 200 years or more, which the local clergy will usually be very glad to let you see (keep in mind that many of these parish registers have been moved to regional town halls and government agencies). Best of all, however, is to seek out professional help. The National Library in Dublin is the best source of information on family names and family crests, and the consultancy service is free. Similarly, the Office of the Registrar General in Dublin's Custom House has details of many births, deaths, and marriages after 1864, and some marriages dating back to 1845 (a substantial part of the records here was destroyed, however, in the Troubles of 1921). The Public Record Office at the Four Courts and the Registry of the Deeds in Henrietta Street, both in Dublin, are two*

other potentially useful sources of information. The National Archives on Bishop Street is a great source of old census information.

Of course, if your great-grandfather's name was Blarney Killakalarney, you should have an easy time sleuthing your family roots. Chances are, however, your name is one of the more prominent surnames in Ireland (⇨ Irish Family Names map, in Chapter 10), so it may take you longer to track down your ancestors among all the Ahernes and O'Briens. If all else fails, try a professional genealogical service.

temporary shows of Irish antiquities. The 18th-century Collins Barracks, near Phoenix Park, houses a collection of glass, silver, furniture, and other decorative arts. ⊠ *National Museum, Kildare St.; Annexe, 7–9 Merrion Row, Southside* ☎ *01/677-7444* ⊕ *www.museum.ie* ⊡ *Free* ☉ *Tues.–Sat. 10–5, Sun. 2–5.*

㉛ Natural History Museum. The famed explorer of the African interior, Dr. Stanley Livingstone (of "Dr. Livingstone, I presume?" fame), inaugurated this museum when it opened in 1857. Today, it is little changed from Victorian times and remains a fascinating repository of mounted mammals, birds, and other flora and fauna. The Irish Room houses the most famous exhibits, skeletons of Ireland's extinct, prehistoric giant "Irish elk." The World Animals Collection includes a 65-foot whale skeleton suspended from the roof. Don't miss the very beautiful Blaschka Collection, finely detailed glass models of marine creatures, the zoological accuracy of which has never been achieved since. The museum is next door to the Government Buildings. ⊠ *Merrion Sq. W, Southside* ☎ *01/ 677–7444* ⊕ *www.museum.ie* ⊠ *Free* ⊙ *Tues.–Sat. 10–5, Sun. 2–5.*

㉙ Number Twenty-Nine. Everything in this carefully refurbished 1794 home, known simply as Number Twenty-Nine, is in keeping with the elegant lifestyle of the Dublin middle class between 1790 and 1820, the height of the Georgian period, when the house was owned by a wine merchant's widow. From the basement to the attic, in the kitchen, nursery, servant's quarters, and the formal living areas, the National Museum of Ireland has re-created the period's style with authentic furniture, paintings, carpets, curtains, paint, wallpapers, and even bellpulls. ⊠ *29 Lower Fitzwilliam St., Southside* ☎ *01/702–6165* ⊕ *www.esb.ie/education* ⊠ *€3.15* ⊙ *Tues.–Sat. 10–5, Sun. 2–5.*

㊳ Royal Irish Academy. The country's leading learned society houses important manuscripts in its 18th-century library, including a large collection of ancient Irish manuscripts, such as the 11th- to 12th-century *Book of the Dun Cow,* and the library of the 18th-century poet Thomas Moore. ⊠ *19 Dawson St., Southside* ☎ *01/676–2570* ⊕ *www.ria.ie* ⊠ *Free* ⊙ *Weekdays 9:30–5.*

㊲ St. Ann's Church. St. Ann's plain, neo-Romanesque granite exterior, built in 1868, belies the Church of Ireland's rich Georgian interior, which Isaac Wills designed in 1720. Highlights of the interior include polished-wood balconies, ornate plasterwork, and shelving in the chancel dating from 1723—and still in use for distributing bread to the parish's poor. ⊠ *Dawson St., Southside* ☎ *01/676–7727* ⊠ *Free* ⊙ *Weekdays 10–4, Sun. for services.*

off the beaten path

SHAW BIRTHPLACE – "Author of many plays" is the simple accolade to George Bernard Shaw (1856–1950) on the plaque outside his birthplace. The Nobel laureate was born here to a once prosperous family fallen on harder times. Shaw lived in this modest, Victorian terrace house until he was 10 and remembers it as having a "loveless" feel. The painstaking restoration of the little rooms highlights the cramped claustrophobic atmosphere. All the details of a family home—wallpaper, paint, fittings, curtains, furniture, utensils, pictures, rugs—remain, and it appears as if the family has just gone out for the afternoon. You can almost hear one of Mrs. Shaw's musical recitals in the tiny front parlor. The children's bedrooms are dotted with photographs and original documents and letters that throw light on Shaw's career. ⊠ *33 Synge St., Southside* ☎ *01/475– 0854* ⊕ *www.visitdublin.com* ⊠ *€6* ⊙ *May–Sept., Mon.–Sat. 10–5, Sun. 2–6.*

Temple Bar

More than any other neighborhood in the city, Temple Bar represents the dramatic changes (good and bad) and ascending fortunes of Dublin that came about in the last decade of the 20th century. The area, which takes its name from one of the streets of its central spine, was targeted for redevelopment in 1991–92 after a long period of neglect, having survived widely rumored plans to turn it into a massive bus depot and/or a giant parking lot. Temple Bar took off *fast* into Dublin's version of New York's SoHo, Paris's Bastille, London's Notting Hill—a thriving mix of high and alternative culture distinct from what you'll find in every other part of the city. Dotting the area's narrow cobblestone streets and pedestrian alleyways are new apartment buildings (inside they tend to be small and uninspired, with sky-high rents), vintage-clothing stores, postage-stamp-size boutiques selling €250 sunglasses and other expensive gewgaws, art galleries galore, a hotel resuscitated by U2, hip restaurants, pubs, clubs, European-style cafés, and a smattering of cultural venues.

Temple Bar's regeneration was no doubt abetted by that one surefire real estate asset: location, location, location. The area is bordered by Dame Street to the south, the Liffey to the north, Fishamble Street to the west, and Westmoreland Street to the east. In fact, Temple Bar is situated so perfectly between everywhere else in Dublin that it's difficult to believe this neighborhood was once largely forsaken. It's now sometimes called the "playing ground of young Dublin," and for good reason: on weekend evenings and daily in the summer it teems with young people—not only from Dublin but from all over Europe—who fly into the city for the weekend, drawn by its pubs, clubs, and lively *craic* (good conversation and fun). The area has become a favorite of young Englishmen on "stag" weekends, 48-hour bachelor parties heavy on drinking and debauching. Some who have witnessed Temple Bar's rapid gentrification and commercialization complain that it's losing its artistic soul—*Harper's Bazaar* said it was in danger of becoming "a sort of pseudoplace," like London's Covent Garden Piazza or Paris's Les Halles. Over the next few years the planned Smithfield development may replace Temple Bar at the cutting edge of Dublin culture, but for the moment there's no denying that this is one of the best places to get a handle on the city.

Numbers in the text correspond to numbers in the margin and on the Dublin Southside map.

a good walk

Start at O'Connell Bridge and walk down Aston Quay, taking in the terrific view west down the River Liffey. Alleys and narrow roads to your left lead into Temple Bar, but hold off turning in until you get to **Ha'penny Bridge** 40 ▶, a Liffey landmark. Turn left and walk through Merchant's Arch, the symbolic entry into Temple Bar (see if you can spot the surveillance cameras up on the walls), which leads you onto the area's long spine, named Temple Bar here but also called Fleet Street (to the east) and Essex Street (to the west). You're right at Temple Bar Square, one of the two largest plazas in Temple Bar. Just up on the right are two of the area's leading art galleries, the Temple Bar Gallery (at Lower Fownes Street) and, another block up, the Original Print Gallery and Black Church Print Studios. Walk west along Temple Bar and turn left onto Eustace Street. If you have children, you may want to go to **the Ark** 41, a children's cultural center. Across the street from the Ark, stop in at the Temple Bar Information Centre and pick up a handy *Temple Bar Guide*. Farther down Eustace Street is the **Irish Film Centre** 42, Temple Bar's leading cultural venue and a great place to catch classic or new indie films. In summer, the center organizes Saturday-night outdoor screenings on **Meeting House Square** 43, behind the Ark, accessed via Curved Street. The **National Photographic Archive** 44 and the nearby **Gallery of Photography** 45, Dublin's leading photography gallery, are also here. Walk a few steps west to the narrow cobbled Sycamore Street, and then turn left and walk to Dame Street, where you'll find the **Olympia Theatre** 46. Farther east along Dame Street, the ultramodern **Central Bank** 47 rises above the city.

TIMING You can easily breeze through Temple Bar in an hour or so, but if you've got the time, plan to spend a morning or afternoon here, drifting in and out of the dozens of stores and galleries, relaxing at a café over a cup of coffee or at a pub over a pint, or maybe even watching a film, if you're looking for a change from sightseeing.

What to See

41 **The Ark.** If you're traveling with children and looking for something fun to do, stop by the Ark, Ireland's cultural center for children, housed in a former Presbyterian church. Its theater opens onto Meeting House Square for outdoor performances in summer. A gallery and workshop space host ongoing activities. ⊠ *Eustace St., Temple Bar* ☎ *01/670–7788* ⊕ *www.ark.ie* ⊠ *Free* ⊘ *Weekdays 9:30–5:30, weekends only if there is a show.*

47 **Central Bank.** Everyone in Dublin seems to have an opinion on the Central Bank. Designed by Sam Stephenson in 1978, the controversial, ultramodern glass-and-concrete building suspends huge concrete slabs around a central axis. It was originally one floor taller, but that had to be lopped off as a hazard to low-flying planes. Skateboarders and inline skaters have taken up residence on the little plaza in front of the building. ⊠ *Dame St., Temple Bar* ☎ *01/671–6666* ⊕ *www.centralbank. ie* ⊘ *Weekdays 10–6.*

45 **Gallery of Photography.** Dublin's premier photography gallery has a permanent collection of early-20th-century Irish photography and also puts on monthly exhibits of contemporary Irish and international photographers. The gallery is an invaluable social record of Ireland. The bookstore is the best place in town to browse for photography books and pick up arty postcards. ⊠ *Meeting House Sq. S, Temple Bar* ☎ *01/ 671–4654* ⊕ *www.irish-photography.com* ⊠ *Free* ⊘ *Tues.–Sat. 11–6.*

40 **Ha'penny Bridge.** Every Dubliner has a story about meeting someone on this cast-iron Victorian bridge, a heavily trafficked footbridge that crosses the Liffey at a prime spot—Temple Bar is on the south side, and the bridge provides the fastest route to the thriving Mary and Henry Street shopping areas to the north. Until early in the 20th century, a halfpenny toll was charged to cross it. Yeats was one among many Dubliners who found this too high a price to pay—more a matter of principle than of finance—and so made the detour via O'Connell Bridge. Congestion on the Ha'penny has been relieved with the opening of the Millennium Footbridge a few hundred yards up the river. A refurbishment, including new railings, a return to the original white color, and tasteful lighting at night, has given the bridge a new lease on life.

42 **Irish Film Centre (IFC).** The opening of the IFC in a former Quaker meetinghouse helped to launch the revitalization of Temple Bar. It has two comfortable art-house cinemas showing revivals and new independent films, the Irish Film Archive, a bookstore for cineastes, and a popular bar and restaurant-café, all of which make this one of the neighborhood's most vital cultural institutions and *the* place to be seen. On Saturday nights in the summer, the center screens films outside on Meeting House Square. ⊠ *6 Eustace St., Temple Bar* ☎ *01/679–5744* ⊕ *www.fii.ie* ⊠ *Free* ⊘ *Weekdays 9:30–late, weekends 11–late.*

need a break? The trendy **Irish Film Centre Café** (⊠ 6 Eustace St., Temple Bar ☎ 01/679–5744) is a pleasant place for a lunchtime break. Sandwiches are large and healthful, with plenty of vegetarian choices, and the people-watching is nonpareil.

43 **Meeting House Square.** The square, which is behind the Ark and accessed via Curved Street, takes its name from a nearby Quaker meetinghouse. Now it's something of a gathering place for Dublin's youth and artists. Numerous summer events—classic movies (Saturday nights), theater, games, and family programs—take place here. (Thankfully, seats are installed.) The square is also a favorite site for the continuously changing street sculpture that pops up all over Temple Bar (artists commissioned by the city sometimes create oddball pieces, such as a half of a Volkswagon protruding from a wall). Year-round, the square is a great spot to sit, people-watch, and take in the sounds of the buskers who swarm to the place. There's also an organic food market here every Saturday morning.

44 **National Photographic Archive.** Formerly housed in the National Library's main building, the National Photographic Archive now has a stylish home in Temple Bar. The total collection comprises approximately 300,000 photographs, most of which are Irish, making up a priceless visual history of the nation. Although most of the photographs are historical, dating as far back as the mid-19th century, there's also a large number of contemporary pictures. Subject matter ranges from topographical views to studio portraits, from political events to early tourist photographs. You can also buy a print of your favorite photo. ⊠ *Meeting House Sq., Temple Bar* ☎ *01/603–0371* ⊕ *www.nli.ie* ⊠ *Free* ☉ *Weekdays 10–5, Sat. 10–2.*

★ **46** **Olympia Theatre.** One of the best places anywhere in Europe to see live musical acts, the Olympia is Dublin's second oldest and one of its busiest theaters. This classic Victorian music hall, built in 1879, has a gorgeous red wrought-iron facade. The Olympia's long-standing Friday and Saturday series, "Midnight at the Olympia," has brought numerous musical performers to Dublin, and the theater has also seen many notable actors strut on its stage, including Alec Guinness, Peggy Ashcroft, Noël Coward, and even Laurel and Hardy. Big-name performers like Van Morrison often choose the intimacy of the Olympia over a larger venue. It's really a hot place to see some fine performances, so if you have a chance, by all means go. Conveniently, there are two pubs here—through doors directly off the back of the theater's orchestra section. ⊠ *72 Dame St., Temple Bar* ☎ *01/677–7744.*

> **need a break?** The creamiest, frothiest coffees in all of Temple Bar can be had at the **Joy of Coffee/Image Gallery Café** (⊠ 25 E. Essex St., Temple Bar ☎ 01/679–3393); the wall of windows floods light onto the small gallery with original photographs adorning the walls.

The Grand Canal & Ballsbridge

At its completion in 1795, the 547-km (340-mi) Grand Canal was celebrated as the longest in Britain and Ireland. It connected Dublin to the River Shannon, and horse-drawn barges carried cargo (mainly turf) and passengers to the capital from all over the country. By the mid-19th century the train had arrived and the great waterway slowly fell into decline, until the last commercial traffic ceased in 1960. But the 6-km (4-mi) loop around the capital is ideal for a leisurely stroll.

The Grand Canal defines the southern border of the city center. Directly below the canal lies exclusive Ballsbridge, a leafy suburb whose northern reaches contain several of the city's best hotels and restaurants. Its major cultural attractions, however, are considerably farther south—a bit too far to reach on foot unless you're really an ambitious walker. You can hop a cab or take the DART train to Sydney Parade, or Bus 7 or Bus 8 from Burgh Quay (on the south bank of the Liffey, just east of O'Connell Bridge).

Numbers in the text correspond to numbers in the margin and on the Dublin Southside map.

a good walk

Begin by walking east along the Pearse Street side of Trinity College until you arrive at the Ringsend Road Bridge. Raised on stilts above the canal is the **Waterways Visitors Centre** (48) ⚑. Head south and then southwest along the bank until you reach the **Mount Street Bridge** (49). On the southeast side of the canal is Percy Place, a street with elegant, three-story terrace houses. On the northwest side, a small lane leads up to the infamous **Scruffy Murphy's** (50) pub. At this point you can take a detour along Northumberland Street and make a left onto Landsdowne Road. From here you can catch the DART one stop to Sandymount Avenue, which leads east to the beach at Sandymount Strand.

Back at Scruffy Murphy's walk southwest along Herbert Place. You can get really close to the dark green water here as it spills over one of the many wood-and-iron locks (all still in working order) that service the canal. James Joyce lost his virginity to a prostitute on the next stretch of the Canal, around Lower Baggot Street Bridge, but these banks belong to the lonesome ghost of another writer, Patrick Kavanagh. A life-size **statue of Patrick Kavanagh** (51) sits here, contemplative, arms folded, legs crossed on a wooden bench. Less than 2 km (1 mi) past Kavanagh's statue the canal narrows as it approaches Richmond Bridge. Just beyond the bridge is the **Irish Jewish Museum** (52). To finish your walk in style, retrace your steps to Richmond Street, make a left, and stroll past a few antiques stores until you arrive at **Bambrick's** (53), a public house in the best tradition of Dublin.

TIMING You could walk this section of the canal in half an hour if you hurried (and didn't make the detour to the Sandymount Strand), but a leisurely pace best suits a waterside walk, so give yourself a couple of hours to visit the Jewish Museum and explore the old streets off the canal.

What to See

(53) **Bambrick's.** This is a pub in the best Irish tradition: half-empty, frequented mostly by men over 50, and with a long, dark-wood bar and a staff whose sharp grinning humor verges on rudeness. ✉ *11 Richmond St. S, Grand Canal* ☎ *01/475–4402* ⏲ *Daily 11 AM–midnight.*

(52) **Irish Jewish Museum.** Roughly 5,000 European Jews fleeing the pogroms of Eastern Europe arrived in Ireland in the late 19th and early 20th centuries. Today the Jewish population hovers around 1,800. The museum, opened in 1985 by Israeli president Chaim Herzog (himself Dublin-educated), includes a restored synagogue and a display of photographs, letters, and personal memorabilia culled from Dublin's most prominent Jewish families. Exhibits trace the Jewish presence in Ireland back to 1067. In homage to Leopold Bloom, the Jewish protagonist of Joyce's *Ulysses,* every Jewish reference in the novel has been identified. The museum is a 20-minute walk or so southwest from St. Stephen's Green. ✉ *3–4 Walworth Rd., Grand Canal* ☎ *01/453–1797* *Free* ⏲ *May–Sept., Tues., Thurs., and Sun. 11–3:30; Oct.–Apr., Sun. 10:30–2:30; also by appointment.*

(49) **Mount Street Bridge.** The bridge has a wooden lock on either side and is the perfect spot to watch these original gateways to the canal in operation. On the southwest corner of the bridge a small stone monument commemorates the battle of Mount Street Bridge in 1916 and the Irish Volunteers who died on this spot.

off the beaten path

SANDYMOUNT STRAND – The Sandymount Strand, a few blocks west of the Sydney Parade DART station, stretches for 5 km (3 mi) from Ringsend to Booterstown. It was cherished by James Joyce and his beloved from Galway, Nora Barnacle, and it figures as one of the settings in *Ulysses.* (The beach is "at the lacefringe of the tide," as Joyce put it.) When the tide recedes, the beach extends for 1½ km (1 mi) from the foreshore, but the tide sweeps in again very quickly. A sliver of a park lies between Strand Road and the beach, which is not suitable for swimming.

50 Scruffy Murphy's. Many a backroom deal by the country's political power brokers has been made in the back room of this classy wood-and-brass pub. It's the perfect spot for a pint and a snack. ⊠ *Lower Mount St., Grand Canal* ☎ *01/661–5006* ⊙ *Daily 11 AM–midnight.*

51 Statue of Patrick Kavanagh. Patrick Kavanagh (1905–67)—Ireland's great rural poet who in 1942 published his best-known poem, *The Great Hunger,* about farming and poverty—spent the later years of his life sitting on a bench here writing about the canal, which flowed from his birthplace in the Midlands to the city where he would die. In one such poem he tells those who outlive him, "O commemorate me with no hero-courageous tomb, just a canal-bank seat for the passerby." Acknowledging Kavanagh's devotion to this spot, his friends commissioned a life-size bronze of the poet here. ⊠ *Canal bank along Wilton Terr., Grand Canal.*

▶ **48 Waterways Visitors Centre.** In this airy wood-and-glass building you can learn about the history of Irish rivers and canals through photos, videos, and models. ⊠ *Grand Canal Quay, Grand Canal* ☎ *01/677-7501* 🎫 *€2.55* ⊙ *June–Sept., daily 9:30–5:30; Oct.–May, Wed.–Sun. 12:30–5:30.*

Dublin West

This section of Dublin takes you from the 10th-century crypt at Christ Church Cathedral—the city's oldest surviving structure—to the modern plant of the Guinness Brewery and its Storehouse museum. It also crosses the Liffey for a visit to Smithfield, the old market area being billed as the next hot location in the city. Dublin is so compact, however, that to separate out the following sights from those covered in the other city-center Southside walks is potentially to mislead—by suggesting that this area is at some remove from the heart of the city center. In fact, this tour's starting point, City Hall, is just across the street from the Thomas Read pub, and Christ Church Cathedral is a very short walk farther west. The westernmost sights covered here—notably the Royal Hospital and Kilmainham Gaol—*are,* however, at some distance, so if you're not an enthusiastic walker, you may want to drive or catch a cab or a bus out to them.

Numbers in the text correspond to numbers in the margin and on the Dublin West map.

a good walk

Begin with a brief visit to **City Hall** 54 ▶, and then walk up Cork Hill to the Castle Street entrance to **Dublin Castle** 55, whose highlights—the grand salons that show off Viceregal Dublin at its most splendid—are only visitable via a guided tour. In the castle you'll also find the **Chester Beatty Library** 56, a world-renowned collection of Asian art and manuscripts. Leave via the same gate, turn left, and walk west along Castle Street to the ancient, picturesque **Christ Church Cathedral** 57, on one of the city's few hills. At the southwest corner of the cathedral, connected via an utterly beguiling Victorian-era bridge, **Dublinia** 58 gives you a chance to experience life in medieval Dublin. Just down Nicholas Street is—begorrah!—**St. Patrick's Cathedral** 59. If you're eager to venture back to the 17th century or love old books, visit the quaint **Marsh's Library** 60, next door to St. Patrick's. You can then stroll through the old artisan redbrick dwellings in the Liberties neighborhood, home to the heaviest concentration of the city's antiques stores, to Thomas Street and—just follow your nose—the **Guinness Brewery and Storehouse** ⑥ , where you can keep up your spirits in more ways than one. At this point, if you want to see more architecture and modern art, proceed farther west to the Irish Museum of Modern Art in the elegant 17th-century **Royal Hospital Kilmainham** ⑫ , and the **Kilmainham Gaol** ⑬ . If you don't elect to head this way, walk back down Thomas Street and make a left at Bridge Street, which you'll follow across the Liffey; north of the river the street becomes Church Street. On your right is the **Four Courts** ⑭ . A little farther up on the left is **St. Michan's Church** ⑮ and the beginning of the Smithfield area. A quick jog to the west to Bow Street (via Mary's Lane) brings you to the **Old Jameson Distillery** ⑯ —here you'll learn all there is to learn about Irish whiskey. End your walk with a thrilling ride up the glass elevator to the top of **The Chimney** ⑰ .

TIMING   Allow yourself a few hours for this tour, especially if you want to include the Guinness Brewery and Storehouse and the Irish Museum of Modern Art at the Royal Hospital. Keep in mind that if you want to cover the easternmost sights—Dublin Castle, City Hall, Christ Church Cathedral, and environs—you can easily append them to a tour of Temple Bar.

What to See

⑤⑥ Chester Beatty Library. After Sir Alfred Chester Beatty (1875–1968), a Canadian mining millionaire, assembled one of the most significant collections of Islamic and Far Eastern art in the Western world, he donated them to Ireland. Housed in the gorgeous clock tower building of Dublin Castle, and voted European Museum of the Year in 2002, this is one of Dublin's real gems. Among the library's exhibits are clay tablets from Babylon dating from 2700 BC, Japanese color wood-block prints, Chinese jade books, and Turkish and Persian paintings. The second floor, dedicated to the major religions, houses 250 manuscripts of the Koran from across the Muslim world, as well as one of the earliest gospels. Life-size Buddhas from Burma and rhino cups from China are among the other curios on show. Guided tours of the library are available on Tuesday and Saturday at 2:30 PM. On sunny days the garden is one of the most tranquil places in central Dublin. ⊠ *Castle St., Dublin West* ☎ *01/407–0750* ⊕ *www.cbl.ie* ⊠ *Free* ⊙ *May–Sept., weekdays 10–5, Sat. 11–5, Sun. 1–5; Oct.–Apr., Tues.–Fri. 10–5, Sat. 11–5, Sun. 1–5.*

FodorśChoice ★

⊙ ⑰ The Chimney. Just in front of the Chief O'Neill hotel stands one of the original brick chimneys, built in 1895, of the Old Jameson Distillery, which has been turned into a 185-foot observation tower with the first 360-degree view of Dublin. The redbrick chimney now has a two-tier, glass-enclosed platform at the top. The ride up in the glass elevator is just as thrilling as the view. ⊠ *Smithfield Village, Dublin West* ☎ *01/817–3820* ⊕ *www. chiefoneills.com* ⊠ *€5* ⊙ *Mon.–Sat. 10–5:30, Sun. 11–5:30.*

★ ⑤⑦ Christ Church Cathedral. You'd never know from the outside that the first Christianized Danish king built a wooden church at this site in 1038; thanks to the extensive 19th-century renovation of its stonework and trim, the cathedral looks more Victorian than Anglo-Norman. Construction on the present Christ Church—the flagship of the Church of Ireland and one of two Protestant cathedrals in Dublin (the other is St. Patrick's just to the south)—was begun in 1172 by Strongbow, a Norman baron and conqueror of Dublin for the English crown, and went on for 50 years. By 1875 the cathedral had deteriorated badly; a major renovation gave it much of the look it has today, including the addition

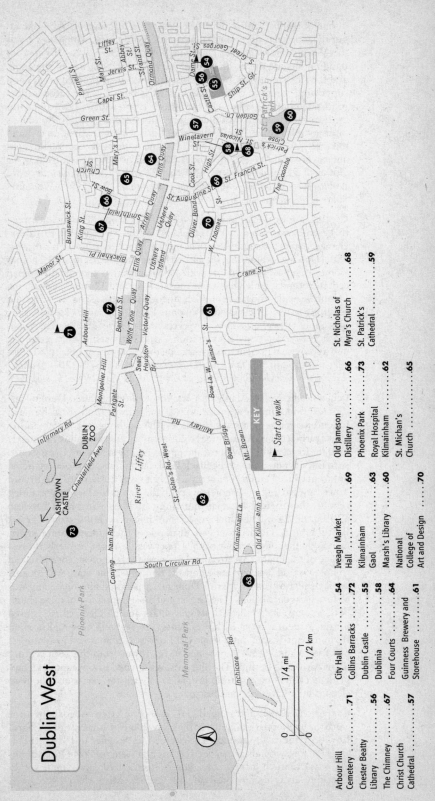

Dublin West

KEY

▲ *Start of walk*

of one of Dublin's most charming structures: a Bridge of Sighs–like affair that connects the cathedral to the old Synod Hall, which now holds the Viking extravaganza, Dublinia. Remains from the 12th-century building include the north wall of the nave, the west bay of the choir, and the fine stonework of the transepts, with their pointed arches and supporting columns. Strongbow himself is buried in the cathedral beneath an impressive effigy. The vast, sturdy **crypt**, with its 12th- and 13th-century vaults, is Dublin's oldest surviving structure and the building's most notable feature. The Treasures of Christ Church exhibition includes manuscripts, various historic artifacts, and impressive examples of gold and silverware. At 6 PM on Wednesday and Thursday you can enjoy the glories of a choral evensong. ⊠ *Christ Church Pl. and Winetavern St., Dublin West* ☎ *01/677–8099* ⊕ *www.cccdub.ie* ⊠ *€3.55* ⊙ *Weekdays 9:45–5, weekends 10–5.*

➤ 54 **City Hall.** Facing the Liffey from Cork Hill at the top of Parliament Street, this grand Georgian municipal building (1769–79), once the Royal Exchange, marks the southwestern corner of Temple Bar. Today it's the seat of the Dublin Corporation, the elected body that governs the city. Thomas Cooley designed the building with 12 columns that encircle the domed central rotunda, which has a fine mosaic floor and 12 frescoes depicting Dublin legends and ancient Irish historical scenes. The 20-foot-high sculpture to the right is Daniel O'Connell, the "Liberator." He looks like he's about to begin the famous speech he gave here in 1800. The building houses a multimedia exhibition—with artifacts, kiosks, graphics, and audiovisual presentations—tracing the evolution of Ireland's 1,000-year-old capital. ⊠ *Dame St., Dublin West* ☎ *01/672–2204* ⊕ *www.dublincity.ie/cityhall/home.htm* ⊠ *€4* ⊙ *Mon.–Sat. 10–5:15, Sun. 2–5.*

55 **Dublin Castle.** Neil Jordan's film *Michael Collins* captured Dublin Castle's near indomitable status well: seat and symbol of the British rule of Ireland for more than seven centuries, the castle figured largely in Ireland's turbulent history early in the 20th century. It's now, however, mainly used for Irish and EU governmental purposes. The sprawling Great Courtyard is the reputed site of the Black Pool (Dubh Linn, pronounced *dove*-lin) from which Dublin got its name. In the Lower Castle Yard, the Record Tower, the earliest of several towers on the site, is the largest remaining relic of the original Norman buildings, built by King John between 1208 and 1220. The clock tower building now houses the Chester Beatty Library. Guided tours are available of the principal State Apartments (on the southern side of the Upper Castle Yard), formerly the residence of the English viceroys and now used by the president of Ireland to host visiting heads of state and EU ministers. The State Apartments are lavishly furnished with rich Donegal carpets and illuminated by Waterford glass chandeliers. The largest and most impressive of these chambers, St. Patrick's Hall, with its gilt pillars and painted ceiling, is used for the inauguration of Irish presidents. The Round Drawing Room, in Bermingham Tower, dates from 1411 and was rebuilt in 1777; numerous Irish leaders were imprisoned in the tower from the 16th century to the early 20th century. The blue oval Wedgwood Room contains Chippendale chairs and a marble fireplace. The Castle Vaults now hold an elegant little patisserie and bistro.

Carved oak panels and stained glass depicting viceroys' coats of arms grace the interior of the Church of the Holy Trinity (formerly called Chapel Royal), on the castle grounds. The church was designed in 1814 by Francis Johnston, who also designed the original General Post Office building on O'Connell Street. Once you're inside, look up—you'll see an elaborate array of fan vaults on the ceiling. More than 100 carved

41

heads adorn the walls outside: St. Peter and Jonathan Swift preside over the north door, St. Patrick and Brian Boru over the east.

One-hour guided tours of the castle are available every half hour, but the rooms are closed when in official use, so call ahead. The easiest way into the castle is through the Cork Hill Gate, just west of City Hall. ⊠ *Castle St., Dublin West* ☎ *01/677–7129* ⊕ *www.dublincastle.ie* ⊠ *State Apartments €4.50, including tour* ⊙ *Weekdays 10–5, weekends 2–5.*

☪ ❺❽ **Dublinia.** Dublin's Medieval Trust has set up an entertaining and informative reconstruction of everyday life in medieval Dublin. The main exhibits use high-tech audiovisual and computer displays; you can also see a scale model of what Dublin was like around 1500, a medieval maze, a life-size reconstruction based on the 13th-century dockside at Wood Quay, and a fine view from the tower. For a more modern take on the city, check out the James Malton series of prints of 18th-century Dublin, hanging on the walls of the coffee shop. Dublinia is in the old Synod Hall (formerly a meeting place for bishops of the Church of Ireland), attached via a covered stonework Victorian bridge to Christ Church Cathedral. ⊠ *St. Michael's Hill, Dublin West* ☎ *01/679–4611* ⊕ *www. dublinia.ie* ⊠ *Exhibit €5.75* ⊙ *Apr.–Sept., daily 10–5; Oct.–Mar., Mon.–Sat. 11–4, Sun. 10–4:30.*

❻❹ **Four Courts.** The stately Corinthian portico and the circular central hall warrant a visit here, to the seat of the High Court of Justice of Ireland. The distinctive copper-covered dome on a colonnaded rotunda makes this one of Dublin's most instantly recognizable buildings. The view from the rotunda is terrific. Built between 1786 and 1802, the Four Courts are James Gandon's second Dublin masterpiece—close on the heels of his Custom House, downstream on the same side of the River Liffey. In 1922, during the Irish Civil War, the Four Courts was almost totally destroyed by shelling—the adjoining Public Records Office was gutted, and many priceless legal documents, including innumerable family records, were destroyed. Restorations took 10 years. There is no tour of the building, but you are welcome to sit in while the courts are in session. ⊠ *Inns Quay, Dublin West* ☎ *01/872–5555* ⊕ *www.courts.ie* ⊙ *Daily 10–1 and 2:15–4.*

★ ❻❶ **Guinness Brewery and Storehouse.** Ireland's all-dominating brewer— founded by Arthur Guinness in 1759 and at one time the largest stout-producing brewery in the world—spans a 60-acre spread west of Christ Church Cathedral. Not surprisingly, it's the most popular tourist destination in town—after all, the Irish national drink is Guinness stout, a dark brew made with roasted malt. The brewery itself is closed to the public, but the Guinness Storehouse is a spectacular attraction, designed to woo you with the wonders of the "dark stuff." In a 1904, cast-iron-and-brick warehouse, the museum display covers six floors built around a huge central glass atrium. Beneath the glass floor of the lobby you can see Arthur Guinness's original lease on the site, for a whopping 9,000 years. The exhibition elucidates the brewing process and its history, with antique presses and vats, a look at bottle and can design through the ages, a history of the Guinness family, and a fascinating archive of Guinness advertisements. You might think it's all a bit much (it's only a drink, after all), and parts of the exhibit do feel a little over-the-top. The star attraction is undoubtedly the top-floor Gravity Bar, with 360-degree floor-to-ceiling glass walls that offer a nonpareil view out over the city at sunset while you sip your free pint. One of the bar's first clients was one William Jefferson Clinton. The funky Guinness Shop on the ground floor is full of lifestyle merchandise associated with the "black stuff." ⊠ *St. James' Gate, Dublin West* ☎ *01/408–4800* ⊕ *www. guinness.com* ⊠ *€13.50* ⊙ *Daily 9:30–5.*

⑥③ Kilmainham Gaol. Leaders of the 1916 Easter Uprising, including Pádrig Pearse and James Connolly, were held in this grim, forbidding structure before being executed in the prison yard. Other famous inmates included the revolutionary Robert Emmet and Charles Stewart Parnell, a leading politician. You can only visit the prison as part of a guided tour, which leaves every hour on the hour. The cells are a chilling sight, while the guided tour and a 30-minute audiovisual presentation relate a graphic account of Ireland's political history over the past 200 years—from a Nationalist viewpoint. A small tearoom is on the premises. ⊠ *Inchicore Rd., Dublin West* ☎ *01/453–5984* ⊕ *www.heritageireland.ie* ⌑ *€5* ⊙ *Apr.–Sept., daily 9:30–5; Oct.–Mar., Mon.–Sat. 9:30–4, Sun. 10–5.*

⑥⓪ Marsh's Library. When Ireland's first public library was founded and endowed in 1701 by Narcissus Marsh, the Archbishop of Dublin, it was open to "All Graduates and Gentlemen." The two-story brick Georgian building has remained virtually the same since then. It houses a priceless collection of 250 manuscripts and 25,000 15th- to 18th-century books. Many of these rare volumes are locked inside cages, as are the readers who wish to peruse them. The cages were to discourage students who, often impecunious, may have been tempted to make the books their own. The library has been restored with great attention to its original architectural details, especially in the book stacks. The library is a short walk west from St. Stephen's Green and accessed through a charming little cottage garden. ⊠ *St. Patrick's Close off Patrick St., Dublin West* ☎ *01/454–3511* ⊕ *www.marshlibrary.ie* ⌑ *€2.50* ⊙ *Mon. and Wed.–Fri. 10–12:45 and 2–5, Sat. 10:30–12:45.*

⑥⑥ Old Jameson Distillery. Founded in 1791, this distillery produced one of Ireland's most famous whiskeys for nearly 200 years, until 1966, when local distilleries merged to form Irish Distillers and moved to a purpose-built, ultramodern distillery in Middleton, County Cork. Part of the complex was converted into the group's head office, and the distillery itself became a museum. There's a short audiovisual history of the industry, which had its origins 1,500 years ago in Middle Eastern perfume making. You can also tour the old distillery, and learn about the distilling of whiskey from grain to bottle, or view a reconstruction of a former warehouse, where the colorful nicknames of former barrel makers are recorded. The 40-minute tour includes a complimentary tasting (remember: Irish whiskey is best drunk without a mixer—try it straight or with water); four attendees are invited to taste different brands of Irish whiskey and compare them against bourbon and Scotch. If you have a large group and everyone wants to do this, phone in advance to arrange it. ⊠ *Bow St., Dublin West* ☎ *01/807–2355* ⊕ *www.irish-whiskey-trail. com* ⌑ *€7* ⊙ *Daily 9–6; tours every ½ hr.*

★ ⑥② Royal Hospital Kilmainham. This replica of Les Invalides in Paris is regarded as the most important 17th-century building in Ireland. Commissioned as a hospice for disabled and veteran soldiers by James Butler—the duke of Ormonde and viceroy to King Charles II—the building was completed in 1684, making it the first building erected in Dublin's golden age. It survived into the 1920s as a hospital, but after the founding of the Irish Free State in 1922, the building fell into disrepair. The entire edifice has since been restored to what it once was.

The structure's four galleries are arranged around a courtyard; there's also a grand dining hall—100 feet long by 50 feet wide. The architectural highlight is the hospital's Baroque chapel, distinguished by its extraordinary plasterwork ceiling and fine wood carvings. "There is nothing in Ireland from the 17th century that can come near this masterpiece," raved cultural historian John FitzMaurice Mills. The Royal

Hospital also houses the **Irish Museum of Modern Art,** which concentrates on the work of contemporary Irish artists such as Richard Deacon, Richard Gorman, Dorothy Cross, Sean Scully, Matt Mullican, Louis Le Brocquy, and James Colman. The museum also displays works by some non-Irish, 20th-century greats, including Picasso and Miró, and regularly hosts touring shows from major European museums. The Café Musée serves light fare such as soups and sandwiches. The hospital is a short ride by taxi or bus from the city center. ⊠ *Kilmainham La., Dublin West* ☎ *01/612–9900* ⊕ *www.modernart.ie* ⊠ *Royal Hospital free; individual art shows may have separate charges; museum free, small charge for special exhibitions* ☉ *Royal Hospital Tues.–Sat. 10–5:30, Sun. noon–5:30; tours every ½ hr. Museum Tues.–Sat. 10–5:30, Sun. noon–5:30; tours Wed. and Fri. at 2:30, Sat. at 11:30.*

65 **St. Michan's Church.** However macabre, St. Michan's main claim to fame is down in the vaults, where the totally dry atmosphere has preserved several corpses in a remarkable state of mummification. They lie in open caskets. Most of the preserved bodies are thought to have been Dublin tradespeople (one was, they say, a religious crusader). Except for its 120-foot-high bell tower, this Anglican church is architecturally undistinguished. The church was built in 1685 on the site of an 11th-century Danish church (Michan was a canonized Danish saint). Another reason to come is to see the 18th-century organ, which Handel supposedly played for his first performance of the *Messiah.* Don't forget to check out the Stool of Repentance—the only one still in existence in the city. Parishioners judged to be "open and notoriously naughty livers" used it to do public penance. ⊠ *Lower Church St., Dublin West* ☎ *01/872–4154* ⊠ *€3.50* ☉ *Apr.–Oct., weekdays 10–12:45 and 2–4:45, Sat. 10–12:45, Sun. service at 10 AM; Nov.–Mar., weekdays 12:30–3:30, Sat. 10–12:45, Sun. service at 10 AM.*

59 **St. Patrick's Cathedral.** The largest cathedral in Dublin and also the national cathedral of the Church of Ireland, St. Patrick's is the second of the capital's two Protestant cathedrals. (The other is Christ Church, and the reason Dublin has two cathedrals is because St. Patrick's originally stood outside the walls of Dublin, while its close neighbor was within the walls and belonged to the see of Dublin.) Legend has it that in the 5th century St. Patrick baptized many converts at a well on the site of the cathedral. The original building, dedicated in 1192 and early English Gothic in style, was an unsuccessful attempt to assert supremacy over Christ Church Cathedral. At 305 feet, this is the longest church in the country, a fact Oliver Cromwell's troops—no friends to the Irish—found useful as they made the church's nave into their stable in the 17th century. They left the building in a terrible state; its current condition is largely due to the benevolence of Sir Benjamin Guinness—of the brewing family—who started financing major restoration work in 1860.

Make sure you see the gloriously heraldic Choir of St. Patrick's, hung with colorful medieval banners, and find the tomb of the most famous of St. Patrick's many illustrious deans, Jonathan Swift, immortal author of *Gulliver's Travels,* who held office from 1713 to 1745. Swift's tomb is in the south aisle, not far from that of his beloved "Stella," Mrs. Esther Johnson. Swift's epitaph is inscribed over the robing-room door. Yeats—who translated it thus: "Swift has sailed into his rest; Savage indignation there cannot lacerate his breast"—declared it the greatest epitaph of all time. Other memorials include the 17th-century Boyle Monument, with its numerous painted figures of family members, and the monument to Turlough O'Carolan, the last of the Irish bards and one of the country's finest harp players. Immediately north of the cathedral is a small park, with statues of many of Dublin's literary figures and St. Patrick's Well. "Living Stones" is the cathedral's permanent exhibition celebrating St. Patrick's place in the life of the city. If you're a music lover, you're in for a treat; matins (9:45 AM) and evensong (5:35 PM) are still sung on most days. ⊠ *Patrick St., Dublin West* ☎ *01/453–9472* ⊕ *www. stpatrickscathedral.ie* 🎫 *€4* ⊙ *May and Sept.–Oct., weekdays 9–6, Sat. 9–5, Sun. 10–11 and 12:45–3; June–Aug., weekdays 9–6, Sat. 9–4, Sun. 9:30–3 and 4:15–5:15; Nov.–Apr., weekdays 9–6, Sat. 9–4, Sun. 10–11 and 12:45–3.*

The Liberties

A stroll through the Liberties puts you in square working-class Dublin, past and present, good and bad. The name derives from Dublin of the Middle Ages, when the area south and west of Christ Church Cathedral was outside the city walls and free from the jurisdiction of the city rulers. A certain amount of freedom, or "liberty," was enjoyed by those who settled here, which attracted people on the fringes of society, especially the poor.

Numbers in the text correspond to numbers in the margin and on the Dublin West map.

a good walk Start on Patrick Street, in the shadow of St. Patrick's Cathedral. Look down the street toward the Liffey and take in the glorious view of Christ Church. Go west on Dean Street, where you'll find John Fallons pub. Take a right off Dean Street onto Francis Street and walk uphill. Several quality antiques shops line both sides of the thoroughfare. Halfway up Francis Street, on the right, behind hefty wrought-iron gates, is one of Dublin's most-overlooked treasures: **St. Nicholas of Myra's Church** ❻❽▶. Continue up Francis Street and take the next right onto Thomas Davis Street, named after a famous patriot and revolutionary (the Liberties area has long had a close association with Irish Nationalism). The street is full of classic, two-story redbrick houses. The area, once the heart of "Darlin' Dublin" and the holy source of its distinctive accent, is rapidly becoming yuppified. Back on Francis Street, in an old factory building with its chimney stack intact, you'll find an exciting market, **Iveagh Market Hall** ❻❾. At the top of Francis Street turn left onto Thomas Street. Across the road, on your right side, stands the wonderfully detailed exterior of St. Augustine and St. John, with its grandiose spire stretching above it. You'll notice churches all over the Liberties; the bishops thought it wise to build holy palaces in the poorest areas of the city as tall, shining beacons of comfort and hope. Farther up Thomas Street in another converted factory is the **National College of Art and Design** ❼⓪.

TIMING Unless you intend on doing some serious antiques shopping, this is a relatively quick stroll—perhaps two hours—as the Liberties is a compact area of small, winding streets.

What to See

❻❾ **Iveagh Market Hall.** One of numerous buildings bestowed upon the city of Dublin by Lord Iveagh of the Guinness family, the cavernous, Victorian, redbrick-and-granite Iveagh Market Hall holds an eclectic market—with books, vintage clothes, records, and jewelry—from Tuesday to Saturday. ⊠ *Francis St., The Liberties* 🎫 *Free* ⊙ *Tues.–Sat. 9–5.*

❼⓪ **National College of Art and Design.** The delicate welding of glass and iron onto the redbrick Victorian facade of this onetime factory makes this school worth a visit. Walk around the cobblestone central courtyard, where there's always the added bonus of viewing some of the students working away in glass, clay, metal, and stone. ⊠ *Thomas St., The Liberties* ☎ *01/671–1377* ⊕ *www.ncad.ie* ✉ *Free* ⊙ *Weekdays 9–7.*

▶ **68** **St. Nicholas of Myra's Church.** A grand neoclassical style characterizes this church, completed in 1834. The highly ornate chapel inside includes ceiling panels of the 12 apostles, and a pietà raised 20 feet above the marble altar, guarded on each side by angels sculpted by John Hogan while he was in Florence. The tiny nuptial chapel to the right has a small Harry Clarke stained-glass window. ⊠ *St. Nicholas St., The Liberties* ✉ *Free* ⊙ *Hrs vary.*

Phoenix Park & Environs

Far and away Dublin's largest park, Phoenix Park (the name is an anglicization of the Irish *Fionn Uisce,* meaning clear water) is a vast, green arrowhead-shape oasis north of the Liffey, about a 20-minute walk from the city center. Dubliners flock here to "take it aisy." It remains the city's main lung, escape valve, sports center (cricket, football, Gaelic games, and polo), and the home of the noble creatures of the Dublin Zoo. A handful of other cultural sights near the park are also worth visiting, but to combine a visit to any of them with any of the other walks in this chapter would be a bit difficult. The Smithfield area and the Old Jameson Distillery, at the end of the Dublin West walk, are the sights closest (the Guinness Brewery and Storehouse, across the river, is also fairly close). So if you do make it to any of those, think about whether you have enough time to append a visit to one or another of these sights. Otherwise, plan to make a special trip out here—walk if you're up to it, or take a car or cab.

Numbers in the text correspond to numbers in the margin and on the Dublin West map.

a good walk
Beginning at the Custom House, walk west along the quays on the north side of the Liffey until you come to Blackhall Place. Turn right and walk north on Blackhall Place and then make a left onto Arbour Hill: the **Arbour Hill Cemetery** **71** ▶ will be on your right. Directly across Arbour Hill are the **Collins Barracks** **72** now a branch of the National Museum (the main entrance is on Benburb Street on the south side). On its west side Benburb becomes Parkgate Street, and it's just a short stroll farther down to the main entrance of **Phoenix Park** **73**.

TIMING Phoenix Park is *big*; exploring it on foot could easily take the better part of a day. If you're looking for a little exercise, head here: jogging, horseback riding, and bicycling are the ideal ways to explore the park more quickly than you can simply by strolling.

What to See

▶ **71** **Arbour Hill Cemetery.** All 14 Irishmen executed by the British following the 1916 Easter Uprising are buried here, including Pádrig Pearse, who led the rebellion; his younger brother Willie, who played a minor role in the uprising; and James Connolly, a socialist and labor leader wounded in the battle. Too weak from his wounds to stand, Connolly was tied to a chair and then shot. The burial ground is a simple but formal area, with the names of the dead leaders carved in stone beside an inscription of the proclamation they issued during the uprising. ⊠ *Arbour Hill, Dublin West* ✉ *Free* ⊙ *Mon.–Sat. 9–4:30, Sun. 9:30–noon.*

72 **Collins Barracks.** The huge Collins Barracks, named for the assassinated republican leader Michael Collins (1890–1922), houses the National Museum's collection of glass, silver, furniture, and other decorative arts; exhibitions on Irish military history; and an exhibition of 200 years of Irish costumes and jewelry. A prize exhibit is a 2,000-year-old Japanese ceremonial bell. ⊠ *Benburb St., Dublin West* ☎ *01/677-7444* ⊕ *www. museum.ie* 🖃 *Free* 🕓 *Tues.–Sat. 10–5, Sun. 2–5.*

🖑 ⑦ **Phoenix Park.** Europe's largest public park, which extends about 5 km (3 mi) along the Liffey's north bank, encompasses 1,752 acres of verdant green lawns, woods, lakes, and playing fields. Sunday is the best time to visit: games of cricket, football (soccer), polo, baseball, hurling (a combination of lacrosse, baseball, and field hockey), and Irish football are likely to be in progress. Old-fashioned gas lamps line both sides of Chesterfield Avenue, the main road that bisects the park for 4 km (2½ mi), which was named for Lord Chesterfield, a lord lieutenant of Ireland, who laid out the road in the 1740s. To the right as you enter the park is the People's Garden, a colorful flower garden designed in 1864.

Among the park's major monuments are the Phoenix Column, erected by Lord Chesterfield in 1747, and the 198-foot obelisk, built in 1817 to commemorate the Duke of Wellington, the Irish general who defeated Napoléon for the British. (Wellington was born in Dublin but, true to the anti-Irish prejudice so prevalent in 19th-century England, balked at the suggestion that he was Irish: "If a man is born in a stable, it doesn't mean he is a horse," he is reputed to have said.) A tall white cross marks the spot where Pope John Paul II addressed more than a million people during his 1979 visit to Ireland. Wild deer can be seen grazing in the many open spaces of the park, especially near here.

You're guaranteed to see wildlife at the **Dublin Zoo,** the third-oldest public zoo in the world, founded in 1830, and just a short walk beyond the People's Garden. The place looks a little dilapidated, but the government has allocated money for a five-year renovation that is now under way and scheduled for completion in 2006. Animals from tropical climes are kept in barless enclosures, and Arctic species swim in the lakes close to the reptile house. Interestingly, the zoo is one of the few places in the world where lions will breed in captivity. Some 700 lions have been bred here since the 1850s, one of whom became familiar to movie fans the world over when MGM used him for its trademark. (As they will tell you at the zoo, he is in fact yawning in that familiar shot: an American lion had to be hired to roar and the "voice" was dubbed.) An African Plains area houses the zoo's larger species. The Pets Corner and City Farm has goats, guinea pigs, and lambs. In summer the Lakeside Café serves ice cream and drinks. ⊠ *Phoenix Park, Dublin West* ☎ *01/677-1425* ⊕ *www.dublinzoo.ie* 🖃 *€10.10* 🕓 *Mar.–Sept., Mon.–Sat. 9:30–6, Sun. 10:30–6; Oct.–Feb., Mon.–Sat. 9:30–5, Sun. 10:30–5.*

Both the president of Ireland and the U.S. ambassador have official residences in the park (the president's is known as Aras an Uachtarain), but neither building is open to the public. Also within the park is a **visitor center,** in the 17th-century fortified Ashtown Castle; it has information about the park's history, flora, and fauna. ⊠ *Phoenix Park, Dublin West* ☎ *01/677-0095* ⊕ *www.heritageireland.ie* 🖃 *€2.75* 🕓 *Visitor center: mid-Mar.–Sept., daily 10–6; Oct., daily 10–5; Nov.–mid-Mar., weekends 10–5.*

need a break?

Ryan's Pub (⊠ 28 Parkgate St., Dublin West ☎ 01/677-6097), one of Dublin's last remaining genuine late-Victorian-era pubs, has changed little since its last remodeling—in 1896. It's right near the entrance to Phoenix Park.

WHERE TO EAT

Revised by
Muriel Bolger
and Naomi
Coleman

Dining out has become something of a national pastime in Ireland. With the blossoming economy of the past decade, 30% of all food eaten is consumed outside the home—a trend that's not confined to Dublin. The dining experience has changed, too, with much greater variety. Although pubs have always been an intrinsic part of Irish life, it has only been in this same period that food has become a real feature of these haunts. Now pub goers can combine the ubiquitous Guinness and Irish whiskey with good, wholesome pub grub.

Irish dining has undergone something of a transition, with ethnic restaurants springing up and more and more global influences appearing on menus. If you want ethnic food, you'll have no trouble finding an establishment to suit your palette. You can choose from elegant restaurants, stylish bistros, relaxed hideaways, and late-night eateries. Indulge in superb French or Italian food one day, and fusion the next—menus often reflect a good mix of Asian, Mediterranean, and modern Irish influences. Vegetarian dishes are becoming increasingly more varied and appealing everywhere. This interest in food has also heralded a new wave of internationally trained professionals who have stamped their own *blás* (Irish for gloss) on traditional ingredients.

The Irish dine later than Americans. They stay up later, too, and bookings are usually not taken before 6:30 or 7 PM and are made until around 11 PM. Lunch goes from 12:30 to 2:30. Pubs often serve food all day—until 8:30 or 9 PM. Most pubs are family friendly and welcome children up until 7 PM. The Irish are an informal bunch, so smart casual dress is typical. The more formal restaurants, however, do expect you to wear a jacket and tie. Shorts and sneakers are out here. Check when booking if unsure.

Prices

A word of warning: you will pay for your dining pleasure here. High overhead and staffing costs have pushed up prices, especially in upscale places. The good news is that although Dublin doesn't have Starbucks, there are scores of local inexpensive cafés serving excellent coffee, often with a good sandwich. Other eateries, borrowing trends from all around the world, serve inexpensive pizzas, focaccia, pitas, tacos, and wraps (which are fast gaining popularity over the sandwich).

It's worthwhile to see if the restaurant of your choice offers an early-bird and/or pre- or post-theater menu, with significantly lower set prices at specific times, usually up to 7:30 PM.

Value Added Tax (VAT)—a 13.5% tax on food and a government excise tax on drinks—will automatically be added to your bill. Before paying, check to see whether a service charge has been included on your bill, which is often the case. If so, you can pay the entire bill with a credit card; if not, it's usual to leave the tip in cash (10% to 15%) if paying the main bill by credit card.

WHAT IT COSTS in euros				
$$$$	**$$$**	**$$**	**$**	**¢**
AT DINNER	over €29	€22–€29	€15–€22	€8–€15	under €8

Prices are per person for a main course at dinner.

ON THE MENU

BEING BOTH AN AGRICULTURAL and a maritime country, Ireland benefits from a copious supply of freshly grown and readily available Irish produce and seafood. Excellent Irish beef, pork, ham, and lamb appear on almost every menu. Keep an eye out, too, for seasonal specials, such as wild and farmed quail and pheasant. Rich and delicious seafood harvests mean you'll find fresh and smoked salmon, oysters, mussels, and shellfish in many guises—all vying with tender cuts of meat and an appetizing selection of quality vegetables. Excellent dairy products are also essential to Irish cuisine. Dollops of fresh cream with home-baked desserts promise some exciting conclusions to these feasts— though you may finish a meal with the delicious native cheeses. Leave room for the mature cheddars and luscious blue cheeses, the slightly sweet Dubliner, St. Tola goat's cheese from Clare, and

Carrigburne Brie from Wexford—only a few of the many fine artisan cheeses produced around the country.

The humble potato still plays an important role in Irish dining, and you'll find this valued vegetable accompanying wild salmon and other seafood, tender lamb, beef, and pork. They're also important in dishes like potato cakes and boxty (potato-and-flour pancake), as well as in colcannon, a traditional Irish dish—with bacon and corned beef—that's a must.

While you're in Dublin, do indulge at least once in the traditional Irish breakfast, which is often served until lunchtime. It includes rashers (bacon), sausages, black and white pudding (types of sausage), mushrooms, tomatoes, fried bread, and a fried egg—with lots of traditional homemade brown and soda breads and the famous Irish creamery butter.

North of the Liffey

Contemporary

$$$–$$$$ ✕ **Chapter One.** In the vaulted, stone-wall basement of the Dublin Writers Museum, just down the street from the Dublin City Gallery, The Hugh Lane, is one of the most notable restaurants on the Northside. Typical dishes include roasted venison with mustard and herb lentils, pancetta, chestnut dumplings, and roasted beetroot. The rich bread-and-butter pudding is a stellar dessert. ✉ *18–19 Parnell Sq., Northside* ☎ *01/873–2266* ⌂ *Reservations essential* ▤ *AE, DC, MC, V* ⊘ *Closed Sun. and Mon. No lunch Sat.*

$$$–$$$$ ✕ **23.** The two-story dining room of this modern restaurant within the Gresham Hotel is a sophisticated blend of droplights, tubular tables, and contemporary art against the backdrop of a dramatic glass wall. The brasserie-style cooking makes use of local ingredients in seafood, duck, chicken, steak, and vegetarian dishes. The pavlova trio, crammed with raspberries, blueberries, and strawberries, is a firm favorite, and a short but varied wine list has been well thought out. The breakfast—buffet-style or from a menu that includes eggs and a full Irish breakfast—attracts early rising tourists and locals. ✉ *Gresham Hotel, 23 Upper O'Connell St., Northside* ☎ *01/817–6116* ⌂ *Reservations essential* ▤ *AE, DC, MC, V* ⊘ *Closed Sun. No lunch.*

$$$
Fodor'sChoice
★
✕ **Halo.** This restaurant in the chic Morrison hotel is a hit with the fashion crowd and lawyers from the nearby Four Courts. With a soaring ceiling and minimalist decor, the dramatic dining room, devised by fashion designer John Rocha, looks moody and mysterious by night, and a little forbidding by day. The emphasis is on complex dishes that look as good as they taste: seared, cured salmon on creamed spinach, and

pomme vapour (mashed potatoes) with tomato and coriander are among the ever-changing specialties. Desserts are miniature works of art on enormous china platters. ⊠ *Morrison hotel, Ormond Quay, Northside* ☎ *01/887–2421* ⊟ *AE, DC, MC, V.*

$$–$$$ ✕ **Bond.** Contemporary food such as smoked-duck salad appears on the menu alongside French dishes such as beef bourguignonne, but the real attraction at the informal and stylish Bond is the wine. Order your food before heading downstairs to choose from a cellar crammed with more than 320 wines. By paying retail price plus €6.35 corkage, you can drink the cheapest fine wine in town. Sommelier Julien le Gentil provides expert advice. A lighter menu of cold dishes such as oysters and smoked salmon is served downstairs. ⊠ *5 Beresford Pl., Northside* ☎ *01/855–9244* ⚖ *Reservations essential* ⊟ *AE, DC, MC, V* ☉ *Closed Sun. No lunch Sat.*

$–$$ ✕ **Harbour Master.** The main attraction of this big, airy restaurant and bar in the Irish Financial Services Centre north of the Liffey is the scenery: it overlooks a canal basin. At lunch the place is packed with stockbrokers and lawyers; dinner is more subdued. You can dine bistro-style at the cavernous bar, but it's better to head for the more spacious—and relaxing—dining area. Try the blackened salmon on a basil polenta mash, served with sautéed chorizo and poppy-seed yogurt dressing. ⊠ *Custom House Docks, Northside* ☎ *01/670–1688* ⊟ *AE, DC, MC, V.*

$ ✕ **The Vaults.** This once-neglected space beneath Connolly Station was imaginatively revamped in 2002 to create one of the city's most fashionable spots. Cavernous arches, smooth stone floors, striking furniture, and dramatic lighting create the background for a mostly young business set. Cocktails are a specialty, although it's worth a visit for the food alone. A wide-ranging menu covers light snack options alongside more substantial dishes like "The Vaults" pizza, a blend of tomato, mozzarella, prawns, red onion, and herbs. Be sure to leave room for the excellent homemade ice cream. Note that they stop serving dinner after 8. ⊠ *Harbourmaster Pl., Northside* ☎ *01/605–4700* ⚖ *Reservations essential* ⊟ *AE, DC, MC, V.*

Irish

¢ ✕ **Soup Dragon.** This tiny café and take-out soup shop serves an astonishing array of fresh soups daily. Soups come in three sizes, and you can get vegetarian soup or soups with meat- or fish-based broth. Favorites include red pepper, tomato, and goat cheese soup; fragrant Thai chicken soup; and hearty mussel, potato, and leek soup. The friendly staff makes fine coffee and delicious smoothies. The cost of soup includes bread and a piece of fruit for dessert—an excellent value. ⊠ *168 Capel St., Northside* ☎ *01/872–3277* ⊟ *No credit cards* ☉ *Closed Sun. No dinner.*

Italian

¢–$ ✕ **Milano.** Like the original Milano eatery on the Southside, in Dublin's Georgian Heart, these branches turn out flashy pizzas, salads, and pasta dishes. ⊠ *38–39 Lower Ormond Quay, Northside* ☎ *01/872–0003* ⊠ *IFSC, Clarion Quay, Northside* ☎ *01/611–9012* ⊟ *AE, DC, MC, V.*

Mediterranean

$–$$ ✕ **101 Talbot.** Popular with Dublin's artistic and literary set, and conveniently close to the Abbey and Gate theaters, this comfortable upstairs restaurant showcases an ever-changing exhibition of local artists' work. The creative contemporary food—with Mediterranean and Middle Eastern influences—uses fresh local ingredients. Try the roast pork fillet marinated in orange, ginger, and soy, and served with fried noodles. The cashew and red-pepper *rissole* (turnover) with chili and ginger jam, served

Where to Eat in Dublin

Saint Brendan's Hospital

Trinity College

Dublin Castle

St. Patrick's Park

St. Stephen's Green

Iveagh Garden

Cathal Brugha Barracks

Custom House

Tara St. Station

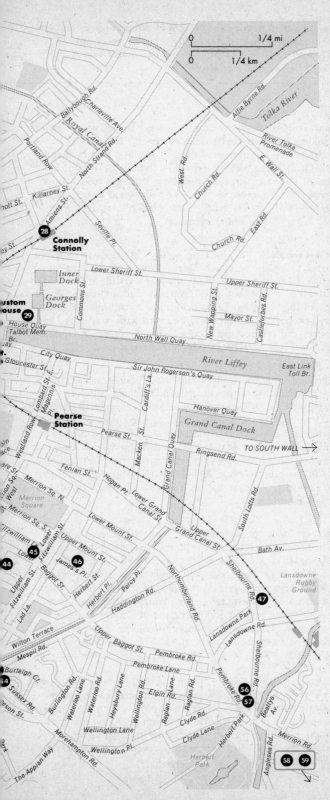

with wild and basmati rice, also impresses. Healthful options and several vegetarian choices make this a highly versatile restaurant. ☒ *101 Talbot St., Northside* ☎ *01/874–5011* ⚿ *Reservations essential* ▤ *AE, DC, MC, V* ☺ *Closed Sun. and Mon.*

City Center

American

\ **$$$$**   ✕**Shanahans.** Dublin's first American-style steak house, in an elegant Georgian building, has proven to be a huge success. It's an old-style place—think large fireplaces, gilt mirrors, a deep carpet, and elegant chandeliers. Certified Irish Angus beef is the star dish, though seafood and lamb are also prized. The basement bar—the Oval Office—is full of Americana and presidential paperwork. ☒ *119 St. Stephen's Green, Southside* ☎ *01/407–0939* ⚿ *Reservations essential* ▤ *AE, DC, MC, V* ☺ *No lunch Mon.–Thurs. and weekends.*

Café

¢   ✕**Busyfeet & Coco Café.** This bustling quirky café emphasizes good
Fodor'sChoice   wholesome food. Organic ingredients play a prominent role on a menu
★   that's laden with delicious salads and sandwiches. Try the grilled goat's cheese salad served with walnut-and-raisin toast and sun-dried-tomato tapenade on a bed of arugula. The delicious homemade hummus sandwich—served on poppy-seed·bread, and topped with roasted red and yellow peppers, red onions, and zucchini—is a favorite. ☒ *41–42 S. William St., Southside* ☎ *01/671–9514* ▤ *No credit cards.*

Continental

$$$$ ✕**Locks.** A genuinely warm welcome awaits you at Claire Douglas's townhouse restaurant, which overlooks the Grand Canal. The dining room is comfortable and old-fashioned, with banquette seating and starched table linens. Hearty portions are served on antique ironstone plates. Classic starters include Locks' special potato skins—dished up with prawns, tomato, and spinach and served with a fabulous hollandaise sauce—and excellent smoked salmon. Choose your main course from the traditional fish dishes, Irish lamb, and venison. ☒ *1 Windsor Terr., Portobello, Southside* ☎ *01/454–3391* ⚿ *Reservations essential* ▤ *AE, DC, MC, V* ☺ *Closed Sun. No lunch Sat.*

French

★ **$$$$**   ✕**Thornton's.** If you are passionate about food, this place is a must—owner Kevin Thornton has forged a reputation as one of the very best chefs in Ireland. His cooking style is light, and his dishes are small masterpieces of structural engineering. A highlight is the braised suckling pig served with trotter and loin in a *poitin* (a kind of Irish whiskey made from potatoes) sauce. Desserts range from banana ice cream to warm chocolate tartlet with raspberries. Sheridans of Dublin supplies the enormous selection of cheeses. The dining room is simple—there's little to distract you from the exquisite food. ☒ *Fitzwilliam Hotel, St. Stephen's Green, Southside* ☎ *01/454–9067* ⚿ *Reservations essential* ▤ *AE, DC, MC, V* ☺ *Closed Sun. and Mon.*

¢   ✕**Lemon Crêpe and Coffee Co.** This place has the best crepes in town, and hungry Dubliners know it. The space is compact, white, and minimalist. A few pavement tables—complete with an outdoor heater—make this a great spot for a tasty snack while you watch Dublin saunter by. To really indulge, follow up savory pancakes with sugar-sweet crepes. Take-out service is swift. ☒ *66 S. William St., Southside* ☎ *01/672–9044* ▤ *No credit cards.*

Indian

$–$$ ✕ **Jaipur.** A spacious room with a sweeping staircase and contemporary
Fodor'sChoice furnishings reflects Jaipur's modern, cutting-edge approach to Indian
★ cooking. Mixed with more traditional dishes, such as chicken tikka masala,
are more unusual preparations, such as *rara gosdh* (lamb slowly cooked
with black-eyed peas). Dishes can be toned down or spiced up to suit
your palate, and service is courteous and prompt. The wine list is well
thought out. ✉ *41 S. Great George's St., Southside* ☎ *01/677–0999*
⌂ *Reservations essential* ▭ *AE, MC, V.*

$–$$ ✕ **Khyber Tandoori.** A short walk from St. Stephen's Green will bring you
to this gem of a restaurant. It specializes in Pakistani cuisine but also serves
a broad selection of Indian dishes. Try the *shami* (Syrian) kebabs—dainty,
spiced patties of minced lamb and lentils—or *kabuli chicken tikka shash-
lik* (marinated, diced chicken with onions and red and green peppers), which
comes bright red and sizzling on an iron platter. Settle in and admire the
richly embroidered wall hangings and the great gusts of steam coming from
the tandoori oven in the glassed-in area. ✉ *44–45 S. William St., Southside* ☎ *01/670–4855* ▭ *AE, DC, MC, V* ☻ *No lunch Sun.*

Italian

$$–$$$ ✕ **Il Primo.** Old wooden tables and chairs give this place a casual air,
and the friendly, if cramped, surroundings attract a devoted clientele.
The Irish-Italian cuisine is both imaginative and reassuring. Among the
main courses, a delicious chicken ravioli in white wine cream, with Parma
ham and wild mushrooms, is a standout. There's a very long wine list
highlighting Italian wines. ✉ *Montague St. off Harcourt St., Southside*
☎ *01/478–3373* ▭ *AE, DC, MC, V* ☻ *No lunch weekends.*

¢–$ ✕ **The Steps of Rome.** Just a few steps from Grafton Street, this Italian
eatery is perfect for a late-night bite or quick lunch (or takeout). Slices
of delicious, homemade thin-crust pizza, with all the traditional toppings,
are the main attraction. The *fungi* (mushroom) pizza is particularly good.
The few tables are usually full, but it's worth waiting for the classic Italian pasta dishes—penne with salmon, and fresh salads with focaccia.
Follow it all up with cheesecake or tiramisu, and good strong espresso.
✉ *1 Chatham Ct., Southside* ☎ *01/670–5630* ▭ *No credit cards.*

Japanese

$–$$ ✕ **Yamamori.** The first of many ramen noodle bars to open in Ireland,
this is one of the best. The meals-in-a-bowl are a splendid slurping experience, and although you'll be supplied with a small Chinese-style soup
spoon, the best approach is with chopsticks. You can also get sushi and
sashimi, plus delicious chicken teriyaki. ✉ *71–72 S. Great George's St.,
Southside* ☎ *01/475–5001* ▭ *AE, MC, V.*

$ ✕ **Wagamama.** Modeled on a Japanese canteen, Wagamama, with its
long wooden tables and benches, ensures a unique communal dining experience. This low-ceilinged basement noodle bar is constantly packed,
but service is swift. Formal courses aren't acknowledged—food is served
as soon as it's ready, and appetizers and main courses arrive together. Choose
from filling bowls of *cha han* (fried rice with chicken, prawns, and vegetables) or chili beef ramen, and wash it down with fresh fruit or vegetable
juice. ✉ *S. King St., Southside* ☎ *01/478–2152* ▭ *AE, DC, MC, V.*

Pan-Asian

$–$$ ✕ **Mao.** Everything is Asian fusion at this bustling café, from the little
Andy Warhol pastiche of Chairman Mao on the washroom door to the
eclectic mix of dishes on the menu, which combine Thai, Vietnamese,
and other Southeast Asian elements. Favorites are the Malaysian chicken
and the *nasi goreng* (Indonesian fried rice with chicken and shrimp). Reservations aren't accepted, so go early to be sure of a seat. There's another

branch in Dun Laoghaire, a 20-minute taxi ride from the city center. ⊠ *2 Chatham Row, Southside* ☎ *01/670–4899* ⊠ *The Pavilion, Dun Laoghaire, South County Dublin* ☎ *01/214–8090* ⌔ *Reservations not accepted* ▭ *MC, V.*

Vegetarian

¢ ✕**Nude.** This sleek fast-food café was such a good idea that owner Norman Hewson—brother of U2's Bono—has opened another branch for takeout only on Upper Leeson Street. The menu is mostly vegetarian, and everything on it is made with organic and free-range ingredients. Choose from homemade soups and vegetable wraps, smoothies, and fresh-squeezed juices. ⊠ *21 Suffolk St., Southside* ☎ *01/677–4804* ⊠ *101 Upper Leeson St., Southside* ☎ *01/661–5650* ▭ *DC, MC, V* ⊘ *Closed weekends. No dinner.*

Dublin's Georgian Heart

Contemporary

$$–$$$ ✕**Dish.** Clever cuisine, a relaxed dining room, and a pleasant staff have secured Dish a loyal following. The large white room with sanded floorboards and long narrow mirrors is a wonderfully stylish space in which to enjoy Gerard Foote's confident cooking. Dishes range from grilled Clonakilty black pudding (sausage with dried pig's blood) with roasted red pepper and borlotti beans to roasted monkfish with bacon, savoy cabbage, beetroot, and cream. The focus is on Irish ingredients. It's popular for Sunday brunch, and the midweek lunch is an excellent value. ⊠ *146 Upper Leeson St., Southside* ☎ *01/664–2135* ⌔ *Reservations essential* ▭ *AE, DC, MC, V.*

★ $–$$$ ✕**La Stampa.** It's one of the most dramatic dining rooms in Dublin, with huge gilt mirrors and elaborate candelabra that are gloriously over the top. This gives even the simplest meal a sense of fun and occasion. The menu changes frequently and reflects the restaurant's eclectic, international style. Try rack of organic lamb with braised beans, tomatoes, and rosemary jus; roasted scallops with artichoke mash and a tomato vinaigrette; or giant prawns served with garlic or mango mayonnaise. Expect brisk but friendly service. ⊠ *35 Dawson St., Southside* ☎ *01/677–8611* ▭ *AE, DC, MC, V.*

Continental

$$$$ ✕**Kevin Arundel at Number Ten.** Chef Kevin Arundel is one of Dublin's rising stars, specializing in modern European cooking. Expect luxury delights such as foie gras, oysters, and truffles served in an intimate, romantic dining room with soft lighting, flowers, and a fireplace. The €45 set dinner menu changes, but might include a starter of *ballotine* (stuffed and shaped into a bundle) of rabbit with shiitake mousse, shallot cream, and caramelized root vegetables followed by West Cork scallops with potato mousseline and garlic butter. The wine list is good, the service is professional, and the quality of cooking offers surprising value for the money. ⊠ *10 Lower Fitzwilliam St., Southside* ☎ *01/676–1367* ⌔ *Reservations essential* ▭ *AE, DC, MC, V* ⊘ *No lunch weekends.*

$$–$$$ ✕**Brownes Brasserie.** Go to this Georgian town house, now a boutique hotel on St. Stephen's Green, if you're looking for a lovely spot in which to share an intimate meal. Huge mirrors reflect the light from crystal chandeliers onto the jewel-color walls and upholstery. The rich and heartwarming food includes such classics as char-grilled swordfish steak with a warm salad of purple potatoes, braised fennel, and salsa verde. The lavender-scented crème brûlée is a lovely finish to a meal. ⊠ *22 St. Stephen's Green, Southside* ☎ *01/638–3939* ⌔ *Reservations essential* ▭ *AE, DC, MC, V* ⊘ *No lunch Sat.*

French

$$$$
Fodor'sChoice
★

Patrick Guilbaud. Expect superb cooking and impeccable service at this fine restaurant with a marvelously lofty dining room hung with paintings from the owners' private collection. The best dishes here are simple—and flawless. Try the house specialty, Châlons duck à l'orange. Follow that, if you can, with the *assiette au chocolat* (a plate of five hot and cold chocolate desserts). The wine list spans 70 pages. ✉ *21 Upper Merrion St., Southside* ☎ *01/676–4192* ⌂ *Reservations essential* 🖃 *AE, DC, MC, V* ☉ *Closed Sun. and Mon.*

Irish

$$–$$$$

Dobbins. Don't be deceived by the sawdust on the floor and the simple furnishings. The combination of cozy booth seating, friendly service, and classic bistro food makes Dobbins popular with businesspeople. Owner John O'Byrne presides over an impressive cellar with hundreds of wines from around the world. Tempura of prawns is a popular starter; boned brace of quail, with black pudding and foie gras stuffing is a typical entrée. There's valet parking, and the staff is expert at summoning taxis. ✉ *15 Stephens La., off Mount St., Southside* ☎ *01/676–4679* ⌂ *Reservations essential* 🖃 *AE, DC, MC, V* ☉ *Closed Sun. and Mon. No lunch Sat.*

$$–$$$

One Pico. Not only is the design sophisticated and modern, but Eamonn O'Reilly's cooking is also decidedly contemporary. Dishes such as fresh chicken and kale-and-bacon mashed potatoes demonstrate a savvy use of Irish ingredients. Follow this with the baked chèvre cheesecake with praline chocolate and orange confit. Service is excellent, and the top-class cooking makes this good value for the money. ✉ *5–6 Molesworth Pl., off Schoolhouse La., Southside* ☎ *01/676–0300* ⌂ *Reservations essential* 🖃 *AE, DC, MC, V* ☉ *Closed Sun.*

¢–$

Kilkenny Kitchen. Take a break from shopping and sightseeing at this big self-service restaurant on the upper floor of the Kilkenny Shop. Homemade soup, casseroles, cold meats, and salads are arranged on a long buffet, along with lots of tasty breads and cakes. Try to get a table by the window overlooking the playing fields of Trinity College. Lunchtime is busy, but it's very pleasant for morning coffee or afternoon tea. ✉ *5–6 Nassau St., Southside* ☎ *01/677–7066* 🖃 *AE, DC, MC, V.*

Italian

¢–$

Milano. The big open kitchen at this bright cheerful place turns out tasty flashy pizzas, with such combinations as tomato and mozzarella, ham and eggs, Cajun with prawns and Tabasco, spinach and egg, and ham and anchovies. There are also simple salads such as tomato and mozzarella with dough balls, and some baked pasta dishes. This is a good place to dine late, with last orders at midnight. Three other branches have opened up: one in Temple Bar, another on Bachelor's Walk, and the third in the Irish Financial Services Centre. ✉ *38 Dawson St., Southside* ☎ *01/670–7744* 🖃 *AE, DC, MC, V.*

Pan-Asian

$–$$$

Diep le Shaker. Comfortable high-back chairs, pristine table linen, and elegant stemware make this big, flamboyant Thai food spot a lovely, and posh, place to dine. It's a place where half the reason for going is to see and be seen. Try the steamed scallops and ginger, or lobster in garlic pepper and Thai herbs. Don't be surprised to see people ordering champagne to go with their meal—there's a permanent party vibe here, which attracts Ireland's wealthy in droves. It's slightly off the beaten track, on a narrow lane off Pembroke Street. ✉ *55 Pembroke La., Southside* ☎ *01/661–1829* 🖃 *AE, DC, MC, V* ☉ *Closed Sun.*

CloseUp

PUB·FOOD

MOST PUBS SERVE FOOD at lunchtime, many throughout the day and into the early evening. The food served is fairly standard, with everything from hearty soups and stews with homemade brown bread for those in a hurry, to chicken curries, pasta dishes, smoked salmon, salads, sandwiches, and good desserts. Many pubs serve a choice of two or three roasted joints and a fish dish with a selection of vegetables. This is an inexpensive way to eat out, and the quality of the food is often quite good. Expect to pay around €4 for soup and brown bread, and €8 to €10 for a main course. Most of the popular pubs take credit cards; tipping is optional.

Many pubs in areas popular with tourists have traditional music sessions, some throughout the week, others on weekends only. It's not necessary to book for these in advance, but if the establishment serves food as well, it's not a bad idea.

Davy Byrne's. James Joyce immortalized this pub in Ulysses. Nowadays it's more akin to a cocktail bar than a Dublin pub, but it's good for fresh and smoked salmon, salads, fresh oysters, and a hot daily special. ⊠ 21 Duke St., Southside ☎ 01/671–1298 ⊟ AE, MC, V.

The Odeon. The converted main building of Harcourt Street's old railway station houses this large, modern bar. Both the lunch and dinner menus include fresh panini, beef and Guinness stew, chicken wings, and homemade sausages. Sunday brunch is served between noon and 5. ⊠ 57 Harcourt St., Southside ☎ 01/478–2088 ⊟ AE, MC, V.

The Old Stand. This pub, one of the oldest in Dublin, is conveniently close to Grafton Street, and serves grilled food, including steaks. ⊠ 37 Exchequer St., Southside ☎ 01/677–7220 ⊟ AE, MC, V.

Stag's Head. Serving one of Dublin's best pub lunches, this place is a favorite among both Trinity students and businesspeople. ⊠ 1 Dame Ct., Southside ☎ 01/679–3701 ⊟ No credit cards.

Zanzibar. This spectacular immense bar on the Northside looks as though it might be more at home in downtown Marrakech. Laze away an afternoon in one of the wicker chairs and enjoy hearty pastas, burgers, salads, and cocktails. ⊠ 34–35 Lower Ormond Quay, Northside ☎ 01/878–7212 ⊟ AE, MC, V.

Temple Bar

American–Casual

$–$$ ✕ **Elephant & Castle.** One of Temple Bar's most popular and established eateries, Elephant & Castle serves traditional American food—charcoal-grilled burgers, salads, omelets, sandwiches, and pasta. Sunday brunch is always packed. When the service is good, the turnover tends to be quick, although you may be inclined to linger. Generous portions of unfussy and well-prepared food, and the casual environment, make this a Dublin stand-out. New Yorkers take note: yes, this is a cousin of the restaurant of the same name in Greenwich Village. ⊠ *18 Temple Bar, Temple Bar* ☎ *01/ 679–3121* ⌂ *Reservations not accepted* ⊟ *AE, DC, MC, V.*

¢–$$ ✕ **Bad Ass Café.** Sinéad O'Connor used to wait tables at this lively café in a converted warehouse between the Central Bank and Ha'penny

Bridge. (A "Rock 'n Stroll" tour plaque notes O'Connor's past here.) Old-fashioned cash shuttles whiz around the ceiling of the barnlike space, with bare floors and primary colors inside and out. You can indulge in some great people-watching behind the wall of glass here. The food—mainly pizzas and burgers—is unexceptional, but the Bad Ass can be a lot of fun and appetites of all ages love it. ⊠ *9–11 Crown Alley, Temple Bar* ☎ *01/671–2596* ▭ *AE, MC, V.*

Cajun–Creole

$–$$ ✕ **Tante Zoe's.** The Deep South comes to Dublin with this dark, bustling restaurant, a firm favorite with vacationers and large parties. Old posters, bamboo, and dark wood set a broody, atmospheric scene for colorful Creole cooking. Seafood fans shouldn't miss the Cajun popcorn—a mountain of spicy baby shrimp coated in bread crumbs and served with a creamy tomato mayonnaise. Spicy blackened chicken with savory rice is another favorite. Desserts are reliably good, particularly the Mississippi mud pie. ⊠ *1 Crow St., Temple Bar* ☎ *01/679–4407* ⊜ *Reservations essential* ▭ *AE, DC, MC, V.*

Contemporary

$$$$ ✕ **The Tea Room.** If you have something to celebrate or you're hoping to spot some celebrities, this is a good bet. It's part of the Clarence hotel, where the stars of stage and screen stay when they're in town. The food is adventurous and consistently good. Typically mouthwatering entrées include risotto of mussels and courgettes (zucchini) with parsley and garlic. The bright, lofty dining room has spectacular flower arrangements and elegant, modern table settings. ⊠ *Clarence hotel, 6–8 Wellington Quay, Temple Bar* ☎ *01/407–0813* ⊜ *Reservations essential* ▭ *AE, DC, MC, V.*

$$–$$$$ ✕ **Mermaid Café.** One of the chef-owners dabbles in fine art, and his tastes in this area are reflected in his artistic and decorative style of bistro cooking. It's not cheap, but the food is quite good. Lunch is an exceptional value—piquant crab cakes, hearty seafood casseroles, rib-eye steak, or radicchio and melted goat's cheese. Good attention to detail and a thoughtful wine list make this modest restaurant with tall windows looking onto busy Dame Street one of the most popular eateries in Temple Bar. ⊠ *69 Dame St., Temple Bar* ☎ *01/670–8236* ▭ *MC, V.*

$$–$$$ ✕ **Pacific.** Temple Bar's most stylish restaurant delivers serious food in slick surroundings. The glass-fronted dining room is matched for drama by a double-story room out back with cream leather seating and sweeping stairs to the Sky Jazz Bar (open weekends only). Despite the name, Pacific isn't primarily a seafood restaurant, and you're as likely to find venison or duck confit on the menu as sea bass and scallops. Chef Nick Woollard's presentation is stunning. Try the lamb shank with caramelized-onion mash, roasted garlic, and port jus. ⊠ *17–19 Sycamore St., Temple Bar* ☎ *01/677–4199* ⊜ *Reservations essential* ▭ *AE, DC, MC, V* ⊗ *No dinner Sun.*

★ $–$$$ ✕ **Eden.** Eden is a happening, trendy place, hip with fashion and media types. It has an open kitchen and a high wall of glass through which you can observe one of Temple Bar's main squares. Patio-style doors lead to an outdoor eating area—a major plus in a city with relatively few alfresco dining spots. Standout dishes include duck leg confit with lentils, and mustard-crusted braised hock of ham served with *champ* (creamy, buttery mashed potatoes with scallions). Desserts include rhubarb crème brûlée and homemade ice creams and sorbets. ⊠ *Meeting House Sq., Temple Bar* ☎ *01/670–5372* ⊜ *Reservations essential* ▭ *AE, DC, MC, V.*

French

★ $$$-$$$$ ✕**Les Frères Jacques.** It brings a little bit of Paris to Temple Bar: old prints of Paris and Deauville hang on the green-papered walls, and the French waiters, dressed in white Irish linen and black bow ties, exude a Gallic charm without being excessively formal. Expect traditional French cooking that nods to the seasons. Seafood is a major attraction, and lobster, fished right from the tank, is a specialty—it's typically roasted and flambéed with Irish whiskey. Also recommended are the meat and game specialties, when in season. A piano player performs Friday and Saturday evenings and the occasional weeknight. ⊠ *74 Dame St., Temple Bar* ☎ *01/679–4555* ⌕ *Reservations essential* ⊟ *AE, MC, V* ☉ *Closed Sun. No lunch Sat.*

Italian

$-$$$ ✕**Osteria Romano.** Members of the Italian community congregate in the evenings at this cheerful eatery, which serves authentic Roman cuisine. Specialties include *melanzane parmigiani,* a delicious dish of baked eggplant and cheese, and the excellent cream-based pastas, such as spaghetti Alfredo and carbonara. Beware of finishing the meal with too many flaming *sambucas* (anise-flavored, semisweet Italian liqueur). The best table, by the window, overlooks the street. ⊠ *5 Crow St., Temple Bar* ☎ *01/ 670–8662* ⊟ *AE, DC, MC, V.*

¢–$ ✕**Milano.** Like the original Milano eatery on the Southside, in Dublin's Georgian Heart, this branch turns out flashy pizzas, salads, and pasta dishes. ⊠ *19 Essex St. E, Temple Bar* ☎ *01/670–3384* ⊟ *AE, DC, MC, V.*

Mediterranean

$$-$$$ ✕**Bruno's.** Experienced French-born restaurateur Bruno Berta has a hit on his hands with his French-Mediterranean bistro on one of the busiest corners in Temple Bar. Simple but stylish dishes range from starters like *feuilleté* of crab meat and saffron sauce to main dishes of roasted scallops with Jerusalem artichoke purée and warm smoked-bacon-and-walnut dressing. The friendly service and relaxed surroundings make this one of the area's best bets. ⊠ *30 Essex St. E, Temple Bar* ☎ *01/ 670–6767* ⊟ *AE, DC, MC, V* ☉ *Closed Sun.*

The Grand Canal & Ballsbridge

Contemporary

$$$-$$$$ ✕**Seasons.** The Four Seasons group prides itself on luxury service and attention to detail, and you should expect no less at the Dublin branch of the hotel's restaurant, with its elegant dining room, silver service, and first-rate cooking. Highly dramatic dishes creatively incorporate Irish, often organic, ingredients. A starter of roasted scallops, cauliflower purée, and raisin and caper dressing might be followed by roasted loin and braised shank of lamb with sauce *paloise* (hollandaise flavored with mint). Sommelier Simon Keegan is one of the best in the country. Sunday brunch has become a ritual for many well-to-do Dublin families. ⊠ *Four Seasons hotel, Simmonscourt Rd., Ballsbridge* ☎ *01/665– 4805* ⌕ *Reservations essential* ⊟ *AE, DC, MC, V.*

$-$$ ✕**O'Connells.** Fresh Irish produce and baked goods are the emphasis in this vast modern space with sleek timber paneling and floor-to-ceiling windows. Try the spit-roasted duck or anything baked in the huge clay oven. Also good are the monkfish with a lemon and garlic sauce, and an omelet made from organic eggs from free-range chickens, peppers, zucchini, and a sweet chili sauce. A tremendous selection of fresh breads is on display in the open kitchen, which turns into a buffet for breakfast and lunch. ⊠ *Merrion Rd., Ballsbridge* ☎ *01/647–3304* ⊟ *AE, DC, MC, V.*

French

$ ✕**French Paradox.** Relaxed, ambitious, and tasteful French Paradox has found a real niche in the Dublin scene. Wine buffs, Francophiles, and gourmets flock here for the traditional fare and Continental environment. Share the *assiette le fond de barrique,* a selection of charcuterie, pâté, and cheese, or perhaps indulge in a smoked-duck salad or a selection from the foie gras menu. Find a nice bottle from the ground-floor wine shop (mostly French labels) and sip it in situ for a mere €8 corkage. Seating is limited, so go on the early side. ⊠ *53 Shelbourne Rd., Ballsbridge* ☎ *01/660–4068* ⌕ *Reservations essential* ▤ *AE, MC, V* ☉ *Closed Sun.*

Philippine

$–$$ ✕**Bahay Kubo.** All dishes are listed in English on the menu at Ireland's only Philippine restaurant, though the basic descriptions fail to capture the true diversity of the cooking. Persevere and you'll find a good selection of authentic Philippine cooking with touches of Chinese. Chicken, beef, and prawns all feature heavily, with red-curry chicken in coconut milk the most popular dish. Desserts have been brought in frozen, so it's best to stick to starters and entrées and finish up with a coffee. ⊠ *14 Bath Ave., Ballsbridge* ☎ *01/660–5572* ⌕ *Reservations essential* ▤ *AE, MC, V* ☉ *Closed Mon. No lunch Sat.–Wed.*

Dublin West

Irish

¢ ✕**Burdock's.** Join the inevitable queue at Dublin's famous take-out fish-and-chips shop, right next door to the Lord Edward pub. You can eat in the gardens of St. Patrick's Cathedral, a 5-minute walk away. ⊠ *2 Werburgh St., Dublin West* ☎ *01/454–0306* ▤ *No credit cards.*

Russian

$$–$$$ ✕**Old Dublin.** This brasserie-style restaurant near St. Patrick's Cathedral specializes in Russian and Scandinavian food. In the evening, glowing fires warm the cozy-but-elegant low-ceiling rooms, and candles light the tables. Blini, borscht, chicken Kiev, and beef Stroganoff figure on the menu, along with a few Irish staples such as roasted lamb and fresh baked salmon. One fine surprise on the menu is planked sirloin Hussar, a steak baked between two oak planks, and served on an oak platter with salad and sweet pickle. ⊠ *90–91 St. Francis St., Dublin West* ☎ *01/454–2028* ▤ *AE, DC, MC, V* ☉ *Closed Sun. No lunch Mon., Tues., Sat.*

The Liberties

Café

¢ ✕**Gallic Kitchen.** Canny Dubliners make regular pilgrimages to Sarah Webb's bakery, where some of the best pastries in town are available daily. There's no seating in this powerhouse patisserie, but long counters allow space for perching your coffee and tucking into the finest sweet and savory treats. Pop in for morning coffee and pear tart; for lunch try quiche or salmon roulade with homemade salsa; and take afternoon tea with a scrumptious scone. Expect queues at lunchtime, and be sure to buy in bulk for the tastiest take-out picnic in town. ⊠ *49 Francis St., The Liberties* ☎ *01/454–4912* ▤ *No credit cards* ☉ *Closed Sun. No dinner.*

Phoenix Park & Environs

Eclectic

$–$$$ ✕**Nancy Hands.** This spot manages to re-create tradition without coming across like a theme bar. A galleylike room juxtaposes old wood, raw brick, and antiques with contemporary art to create a convivial, cozy dining area. The bar food is good, but the upstairs restaurant operates on a more serious level. Specialties include Flanagan's Twist—a mousseline of scallop and crab encased in fresh salmon—and a Mediterranean skewer laden with succulent chicken and beef. The menu includes Thai- and Japanese-style dishes, too. Numerous wines are served by the glass, and the selection of spirits is one of the most impressive in the country. ✉ *30–32 Parkgate St., Dublin West* ☎ *01/677–0149* ✍ *Reservations essential* ▭ *AE, DC, MC, V.*

WHERE TO STAY

"An absolute avalanche of new hotels" is how the *Irish Times* characterized Dublin's hotel boom. New lodgings have sprung up all over the city, including the much-talked-about Westin at College Green, and a few in Ballsbridge, an inner "suburb" that's a 20-minute walk from the city center.

Dublin has a decent selection of inexpensive accommodations, including many moderately priced hotels with basic but agreeable rooms. Many B&Bs, long the mainstay of the economy end of the market, have upgraded their facilities and now provide rooms with private bathrooms or showers, as well as multichannel color televisions and direct-dial telephones.

If you've rented a car and you're not staying at a hotel with secure parking facilities, it's worth considering a location out of the city center, such as Dalkey or Killiney, where the surroundings are more pleasant and you won't have to worry about parking on city streets.

Prices

Demand for rooms means that rates are high at the best hotels by the standards of any major European or North American city (and factoring in the exchange rate means a hotel room can take a substantial bite out of your budget). The recent slump in tourism, however, has caused a few hotels to cut their prices considerably. Service charges range from 15% in expensive hotels to zero in moderate and inexpensive ones. Be sure to inquire when you make reservations.

As a general rule of thumb, lodgings on the north side of the river tend to be more affordable than those on the south. B&Bs charge as little as €46 a night per person, but they tend to be in suburban areas—generally a 15-minute bus ride from the center of the city. This is not in itself a great drawback, and savings can be significant.

Many hotels have a weekend, or "B&B," rate that's often 30% to 40% cheaper than the ordinary rate; some hotels also have a midweek special that provides discounts of up to 35%. These rates are available throughout the year but are harder to get in high season. Ask about them when booking a room (they are available only on a prebooked basis), especially if you plan a brief or weekend stay.

WHAT IT COSTS in euros					
	$$$$	**$$$**	**$$**	**$**	**¢**
FOR 2 PEOPLE	over €230	€180–€230	€130–€180	€80–€130	under €80

Prices are for two people in a standard double room in high season, including VAT and a service charge (often applied in larger hotels).

MORE BANG FOR YOUR BUCK

THE DAYS OF COUNTLESS CHEAP LODGINGS in Dublin are long gone: prices are now comparable to those in Paris and London. So it's more important than ever to get the best deal for your dollar. The **Merrion** is one of the most expensive hotels in the city, but its location between Merrion Square and St. Stephen's Green is perfect, the parking is free, and the rooms are the biggest in town. As an added bonus, staying here secures you the right to brag that you've slept in the Georgian former home of the Duke of Wellington himself. If location is a priority but you don't want to spend a fortune, try the moderately priced, redbrick **Central Hotel**, which lives up to its name: it's literally 100 yards from the front gate of Trinity College. The rooms are small but stylish, and you have easy access to the wonderful Library Bar, the most serene drinking spot in Dublin. To

stay just off the ever-trendy Grafton Street for less than €150 is a real treat, and the **Grafton Guesthouse** also throws in beautifully furnished rooms in a Victorian town house. A pleasant outdoor courtyard, en suite showers, a turf fire, and a delicious all-you-can-eat breakfast—does that sound like a hostel to you? Well, it is—**Globetrotters Tourist Hostel** is the pick of its kind in the city, and it even has a cute B&B next door. Perhaps because the **Hotel Saint George** is on the Northside, its prices do not reflect its opulence. Add in the free parking and oversize rooms and you know you've found a real bargain.

North of the Liffey

In Town

$$$$ **The Morrison.** Halfway between the Ha'penny and Capel Street bridges, the Morrison is no more than a 10-minute walk from Trinity College. The ultramodern interior—designed by John Rocha, Ireland's most acclaimed fashion designer—can be a bit cold. He had the last word on everything, down to the toiletries and staff uniforms. Rooms have unfussy modern furnishings and are high-tech, with top-of-the-line entertainment units and satellite TVs. The Halo restaurant has an Asian fusion theme. ⊠ *Ormond Quay, Northside, 1* ☎ *01/887–2400* ☒ *01/878–3185* ⊕ *www.morrisonhotel.ie* ⤶ *88 rooms with bath, 7 suites* △ *2 restaurants, room service, in-room data ports, minibars, cable TV, in-room VCRs, 2 bars, dry cleaning, laundry service, concierge, business services, meeting rooms, free parking, no-smoking rooms* ⊟ *AE, DC, MC, V* ⦿ *BP.*

$$$–$$$$ **Clarion Hotel IFSC.** Smack in the middle of the International Financial Services Centre, the Clarion—with an office-blocklike exterior—is indistinguishable from many of the financial institutions that surround it. The public spaces are bright and cheery, if a little uninspired, and the bedrooms are all straight lines and contemporary light-oak furnishings. Shades of blue and taupe create a calm environment. Try to get a room at the front with great views out over the Liffey. The hotel mainly caters to business travelers, so weekend bargains are a definite possibility—make sure you ask for them. ⊠ *IFSC, Northside, 1* ☎ *01/433–8800* ☒ *01/433–8811* ⊕ *www.clarionhotelifsc.com* ⤶ *147 rooms with bath, 13 suites* △ *Restaurant, room service, in-room data ports, minibars, cable TV, indoor pool, health club, massage, bar, dry cleaning, laundry service, free parking, no-smoking rooms* ⊟ *AE, DC, MC, V* ⦿ *BP.*

$$$ 🏨 **Royal Dublin Hotel.** O'Connell Street is not what it once was, but this renovated, upmarket hotel has just about a perfect location at the top of the old thoroughfare. All of the Northside's major attractions are nearby, and you can walk south to Trinity College in 10 minutes. The public spaces are well lighted and decorated in glass and brass. Rooms are spacious, and the hotel has built a solid reputation for extra-friendly service. The Georgian Room and Raffles bar try to put on posh English airs (think crisp linens), but the casual warmth of the staff undoes the stuffiness. ⊠ *O'Connell St., Northside, 1* ☎ *01/873–3666* 🖷 *01/873–3120* ⊕ *www.royaldublin.com* ⟿ *117 rooms with bath, 3 suites* ⚭ *Restaurant, room service, in-room data ports, minibars, cable TV, in-room VCRs, bar, dry cleaning, laundry service, no-smoking rooms* ▤ *AE, MC, V* ⦿*I BP, EP.*

$–$$ 🏨 **Charleville Lodge.** It's worth the short commute to the city center (the No. 10 bus takes five minutes, and it's a great walk in good weather) to enjoy the luxury and great value of the Charleville Lodge. It's part of a row of beautifully restored Victorian terraced houses in the historic Phibsborough area of Dublin's Northside. The dramatically lighted residents' lounge, with a working fireplace, is a great spot to chat with other travelers who have dared to stray off the beaten path. Rooms are brightly colored and spacious. ⊠ *268–272 N. Circular Rd., Northside, 7* ☎ *01/838–6633* 🖷 *01/838–5854* ⊕ *www.charlevillelodge. ie* ⟿ *30 rooms with bath* ⚭ *Free parking, no-smoking rooms* ▤ *MC, V* ⦿*I BP, EP.*

$ 🏨 **Clifden Guesthouse.** The Gardiner Street area has a reputation for cheap, poor-quality guest houses, but the Clifden, although still certainly a bargain, is a cut above the rest. The Georgian building has been stylishly refurbished, and the rooms are spacious, with modern furnishings. O'Connell Street is only a 5-minute walk away. As an added bonus, you can park here for free even after you have checked out. ⊠ *32 Gardiner Pl., Northside, 1* ☎ *01/874–6364* 🖷 *01/874–6122* ⊕ *www.clifdenhouse. com* ⟿ *14 rooms with bath* ⚭ *Free parking, no-smoking rooms* ▤ *MC, V* ⦿*I BP.*

$ 🏨 **Hotel Saint George.** Surprisingly opulent for the price, this comfortable Georgian hotel at the top of O'Connell Street has a splendid period staircase, original plasterwork, and beautiful marble fireplaces. Bedrooms are large, with high ceilings and pastel color schemes. On the Northside, the Saint George is close to the airport and numerous cultural highlights; the Abbey and Gate theaters, the Dublin Writers Museum, and the Dublin City Gallery, The Hugh Lane are all within walking distance. ⊠ *7 Parnell Sq. E, Northside, 1* ☎ *01/874–5611* 🖷 *01/874–5582* ⟿ *50 rooms with bath* ⚭ *Free parking, no-smoking rooms* ▤ *MC, V* ⦿*I BP, EP.*

Fodor'sChoice ★

¢–$ 🏨 **Globetrotters Tourist Hostel.** Globetrotters is a giant step up from many Dublin hostels, with a pleasant outdoor courtyard; clean, locking dorm rooms with en suite showers; a turf fire; comfortable bunk beds (with lamps for late-night reading); and a delicious all-you-can-eat breakfast. Plus, you're within walking distance of the city center, one block from the bus station, and two blocks from the train station. The owners also run Town House, a cute B&B in the same building. ⊠ *46 Lower Gardiner St., Northside, 1* ☎ *01/873–5893* 🖷 *01/878–8787* ⊕ *www. townhouse.ie* ⟿ *94 dorm beds, 38 double rooms with bath* ⚭ *Restaurant, no-smoking rooms* ▤ *MC, V* ⦿*I BP, EP.*

¢ 🏨 **Marian Guest House.** The Marian's mighty full Irish breakfast, with black pudding and smoked bacon, is reason enough to stay at this family-run guest house (the whole family can speak Irish, by the way). The place only has six rooms, so you get lots of attention and pampering. Rooms are fairly basic, but clean and pleasant. ⊠ *21 Upper Gardiner*

St., Northside, 1 ☎ *01/874–6364* ⤶ *6 rooms with bath* ⚿ *Free parking* ☰ *MC, V* ⧖ *BP.*

Dublin Airport

$$$–$$$$ ⊞ **Holiday Inn Dublin Airport.** A low-rise redbrick structure with a plain exterior, the Holiday Inn has basic but spacious rooms. The Bistro Restaurant serves fish, meat, and vegetarian dishes; Sampans serves Chinese cuisine at dinner only. There's live music in the bar on weekends. You have access to a nearby health club. ✉ *Dublin Airport, North County Dublin* ☎ *01/808–0500* ☷ *01/844–6002* ⊕ *www.ichotelsgroup. com* ⤶ *247 rooms with bath* ⚿ *2 restaurants, room service, bar, free parking, no-smoking rooms* ☰ *AE, DC, MC, V* ⧖ *BP, EP.*

$$–$$$$ ⊞ **Great Southern Hotel.** *Within* the airport complex, near the main terminal, and next to the main road into the city center is this modern five-story hotel that's part of one of Ireland's most respected chains. The accommodation itself is spacious and comfortable, if a little unexciting, but the service is exceptional. ✉ *Dublin Airport, North County Dublin* ☎ *01/844–6000* ☷ *01/844–6001* ⊕ *www.gsh.ie* ⤶ *229 rooms with bath* ⚿ *Restaurant, room service, bar, free parking* ☰ *AE, DC, MC, V* ⧖ *BP, EP.*

$–$$ ⊞ **Skylon.** On the main road into Dublin city center from the airport stands this modern five-story hotel with a concrete-and-glass facade and generous-size rooms, plainly decorated in cool pastels. Double beds and a pair of easy chairs are almost the only furniture in the rooms. A glass-fronted lobby with a large bar and the Rendezvous Room restaurant dominate the public areas. The cooking is adequate but uninspired, with dishes such as grilled steak, poached cod, and omelets. ✉ *Upper Drumcondra Rd., North County Dublin* ☎ *01/837–9121* ☷ *01/837–2778* ⊕ *www.skylon.org* ⤶ *88 rooms with bath* ⚿ *Restaurant, bar, free parking* ☰ *AE, DC, MC, V* ⧖ *EP.*

City Center

★ $$$$ ⊞ **Le Méridien Shelbourne.** Paris has the Ritz, New York has the Plaza, and Dublin has the Shelbourne. Waterford chandeliers, gleaming old masters on the wall, and Irish Chippendale chairs invite you to linger in the lobby. Each guest room has fine, carefully selected furniture and luxurious drapes, with splendid antiques in the older rooms. Those in front overlook St. Stephen's Green, but rooms in the back, without a view, are quieter. The Lord Mayor's Lounge, off the lobby, is a perfect rendezvous spot and offers a lovely afternoon tea—a real Dublin tradition. ✉ *27 St. Stephen's Green, Southside, 2* ☎ *01/663–4500; 800/543–4300 in the U.S.* ☷ *01/661–6006* ⊕ *www.shelbourne.ie* ⤶ *181 rooms with bath, 9 suites* ⚿ *2 restaurants, room service, indoor pool, health club, hot tub, sauna, 2 bars, free parking, no-smoking rooms* ☰ *AE, DC, MC, V* ⧖ *BP.*

$$$$ ⊞ **Westbury.** This comfortable modern hotel is in the heart of Southside, right off the city's buzzing shopping mecca: Grafton Street. You can join elegantly dressed Dubliners for afternoon tea in the spacious mezzanine-level main lobby, furnished with antiques. Alas, the utilitarian rooms—painted in pastels—don't share the lobby's elegance. More inviting are the suites, which combine European stylings with tasteful Japanese screens and prints. The flowery Russell Room serves formal lunches and dinners; the downstairs Sandbank, a seafood restaurant and bar, looks like a turn-of-the-20th-century establishment. ✉ *Grafton St., Southside, 2* ☎ *01/679–1122* ☷ *01/679–7078* ⊕ *www.jurysdoyle. com* ⤶ *204 rooms with bath, 8 suites* ⚿ *2 restaurants, room service, minibars, cable TV, in-room VCRs, bar, dry cleaning, laundry service, free parking, no-smoking rooms* ☰ *AE, DC, MC, V* ⧖ *BP.*

$$$$ ⊞ **Westin Dublin.** Reconstructed from three 19th-century landmark buildings (including a former bank) across the road from Trinity College, the Westin is all about location. The public spaces re-create a little of the splendor of yesteryear: marble pillars, tall mahogany doorways, blazing fireplaces, and period detailing on the walls and ceilings. The bedrooms, on the other hand, are functional and small, with the crisp, white Indian linen and custom-made beds the only luxurious touches. The rooms that overlook Trinity are a little more expensive, but the engaging view makes all the difference. The restaurant and Mint Bar are in the original vaults of the bank. ⊠ *College Green, Southside, 2* ☎ *01/ 645–1000* 🖶 *01/645–1234* ⊕ *www.westin.com* 🛏 *141 rooms with bath, 22 suites* ⚘ *Restaurant, room service, minibars, cable TV, 2 bars, dry cleaning, laundry service, concierge, business services, meeting rooms, free parking, no-smoking rooms* ▭ *AE, DC, MC, V* ◯ *BP, EP.*

$$$ ⊞ **La Stampa.** This intimate boutique town-house hotel, above the ever-
FodorśChoice   popular La Stampa restaurant and 50 yards from Trinity College, is the
★   classiest new arrival on the Dublin scene. Each suite is individually decorated with an Asian theme—lots of wood, simple color schemes, and velvet bedspreads imported from Paris to add to the luxury. For the price, there are few better spots in town. ⊠ *35 Dawson St., Southside, 2* ☎ *01/677–4444* 🖶 *01/677–4411* ⊕ *www.lastampa.ie* 🛏 *21 suites with bath* ⚘ *Restaurant, room service, minibars, cable TV, in-room VCRs, dry cleaning, laundry service, free parking, no-smoking rooms* ▭ *AE, DC, MC, V* ◯ *BP, EP.*

$–$$$ ⊞ **Drury Court Hotel.** A 2-minute walk from Grafton Street, this small hotel is just around the corner from some of the city's best restaurants. Subtle greens, golds, and burgundies decorate the rooms. In the parquet-floor rathskeller dining room you can get breakfast and dinner; lunch is served in the casual Digges Lane Bar, frequented by many young Dubliners. ⊠ *28–30 Lower Stephens St., Southside, 2* ☎ *01/475–1988* 🖶 *01/ 478–5730* ⊕ *www.drurycourthotel.com* 🛏 *30 rooms with bath, 2 suites* ⚘ *Restaurant, room service, bar, dry cleaning, laundry service, meeting room* ▭ *AE, DC, MC, V* ◯ *EP.*

$–$$ ⊞ **Central Hotel.** This grand, old-style redbrick hotel, established in 1887, is in the heart of the city center, steps from Grafton Street, Temple Bar, and Dublin Castle. Rooms are small but have high ceilings and practical but tasteful furniture. Adjacent to the hotel is Molly Malone's Tavern, a lively hotel-bar with plenty of regulars who come for the atmosphere and the live, traditional Irish music on Friday and Saturday nights. The restaurant and Library Bar—one of the best spots in the city for a quiet pint—are on the first floor. ⊠ *1–5 Exchequer St., Southside, 2* ☎ *01/679–7302* 🖶 *01/679–7303* ⊕ *www.centralhotel.ie* 🛏 *67 rooms with bath, 3 suites* ⚘ *Restaurant, room service, 2 bars, dry cleaning, laundry service, concierge, business services, meeting rooms* ▭ *AE, DC, MC, V* ◯ *BP, EP.*

$–$$ ⊞ **Georgian House Hotel.** The owners of this hotel took three classic Georgian houses near St. Stephen's Green, added a modern extension, and opened one of Dublin's best value hotels. So you get an 18th-century-Dublin experience—high ceilings, fireplaces, antique mirrors—at guesthouse prices. Within the hotel, McGuires is a cozy, unpretentious little pub. ⊠ *18 Lower Bagot St., Southside, 2* ☎ *01/661–8832* 🖶 *01/661– 8834* 🛏 *70 rooms with bath* ⚘ *Restaurant, bar, free parking* ▭ *AE, MC, V* ◯ *BP.*

$–$$ ⊞ **Grafton Guesthouse.** A Victorian Gothic–style building has been tastefully transformed into one of central Dublin's best bargains. It's just a few minutes away from Trinity College and Grafton Street. The rooms are a little cramped, but they are stylishly decorated with cheerful pine furnishings, and the small size of the place ensures warm, friendly service. ✉ 26–27 S. Great George's St., Southside, 2 ☎ 01/679–2041 ℻ 01/677–9715 ⇆ 15 rooms with bath ⚐ No-smoking rooms ▭ AE, MC, V 🍴 BP.

Dublin's Georgian Heart

$$$$ **Conrad Dublin International.** In a seven-story redbrick and smoked-glass building just off St. Stephen's Green, the Conrad, owned by the Hilton Group, firmly aims for international business travelers. Gleaming light marble graces the large formal lobby. Rooms are rather cramped and have uninspiring views of the adjacent office buildings, but are nicely outfitted with natural-wood furnishings, painted in sand colors and pastel greens, and have Spanish marble in the bathrooms. A note to light sleepers: the air-conditioning/heating system can be noisy. The hotel has two restaurants: the informal Plurabelle and the plusher Alexandra Room. ✉ *Earlsfort Terr., Southside, 2* ☎ *01/676–5555* ℻ *01/676–5424* 🌐 *www.conradhotels.com* ⇆ *182 rooms with bath, 9 suites* ⚐ *2 restaurants, room service, in-room data ports, in-room safes, minibars, cable TV, in-room VCRs, gym, bar, concierge, business services, meeting rooms, free parking, no-smoking rooms, no-smoking floor* ▭ *AE, DC, MC, V* 🍴 *BP.*

$$$$ Fodor's Choice ★ **Merrion.** The home of the Duke of Wellington, hero of the Battle of Waterloo, is one of the four exactingly restored Georgian town houses that make up this luxurious hotel. The stately rooms are appointed in classic Georgian style—from the crisp linen sheets to the Carrara-marble bathrooms. Some are vaulted with delicate Adamesque plasterwork ceilings, and others are graced with magnificent, original marble fireplaces. Rooms in the old house are more expensive than those in the new extension. You know this place must be special, because leading Dublin restaurateur Patrick Guilbaud has moved his eponymous restaurant here. ✉ *Upper Merrion St., Southside, 2* ☎ *01/603–0600* ℻ *01/603–0700* 🌐 *www.merrionhotel.com* ⇆ *120 rooms with bath, 25 suites* ⚐ *2 restaurants, room service, in-room data ports, in-room safes, minibars, cable TV, in-room VCRs, indoor pool, health club, hair salon, massage, steam room, 2 bars, dry cleaning, laundry service, concierge, business services, meeting rooms, free parking, no-smoking rooms, no-smoking floor* ▭ *AE, DC, MC, V* 🍴 *BP, EP.*

$$$–$$$$ **Davenport.** The gorgeous, bright-yellow neoclassical facade of this hotel behind Trinity College was originally built in the 1860s to front a church. Tasteful deep colors and functional furnishings characterize the reasonably spacious rooms and larger suites. The hotel restaurant, Lanyon's, serves breakfast, lunch, and dinner amid traditional Georgian surroundings. In the comfortable President's Bar, see how many heads of state you can identify in the photos covering the walls. ✉ *Merrion Sq., Southside, 2* ☎ *01/661–6800; 800/327–0200 in the U.S.* ℻ *01/661–5663* 🌐 *www.ocallaghanhotels.ie* ⇆ *113 rooms with bath, 2 suites* ⚐ *Restaurant, room service, minibars, cable TV, in-room VCRs, bar, dry cleaning, laundry service, concierge, business services, meeting rooms, free parking, no-smoking rooms* ▭ *AE, DC, MC, V* 🍴 *BP, EP, MAP.*

$$–$$$$ **Number 31.** Two Georgian mews strikingly renovated in the early '60s as the private home of Sam Stephenson, Ireland's leading modern architect, are now connected via a small garden to the grand town house they once served. Together they form a marvelous guest house a short walk from St. Stephen's Green. Owners Deirdre and Noel Comer serve made-to-order breakfasts at refectory tables in the balcony dining room. The white-tile sunken living room, with its black leather sectional sofa and modern artwork that includes a David Hockney print, may make you think you're in California. ✉ *31 Leeson Close, Southside, 2* ☎ *01/*

Where to Stay in Dublin

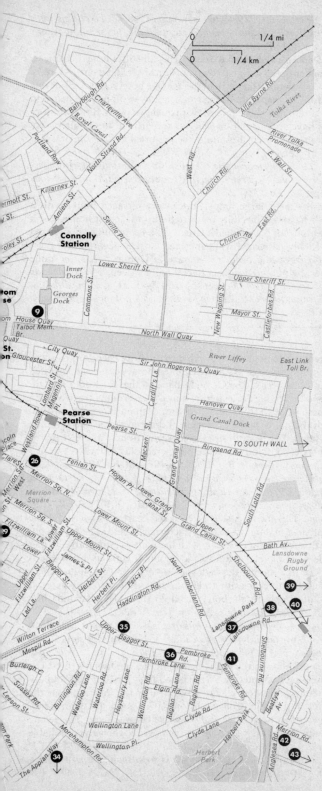

676–5011 🖨 01/676–2929 ⊕ *www.number31.ie* 🛏 *18 rooms with bath* ⟂ *Dry cleaning, laundry service, free parking, no-smoking rooms* ▤ *AE, MC, V* |○| *BP, EP.*

$$$ 🏨 **Clarion Stephen's Hall Hotel & Suites.** This all-suites hotel occupies a tastefully modernized Georgian town house just off St. Stephen's Green. The suites, considerably larger than the average hotel room, include one or two bedrooms, a separate sitting room, a fully equipped kitchen, and bath. They are comfortably equipped with quality modern furniture. Top-floor suites have spectacular city views, and ground-floor suites have private entrances. Morel's Restaurant serves breakfast, lunch, and dinner. ✉ *14–17 Lower Leeson St., Southside, 2* 🕿 *01/661–0585* 🖨 *01/661–0606* ⊕ *www.premgroup.ie* 🛏 *34 suites* ⟂ *Restaurant, room service, kitchens, cable TV, 2 bars, meeting rooms, free parking, no-smoking rooms* ▤ *AE, DC, MC, V* |○| *BP, EP.*

$–$$ 🏨 **Kilronan House.** A large, late-19th-century terraced house with a white facade has been carefully converted into this guest house, just a 5-minute walk from St. Stephen's Green. The furnishings are updated each year. Richly patterned wallpaper and carpets decorate the guest rooms, and orthopedic beds (rather rare in Dublin hotels, let alone guest houses) help to guarantee a restful night's sleep. ✉ *70 Adelaide Rd., Southside, 2* 🕿 *01/475–5266* 🖨 *01/478–2841* ⊕ *www.dublinn.com* 🛏 *12 rooms with bath* ⟂ *Free parking, no-smoking room* ▤ *MC, V* |○| *BP, EP.*

Temple Bar

$$$$ 🏨 **The Clarence.** You might well bump into celebrity friends of co-owners Bono and the Edge of U2 at this contemporary hotel, understated to the point of austerity. The Octagon Bar and the Tea Room Restaurant are popular Temple Bar watering holes. Guest rooms are decorated in a mishmash of earth tones accented with deep purple, gold, cardinal red, and royal blue. With the exception of those in the penthouse suite, rooms are small. The laissez-faire service seems to take its cue from the minimalist style, so if you like to be pampered, stay elsewhere. ✉ *6–8 Wellington Quay, Temple Bar, 2* 🕿 *01/407–0800* 🖨 *01/407–0820* ⊕ *www.theclarence.ie* 🛏 *47 rooms with bath, 3 suites* ⟂ *Restaurant, minibars, cable TV, bar, dry cleaning, laundry service, meeting rooms, free parking, no-smoking rooms* ▤ *AE, DC, MC, V* |○| *BP, EP.*

$$–$$$ 🏨 **Paramount.** This medium-size hotel in the heart of modern Temple Bar has opted to maintain its classy Victorian facade. The foyer continues this theme of solid elegance, with incredibly comfortable leather couches, bleached-blond oak floors, and burgundy curtains. Dark woods and subtle colors decorate the bedrooms—very 1930s (you just know if Bogart and Bacall ever came to Dublin they'd have to stay here). If you're fond of a tipple, try the hotel's art deco Turks Head Bar and Chop House. ✉ *Parliament St. and Essex Gate, Temple Bar, 2* 🕿 *01/417–9900* 🖨 *01/417–9904* ⊕ *www.paramounthotel.ie* 🛏 *70 rooms with bath* ⟂ *Restaurant, in-room data ports, cable TV, bar, laundry service, no-smoking rooms* ▤ *AE, DC, MC, V* |○| *BP, EP.*

$$–$$$ 🏨 **Parliament.** Although the Parliament is in one of Dublin's finest Edwardian buildings, its interior is very much functional, if tidy, and appeals to mainly a business clientele—drawn by the location near the Central Bank and Trinity College. Rooms are a good size, with a simple, slightly monotonous beige and off-white color scheme. The Senate restaurant and Forum bar keep up the democratic theme with reliable selections. ✉ *Lord Edward St., Temple Bar, 2* 🕿 *01/670–8777* 🖨 *01/670–8787* ⊕ *www.regencyhotels.com* 🛏 *63 rooms with bath* ⟂ *Restaurant, cable TV, bar, no-smoking rooms* ▤ *AE, DC, MC, V* |○| *BP, EP.*

$$–$$$ ⌧ **Temple Bar.** A large, old-fashioned cast-iron fireplace, natural-wood furniture, and lots of plants fill this hotel's delightful art deco lobby. Off the lobby are a small cocktail bar and the bright, airy, glass-roof Terrace restaurant, which serves sandwiches, pastas, omelets, and fish all day. Mahogany furnishings and autumn green and rust colors characterize the guest rooms, nearly all of which have double beds (this makes them more than a little cramped). The Boomerang nightclub on the premises is open to both guests and the public. The hotel is in a former bank building, around the corner from Trinity College. ⌧ *Fleet St., Temple Bar, 2* ☎ *01/677–3333* 🖷 *01/677–3088* ⊕ *www.towerhotelgroup. ie/templebar* ⌧ *129 rooms with bath* ⌕ *Restaurant, cable TV, 2 bars, nightclub, parking (fee)* ▭ *AE, DC, MC, V* ⍥ *BP, EP.*

The Grand Canal & Ballsbridge

$$$$ ⌧ **Berkeley Court.** The most quietly elegant of Dublin's large modern hotels, Berkeley Court has a glass-and-concrete exterior that's designed in a modern, blocklike style, and is surrounded by verdant grounds. The vast white-tile and plushly carpeted lobby has roomy sofas and antique planters. Golds, yellows, and greens decorate the large guest rooms, with antiques or period reproductions; bathrooms are tiled in marble. The Berkeley Room restaurant has table d'hôte and à la carte menus; the more informal Conservatory Grill, with large windows, serves grilled food and snacks. ⌧ *Lansdowne Rd., Ballsbridge, 4* ☎ *01/660–1711; 800/550–0000 in the U.S.* 🖷 *01/661–7238* ⊕ *www.jurysdoyle.com* ⌧ *158 rooms with bath, 24 suites* ⌕ *2 restaurants, room service, cable TV, gym, hair salon, some hot tubs, bar, shops, dry cleaning, laundry service, business services, meeting rooms, free parking, no-smoking rooms* ▭ *AE, DC, MC, V* ⍥ *BP, EP.*

$$$$ ⌧ **Burlington.** In high contrast to the hotel's impersonal, 1972 glass-and-concrete facade, the staff here is friendly and attentive. Public rooms, especially the large bar, have mahogany counters and hanging plants that enhance the conservatory-style setting. The generous-size rooms—in a modern minimalist design, with neutral tones—have large picture windows. At night, Annabel's nightclub and the seasonal (summer) Irish cabaret are both lively spots. The Burlington has no sports and health facilities, but the Doyle hotel group, which runs it, has an arrangement that allows you to use the RiverView Sports Club in nearby Clonskeagh for €6.35 a visit. ⌧ *Upper Leeson St., Ballsbridge, 4* ☎ *01/660–5222* 🖷 *01/660–8496* ⊕ *www.jurysdoyle.com* ⌧ *506 rooms with bath* ⌕ *2 restaurants, room service, cable TV, 3 bars, cabaret (May–Oct.), nightclub, shops, dry cleaning, laundry service, business services, meeting rooms, free parking, no-smoking rooms* ▭ *AE, DC, MC, V* ⍥ *BP, EP.*

$$$$ ⌧ **Four Seasons.** Much controversy surrounds the brash postmodern architecture of this hotel. The six-floor building mixes a Victorian and Georgian design with modern glass and concrete. The impressive landscaping makes the hotel seem like an oasis; a big effort has been made to ensure that a bit of greenery can be seen from most rooms. Rooms are spacious, with large windows that allow the light to flood in. A selection of landscapes on the walls gives the place a more human feel. ⌧ *Simmonscourt Rd., Ballsbridge, 4* ☎ *01/665–4000* 🖷 *01/665–4099* ⊕ *www.fourseasons. com* ⌧ *192 rooms with bath, 67 suites* ⌕ *Restaurant, coffee shop, cable TV, indoor pool, hot tub, bar, shop, dry cleaning, laundry service, business services, meeting rooms, free parking, no-smoking rooms* ▭ *AE, DC, MC, V* ⍥ *BP, EP.*

$$$$ ⌧ **Herbert Park Hotel.** Some of the rooms face the park of the same name adjacent to this hotel, which is also beside the River Dodder. Two of the suites have large balconies with views of the park or the leafy suburbs. Relaxing shades of blue and cream predominate in the spacious rooms; all have individually controlled air-conditioning, a large desk, and two telephone lines. The hotel's large lobby has floor-to-ceiling windows and a slanted glass roof. The spacious bar, terrace lounge, and restaurant are Japanese-inspired minimalist in style. You can dine on the restaurant terrace in warm weather. ⊠ *Merrion Rd., Ballsbridge, 4* ☎ *01/667–2200* 📠 *01/667–2595* ⊕ *www. herbertparkhotel.ie* 🛏 *150 rooms with bath, 3 suites* ⚒ *Restaurant, cable TV, gym, bar, business services, free parking, no-smoking rooms* 🖃 *AE, DC, MC, V* 🍽 *BP, EP.*

$$$$ 🏨 **Jurys Ballsbridge and the Towers.** These adjoining seven-story hotels, popular with businesspeople, have more atmosphere than most comparable modern hotels. The Towers has an edge over its older, larger, less-expensive companion, Jurys Ballsbridge. Rooms in the Towers are decorated in blue and gold with built-in, natural-wood furniture; the large beds and armchairs are comfortable. Jurys Ballsbridge, on the other hand, has large, plainly decorated rooms with light walls and brown drapes; furnishings are functional and uninspired. ⊠*Pembroke Rd. (Jurys Ballsbridge) and Lansdowne Rd. (the Towers), Ballsbridge, 4* ☎ *01/660–5000* 📠 *01/ 679–7078* ⊕*www.jurysdoyle.com* 🛏 *Jurys Ballsbridge: 300 rooms with bath, 3 suites. The Towers: 100 rooms with bath, 5 suites* ⚒ *2 restaurants, coffee shop, some kitchenettes, indoor-outdoor pool, hot tub, bar, cabaret (May–Oct.), shop, dry cleaning, laundry service, business services, meeting rooms, free parking* 🖃 *AE, DC, MC, V* 🍽 *BP, EP.*

★ $$$–$$$$ 🏨 **Hibernian.** This early-20th-century Edwardian nurses' home designed by Albert E. Murray—one of the architects of the Rotunda Hospital—now serves as a small, elegant luxury hotel. One of the city's most elegant and intimate hotels, it retains the distinctive red-and-amber brick facade, and has smallish rooms, nicely done in pastels, with deep-pile carpets and comfortable furniture. The public rooms, in cheerful chintz and stripes, include a period-style library and a sun lounge—both comfortable spaces to relax before or after a dinner in the hotel's intimate restaurant, the Patrick Kavanagh Room. ⊠ *Eastmoreland Pl. off Upper Baggot St., Ballsbridge, 4* ☎ *01/668–7666 or 800/414243* 📠 *01/660– 2655* ⊕ *www.hibernianhotel.com* 🛏 *40 rooms with bath* ⚒ *Restaurant, bar, parking (fee)* 🖃 *AE, DC, MC, V* 🍽 *BP, EP.*

$$–$$$ 🏨 **Mount Herbert Hotel.** The Loughran family's sprawling accommodation includes a number of large, Victorian-era houses. The hotel overlooks some of Ballsbridge's fine rear gardens and is right near the main rugby stadium; the nearby DART will have you in the city center in seven minutes. The simple rooms are painted in light shades and contain little besides beds. The lounge is a good place to relax. The restaurant, which overlooks the English-style back garden (floodlighted at night) and children's play area, serves three meals a day; at dinner you can dine on steaks and stews. ⊠ *7 Herbert Rd., Ballsbridge, 4* ☎*01/668–4321* 📠*01/660–7077* ⊕*www. mountherberthotel.ie* 🛏*200 rooms with bath* ⚒ *Restaurant, cable TV, sauna, bar, shop, business services, meeting rooms, free parking, no-smoking rooms* 🖃 *AE, DC, MC, V* 🍽 *BP, EP, MAP.*

$$ 🏨 **Jurys Tara.** On the main coast road 10 to 15 minutes from the Dun Laoghaire ferry terminal and 6½ km (4 mi) from the city center is this unpretentious, informal seven-story hotel. It's also near the Booterstown Marsh Bird Sanctuary. The best rooms are in the original section and face Dublin Bay; rooms in the addition have slightly more modern furnishings. The restaurant serves grilled fish, steaks, and omelets. The hotel staff is very personable. ⊠ *Merrion Rd., Ballsbridge, 4* ☎ *01/269– 4666* 📠 *01/269–1027* ⊕ *www.jurysdoyle.com* 🛏 *114 rooms with bath* ⚒ *Restaurant, bar, dry cleaning, laundry service, free parking, no-smoking rooms* 🖃 *AE, DC, MC, V* 🍽 *BP, EP.*

★ **$$** ☑ **Lansdowne.** The cozy, Georgian-style rooms in this small Ballsbridge hotel have delightful floral-pattern furnishings. Photos of sports personalities hang on the walls of the Green Blazer bar in the basement, a popular haunt for local businesspeople and fans of the international rugby matches held at nearby Lansdowne Road; you can get a bite to eat here all day. Next to the bar is Parker's Restaurant, which specializes in seafood and grilled steaks. ✉ *27 Pembroke Rd., Ballsbridge, 4* ☎ *01/668–2522* 📠 *01/668–5585* 🌐 *www.lansdownehotel.com* 🛏 *38 rooms with bath, 2 suites* ⟁ *Restaurant, bar, free parking* ⊟ *AE, DC, MC, V* ⊙| *BP, EP.*

$–$$ ☑ **Ariel Guest House.** This redbrick 1850 Victorian guest house in a tree-
Fodor'sChoice lined suburb is one of Dublin's finest, just a few steps from a DART
★ stop and a 15-minute walk from St. Stephen's Green. Restored rooms in the main house are lovingly decorated with Victorian and Georgian antiques, Victoriana, and period wallpaper and drapes. The 13 rooms at the back of the house are more spartan, but all are immaculate. A Waterford-crystal chandelier hangs over the comfortable leather and mahogany furniture in the gracious, fireplace-warmed drawing room. Owner Michael O'Brien is an extraordinarily helpful and gracious host. ✉ *52 Lansdowne Rd., Ballsbridge, 4* ☎ *01/668–5512* 📠 *01/668–5845* 🛏 *40 rooms with bath* ⟁ *Free parking* ⊟ *MC, V* ⊙| *BP.*

Dublin West

$$–$$$ ☑ **Chief O'Neill's.** Smallish, high-tech rooms all have in-room data ports and look thoroughly up-to-date, with chrome fixtures and minimalist furnishings, at this hotel, the largest building in Smithfield Village, named after a 19th-century Corkman who became chief of police in Chicago. Top-floor suites have delightful roof-top gardens with views of the city on both sides of the Liffey. The café-bar has live traditional music and contemporary Irish food, and Asian cuisine is available in Kelly & Ping, a bright, airy restaurant off Duck Lane, a shopping arcade that's part of the hotel complex. ✉ *Smithfield Village, Dublin West, 7* ☎ *01/817–3838* 📠 *01/817–3839* 🌐 *www.chiefoneills.com* 🛏 *70 rooms with bath, 3 suites* ⟁ *Restaurant, room service, in-room data ports, minibars, cable TV, in-room VCRs, gym, bar, shops, dry cleaning, laundry service, free parking, no-smoking rooms* ⊟ *AE, DC, MC, V* ⊙| *BP, EP.*

$ ☑ **Jurys Christchurch Inn.** Expect few frills at this functional budget hotel, part of a Jurys minichain that offers a low, fixed room rate for up to three adults or two adults and two children. (The branch at Custom House Quay operates according to the same plan.) The biggest plus is the pleasant location, facing Christ Church Cathedral and within walking distance of most city-center attractions. The rather spartan rooms are decorated in pastel colors and utilitarian furniture. ✉ *Christ Church Pl., Dublin West, 8* ☎ *01/454–0000* 📠 *01/454–0012* 🌐 *www.jurysdoyle. com* 🛏 *182 rooms with bath* ⟁ *Restaurant, bar, parking (fee), no-smoking rooms* ⊟ *AE, DC, MC, V* ⊙| *EP.*

¢ ☑ **Avalon House.** Many young, independent travelers rate this cleverly restored redbrick Victorian building, a 5-minute walk southwest from Grafton Street and five to 10 minutes from some of the city's best music venues, the most appealing of Dublin's hostels. Avalon House has a mix of dormitories, rooms without bath, and rooms with bath. The dorm rooms and en suite quads all have loft areas that offer more privacy than you'd typically find in a multibed room. The Avalon Café serves food until 10 PM but is open as a common room after hours. ✉ *55 Aungier St., Dublin West, 2* ☎ *01/475–0001* 📠 *01/475–0303* 🌐 *www.avalon-house.ie* 🛏 *35 4-bed rooms with bath, 5 4-bed rooms without bath, 4 twin rooms with bath, 4 single rooms without bath, 22 twin rooms without bath, 5 12-bed dorms, 1 10-bed dorm, 1 26-bed dorm* ⟁ *Café, bar; no room TVs* ⊟ *AE, MC, V* ⊙| *CP.*

¢ ⊞ **Bewleys at Newlands Cross.** Stay at this four-story hotel on the south-west outskirts of the city if you're planning to head out of the city early (especially to points in the southwest and west) and don't want to deal with morning traffic. The hotel is emulating the formula popularized by Jurys Inns, in which rooms—here each has a double bed, a single bed, and a sofa bed—are a flat rate for up to three adults or two adults and two children. ⊠ *Newlands Cross, Naas Rd., Dublin West, 22* ☎ *01/464–0140* 🖨 *01/464–0900* ⊕ *www.bewleyshotels.com* 🖙 *256 rooms with bath* ♿ *Café, free parking, no-smoking rooms* ▭ *AE, MC, V* ⍥ *EP.*

NIGHTLIFE & THE ARTS

Long before Stephen Daedalus's excursions into nighttown in Joyce's *A Portrait of the Artist as a Young Man,* Dublin was proud of its lively after-hours scene, particularly its thriving pubs. Lately, however, with the advent of Irish rock superstars (think U2, the Cranberries, Sinéad O'Connor, Bob Geldof) and the resurgence of Celtic music (think *Riverdance,* the sound track to *Titanic*), the rest of the world seems to have discovered that Dublin is one of the most happening places in the world. Most nights the city's pubs and clubs overflow with young cell phone–toting Dubliners and Europeans who descend on the capital for weekend getaways. The city's 900-plus pubs are its main source of entertainment; many public houses in the city center have live music—from rock to jazz to traditional Irish.

Theater has always been taken seriously in the city that was home to O'Casey, Synge, Yeats, and Beckett. Today Dublin has eight major theaters that reproduce the Irish "classics," and newer fare from the likes of Martin Macdonagh and Conon Macpherson. At long last, the Gaiety Theatre has given long-overlooked opera a home in Dublin. There are some two dozen cinema screens in the city center, plus a number of large, multiscreen cinema complexes in the suburbs, which show current releases made in Ireland and abroad.

The visual arts have always been the poor cousin in the Dublin cultural family. In recent years, small galleries have sprung up all over the city, and the development of Temple Bar Galleries has encouraged a whole new generation of painters, photographers, and sculptors.

Check the following newspapers for informative listings: the *Irish Times* publishes a daily guide to what's happening in Dublin and in the rest of the country, and has complete film and theater schedules. The *Evening Herald* lists theaters, cinemas, and pubs with live entertainment. *In Dublin* and the *Big Issue* are weekly guides to all film, theater, and musical events around the city. The *Event Guide,* a weekly free paper that lists music, cinema, theater, art shows, and dance clubs, is available in pubs and cafés around the city. In peak season, consult the free Bord Fáilte (Irish Tourist Board) leaflet "Events of the Week." The **Temple Bar Web site** (⊕ www.temple-bar.ie) provides information about events in the Temple Bar area.

Nightlife

Dubliners have always enjoyed a night out, but in the last decade or so they have turned the pleasure into a work of art. The city has undergone a major nightlife revolution and now, for better or worse, bears more than a passing resemblance to Europe's nightclub hotspot, London. The streets of the city center, once hushed after the pubs had closed, are the scene of what appears to be a never-ending party—you're as likely to find crowds at 2 AM on a Wednesday as you are at the same time on a Saturday. Loud, brash dance clubs, where style and

FROM BONO TO BODHRANS

MUSIC FILLS DUBLIN'S STREETS (especially Grafton Street) and its pubs, where talk of music is as popular as the tunes themselves. Many Dubliners are obsessed with music of every kind and will happily discuss anything from Elvis's earliest recordings (remember Jimmy's father in The Commitments?) to U2's latest incarnation. The city has been the stomping ground of so many big-league rock and pop musicians that Dublin Tourism has created a "Rock 'n Stroll" Trail, which covers 16 spots with musical associations, most of them in the city center and Temple Bar. It includes places like Bewley's Oriental Café, where Bob Geldof and the other members of the Boomtown Rats used to hang out, and the Bad Ass Café, where Sinéad O'Connor once worked. You're forgiven if you think some connections between the trail sites and the musicians seem hokey, but you're not if you don't seek out Dublin's lively, present-day music scene. Several small pubs and larger halls host live music, but the best places are midsize venues—such as the Olympia Theatre and the Temple Bar Music Centre—where you can hear well-established local acts and leading international artists (including world-renowned Irish musicians) playing everything from traditional and folk rock to jazz-funk and "Dubcore," a term coined to describe the city's many noisy alternative bands. Traditional Irish music (or "Trad"), very much a child of rural Ireland, is alive and kicking in the urban sprawl of Dublin. Scores of city bars host impromptu "sessions" and professional gigs with fiddles, banjos, and the beat of the bodhran hand drum. The Cobblestone in lively Smithfield is one of the most famous and atmospheric venues.

swagger rule, have replaced the old-fashioned discos, once the only option for late-night entertainment. The dominant sound in Dublin's clubs is electronic dance music, and the crowd that flocks to them every night of the week is of the trendy, under-30 generation. Leeson Street—just off St. Stephen's Green, south of the Liffey, and known as "the strip"—is a main nightclub area that starts at pub closing time and lasts until 4 AM. It has lost its gloss since a number of lap-dancing establishments have opened. The dress code at Leeson Street's dance clubs is informal, but jeans and sneakers are not welcome. Most of these clubs are licensed only to sell wine, and the prices can be exorbitant (up to €26 for a mediocre bottle); the upside is that most don't charge to get in.

There are plenty of alternatives to the electronic dance scene, including nightclubs where the dominant sounds range from soul to salsa—such as the weekend nightclub at the Gaiety Theatre and the totally Latin Sugar Club. While jazz isn't a big part of the nightlife here, a few regular venues do draw the best of local and international talent. And if you're looking for something more mellow, the city doesn't disappoint: there are brasseries, bistros, cafés, and all manner of other late-night eateries where you can sit, sip, and chat until 2 AM or later.

In another trend, some of Dublin's old classic pubs—arguably some of the finest watering holes in the world—have been "reinvented" as popular spots, with modern interiors and designer drinks to attract a younger, upwardly mobile crowd. Beware Dublin Tourism's "Official Dublin Pub Guide," which has a tendency to recommended many of these bland spots. Despite the changes, however, the traditional pub has steadfastly clung to its role as the primary center of Dublin's social life. The city has nearly 1,000 pubs ("licensed tabernacles," writer Flann O'Brien calls them). And although the vision of elderly men enjoying a chin wag over a creamy pint of stout has become something of a rarity, there are still plenty of places where you can enjoy a quiet drink and a chat. Last drinks are called at 11:30 PM Monday to Wednesday, 12:30 AM Thursday to Saturday, and 11 PM on Sunday. Some city-center pubs have extended opening hours and don't serve last drinks until 1:45 AM.

A word of warning: although most pubs and clubs are extremely safe, the lads can get lively—public drunkenness is very much a part of Dublin's nightlife. Whereas this is for the most part seen as the Irish form of unwinding after a long week (or, well, day), it can sometimes lead to regrettable incidents (fighting, for instance). In an effort to keep potential trouble at bay, bouncers and security guards maintain a visible presence in all clubs and many pubs around the city. At the end of the night, the city center is full of young people trying to get home, which makes for extremely long lines at taxi stands and late-night bus stops, especially on weekends. The combination of drunkenness and impatience can sometimes lead to trouble, so act cautiously. If you need late-night transportation, try to arrange it with your hotel before you go out.

Irish Cabaret, Music & Dancing

CITY CENTER **Harcourt Hotel** (⊠ Harcourt St., Southside ☎ 01/478–3677) is where some of the best traditional musicians gather for wild jam sessions.

BALLSBRIDGE **Burlington hotel** (⊠ Upper Leeson St., Ballsbridge ☎ 01/660–5222) has a high-class lounge featuring a well-performed Irish cabaret—with dancing, music, and song.

Jurys hotel (⊠ Pembroke Rd., Ballsbridge ☎ 01/660–5000) stages a traditional Irish cabaret.

DUBLIN WEST **Castle Inn** (⊠ Christ Church Pl., Dublin West ☎ 01/475–1122) is really just a huge pub that has traditional Irish music and dancing with dinner in a medieval-style banquet hall.

Jazz

JJ Smyth's (⊠ 12 Aungier St., Southside ☎ 01/475–2565) is an old-time jazz venue where Louis Stewart, the granddaddy of Irish jazz, is a regular visitor.

Jurys Ballsbridge (⊠ Pembroke Rd., Ballsbridge ☎ 01/660–5000) attracts the country's top jazz musicians and voices to its lively Sunday-evening sessions.

Nightclubs

CITY CENTER **Lillie's Bordello** (⊠ Grafton St., Southside ☎ 01/679–9204) is a popular spot for a trendy professional crowd, as well as for rock and film stars. **The Pod** (⊠ Harcourt St., Southside ☎ 01/478–0166), also known as the "Place of Dance," qualifies as Dublin's most renowned dance club, especially among the younger set. Whether you get in depends as much on what you're wearing as on your age.

Red Box (⊠ Old Harcourt St. Station, Harcourt St., Southside ☎ 01/478–0166), adjacent to the Pod and the Chocolate Bar, can pack in more than 1,000 people and surround them with state-of-the-art sound and light. It regularly hosts Irish and international rock acts, and celebrity DJs from Europe and the United States. It has full bar facilities.

Renards (⊠ St. Fredrick St., Southside ☎ 01/677–5876) is where you'll find thirtysomethings who like to let their hair down. The music can be a bit predictable, but you might just bump into Bono.

Rí Ra (⊠ Dame Ct., Southside ☎ 01/677–4835) is part of the hugely popular Globe bar. The name means "uproar" in Irish, and on most nights the place does go a little wild. It's one of the best spots in Dublin for fun, no-frills dancing. Upstairs is more low-key.

Sugar Club (⊠ Lower Lesson St., Southside ☎ 01/678–7188) is a refreshing mix of cocktail bar, nightclub, and performance venue. The place is known for its smooth Latin sounds and plush surroundings.

TEMPLE BAR **Temple Bar Music Centre** (⊠ Curved St., Temple Bar ☎ 01/670–9202) claims to provide a different sound every night, including house, tribute bands, guitar-driven rock, and Latin music.

Viper Room (⊠ 5 Aston Quay, Temple Bar ☎ 01/672–5566), decorated in rich reds and purples, is a delightfully decadent late-night club that plays funk, chart, and rhythm and blues. Downstairs there's live jazz and salsa.

Pubs

NORTH OF THE LIFFEY **The Flowing Tide** (⊠ Lower Abbey St., Northside ☎ 01/874–0842), directly across from the Abbey Theatre, draws a lively pre- and post-theater crowd. No TVs, quality pub talk, and a great pint of Guinness make it a worthwhile visit.

GUBU (⊠ Capel St., Northside ☎ 01/874–0710), run by the hugely successful owners of the Globe, is a mixed gay and straight bar. The music is loud and dance-driven, and the downstairs pool table is an added bonus.

The Vaults (⊠ Harbourmaster Pl., Northside ☎ 01/678–8867) is in a wonderful stone cellar under Connolly Station. The classy wood-and-leather booths and tasty pub grub make it popular with office workers from the nearby IFSC during the week.

CITY CENTER **Cassidy's** (⊠ 42 Lower Camden St., Southside ☎ 01/475–1429) is a quiet neighborhood pub with a pint of stout so good that former president Bill Clinton dropped in for one during a visit to Dublin.

Cellar Bar (⊠ 24 Upper Merrion St., Southside ☎ 01/603–0600), at the Merrion Hotel, is in a stylish 18th-century wine vault with bare brick walls and vaulted ceilings. It tends to draw a well-heeled crowd.

Davy Byrne's (⊠ 21 Duke St., Southside ☎ 01/671–1298) is a pilgrimage stop for Joyceans. In *Ulysses,* Leopold Bloom stops in here for a glass of burgundy and a Gorgonzola-cheese sandwich. He then leaves the pub and walks to Dawson Street, where he helps a blind man cross the road. The pub is unrecognizable from Joyce's day, but it still serves some fine pub grub.

Dockers (⊠ 5 Sir John Rogerson's Quay, Southside ☎ 01/677–1692), a trendy quayside spot east of the city center, is just around the corner from Windmill Lane Studios—where U2 and other noted bands record. At night the area is a little dicey, so it's best to visit during the day.

Doheny & Nesbitt (⊠ 5 Lower Baggot St., Southside ☎ 01/676–2945), a traditional spot with snugs, dark wooden furnishings, and smoke-darkened ceilings, has hardly changed over the decades.

Doyle's (⊠ 9 College St., Southside ☎ 01/671–0616), a small cozy pub, is a favorite with journalists from the *Irish Times* office, just across the street.

George (⊠ 89 S. Great George's St., Southside ☎ 01/478–2983), Dublin's two-floor main gay pub, draws an almost entirely male crowd; its nightclub stays open until 2:30 AM nightly except Tuesday. The "alternative bingo night," with star drag act Miss Shirley Temple Bar, is a riot of risqué fun.

Globe (⊠ 11 S. Great George's St., Southside ☎ 01/671–1220), one of the hippest café-bars in town, draws arty, trendy Dubliners who sip espresso drinks by day and pack the place at night. There's live jazz on Sunday.

FodorśChoice ★ **Grogans** (⊠ 15 S. William St., Southside ☎ 01/677–9320), also known as the Castle Lounge, is a small place packed with creative folk. Owner Tommy Grogan is known as a patron of local artists, and his walls are covered with their work.

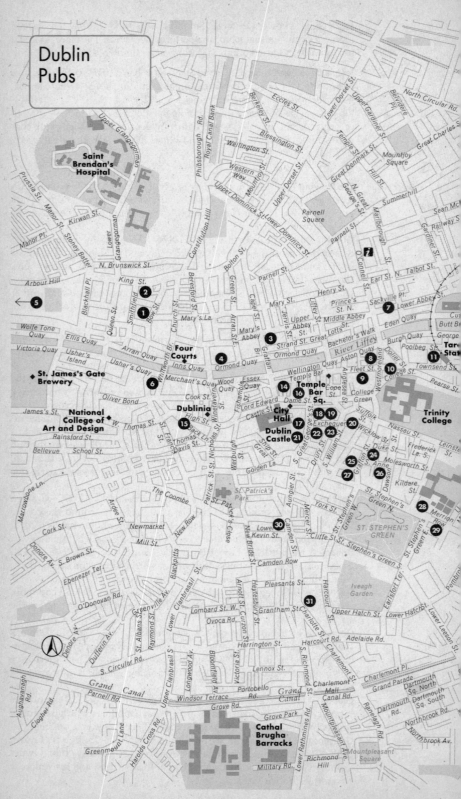

Dublin Pubs

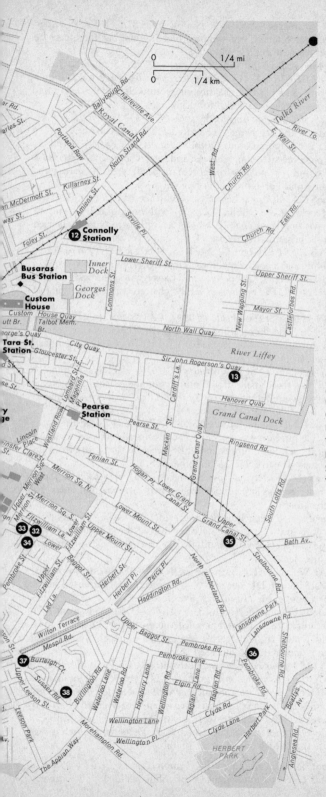

Hogan's (⊠ 35 Great St. George's St., Southside ☎ 01/677–5904), a huge floor space on two levels, gets jammed most nights, but the old place maintains its style through it all.

Horseshoe Bar (⊠ Le Méridien Shelbourne, 27 St. Stephen's Green, Southside ☎ 01/676–6471) is a popular meeting place for Dublin's businesspeople and politicians, though around the semicircular bar there's comparatively little space for drinkers.

Kehoe's (⊠ 9 S. Anne St., Southside ☎ 01/677–8312) is popular with Trinity students and academics. The tiny back room is cozy.

Kitty O'Shea's (⊠ Upper Grand Canal St., Southside ☎ 01/660–9965) has Pre-Raphaelite–style stained glass, and lots of sports paraphernalia on the walls, and is popular with sports fans of all types. Its sister pubs are in Brussels and Paris; this is the original.

Lesson Lounge (⊠ 148 Upper Lesson St., Southside ☎ 01/660–3816) has the look of a classic old Dublin "boozer," with one notable exception: it has a television. The Lesson is known as a place to watch televised sports of all kinds, and it's always pleasant and inclusive.

Long Hall Pub (⊠ 51 S. Great George's St., Southside ☎ 01/475–159), one of Dublin's most ornate traditional taverns, has Victorian lamps, a mahogany bar, mirrors, chandeliers, and plasterwork ceilings, all more than 100 years old. The pub serves sandwiches and an excellent pint of Guinness.

McDaid's (⊠ 3 Harry St., Southside ☎ 01/679–4395) attracted boisterous Brendan Behan and other leading writers in the 1950s; its wild literary reputation still lingers, although the bar has been discreetly modernized and is altogether quieter.

Mulligan's (⊠ 8 Poolbeg St., Southside ☎ 01/677–5582) is synonymous in Dublin with a truly inspirational pint of Guinness. Until a few years ago no women were admitted. Today journalists, locals, and students of both genders flock here for the perfect pint.

Neary's (⊠ 1 Chatham St., Southside ☎ 01/677–7371), with an exotic, Victorian-style interior, was once the haunt of music-hall artists and a certain literary set, including Brendan Behan. Join the actors from the adjacent Gaiety Theatre for a good pub lunch.

O'Donoghue's (⊠ 15 Merrion Row, Southside ☎ 01/676–2807), a cheerful smoky hangout, has impromptu musical performances that often spill out onto the street.

The Old Stand (⊠ 37 Exchequer St., Southside ☎ 01/677–7220), one of the oldest pubs in the city, is named after the old stand at Landsdowne Road, home to Irish rugby and football. The place is renowned for great pints and fine steaks.

Solas (⊠ 31 Wexford St., Southside ☎ 01/470–0583) offers not only some of Dublin's top DJs but also a wide selection of imported beers. The result: a young, hip crowd that likes to dance.

Fodor'sChoice ★ **Stag's Head** (⊠ 1 Dame Ct., Southside ☎ 01/679–3701) dates from 1770 and was rebuilt in 1895; theater people from the nearby Olympia, journalists, and Trinity students gather around the unusual counter, fashioned from Connemara red marble.

Toner's (⊠ 139 Lower Baggot St., Southside ☎ 01/676–3090), though billed as a Victorian bar, actually goes back 200 years, with an original flagstone floor to prove its antiquity, as well as wooden drawers running up to the ceiling—a relic of the days when bars doubled as grocery shops. Oliver St. John Gogarty, who was the model for Buck Mulligan in James Joyce's *Ulysses,* accompanied W. B. Yeats here, in what was purportedly the latter's only visit to a pub.

TEMPLE BAR **Front Lounge** (⊠ 33 Parliament St., Temple Bar ☎ 01/679–3988), a modern pub, caters to a mixed crowd of young professionals, both gay and straight.

Oliver St. John Gogarty (⊠ 57 Fleet St., Temple Bar ☏ 01/671–1822) is a lively bar that attracts all ages and nationalities; it overflows with patrons in summer. On most nights there is traditional Irish music upstairs. **Palace Bar** (⊠ 21 Fleet St., Temple Bar ☏ 01/677–9290), scarcely changed since the 1940s, is tiled and rather barren looking, but is popular with journalists and writers. (The *Irish Times* is nearby.) The walls are lined with cartoons drawn by the illustrators who used to spend time here.

The Porterhouse (⊠ 16–18 Parliament St., Temple Bar ☏ 01/679–8847) is one of the few bars in Ireland to brew its own beer. The Plain Porter has won the best stout at the "Brewing Oscars," beating out the mighty Guinness. The tasteful interior is all dark woods and soft lighting.

BALLSBRIDGE **Dubliner Pub** (⊠ Jurys hotel, Pembroke Rd., Ballsbridge ☏ 01/660–5000), an old-fashioned Irish pub, is a busy meeting place during lunch and after work.

O'Brien's (⊠ Sussex Terr., Ballsbridge ☏ 01/668–2594), beside the Doyle Burlington hotel, is a little antique gem of a pub, scarcely changed since the 1950s, with traditional snugs.

DUBLIN WEST **Brazen Head** (⊠ Bridge St., Dublin West ☏ 01/677–9549), Dublin's oldest pub (the site has been licensed since 1198), has stone walls and open fires—it has hardly changed over the years. The pub is renowned for traditional-music performances and lively sing-along sessions on Sunday evenings. On the south side of the Liffey quays, it's a little difficult to find—turn down Lower Bridge Street and make a right into the old lane.

Chief O'Neill's (⊠ Smithfield Village, Dublin West ☏ 01/817–3838), a Dublin hotel, has a large bar-café that's open and airy; it often hosts traditional Irish sessions.

Cobblestone (⊠ N. King St., Dublin West ☏ 01/872–1799) is a glorious house of ale in the best Dublin tradition, popular with Smithfield-market workers. Its chatty imbibers and live traditional music are attracting a wider, younger crowd from all over town.

Mother Redcap's Tavern (⊠ Back La., Dublin West ☏ 01/453–8306) is an authentic re-creation of a 17th-century Dublin tavern, with stone walls from an old flour mill, beams, and old prints of the city.

Out on the Liffey (⊠ 27 Ormond Quay, Dublin West ☏ 01/872–2480) is Dublin's second gay pub; it draws a mixed gay and straight crowd of both men and women.

Ryan's Pub (⊠ 28 Parkgate St., Dublin West ☏ 01/677–6097) is one of Dublin's last genuine, late-Victorian-era pubs, and has changed little since its last (1896) remodeling.

The Arts

Art Galleries

NORTH OF THE LIFFEY **The Bridge,** a restored 18th-century Georgian house on the river, has an impressive, open-plan gallery. An internal bridge leads from the gallery shop to the big space at the back with exhibits of established and rising Irish artists in all media. ⊠ *6 Upper Ormond Quay, Northside* ☏ *01/872–9702* ☉ *Mon.–Sat. 10–6, Sun. 2–5.*

CITY CENTER **Green on Red Galleries,** a rather unprepossessing gallery near the back of Trinity College, is one of Dublin's best. The constantly changing exhibitions showcase the work of some of the country's—and Britain's—most promising up-and-coming artists. ⊠ *26–28 Lombard St. E, Southside* ☏ *01/671–3414* ☉ *Weekdays 11–6, Sat. 11–5.*

Kerlin Gallery, perhaps Dublin's most important commercial gallery, exhibits the work of many of Ireland's important contemporary artists, including such internationally recognized figures as New York–based Sean Scully, Kathy Prendergast, Paul Seawright, and Stephen McKenna. This large space is behind Grafton Street. ⊠ *Anne's La., S. Anne St., Southside* ☎ *01/670–9093* ☉ *Weekdays 10–5:45, Sat. 11–4:30.*

Rubicon Gallery, a second-floor gallery overlooking St. Stephen's Green, holds yearly exhibitions in all media. ⊠ *10 St. Stephen's Green, Southside* ☎ *01/670–8055* ☉ *Mon.–Sat. 11–5:30.*

Solomon Gallery, although not exactly a risk taker, has slowly developed a reputation as one of Dublin's leading fine-art galleries. ⊠ *Powerscourt Townhouse Centre, S. William St., Southside* ☎ *01/679–4237* ☉ *Mon.–Sat. 10–5:30.*

TEMPLE BAR **National Photographic Archive** is a trove of Irish photographs from the late 19th and early 20th centuries. The Archive also hosts exhibits of work from contemporary Irish photographers—north and south. ⊠ *Meeting House Sq., Temple Bar* ☎ *01/603–0200* ☉ *Weekdays 10–5, Sat. 10–2.*

Original Print Gallery, in an ultramodern building by the same prominent Dublin architect who designed Temple Bar Gallery, specializes in handmade limited editions of prints by Irish artists. Also in the building, the **Black Church Print Studio** (☎ 01/677–3629) exhibits prints. ⊠ *4 Temple Bar, Temple Bar* ☎ *01/677–3657* ☉ *Tues.–Fri. 10:30–5:30, Sat. 11–5, Sun. 2–6.*

Temple Bar Gallery is the flagship of the Temple Bar redevelopment project. Expect to see the work of emerging Irish photographers, painters, sculptors, and other artists. Shows are on monthly rotating schedules. ⊠ *5–9 Temple Bar, Temple Bar* ☎ *01/671–0073* ☉ *Mon.–Sat. 11–6, Sun. 2–6.*

DUBLIN WEST **5th** is the gallery in which every Irish artist wants to be shown. The location is spectacular: it's on the fifth floor of the impressive Guinness Storehouse. Regularly changing exhibits include painting and sculpture, but the emphasis is on innovative installation and Web art from all over the world. ⊠ *St. James Gate, Dublin West* ☎ *01/408–4800* ☉ *Daily 9–5:30.*

Classical Music & Opera

CITY CENTER **The Bank of Ireland Arts Center** (⊠ Foster Pl. S, Southside ☎ 01/671–1488) is great at lunchtime, when classical music and opera recitals take place.

National Concert Hall (⊠ Earlsfort Terr., Southside ☎ 01/475–1666), just off St. Stephen's Green, is Dublin's main theater for classical music of all kinds, from symphonies to chamber groups. It houses the National Symphony Orchestra of Ireland.

Opera Ireland (⊠ John Player House, 276–288 S. Circular Rd., Southside ☎ 01/453–5519) performs at the Gaiety Theatre; call to find out what's on and when.

St. Stephen's Church (⊠ Merrion Sq., Southside ☎ 01/288–0663) stages a regular program of choral and orchestral events under its glorious "pepper canister" cupola.

TEMPLE BAR **Opera Theatre Company** (⊠ Temple Bar Music Centre, Curved St., Temple Bar ☎ 01/679–4962) is Ireland's only touring opera company. They perform at venues in Dublin and throughout the country.

DUBLIN WEST **Royal Hospital Kilmainham** (⊠ Military Rd., Dublin West ☎ 01/671–8666) presents frequent classical concerts in its magnificent 17th-century interior.

Film

NORTH OF THE LIFFEY **Savoy Cinema** (⊠ O'Connell St., Northside ☎ 01/874–6000), just across from the General Post Office, is a four-screen theater with the largest screen in the country.

UGC Multiplex (✉ Parnell Center, Parnell St., Northside ☎ 01/872–8400), a 12-screen theater just off O'Connell Street, is the city center's only multiplex movie house; it shows the latest commercial features.

TEMPLE BAR   **Irish Film Centre** (✉ 6 Eustace St., Temple Bar ☎ 01/677–8788) shows classic and new independent films.

CITY CENTER   **Screen Cinema** (✉ 2 Townsend St., Southside ☎ 01/671–4988), between Trinity College and O'Connell Street Bridge, is a popular three-screen art-house cinema.

Rock & Contemporary Music

NORTH OF THE LIFFEY   **The Ambassador** (✉ 1 Parnell Sq., Northside ☎ 01/889–9403) was once a cinema attached to the Gate Theatre. The plush interior and seats have been removed, and the stripped-down venue now houses visiting bands and "school-disco" nights with music from the '70s and '80s.

The Point (✉ Eastlink Br., Northside ☎ 01/836–3633), a 6,000-capacity arena about 1 km (½ mi) east of the Custom House on the Liffey, is Dublin's premier venue for internationally renowned acts. Call or send a self-addressed envelope to receive a list of upcoming shows; tickets can be difficult to obtain, so book early.

CITY CENTER   **International Bar** (✉ Wicklow St., Southside ☎ 01/677–9250) has a long-established, tiny, get-close-to-the-band venue upstairs. It hosts theater in the afternoons.

Whelan's (✉ 25 Wexford St., Southside ☎ 01/478–0766), just off the southeastern corner of St. Stephen's Green, is one of the city's best—and most popular—music venues. Well-known performers play everything from rock to folk to traditional music.

TEMPLE BAR   **Olympia Theatre** (✉ 72 Dame St., Temple Bar ☎ 01/677–7744) puts on its "Midnight from the Olympia" shows every Friday and Saturday from midnight to 2 AM, with everything from rock to country.

Temple Bar Music Centre (✉ Curved St., Temple Bar ☎ 01/670–0533) is a music venue, rehearsal space, television studio, and pub rolled into one. It buzzes with activity every day of the week. Live acts range from rock bands to world music to singer-songwriters.

DUBLIN WEST   **Vicar Street** (✉ 58–59 Thomas St., Dublin West ☎ 01/454–5533), just across from Christ Church Cathedral, is a seated venue for intimate concerts. It often plays host to folk music, jazz, and comedy, as well as rock performances.

Theater

NORTH OF THE LIFFEY   **Abbey Theatre** (✉ Lower Abbey St., Northside ☎ 01/878–7222), the home of Ireland's national theater company, stages mainstream, mostly Irish traditional, plays. Its sister theater at the same address, the Peacock, offers more experimental drama. In 1904 W. B. Yeats and his patron, Lady Gregory, opened the theater, which became a major center for the Irish literary renaissance—the place that first staged works by J. M. Synge and Sean O'Casey, among many others. The original theater burned down in 1951, but it reopened with a modern design in 1966.

Gate Theatre (✉ Cavendish Row, Parnell Sq., Northside ☎ 01/874–4045), an intimate 371-seat theater in a jewellike Georgian assembly hall, produces the classics and contemporary plays by leading Irish writers.

CITY CENTER   **Andrew's Lane Theatre** (✉ 9–11 Andrew's La., Southside ☎ 01/679–5720) presents experimental productions.

Gaiety Theatre (✉ S. King St., Southside ☎ 01/677–1717) is the home of Opera Ireland when it's not showing musical comedy, drama, and revues. Weekends this elegant theater is taken over by a nightclub with live music and cabaret.

Samuel Beckett Centre (⊠ Trinity College, Southside ☎ 01/608–2266) is home to Trinity's Drama Department, as well as visiting groups from around Europe. Dance is often performed here by visiting troupes.

TEMPLE BAR   **New Project Arts Centre** (⊠ 39 E. Essex St., Temple Bar ☎ 01/671–2321) is a theater and performance space right in the center of Temple Bar. Fringe and mainstream theater, contemporary music, and experimental art have all found a home here.

Olympia Theatre (⊠ 72 Dame St., Temple Bar ☎ 01/677–7744) is Dublin's oldest and premier multipurpose theatrical venue. In addition to its high-profile musical performances, it has seasons of comedy, vaudeville, and ballet.

DUBLIN WEST   **Tivoli** (⊠ 135–138 Francis St., Dublin West ☎ 01/454–4472) brings culture to the heart of old working-class Dublin, the Liberties. Comedy-based shows and the occasional Shakespeare play are favored.

SPORTS & THE OUTDOORS

Health clubs have really caught on in Dublin and seem to be sprouting up in every corner of the city. But Dublin has no dearth of opportunities for getting out and moving about. It's true you'll have to travel to the suburbs north and south to enjoy most of them, but it's well worth it for the chance to explore a beach, horseback-ride through a forest, or bike through Phoenix Park.

Beaches

The main beach for swimming on the south side of Dublin is at **Killiney** (⊠ 13 km [8 mi] south of the city center, South County Dublin), a 3-km-long (2-mi-long) shingle (pebbly) beach. The DART train station is right by the beach; get off at Killiney. **Malahide,** a charming village on the Northside DART line, has a clean and easily accessible beach, though the current can be strong. To the north of Dublin city is **North Bull Island,** created over years by the action of the tides. The fine sand here stretches for almost 3 km (2 mi). Bus 130 from Lower Abbey Street stops by the walkway to the beach. Near Dublin city center, **Sandymount Strand** is a long expanse of fine sand where the tide goes out nearly 3 km (2 mi), but it's not suitable for swimming or bathing because the tide races in so fast. The strand can be reached easily by the DART train.

Bicycling

It's not a good idea to ride bicycles in the city center—traffic is heavy, and most roads don't have shoulders, much less bike lanes. Phoenix Park and some suburbs (especially Ballsbridge, Clontarf, and Sandymount), however, are pleasant once you're off the main roads. There's plenty of challenging terrain immediately south of the city, in the Dublin and Wicklow mountains. Don't forget to secure your bicycle if you leave it unattended.

You can rent bicycles for about €57 a week; an equivalent amount will be charged for deposit. Nearly 20 companies in the Dublin region rent bicycles; Tourist Information Offices (TIOs) have a full list. **McDonald's** (⊠ 38 Wexford St., Southside ☎ 01/475–2586) is a central bike-repair and -rental shop. **Mike's Bike Shop** (⊠ Dun Laoghaire Shopping Center, Dun Laoghaire, South County Dublin ☎ 01/280–0417) is a long-established bike outfit in the southern suburbs of Dublin. **Tracks Cycles** (⊠ 8 Botanic Rd., North County Dublin ☎ 01/873–2455) has an established reputation for being trustworthy in repairs, sales, and rentals of all types of bikes.

Bowling

Bowling is a popular sport in Dublin. Two kinds are played locally. The sedate, exclusive, outdoor variety known as crown-green bowling is played at a number of locations in the suburbs. Dublin also has six indoor 10-pin bowling centers.

Bray Leisure Bowl (⊠ Quinsboro Rd., Bray ☎ 01/286–4455), an indoor bowling center, serves the area near the Wicklow border. **Herbert Park** (⊠ Ballsbridge ☎ 01/660–1875) has a splendid, baby-soft bowling green. **Kenilworth Bowling Club** (⊠ Grosvenor Sq., Rathmines ☎ 01/497–2305) welcomes paying visitors, and lessons are available. The green is half the size of a football pitch, and smooth as a carpet. **Leisureplex Coolock** (⊠ Malahide Rd., Coolock, North County Dublin ☎ 01/848–5722 ⊠ Village Green Center, Tallaght ☎ 01/459–9411) is popular with bowlers from both sides of the city, as it has plenty of lanes and is easy to reach.

Metro Bowl (⊠ 149 N. Strand Rd., North County Dublin ☎ 01/855–0400) tends to attract the more serious bowlers. **Stillorgan Bowl** (⊠ Stillorgan Rd., Stillorgan ☎ 01/288–1656) is the oldest 10-pin center in Ireland. **Superdome** (⊠ Palmerston Shopping Centre, Palmerston ☎ 01/626–0700) draws big crowds of teenage and family bowlers.

Football

Soccer—called football in Europe—is very popular in Ireland, largely due to the euphoria resulting from the national team's successes since the late 1980s. However, the places where you can watch it aren't ideal—they tend to be small and out-of-date. **Lansdowne Road Stadium** (⊠ 62 Lansdowne Rd., Ballsbridge ☎ 01/668–4601), a vast rugby stadium, is the main center for international matches.

League of Ireland matches take place throughout the city every Sunday from September to May. For details, contact the **Football Association of Ireland** (⊠ 80 Merrion Sq. S, Southside ☎ 01/676–6864).

Gaelic Games

The traditional games of Ireland, Gaelic football and hurling, attract a huge following, with roaring crowds cheering on their county teams. Games are held at Croke Park, the national stadium for Gaelic games, just north of the city center. For details of matches, contact the **Gaelic Athletic Association (GAA)** (⊠ Croke Park, North County Dublin ☎ 01/836–3222 ⊕ www.gaa.ie).

Golf

Think idyllic. The Dublin region is a great place for golfers—it has 32 18-hole courses, 16 9-hole courses, and several more 18-hole courses on the way. Below are only some of the major 18-hole courses around Dublin.

Deer Park (⊠ Deer Park Hotel, Howth, North County Dublin ☎ 01/832–6039) is a top-quality parkland golf course. It has 48 holes, and the longest 18-hole course is 6,830 yards. **Edmonstown** (⊠ Rathfarnham, South County Dublin ☎ 01/493–2461), a beautiful golf course, serves an upscale clientele. The championship 18-hole course is 6,011 yards long. Expert tuition is available. **Elm Park** (⊠ Donnybrook, South County Dublin ☎ 01/269–3438) welcomes visiting golfers and beginners. **Foxrock** (⊠ Torquay Rd., Foxrock, South County Dublin ☎ 01/289–3992) is a tough 9-hole golf course with a gorgeous location in the Southside suburbs.

The 18-hole, 6,010-yard **Hermitage** (✉ Lucan, North County Dublin ☎ 01/626–4781) is one of the city's more difficult golf courses. **Newlands** (✉ Clondalkin, South County Dublin ☎ 01/459–2903) attracts golfers from the Southside of the city. The 18-hole course is 6,100 yards. The golf course at **Sutton** (✉ Sutton, South County Dublin ☎ 01/832–3013) has only 9 holes, but they're top quality and the course is as exclusive and as pricey as everything else in this wealthy suburb. **Woodbrook** (✉ Bray, South County Dublin ☎ 01/282–4799) is worth the trip out of the city for a day of golf by the sea. The very long 18-hole course is 6,836 yards.

At **Golf D2** (✉ Cow St., Temple Bar ☎ 01/672–6181) you can practice even if it's raining. You strike a real ball with a real club against a huge screen, which tracks the virtual course of your shot. It's a cool idea, and it works. You can play 34 of the world's most famous courses, including St. Andrews and Pebble Beach. It costs €19.05 for a half hour, and you must book ahead.

Greyhound Racing

Greyhound racetracks are among the best places to see Dubliners at their most passionate and full of wicked humor. Although it's a somewhat dilapidated greyhound racing track, **Harolds Cross** (✉ Harolds Cross, South County Dublin ☎ 01/497–1081) serves its purpose with racing year-round. **Shelbourne Park** (✉ Shelbourne Park, South County Dublin ☎ 01/668–3502) is a relatively stylish place to watch greyhound racing year-round. You can book a table in the restaurant that overlooks the track.

Health Clubs

Not far from the Ballsbridge hotels, **Equinox Leisure** (✉ St. John's Rd. E, near Sydney Parade DART station, Ballsbridge ☎ 01/269–5764) has a full gym and nightly fitness classes of all levels. The **Iveagh Fitness Club** (✉ Christ Church St., Dublin West ☎ 01/454–6555) is next to Christ Church Cathedral, in a complex of beautiful old redbrick buildings. It has a pool, sauna, and full weight room. Just off Grafton Street, the **Jackie Skelly Fitness Centre** (✉ 41–42 Clarendon St., Southside ☎ 01/677–0040) is perfect if you're staying in a city-center hotel without a gym. In Rathgar village, the **Orwell Club** (✉ 75 Orwell Rd., Rathgar, South County Dublin ☎ 01/492–3146) is not far from many of the Southside hotels. The city-center **Riverside Fitness Centre** (✉ Eden Quay, Northside ☎ 01/878–7303) even has baby-sitting facilities for young children while you work out.

Horse Racing

Horse racing—from flat to hurdle to steeplechase—is one of the great sporting loves of the Irish. The sport is closely followed and betting is popular, but the social side of attending races is equally important to Dubliners. The main course in Dublin is **Leopardstown** (✉ Leopardstown Rd., Southside ☎ 01/289–3607 ⊕ www.leopardstown.com), an ultramodern course that hosts the Hennessey Gold Cup in February, Ireland's most prestigious steeplechase. Summertime is devoted to flat racing, and the rest of the year to racing over fences. You can also nip in for a quick meal at the restaurant.

The **Curragh** (☎ 045/441–205 ⊕ www.curragh.ie), southwest of Dublin off M7, hosts the five Classics, the most important flat races of the season, from May to September. There are numerous bars here and two restaurants. **Fairyhouse** (✉ Co. Meath ☎ 01/825–6167) hosts the Grand National, the most popular steeplechase of the season, every Easter Monday. **Punchestown** (☎ 045/897–704), outside Naas, County Kildare, is the home of the ever-popular Punchestown National Hunt Festival in April.

Horseback Riding

Stables on the outskirts of the city give you immediate access to some excellent riding areas—Counties Dublin, Kildare, Louth, Meath, and Wicklow all have unspoiled country territory. In the city itself, you'll find superb, quiet riding conditions at Phoenix Park, away from the busy main road that bisects the park. About 20 riding stables in the greater Dublin area have horses for hire by the hour or day, both for novices and for experienced riders; a few also operate as equestrian centers and offer lessons. Outside Dublin, **Brittas Lodge Riding Stables** (⊠ Brittas, South County Dublin ☎ 01/458–2726) has fantastic facilities, and, wonderfully, is right next to one of the nicest beaches on the East Coast. Horseback riders at the **Deerpark Riding Center** (⊠ Castleknock Rd., Castleknock, North County Dublin ☎ 01/820–7141) canter in Dublin's massive Phoenix Park.

Rugby

For details about rugby in Ireland, contact the **Irish Rugby Football Union** (☎ 01/647–3800 ⊕ www.irishrugby.ie). International rugby matches run during the winter and spring at the vast **Lansdowne Road Stadium** (⊠ 62 Lansdowne Rd., Ballsbridge ☎ 01/668–4601). Local matches are also played every weekend during that time.

Running

Traffic in Dublin, heavy from early morning until late at night, is getting worse, so if you jog here, expect to dodge vehicles and stop for lights. (Remember *always* to look to your right *and* your left before crossing a street.) If you're staying in Temple Bar or on the western end of the city and you can run 9 km (5½ mi), head to Phoenix Park, easily the nicest place in Dublin for a jog. If you're on the Southside, Merrion Square, St. Stephen's Green, and Trinity College are all good places for short jogs, though be prepared to dodge pedestrians; if you're looking for a longer route, ask your hotel to direct you to the Grand Canal, which has a pleasant path you can run along as far east as the Grand Canal Street Bridge.

Swimming

The private pool at **Dundrum Family Recreation Center** (⊠ Meadowbrook, Dundrum, South County Dublin ☎ 01/298–4654) is open to the public for a small fee. There are usually two lanes open for lap swimming, and the showers and changing rooms are clean. For a hardy dip, there's year-round sea swimming at the **Forty Foot Bathing Pool,** a traditional sea-bathing area—in use for more than a century (and popular with older nude men)—in Sandycove. It's deep and nicely sheltered from the wind. Steps lead down into the water. **St. Vincent's** (⊠ Navan Rd., North County Dublin ☎ 01/838–4906) is a public pool in the northern suburbs of the city. Two lanes are available for laps in the morning, at lunchtime, and in the late evening. Changing rooms have good showers, but you have to take your clothes into the pool area.

Terenure College (⊠ Templeogue Rd., Terenure, South County Dublin ☎ 01/490–7071) is a high school with a pool that's open to the public when school's not in session and competitions aren't taking place. The modern changing rooms have lockers with locks, and there are usually a couple of lanes open for lap swimming. One of the best of Dublin's 12 public pools is **Townsend Street** (⊠ Townsend St., Southside ☎ 01/672–9121). Six lanes are available for laps every evening from 5 to 7. Lockers and showers are provided. **Williams Park** (⊠ Williams Rd.,

Rathmines, South County Dublin ☎ 01/496–1275) is a quality public pool in the southern suburbs. Five lanes are available for early morning laps on Tuesday and Thursday. Showers are provided, and you bring your clothes with you poolside in a basket.

Tennis

Tennis is one of Dublin's most popular participant sports, and some public parks have excellent tennis facilities open to the public. For information about playing tennis in Dublin, contact **Tennis Ireland** (✉ 22 Argyle Sq., Donnybrook, South County Dublin ☎ 01/668–1841).

Bushy Park (✉ Terenure, South County Dublin ☎ 01/490–0320) has well-maintained public tennis courts. The 12 asphalt courts are available for €1.50 an hour and are open daily from 10 to dusk. Thanks to its excellent facilities, **Herbert Park** (✉ Ballsbridge ☎ 01/668–4364) attracts some serious tennis players to its public courts. The 12 asphalt courts cost €2.50 an hour and are open daily from 8 to dusk. **Kilternan Tennis Centre** (✉ Kilternan Golf and Country Club Hotel, Kilternan, South County Dublin ☎ 01/295–3729) has everything a tennis player could want—lessons, serving machines, racket stringing—at a price. Four indoor and four outdoor floodlighted Savannah-grass courts are available for €14 an hour. It's open daily 9 to 10. **St. Anne's Park** (✉ Dollymount Strand, North County Dublin ☎ 01/833–8898) has 12 quality asphalt courts within sniffing distance of the ocean. The courts cost €3 an hour and are open from 10 until an hour before dusk every day. **West Wood Lawn Tennis Club** (✉ Leopardstown Racecourse, Foxrock, South County Dublin ☎ 01/289–2911) is popular with young, serious-minded players. Lessons are offered for €5 an hour on the 11 indoor and four outdoor courts. It's open daily 8 to 10.

SHOPPING

The only known specimens of leprechauns or shillelaghs in Ireland are those in souvenir-shop windows, and shamrocks mainly bloom around the borders of Irish linen handkerchiefs and tablecloths. But today you'll find much more than kitschy designs. There's a tremendous variety of stores in Dublin, many of which are quite sophisticated—as a walk through Dublin's central shopping area, from O'Connell to Grafton Street, will prove. Department stores stock internationally known fashion-designer goods and housewares, and small (and often pricey) boutiques sell Irish crafts and other merchandise. But don't expect too many bargains here. And be prepared, if you're shopping in central Dublin, to push through crowds—especially in the afternoons and on weekends. Most large shops and department stores are open Monday to Saturday 9 to 6. Although nearly all department stores are closed on Sunday, some smaller specialty shops stay open. Those with later closing hours are noted below. You're particularly likely to find sales in January, February, July, and August.

Shopping Streets

Dublin's dozen or so main shopping streets each have a different character. Visit them all to appreciate the wide selection of items for sale here. The main commercial streets north of the river have both chain and department stores that tend to be less expensive (and less design-conscious) than their counterparts in the city center on the other side of the Liffey.

North of the Liffey

Henry Street, where cash-conscious Dubliners shop, runs westward from O'Connell Street. Arnotts department store is the anchor here; smaller, specialty stores sell CDs, footwear, and clothing. Henry Street's continuation, Mary Street, has a branch of Marks & Spencer and the Jervis Shopping Centre.

O'Connell Street, the city's main thoroughfare, while more downscale than Southside city streets (such as Grafton Street), is still worth a walk. One of Dublin's largest department stores, Clery's, is here, across from the GPO. On the same side of the street as the post office is Eason's, a large book, magazine, and stationery store.

City Center

Dawson Street, just east of Grafton Street between Nassau Street to the north and St. Stephen's Green to the south, is the city's primary bookstore avenue. Waterstone's and Hodges Figgis face each other on different sides of the street.

Francis Street and surrounding areas, such as the Coombe, have plenty of shops where you can browse. It's all part of the Liberties, the oldest part of the city and the hub of Dublin's antiques trade. If you're looking for something in particular, dealers will gladly recommend the appropriate store to you.

Grafton Street, Dublin's bustling pedestrian-only main shopping street, has two upscale department stores: Marks & Spencer and Brown Thomas. The rest of the street is taken up by smaller shops, many of them branches of international chains, such as the Body Shop and Bally, and many British chains. This is also the spot to buy fresh flowers, available at reasonable prices from outdoor stands. On the smaller streets off Grafton Street—especially Duke Street, South Anne Street, and Chatham Street—are worthwhile crafts, clothing, and designer housewares shops.

Nassau Street, Dublin's main tourist-oriented thoroughfare, has some of the best-known stores selling Irish goods, but you won't find many locals shopping here. Still, if you're looking for classic Irish gifts to take home, you should be sure at least to browse along here.

Temple Bar, Dublin's hippest neighborhood, is dotted with small precious boutiques—mainly intimate quirky shops that traffic in a small selection of *très* trendy goods, from vintage wear to some of the most avant-garde Irish clothing you'll find anywhere in the city.

Shopping Centers

North of the Liffey

Ilac Center (✉ Henry St., Northside) was Dublin's first large, modern shopping center, with two department stores, hundreds of specialty shops, and several restaurants. The stores are not as exclusive as those at some of the other centers, but there's plenty of free parking.

Jervis Shopping Centre (✉ Jervis and Mary Sts., Northside ☎ 01/878-1323) is a slightly high-end center, with some of the major British chain stores. It has a compact design and plenty of parking space.

City Center

Powerscourt Townhouse Centre (✉ 59 S. William St., Southside), the former town home of Lord Powerscourt, built in 1771, has an interior courtyard that has been refurbished and roofed over; a pianist often plays on the dais at ground-floor level. Coffee shops and restaurants share space with a mix of antiques and crafts stores, including the HQ Gallery, the main showcase of the Irish Craft Council and one of the finest places in Dublin to buy contemporary crafts. You can also buy original Irish fashions here by young designers, such as Gráinne Walsh.

Royal Hibernian Way (✉ off Dawson St. between S. Anne and Duke Sts., Southside ☎ 01/679–5919) is on the former site of the two-centuries-old Royal Hibernian Hotel, a coaching inn that was demolished in 1983. The pricey stylish shops—about 20 or 30, many selling fashionable clothes—are small in scale and include a branch of Leonidas, the Belgian chocolate firm.

St. Stephen's Green Centre (✉ northwest corner of St. Stephen's Green, Southside ☎ 01/478–0888), Dublin's largest and most ambitious shopping complex, resembles a giant greenhouse, with Victorian-style ironwork. On three floors overlooked by a vast clock, the 100 mostly small shops sell crafts, fashions, and household goods.

Tower Design Centre (✉ Pearse St., Southside ☎ 01/677–5655), east of the heart of the city center (near the Waterways Visitors Centre), has more than 35 separate crafts shops in a converted 1862 sugar-refinery tower. On the ground floor there are workshops devoted to heraldry and Irish pewter; the other six floors have stores that sell hand-painted silks, ceramics, hand-knit items, jewelry, and fine-art cards and prints.

Westbury Mall (✉ Westbury Hotel, off Grafton St., Southside) is an upmarket shopping mall where you can buy designer jewelry, antique rugs, and decorative goods.

Department Stores

Arnotts (✉ Henry St., Northside ☎ 01/872–1111 ✉ Grafton St., Southside ☎ 01/872–1111), on three floors, stocks a wide selection of clothing, household, and sporting goods. The smaller Grafton Street branch sells new fashion and footwear.

A-Wear (✉ Grafton St., Southside ☎ 01/671–7200 ✉ Henry St., Northside ☎ 01/872–4644) specializes in fashion for men and women. Many of the items are seasonal and closely follow the ever-changing trends. Leading Irish designers, including John Rocha, supply A-Wear with a steady stream of clothing.

Brown Thomas (✉ Grafton St., Southside ☎ 01/679–5666), Dublin's most exclusive department store, stocks the leading designer names (including many Irish designers) in clothing and cosmetics, plus lots of stylish accessories. There's also a good selection of crystal.

Clery's (✉ O'Connell St., Northside ☎ 01/878–6000), once the city's most fashionable department store, is still worth a visit. You'll find all kinds of merchandise—from fashion to home appliances—on its four floors. Note that goods sold here reflect a distinctly modest, traditional sense of style.

Dunnes Stores (✉ St. Stephen's Green Centre, Southside ☎ 01/478–0188 ✉ Henry St., Northside ☎ 01/872–6833 ✉ Ilac Center, Mary St., Northside ☎ 01/873–0211) is Ireland's largest chain of department stores. All of the branches stock fashion, household, and grocery items, and have a reputation for value and variety.

Eason's (✉ O'Connell St., Northside ☎ 01/873–3811 ✉ Ilac Center, Mary St., Northside ☎ 01/872–1322) is known primarily for its large selection of books, magazines, and stationery; the larger O'Connell Street branch sells tapes, CDs, records, videos, and other audiovisual goodies.

Marks & Spencer (✉ Grafton St., Southside ☎ 01/679–7855 ✉ Henry St., Northside ☎ 01/872–8833), perennial competitor to Brown Thomas, stocks everything from fashion (including lingerie) to tasty unusual groceries. The Grafton Street branch even has its own bureau de change, which doesn't charge commission.

Roches Stores (✉ Henry St., Northside ☎ 01/873–0044) is where sensible Dubliners have shopped for generations. Household goods are the specialty, but you'll also find great value on clothes.

Outdoor Markets

Liberty Market, on the north end of Meath Street in the Liberties section of Southside, sells bric-a-brac Friday and Saturday from 10 to 6, and Sunday from noon to 5:30. Listening to the banter between buyers and sellers can be lots of fun.

Meeting House Square Market, held Saturday mornings at the heart of Temple Bar, is a good place to buy homemade foodstuffs: breads, chocolate, and organic veggies.

Moore Street, on the Northside behind the Ilac Center, is open Monday through Saturday from 9 to 6. Stalls, which line both sides of the street, sell fruits and vegetables; this is also a good place to buy shoes and boots. Moore Street vendors are known for their sharp wit, so expect the traditional Dublin repartee when you're shopping.

Specialty Shops

Antiques

Dublin is one of Europe's best cities in which to buy antiques, largely due to a long and proud tradition of restoration and high-quality craftsmanship. The Liberties, Dublin's oldest district, is, fittingly, the hub of the antiques trade, and is chockablock with shops and traders. Bachelor's Walk, along the quays, also has some decent shops. It's quite a seller's market, but bargains are still possible.

Antiques and collectibles fairs take place at **Newman House** (⊠ 85–86 St. Stephen's Green, Southside ☎ 01/670–8295) every second Sunday throughout the year.

Conlon Antiques (⊠ 21 Clanbrassil St., Dublin West ☎ 01/453–7323) sells a diverse selection of antiques, from sideboards to fanlights.

Ha'penny Bridge Galleries (⊠ 15 Bachelor's Walk, Northside ☎ 01/872–3950) has four floors of curios, with a particularly large selection of bronzes, silver, and china.

O'Sullivan Antiques (⊠ 43–44 Francis St., Dublin West ☎ 01/454–1143 or 01/453–9659) specializes in 18th- and 19th-century furniture and has a high-profile clientele, including Mia Farrow and Liam Neeson.

Books

You won't have any difficulty weighing down your suitcase with books. Ireland, after all, produced four Nobel literature laureates in just under 75 years. If you're at all interested in modern and contemporary literature, be sure to leave yourself time to browse through the bookstores, as you're likely to find books available here you can't find back home. Best of all, thanks to an enlightened national social policy, there's no tax on books, so if you only buy books, you don't have to worry about getting VAT slips.

Books Upstairs (⊠ 36 College Green, Southside ☎ 01/679–6687) carries an excellent selection of special-interest books, including gay and feminist literature, psychology, and self-help books.

Cathach Books (⊠ 10 Duke St., Southside ☎ 01/671–8676) sells first editions of Irish literature and many other books of Irish interest, plus old maps of Dublin and Ireland.

Dublin Bookshop (⊠ 24 Grafton St., Southside ☎ 01/677–5568) is an esteemed, family-owned store that sells mass-market books.

Eason's/Hanna's (⊠ 29 Nassau St., Southside ☎ 01/677–1255) sells secondhand and mass-market paperbacks and hardcovers, and has a good selection of works on travel and Ireland.

Flying Pig Bookshop (✉ 17 Crow St., Temple Bar ☎ 01/679–5099) stocks Ireland's largest selection of secondhand science fiction and fantasy books.

Greene's (✉ Clare St., Southside ☎ 01/676–2544) carries an extensive range of secondhand volumes and new educational and mass market books.

Hodges Figgis (✉ 56–58 Dawson St., Southside ☎ 01/677–4754), Dublin's leading independent bookstore, stocks 1½ million books on three floors. There's a pleasant café on the first floor.

Hughes & Hughes (✉ St. Stephen's Green Centre, Southside ☎ 01/478–3060) has strong travel and Irish-interest sections. There's also a store at Dublin Airport.

Waterstone's (✉ 7 Dawson St., Southside ☎ 01/679–1415), a large two-story branch of the British chain, features a fine selection of Irish and international books.

Winding Stair (✉ 40 Ormond Quay, Northside ☎ 01/873–3292) is a charming new- and used-book store overlooking the Liffey. The little upstairs café is the perfect spot for an afternoon of reading.

China, Crystal, Ceramics & Jewelry

Ireland is *the* place to buy Waterford crystal, which is available in a wide selection of products, including relatively inexpensive items. Other lines are now gaining recognition, such as Cavan, Galway, and Tipperary crystal.

Blarney Woollen Mills (✉ 21–23 Nassau St., Southside ☎ 01/671–0068) is one of the best places for Belleek china, Waterford and Galway crystal, and Irish linen.

China Showrooms (✉ 32–33 Lower Abbey St., Northside ☎ 01/878–6211), which has been operating since 1942, carries all the top brand names in fine china, including Aynsley, Royal Doulton, and Belleek. It also stocks Waterford, Tyrone, and Tipperary hand-cut crystal.

Crafts Centre of Ireland (✉ St. Stephen's Green Centre, Southside ☎ 01/475–4526) carries an impressive inventory of Ireland's most famous contemporary designers, including Michael Kennedy and Diane McCormick (ceramics), Glen Lucas (wood turning), and Jerpoint Glass (glassworks).

Crannóg (✉ Crown Alley, Temple Bar ☎ 01/671–0805) specializes in ceramics and contemporary Irish jewelry, especially silver pendants and rings.

Designyard (✉ E. Essex St., Temple Bar ☎ 01/677–8453) carries beautifully designed Irish and international tableware, lighting, small furniture, and jewelry.

House of Ireland (✉ 37–38 Nassau St., Southside ☎ 01/671–6133) has an extensive selection of crystal, jewelry, tweeds, sweaters, and other upscale goods.

Kilkenny Shop (✉ 5–6 Nassau St., Southside ☎ 01/677–7066) specializes in contemporary Irish-made ceramics, pottery, and silver jewelry, and regularly holds exhibits of exciting new work by Irish craftspeople.

McDowell (✉ 3 Upper O'Connell St., Northside ☎ 01/874–4961), a jewelry shop popular with Dubliners, has been in business for more than 100 years.

Tierneys (✉ St. Stephen's Green Centre, Southside ☎ 01/478–2873) carries a good selection of crystal and china. Claddagh rings (composed of two hands clasped around a heart with a crown above it), pendants, and brooches are popular.

Weir & Sons (✉ 96 Grafton St., Southside ☎ 01/677–9678), Dublin's most prestigious jeweler, sells not only jewelry and watches, but also china, glass, lamps, silver, and leather.

Clothing Stores

Costume (✉ 10 Castel Market, Southside ☎ 01/679–4188) is a classy boutique where Dubliners with fashion sense and money like to shop for colorful, stylish clothes. Local designers include Leigh, Helen James, and Antonia Campbell-Hughes; Temperley and Preen are among the international designers featured.

Platform (✉ 50 S. William St., Southside ☎ 01/677–7380), with its modern, sleek clothing, is run by the unique Joan Woods, who always seems to have her little dog in tow. You enter the narrow cozy shop through a set of beautiful stone arches. Scandinavian and Dutch labels are sold alongside Ireland's Tim Ryan and hats by Philip Tracy.

Museum Stores

National Gallery of Ireland Shop (✉ Merrion Sq. W, Southside ☎ 01/678–5450) has a terrific selection of books on Irish art, plus posters, postcards, notecards, and lots of lovely bibelots.

National Museum Shop (✉ Kildare St., Southside ☎ 01/677–7444 Ext. 327) carries jewelry based on ancient Celtic artifacts in the museum collection, contemporary Irish pottery, a large selection of books, and other gift items.

Trinity College Library Shop (✉ Old Library, Trinity College, Southside ☎ 01/608–2308) sells Irish-theme books, *Book of Kells* souvenirs, clothing, jewelry, and lovely Irish-made items.

Music

Celtic Note (✉ 12 Nassau St., Southside ☎ 01/670–4157) is aimed at the tourist market, with lots of compilations and greatest hits formats.

Claddagh Records (✉ 2 Cecilia St., Temple Bar ☎ 01/679–3664) has a good selection of traditional and folk music.

Gael Linn (✉ 26 Merrion Sq., Southside ☎ 01/676–7283) specializes in traditional Irish-music and Irish-language recordings; it's where the aficionados go.

HMV (✉ 65 Grafton St., Southside ☎ 01/679–5334 ✉ 18 Henry St., Northside ☎ 01/872–2095) is one of the larger record shops in town.

McCullogh Piggott (✉ 25 Suffolk St., Southside ☎ 01/677–3138) is the best place in town to buy instruments, sheet music, scores, and books about music.

Tower Records (✉ 6–8 Wicklow St., Southside ☎ 01/671–3250) is the best-stocked international chain.

Virgin Megastore (✉ 14–18 Aston Quay, Southside ☎ 01/677–7361) is Dublin's biggest music store and holds in-store performances by Irish bands.

Sweaters & Tweeds

Don't think Irish woolens are limited to Aran sweaters and tweed jackets. You can choose souvenirs from a wide selection of hats, gloves, scarves, blankets, and other goods here. If you're traveling outside of Dublin, you may want to wait to make purchases elsewhere, but if Dublin is it, you still have plenty of good shops from which to choose. The tweed sold in Dublin comes from two main sources: Donegal and Connemara. Labels inside the garments guarantee their authenticity. The following are the largest retailers of traditional Irish woolen goods in the city.

An Táin (✉ 13 Temple Bar Sq. N, Temple Bar ☎ 01/679–0523) carries hyperstylish handmade Irish sweaters, jackets, and accessories.

Blarney Woollen Mills (✉ 21–23 Nassau St., Southside ☎ 01/671–0068) stocks a good selection of tweed, linen, and woolen sweaters in all price ranges.

Cleo Ltd. (✉ 18 Kildare St., Southside ☎ 01/676–1421) sells hand-knit sweaters and accessories made only from natural fibers; it also carries its own designs.

Dublin Woollen Mills (✉ Metal Bridge Corner, Northside ☎ 01/677–5014) at Ha'penny Bridge has a good selection of hand-knit and other woolen sweaters at competitive prices.

Kevin and Howlin (✉ 31 Nassau St., Southside ☎ 01/677–0257) specializes in handwoven tweed men's jackets, suits, and hats, and also sells tweed fabric.

Monaghan's (✉ Grafton Arcade, 15–17 Grafton St., Southside ☎ 01/677–0823) specializes in cashmere.

Vintage

Flip (✉ 4 Upper Fownes St., Temple Bar ☎ 01/671–4299), one of the original stores in Temple Bar, sells vintage and retro clothing from the '50s, '60s, and '70s.

Jenny Vander (✉ Georges Street Arcade, Southside ☎ 01/677–0406) is the most famous name in Irish vintage and retro clothing. Just browsing through her collection is a pleasure.

SIDE TRIPS

Dubliners are undeniably lucky. Few populaces enjoy such glorious—and easily accessible—options for day trips. Just outside the city lie some of the region's most unique sights, including the James Joyce Martello Tower, Marino Casino, and Malahide Castle.

Beyond the southern neighborhood of Ballsbridge, sights are too spread out to cover on foot, and it's necessary to use either a car or public transportation (the bus or DART). If you have a car, then head to Rathfarnham, directly south of the city. Alternatively, head east and follow the coast road south to Dun Laoghaire and points even farther south. Traveling to and from each of the suburbs will take up most of a day, so you need to pick and choose the excursions you prefer.

South County Dublin

Dublin's southern suburbs are home to its more affluent and well-heeled citizens. As is usually the case, the wealthy folk have chosen some of the most scenic parts of the city, with the beautiful coastline to the east and Wicklow and its mountains to the south.

Numbers in the text correspond to numbers in the margin and on the South County Dublin map.

Rathfarnham

❶ *Bus 47A from Hawkins St. in the city center goes to both parks in Rathfarnham. Or drive, leaving the city center via Nicholas St. just west of Christ Church Cathedral and following it south through Terenure.*

Two parks lie in the suburb of Rathfarnham, due south of the city at the edge of the Dublin Mountains. The 18th-century house in **St. Enda's National Historic Park** has been turned into the **Pearse Museum,** commemorating Pádrig Pearse, leader of Dublin's 1916 Easter Uprising. In the early 20th century, the house was an Irish-language boys' school, which Pearse and his brother Willie founded. The museum preserves Pearse-family memorabilia, documents, and photographs. A lake and nature trails are also on the park's 50-acre grounds, and guides are available for tours of the park or simply for information. ✉ *Grange Rd., South County Dublin* ☎ *01/493–4208* 💷 *Free* ☉ *Park daily 8:30–dusk. Museum May–Aug., daily 10–1 and 2–5:30; Sept.–Apr., daily 10–1 and 2–4.*

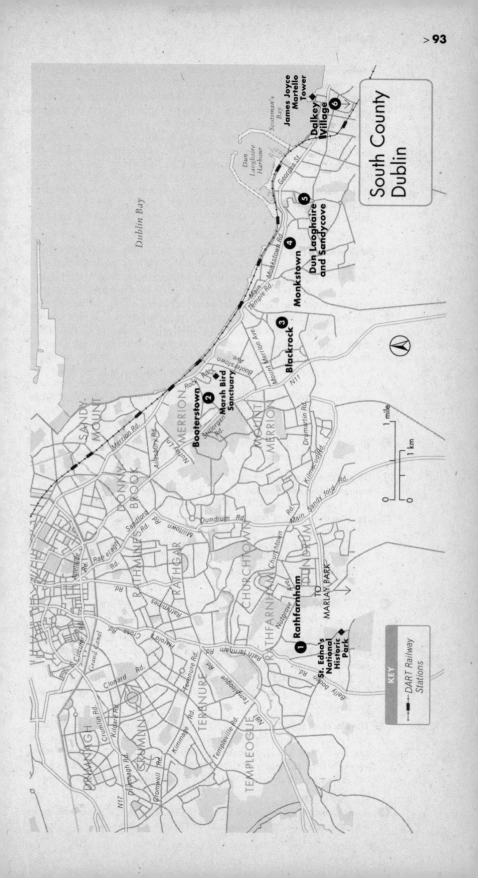

South County Dublin

James Joyce Martello Tower

6 Dalkey Village

Scotsman's Bay

Dun Laoghaire Harbour

Georges St.

5 Dun Laoghaire and Sandycove

Monkstown Rd.

4 Monkstown

Main Temple Rd.

Dublin Bay

Mount Merrion Ave.

3 Blackrock

N11

Rock Rd.

Booterstown Ave.

2 Booterstown

MERRION

Stillorgan Marsh Bird Sanctuary Rd.

Merrion Rd.

SANDY MOUNT

Nutley Ln.

Ailesbury Rd.

MOUNT MERRION

Drumartin Rd.

Kilmacud Rd.

DONNY BROOK

Sandford Rd.

Milltown

RANELAGH

Dundrum Rd.

Main Sandy ford Rd.

1 mile

1 km

0

Anglesea Rd.

Rd.

RATHMINES

Rathmines Rd.

RATHGAR

CHURCHTOWN

Churchtown

DUNDRUM

TO MARLAY PARK

1 Rathfarnham

Nutgrove Ave.

Rath farnham Rd.

S. Circular Rd.

Grand Canal

Harold's Cross Rd.

Clonard Rd.

Kimmage Cross Rd.

RATHGAR

RATH FARNHAM

St. Enna's National Historic Park

Bally boden Rd.

DRIMNAGH

Crumlin Rd.

Kildare Rd.

CRUMLIN

Dolphin Rd.

Cromwell Fort

N17

TERENURE

Terenure Rd.

Fortfield Rd.

Templeville Rd.

Kimmage Rd.

TEMPLEOGUE

Templeogue Rd.

N81

KEY

━━ DART Railway Stations

Marlay Park marks the start of the Wicklow Way, a popular walking route that crosses the Wicklow Mountains for 137 km (85 mi), through some of the most rugged landscapes in Ireland. In addition to its woodlands and nature walks, the 214-acre park has a cobbled courtyard, home to brightly plumaged peacocks. Surrounding the courtyard are crafts workshops, where you're welcome to observe bookbinding, jewelry making, and furniture making in process. Every Saturday from 3 to 5, kids can take a free ride on the model steam railway. To get here, leave St. Enda's Park via Grange Road and walk up the hill for about 1 km (½ mi), turning left at the T junction and continuing another ½ km (¼ mi). ⊠ *Grange Rd., South County Dublin* ☎ *01/493–4059* ⊠ *Free* ☉ *Feb. and Mar., daily 10–6; Apr. and Sept., daily 10–8; May–Aug., daily 10–9; Oct., daily 10–7; Nov.–Jan., daily 10–5.*

NIGHTLIFE **Johnnie Fox's** (⊠ Glencullen, South County Dublin ☎ 01/295–5647), 12 km (7½ mi) from the city center and 1½ km (1 mi) from Rathfarnam, sits 1,000 feet up in the Dublin Mountains, making it the highest licensed premises in Ireland. You approach it by a winding and steeply climbing route that turns off the main Dublin–Enniskerry road at Stepaside. Refusing to bow to the whims of modernization, it has steadfastly maintained its traditional character—oak tables, rough-stone floor flags strewn with sawdust, and ancient bric-a-brac, including copper kettles, crockery, old prints, and guns—and appears very much as it did in the early 19th century, when Daniel O'Connell used it as a safe house for his seditious meetings. You can get lunch and dinner here; the specialty is seafood, and it alone is worth the journey. In the evenings expect to hear traditional Irish music.

Booterstown

② *Take the DART local train from either Tara St. or Pearce St. Or take R118 from the corner of Lower Merrion St. and Merrion Sq.*

Booterstown stretches along Dublin Bay south of Sandymount. The **Booterstown Marsh Bird Sanctuary** is the largest wildlife preserve in the Dublin area. Curlews, herons, kingfishers, and other fairly rare migratory species come to nest here; information boards along the road describe the birds. Also on this main road is Glena, the house where Athlone-born John McCormack, one of the best and most popular tenors in the first quarter of the 20th century, died on September 16, 1945. ⊠ *Between the DART line and Rock Rd.* ☎ *01/454–1786.*

Blackrock

③ *3 km (2 mi) south of Booterstown. Take the DART line from the city center to Blackrock.*

Fine sea views, swimming, a weekend market, and a major shopping center draw Dubliners down to Blackrock, a bedroom community where James Joyce's parents lived with their large brood for most of 1892. Above the Blackrock DART station, at **Idrone Terrace**—lined with restored, old-fashioned lamps—you can take in a lovely view across the bay to Howth Peninsula.

SHOPPING The **Blackrock** (☎ 01/283–1660) is one of the most customer-friendly shopping centers around. It's built on two levels, looking onto an inner courtyard, with the giant Superquinn Foodstore, cafés, and restaurants, as well as shops selling clothes, electronics, and crafts. Blackrock can be reached conveniently on the DART train line; it has its own stop.

Monkstown

④ *3 km (2 mi) south of Blackrock on R119. Take the DART train from the city center to the Monkstown and Seapoint stations.*

One of Dublin's most exclusive suburbs, Monkstown is known for its two architectural curiosities. John Semple, the architect of Monkstown's **Anglican parish church,** built in 1833, was inspired by two entirely different styles, the Gothic and the Moorish, which he joined into an unlikely hybrid of towers and turrets. The church, which is in the town's main square, is only open during Sunday services. The well-preserved ruins of **Monkstown Castle** lie about 1 km (½ mi) south of the suburb; it's a 15th-century edifice with a keep, a gatehouse, and a long wall section, all surrounded by greenery. The **Lambert Puppet Theatre** (⌂ Clifton La., South County Dublin ☎ 01/280–0974), which stages regular puppet shows, houses a puppetry museum.

NIGHTLIFE **Comhaltas Ceoltóiri Éireann** (⌂ 35 Belgrave Sq., South County Dublin ☎ 01/280–0295) is the place to go for a boisterous summer evening of Irish music and dancing.

Dun Laoghaire & Sandycove

⑤ *2½ km (1½ mi) southeast along Monkstown along R119, the Monkstown Crescent.*

After the British monarch King George IV disembarked for a brief visit in 1821, Dun Laoghaire (pronounced dun *lear*-ee) was renamed Kingstown, but it reverted to its original Irish name 99 years later. Its Irish name refers to Laoghaire, the High King of Tara who in the 5th century permitted St. Patrick to begin converting Ireland to Christianity. The town was once a Protestant stronghold of the old ruling elite; in some of the neo-Georgian squares and terraces behind George's Street, the main thoroughfare, a little of the community's former elegance can still be seen.

Dun Laoghaire has long been known for its great harbor, enclosed by two piers, each 2½ km (1½ mi) long. The harbor was constructed between 1817 and 1859 using granite quarried from nearby Dalkey Hill; the west pier has a rougher surface and is less favored for walking than the east pier, which has a bandstand where musicians play in summer. The workaday business here includes passenger-ship and freight-services sailings to Holyhead in north Wales, 3½ hours away. Dun Laoghaire is also a yachting center, with the members-only Royal Irish, National, and Royal St. George yacht clubs, all founded in the 19th century, lining the harbor area.

A 15-minute walk south of Dun Laoghaire along the coast road brings you to the village of Sandycove, with a lovely little beach and the famous Martello Tower.

The **National Maritime Museum,** west of the harbor and across from the Gresham Royal Marine Hotel and the People's Park, is in the former Mariners' church. Its nave makes a strangely ideal setting for exhibits like the French longboat captured during an aborted French invasion at Bantry, County Cork, in 1796. A particularly memorable exhibit is the old optic from the Baily Lighthouse on Howth Head, across Dublin Bay; the herringbone patterns of glass reflected light across the bay until several decades ago. ⌂ *Haigh Terr., South County Dublin* ☎ *01/280–0969* ⌂ *€1.90* ⊙ *May–Sept., Tues.–Sun. 1–5.*

From the harbor area Marine Parade leads alongside Scotsmans Bay for 1¼ km (¾ mi), as far as Sandycove and the **Forty Foot Bathing Pool,** a traditional bathing area that attracts mostly nude older men. Women were once banned from here, but now hardy swimmers of both genders are free to brave its cold waters.

Originally built in 1804, when Napoléon's invasion seemed imminent, the **James Joyce Martello Tower** was demilitarized in the 1860s along with most of the rest of the 34 Martello towers that ring Ireland's coast. Martello towers were first built in Italy to protect the coastline against the possibility of a Napoleonic naval invasion. In Ireland, they were built by the British to protect Irish shores from the same threat and were re-markable for their squat and solid construction, rotating cannon at the top, and—most importantly—their proximity to one another, so that each one is within visible range of the one next to it. In 1904, this tower was rented to Oliver St. John Gogarty, a medical student who was known for his poetry and ready wit, for £8 a year. He wanted to create a nurturing environment for writers and would-be literati. Joyce spent a week here in September 1904 and described it in the first chapter of *Ulysses*, using his friend as a model for the character Buck Mulligan. The tower now houses the **Joyce Museum**, founded in 1962 thanks to Sylvia Beach, the Paris-based first publisher of *Ulysses*. The exhibition hall contains first editions of most of Joyce's works. Joycean memora-bilia include his waistcoat, embroidered by his grandmother, and a tie that he gave to Samuel Beckett (who was Joyce's onetime secretary). The gunpowder magazine stores the Joyce Tower Library, including a death mask of Joyce taken on January 13, 1941. The tower stands a few steps away from the Forty Foot Bathing Pool. ⊠ *Sandycove* ☎ *01/280–9265* ⊕ *www.visitdublin.com* 🎫 *€6* ⏱ *Apr.–Oct., Mon.–Sat. 10–1 and 2–5, Sun. 2–6; Nov.–Mar. by appointment.*

$$–$$$ ✕ **Brasserie Na Mara.** Chef Derek Breen serves Irish dishes with a mod-ern twist in this brasserie. *Na mara* means "of the sea" in Gaelic, and although he kept the name, he jettisoned the emphasis on seafood. Fish, is, nonetheless, one specialty, and baked monkfish tops the list. The build-ing has an unusual history: the first railway in Ireland, opened in 1834, was built from Westland Row (now Pearse Station) in Dublin to Dun Laoghaire. Much of the original station's entrance and ticketing area has been converted into this restaurant—now tall Georgian windows overlook the busy Dun Laoghaire ferryport. Reservations are essential on weekends. ⊠ *Dun Laoghaire Harbour, Dun Laoghaire, South County Dublin* ☎ *01/280–6767* 🖃 *AE, DC, MC, V* ⏱ *No lunch Sat. No dinner Sun.*

$$ ✕ **Caviston's.** Stephen Caviston and his family have been dispensing fine food for years from their fish counter and delicatessen in Sandy-cove. The fish restaurant next door is an intimate place. Typical en-trées include panfried scallops served in the shell with a thermidor sauce, and steamed Dover sole with mustard sauce. You can also get a halved lobster with a simple butter sauce for an exceptionally good price. ⊠ *58–59 Glasthule Rd., Sandycove, South County Dublin* ☎ *01/ 280–9120* 🖃 *MC, V* ⏱ *Closed Sun., Mon., and late Dec.–early Jan. No dinner.*

$–$$ ✕ **Duzy's Café.** This stylish Mediterranean restaurant sits above the Eagle House pub on the north side of Dun Laoghaire. The summery Mediterranean colors and striking paintings—which are large and spe-cially commissioned—create a dashing impression. The panfried scal-lops in a sesame-lime dressing is terrific. ⊠ *18 Glasthule Rd., Sandycove, South County Dublin* ☎ *01/230–0210* 🖃 *AE, DC, MC, V* ⏱ *No lunch Sat.*

$$$ 🏨 **Gresham Royal Marine Hotel.** This 1870 seaside hotel has comfortable, spacious rooms with contemporary furnishings. The lofty ceilings from the original building are preserved in the suites, with four-poster beds and sitting rooms. Ask for a room at the front of the hotel, facing Dun Laoghaire harbor. ⊠ *Marine Rd., Dun Laoghaire, South County Dublin*

☎ 01/280–1911 🖷 01/280–1089 ⊕ *www.gresham-hotels.com* 🔑 *95 rooms with bath, 8 suites* ♨ *Restaurant, room service, 2 bars, business services, free parking, no-smoking rooms* ⊟ *AE, DC, MC, V* ⦿ *BP, EP.*

Dalkey Village

6 *From the James Joyce Martello Tower in Sandycove, it's an easy walk or quick drive 1 km (½ mi) south to Dalkey. Or take the DART line from the city center to Dalkey.*

Along Castle Street, the town's main thoroughfare, are the substantial stone remains, resembling small, turreted castles, of two 15th- and 16th-century fortified houses. From the mainland's Vico Road, beyond Coliemore Harbour, are astounding bay views as far as Bray in County Wicklow. On Dalkey Hill stands **Torca Cottage,** home of the Nobel Prize–winning writer George Bernard Shaw from 1866 to 1874. You can return to Dalkey Village by Sorrento Road. The cottage is closed to the public. The **Heritage Centre** attached to Dalkey Castle has exhibits on local history, including a script written by playwright and local resident Hugh Leonard. ⊠ *Castle St., South County Dublin* ☎ *01/285–8366* 🖃 *Free* ⊙ *Apr.–Oct., weekdays 9:30–5:50, weekends 11–5; Nov.–Mar., weekends 11–5.*

In summer, small boats make the 15-minute crossing from Coliemore Harbour to **Dalkey Island,** covered with long grass, uninhabited except for a herd of goats, and graced with its own Martello tower—and an excellent bird sanctuary. The 8th-century ruins of St. Begnet's church sit right beside the bird sanctuary.

WHERE TO STAY
★ $$$–$$$$
⛻ **Fitzpatrick Castle Dublin.** For its sweeping views over Dun Laoghaire and Dublin Bay, the Fitzpatrick is worth the 15-km (9-mi) drive from the Dublin city center. The original part of the hotel is an 18th-century stone castle, with a substantial modern addition housing rooms; many are furnished with antiques and four-poster beds, and have large bathrooms. The hotel is convenient to golfing, horseback riding, and fishing, and the fitness facilities include a heated pool. The views from Killiney Hill, behind the hotel, are spectacular, and the seaside village of Dalkey and Killiney Beach are both within walking distance. ⊠ *Killiney, South County Dublin* ☎ *01/230–5400* 🖷 *01/230–5466* ⊕ *www.fitzpatrickhotels.com* 🔑 *113 rooms with bath* ♨ *Restaurant, cable TV, indoor pool, health club, bar, meeting rooms, free parking* ⊟ *AE, DC, MC, V* ⦿ *BP, EP.*

North County Dublin

Dublin's northern suburbs remain predominantly working class and largely residential, but there are a few places worth the trip, such as the architectural gem Marino Casino. As with most other suburban areas, walking may not be the best way to get around. It's good, but not essential, to have a car. Buses and trains serve most of these areas—the only drawback is that to get from one suburb to another by public transportation, you have to backtrack through the city center. Even if you're traveling by car, visiting all these sights will take a full day, so plan your trip carefully before setting off.

Numbers in the text correspond to numbers in the margin and on the North South County Dublin map.

Glasnevin

7 *Drive from the north city center by Lower Dorset St., as far as the bridge over the Royal Canal. Turn left, go up Whitworth Rd., by the side of the canal, for 1 km (½ mi); at its end, turn right onto Prospect Rd. and then left onto the Finglas road, N2. You can also take Bus 40* *or Bus 40A from Parnell St., next to Parnell Sq., in the northern city center.*

Glasnevin Cemetery, on the right-hand side of the Finglas road, is the best-known burial ground in Dublin. It's the site of the graves of many distinguished Irish leaders, including Eamon De Valera, a founding father of modern Ireland and a former Irish *taoiseach* (prime minister) and president, and Michael Collins, the celebrated hero of the Irish War of Independence. Other notables interred here include the late-19th-century poet Gerard Manley Hopkins and Sir Roger Casement, an Irish rebel hanged for treason by the British in 1916. The large column to the right of the main entrance is the tomb of "The Liberator" Daniel O'Connell, perhaps Ireland's greatest historical figure, renowned for his nonviolent struggle for Catholic rights and emancipation, which he achieved in 1829. The cemetery is freely accessible all day.

The **National Botanic Gardens,** on the northeastern flank of Glasnevin Cemetery, date from 1795 and have more than 20,000 different varieties of plants, a rose garden, and a vegetable garden. The main attraction is the Curvilinear Range—400-foot-long greenhouses designed and built by a Dublin ironmaster, Richard Turner, between 1843 and 1869. The Palm House, with its striking double dome, was built in 1884 and houses orchids, palms, and tropical ferns. ⊠ *Glasnevin Rd., North County Dublin* ☎ *01/837–4388* 🎫 *Free* ◷ *Apr.–Sept., Mon.–Sat. 10–6, Sun. 11–6; Oct.–Mar., Mon.–Sat. 10–4:30, Sun. 11–4:30.*

Marino Casino

8 *Take the Malahide road from Dublin's north city center for 4 km (2½ mi). Or take Bus 20A or Bus 24 to the Casino from Cathal Brugha St. in the north city center.*

One of Dublin's most exquisite, yet also most underrated, architectural landmarks, the Marino Casino (the name has nothing to do with gambling—it means "little house by the sea," and the building overlooks Dublin Harbour) is a small-scale, Palladian-style Greek temple, built between 1762 and 1771 from a plan by Sir William Chambers. Often compared to the Petit Trianon at Versailles, it was commissioned by the great Irish grandee Lord Charlemont as a summerhouse. Although the grand mansion on Charlemont's estate was tragically demolished in 1921, this sublime casino was saved and lovingly restored (Sir William's original plans survived). Inside, highlights are the china-closet boudoir, the huge golden sunset in the ceiling of the main drawing room, and the signs of the zodiac in the ceiling of the bijou-size library. When you realize that the structure has, in fact, 16 rooms—there are bedrooms upstairs—Sir William's sleight-of-hand is readily apparent: from its exterior, the structure seems to contain only one room. The tricks don't stop there: the freestanding columns on the facade are hollow so they can drain rainwater, and the elegant marble urns on the roof are chimneys. Last but not least, note the four stone lions on the outside terrace—they were carved by Joseph Wilson, who created the famous British royal coronation coach back in London. All in all, this remains, to quote scholar Desmond Guinness, "one of the most exquisite buildings in Europe." It makes a good stop on the way to Malahide, Howth, or North Bull Island. ⊠ *Malahide Rd., Marino, North County Dublin* ☎ *01/833–1618* ⊕ *www.heritageireland.ie* 🎫 *€2.75* ◷ *Feb., Mar., and Nov., Sun. and Thurs. noon–4; Apr., Sun. and Thurs. noon–5; May and Oct., daily 10–5; June–Sept., daily 10–6.*

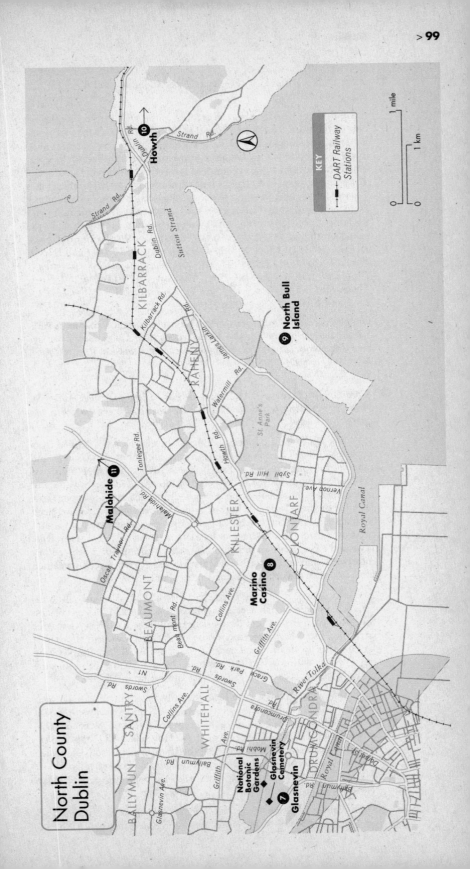

North County Dublin

KEY

DART Railway
Stations

1 mile

1 km

10 Howth

Strand Rd.

Dublin Rd.

Strand Rd.

KILBARRACK

Dublin Rd.

Kilbarrack Rd.

Kilbarrack Rd.

Sutton Strand

RAHENY

James Larkin Rd.

Watermill Rd.

9 North Bull
Island

St. Anne's
Park

Howth Rd.

Sybil Hill Rd.

Vernon Ave.

CLONTARF

Royal Canal

11 Malahide

Tonlegee Rd.

Oscar Traynor Rd.

Malahide Rd.

KILESTER

Collins Ave.

Beaumont Rd.

BEAUMONT

8 Marino
Casino

Griffith Ave.

Grace Park Rd.

Swords Rd.

River Tolka

SANTRY

N1

Collins Ave.

Ballymun Rd.

WHITEHALL

Griffith Ave.

Mobhi Rd.

Drumcondra Rd.

DRUMCONDRA

Royal Canal

Dublin Rd.

Ballymun Rd.

BALLYMUN

Glasnevin Ave.

Glasnevin Rd.

Griffith

National
Botanic
Gardens

♦ Glasnevin
Cemetery

7 Glasnevin

North Bull Island

❾ *From Dublin's north city center, take the Clontarf road for 4 km (2½ mi) to the causeway.*

A 5-km-long (3-mi-long) island created in the 19th century by the action of the tides, North Bull Island is one of Dublin's wilder places—it's a nature conservancy with vast beach and dunes. The island is linked to the mainland via a wooden causeway that leads to Bull Wall, a 1½-km (1-mi) walkway that stretches as far as the North Bull Lighthouse. The island is also accessible via a second, northerly causeway, which takes you to Dollymount Strand. (The two routes of entry don't meet at any point on the island.) You can reach this causeway from the mainland via James Larkin Road. The small **visitor center** here largely explains the island's bird life. ⊠ *Off the northerly causeway, North County Dublin* ☎ *01/833–8341* ⊠ *Free* ☉ *Mar.–Oct., Mon.–Wed. 10:15–1 and 1:30–4, Thurs. 10:15–1 and 1:30–3:45, Fri. 10:15–1 and 1:30–2:30, weekends 10–1 and 1:30–5:30; Nov.–Feb., Mon.–Wed. 10:15–1 and 1:30–4, Thurs. 10:15–1 and 1:30–3:45, Fri. 10:15–1 and 1:30–2:30, weekends 10–1 and 1:30–4:30.*

On the mainland directly across from North Bull Island is **St. Anne's Park**, a public green with extensive rose gardens (including many prize hybrids) and woodland walks. ⊠ *James Larkin Rd. and Mt. Prospect Ave., North County Dublin.*

Howth

❿ *From Dublin, take the DART train, or Bus 31B from Lower Abbey St. in the city center. Or, by car, take the Howth road from the north city center for 16 km (10 mi).*

A fishing village at the foot of a long peninsula, Howth (derived from the Norse *hoved*, meaning head; it rhymes with "both") was an island inhabited as long ago as 3250 BC. Between 1813 and 1833, Howth was the Irish terminus for the sea crossing to Holyhead in north Wales, but it was then superseded by the newly built harbor at Kingstown (now Dun Laoghaire). Today, its harbor, which supports a large fishing fleet, includes a marina. Both arms of the harbor pier form extensive walks. Separated from Howth Harbour by a channel nearly 1½ km (1 mi) wide is **Ireland's Eye,** with an old stone church on the site of a 6th-century monastery, and an early-19th-century Martello tower. In calm weather, local boatmen make the crossing to the island.

At the King Sitric restaurant on the East Pier, a 2½-km (1½-mi) cliff walk begins, leading to the white **Baily Lighthouse,** built in 1814. In some places, the cliff path narrows and drops sheerly to the sea, but the views out over the Irish Sea are terrific. Some of the best views in the whole Dublin area await from the parking lot above the lighthouse, looking out over the entire bay as far south as Dun Laoghaire, Bray, and the north Wicklow coast. You can also see quite a bit of Dublin.

Until 1959, a tram service ran from the railway station in Howth, over Howth Summit, and back down to the station. One of the open-top Hill of Howth trams that plied this route is now the star at the **National Transport Museum,** a short, 800-yard walk from Howth's DART station. Volunteers spent several years restoring the tram, which stands alongside other unusual vehicles, including old horse-drawn bakery vans. ☎ *01/848–0831 or 01/847–5623* ⊠ *€3* ☉ *June–Aug., daily 10–5; Sept.–May, weekends 2–5.*

The **Howth Castle Gardens**, next door to the Transport Museum and accessible from the Deer Park Hotel, were laid out in the early 18th century. The many rare varieties of its fine rhododendron garden are in full flower April through June; there are also high beech hedges. The rambling castle, originally built in 1654 and considerably altered in the intervening centuries, is not open to the public, but you can access the ruins of a tall, square 16th-century castle and a Neolithic dolmen. ⊠ *Deer Park Hotel, North County Dublin* ☎ *01/832–2624* ≌ *Free* ☉ *Daily 8–dusk.*

WHERE TO EAT ✕ **King Sitric.** This well-known seafood restaurant is one of Howth's
$$$$ main attractions. It's in a Georgian house on the harborfront, with the yacht marina and port on one side and with sea views from the upstairs seafood bar, where informal lunches are served in summer. A house specialty is black sole meunière, grilled and finished with a nut-brown butter sauce, but lobster, caught just yards away in Balscadden Bay, is the big treat—it's best at its simplest, in butter sauce. Crab is equally fresh, dressed with mayonnaise or Mornay sauce. ⊠ *East Pier, North County Dublin* ☎ *01/832–5235* ▭ *AE, DC, MC, V* ☉ *Closed Sun. No lunch Sat.*

$$–$$$$ ✕ **Abbey Tavern.** The original stone walls, flagged floors, blazing turf fires, and old gaslights of the 16th-century building that houses this old-world tavern may make you feel like you're in a time gone by. The upstairs restaurant serves traditional Irish and Continental cuisine, and specializes in fish dishes. Sole Abbey (filleted and stuffed with prawns, mushrooms, and herbs) is a house specialty, and fresh Dublin Bay prawns can be cooked to order. Traditional Irish music is performed in a different part of the building. The restaurant is a 5-minute walk from the DART station; call for directions. ⊠ *Abbey St., North County Dublin* ☎ *01/839–0307* ⚠ *Reservations essential* ▭ *AE, DC, MC, V* ☉ *No dinner Sun.*

Malahide

🕚 *By car, drive from the north city center on R107 for 14½ km (9 mi). Or catch the hourly train from Connolly Station. Or board Bus 42 to Malahide, which leaves every 15 mins from Beresford Pl. behind the Custom House.*

★ ☽ Malahide is chiefly known for **Malahide Castle,** a picture-book castle occupied by the Anglo-Irish and aristocratic Talbot family from 1185 until 1976, when it was sold to the Dublin County Council. The great expanse of parkland around the castle includes a botanical garden with more than 5,000 species and varieties of plants, all clearly labeled. The castle itself combines different styles and periods; the earliest section, the three-story tower house, dates from the 12th century. The medieval great hall is the only one in Ireland that is preserved in its original form, while the National Portrait Gallery has many fine paintings of the Talbot family and 18th- and 19th-century Irish notables. Authentic 18th-century pieces furnish the other rooms. Within the castle, the **Fry Model Railway Museum** houses rare, handmade models of the Irish railway. Children always marvel at one of the world's largest miniature railways, which covers an area of 2,500 square feet. The castle's self-service restaurant serves good homemade food all day. ⊠ *10 km (6 mi) north of Howth on the Coast Rd., North County Dublin* ☎ *01/846–2184* ⊕ *www.malahide.ie* ≌ *€6* ☉ *Apr.–Oct., Mon.–Sat. 10–5, Sun. 11–6; Nov.–May, Mon.–Sat. 10–5, Sun. 11–5.*

☽ **Newbridge House,** in nearby Donabate, was built between 1740 and 1760 for Charles Cobbe, Archbishop of Dublin. The Cobbe family owned the house until 1985, when it, along with most of its furnishings, was purchased by the state. One of the finest Georgian interiors in Ireland, the Red Drawing Room is hung with dozens of paintings and decorated with many fine antiques. The kitchens of the house still have their original utensils. Crafts workshops and some examples of old-style transportation, such as coaches, are in the courtyard. Beyond the walled garden are 366 acres of parkland and a restored 18th-century animal farm. Tara's Palace, a dollhouse that was made to raise funds for children's charities, is also here; it has 25 rooms, all fully furnished in miniature. The exterior of the dollhouse is based on the facades of three great Irish houses—Carton, Castletown, and Leinster. The coffee shop is renowned for the quality and selection of its homemade goods. You can travel from Malahide to Donabate by train, which takes about 10 minutes. From the Donabate train station, it's a 15-minute walk to the Newbridge House grounds. ✉ *Donabate, 8 km (5 mi) north of Malahide, signposted from N1, North County Dublin* ☎ *01/843–6534* ✉ *€5.50* ⊘ *Apr.–Sept., Tues.–Sat. 10–5, Sun. 2–6; Oct.–Mar., weekends 2–5.*

WHERE TO EAT
$$$–$$$$

✕ **Bon Appetit.** The striking floral decor creates a cozy traditional air, an impression heightened by the staff of black-jacketed waiters. Owner-chef Patsy McGuirk's traditional Continental menu includes such entrées as warm salad of Dublin Bay king prawns with pine nuts, prawn oil, and shavings of Parmesan and a generous selection of desserts. Especially fine is sole McGuirk—filleted, stuffed with prawns and turbot, and baked with white wine and cream. ✉ *9 James's Terr., North County Dublin* ☎ *01/845–0314* ▭ *AE, DC, MC, V* ⊘ *Closed Sun. No lunch Sat.*

DUBLIN A TO Z

To research prices, get advice from other travelers, and book travel arrangements, visit www.fodors.com.

AIR TRAVEL

There are daily services to Dublin from all major London airports. Flights to Dublin also leave from Birmingham, Bristol, East Midlands, Liverpool, Luton, Manchester, Leeds/Bradford, Newcastle, Edinburgh, and Glasgow. Prices vary a great deal between companies and at different seasons. There are also numerous flights from Europe and North America.

From the United Kingdom, six airlines serve destinations in Ireland: Aer Lingus, British Airways, British Midland, City Jet, Go, and Ryanair. Aer Lingus operates 12 flights from Heathrow and Gatwick Airports. British Airways has a regular schedule out of Heathrow. British Midland operates 10 flights to Dublin from Heathrow. City Jet flies from the very central London City Airport. Go flies from Edinburgh. Ryanair operates several no-frills, low-price flights from Luton and Stanstead airports—Ryanair is known for being the cheapest, but this means cutting back on comfort and services.

Major European carriers, such as Air France, Alitalia, Lufthansa, Sabena, and SAS, run direct services to Dublin from most European capital cities and major regional airports, especially those in Germany.

Three airlines have regularly scheduled flights from the United States to Dublin. Aer Lingus flies direct from New York, Boston, Los Angeles, Baltimore, and Chicago to Dublin. Continental flies from New York (Newark Liberty International Airport) to Dublin. Delta flies from Atlanta to Dublin via New York.

Within Ireland, Aer Lingus operates flights from Dublin to Belfast, Cork, Derry, Kerry, Shannon, Galway, Knock in County Mayo, Donegal, and Sligo. Ryanair flies to Belfast.

🛦 Carriers **Aer Lingus** 🕾 01/844-4747. **British Airways** 🕾 800/626-747. **British Midland** 🕾 01/283-8833. **City Jet** 🕾 01/844-5566. **Continental** 🕾 1890/925-252. **Delta** 🕾 01/844-4166 or 01/676-8080. **Go** 🕾 1890/923-922. **Ryanair** 🕾 01/844-4411.

AIRPORTS

Dublin Airport, 10 km (6 mi) north of the city center, serves international and domestic airlines.

🛦 Airport Information **Dublin Airport** 🕾 01/844-4900.

TRANSFERS Dublin Bus operates a shuttle service between Dublin Airport and the city center, with departures outside the arrivals gateway; you pay the driver inside the bus. The single fare is €5. Service runs from 5:45 AM to 11:30 PM, at intervals of about 20 minutes (after 8 PM buses run every hour), to as far as Dublin's main bus station (Busaras), behind the Custom House on the Northside. Journey time from the airport to the city center is normally 30 minutes, but it may be longer in heavy traffic. If you have time, you can save money by taking a regular bus for €1.30.

A taxi is a quicker alternative than the bus to get from the airport to Dublin center. A line of taxis waits by the arrivals gateway; the fare for the 30-minute journey to any of the main city-center hotels is about €17 to €19 plus tip (tips don't have to be large but they are increasingly expected). Ask about the fare before leaving the airport.

🛦 **Busaras** 🕾 01/830-2222. **Dublin Bus** 🕾 01/873-4222.

BOAT & FERRY TRAVEL

Irish Ferries runs a regular car and passenger service directly into Dublin port from Holyhead in Wales. Stena Sealink docks in Dublin port and has service to Holyhead (3½ hours) and to Dun Laoghaire (High Speed Service, known as "HSS," which takes 99 minutes). Prices and departure times vary according to season, so call to confirm. In summer reservations are strongly recommended. Dozens of taxis wait to take you into town from both ports, or you can take DART or a bus to the city center.

🛦 Boat & Ferry Lines **Irish Ferries** ✉ Merrion Row, Southside 🕾 01/661-0511. **Stena Sealink** ✉ Ferryport, Dun Laoghaire, South County Dublin 🕾 01/204-7777.

BUS TRAVEL

Busaras, just behind the Custom House on the Northside, is Dublin's main station for buses to and from the city. In town, there's an extensive network of buses, most of which are green double-deckers. Some bus services run on cross-city routes, including the smaller "Imp" buses, but most buses start in the city center. Buses to the north of the city begin in the Lower Abbey Street–Parnell Street area, while those to the west begin in Middle Abbey Street and in the Aston Quay area. Routes to the southern suburbs begin at Eden Quay and in the College Street area. Several buses link the DART stations, and another regular bus route connects the two main provincial railway stations, Connolly and Heuston. If the destination board indicates AN LÁR, that means that the bus is going to the city center.

Museumlink is a shuttle service that links up the Natural History Museum, National Museum, and Collins Barracks. You can catch it outside any of the three museums.

FARES & Timetables (€3.20) are available from Dublin Bus, staffed weekdays
SCHEDULES 9–5:30, Saturday 9–1. Fares begin at 70 cents and are paid to the driver, who will accept inexact fares, but you'll have to go to the central office

in Dublin to pick up your change as marked on your ticket. Change transactions and the city's heavy traffic can slow service down considerably.

Late-night buses run Monday to Saturday until 3 AM on all major routes; the fare is €4–€6.

🔢 **Busaras** ☎ 01/830-2222. **Dublin Bus** ✉ 59 Upper O'Connell St., Northside ☎ 01/873-4222 ⊕ www.dublinbus.ie.

BUSINESS HOURS

Dublin is gradually becoming a 24-hour city, even though the bus and DART train services close down for the night at 11:30. (A few lines run until dawn on the weekends, and late buses go until 3 AM.) Many taxis run all night, but the demand, especially on weekends (and particularly near clubs on the Leeson Street strip and elsewhere, which stay open until 4 AM or later), can make for long lines at taxi stands.

Banks are open weekdays 10–4 and remain open on Thursday until 5. All stay open at lunchtime. Most branches have ATMs that accept bank cards and MasterCard and Visa credit cards.

Museums are normally open Tuesday–Saturday and Sunday afternoon.

Stores are open Monday–Saturday 9–5:30 or 9–6, except on Thursday, when they're open until 8. Smaller city-center specialty stores open on Sunday as well, usually 10–6. Most department stores are closed on Sunday.

Most pubs open Monday–Saturday at 10:30 AM and 12:30 PM on Sunday. They must stop serving at 11:30 PM Monday–Wednesday, 12:30 AM Thursday–Saturday, and 11 PM on Sunday, but take another hour to empty out. A number of bars in the city center have permission to serve until 2 AM on weekend nights.

CAR RENTAL

Renting a car in Dublin is very expensive, with high rates and a 12½% local tax. Gasoline is also expensive by U.S. standards, at around €1 a liter. Peak-period car-rental rates begin at around €260 a week for the smallest stick models, like a Ford Fiesta. Dublin has many car-rental companies, and it pays to shop around and to avoid "cowboy" outfits without proper licenses.

A dozen car-rental companies have desks at Dublin Airport; all the main national and international firms also have branches in the city center. Some reliable agencies are listed below.

🔢 Agencies **Avis** ✉ 1 Hanover St. E, Southside ☎ 01/677-5204 ✉ Dublin Airport, North County Dublin ☎ 01/844-5204. **Budget** ✉ 151 Lower Drumcondra Rd., North County Dublin ☎ 01/837-9802 ✉ Dublin Airport, North County Dublin ☎ 01/844-5919. **Dan Dooley** ✉ 42–43 Westland Row, Southside ☎ 01/677-2723 ✉ Dublin Airport, North County Dublin ☎ 01/844-5156. **Hertz** ✉ Leeson St. Bridge, Southside ☎ 01/660-2255 ✉ Dublin Airport, North County Dublin ☎ 01/844-5466. **Murray's Rent-a-Car** ✉ Baggot St. Bridge, Southside ☎ 01/668-1777 ✉ Dublin Airport, North County Dublin ☎ 01/844-4179.

CAR TRAVEL

Traffic in Ireland has increased exponentially in the last few years, and nowhere has the impact been felt more than in Dublin, where the city's complicated one-way streets are congested not only during the morning and evening rush hours but often during much of the day. If possible, avoid driving a car except to get in and out of the city (and be sure to ask your hotel or guest house for clear directions to get you out of town).

EMBASSIES

Embassies are open weekdays 9–1 and 2–5.

🚩 **Australia** ✉ Fitzwilton House, Wilton Terr., Southside ☎ 01/676–1517. **Canada** ✉ 65 St. Stephen's Green, Southside ☎ 01/478–1988. **United Kingdom** ✉ 29 Merrion Rd., Southside ☎ 01/205–3700. **United States** ✉ 42 Elgin Rd., Southside ☎ 01/668–8777.

EMERGENCIES

Call the Eastern Help Board for the names of doctors in the area. The Dublin Dental Hospital has emergency facilities and lists of dentists who provide emergency care. Hamilton Long, a Dublin pharmacy, is open Monday–Wednesday and Saturday 8:30–6, Thursday 8:30–8, and Friday 8:30–7. Temple Bar Pharmacy is open Monday–Wednesday, Friday, and Saturday 9–7, Thursday 9–8.

🚩 Doctors & Dentists **Dublin Dental Hospital** ✉ 20 Lincoln Pl., Southside ☎ 01/662–0766. **Eastern Help Board** ☎ 01/679–0700.

🚩 Emergency Services **Ambulance, fire, police (gardai)** ☎ 999.

🚩 Hospitals **Beaumont** ✉ Beaumont Rd., North County Dublin ☎ 01/837–7755. **Mater** ✉ Eccles St., Northside ☎ 01/830–1122. **St. James's** ✉ 1 James St., Dublin West ☎ 01/453–7941. **St. Vincent's** ✉ Elm Park, South County Dublin ☎ 01/269–4533.

🚩 Late-Night Pharmacies **Hamilton Long** ✉ 5 Upper O'Connell St., Northside ☎ 01/874–8456. **Temple Bar Pharmacy** ✉ 20 E. Essex St., Temple Bar ☎ 01/670–9751.

INTERNET CAFÉS

In the city center are a number of Internet cafés, which all charge between €3 and €6 an hour. Some of the cheapest places are on Thomas Street, as it's not smack in the center of town.

Central Cybercafe is popular with students. Planet Cyber Café is the city's best, with top-notch computers and a good coffee bar.

🚩 **Central Cybercafe** ✉ 6 Grafton St., Southside ☎ 01/677–8298. **Planet Cyber Café** ✉ 13 Andrews St., Southside ☎ 01/670–5182.

MAIL & SHIPPING

Post offices are open weekdays 9–1 and 2–5:30, Saturday 9–12:30. Main post offices are open Saturday afternoons, too (look for green signs that say "An Post"). The General Post Office (GPO) on O'Connell Street, which has foreign exchange and general delivery facilities, is open Monday–Saturday 8–8, Sunday 10:30–6:30.

SIGHTSEEING TOURS

BUS TOURS   Dublin Bus has 3- and 4-hour tours of the city center that include Trinity College, the Royal Hospital Kilmainham, and Phoenix Park. The 1-hour City Tour, with hourly departures, allows you to hop on and off at any of the main sights. Tickets are available from the driver or Dublin Bus. There's also a continuous guided open-top bus tour (€12), run by Dublin Bus, that allows you to hop on and off the bus as often as you wish and visit some 15 sights along its route. The company also conducts a north-city coastal tour, going to Howth, and a south-city tour, traveling as far as Enniskerry.

Gray Line Tours runs city-center tours that cover the same sights as the Dublin Bus itineraries. Bus Éireann organizes day tours out of Busaras, the main bus station, to country destinations such as Glendalough.

🚩 **Bus Éireann** ☎ 01/836–6111. **Dublin Bus** ☎ 01/873–4222. **Gray Line Tours** ☎ 01/670–8822.

CARRIAGE TOURS   Horse-drawn-carriage tours are available around Dublin and in Phoenix Park. For tours of the park, contact the Department of the Arts, Culture and the Gaeltacht. Carriages can be hired at the Grafton Street corner of St. Stephen's Green, without prior reservations.

🚩 **Department of the Arts, Culture and the Gaeltacht** ☎ 01/661–3111.

PUB & MUSICAL TOURS   Dublin Tourism has a booklet to its self-guided "Rock 'n Stroll" Trail, which covers 16 sights with associations to such performers as Bob Geldof, Christy Moore, Sinéad O'Connor, and U2. Most of the sights are in the city center and Temple Bar. The Traditional Musical Pub Crawl begins at Oliver St. John Gogarty and moves on to other famous Temple Bar pubs. Led by two professional musicians who perform songs and tell the story of Irish music, the tour is given May–October, daily at 7:30 PM; the cost is €9. The Comedy Coach is a nightly hop-on, hop-off tour of Dublin pubs, clubs, and restaurants. There is nonstop entertainment on the bus—musicians and comics keep everyone happy between pints. A ticket costs around €15.

Colm Quilligan arranges highly enjoyable evening walks of the literary pubs of Dublin, where "brain cells are replaced as quickly as they are drowned." The *Dublin Literary Pub Crawl* is a 122-page guide to those Dublin pubs with the greatest literary associations; it's widely available in Dublin bookstores.
🎵 **Colm Quilligan** ☎ 01/454-0228. **Comedy Coach** ☎ 01/280-1899. **Oliver St. John Gogarty** ✉ 57 Fleet St., Temple Bar ☎ 01/671-1822. **Traditional Musical Pub Crawl** ✉ Discover Dublin, 20 Lower Stephens St., Southside ☎ 01/478-0191.

TRAIN TOURS   Guided tours of Dublin using the DART system are organized by Views Unlimited.
🎵 **Views Unlimited** ✉ 8 Prince of Wales Terr., Bray, South County Dublin ☎ 01/286-0164 or 01/285-6121.

WALKING TOURS   Historical Walking Tours of Dublin, run by Trinity College history graduate students, are excellent 2-hour introductions to the city. The Bord Fáilte–approved tours take place from May to September, starting at the front gate of Trinity College, daily at 11 AM and 3 PM, with an extra tour on weekends at noon; tours are also available October–April Friday–Sunday at noon. The cost is €10.

A Georgian/Literary Walking Tour leaves from the Grafton Street branch of Bewley's Oriental Café June–September daily at 11; each tour lasts approximately two hours and costs €9. Trinity Tours organizes walks of the Trinity College campus on weekends from March 17 (St. Patrick's Day) through mid-May and from mid-May to September daily. The half-hour tour costs €7.60 and includes admission to the *Book of Kells*; tours start at the college's main gate. The Zozimus Experience is an enjoyable walking tour of Dublin's medieval past, with a particular focus on the seedy, including great escapes, murders, and mythical happenings. Tours, which are led by a guide in costume, are by arrangement only and start at the main gate of Dublin Castle at 6:45 PM; it costs €10 per person. (Prepare yourself for a surprise.)
🎵 **Georgian/Literary Walking Tour** ☎ 01/496-0641. **Historical Walking Tours of Dublin** ☎ 01/878-0227. **Trinity Tours** ☎ 01/608-2320. **Zozimus Experience** ☎ 01/661-8646.

SAFETY
What crime there is in Dublin is often drug-related. Sidestreets off O'-Connell Street can be dangerous, especially at night. When you park your car, *do not* leave any valuables inside, even under a raincoat on the back-seat or in the trunk; be especially careful parking around the Guinness Brewery and the Old Jameson Distillery.

TAXIS
Official licensed taxis, metered and designated by roof signs, do not cruise. There are taxi stands beside the central bus station, and at train stations, O'Connell Bridge, St. Stephen's Green, College Green, and near major

hotels; the Dublin telephone directory has a complete list. The initial charge is €2.30, with an additional charge of about €2 per kilometer thereafter. The fare is displayed on a meter (make sure it's on). You may, instead, want to phone a taxi company and ask for a cab to meet you at your hotel, but this may cost up to €2.55 extra. Hackney cabs, which also operate in the city, have neither roof signs nor meters and will sometimes respond to hotels' requests for a cab. Negotiate the fare before your journey begins. Although the taxi fleet in Dublin is large, the cabs are nonstandard and some cars are neither spacious nor in pristine condition. Cab Charge has a reliable track record. Metro is one of the city's biggest but also the busiest. VIP Taxis usually has a car available for a longer trip.

🚖 Taxi Companies **Cab Charge** ☎ 01/677-2222. **Metro** ☎ 01/668-3333. **VIP Taxis** ☎ 01/478-3333.

TRAIN TRAVEL

Connolly Station provides train service to and from the east coast, Belfast, the north (with stops in Malahide, Skerries, and Drogheda), the northwest, and some destinations to the south, such as Wicklow and Arklow. Heuston Station is the place for trains to and from the south and west; trains run from here to Kildare Town, west of Dublin, via Celbridge, Sallins, and Newbridge. Pearse Station is for Bray and connections via Dun Laoghaire to the Liverpool-Holyhead ferries. Contact the Irish Rail Travel Centre for information.

An electric railway system, the Dublin Area Rapid Transit (DART), connects Dublin with Howth to the north and Bray to the south on a fast efficient line. There are 25 stations on the route, which is the best means of getting to seaside destinations, such as Howth, Blackrock, Dun Laoghaire, Dalkey, Killiney, and Bray.

FARES & SCHEDULES DART service starts at 6:30 AM and runs until 11:30 PM; at peak periods, 8–9:30 AM and 5–7 PM, trains arrive every five minutes. At other times of the day, the intervals between trains are 15 to 25 minutes. Call ahead to check precise departure times (they do vary, especially on bank holidays). Tickets can be bought at stations, but it's also possible to buy weekly rail tickets, as well as weekly or monthly "rail-and-bus" tickets, from the Irish Rail Travel Centre. Individual fares begin at €1 and range up to €4. You'll pay a heavy penalty for traveling the DART without a ticket.

🚆 Train Information **Connolly Station** ✉ Amiens St., Northside. **DART** ☎ 01/836-6222 ⊕ www.irishrail.ie/dart. **Heuston Station** ✉ end of Victoria Quay, Dublin West. **Irish Rail Travel Centre** ✉ 35 Lower Abbey St., Northside ☎ 01/836-6222 ⊕ www.irishrail.ie. **Pearse Station** ✉ Westland Row, Southside.

TRAVEL AGENCIES

🧳 Local Agents **American Express** ✉ 116 Grafton St., Southside ☎ 01/677-2874. **Thomas Cook** ✉ 118 Grafton St., Southside ☎ 01/677-1721.

VISITOR INFORMATION

Bord Fáilte, the Irish Tourist Board, has its own visitor information offices in the entrance hall of its headquarters at Baggot Street Bridge; it's open weekdays 9:15–5:15. A suburban tourist office in Tallaght is open March–December, daily 9:30–5.

The main Dublin Tourism center on Suffolk Street is open July–September, Monday–Saturday 8:30–6, Sunday 11–5:30, and October–June, daily 9–6. The Dublin Airport branch is open daily 8 AM–10 PM; the branch at the Ferryport, Dun Laoghaire, is open daily 10–9.

The Temple Bar Information Centre produces the easy-to-use, annually updated *Temple Bar Guide,* which provides complete listings of the area's stores, pubs, restaurants, clubs, galleries, and other cultural venues.

🖪 Tourist Information **Bord Fáilte** ✉ Baggot St. Bridge, Southside ☎ 01/602–4000 in Dublin; 1850/230–330 in the rest of Ireland ✉ The Square, Tallaght ☎ 1850/230–330 ⊕ www.ireland.travel.ie. **Dublin Tourism** ✉ Suffolk St., off Grafton St., Southside ☎ 01/605–7700 in Dublin; 1850/230330 in rest of Ireland ⊕ www.visitdublin.com. **Temple Bar Information Centre** ✉ 18 Eustace St., Temple Bar ☎ 01/671–5717.

DUBLIN ENVIRONS

FODOR'S CHOICE
Barberstown Castle, *hotel in Straffan*
Castletown House, *estate in Celbridge*
Glendalough, *monastery in County Wicklow*
Kildare Hotel and Country Club, *Straffan*
Newgrange, *prehistoric tombs in Donore*
Poppies Country Cooking, *Enniskerry*
Rathsallagh House, *restaurant (and hotel) in Dunlavin*

HIGHLY RECOMMENDED
HOTELS Kilkea Castle, *Castledermot*
Tinakilly House, *Rathnew*

RESTAURANTS Roundwood Inn, *Roundwood*
Tree of Idleness, *Bray*

SIGHTS Japanese Gardens, *Kildare Town*
Mount Usher Gardens, *Ashford*
Powerscourt House, Gardens, and Waterfall, *Enniskerry*
Roundwood, *scenic village in County Wicklow*

By Anto
Howard

ONE OF THE LOVELIEST REGIONS in Ireland, the Pale—the counties immediately north, south, and west of Dublin—is a kind of open-air museum filled with legendary Celtic sites, grand gardens, and elegant Palladian country estates. France has its châteaux of the Loire Valley, England the treasure houses of Kent and Sussex, Germany its castles of the Rhine, but the grand estates of the Pale rank pretty high in the galaxy of stately style.

The Dublin environs include three basic geographical regions: County Wicklow's coast and mountains, the Boyne Valley, and County Kildare. Lying tantalizingly close to the south of Dublin is the mountainous county of Wicklow, which contains some of the most *et-in-Arcadia-ego* scenery in the Emerald Isle. Here, the gently rounded Wicklow Mountains—to some tastes Ireland's finest—contain the evocative monastic settlement at Glendalough, many later abbeys and churches, and such noted 18th-century estates as Powerscourt and Russborough. Nearby is an impressive eastern coastline that stretches from Counties Wicklow to Louth, punctuated by delightful harbor towns and fishing villages. The coast is virtually unspoiled for its entire length.

North of Dublin lies the Boyne Valley, with its abundant ruins of Celtic Ireland extending from Counties Meath to Louth. Some of the country's most evocative Neolithic ruins—including the famous passage graves at Newgrange—are nestled into this landscape, where layer upon layer of history penetrates down into earlier, unknowable ages. It was west of Drogheda—a fascinating town settled by the Vikings in the early 10th century—that the Tuatha De Danann, onetime residents of Ireland, went underground when defeated by the invading Milesians and became, it is said, "the good people" (or fairies) of Irish legend. In pagan times this area was the home of Ireland's high kings, and the center of religious life. In those days, all roads led to Tara, the fabled Hill of Kings, the royal seat and the place where the national assembly was once held. Today, time seems to stand still there—and you should do so, too, for it is almost sacrilegious to introduce a note of urgency.

Southwest of Dublin are the flat pastoral plains of County Kildare; the plains stretch between the western Midlands and the foothills of the Dublin and Wicklow mountains—both names actually refer to one mountain, but each marks its county's claim to the land. Kildare is the flattest part of Ireland, a playing field for the breeding, training, and racing of some of the world's premier Thoroughbreds.

Of all the artistic delights that beckon both north and south of Dublin, few enchant as much as the imposing country estates of County Wicklow. Here, during the "glorious eighteenth," great Anglo-Irish estates were built by Irish "princes of Elegance and Prodigality." Only an hour or two from Dublin, these estates were profoundly influenced by the country villas of the great Italian architect Andrea Palladio, who erected the estates of the Venetian aristocracy only a short distance from the city on the lagoon. As in other parts of Ireland, the ancestral homes of the dwindling members of the Anglo-Irish ascendancy dot the landscape in the Pale. Today, lords and baronets down on their luck have turned into hoteliers who welcome guests to castle holidays with adaptable grace.

Exploring Dublin Environs

All of the towns and sights in the Dublin environs region can be visited on a day trip from the city. This chapter is organized into three different sections, each of which makes a reasonable day trip. Keep in mind that it's easy to lose an hour or so making detours, chatting with locals,

Numbers in the text correspond to numbers in the margin and on the Dublin Environs map.

If you have 3 days

Travel south from Dublin along N11 to **Powerscourt House, Gardens, and Waterfall** ⑲ ⌐. Follow the road up to **Roundwood** ⑳, the highest village in Ireland. Move on to the monastic settlement of **Glendalough** ㉑. Follow R752 south to Rathnew and proceed to **Avoca** ㉕, home of Ireland's oldest mill. End your day in ☒ **Wicklow Town** ㉓, north of Avoca on R754; or, if you want to remain Dublin based, return to the capital via N11.

Begin your second day with a visit to **Castletown House** ㉗ near Celbridge, easily reached via N4 and R403. Continue south and turn left at Clane until you reach **Naas** ㉙. From here head southeast along R410 and go the short distance to **Russborough House** ㉚. Or, continue west toward **Kildare Town** ㉝, an elegant, prosperous town surrounded by the broad, flat plains of **the Curragh** ㉜. The National Stud and Japanese Gardens, just outside Kildare Town, are area highlights. (If you spent your first night in Wicklow, return to Glendalough and proceed toward Kildare via the Wicklow Gap, a maze of winding roads that take you through the villages of Granabeg, Hollywood, and Kilcullen.) Spend your second night in ☒ **Straffan** ㉘ or back in ☒ **Dublin.**

On your third day, head north of Dublin to Counties Meath and Louth via N3, which will take you to the **Hill of Tara** ②, an important Celtic site. Travel back another 2,000 years with a visit to **Newgrange** ⑤. On your way north to **Monasterboice** ⑩, with its fine high cross, visit the small Georgian village of **Slane** ⑥. Make a stop along N51 at **King William's Glen** ⑦, site of the Battle of the Boyne in 1690.

If you have 5 days

Driving south from Dublin, stop off in the coastal town of **Bray** ⑱ ⌐, a Victorian seaside resort, before heading toward **Powerscourt House, Gardens, and Waterfall** ⑲; **Roundwood** ⑳; and **Glendalough** ㉑. For a taste of more recent history, follow N11 a few miles south to Rathnew and drive inland on R752 until you reach **Avondale House and Forest Park** ㉔, the home of the 19th-century Irish leader Charles Stewart Parnell. Overnight in ☒ **Wicklow Town** ㉓ or near the ☒ **Poulaphouca Reservoir** ㉛, home of the wonderful Rathsallagh House. If you have time, visit the seaside resort of **Arklow** ㉖ or the **Mount Usher Gardens** ㉒ northwest of Wicklow Town. Spend your second day visiting the broad flatland of County Kildare, venturing as far south as **Ballytore** ㉟ and **Castledermot** ㊱ before spending the night in ☒ **Straffan** ㉘. On your third day, set off for the Celtic and prehistoric sights of County Meath. Be sure to visit the 12th-century remains of **Mellifont Abbey** ⑨, near **Slane** ⑥, and the town of **Kells** ④, a former monastic community. Overnight in historic ☒ **Drogheda** ⑧. The following morning, travel north to **Dundalk** ⑭, the border town of **Omeath** ⑰, and **Inniskeen** ⑬, home of poet Patrick Kavanagh. After lunch, take the **Cooley Peninsula Drive** ⑮ and visit the medieval fishing town of **Carlingford** ⑯. Spend the night in Drogheda, returning to Dublin the next day via the ancient town of **Louth** ⑫ and the market town of **Ardee** ⑪.

and otherwise enjoying the unexpected. The itineraries below cover the area's highlights; if you have fewer than three days, use parts of each day's suggested itinerary to plan your excursion. A car is essential for visiting most sights—and don't plan on visiting both the north and south of Dublin in the same day. You can also reach some points of interest by public transport: bus tours from Dublin cover County Wicklow as far as Glendalough in the southwest and the Boyne Valley to the north; suburban bus services reach into the foothills of the Dublin Mountains; and Bus Éireann services take in the outlying towns. Some popular sights have direct connections to Dublin, including Enniskerry and Powerscourt Estate, which can be reached by taking the No. 44 bus from the Dublin quays area.

About the Restaurants

Dining out in the area is essentially a casual affair, but the innovations and experimentation of Dublin's top restaurateurs are influencing the cooking—and the prices—at the finer establishments outside the capital. As in the Southwest, chefs hereabouts have a deep respect for fresh, locally grown and raised produce. You'll find everything from Continental-style meals to hearty ploughman's lunches.

About the Hotels

In Counties Wicklow and Kildare there are excellent accommodations, even if the choice may not be vast. If you have only a night or two outside Dublin, try to stay at least one night in one of the area's country-house or manor-house hotels, where some of Ireland's finest hosts welcome you into sometimes glorious, sometimes rustic, but almost invariably comfortable homes. Old-style hotels in Counties Meath and Louth are showing signs of improvement and are becoming ever more popular. Bed-and-breakfasts, as elsewhere in Ireland, are always a delightful option. Accommodations throughout the region can book up in July and August, so be sure to reserve far ahead if you're visiting during this time.

WHAT IT COSTS In Euros					
	$$$$	**$$$**	**$$**	**$**	**¢**
RESTAURANTS	over €29	€22–€29	€15–€22	€8–€15	under €8
HOTELS	over €230	€180–€230	€130–€180	€80–€130	under €80

Restaurant prices are per person for a main course at dinner. Hotel prices are for two people in a double room, including VAT and a service charge (often applied in larger hotels).

Timing

The wild mountains of Wicklow and the flat pasturelands of Kildare are at their best in spring and summer. However, the rainfall is often higher in March and April. If you're planning to tour the towns and historic sites, come in winter to avoid the crush. Bring warm clothing and boots, and be prepared for light snow on the hills.

THE BOYNE VALLEY

The great prehistoric, pagan, and Celtic monuments of the wide arc of fertile land known as the Boyne Valley invariably evoke a grand sense of wonder. You don't have to be an archaeologist to be awed by Newgrange and Knowth—set beside the River Boyne—or the Hill of Tara, Mellifont Abbey, and the high cross of Monasterboice.

One way to approach exploring this area is to start at the town of Trim, the locale closest to Dublin, and work your way north. Keep in mind

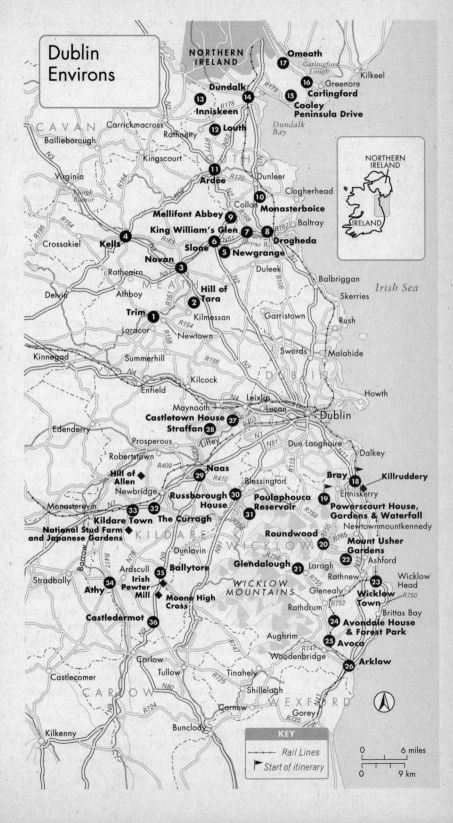

Dublin Environs

NORTHERN IRELAND

Omeath 17

Carlingford 16

Dundalk 14

Inniskeen 13

Louth 12

Ardee 11

Monasterboice 10

Mellifont Abbey 9

King William's Glen 7

Slane 6

Newgrange 5

Navan 3

Hill of Tara 2

Trim 1

Kells 4

Carlingford 15

Cooley Peninsula Drive

Drogheda 8

Dundalk Bay

Carlingford Lough

Greenore

Kilkeel

Irish Sea

Balbriggan

Skerries

Rush

Malahide

Swords

Howth

Dublin

Dun Laoghoire

Dalkey

Castletown House 27

Straffan 28

Naas 29

Hill of Allen

Russborough House 30

The Curragh

Kildare Town 33 32

National Stud Farm and Japanese Gardens

Athy 34

Irish Pewter Mill 35

Ballytore

Moone High Cross

Castledermot 36

Poulaphouca Reservoir 31

Roundwood

Glendalough

Bray 18

Killruddery

Powerscourt House, Gardens & Waterfall 19

Mount Usher Gardens 22

Avondale House & Forest Park 24

Avoca 25

Arklow 26

Wicklow Town 23

Wicklow Head

Brittas Bay

Wicklow Mountains

NORTHERN IRELAND

IRELAND

KEY

Rail Lines

Start of itinerary

0   6 miles

0   9 km

that Omeath and the scenic Cooley Peninsula at the end of this section are on the border of Northern Ireland. (If you make it this far north, consult Chapter 8, particularly the coverage of the Mountains of Mourne, which are just across Carlingford Lough.)

Trim

❶ *51 km (32 mi) northwest of Dublin via N3 to R154.*

The heritage town of Trim, on the River Boyne, contains some of the finest medieval ruins in Ireland. In 1359, on the instructions of King Edward III, the town was walled and its fortifications strengthened. In the 15th century several parliaments were held here. Oliver Cromwell massacred most of its inhabitants when he captured the town in 1649. **Trim Castle,** the largest Anglo-Norman fortress in Ireland, dominates present-day Trim from its 2½-acre site, which slopes down to the river's placid waters. Built by Hugh de Lacy in 1173, the castle was soon destroyed and then rebuilt from 1190 to 1220. The ruins include an enormous keep with 70-foot-high turrets flanked by rectangular towers. The outer castle wall is almost 500 yards long, and five D-shape towers survive. The admission price includes a tour. ✉ *Trim, Co. Meath* ☎ *046/38619* ⊕ *www.heritageireland.ie* ✉ *Keep and grounds €3.10, grounds only €1.20* ☉ *May–Oct., daily 10–6.*

Facing the river is the **Royal Mint,** a ruin that illustrates Trim's political importance in the Middle Ages.

The **Yellow Steeple** overlooks Trim from a ridge opposite the castle. The structure was built in 1368 and is a remnant of the Augustinian abbey of St. Mary's, founded in the 13th century, which itself was the site of a great medieval pilgrimage to a statue of the Blessed Virgin. Much of the tower was destroyed in 1649 to prevent its falling into Cromwell's hands, and today only the striking, 125-foot-high east wall remains. The Church of Ireland **St. Patrick's Cathedral** (✉ Loman St.) dates from the early 19th century, but the square tower belongs to an earlier structure built in 1449. In the old town hall, the **visitor center**'s "The Power and the Glory" audiovisual display tells the story of the arrival of the Normans and of medieval Trim. ✉ *Castle St.* ☎ *046/37227* ⊕ *www. meathtourism.ie* ✉ *€3.50* ☉ *Mon.–Sat. 10–5, Sun. noon–5:30.*

If your ancestors are from County Meath, take advantage of the family-history tracing service at the **Meath Heritage and Genealogy Center.** ✉ *Castle St.* ☎ *046/36633* ✉ *Free* ☉ *Weekdays 9–1 and 1:30–5.*

At **Newtown,** 1¼ km (¾ mi) east of Trim on the banks of the River Boyne, are the ruins of what was the largest cathedral in Ireland, built beginning in 1210 by Simon de Rochfort, the first Anglo-Norman bishop of Meath. At **Laracor,** 3 km (2 mi) south of Trim on R158, a wall to the left of the rectory is where Jonathan Swift (1667–1745), the satirical writer, poet, and author of *Gulliver's Travels,* was rector from 1699 until 1714, when he was made dean of St. Patrick's Cathedral in Dublin. Nearby are the walls of the cottage where Esther Johnson, the "Stella" who inspired much of Swift's writings, once lived. One of the most pleasant villages of south County Meath, **Summerhill,** 8 km (5 mi) southeast of Laracor along R158, has a large square and a village green with a 15th-century cross. **Cnoc an Linsigh,** an attractive area south of Summerhill with forest walks and picnic sites, is ideal for a half day of meandering. Many of the lanes that crisscross this part of County Meath provide delightful driving between high hedgerows and afford occasional views of the lush, pastoral countryside.

off the beaten path

RATHCAIRN – This town is the only Gaeltacht (Irish-speaking) region in Leinster. Thanks to a 1930s social experiment, a number of Connemara Irish-speaking families were transported to this fertile part of County Meath. They flourished, and Rathcairn is proud to be the only expanding Gaeltacht area. Spend a few hours in the sleepy town and the surrounding land, where, charmingly, everything is conducted in Irish. To get here from Trim, follow R154 12 km (7½ mi) northwest; you'll enter the town a few miles before you hit Athboy.

Where to Stay & Eat

¢ ✕ 🔲 **Brogan's.** The modern bedrooms are spacious and comfortable at this family-run guest house on High Street in the heart of Trim. Made with the freshest local produce, the food at the pub-restaurant ($) on the ground floor is better than typical pub fare. The joint of lamb is a treat. ⊠ *High St., Co. Meath* ☎ *046/31237* 🗐 *046/37648* 🗩 *14 rooms with bath* ⚲ *Restaurant, bar* 🖃 *AE, MC, V* ⦿ *BP.*

¢ 🔲 **Tigh Catháin.** The "House of Ó Catháin" is a Tudor-style country cottage about 1 km (½ mi) outside of town on the Longwood road. Owner Marie Keane has artfully decorated the three large bedrooms in different color schemes based on the natural colors of the region. But the real wonders here are the lovely gardens out back and in front, perfect for lounging around in the sun. ⊠ *High St., Co. Meath* ☎ *046/31996* 🗩 *3 rooms with bath* ⦿ *BP.*

Hill of Tara

➋ *14½ km (9 mi) east of Trim, 33 km (20½ mi) northwest of Dublin on N3.*

At the meeting point of the five ancient roads of Ireland and known in popular folklore as the seat of the High Kings of Ireland, the Hill of Tara is one of the country's most important historical sites. The 19th-century ballad by Thomas Moore, "The Harp That Once Through Tara's Halls," was a factor in the long over-romanticized view of Tara. Systematic excavation by 20th-century archaeologists has led to the less exciting conclusion that the remains are those of an Iron Age fort that had multiple ring forts, some of which were ruined in the 19th century by religious zealots from England who believed they would find the Ark of the Covenant here. The "Mound of the Hostages," a Neolithic passage grave, most likely gave the place its sacred air. During the hill's reign as a royal seat, which lasted to the 11th century, a great *feis* (national assembly) was held here every three years, during which time laws were passed and tribal disputes were settled. Tara's decline was predicted one eventful Easter Eve in the 5th century on a night when, according to the Druid religion, no fires could be lit. Suddenly on a hillside some miles away, flames were spotted. "If that fire is not quenched now," said a Druid leader, "it will burn forever and will consume Tara." The fire seen by the court at Tara was lit by St. Patrick (circa 5th century) at Slane to celebrate the Christian rites of the Paschal. Tara's influence waned with the arrival of Christianity; the last king to live here was Malachy II, who died in 1022.

But like so many of the most prominent sites of the pagan, pre-Christian era, Christianity remade Tara in its own image. Today a modern statue of St. Patrick stands here, as does a pillar stone that may have been the coronation stone (it was reputed to call out in approval when a king was crowned). In the graveyard of the adjacent Anglican church is a pillar with the worn image of a pagan god and a Bronze Age stone standing on end.

The main attraction of a visit here is the Hill of Tara's height: it rises more than 300 feet above sea level, and from its top on a clear day you can see across the flat central plain of Ireland, with the mountains of east Galway rising nearly 160 km (100 mi) away. In the mid-19th century, the nationalist leader Daniel O'Connell staged a mass rally here that supposedly drew more than a million people—nearly a third of Ireland's current population. In an old Church of Ireland church on the hillside, the Interpretative Center tells the story of Tara and its legends. This can be truly informative, for without expert assistance, it's difficult to identify many of the earthworks at Tara. ⊠ *Hill of Tara* ☎ *046/ 25903* ⊕ *www.heritageireland.ie* ☜ *€1.90* ☺ *May–Oct., daily 10–6.*

Navan

❸ *10 km (6 mi) northwest of the Hill of Tara on N3, 48 km (30 mi) north of Dublin on N3.*

Navan, at the crucial juncture of the Rivers Blackwater and Boyne, is a busy market and mining town with evidence of prehistoric settlements. It took off in the 12th century, when Hugh de Lacy, lord of Trim, had the place walled and fortified, making it a defensive stronghold of the English Pale in eastern Ireland. It is now the administrative center of Meath. At **St. Mary's Church**, built in 1839, you'll find a late-18th-century wood carving of the Crucifixion, the work of a local artist, Edward Smyth—who at the time was the greatest sculptor Ireland had produced since the Middle Ages. On Friday, the **Fair Green**, beside the church, hosts a bustling outdoor market. ⊠ *Trimgate St.* ☜ *Free* ☺ *Daily 8–8.*

The best views of town and the surrounding area are from the top of the **Motte of Navan**, a grassy mound said to be the tomb of Odhbha, the deserted wife of a Celtic king who, the story goes, died of a broken heart. D'Angulo, the Norman baron, adapted it into a motte and bailey (a type of medieval Norman castle).

Where to Stay & Eat

$–$$ ✕☷ **Mountainstown House.** A real gem at a great price, this restored Queen Anne and Georgian house and courtyard has been in the Pollock family since 1796. Eight hundred acres of parkland surround the grand old manor, with horses, donkeys, poultry, and peacocks all basking in the rolling landscape. The six rooms all face south, and the three with en suite bathrooms are very large. The splendidly ornamental restaurant ($$$$) serves a wonderful set-menu meal, which changes every night but always involves local meats and produce. ⊠ *Castletown, Co. Meath* ☎ *046/54154* ☐ *046/54154* ☜ *6 rooms, 3 with bath* ☐ *Restaurant, bar* ☐ *AE, MC, V* ☉ *BP, FAP, MAP.*

Kells

❹ *16 km (10 mi) northwest of Navan on N3.*

In the 9th century, a group of monks from Iona in Scotland took refuge at Kells (Ceanannus Mór) after being expelled by the Danes. St. Columba had founded a monastery here 300 years earlier, and although some historians think the indigenous monks wrote and illustrated the *Book of Kells*—the Latin version of the four Gospels and one of Ireland's greatest medieval treasures—most scholars now believe that the Scottish monks brought it with them. Reputed to have been fished out of a watery bog at Kells, the legendary manuscript was removed for safekeeping during the Cromwellian wars to Trinity College, Dublin, where it remains. A large exhibit is now devoted to it in the college's Old Library, where a few of the original pages at a time are on view. A copy of the

Book of Kells is on display in the Church of Ireland **St. Columba's** in Kells; it's open until 5 on weekdays and until 1 on Saturdays. Four elaborately carved high crosses stand in the church graveyard; you'll find the stump of a fifth in the marketplace—during the 1798 uprising against British rule it was used as a gallows.

Similar in appearance to St. Kevin's Church at Glendalough and Cormac's Chapel at Cashel, **St. Colmcille's House** is a small, two-story, 7th-century church measuring about 24 feet square and nearly 40 feet high, with a steeply pitched stone roof. The nearly 100-foot-high **round tower**, adjacent to St. Colmcille's House, dates prior to 1076 and is in almost perfect condition. Its top story has five windows, each facing an ancient entrance to the medieval town.

Where to Stay

¢ ⊡ **Lennoxbrook.** This fine, 200-year-old-plus farmhouse is run by Pauline Mullan, whose children are the fifth generation of the family to occupy the home. A casual, friendly mood prevails throughout the house. Upstairs, finely patterned wallpaper and period furniture decorate the rooms. Lamb is a typical dinner entrée (€20 extra). The house, 5 km (3 mi) north of Kells on N3, is also convenient to Newgrange. The prehistoric forts, passage graves, and other remains dating from 2000 BC on the Loughcrew Hills are a 15-minute drive away. ⊠ *Co. Meath* ☏ *046/ 45902* ➴ *4 rooms with bath* ⚅ *Dining room* ▤ *MC, V* ⦿ *BP, FAP.*

Newgrange

⑤ *11 km (7 mi) east of Navan on N51, 24 km (15 mi) east of Kells.*

FodorśChoice
★

Expect to see no less than one of the most spectacular prehistoric tombs in Europe when you come to Newgrange. Built in the 4th millennium BC—which makes it roughly 1,000 years older than Stonehenge—Newgrange was constructed with some 250,000 tons of stones, much of which came from the Wicklow Mountains, 80 km (50 mi) to the south. How the people who built this tumulus transported the stones here remains a mystery. The mound above the tomb measures more than 330 feet across and reaches a height of 36 feet at the front. White quartz stones were used for the retaining wall, and egg-shape gray stones were studded at intervals. The passage grave may have been the world's earliest observatory. It was so carefully constructed that, for five days on and around the winter solstice, the rays of the rising sun still hit a roof box above the lintel at the entrance to the grave. The rays then shine for about 20 minutes down the main interior passageway to illuminate the burial chamber. The site was restored in 1962 after years of neglect and quarrying. A visit to the passage grave during the winter solstice is considered to be the most memorable experience of all, in part due to the luck needed to witness the illumination. You'll have to get on the nine-year waiting list to reserve one of the 24 places available on each of the five mornings (December 19–23). And even if you have a place, there's no guarantee that clouds won't be obscuring the sun. But if you visit the interior of this Bronze Age tomb you can see the effect artificially re-created. The geometric designs on some stones at the center of the burial chamber continue to baffle experts.

The prehistoric sites of nearby Dowth and Knowth have been under excavation since 1962, and although Dowth is still closed to the public, **Knowth** is open at last. The great tumulus at Knowth is comparable in size and shape to Newgrange, standing at 40 feet and having a diameter of approximately 214 feet. Some 150 giant stones, many of them beautifully decorated, surrounded the mound. However, the mound itself is different in its composition from that of Newgrange, consisting of layers of stones, turf, and clay. More than 1,600 boulders, each weighing from one to several tons, were used in the construction. The earliest tombs and carved stones date from the Stone Age (3000 BC), although the site was in use until the early 14th century. In the early Christian era (4th–8th centuries AD) it was the seat of the High Kings of Ireland. Much of the site is still under excavation, and you can often watch archaeologists at work here. Access to Newgrange and Knowth is solely via **Brú na Bóinne** ("Palace of the Boyne"), the Boyne Valley visitor center. Arrive early if possible, because Newgrange often sells out. ⊠ *Donore, off N2, signposted from Slane* ☎ *041/982–4488* ⊕ *www.heritageireland.ie* ⊠ *Newgrange and interpretive center €5; Knowth and interpretive center €3.80; Newgrange, Knowth, and interpretive center €8.80* ⊘ *Newgrange May, daily 9:30–6:30; June–mid-Sept., daily 9:30–7; mid-Sept.–Feb., daily 10–4:30; Mar. and Apr., daily 10–5. Knowth June–mid-Sept., daily 9–7; May and mid-Sept.–end of Sept., daily 9–6:30; Mar., Apr., and Oct., daily 9:30–5:30; Nov.–Feb., daily 9:30–5.*

Slane

❻ *2½ km (1½ mi) north of Newgrange, 46 km (29 mi) northwest of Dublin on N2.*

Slane Castle is the draw at this small, Georgian village, built in the 18th century around a crossroads on the north side of the River Boyne. The 16th-century building known as the **Hermitage** was constructed on the site where St. Erc, a local man who was converted to Christianity by St. Patrick, led a hermit's existence. All that remains of his original monastery is the faint trace of the circular ditch that surrounded it.

The stately 18th-century **Slane Castle** is beautifully situated overlooking a natural amphitheater. Back in 1981, the castle's owner, Anglo-Irish Lord Henry Mountcharles, staged the first of what have been some of Ireland's largest outdoor rock concerts; U2, still only one album old, had second billing to Thin Lizzy that year. Most of rock's greatest names have performed here since, including Bob Dylan, Bruce Springsteen, David Bowie, and the Rolling Stones—REM's show holds the record for attendance, with 70,000. In 2001, after a decade of renovation following a devastating fire, the castle reopened to the public for tours, which take in the main hall, a ballroom, and other rooms. ☎ *041/988–4400* ⊕ *www.slanecastle.ie* ⊠ *€7* ⊘ *Tours late May–early Sept., Mon.–Thurs. noon–5.*

North of Slane town is the 500-foot-high **Slane Hill**, where St. Patrick proclaimed the arrival of Christianity in 433 by lighting the Paschal Fire. From the top, you have sweeping views of the Boyne Valley. On a clear day, the panorama stretches from Trim to Drogheda, a vista extending 40 km (25 mi).

A two-hour tour of farmer Willie Redhouse's fully functioning arable ☾ and livestock **Newgrange Farm** includes feeding the ducks, bottle-feeding the lambs, a tour of the aviaries with their exotic birds, and a donkey ride for the kids. Demonstrations of sheepdog work, threshing, and horseshoeing are given. Every Sunday at 3 PM the weekly "Sheep Derby" takes place, with teddy bears tied to the animals in the place of jockeys. Visiting children are made "owners" of individual sheep for the duration of the race. The farm lies 3 km (2 mi) east of Slane on N51. ☎ *041/982–4119* ⊠ *€5* ⊘ *Easter–Aug., daily 10–5.*

IRELAND'S ANCIENT HEART

The Boyne Valley, which straddles the county of Louth and runs through the flat heartland of Meath, holds 10% of all prehistoric monuments in Ireland. Foremost among these is Neolithic Newgrange, passage graves built in the 4th millennium BC. The Hill of Tara, one of the focal points for the ancient high kings of Ireland, was where disputes between clans were settled, new laws were passed, and, eventually, Christianity was proclaimed from the summit by St. Patrick. The advent of Christianity led to the construction of County Wicklow's Glendalough monastery, founded by one of St. Patrick's followers, St. Kevin. Later, in the 12th century, the first Cistercian house in Ireland, the monastery of Mellifont, was founded. North of Mellifont are the ruins of Monasterboice, another monastic site where one of the finest high crosses in Ireland stands in the shadow of a 9th-century round tower.

Where to Stay & Eat

$ ✕🍽 **Conyngham Arms Hotel.** Built in the mid-19th century, the Conyngham Arms, at the crossroads in Slane, maintains its village-inn look to this day. Four-poster beds in the guest rooms let you imagine what it's like to sleep like the aristocracy. The Gamekeeper's Lodge Bistro ($$) serves simple but delightful fresh meat and fish dishes. Try the salmon in season. ✉ *Co. Meath* 🕾 *041/988–4444* 🖷 *041/982–4205* 🛏 *14 rooms with bath* 🖧 *Restaurant, bar* 🖃 *AE, MC, V* 🍽 *BP, FAP, MAP.*

King William's Glen

❼ *7½ km (4½ mi) east of Slane on N51.*

On the northern bank of the River Boyne, King William's Glen is where a portion of King William of Orange's Protestant army hid before the Battle of the Boyne in 1690. They won by surprising the Catholic troops of James II, who were on the southern side, but many of the Protestant-Catholic conflicts in present-day Northern Ireland can be traced to the immediate aftermath of this battle. The site is marked with an orange and green sign; part of the site is also incorporated in the nearby, early 19th-century **Townley Hall Estate,** which has forest walks and a nature trail (the house is not open to the public).

Drogheda

❽ *6½ km (4 mi) east of King William's Glen on N51, 45 km (28 mi) north of Dublin on N1.*

Drogheda (pronounced draw-*hee*-da) is one of the most enjoyable and historic towns on the east coast of Ireland—and a setting for one of the most tragic events in Irish history (⇨ Bloody Cromwell! box). It was colonized in 911 by the Danish Vikings; two centuries later, the town was taken over by Hugh de Lacy, the Anglo-Norman lord of Trim, who was responsible for fortifying the towns along the River Boyne. At first, two separate towns existed on the northern and southern banks of the river. In 1412, already heavily walled and fortified, Drogheda was unified, making it the largest English town in Ireland. Today, large 18th-century warehouses line the northern bank of the Boyne. In the center of the town, around West Street, is the historic heart of Drogheda. Towering over the river is the long **railway viaduct.** Built around 1850 as part of the railway line from Dublin to Belfast, it is still used and is a splendid example of Victorian engineering. Because of its height above the river, the viaduct remains Drogheda's most prominent landmark.

The bank building on the corner of West and Shop streets, called the **Tholsel,** is an 18th-century square granite edifice with a cupola. The 13th-century **St. Laurence's Gate,** one of the two surviving entrances from Drogheda's original 11 gates in its town walls, has two four-story drum towers and is one of the most perfect examples in Ireland of a medieval town gate. **Butler's Gate,** near the Millmount Museum, predates St. Laurence's Gate by 50 years or more.

The Gothic Revival, Roman Catholic **St. Peter's Church** (⊠ West St.) houses the preserved head of St. Oliver Plunkett. Primate of all Ireland, he was martyred in 1681 at Tyburn in London; his head was pulled from the execution flames. A severe, 18th-century church within an enclosed courtyard, the Anglican **St. Peter's** (⊠ Fair St.) is rarely open except for Sunday services. It's worth a peek for its setting and the fine views over the town from the churchyard.

The **Millmount Museum and Martello Tower,** off the Dublin road (N1) south of Drogheda, shares space in a renovated British Army barracks with crafts workshops, including a pottery and picture gallery and studio. Relics of eight centuries of Drogheda's commercial and industrial past are on display, including painted banners of the old trade guilds, a circular willow and leather coracle (the traditional fishing boat on the River Boyne), and many instruments and utensils from domestic and factory use. There are also mementos of the most infamous episode in Drogheda's history, the 1649 massacre of 3,000 people by Oliver Cromwell. The exhibit inside the Martello Tower adjacent to the museum focuses on the military history of Drogheda. ⊠ Millmount ☎ 041/983–3097 ⊠ Museum €3, tower €2.50 ⊙ Mon.–Sat. 10–5:30, Sun. 2:30–5:30.

Across the Meath border in County Dublin, 18 km (11 mi) south of Drogheda, is **Ardgillan Demesne,** one of the prettiest parks along the coast. Its 194 acres consist of rolling pastures, mixed woodland, and gardens overlooking the Bay of Drogheda, with splendid views of the coastline. The castle here, built in 1738 for a landowning family, rises two stories. Ground-floor rooms are decorated in Georgian and Victorian styles; first-floor rooms house a permanent display of 17th-century maps, and host an annual program of exhibitions. ⊠ Balbriggan ☎ 01/849–2212 ⊕ www.fingalcoco.ie ⊠ €3.80 ⊙ Apr.–June and Sept., Tues.–Sun. 11–6; Oct.–Mar., Tues.–Sun. 11–4:30; July–Aug., daily 11–dusk.

off the beaten path

BALTRAY AND CLOGHERHEAD – Two pleasant villages are within easy reach of Drogheda. From Drogheda's center, follow R167 northeast along the northern bank of the River Boyne for 11 km (7 mi) to Baltray, a fishing village that still looks much as it did in the 18th century. From here, continue north another 8 km (5 mi) to the fishing village of Clogherhead. Take a walk above the local harbor to the heights of Clogher Head for outstanding views north to the Mountains of Mourne and south to Skerries.

Where to Stay & Eat

¢–$ ✕ **Monk's.** This little café on the river is always full of locals looking for healthful food at a decent price. Monk's specializes in delicious, somewhat off-center sandwiches, including a wonderful goat-cheese bruschetta and a spicy Mexican chicken sandwich. The hot breakfasts are a treat, with chunky French toast and fruit the most popular dish. ⊠ North Quay ☎ 041/984–5630 ⊟ MC, V.

BLOODY CROMWELL!

N MUCH OF THE *English-speaking world Oliver Cromwell is regarded as something of a hero, a deeply religious self-made man, master general, and leader of the victorious parliamentary side in the English Civil Wars. In Ireland the Lord Protector's name is usually followed by a spit and a curse. In 1649 Old Ironsides arrived in Ireland to subdue a royalist and Catholic rebellion once and for all. His methods were simple: burn every building, and kill every person that stood in his way. "To Hell or to Connaught" was the dire choice he offered the native population as he drove them ever westward and off the more fertile lands of the east and south. When he approached the walled town of Drogheda, the gates were closed to him. Led by the Anglo-Irish Sir Arthur Aston, the native Catholic population bravely defended their town against Cromwell's relentless siege, twice driving back the advancing army. On the third attempt the town fell, and the order went out that no mercy was to be shown. It is estimated that up to 3,500 men, women, and children were slaughtered. One group hid in the steeple of St. Peter's church, so Cromwell burned it down with them all inside. Sir Arthur was beaten to death with his own wooden leg!*

$–$$ ✕▦ **Boyne Valley Hotel and Country Club.** A 1-km (½-mi) drive leads to this 19th-century mansion on 16 acres that was once owned by a Drogheda brewing family. The newer wing of the hotel has double rooms, all with contemporary furnishings. A large conservatory houses a bar and overlooks the grounds, while a spacious hall is decorated with antiques and comfy chairs. The Cellar Restaurant specializes in fresh fish. ✉ *Dublin Rd., Co. Louth* ☎ *041/983–7737* 🖷 *041/983–9188* ⊕ *www.boyne-valley-hotel.ie/* ⇱ *37 rooms with bath* ⌂ *Restaurant, 18-hole golf course, 2 tennis courts, indoor pool, health club, bar* ▤ *AE, DC, MC, V* ⦿ *BP.*

Mellifont Abbey

❾ *8 km (5 mi) west of Drogheda on R168, 11 km (7 mi) north of Newgrange on N2.*

On the eastern bank of the River Mattock, which creates a natural border between Counties Meath and Louth here, lie the remains of Mellifont Abbey, the first Cistercian monastery in Ireland. Founded in 1142 by St. Malachy, archbishop of Armagh, it was inspired by the formal structure around a central courtyard of St. Bernard of Clairvaux's monastery, which St. Malachy had visited. Among the substantial ruins are the two-story chapter house, built in 12th-century English-Norman style and once a daily meeting place for the monks; it now houses a collection of medieval glazed tiles. Four walls of the 13th-century octagonal lavabo, or washing place, still stand, as do some arches from the Romanesque cloister. At its peak Mellifont presided over almost 40 other Cistercian monasteries throughout Ireland, but all were suppressed by Henry VIII in 1539 after his break with the Catholic Church. Adjacent to the car park is a small **architectural museum** depicting the history of the abbey and the craftsmanship that went into its construction. ⊠ *Near Collon* ☎ *041/982–6459* 🎫 *€2* ⊙ *May–mid-June and mid-Sept.–Oct., daily 10–5; mid-June–mid-Sept., daily 9:30–6:30.*

Where to Eat

$$–$$$ ✕ **Forge Gallery Restaurant.** Warm rose and plum tones and antique furnishings decorate this well-established restaurant in a converted forge, and an old fireplace creates a comforting warmth and light. The cuisine mixes French Provençale with a strong hint of traditional Irish cooking. Two popular specialties are salmon and crab in phyllo pastry, and prawns and scallops in a cream and garlic sauce. Make sure you try one of the seasonal homemade soups. Paintings by local artists hang in the reception area and are for sale. Reservations are essential on weekends. ⊠ *North of Slane on N2, Collon* ☎ *041/982–6272* ▭ *AE, DC, MC, V* ⊙ *Closed Sun., Mon. and second wk in Jan.*

Monasterboice

10 *8 km (5 mi) northeast of Mellifont Abbey on N1, 8 km (5 mi) north of Drogheda.*

Ireland has more carved-stone high crosses than any other European country, and an outstanding collection is in the small, secluded village of Monasterboice, a former monastic settlement. Dating to AD 923, the **Muireadach Cross** stands nearly 20 feet high and is considered to be the best-preserved example of a high cross anywhere in Ireland. Its elaborate panels depict biblical scenes, including Cain slaying Abel, David and Goliath, and a centerpiece of the Last Judgment. (Figurative scenes are not a characteristic of earlier high crosses, such as those found in Ahenny, County Clare, which are elaborately ornamented but without figures.) From the adjacent, 110-foot-high **round tower,** the extent of the former monastic settlement at Monasterboice is apparent. The key to the tower door is kept at the nearby gate lodge.

Ardee

11 *14½ km (9 mi) northwest of Monasterboice on N2.*

In this market town, formerly at the northern edge of the Pale (originally the Pale referred to the area of eastern Ireland ruled directly by the Normans), stand two 13th-century castles: Ardee Castle and Hatch's Castle. The town of Ardee (Baile Átha Fhirdia or Ferdia's Ford), interestingly, was named after the ford where the mythical folk hero Cuchulainn fought his foster brother Ferdia. There's a statue depicting this battle at the start of the riverside walk. **Ardee Castle** (the one with square corners) was converted into a courthouse in the 19th century. The castle faces north—built to protect the Anglo-Irish Pale from the Celtic Tribes beyond. **Hatch's Castle** (with rounded corners) is a private residence and not open to the public. **St. Mary's Church of Ireland** on Main Street incorporates part of a 13th-century Carmelite church burned by Edward Bruce in 1316.

Where to Eat

$–$$ ✕ **Gables House and Restaurant.** At this family-run spot off N2, not far from the Dundalk junction, expect a French-influenced cooking style, generous portions, and a fine catch of the day—often monkfish, halibut, or sole. The restaurant has lush, traditional-style furnishings: antique mahogany furniture, deep-burgundy velvet curtains, and oil paintings by local artists. Polished tables, silver cutlery, linen napkins, lace coasters, and gleaming leaded-crystal glasses add an elegant touch.

For dessert, satisfy your sugar craving with the Gables Medley: cheese-cake, profiteroles, and homemade ice cream. ⊠ *Dundalk Rd.* ☎ *041/685–7389* ☰ *MC, V.*

Louth

12 *11½ km (7 mi) north of Ardee on R171.*

Louth warrants a visit, if only for the splendidly preserved oratory here. St. Patrick, Ireland's patron saint, was reputed to have built his first church (which is no longer here) in this hilltop village in the 5th century. He also made St. Mochta (d. 534) the first bishop of Louth. Standing at the center of the village is the excellently preserved **St. Mochta's House,** an oratory dating from the 11th century, which has a steeply pitched stone roof that can be reached by a stairway. The house is freely accessible—but watch out for cattle in the surrounding field.

Inniskeen

13 *6½ km (4 mi) north of Louth.*

On the road to Dundalk and just over the Louth county boundary in Monaghan, lies Inniskeen, a small farming town that doubles as a so-cial hearth for the area's far-flung community. Patrick Kavanagh (1906–69), the area's most famous poet, is commemorated at the **Inniskeen Folk Museum,** housed in a converted church next to a round tower. Born and raised here, Kavanagh immortalized the town in his early poem "Inniskeen Road"—where as a child he spied on young lovers and their "wink and elbow language of delight"—before becoming one of Ireland's leading poets. He was brought back to the village for burial. ☎ *042/937-8109* ⊠ *Donations accepted* ☉ *May–Sept., Sun. 3–6, or by appointment.*

Dundalk

14 *14½ km (9 mi) east of Inniskeen, 80 km (50 mi) north of Dublin on N1.*

Dundalk is a thriving, if uninspiring, frontier town—only 9½ km (6 mi) from the Northern Ireland border—with some fine historic buildings. It's the main town of County Louth (Ireland's smallest county), and it dates from the early Christian period, around the 7th century. The area near the town is closely connected with Cuchulainn (pronounced *coo-*lain)—"a greater hero than Hercules or Achilles," as Frank McCourt, in *Angela's Ashes,* recalls his father claiming. Cuchulainn, the warrior of the old Irish epic *Táin Bó Cuailnge* (Cattle Raid of Cooley), was the hero of ancient Ulster—which then included the Dundalk area—and de-fended her borders and interests against newcomers.

On Mill Street, the **bell tower** of a Franciscan monastery with Gothic windows dates from the 13th century. The Catholic **St. Patrick's Cathedral** was built between 1835 and 1847, when the Gothic Revival was at its height. With its buttresses and mosaics lining the chancel and the side chapel walls, the cathedral was modeled on the 15th-century King's College Chapel at Cambridge, England. The fine exterior was built in Newry granite, and the high altar and pulpit are of carved Caen stone. ⊠ *Town center* ☉ *Daily 8–6.*

The Market House, the Town Hall, and the Courthouse are examples of the town's 19th-century heritage; the **Courthouse** is the most impres-sive of the three, built in the 1820s in a severe Greek Revival style, with Doric columns supporting the portico. It stands north of St. Patrick's Cathedral.

The **Dundalk County Museum** is dedicated to preserving the history of the dying local industries, such as beer brewing, cigarette manufacturing, shoe and boot making, and railway engineering. Other exhibits deal with the history of Louth from 7500 BC to the present. ⊠ *Joycelyn St.* ☎ *042/932–7056* ⊕ *www.louthcoco.ie* ⊠ *€3.80* ⊙ *Tues.–Sat. 10:30–5:30, Sun. 2–6.*

Where to Stay & Eat

$$–$$$ ✕⊡ **Ballymascanlon House Hotel.** On 130 acres on the scenic Cooley Peninsula just north of Dundalk, you'll find this converted Victorian mansion with a reputation for comfort and good cuisine. Reproduction period pieces fill the large guest rooms. The restaurant serves a set menu of Irish and French cuisine; it specializes in fresh seafood, such as lobster in season. Vegetarian plates are also available. ⊠ *Dundalk, Co. Louth* ☎ *042/935–8200* 🖶 *042/937–1598* ⊕ *www.ballymascanlon.com* ⇗ *74 rooms with bath* ⚭ *Restaurant, 18-hole golf course, 2 tennis courts, indoor pool, health club, 2 bars* ⊟ *AE, DC, MC, V* ⎇ *BP.*

¢–$ ⊡ **Balrobin House.** This Georgian house was the former home of Sir Lionel Harty and his wife Lady Lucy, who in the late 19th century would wine and dine Ireland's elite in its lush surroundings. A marble fireplace, a walled garden, and antique gates are among the many original features of the house. The rooms maintain a period look with high, plasterwork ceilings and ornate furnishings. ⊠ *Kilkerley, Co. Louth* ☎ *042/937–7701* ⇗ *4 rooms with bath* ⊟ *MC, V* ⎇ *BP.*

Cooley Peninsula Drive

⑮ *Beginning in Dundalk, 80 km (50 mi) north of Dublin.*

If you have a car and three or four free hours, go for a scenic drive around the Cooley Peninsula and indulge in some of the finest views of the east coast of Ireland. This is a 64-km (40-mi) round-trip beginning and ending in Dundalk. Beyond the Carlingford Lough on the north side of the peninsula, the Mountains of Mourne rise in the distance. From **Gyles Quay,** a small coastal village with a clean, safe beach, you can take in excellent views southward along the County Louth coast to Clogher Head. A road winds east around the Cooley Peninsula to **Greenore,** a town built in Victorian times as a ferryboat terminal. Today it's a port for container traffic.

Carlingford

⑯ *21 km (13 mi) east of Dundalk, 6½ km (4 mi) south of Omeath on R173.*

The small, medieval fishing town of Carlingford appeals for its natural scenery, as well as its striking whitewashed, thatched cottages. The mountains of the Cooley Peninsula back right up to the town, the Carlingford Lough lies at its feet, and the Mountains of Mourne rise only 5 km (3 mi) away across the lough.

Some remnants from the area's medieval days include a tower from the town wall and one of its gates, which later became the town hall. The 15th-century **Mint Tower House,** in an alley off Market Square, is notable for its mullioned, limestone windows. **Taaffe's Castle,** a 16th-century fortified town house on the quay, has classic Norman defensive features. A massive, 13th-century fortress that rises up over the entrance to Carlingford Lough, **King John's Castle** has an unusual trait: its west gateway is only wide enough to admit one horseman. It was built in the 1190s and named for the English king who paid a brief visit in 1210.

The highlight of the **Holy Trinity Heritage Centre,** in a former church, is a mural depicting the village at the height of the Middle Ages. An audiovisual display focuses on village history and the efforts to preserve

Carlingford's medieval heritage. ⊠ *Churchyard Rd.* ☎ *042/937–3888*
☞ *€2* ☉ *Weekdays 10–12:30 and 2–4:30.*

Omeath

⑰ *6½ km (4 mi) northwest of Carlingford on R173.*

This northernmost town on Cooley Peninsula is blessed not only with
a stunning landscape, but also with the distinction of having unusual
pictures—stations of the cross—that Catholics pray before in a solemn
procession every Good Friday. Omeath was the last main Gaeltacht (Irish-
speaking) village in this part of Ireland (most extant Gaeltacht villages
are in the Southwest and the West). There's a narrow road that climbs
the mountains behind Omeath. As you ascend, the views become ever
more spectacular, stretching over the Mountains of Mourne in the north
and as far south as Skerries, 32 km (20 mi) north of Dublin. This narrow road leads back to Dundalk.

On the eastern side of the Omeath, on the outside of a shrine, are the
open-air **stations of the cross**—the 14 pictures of the key moments during Christ's last days—at the monastery of the Rosminian Fathers.
Jaunting cars (traps pulled by ponies) take visitors to the site from the
quayside. Daily from June to September, stalls at the **quay** sell all kinds
of shellfish, including oysters and mussels, from the nearby lough. In
July and August, a ferry service runs until 6 PM from here to Warrenpoint, across the lough in Northern Ireland; the trip takes five minutes.

COUNTY WICKLOW

Make your way to the fourth or fifth story of almost any building in
Dublin that faces south and you'll see off in the distance—amazingly,
though, not *that* far off in the distance—the green, smooth hills of the
Dublin and Wicklow mountains. On a clear day the mountains are even
visible from some streets in and around the city center. If your idea of
solace is green hills, and your visit to Ireland is otherwise limited to Dublin,
County Wicklow—or Cill Mhantain (pronounced kill *wan*-tan), as it is
known in Irish—should be on your itinerary.

Not that the secret isn't out: rugged and mountainous with dark, wooded
forests, central Wicklow, known as the "garden of Ireland," is a popular picnic area among Dubliners. It has some of Ireland's grandest 18th-
century mansions, and cradles one of the country's earliest Christian
retreats: Glendalough. Nestled in a valley of dense woods and placid
lakes, Glendalough and environs can seem (at least during the off-season) practically untouched since their heyday 1,000 years ago. The
same granite mountains that have protected Glendalough all these years
run into the sea along the east coast, which has several popular sandy
beaches. Journey from Dublin down to Arklow, sticking to the east side
of the Wicklow Mountains. A quick note about getting here: it takes
stamina to extract yourself from the unmarked maze of the Dublin ex-
urbs (your best bet is to take N11, which becomes M11, and then again
N11), but once you've accomplished that feat, this gorgeous, mysterious terrain awaits.

Bray

▶ **⑱** *22 km (14 mi) south of Dublin on N11, 8 km (5 mi) east of Enniskerry
on R755.*

One of Ireland's oldest seaside resorts, Bray is a trim village known for
its dilapidated summer cottages and sand-and-shingle beach, which

stretches for 2 km (1 mi). When the trains first arrived from Dublin in 1854, Bray became the number one spot for urban vacationers and subsequently took on the appearance of an English oceanfront town. Some Dubliners still flock to the faded glory of Bray's boardwalk to push baby carriages and soak up the sun. It's the terminus of the DART train from Dublin, so it's easy to get here without a car. Uncrowded hiking and mountain-bike trails crisscross the mountains bordering Bray to the south. One of the best is a well-marked path leading from the beach to the 10-foot-tall cross that crowns the spiny peak of Bray Head, a rocky outcrop that rises 791 feet from the sea. The semi-difficult, one-hour climb affords stunning views of Wicklow Town and Dublin Bay.

The **Heritage Centre,** opposite the Royal Hotel, in the old courthouse, houses on its lower level a re-created castle dungeon with a 1,000-years-of-Bray exhibition. Upstairs is a huge model railway and a display about modern Bray. ⊠ *Lower Main St.* ☎ *01/286–6796* ☎ *€3.80* ☉ *June–Sept., weekdays 9–5, Sat. 10–4, Sun. noon–5; Oct.–May, weekdays 9:30–4:30, Sat. 10–4:30.*

One Martello Terrace (☎ 01/286–8407), at the harbor, is Bray's most famous address. James Joyce (1882–1941) lived here between 1887 and 1891 and used the house as the setting for the Christmas dinner in *A Portrait of the Artist as a Young Man.* Today the house is privately owned by an Irish Teachta Dála (member of Parliament, informally known as a "TD"). The phone number listed above rings at her constituency office; someone there should be able to help scholars and devotees arrange a visit. Call on a Thursday between 10 AM and 1 PM. Although the residence has been renovated, the dining room portrayed in Joyce's novel still maintains the spirit of his time.

National Sealife is an aquarium and museum dedicated to the creatures of the sea, with an emphasis on those that occupy the waters around Ireland. Besides massive sea tanks that contain all manner of swimming things, there's a major conservation project with captive breeding of sea horses. **FinZone** is an undersea adventure trail perfect for kids, with puzzles to solve. Touch-screen computers and video games give the whole thing a high-tech feel. In winter call to confirm opening times before visiting. ⊠ *Strand Rd.* ☎ *01/286–6939* ⊕ *www.sealife.ie* ☎ *€8* ☉ *Daily 10–5.*

The 17th-century formal gardens at **Killruddery House** are precisely arranged, with fine beech hedges, Victorian statuary, and a parterre of lavender and roses. The Brabazon family, the earls of Meath, have lived here continuously since 1618. In 1820 they hired William Morris to remodel the house as a revival Elizabethan mansion. The estate also has a Crystal Palace conservatory modeled on those at the botanic gardens in Dublin. ⊠ *Killruddery, off the Bray–Greystones Rd., 3 km (2 mi) south of Bray* ☎ *01/286–2777* ☎ *House and gardens €6.50, gardens only €4.50* ☉ *Gardens Apr.–Sept., daily 1–5; house May–June and Sept., daily 1–5; by appointment at other times.*

Where to Eat

★ **$$–$$$** ✕ **Tree of Idleness.** This Greek-Cypriot restaurant, a 10-minute walk from Bray's DART train station, is a pleasant dining spot on the ground floor of a Victorian house along the seafront. It specializes in classic dishes, such as moussaka (eggplant and ground meat) and *keftedes* (meatballs). You can also order the excellent roast suckling pig with caramelized apples. Whatever you choose from the menu, expect tasty, hearty portions. The extensive wine list includes Greek and Cypriot house wines, as well as plenty of French, Italian, and New World wines. ⊠ *Seafront* ☎ *01/*

286–3498 ⊟ *AE, MC, V* ⊘ *Closed Mon., last wk in Aug., and 1st wk in Sept. No lunch.*

¢–$ ✕ **Summerville Country Cooking.** This restaurant is in Greystones, an old-fashioned seaside resort a couple miles south of Bray. The ceilings are high, the space is airy and bright, and the food—ranging from shepherd's pie to vegetarian quiche—tastes absolutely delicious. If you can, dine here in summer, when you can take advantage of the sun-drenched garden terrace. ⊠ *1 Trafalgar Rd., Greystones* ☎ *01/287–4228* ⊟ *V.*

Powerscourt House, Gardens & Waterfall

★ ♨ ⌐ ⑲ *25 km (16 mi) south of Dublin on R117, 22 km (14 mi) north of Glendalough on R755.*

Within the shadow of the famous Sugar Loaf mountain and one of the prettiest villages in Ireland, Enniskerry is built around a sloping central triangular square and surrounded by the wooded Wicklow Mountains. From Dublin you can get to Enniskerry directly by taking the No. 44 bus from the Dublin quays area. The main reason to visit the area around Enniskerry is the **Powerscourt Estate.** The grounds were originally granted to Sir Richard Wingfield, the first viscount of Powerscourt, by King James I of England in 1609. Richard Castle (1690–1751), the architect of Russborough House, designed Powerscourt House in a grand Palladian style, and it was constructed between 1731 and 1743. The original ballroom on the first floor—once "the grandest room in any Irish house," according to historian Desmond Guinness—still gives a sense of the house's former life.

Powerscourt Gardens, considered among the finest in Europe, were first laid out from 1745 to 1767 following the completion of the house—and then were radically redesigned in the Victorian style, from 1843 to 1875. The redesign was the work of the eccentric, boozy Daniel Robertson, who liked to be tootled around the gardens-in-progress in a wheelbarrow while nipping at his bottle of sherry. The Villa Butera in Sicily inspired him—which is why you'll find in the gardens sweeping terraces, antique sculptures, and a circular pond and fountain flanked by winged horses. There's a celebrated view of the Italianate patterned ramps, lawns, and pond across the beautiful, heavily wooded Dargle Valley, which stair-steps to the horizon and the noble profile of Sugar Loaf mountain. The grounds include many specimen trees (plants grown for exhibition), an avenue of monkey puzzles, a parterre of brightly colored summer flowers, and a Japanese garden. The kitchen gardens, with their modest rows of flowers, are a striking antidote to the classical formality of the main sections. A self-serve restaurant, crafts center, garden center, and a children's play area are also on the grounds. ⊠ *Enniskerry* ☎ *01/204–6000* ⊕ *www.powerscourt.ie* ⊡ *House €2, gardens €6* ⊘ *Mar.–Oct., daily 9:30–5:30; Nov.–Feb., daily 9:30–dusk.*

One of the most inspiring sights to the writers and artists of the Romantic generation, the 400-foot **Powerscourt Waterfall,** 5 km (3 mi) south of the gardens, is the highest in the British Isles. ⊠ *Enniskerry* ⊡ *€3.50* ⊘ *June–Aug., daily 9:30–7; Sept.–mid-Dec. and late Dec.–May, daily 10:30–dusk.*

Where to Eat

¢–$ ✕ **Poppies Country Cooking.** This cozy café—with a pine-paneled ceiling,
Fodor'sChoice farmhouse furniture, and paintings of poppies on the walls—is a great
★ place for breakfast, lunch, or late-afternoon tea. Expect potato cakes, shepherd's pie, lasagna, vegetarian quiche, house salads, and soup. But the most popular dishes are Poppies chicken (a casserole-like concoc-

tion) and homity pie (pot pie with potatoes, onion, garlic, and cream cheese). For dessert try the apple pie or the rhubarb crumble, which is so good that the Irish rugby team stops by for it after practice. ⊠ *The Square, Enniskerry* ☎ *01/282–8869* ⊟ *MC, V* ⊘ *No dinner.*

Roundwood

★ ❷ *18 km (11 mi) south of Enniskerry on R755.*

At 800 feet above sea level, Roundwood is the highest village in Ireland. It's also surrounded by some pretty spectacular mountain scenery. The Sunday-afternoon market in the village hall, where cakes, jams, and other homemade goods are sold, livens up what is otherwise a sleepy place. From the broad main street, by the Roundwood Inn, a minor road leads west for 8 km (5 mi) to two lakes, Lough Dan and Lough Tay, lying deep between forested mountains like Norwegian fjords.

Where to Eat

★ **$$–$$$** ✕ **Roundwood Inn.** Definitely check out this 17th-century inn, furnished in a traditional style, with wooden floors, dark furniture, and diamond-shape windows. It's best known for its good, reasonably priced bar food—eaten at sturdy tables beside an open fire. The restaurant offers a combination of Continental and Irish cuisines, reflecting the traditions of the German proprietor, Jurgen Schwalm, and his Irish wife, Aine. The separate bar and lounge also serve an excellent menu that includes a succulent seafood platter of salmon, oysters, lobster, and shrimp. ⊠ *Main St., Roundwood village center* ☎ *01/281–8107* ⚑ *Reservations essential* ⊟ *AE, MC, V* ⊘ *Closed Mon.–Tues. No dinner Sun.*

Glendalough

❷ *9½ km (6 mi) southwest of Roundwood, 54 km (33 mi) south of Dublin on R117 and R755.*

Fodor'sChoice ★

Nestled in a lush, quiet valley deep in the rugged Wicklow Mountains, among two lakes, evergreen and deciduous trees, and acres of windswept heather, Glendalough is one of Ireland's premier monastic sites. It flourished as a monastic center from the 6th century until 1398, when English soldiers plundered the site, leaving the ruins that you see today. (The monastery survived earlier 9th- and 10th-century Viking attacks.) The monastery was founded by St. Kevin (Coemghein, or "fair begotten" in Irish [d. 618]), a descendant of the royal house of Leinster, who renounced the world and came here to live as a hermit before opening the monastery in 550. Note that in high season, hordes of visitors to Glendalough make it difficult to appreciate the quiet solitude that brought St. Kevin to this valley. The visitor center is a good place to orient yourself and pick up a useful pamphlet. Many of the ruins are clumped together beyond the visitor center, but some of the oldest surround the Upper Lake, where signed paths direct you through spectacular scenery absent of crowds. Most ruins are open all day and are freely accessible.

Probably the oldest building on the site, presumed to date from St. Kevin's time, is the **Teampaill na Skellig** (Church of the Oratory), on the south shore of the Upper Lake. A little to the east is **St. Kevin's Bed,** a tiny cave in the rock face, about 30 feet above the level of the lake, where St. Kevin lived his hermit's existence. It's not easily accessible; you approach the cave by boat, but climbing the cliff to the cave can be dangerous so it isn't a great idea. At the southeast corner of the Upper Lake is the 11th-century **Reefert Church,** with the ruins of a nave and a chancel. The saint also lived in the adjoining, ruined beehive hut with five crosses, which marked the original boundary of the monastery. You get a superb view of the valley from here.

The ruins by the edge of the Lower Lake are the most important of those at Glendalough. The **gateway,** beside the Glendalough Hotel, is the only surviving entrance to an ancient monastic site anywhere in Ireland. An extensive **graveyard** lies within, with hundreds of elaborately decorated crosses, as well as a perfectly preserved six-story **round tower.** Built in the 11th or 12th century, it stands 100 feet high, with an entrance 25 feet above ground level.

The largest building at Glendalough is the substantially intact 7th- to 9th-century **cathedral,** where you'll find the nave (small for a large church, only 30 feet wide by 50 feet long), chancel, and ornamental oolite limestone window, which may have been imported from England. South of the cathedral is the 11-foot-high Celtic **St. Kevin's Cross.** Made of granite, it is the best-preserved such cross on the site. **St. Kevin's Church** is an early barrel-vaulted oratory with a high-pitched stone roof.

A note about getting here directly from Dublin: you can take the St. Kevin's bus service. If you're driving from Dublin, consider taking the scenic route along R155, which includes awesome, austere mountaintop passes. Don't drive this route if you're in a hurry, and don't look for a lot of signage—just concentrate on the glorious views. ☎0404/45325 ⊕ *www. heritageireland.ie* ☑ *€2.50* ☉ *Mid-Mar.–mid-Oct., daily 9:30–6; mid-Oct.–mid-Mar., daily 9:30–5; last admission 45 mins before closing.*

Where to Stay & Eat

$$ ✕⌂ **Glendalough Hotel.** Purists object to the proximity of this old-fashioned, early 19th-century hotel to the ruins at Glendalough, but to others it's a convenience. Some of the bedrooms, decorated in pastel colors, overlook the monastery and the wooded mountain scenery; others face the grounds. The burble of running water from the Glendassan River audibly enhances the experience. The restaurant ($$–$$$) also has views of the lawn. The Irish menu is simple, but portions are hearty and the pub is the only one for miles around. ⊠ *Co. Wicklow* ☎ *0404/45135* 🖷 *0404/ 45142* ⊕ *www.glendaloughhotel.com* ⊅ *40 rooms with bath* ⌂ *Restaurant, fishing, bar* ⊟ *AE, DC, MC, V* ☉ *Closed Dec. and Jan.* ⫶⊙⫶ *BP.*

Mount Usher Gardens

★ ㉒ *13 km (8 mi) east of Glendalough, 14½ km (9 mi) southeast of Roundwood on R764.*

Settled into more than 20 acres on the banks of the River Vartry, the gardens here were first laid out in 1868 by textile magnate Edward Walpole. Succeeding generations of the Walpole family further planted and maintained the grounds, which today have more than 5,000 species. The gardener has made the most of the riverside locale by planting eucalypti, azaleas, camellias, and rhododendrons. The river is visible from nearly every place in the gardens; miniature suspension bridges bounce and sway underfoot as you cross the river. There's a cluster of crafts shops, including a pottery workshop, as well as a bookstore and self-service restaurant, at the entrance. The twin villages of Ashford and Rathnew are to the south and east, and Newtownmountkennedy is to the north. ⊠ *Ashford* ☎ *0404/40205* ⊕ *www.mount-usher-gardens.com* ☑ *€6* ☉ *Mid-Mar.–Oct., daily 10:30–6.*

Where to Stay & Eat

★ **$$$–$$$$** ✕⌂ **Tinakilly House.** William and Bee Power have beautifully restored this Victorian-Italianate mansion, built in the 1870s by Captain Robert

Halpin (1836–94). The lobby has mementos of Captain Halpin and his nautical exploits, including paintings and ship models; Victorian antiques fill the house. Some bedrooms have four-poster beds, sitting areas, and views of the Wicklow landscape, the Irish Sea, or the lovely gardens on the 7-acre grounds. In the dining room ($$$), expect to be served French-influenced Irish cuisine, with fresh vegetables from the garden. Brown and fruit breads are baked daily. ⊠ *Rathnew, Co. Wicklow* ☎ *0404/69274* 🖷 *0404/67806* ⊕ *www.tinakilly.ie* ⤳ *52 rooms with bath, 5 suites* ♧ *Restaurant, tennis court, some hot tubs, bar* ▱ *AE, DC, MC, V* ⭄ *BP.*

Wicklow Town

㉓ *26 km (16 mi) east of Glendalough on R763, 51 km (32 mi) south of Dublin on N11.*

At the entrance to the attractive, tree-lined Main Street of Wicklow Town—its name, from the Danish *wyking alo,* means "Viking meadow"— sprawl the extensive ruins of a 13th-century Franciscan friary. The **friary** was closed down during the 16th-century dissolution of the monasteries in the area, but its ruins are a reminder of Wicklow's stormy past, which began with the unwelcome reception given to St. Patrick on his arrival in AD 432. Inquire at the nearby **priest's house** (⊠ Main St. ☎ 0404/67196) to see the ruins.

The old town jail, just above Market Square, has been converted into a museum and **Heritage Centre,** where it's possible to trace your genealogical roots in the area. Computer displays and life-size models tell the gruesome history of the jail, from the local rebellion in 1798 right up to the late 19th century. ⊠ *Market Sq.* ☎ *0404/61599* ⊕ *www. wicklow.ie* 🖾 €5.70 ⊙ *Apr.–Dec., daily 10–5.*

The **harbor** is Wicklow Town's most appealing area. Take Harbour Road down to the pier; a bridge across the River Vartry leads to a second, smaller pier, at the northern end of the harbor. From this end, follow the shingle beach, which stretches for 5 km (3 mi); behind the beach is the broad lough, a lagoon noted for its wildfowl. Immediately south of the harbor, perched on a promontory that has good views of the Wicklow coastline, is the ruin of the **Black Castle.** This structure was built in 1169 by Maurice Fitzgerald, an Anglo-Norman lord who arrived with the English invasion of Ireland. The ruins (freely accessible) extend over a large area; with some difficulty, you can climb down to the water's edge.

Between one bank of the River Vartry and the road to Dublin stands the Protestant **St. Lavinius Church,** which incorporates various unusual details: a Romanesque door, 12th-century stonework, fine pews, and an atmospheric graveyard. The church is topped off by a copper, onion-shape cupola, added as an afterthought in 1771. 🖾 *Free* ⊙ *Daily 10–6.*

Where to Stay & Eat

¢–$ ✕ **Pizza del Forno.** Take advantage of this great spot for people-watching on Main Street. The place has red-and-white-check tablecloths, low lighting, and a pizza oven blazing away. The inexpensive pizzas, pasta, steaks, and vegetarian dishes appeal to a wide array of appetites. ⊠ *Main St.* ☎ *0404/67075* ▱ *AE, MC, V* ⊙ *Closed Christmas–mid-Feb.*

$$$ 🏠 **Wicklow Head Lighthouse.** This 95-foot-high stone tower—first established in 1781—once supported an eight-sided lantern, and has been renovated by the Irish Landmark Trust as a lodging. It sleeps four to six people in two delightfully quirky octagonal bedrooms and one

double sofa bed in the sitting room. The kitchen–dining room at the top has stunning views out over the coast. Don't forget anything in the car; it's a long way down. You rent the entire lighthouse, and you must book for at least two nights. The old lighthouse is just south of town on Wicklow Head, right next to the new, automated one. ⌂ *Wicklow Head, Co. Wicklow* ☎ *01/670–4733* 🖷 *01/670–4887* ⌨ *Lighthouse sleeps 4–6, 2 baths* ☰ *MC, V* ⍾ *EP.*

$ 🏠 **Old Rectory Country House.** Once a 19th-century rectory, this charming Greek Revival country house—only open in the summer—now serves as a B&B. Black-and-white marble fireplaces, bright colors, original oil paintings, and antique and contemporary furniture fill the house; the light, spacious guest rooms are decorated in white and pastel shades, and have antique Victorian and country-house pieces. The Old Rectory is perched on a hillside just off the main road from Dublin on the approach to Wicklow Town. ⌂ *Wicklow Town, Co. Wicklow* ☎ *0404/ 67048* 🖷 *0404/69181* ⌨ *8 rooms with bath* ☰ *AE, MC, V* ⍾ *Closed Sept.–May* ⍾ *BP.*

Avondale House & Forest Park

㉔ *17 km (10½ mi) southwest of Wicklow Town on R752.*

Outside the quaint village of Rathdrum, on the west bank of the Avondale River, is the 523-acre **Avondale Forest Park.** Part of a then-burgeoning movement to preserve and expand the Irish forest, it was, in 1904, the first forest in Ireland to be taken over by the state. There's a fine 5½-km (3½-mi) walk along the river, as well as pine and exotic-tree trails. **Avondale House,** on the grounds of the park, resonates with Irish history. The house was the birthplace and lifelong home of Charles Stewart Parnell (1846–91), the "Uncrowned King of Ireland," the country's leading politician of the 19th century and a wildly popular campaigner for democracy and land reform. His career came to a halt after he fell in love with a married woman, Kitty O'Shea—her husband started divorce proceedings and news of the affair ruined Parnell's political career. He died a year later. (Joyce dramatized the controversy, in *A Portrait of the Artist as a Young Man,* as a keenly contested argument during the Daedalus family dinner.) Parnell's house, built in 1779, has been flawlessly restored—except for the reception and dining rooms on the ground floor, which are filled with Parnell memorabilia, including some of his love letters to Kitty O'Shea and political cartoons portraying Parnell's efforts to secure home rule for Ireland. ☎ *0404/46111* ⊕ *www. coillte.ie* 🎫 *House €4.45, parking €5* ⍾ *Mar.–Oct., daily 11–6.*

Avoca

㉕ *6½ km (4 mi) south of Avondale Forest Park on R754.*

Heavily forested hills surround the small, lovely hamlet of Avoca, at the confluence of the Rivers Avonbeg and Avonmore. Beneath a riverside tree here, the Irish Romantic poet Thomas Moore (1779–1852) composed his 1807 poem, "The Meeting of the Waters." There are some pleasant forest walks nearby, with scenic views of the valley. The oldest hand-weaving mill in Ireland, dating to 1723, **Avoca Handweavers** offers a short tour of the mill, which is still operating. The store sells a wide selection of its own superb fabrics and woven and knit apparel, some of which is difficult to find elsewhere. ☎ *0402/35105* 🎫 *Free* ⍾ *Shop mid-Mar.–Oct., daily 9:30–6; Nov.–mid-Mar., daily 9:30–5:30. Mill mid-Mar.–Oct., daily 8–4:30; Nov.–mid-Mar., weekdays 8–4:30.*

Arklow

㉖ *11 km (7 mi) southeast of Avoca on R754.*

An ideal point to access the intensely pastoral Vale of Avoca, the small beach town of Arklow is wrapped around an old port. The **Maritime Museum,** in the public library building near the railway station, traces Arklow's distinguished seafaring tradition. Exhibits include old photographs, some original boats, and the logs of long-dead captains. To get here, take a left at St. Peter's Church as you're heading out of town in the direction of Gorey and Wexford. ⊠ *St. Mary's Rd.* 🕾 *0402/32868* 🖃 *€5* ☉ *May–Sept., Mon.–Sat. 10–1 and 2–5; Oct.–Apr., weekdays 10–1 and 2–5.*

☺ Immediately north of Arklow is **Brittas Bay,** an expanse of white sand, quiet coves, and rolling dunes—perfect for adventurous kids. In summer it's popular with vacationing Dubliners.

Shopping

If you love bread or have a sweet tooth, stop in at **Stone Oven Bakery** (⊠ 65 Lower Main St. 🕾 0402/39418) at the bottom of the hill. The German-born baker, Egon Friedrich, prepares sourdough breads and delicious sweet treats, including hazelnut-chocolate triangles. You can also get simple cheese-and-bread sandwiches to go—or you can eat in the tiny, slightly haphazard café.

COUNTY KILDARE & WEST WICKLOW

Horse racing is a passion in Ireland—just about every little town has at least one betting shop—and County Kildare is the country's horse capital. Nestled between the basins of the River Liffey to the north and the River Barrow to the east, its gently sloping hills and grass-filled plains are perfect for breeding and racing Thoroughbreds. For first-time visitors, the National Stud just outside Kildare Town provides a fascinating glimpse into the world of horse breeding. The Japanese Gardens, adjacent to the National Stud, are among Europe's finest, while Castletown House, in Celbridge to the north, is one of Ireland's foremost Georgian treasures. You may want to pick up this leg from Glendalough—the spectacular drive across the Wicklow Gap, from Glendalough to Hollywood, makes for a glorious entrance into Kildare. One last note: consult Chapter 4, the Southeast, if you make it as far south as Castledermot, because Carlow and environs are only 10 km (6 mi) farther south.

Castletown House

㉗ *24 km (15 mi) southwest of Dublin via N7 to R403, 6½ km (4 mi) south*
Fodor'sChoice *of Maynooth.*
★

In the early 18th century, a revival of the architectural style of Andrea Palladio (1508–80) swept through England. Architects there built dozens of houses reinterpreting that style. The rage took hold of Ireland's Anglo-Irish aristocracy as well. Arguably the largest and finest example of an Irish Palladian–style house is Castletown, begun in 1722 for William Conolly (1662–1729), the Speaker of the Irish House of Commons and at the time the country's wealthiest man. Conolly hired the Italian architect Alessandro Galilei, who designed the facade of the main block; in 1724, the young Irish architect Sir Edward Lovett Pearce completed the design of the house by adding the colonnades and side pavilions. Conolly's death brought construction to a halt; it wasn't until his great-nephew, Thomas Conolly, and his wife, Lady Louisa (née Lennox), took up residence in 1758 that work on the house picked up again. Today Castletown is the largest house built as a private residence. (The American poet Robert Lowell lived here for a time in the 1960s.) The house was rescued in 1967 by Desmond Guinness, of the brewing family—the then president of the Irish Georgian Society. Now the Irish state owns the property. It's also the headquarters of the Irish Georgian Society and contains many pieces of the original furniture.

Within the house, the hall plasterwork was done by the Lafranchini brothers, Swiss-Italian craftsmen who worked in Dublin in the mid-18th century. The ground-floor Print Room is the only 18th-century example in Ireland of this elegant fad—like oversize postage stamps in a giant album, black-and-white prints were glued to the walls by fashionable young women. Upstairs at the rear of the house, the Long Gallery, almost 80 feet by 23 feet, is the most notable of the public rooms—it's decorated in Pompeian style and has three Venetian Murano glass chandeliers. ☒ *Celbridge* ☎ *01/628–8252* ⊕ *www.heritageireland.ie* ☒ €4 ☉ *Apr.–Sept., weekdays 10–6, weekends 1–6; Oct., weekdays 10–5, Sun. 1–5; Nov., Sun. 1–5.*

In Maynooth, a tiny Georgian town slightly to the west of Castletown House, you'll find **St. Patrick's College.** What was once a center for the training of Catholic priests is now one of Ireland's most important lay universities. The visitor center chronicles the college's history and that of the Catholic Church in Ireland. Stroll through the university gardens— the Path of Saints or the Path of Sinners. At the entrance to St. Patrick's College are the ruins of **Maynooth Castle,** the ancient seat of the Fitzgerald family. The Fitzgeralds' fortunes changed for the worse when they led the rebellion of 1536 (it failed). The castle keep, which dates from the 13th century, and the great hall are still in decent condition. Mrs. Saults at 9 Parson Street has the key; admission is free. ☎ *01/628–5222* ⊕ *www.may.ie* ☉ *St. Patrick's May–Sept., Mon.–Sat. 11–5, Sun. 2–6; guided tours every hr.*

Where to Stay & Eat

$$$$ ✕▥ **Moyglare Manor.** Owner Nora Devlin has exuberantly decorated this majestic Georgian manor house with her renowned antiques collection. Velvet chairs, oil paintings, and thickly draped windows furnish the drawing room, and the grand bedrooms have four-poster canopy beds, roomy wardrobes, marble fireplaces, and comfortable, chintz-covered armchairs. Lamp-shaded wall sconces add a romantic touch to the formal dining room, where a traditional French five-course set menu is served. The manor, which occupies 16 pastoral acres dotted with sheep and cows, is 29 km (18 mi) west of Dublin. ☒ *Maynooth, Co. Kildare* ☎ *01/628–6351* 🖷 *01/628–5405* ⊕ *www.moyglaremanor.ie* ⇆ *17 rooms with bath* ⟂ *Restaurant, 2 bars* ▤ *AE, DC, MC, V* ⊠ *BP, MAP.*

Straffan

❷⑧ *5 km (3 mi) southwest of Castletown House on R403, 25½ km (16 mi) southwest of Dublin.*

Its attractive location on the banks of the River Liffey, its unique butterfly farm, and the Kildare Hotel and Country Club—where Arnold Palmer designed the K Club, one of Ireland's most renowned 18-hole golf courses—are what make Straffan so appealing. The only one of its kind in Ireland, the **Straffan Butterfly Farm** has a tropical house with exotic plants, butterflies, and moths. Mounted and framed butterflies are for sale. ☎ *01/627–1109* ☒ €4 ☉ *June–Sept., daily noon–5:30.*

The **Steam Museum** covers the history of Irish steam engines, handsome machines used both in industry and agriculture—churning butter, threshing corn. There's also a fun collection of model locomotives. Engineers are present on "live steam days"; phone in advance to confirm. ⊠ *Lodge Park* ☎ *01/627-3155* ✆ *Live steam days €5.10, other times €4* ⊙ *Easter–May and Sept., Sun. 2–6; June–Aug., Tues.–Sun. 2–6.*

Where to Stay & Eat

$$$$ ✕⊡ **Kildare Hotel and Country Club.** Manicured gardens and the renowned
Fodor'sChoice Arnold Palmer–designed K Club golf course surround this mansard-roofed
★ country mansion. The spacious, comfortable guest rooms are each uniquely decorated with antiques, and have large windows that overlook either the Liffey or the golf course. (The rooms in the old house are best.) The hotel also has a leasing agreement with several privately owned cottages on the property. Chef Michel Flamme serves an unashamedly French menu—albeit with the hint of an Irish flavor—at the Byerly Turk Restaurant (named after a famous racehorse). ⊠ *Co. Kildare* ☎ *01/601-7200* ☒ *01/601-7299* ⊕ *www.kclub.ie* ✆ *69 rooms with bath, 26 apartments* ⅋ *2 restaurants, 18-hole golf course, 4 tennis courts, indoor pool, hair salon, fishing, horseback riding, squash, 3 bars* ▭ *AE, DC, MC, V* ⬦ *BP, MAP.*

$$–$$$ ✕⊡ **Barberstown Castle.** With a 13th-century castle keep at one end,
Fodor'sChoice an Elizabethan central section, and a large Georgian country house at
★ the other, Barberstown represents 750 years of Irish history. Turf fires blaze in ornate fireplaces in the three sumptuously decorated lounges. Reproduction pieces fill the bedrooms, some of which have four-poster beds. The restaurants—one Georgian, one medieval (the latter on the ground floor of the castle keep)—serve creatively prepared French food. ⊠ *Co. Kildare* ☎ *01/628-8157* ☒ *01/627-7027* ⊕ *www. barberstowncastle.ie* ✆ *22 rooms with bath* ⅋ *Restaurant, bar* ▭ *AE, DC, MC, V* ⬦ *BP, MAP.*

en route County Kildare has two major canal systems that connect Dublin with the Rivers Shannon and Barrow and the interior Lakelands. Sixteen kilometers (10 mi) southwest of Straffan on R403, **Robertstown** sits on the **Grand Canal** (the other major canal is the **Royal,** which heads to the northeast from Dublin), where you can take scenic walks and, during the summer, barge trips. Built in the early 19th century to accommodate passengers on the canal, the **Grand Canal Hotel** (⊠ Robertstown ☎ 045/870–005) offers candlelit dinners and musical entertainment.

Naas

㉙ *13 km (8 mi) south of Straffan on R407, 30 km (19 mi) southwest of Dublin on N7.*

The seat of County Kildare and a thriving market town in the heartland of Irish Thoroughbred country, Naas (pronounced nace) is full of pubs with high stools where short men (trainee jockeys) discuss the merits of their various stables. Naas has its own small racecourse, but **Punchestown Racecourse** (⊠ 3 km [2 mi] south of Naas on R411 ☎ 045/ 897–704) has a wonderful setting amid rolling plains, with the Wicklow Mountains a spectacular backdrop. Horse races are held regularly here, but the most popular event is the Punchestown National Hunt Festival in April.

Russborough House

30 *16 km (10 mi) southeast of Naas on R410.*

One of the highlights of the western part of County Wicklow, Russborough House is among the finest of the many Palladian-style villas built in Ireland by the Anglo-Irish ascendancy in the first half of the 18th century. (Castletown House, Emo Court, and Castle Coole are the other stars in this constellation.) In 1741, a year after Joseph Leeson inherited a vast fortune from his father, a successful Dublin brewer, he commissioned Richard Castle (architect of Leinster House and Powerscourt) to build this palatial home. Castle worked on it until his death, after which time his associate Francis Bindon took over. They pulled out all the stops to create a confident, majestic house with a silver-gray Wicklow granite facade that extends for more than 700 feet and encompasses a seven-bay central block, off which radiate two semicircular loggias connecting the flanking wings.

Baroque exuberance reigns in the house's main rooms, especially in the lavishly ornamented plasterwork ceilings executed by the Lafranchini brothers, who also worked at Castletown House. After a long succession of owners, Russborough was bought in 1952 by Sir Alfred Beit, the nephew of the German cofounder (with Cecil Rhodes) of the De Beers diamond operation, and it now belongs to Lady Beit, his widow. In 1988, after two major robberies, the finest works in the Beits' art collection were donated to the National Gallery of Ireland in Dublin. However, works by Gainsborough, Guardi, Murillo, Reynolds, and Rubens remain, as well as bronzes, silver, and porcelain. The views from Russborough's windows take in the foothills of the Wicklow Mountains and a small lake in front of the house; the extensive woodlands on the estate are open for exploration. ⊠ *Blessington, off N81* ☎ *045/865–239* ⊠ *€6, up-stairs bedrooms €3.50* ☺ *May–Sept., daily 10:30–5:30; Apr. and Oct., Sun. 10:30–5:30.*

Poulaphouca Reservoir

31 *3 km (2 mi) southeast of Russborough House, 33 km (21 mi) north-west of Glendalough on R758 via R756.*

Known locally as the Blessington Lakes, Poulaphouca (pronounced pool-a-*fook*-a) Reservoir is a large, meandering artificial lake that provides Dublin's water supply minutes from Russborough House. You can drive around the entire perimeter of the reservoir on minor roads; on its southern end lies Hollywood Glen, a particularly beautiful natural spot.

On the western shore of the lakes, the small market town of **Blessington,** with its wide main street lined on both sides by tall trees and Georgian buildings, is one of the most charming villages in the area. It was founded in the late 17th century, and was a stop on the Dublin–Waterford mail-coach service in the mid-19th century. Until 1932, a steam train ran from here to Dublin.

Beyond the southern tip of the Poulaphouca Reservoir, 13 km (8 mi) south of Blessington on N81, look for a small sign for the **Piper's Stones,** a Bronze Age stone circle that was probably used in a ritual connected with worship of the sun. It's just a short walk from the road.

You can take in splendid views of the Blessington Lakes from the top of **Church Mountain,** which you reach via a vigorous walk through Woodenboley Wood, at the southern tip of Hollywood Glen. Follow the main forest track for about 20 minutes and then take the narrow path that heads up the side of the forest to the mountaintop.

Where to Stay & Eat

$$$$ ✕🔲 **Rathsallagh House.** At the end of a long drive that winds through a
Fodor'sChoice golf course, and set in 530 acres of parkland is Rathsallagh House, which
★ came into being when low-slung, ivy-covered Queen Anne stables were converted into a farmhouse in 1798. Enveloping couches and chairs, fresh flower arrangements, large windows, fireplaces, and lots of lamps furnish the two drawing rooms. Kay's outstanding haute-Irish dinner menu changes daily. Specialties include paupiette of herb-filled salmon with onion and chive beurre blanc. ✉ *Dunlavin, Co. Wicklow* ☎ *045/403–112* 🖶 *045/403–343* ⊕ *www.rathsallagh.com* ⇒ *29 rooms with bath* ⟨ *Restaurant, 18-hole golf course, tennis court, indoor pool, massage, sauna, croquet, bar, meeting rooms* ⊟ *AE, DC, MC, V* ⦿| *BP, MAP.*

The Curragh

③2 *8 km (5 mi) southwest of Naas on M7, 25½ km (16 mi) west of Poulaphouca Reservoir.*

The broad plain of the Curragh, bisected by the main N7 road, is the biggest area of common land in Ireland, encompassing about 31 square km (12 square mi) and devoted mainly to grazing. This is Ireland's major racing center, home of the **Curragh Racecourse** (✉ N7 ☎ 045/441–205); the Irish Derby and other international horse races are run here.

The **Curragh Main Barracks,** a large camp where the Irish Army trains, has a small museum. One of its prize relics is the armored car once used by Michael Collins, the former head of the Irish Army—in December 1921, Collins signed the Anglo-Irish Treaty, designating a six-county North to remain in British hands in exchange for complete independence for Ireland's remaining 26 counties. The car can be seen with permission from the commanding officer. ☎ *045/445–161, ask for the command adjutant* ✉ *Free.*

Kildare Town

③3 *5 km (3 mi) west of the Curragh on M7, 51 km (32 mi) southwest of Dublin via N7 and M7.*

Horse breeding is the cornerstone of County Kildare's thriving economy, and Kildare Town is the place to come if you're crazy about horses. Right off Kildare's main market square, the **Silken Thomas** (☎ 045/522–232) pub re-creates an old-world atmosphere with open fires, dark wood, and leaded lights; it's a good place to stop for lunch before exploring the sights here.

The Church of Ireland **St. Brigid's Cathedral** is where the eponymous saint founded a religious settlement in the 5th century. The present cathedral, with its stocky tower, is a restored 13th-century structure. It was partially rebuilt around 1686, but restoration work wasn't completed for another 200 years. The stained-glass west window of the cathedral depicts three of Ireland's greatest saints: Brigid, Patrick, and Columba. In pre-Christian times druids gathered around a sacred oak that stood on the grounds and from which Kildare (*Cill Dara*), or the "Church of the Oak," gets its name. Also on the grounds is a restored fire pit reclaimed from the time of Brigid, when a fire was kept burning—by a chaste woman—in a female-only fire temple. Interestingly, Brigid started the place for women, but it was she who asked monks to move here as well. ✉ *Off Market Sq.* ☎ *No phone* ✉ *€80* ☉ *Daily 10–6.*

The 108-foot-high **round tower,** in the graveyard of St. Brigid's Cathedral, is the second highest in Ireland. It dates from the 12th century. Extraordinary views across much of the Midlands await you if you're energetic enough to climb the stairs to the top. ☎ *045/521–229* ☒ *€2.55* ☉ *May–Sept., daily 10–1 and 2–5.*

If you're a horse aficionado, or even just curious, check out the **National Stud Farm,** a main center of Ireland's racing industry. The Stud was founded in 1900 by brewing heir Colonel William Hall-Walker, and transferred to the Irish state in 1945. It's here that breeding stallions are groomed, exercised, tested, and bred. Spring and early summer, when mares will have foals, are the best times to visit. Besides being crazy about horses, Walker may just have been crazy, or at least a little eccentric—he believed in astrology, so foals had their charts done. Those with unfavorable results were sold right away. He even built the stallion boxes with lantern roofs that allow the moon and stars to work their magic on the occupants. The **National Stud Horse Museum,** also on the grounds, recounts the history of horses in Ireland. Its most outstanding exhibit is the skeleton of Arkle, the Irish racehorse that won major victories in Ireland and England during the late 1960s. The museum also contains medieval evidence of horses, such as bones from 13th-century Dublin, and some early examples of equestrian equipment. ☒ *About ½ km (⅓ mi) south of Kildare Town* ☎ *045/521–617* ⊕ *www.irish-national-stud.ie* ☒ *€8.50 (includes entry to Japanese Gardens)* ☉ *Mid-Feb.–mid-Nov., daily 9:30–6.*

★ Adjacent to the National Stud Farm, the **Japanese Gardens** were created between 1906 and 1910 by the Stud's founder, Colonel Hall-Walker, and laid out by a Japanese gardener, Tassa Eida, and his son Minoru. The gardens are recognized as among the finest in Europe, although they're more of an East–West hybrid rather than authentically Japanese. The Scots pine trees, for instance, are an appropriate stand-in for traditional Japanese pines, which signify long life and happiness. The gardens symbolically chart the human progression from birth to death, although the focus is on the male journey. A series of landmarks runs along a meandering path: the Tunnel of Ignorance (No. 3) represents a child's lack of understanding; the Engagement and Marriage bridges (Nos. 8 and 9) span a small stream; and from the Hill of Ambition (No. 13), you can look back over your joys and sorrows. It ends with the Gateway to Eternity (No. 20), beyond which lies a Buddhist meditation sand garden. This is a worthwhile destination any time of the year, though it's particularly glorious in spring and fall. ☒ *About 2½ km (1½ mi) south of Kildare Town, clearly signposted off market square* ☎ *045/521–617* ⊕ *www.irish-national-stud.ie* ☒ *€8.50 (includes entry to National Stud)* ☉ *Mid-Feb.–mid-Nov., daily 9:30–6.*

Athy

❸❹ *24 km (15 mi) south of Kildare Town on R417, 33½ km (21 mi) southwest of Naas.*

The River Barrow widens considerably at the industrial town of Athy, whose designation as a heritage town has spiffed things up—especially the 18th-century town houses and the castle here. Overlooking the river, by the bridge, 16th-century **White's Castle,** now a private home that's closed to the public, was built by the earl of Kildare to defend this strategic crossing.

The modern pentagonal **Catholic church** (1963–65) in the middle of town has a striking interior with statues, a crucifix by local artist Brid ni Rinn on the high altar, and stations of the cross by the well-known painter and member of the Royal Hibernian Academy, George Campbell (1917–79). ✉ *Free* ☉ *Daily 8–6.*

Ballytore

㉟ *8 km (5 mi) east of Athy, 26 km (16 mi) south of Naas on N9.*

In the 18th and 19th centuries, Ballytore was a Quaker settlement—one of few in Ireland. An old schoolhouse is now a small **Quaker Museum.** Among the pupils at the school was Edmund Burke (1729–97), the orator and political philosopher who was close to Samuel Johnson and Sir Joshua Reynolds. ✉ *The Library* ☎ *045/431–109* ✉ *Free* ☉ *Tues.–Fri. 11–6, Sat. 11–1.*

An old mill was converted into the **Crookstown Heritage Centre,** a museum of the flour-milling and baking industries with a functioning water mill. Built in 1840, the center helped reduce the effects of the Great Famine in this area. You can get a quick bite in its coffee shop. ✉ *The Mill* ☎ *0507/ 23222* ✉ *€3.20* ☉ *Apr.–Sept., daily 10–7; Oct.–Mar., Sun. 2–5:30.*

Where to Eat

$–$$ ✕ **Moone High Cross Inn.** A cornucopia of local artifacts, newspaper clippings, and old photographs decorates this old pub, which makes for fascinating browsing while you nosh on the bar food—steak, salmon, and bacon and cabbage. Save room for the homemade apple pie. On sunny days, you can sit outside and admire the old signs in the beer garden. The inn is down the road from the Moone High Cross, about 7½ km (5 mi) south of Ballytore. ✉ *Bolton Hill, Moone* ☎ *0507/24112* ▬ *MC, V.*

en route From Ballytore take the main N9 road south for 3 km (2 mi) to Timolin, where the **Irish Pewter Mill** pays splendid tribute to an old Irish craft with its showrooms, factory, and museum. Jugs, plates, and other pewter items are for sale. ☎ *0507/24164* ✉ *Free* ☉ *May–Sept., weekdays 9:30–5, weekends 11–4.*

Several well-preserved high crosses stand among monastic ruins in South Kildare. On N9, 1½ km (1 mi) beyond Timolin, take the signposted right turn at the Moone Post Office and continue for 3 km (2 mi) to the **Moone High Cross,** an ancient Celtic cross that stands 17½ feet high. Its 51 sculptured panels depict scriptural scenes.

Castledermot

㊱ *13 km (8 mi) south of Ballytore on N9.*

On the left side of the village of Castledermot stand an almost perfectly preserved 10th-century round tower together with two 10th-century high crosses, equally well preserved, on the grounds of the local church. From the church gate, you can walk back to the main road along the footpath, which is totally enclosed by trees. It's a splendid, serene walk. On the right side of the road in the village are the substantial ruins of a Franciscan friary, most of which date from the 14th century.

Where to Stay & Eat

★ $$$–$$$$ ✕▥ **Kilkea Castle.** This is a wonderfully elegant place to stay. Built in 1180 as a defensive Anglo-Norman castle, Kilkea is steeped in history and populated with the ghosts of the Fitzgerald family. The 11 rooms in the castle itself are more luxuriously furnished than those surrounding the adjacent courtyard. The Irish dishes served in the restaurant, in what was the great hall of the castle, are based on seasonal produce, some of it from the old, walled gardens below. The hotel has an extensive sports complex, including a golf course and clubhouse. ⊠ *Castle-dermot, Co. Kildare, near Athy* ☎ *0503/45156* 🖷 *0503/45187* 🛏 *36 rooms with bath* ♿ *Restaurant, 18-hole golf course, 2 tennis courts, indoor pool, health club, fishing, archery, 2 bars* ▤ *AE, DC, MC, V* ⏧ *BP, MAP.*

DUBLIN ENVIRONS A TO Z

To research prices, get advice from other travelers, and book travel arrangements, visit www.fodors.com.

BUS TRAVEL

Bus services link Dublin with the main and smaller towns in the area. All buses for the region depart from Dublin's Busaras, the central bus station, at Store Street. For bus inquiries, contact Bus Éireann. You can reach Enniskerry and the Powerscourt Estate by taking Dublin Bus No. 44 from the Dublin quays area.

St. Kevin's, a private bus service, runs daily from Dublin (outside the Royal College of Surgeons on St. Stephen's Green) to Glendalough, stopping off at Bray, Roundwood, and Laragh en route. Buses leave Dublin daily at 11:30 AM and 6 PM (7 PM on Sunday); buses leave Glendalough weekdays at 7:15 AM and 4:15 PM (9:45 AM and 4:15 PM on Saturday; 9:45 AM and 5:30 PM on Sunday). One-way fare is €9; a round-trip ticket costs €15.

🚹 Bus Information **Bus Éireann** ☎ 01/836-6111 ⊕ www.buseireann.ie. **Dublin Bus** ☎ 01/873-4222 ⊕ www.dublinbus.ie. **St. Kevin's** ☎ 01/281-8119 ⊕ www.glendaloughbus.com.

CAR TRAVEL

The easiest and best way to tour Dublin's environs is by car, because many sights are not served by public transportation, and what service there is, especially to outlying areas, is infrequent. (⇨ If you need to rent a car, *see* Car Rental *in* Dublin A to Z *in* Chapter 1.) To visit destinations in the Boyne Valley, follow N3, along the east side of Phoenix Park, out of the city and make Trim and Tara your first stops. Alternatively, leave Dublin via N1/M1 toward Belfast. Try to avoid the road during weekday rush hours (8 AM–10 AM and 5 PM–7 PM); stay on it as far as Drogheda and start touring from there.

To reach destinations in County Kildare, follow the quays along the south side of the River Liffey (they are one-way westbound) to St. John's Road West (N7); in a matter of minutes, you're heading for open countryside. Avoid traveling this route during the evening peak rush hours, especially on Friday, when Dubliners are themselves making their weekend getaways.

To reach destinations in County Wicklow, N11/M11 is the fastest and most clearly marked route. The two more scenic routes to Glendalough are R115 to R759 to R755, or R177 to R755.

EMERGENCIES

🚹 **Ambulance, fire, police** ☎ 999.

TOURS

Bus Éireann runs guided bus tours to many of the historic and scenic locations throughout the Dublin environs daily during the summer. Visits include trips to Glendalough in Wicklow; Boyne Valley and Newgrange in County Louth; and the Hill of Tara, Trim, and Navan in County

Meath. All tours depart from Busaras Station, Dublin; information is available by phone Monday–Saturday 8:30–7, Sunday 10–7. Gray Line, a privately owned touring company, also runs many guided bus tours throughout the Dublin environs between May and September. Wild Coach Tours has half- and full-day trips to Glendalough, Powerscourt House and Garden, and Malahide Castle in small Mercedes coaches. Prices start at €20.

Wicklow Trail Rides takes experienced adult horseback riders on week-long rides through the Wicklow Mountains (May–September), with overnight stays in country homes and guest houses. Instructional holidays for children and adults at the riding center are also available.

The Wicklow Way is Ireland's most popular walking route, a 137-km (85-mi) trek through the Dublin and Wicklow mountains. The walk begins in Marlay Park, just south of Dublin city center, where there is a selection of different trails. County Wicklow also sponsors three annual walking festivals. The two-day Rathdrum Easter Walking Festival includes hill walks of varying lengths over Easter weekend. The first weekend of May, the Wicklow Mountains May Walking Festival is centered on Blessington. The Wicklow Mountains Autumn Walking Festival is based in the Glenmalure area.

🚍 Bus Tours **Bus Éireann** ☎ 01/836-6111. **Gray Line** ☎ 01/661-9666. **Wild Coach Tours** ☎ 01/280-1899.

🏇 Horseback-Riding Tours **Wicklow Trail Rides** ✉ Grainne Sugars, Calliaghstown Riding Center, Ratcoole, Co. Dublin ☎ 01/458-9236 🖶 01/458-8171.

🚶 Walking Tours & Events **Rathdrum Easter Walking Festival** ☎ 0404/46262. **Wicklow Mountains Autumn Walking Festival** ☎ 0404/66058. **Wicklow Mountains May Walking Festival** ☎ 0404/66058. **Wicklow Way Information** ☎ 01/493-4059.

TRAIN TRAVEL

Irish Rail (Iarnród Éireann) trains run the length of the east coast, from Dundalk to the north in County Louth to Arklow along the coast in County Wicklow. Trains make many stops along the way; there are stations in Drogheda, Dublin (the main stations are Connolly Station and Pearse Station), Bray, Greystones, Wicklow, and Rathdrum. From Heuston Station, the Arrow, a commuter train service, runs westward to Celbridge, Naas, Newbridge, and Kildare Town. Contact Irish Rail for schedule and fare information.

🚆 Train Information **Connolly Station** ✉ Amiens St., Northside, Dublin. **Heuston Station** ✉ Victoria Quay and St. John's Road W, Dublin West, Dublin. **Irish Rail** ☎ 01/836-6222. **Pearse Station** ✉ Westland Row, Southside, Dublin.

VISITOR INFORMATION

For information on travel in the Dublin environs and for help in making lodging reservations, contact one of the following Tourist Information Offices (TIOs) year-round: Dublin Tourism and Bord Fáilte, Dundalk, Mullingar, Trim, or Wicklow Town. Mullingar is the head office of tourism for Counties Louth, Meath, and Kildare; it can give you contact information for temporary TIOs in these areas. During the summer, temporary TIOs are open throughout the environs, in towns such as Arklow and Avoca in County Wicklow, Drogheda and Dundalk in County Louth, and Kildare Town in County Kildare.

🛈 Tourist Information **Bord Fáilte** ☎ 1850/230-330 in Ireland; 800/223-6470 in the U.S. and Canada; 800/039-7000 in the U.K.; 02/9299-6177 in Australia; 09/379-8720 in New Zealand. **Dublin Tourism** ☎ 01/605-7700 or 01/602-4129. **Dundalk** ☎ 042/933-5484. **Mullingar** ☎ 044/48761. **Trim** ☎ 046/37227. **Wicklow Town** ☎ 0404/69117.

THE MIDLANDS

FODOR'S CHOICE

Castle Leslie, *hotel in Glaslough*

Clonmacnoise, *ancient monastery near Shannonbridge*

Crookedwood House, *hotel in Mullingar*

Strokestown Park House, *estate in Strokestown*

Wineport Lodge, *restaurant in Glasson*

HIGHLY RECOMMENDED

HOTELS   Hilton Park, *Clones*

Hodson Bay Hotel, *Athlone*

Nuremore Hotel and Country Club, *Carrickmacross*

Slieve Russell Hotel and Country Club, *Ballyconnell*

SIGHTS   Belvedere House Gardens, *Mullingar*

Birr Castle Demesne, *Birr*

Emo Court and Gardens, *Emo*

Updated by
Alannah
Hopkin

IRISH SCHOOLCHILDREN WERE ONCE TAUGHT to think of their country as a saucer, with mountains around the edge and a dip in the middle. The dip is the Midlands—or the Lakelands, as it is sometimes also referred to—and this often-overlooked region comprises nine counties: Cavan, Laois (pronounced leash), Westmeath, Longford, Offaly, Roscommon, Monaghan, Leitrim, and Tipperary. Unspectacular and unsung, the flat plains of the Midlands form the geographical heart of Ireland. Among the highlights are Clonmacnoise, Ireland's most important monastic ruins; historic towns with age-old industries, such as lace making and crystal making; the gardens of Birr Castle; and some of Ireland's finest Anglo-Irish houses—Strokestown Park House, Castle Leslie, and Emo Court.

A fair share of Ireland's 800 bodies of water speckle this lush countryside. Many of the lakes formed by glacial action some 10,000 years ago are quite small, especially in Cavan and Monaghan. Anglers have learned to expect to have a lake to themselves. Because of all the water, much of the landscape lies under blanket bog, a unique ecosystem that's worth exploring. The River Shannon, one of the longest rivers in Europe and the longest in the British Isles, bisects the Midlands from north to south, piercing a series of loughs (lakes): Lough Allen, Lough Ree, and Lough Derg. The Royal Canal and the Grand Canal cross the Midlands from east to west, ending in the Shannon north and south of Lough Ree.

The main roads from Dublin to the south and the west cross the area—and these roads ultimately came to eclipse the Shannon and the canals as important transportation arteries—but there is also a network of minor roads linking the more scenic areas. The Laois Heritage Trail, a day-long drive, leads to some of the region's less frequented villages, where visitors still have some novelty value. Wilderness hiking and horseback-riding trails run through the Slieve Bloom Mountains, on the Laois-Offaly border, to pretty villages and across bogland and woodlands, often with sweeping views of unspoiled countryside. Attractive hill and lake scenery can be found in the forest parks of Killykeen and Lough Key. The towns themselves—including Nenagh, Roscommon, Athlone, Boyle, Mullingar, Tullamore, Longford, and Cavan—are not among Ireland's most distinctive, but they are likely to appeal to people hungry for a time when the pace of life was slower and every neighbor's face was familiar. A Midland town's main hotel is usually the social center, a good place from which to experience life as the locals do. Night owls and thrill seekers should head elsewhere.

Exploring the Midlands

This chapter is organized into three sections: the eastern Midlands, the northern Midlands, and the western Midlands. The first two areas can easily be covered in an extended visit to the Midlands, as they chart a course almost due north from the initial starting point in Abbeyleix, County Laois. The third section includes sights west of those in the first two, which means they can easily be visited if you're flying into Shannon and beginning your explorations of Ireland in the western half of the country. In fact, because the Midlands border virtually every major county of Ireland, there are three places in this chapter where you should be alert to nearby locales covered in other chapters: the easternmost sights in the Midlands (Emo Court and Coolbanagher) are within a few miles of the westernmost sites in Dublin Environs; the westernmost sights in the Midlands (Boyle and Lough Key Forest Park) are just across the border from County Sligo; and the northernmost sights and towns of the Midlands are just across the border from Northern Ireland.

Numbers in the text correspond to numbers in the margin and on the Midlands map.

If you have 3 days

Heading east from Shannon Airport, turn off the N7 Limerick–Dublin road for ⬛ **Birr** ⓴ ►, a quiet Georgian town built around its magnificent castle and gardens. Then take the Bord na Mona Bog Rail Tour, near Shannonbridge, a good introduction to the flora and fauna of Ireland's many bogs. While you're in the area, stop at **Clonmacnoise** ⑱, Ireland's most important monastic settlement, and return to Birr for the night. The next day head for **Strokestown** ⑮ and its namesake house, where a museum documents the causes and effects of the 1845–49 Great Famine. If you have time, drive east to **Longford** ⑨ and visit the nearby Carrigglas Manor, a romantic 1837 Tudor-Gothic house that has Jane Austen associations. Head to ⬛ **Boyle** ⑭, a good place to stay overnight. If the weather is good on the next day, take some fresh air in Lough Key Forest Park, or just take time to explore this old-fashioned town. From here you'll be well positioned to explore western and northwestern Ireland.

3

If you have 5 days

Heading from Dublin or from points east in Wicklow and Kildare, start at **Portarlington** ③ ►, making sure to visit the nearby Emo Court and Gardens, a large-scale country house designed by James Gandon, the architect responsible for much of Georgian Dublin. Move north to the Charleville Forest Castle outside **Tullamore** ④, then to **Kilbeggan** ⑤, where you can learn about whiskey making at Locke's Distillery; if you have time, stop in at the beautiful Belvedere House Gardens to the north. Stay in or around ⬛ **Mullingar** ⑥ for the night. On the morning of the second day, briefly explore Mullingar, and then head north on scenic R394 to **Castlepollard** ⑦ and the massive Tullynally Castle and Gardens. Crystal aficionados should stop in **Cavan** ⑩, while nature buffs can easily spend the afternoon exploring the nearby water-laced Killykeen Forest Park. Spend the night in ⬛ **Cootehill** ⑪, an old-fashioned, friendly County Cavan town popular with anglers. On your third day you can either jump across the border to explore the southernmost sights in Northern Ireland or head southwest, making a brief stop at Rossmore Forest Park on your way to the border town of ⬛ **Clones** ⑬, a lace-making center. On your fourth day, return to Cavan and pick up the road to **Longford** ⑨. To the west lies **Strokestown** ⑮ and its namesake house. ⬛ **Athlone** ⑰ is a convenient place to spend the night—from here you're well positioned for an early morning visit to **Clonmacnoise** ⑱, the most important early Christian monastic site in Ireland. Take in the Bord na Mona Bog Rail Tour near Shannonbridge on your way to **Banagher** ⑲, where you can either take a two-hour Shannon cruise (a great trip in good weather) or drive around **Lough Derg** ㉑. You can choose to end up in either ⬛ **Birr** ⓴, **Roscrea** ㉒, or ⬛ **Nenagh** ㉓; from any of these towns you're not far from Shannon Airport and points to the west and southwest.

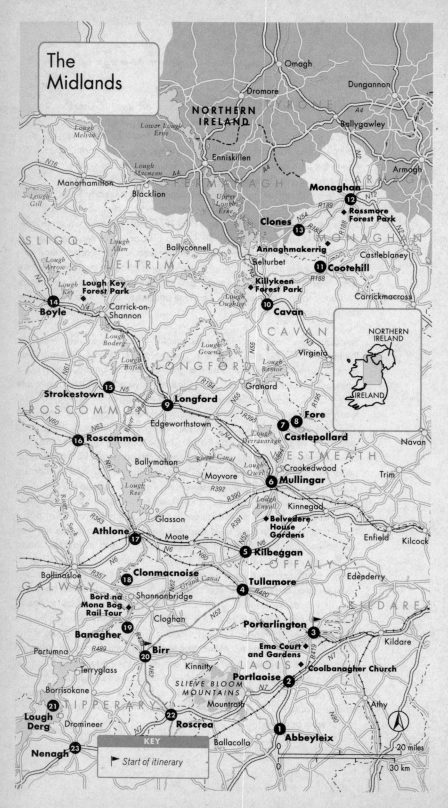

The Midlands

NORTHERN IRELAND

Omagh
Dromore
Dungannon
Ballygawley
A4
Enniskillen
Lower Lough Erne
Lough Melvin
Manorhamilton
Lough Gill
Blacklion
Upper Lough Erne
Monaghan
12
N12
Rossmore Forest Park
SLIGO
LEITRIM
Ballyconnell
Belturbet
Clones **13**
N54
R183
Annaghmakerrig
Castleblaney
11 Cootehill
R188
Carrickmacross
Lough Arrow
N4
Lough Allen
Lough Key Forest Park
14 Boyle
N4
Carrick-on-Shannon
Lough Bodery
Lough Bofin
Killykeen Forest Park
Lough Oughter
10 Cavan
CAVAN
N3
Virginia
NORTHERN IRELAND
IRELAND

LONGFORD
Lough Gowna
Lough Ramor
Granard
R194
N55
Lough Kinale
R395
Fore
7 **8**
Castlepollard
Navan
Strokestown **15**
N5
9 Longford
Edgeworthstown
ROSCOMMON
N63
N60
16 Roscommon
N61
Ballymahon
Royal Canal
Moyvore
Lough Owel
Crookedwood
WESTMEATH
Trim
R392
R390
6 Mullingar
N4
Lough Derravaragh
Lough Ennell
Kinnegad
Enfield
Kilcock
Glasson
Lough Ree
R363
Athlone **17**
Moate
R391
N52
Belvedere House Gardens
N6
5 Kilbeggan
N6
Ballinasloe
R357
GALWAY
18 Clonmacnoise
Shannonbridge
Grand Canal
N52
Tullamore **4**
R420
OFFALY
Edenderry
N6
Bord na Mona Bog Rail Tour
Cloghan
Portarlington
3
KILDARE
Kildare
Banagher **19**
R489
20 Birr
N62
Kinnitty
Emo Court and Gardens
R419
N7
Coolbanagher Church
Portumna
Terryglass
SLIEVE BLOOM MOUNTAINS
LAOIS
Portlaoise
2
N7
Athy
N80
Borrisokane
TIPPERARY
Dromineer
Mountrath
Lough Derg **21**
22
Roscrea
Ballacolla
1 Abbeyleix
Nenagh **23**

KEY

⚑ Start of itinerary

0 ————— 20 miles

0 ————— 30 km

About the Restaurants

Most restaurants are simple eateries, ranging in price from inexpensive ($) to moderate ($$), and are often attached to family hotels. Mullingar, in the center of the Midlands, is the beef capital of Ireland, and the many lakes and rivers of the region provide an abundance of fresh salmon and trout. No place is more than an hour and a half from the sea, so expect to find lots of fresh ocean fish.

About the Hotels

There are some opulent country-house hotels in the region, but accommodations are for the most part modest affairs. The choice is usually between a small-town hotel offering a reasonable standard of basic comfort or a scenic country-house bed-and-breakfast. In summer, reserve far ahead for boating resorts on the Shannon and its loughs.

WHAT IT COSTS In Euros				
$$$$	**$$$**	**$$**	**$**	**¢**
RESTAURANTS over €29	€22–€29	€15–€22	€8–€15	under €8
HOTELS over €230	€180–€230	€130–€180	€80–€130	under €80

Restaurant prices are per person for a main course at dinner. Hotel prices are for two people in a double room, including VAT and a service charge (often applied in larger hotels).

Timing

The Midlands are a good year-round choice because, unlike those in the more popular destinations in western and southwestern Ireland, the restaurants, accommodations, and major attractions stay open all year. The area is usually quiet, except at the boating resorts on the Shannon and its loughs, which are heavily booked by Irish vacationers in July and August.

THE EASTERN MIDLANDS

The eastern fringe of the Midlands is about an hour's drive from Dublin, and a visit to the area could easily be grafted onto a trip to the Dublin environs. A good tour begins at Abbeyleix and moves northwest to Castlepollard and environs, stopping just short of Longford, the jumping-off point for the northern Midlands.

Abbeyleix

❶ *99 km (61 mi) southwest of Dublin.*

Abbeyleix is an attractive village, built from scratch by the local landlord, the viscount de Vesci, in the 18th century with a broad main street and well-proportioned Georgian town houses. **Morrissey's Pub and Grocery Store** (⊠ Main St. ☎ 0502/31281) dates from 1775 and is one of the most famous pubs in the country. Its interior—with antique bar fittings, an ancient potbellied stove, and collections of old cash registers and antique biscuit tins—makes it a gem among Irish pubs.

The **Heritage House,** a former Patrician Brothers School, has informative displays on the de Vesci family and the history of Abbeyleix. ⊠ *Top of town* ☎ *0502/31653* ⊕ *www.laois.local.ie* ⊠ *€3.50* ☉ *May–Sept., weekdays 9–5, weekends 9–1; Oct.–Apr., weekdays 9–5.*

Ballinakill, a pretty Georgian village about 5 km (3 mi) south of Abbeyleix built on a sloping street, contains the **Heywood Gardens,** designed by the English architect Sir Edward Lutyens in the early 20th century within an existing 18th-century park. The Lutyens' house burned down, but the gardens, regarded as among his finest, are undergoing ongoing restoration. A formal lawn flanked by traditional herbaceous borders leads to a sunken Italian garden. ⊠ *Ballinakill* ☎ *0502/33563* ⊕ *www. laois.local.ie* 🖃 *Free* ⊘ *Daily 9–dusk.*

Where to Stay & Eat

$ ✕🖼 **Preston House.** This ivy-clad Georgian schoolhouse on the main Cork–Dublin road is a popular lunch and coffee stop by day, renowned for home-baked goods, although in the evening the restaurant ($–$$; closed Sunday and Monday) takes on a more formal aspect. Owner Allison Dowling prepares local beef and lamb in traditional Irish style—roasted or grilled—and also serves lighter dishes, including baked cheese soufflé and warm chicken salad. The guest rooms are spacious, furnished with solid Victorian antiques, and all have working fireplaces. They also have views of the long back gardens and fields beyond. ⊠ *Main St., Co. Laois* 🖼🖼 *0502/31432* 🔖 *4 rooms with bath* ⅋ *Restaurant, some pets allowed, no smoking* ⊟ *MC, V* ⅋⊙⅋ *BP.*

¢ 🖼 **Foxrock Inn.** A friendly red setter called Grouse greets new arrivals at this modest, modern house attached to the pub Mary's Bar. The peaceful countryside and the genuinely warm welcome are the main attractions here. Sean and Mary Hyland, an enthusiastic young couple, can advise you on hiking in the Slieve Bloom Mountains and can organize golf and angling packages. Rooms are plain but clean and comfortable. Simple, home-cooked dinners and packed lunches are available. It's in the tiny village of Ballacolla, tucked away on a back road 8 km (5 mi) east of Abbeyleix (signposted off the R434 road to Borris-in-Ossory). ⊠ *Clough, Ballacolla, Co. Laois* 🖼🖼 *0502/38637* ⊕ *www.foxrockinn. com* 🔖 *5 rooms with bath* ⅋ *Dining room* ⊟ *V* ⅋⊙⅋ *BP.*

Shopping

Rural Ireland may seem an unlikely place to buy designer labels, but Calvin Klein, Ralph Lauren, and DKNY are among the brands sold at Ireland's first designer outlet store, **Brandcentral** (⊠ Rathdowney ☎ 0505/48900 ⊕ www.brandcentral.ie). This huge indoor mall carries name-brand end-of-season goods at discounts ranging from 30% to 70%. Clothing predominates, but you can also buy footwear, luggage, books, housewares, and videos and DVDs. To get here from Abbeyleix, follow R433 west for 19 km (12 mi) to Rathdowney.

Portlaoise

❷ *14 km (9 mi) north of Abbeyleix.*

The rich farmland south and west of Portlaoise, an hour by train or car from Dublin, is one of Ireland's undiscovered gems. Even the Irish themselves talk of County Laois as one of Ireland's best-kept secrets. Golf, coarse fishing, hiking, and horseback riding are traditional sports hereabouts, and the development of the Grand Canal for recreational purposes is adding to the area's attractions. Explore the pretty villages and romantic ivy-covered ruins by car, or follow one of the many hiking trails.

Though Portlaoise itself may be best known for its high-security prison, which looms menacingly over the whole town, great efforts have been made to spruce up the area. The town center is now largely for pedestrians, and it has been greatly improved by an imposing new hotel and a lively arts center. In addition to being a good base for exploring the surrounding countryside, Portlaoise is a good place to stay to avoid the heavy traffic that can clog up the main N7 Dublin road, if you're heading for Cork or Limerick.

At the Tourist Information Office in Portlaoise you can pick up a map of the **Laois Heritage Trail**, a signposted, day-long drive on quiet, back roads that takes in 13 heritage sites; the circular trail starts in Borris-in-Ossary on N7.

The famous **Rock of Dunamase** is a knobbly mound, a dramatic 150-foot limestone outcrop with a long history serving as a fortification. It was in use as early as AD 140, and was occupied in turn by the Vikings, Normans, Irish, and English. Today it is crowned by the ruins of a 12th-century castle, once home to Dermot Mac Murrough, King of Leinster, who precipitated the Norman invasion when he invited Strongbow to Ireland to marry his daughter, whose dowry included the Rock. Some of the castle's thick walls still stand. The main reason for visiting the Rock today is to take the short walk to its summit to enjoy the view of the Slieve Bloom Mountains to the north and the Wicklow Mountains to the south. ⊠ *5 km (3 mi) east of Portlaoise on the N80 Stradbally road.*

Where to Stay & Eat

$ ✕ **Kingfisher.** The high-ceiling room was once a banking hall, but now its softly lighted walls glow with warm terra-cotta tones, the perfect complement to the spicy-but-not-too-spicy Punjabi cuisine. *Pappadams* (crunchy lentil-flour bread) and condiments appear before you order, and the friendly staff in traditional dress will guide you expertly through the long menu. Dishes vary from mild and creamy *kormas* (curried meat dishes) to fresh cod with a mild blend of spices and lemon juice to chicken "cooked with angry green chillies." People travel from miles around to dine at this lively and stylish venue in the town center. ⊠ *Old AIB Bank, Main St.* ☎ *0502/62500* ⊟ *AE, MC, V* ☉ *No lunch Sat.–Tues.*

$$–$$$$ ▥ **The Heritage.** Imagine a hotel so imposing that it does not need a street address and you're getting close to the ambitious scale of The Heritage. A six-pillar classic portico dominates the massive facade, which helped transform the town center from run-down to swanky. The best of modern Irish design—handmade rugs and specially crafted wood paneling—decorates the public rooms. The guest rooms are spacious and restful, with plain, warm-color walls and custom-made Victorian-style furniture. A shuttle service is provided to the 18-hole golf club, designed by Seve Ballesteros. ⊠ *Co. Laois* ☎ *0502/78588* ⊞ *0502/78577* ⊕ *www.theheritagehotel.com* ↵ *102 rooms with bath, 8 suites* ♨ *2 restaurants, coffee shop, in-room data ports, cable TV, golf privileges, indoor pool, health club, hot tub, massage, sauna, steam room, 3 bars, nightclub* ⊟ *AE, DC, MC, V* ❑ *BP.*

$ ▥ **Ivyleigh House.** An elegant, early Georgian town house in the center of Portlaoise (follow signs for the multistory car park), this gracious residence has been lovingly restored by hosts Dinah and Jerry Campion. Plump sofas, Regency-style striped wallpaper, crystal chandeliers, and elaborate antique mantels decorate the two sitting rooms, one of which is a TV-free zone. Luxurious drapes hang on the sash windows of the spacious bedrooms. The beds are Victorian, the sheets Irish linen, and the mattresses orthopedic. Dinah's breakfasts are legendary; try perfect porridge with cream followed by scrambled eggs with smoked salmon. Room TVs are available by request. ⊠ *Bank Pl., Co. Laois* ☎ *0502/22081* ⊞ *0502/63343* ⊕ *www.ivyleigh.com* ↵ *4 rooms with bath* ♨ *No room TVs, no kids under 8, no smoking* ⊟ *MC, V* ❑ *BP.*

Nightlife & the Arts

Also known as Turley's bar, the canalside **Anchor Inn** (⊠ Grand Canal, Vicarstown, near Stradbally ☎ 0502/25189), 10 km (6 mi) east of Portlaoise on N80, is popular for its lively Monday-night traditional-music sessions, which start around 9. Sessions take place more frequently in the summer.

The lively **Dunamaise Arts Centre** (✉ Main St. ☎ 0502/63355 ⊕ www. dunamaisetheatre.com), formerly the town jail, built into the back of the 18th-century stone courthouse, has a 238-seat theater, an art gallery, and a friendly coffee shop (open 8:30–5:30). You may catch a professional production on tour or a local amateur show. The art exhibits, usually by contemporary Irish artists, are of a high standard. It's on a corner between a multistory car park and the Heritage hotel.

Sports & the Outdoors

The **Heath Golf Club** (✉ 5 km [3 mi] northeast of Portlaoise on main Dublin road ☎ 0502/46533) is a challenging 18-hole parkland course. The Seve Ballesteros–designed **Heritage Golf & Heritage Club** (✉ Killenard ☎ 0502/ 45994), just off the main Dublin–Cork road, is an 18-hole, par-72 course.

Portarlington

▶ ❸ *13 km (8 mi) northeast of Portlaoise.*

Built on the River Barrow in the late 17th century, Portarlington was originally an English settlement. Later on, a Huguenot colony developed here; French surnames are still common in the area. Some good examples of Georgian architecture can be seen in the town. A quintessential landmark of Irish Palladian elegance lies just 7 km (4½ mi) south of Portarlington: **Emo Court and Gardens,** one of the finest large-scale country houses near Dublin open to the public. If you elect to skip over much of the Midlands, at least try to tack on a visit to Emo, especially if you're in County Kildare or Wicklow. To come upon the house from the main drive, an avenue lined with magisterial Wellingtonia trees, is to experience one of Ireland's great treasure-house views. Begun in 1790 by James Gandon, architect of the Custom House and the Four Courts in Dublin, Emo (the name derives from the Italian version of the original Irish name Imoe) is thought to be Gandon's only domestic work on as grand a scale as his Dublin civic buildings. Construction continued on and off for 70 years, as family money troubles followed the untimely death of Emo's first patron and owner, the first earl of Portarlington.

In 1996, Emo's English-born owner, Mr. Cholmeley Dering Cholmeley-Harrison, donated the house to the Irish nation. The ground-floor rooms have been beautifully restored and decorated. Among the highlights are the entrance hall, with trompe l'oeil in the apses on each side, and the library, which has a carved Italian marble mantle with putti frolicking among grapevines. But the showstopper, and one of the finest rooms in Ireland, is the domed rotunda—in fact the work of one of Gandon's successors, the Irish architect William Caldbeck—inspired by the Roman Pantheon. Marble pilasters with gilded Corinthian capitals support the rotunda's blue-and-white coffered dome. Emo's 55 acres of grounds include a 20-acre lake, lawns planted with yew trees, a small garden (the Clocker) with Japanese maples, and a larger one (the Grapery) with rare trees and shrubs. ✉ Emo ☎ 0502/26573 ⊕ *www.heritageireland.ie* ☞ *Gardens free, house €2.50* ⊙ *Gardens daily 10:30–5:30; house mid-June–mid-Sept., Tues.–Sun. 10–6 (last tour at 5:15).*

Coolbanagher Church, the familiar name for the exquisite Church of St. John the Evangelist, was, like Emo Court and Gardens, designed by James Gandon. On view inside are Gandon's original 1795 plans; there's also an elaborately sculpted 15th-century font from an earlier church that once stood nearby. Adjacent to the church is Gandon's mausoleum for

Lord Portarlington, his patron at Emo. The church is open daily spring through autumn; during other months, ask around in the tiny village for a key, or call the rectory, a 10-minute drive away. ⊠ *8½ km (5 mi) south of Portarlington on R419* ☎ *0502/24143 rectory* 🖃 *Free* ⊙ *May–Oct., daily 9–6.*

$$ 🏨 **Roundwood House.** Behind the Palladian facade of this relaxed, classically beautiful 1730s house is a simple interior with family antiques and Persian rugs. You can stay in one of the large rooms in the main house or in a smaller, cozy room in the original house, which dates from 1650 and is behind the herb garden. Just off N7 in the Slieve Bloom Mountains, the house sits amid 18 acres of woodland and is ideal for hiking. Hosts Frank and Rosemarie Kennan often share your table at dinner (for residents only), which consists of a multicourse set menu of Continental cuisine. ⊠ *Mountrath, Co. Laois* ☎ *0502/32120* 🖷 *0502/ 32711* ⇨ *10 rooms with bath* ⅏ *Dining room; no room phones, no room TVs* 🖃 *AE, DC, MC, V* ⅋⅋ *BP.*

¢ 🏨 **Eskermore House.** Though this 1745 farmhouse, on a 150-acre farm dedicated to cattle grazing and grass production, has been modernized, it still has roses over the front door and a chiming grandfather clock. Located 8 km (5 mi) north of Portarlington on R402, this is a good base for hiking in the Slieve Bloom Mountains. The guest rooms are simply but comfortably furnished and face south over a beech-tree-lined avenue and semiwild gardens; room TVs are available on request. The sitting room has an open turf fire, a piano, and cable TV. Host Ann Mooney will prepare a wholesome dinner with advance notice. ⊠ *Mount Lucas, Edenderry, Co. Offaly* ☎ *0506/53079* ⊕ *www.eskermore.com* ⇨ *3 rooms with bath* ⅏ *No room TVs* 🖃 *MC, V* ⅋⅋ *BP.*

Tullamore

❹ *27 km (17 mi) northwest of Portarlington.*

Tullamore, the county seat of Offaly, is a big country town on the Grand Canal. **Charleville Forest Castle** is a castellated, Georgian–Gothic Revival manor house on about 30 acres of woodland walks and gardens. This magnificent building dates from 1812 and is a fine example of the work of architect Francis Johnston, who was responsible for many of Dublin's stately Georgian buildings. Look for the William Morris–designed dining room with its original wallpaper. Guided tours of the interior are available. ⊠ *1½ km (1 mi) outside Tullamore on N52 to Birr* ☎ *0506/21279* 🖃 *€5* ⊙ *May, weekends 2–5; June–Sept., Wed.–Sun. 2–5; Oct.–Apr., groups of 4 or more by appointment.*

BOATING Exploring the inland waterways aboard your own boat is a leisurely way to discover the unspoiled scenery, hidden villages, and abundant wildlife of Ireland's interior. You can rent a river cruiser for a floating holiday from **Celtic Canal Cruisers Ltd.** (⊠ 24th Lock ☎ 0506/21861).

GOLF **Esker Hills Golf & Country Club** (⊠ 5 km [3 mi] north of Tullamore on N80 ☎0506/55999) is a challenging 18-hole, par-71 championship course with natural lakes and woodlands.

Kilbeggan

❺ *11 km (7 mi) north of Tullamore.*

Kilbeggan is known mainly for **Locke's Distillery,** which was established in 1757 to produce a traditional Irish malt whiskey. It closed down in

1954 and was reopened in 1987 by Cooley Distillery, which now makes its whiskey in County Louth but brings it here to be matured in casks. The distillery has been restored as a museum of industrial archaeology illustrating the process of Irish pot-whiskey distillation and the social history of the workers' lives. ☎ *0506/32134* ⊕ *www. lockesdistillerymuseum.com* ☞ *€4* ⊙ *Apr.–Oct., daily 9–6; Nov.–Mar., daily 10–4.*

Mullingar

❻ *24 km (15 mi) northeast of Kilbeggan.*

Irish farmers describe a good young cow as "beef to the ankle, like a Mullingar heifer." In this area of rich farmland, Mullingar is known as Ireland's beef capital. It's also County Westmeath's major town—a busy commercial and cattle-trading center on the Royal Canal, midway between two large, attractive lakes, Lough Owel and Lough Ennel. Buildings here date mostly from the 19th century.

Finely carved stonework decorates the front of the large, Renaissance-style Catholic **Cathedral of Christ the King,** completed in 1939. Mosaics of St. Patrick and St. Anne by the Russian artist Boris Anrep adorn the spacious interior. ⊠ *Mary St.* ☎ *044/48391* ⊙ *Daily 9–5:30.*

Mullingar Bronze and Pewter Centre offers free tours of its workshop, where the age-old craft of pewter making is still practiced. Sculptured bronze figures are also being made here—by Genesis Fine Art. You can purchase both pewter and bronze in the showroom. There's a coffee shop on the premises. ⊠ *Great Down, The Downs* ☎ *044/44948* ☞ *Free* ⊙ *Weekdays 9:30–5:30, Sat. 10–5:30.*

★ ☺ **Belvedere House Gardens** occupies a beautiful spot: the northeast shore of Lough Ennel. Access to this stately mid-18th-century hunting lodge with extensive gardens is through the servants' entrance—so you can see what life behind the scenes was like back then. Within the gardens is a Victorian glass house. The parkland beyond slopes down to the lake and provides a panoramic view of its islands. You can tour the 160 acres of the estate and woodland trails on the Belvedere tram. Also on the estate are a coffee shop, an animal sanctuary, and a children's play area. ⊠ *4 km (2½ mi) south of Mullingar on N52* ☎ *044/40861* ⊕ *www. belvedere-house.ie* ☞ *House and parkland €6, tram €1.30* ⊙ *Nov.–Mar., daily 10:30–4; Apr.–Aug., daily 10:30–7; Sept. and Oct., daily 10:30–6:30.*

Where to Stay & Eat

$–$$ ✕▦ **Crookedwood House.** This large rectory, more than 200 years old,
FodorsChoice overlooks Lough Derravaragh. There are spacious bedrooms here, but
★ the main attraction is the food ($$$–$$$$). Chef-owner Noel Kenny has earned a reputation for his German-inspired take on modern Irish cuisine. In winter, try the Hunter's Plate—a selection of venison, pheasant, wild duck, and pigeon. Also irresistible is the trio of salmon, sole, and scallops with lobster sauce. The unusual combination of honey-roasted pork steak and salmon is wrapped in phyllo pastry and baked with grapes. The house is 13 km (8 mi) north of Mullingar on the R394 Castlepollard road. ⊠ *Co. Westmeath* ☎ *044/72165* 🖶 *044/72166* ⊕ *www. crookedwoodhouse.com* ⇦ *18 rooms with bath* ☺ *Restaurant, cable TV* ▭ *AE, DC, MC, V* ⦿ *BP* ⊙ *Closed 2 wks in Nov.; no dinner Mon.*

$$$ ▦ **Temple.** The Fagan family will warmly welcome you into their superb Victorian farmhouse, surrounded by 100 acres of parkland. Modest antiques fill the large guest rooms. This is a good place to stay if you have kids, as they can enjoy watching a working sheep farm while you indulge in a luscious relaxation program. The 24-hour rate includes yoga and one hour-long spa treatment, plus the delicious, freshly prepared food from Bernadette Fagan's kitchen. Temple is along N6, almost equidistant from Mullingar, Tullamore, and Athlone. ✉ *Horseleap, Moate, Co. Westmeath* ☎ *0506/35118* 📠 *0506/35008* 🌐 *www.templespa.ie/* *8 rooms with bath* *Massage, sauna, spa, steam room, bicycles, no-smoking rooms; no room TVs* 💳 *AE, MC, V* *Closed 1 wk at Christmas* *AI.*

$$–$$$ **Bloomfield House Hotel.** A rambling two-story former convent with a castellated roof on the shores of Lough Ennel has been converted into a comfortable hotel with an excellent fitness center. The style here is cheerful—modern furniture in warm shades of plaid. The rooms are spacious, and all have peaceful country views. The Brinsley Restaurant has tall Georgian-style windows overlooking the lake, and serves local beef and seafood. The hotel lies 3 km (2 mi) south of Mullingar on N52. ✉ *Tullamore Rd., Co. Westmeath* ☎ *044/40894* 📠 *044/43767* 🌐 *www.bloomfieldhouse.com* *65 rooms with bath* *Restaurant, cable TV, indoor pool, gym, hot tub, sauna, steam room, bar, meeting rooms* 💳 *AE, DC, MC, V* *BP.*

Sports & the Outdoors

GOLF **Delvin Castle Golf Club** (✉ Delvin ☎ 044/64315) is a 9-hole course. **Mullingar Golf Club** (✉ Belvedere ☎ 044/48629) is an 18-hole parkland course.

HORSEBACK RIDING **Mullingar Equestrian Centre** (✉ Athlone Rd. ☎ 044/48331) has riding on the shores of Lough Derravaragh and lessons at all levels. The center also organizes residential riding holidays.

Castlepollard

❼ *21 km (13 mi) north of Mullingar.*

Castlepollard is a pretty village of multihued, 18th- and 19th-century houses laid out around a large, triangular green. **Tullynally Castle and Gardens** is the largest castle in Ireland that still functions as a family home. The total circumference of the building's masonry adds up to nearly ½ km (¼ mi)—an astonishing agglomeration of towers, turrets, and battlements that date from the first early fortified building, circa 1655, up through the mid-19th century, when additions in the Gothic Revival style went up one after another. Two wings designed by Sir Richard Morrison in 1840 that joined the main block to the stable court had dramatically different purposes: one was given over entirely to luxurious quarters for the dowager countess; the other housed 40 *indoor* servants. This was one of the first houses in the British Isles to have central heating.

The house is closed to the public, but you can roam about the lovely grounds. The rolling parkland was first laid out in 1760, much along the lines you see today, with fine rhododendrons, numerous trees, and a lake. A garden walk through the grounds in front of the castle leads to a spacious flower garden, a pond, and walled gardens. The kitchen garden here is one of the largest in Ireland, with a row of old Irish yew trees. Don't miss the forest path, which takes you around the perimeter of the parkland and affords excellent views back to the romantic castle.

Tullynally—the name, literally translated, means "Hill of the Swans"—has been the home of 10 generations of the literary Pakenham family and the seat of the earls of Longford. Among the living Pakenhams are the historical biographer Antonia Fraser, wife of the playwright Harold Pinter, and her brother Thomas, a historian and lover of trees. He is the current earl, following the death of his father, a well-known prison reformer, in 2002, but does not use the title. ✉ *1½ km (1 mi) west of Castle-*

*pollard on the R395 road to Granard ☎ 044/61159 ⊕ www.
tullynallycastle.com ✉ €5 ☉ May–Aug., daily 2–6.*

Fore

❽ *5 km (3 mi) east of Castlepollard.*

Irish myth permeates this village known for its "seven wonders"; it's
worth a fun walk to discover "the water that runs uphill" or "the stone
raised by St. Fechin." The monk founded a monastery here, in the 7th
century, and the village is now known not only for its legend, but also
for its medieval church and the remains (supposedly the largest in Ireland) of a Benedictine abbey. The remains of **Fore Abbey** dominate the
simple village. St. Fechin's Church, dating from the 10th century, has a
massive, cross-inscribed lintel stone. Nearby are the remains of a 13th-
century Benedictine abbey, whose imposing square towers and loophole
windows resemble a castle rather than an abbey.

THE NORTHERN MIDLANDS

This section starts in Longford and works its way north, leaving the ancient kingdom of Leinster for Ulster's two most southerly counties,
Cavan and Monaghan. (Ulster's other counties now constitute Northern Ireland.) The land north of Cavan is characterized by small, round
hills called drumlins and is known as "drumlin country."

Longford

❾ *37 km (23 mi) west of Castlepollard, 124 km (77 mi) northwest of Dublin.*

Longford, the seat of County Longford and a typical little market-town
community, is a draw for Jane Austen fans. If Jane Austen intrigues you,
consider visiting **Carrigglas Manor.** The romantic Tudor-Gothic house,
built in 1837 by Thomas Lefroy, offers a glimpse into gracious country
living in 19th-century surroundings. Lefroy's descendants, who still live
here, note that as a young man in England he was romantically involved
with the novelist. Why they never married is a mystery, but it is believed
that Austen based the character of Mr. Darcy in *Pride and Prejudice* on
Mr. Lefroy. The house still has high-quality plasterwork and many of
its original mid-19th-century furnishings. A magnificent stable yard, part
of an earlier house on the site, was designed in 1790 by James Gandon,
architect of Dublin's Custom House and Four Courts. Go into the stable yard and gardens to enter the small costume museum, which displays mostly 18th-century apparel found in the house. There's also an
outdoor tea room in the plush period gardens. ⊠ *5 km (3 mi) northeast of Longford on the R194 road to Granard ☎ 043/45165 ⊕ www.
carrigglas.com ✉ Stable yard, gallery, and shop free; gardens and museum €6 ☉ Stable yard, gardens, and museum daily 11–3; house, by
appointment only, May–Sept., Mon., Tues., Fri., and Sat. 2–6.*

Cavan

❿ *53 km (33 mi) northeast of Longford, 114 km (71 mi) northwest of
Dublin.*

A small, quiet, undistinguished town serving the local farming community,
Cavan is also, increasingly, known for its crystal factory. There are two
central streets. With its pubs and shops, Main Street is like many other
streets in similar Irish towns. Farnham Street has Georgian houses,
churches, and a courthouse. **Cavan Crystal** is an up-and-coming rival to
Waterford in the cut-lead-crystal line; the company offers guided fac-

tory tours and access to its factory shop. This is a good opportunity to watch skilled craftspeople at work if you can't make it to Waterford. A major building attached to the factory houses a visitor center, glass museum, restaurant, and coffee shop. ☒ *Dublin Rd.* ☎ *049/433–1800* ⊕ *www.cavancrystaldesign.com* ☒ *Free* ☉ *Guided tours weekdays at 9:30, 10:30, and 11:30.*

off the beaten path

KILLYKEEN FOREST PARK – This park is part of the beautiful, mazelike network of lakes called Lough Oughter. Within the park's 600 acres are a number of signposted walks and nature trails, stables offering horseback riding, and boats and bicycles for rent. Twenty-eight fully outfitted two- and three-bedroom cottages are available for weeklong, weekend, or midweek stays; everything is provided except towels. Rates vary according to the season; call for details. ☒ *11 km (7 mi) north of Cavan* ☎ *049/433–2541* ⊕ *www.coillte.ie* ☒ *Free, parking €1.90* ☉ *Feb.–Dec., daily 9–5.*

Where to Stay & Eat

★ **$$$–$$$$** ✕☒ **Slieve Russell Hotel and Country Club.** The fitness facilities are outstanding, and many people stay for the golfing and the excellent freshwater and trout fishing at this palatial modern country hotel on 300 acres. The luxurious bedrooms have chunky, art deco–style furniture. White linens and wrought-iron chandeliers decorate the formal Conall Cearnach restaurant, where the extensive menu includes traditionally prepared seafood dishes such as black sole on the bone or salmon hollandaise. The Brackley Buttery restaurant ($$–$$$$) is more informal. The hotel, which is 26 km (16 mi) west of Cavan, is a convenient place to break a journey between Dublin and Sligo. ☒ *Ballyconnell, Co. Cavan* ☎ *049/952–6444* ☒ *049/952–6474* ⊕ *www.quinn-group.com* ⇆ *141 rooms with bath, 10 suites* ♨ *2 restaurants, in-room data ports, cable TV, 9- and 18-hole golf courses, 4 tennis courts, 2 indoor pools, health club, hot tub, sauna, fishing, horseback riding, Ping-Pong, squash, 2 bars, meeting rooms* ☰ *AE, DC, MC, V* ¶⊙¶ *BP.*

$–$$$ ✕☒ **Cabra Castle.** With its crenellations and Gothic windows, this enormous gray-stone castle could have been designed in Hollywood. In fact, it was built in 1699 as the centerpiece of a 1,000-acre estate, most of which now belongs to the Dun a Ri National Park. For the full effect, ask for a "castle room," furnished with especially elaborate Victorian antiques. The Victorian-Gothic theme is carried through in the bar and the restaurant (fixed-price Continental menu) with varying degrees of success. Don't miss the castle gallery, which has hand-painted ceilings and leaded-glass windows. ☒ *Kingscourt, 65 km (40 mi) south of Cavan, Co. Cavan* ☎ *042/966–7030* ☒ *042/966–7039* ⊕ *www.cabracastle.com* ⇆ *29 rooms with bath* ♨ *Restaurant, cable TV, 9-hole golf course, fishing, horseback riding, bar, meeting rooms* ☰ *AE, MC, V* ¶⊙¶ *BP.*

¢ ✕☒ **MacNean House & Bistro.** Food lovers seeking the inspired Continental cuisine of Neven Maguire make pilgrimages to this simple guest house and bistro ($$–$$$) tucked away on the Cavan–Fermanagh border. Among the seafood and game dishes are steamed turbot with spinach in a basil-butter sauce, and saddle of hare stuffed with chicken and pesto mousse on a parsnip purée with rosemary jus. Desserts are Neven's specialty—try the hazelnut nougat glacé. Given the remoteness of Blacklion, you might want to book a room when reserving a table. The 65-km (40-mi) detour makes sense if you are heading from Dublin northwest to Sligo or Donegal. ☒ *Blacklion, Co. Cavan* ☎ *072/53022* ☒ *072/53404* ⇆ *5 rooms with bath* ♨ *Restaurant* ☰ *MC, V* ¶⊙¶ *BP.*

Sports & the Outdoors

Visitors are welcome at the 18-hole **County Cavan Golf Club** (⊠ Arnmore House ☎ 049/433–1283). There are two golf courses at the **Slieve Russell Hotel** (⊠ Ballyconnell ☎ 049/952–6444), a 9-hole parkland course and an 18-hole championship course.

Cootehill

⑪ *26 km (16 mi) northeast of Cavan.*

One of the most underestimated small towns in Ireland, Cootehill commands a lovely outpost on a wooded hillside in the heart of County Cavan. Its wide streets, with intriguing old shops, are always busy without being congested. Most who come here are anglers from Europe, the United Kingdom, and the rest of Ireland.

Only pedestrians are allowed through the gates of Bellamont Forest. After about a mile of woodlands, a trail leads to the exquisite, hilltop **Bellamont House,** designed in 1728 by Edward Lovett Pearce, architect of Dublin's Bank of Ireland. Small but perfectly proportioned, it has remained virtually unaltered since it was built and is considered one of Ireland's finest Palladian-style houses. It's now a private home—but is occasionally opened to the public. If you're interested, inquire locally or at the Tourist Information Office (TIO) in Cavan. Walk up the main street of Cootehill to "the top of the town" (past the White Horse hotel), and you'll see the entrance to the forest.

Where to Stay & Eat

$ ✕ **The White Horse.** This typical market-town hotel serves as a lively gathering place for the community, and is particularly popular with visiting anglers. Some rooms in the rambling Victorian building are a bit small; all are plainly decorated. The quieter rooms are in the back. The restaurant ($–$$$), a softly lighted room with mahogany furniture, is popular with locals, who head here for generous portions and simply cooked Irish dishes. ⊠ *Market St., Co. Cavan* ☎ *049/555–2124* 🖶 *049/555–2407* 🛏 *30 rooms, 24 with bath* ♦ *Restaurant, 2 bars* ▤ *MC, V* ⦿ *BP.*

¢ **Riverside House.** Both serious anglers and nonsporting types appreciate the genuine, old-fashioned Irish hospitality at Joe and Una Smith's farm. Their substantial Victorian house on 100 acres overlooks the River Annalee. All rooms have peaceful views and are individually decorated with modest antiques and family hand-me-downs. Dinner can be served by arrangement. Bring your boots if you want to explore around this working dairy farm. The lodging is signposted 1 km (½ mi) outside town off R188. ⊠ *Co. Cavan* ☎ *049/555–2150* 🖶 *049/555–2150* ⊕ *www.irishfarmholidays.com* 🛏 *6 rooms, 5 with bath* ♦ *Dining room, boating, fishing; no room phones* ▤ *MC* ⦿ *BP.*

Monaghan

⑫ *24 km (15 mi) north of Cootehill.*

This former British garrison town is built around a central square known as the Diamond. On the square, the town's old **Market House,** elegantly constructed of limestone in 1792, is now the tourist office. The **County Museum** traces the history of Monaghan from earliest times to the present through archaeological finds, traditional crafts, artwork, and other historical artifacts. ⊠ *Hill St., Co. Monaghan* ☎ *047/82928* ⊕ *www.monaghan.ie* ⊘ *June–Sept., Tues.–Sat. 11–5; Oct.–May, Tues.–Sat. 11–1 and 2–5.*

THE GREAT HUNGER

N HIS EPIC POEM The Great Hunger, generally regarded as one of the masterpieces of Irish literature, poet Patrick Kavanagh (1904–67) summed up his native Monaghan as a place whose peasant populace remained "locked in a stable with pigs and cows forever." The intellectual and sexual paralysis reflected in the work is undoubtedly a thing of the past, but the unremitting barrenness of Kavanagh's vision is still evident in the county's unvarying landscape. Given the acerbic nature of the poem, it's rather ironic that Kavanagh-centered tourism is big business in the region. Kavanagh worked on the family farm in his youth: though closed to the public, the farmhouse, a plain building dating from 1791, is signposted off the R179 Carrickmacross road. Kavanagh's bittersweet relationship with Monaghan led to self-imposed exile in Dublin. A lover

of controversy in his lifetime, Kavanagh in death remains a source of conflict and debate: in 1998, 31 years after he died, a monument at his grave in memory of his widow, Katherine, was extensively damaged and anonymously replaced by an old wooden cross and stepping stones removed from the garden of his family home at Mucker, a short distance from the village in which he was reared.

---

off the beaten path

ROSSMORE FOREST PARK – For fresh air in pleasant surroundings, head to this park with 691 acres of low hills, small lakes, and pleasant forest walks through rhododendron groves. Nature trails are signposted. The park is just outside Monaghan, on the R189 Newbliss road.

Where to Stay & Eat

$$$–$$$$
Fodor$Choice
★

✕ **Castle Leslie.** The 1870 Castle Leslie, a mix of Gothic and Italianate styles, sits on the shores of beautiful Glaslough, whose waters are mirrorlike on sunny days. The large bedrooms are decked out in Victorian splendor with original furniture, some of it dating to 1660. A four-course fixed-price dinner of Continental food is served by candlelight in the dining room, with waitresses in Victorian dress. Entrées may include braised partridge in season or salmon with sesame and ginger vinaigrette. The castle's popularity increased greatly after ex-Beatle Paul McCartney and Heather Mills married here in 2002, so reserve far ahead. ✉ Glaslough, 11 km (7 mi) northeast of Monaghan, Co. Monaghan ☎ 047/88109 ☐ 047/88256 ⊕ www.castleleslie.com ➪ 14 rooms with bath ⌂ Dining room, boating, fishing; no room phones, no room TVs, no kids, no smoking ⊟ MC, V ⊖ BP.

★ **$$$–$$$$**
✕ **Nuremore Hotel and Country Club.** This Victorian country house, now a luxury hotel, has excellent sporting facilities, including its own trout lake. Open fires blaze in the large lounge, which is furnished with plump armchairs and Victorian tables. Mahogany Victorian furniture fills the bedrooms. The formal restaurant ($$–$$$) serves a rich, luxurious French-Irish cuisine—Irish Angus beef, fresh foie gras, lobster, and classic desserts, including a pear and almond tart with fresh cream. Only 80 km (50 mi) from both Dublin and Belfast, Nuremore is a popular

CloseUp

THE CONTRIBUTION OF CLONES

Although in terms of its population Clones is a relatively unimportant Midlands town, culturally it has had an impact far beyond its size. Among the more famous citizens of the town are Barry McGuigan, former World Featherweight Boxing Champion and one of the most popular sports figures ever to emerge in Ireland; Thomas Bracken, the man who penned New Zealand's national anthem; and, currently the area's most celebrated citizen, novelist Patrick McCabe, whose novels perfectly

capture the vaguely time-locked quality of life in the town. McCabe's novel The Butcher Boy put Clones on the map internationally, particularly when Neil Jordan, Ireland's preeminent movie director, filmed the book in and around the town. As he was quoted saying, "If I ever want to quantify anything, I measure it against Clones. There is nothing you will ever encounter in life you haven't seen in some form in Clones."

weekend retreat for city dwellers. ⊠ *Carrickmacross, 32 km (20 mi) south of Monaghan on N2, Co. Monaghan* ☎ *042/966–1438* 🖷 *042/ 966–1853* ⊕ *www.nuremore-hotel.ie* ⮑ *65 rooms with bath, 5 suites* ⚘ *Restaurant, cable TV, 18-hole golf course, 2 tennis courts, indoor pool, health club, sauna, steam room, fishing, horseback riding, squash, bar, meeting rooms* ⊟ *AE, DC, MC, V* ⦿ *BP.*

Clones

⑬ *24 km (15 mi) southwest of Monaghan.*

Nowadays Clones (pronounced clo-*nez*), a small, agricultural market town 1 km (½ mi) from the Northern Ireland border, is one of two lace-making centers in County Monaghan (the other is Carrickmacross). It also has some ruins worth seeing. In early Christian times Clones was the site of a monastery founded by St. Tighearnach, who died here in AD 458. An **Augustinian abbey** replaced the monastery in the 12th century, and its remains can still be seen near the 75-foot round tower on Abbey Street. A 10th-century Celtic **high cross**, with carved panels depicting scriptural scenes, stands in Clones's central diamond. In an attempt to bring in some income in the 19th century, the wives of local rectors took up lace-making. Crochetwork and small raised dots are two hallmarks of Clones lace. A varied selection of Clones lace is on display around town and can be purchased at the **Clones Lace Centre.** ⊠ *Cara St.* ☎ *047/52125* ☉ *Mon. and Wed.–Sat. 10–6.*

> **off the beaten path**

ANNAGHMAKERRIG – This small forest park with a lake is the site of Annaghmakerrig House, home of the Shakespearian stage director Sir Tyrone Guthrie until his death in 1971. He left it to the nation as a residential center for writers, artists, and musicians. It's not officially open to the public, but if you have a special interest in the arts or in its previous owner, do ask to be shown around. You can wander through and picnic on its grounds. ⊠ *13 km (8 mi) southeast of Clones* ☎ *047/54003* ⊕ *www.tyroneguthrie.ie.*

Where to Stay

★ **$$$–$$$$** ⌂ **Hilton Park.** In addition to a stately Georgian mansion, the 500-acre grounds here include three lakes, a working sheep farm, and an organic market garden. Johnny and Lucy Madden, the friendly hosts, run their house with stylish informality. All rooms are individually decorated with antiques and have lovely views; some have four-poster beds. A dinner of home-grown fruit and vegetables, combined with local meat and fish, is available for guests only. Next door is the Clones Golf Club. To find Hilton Park, look for large black gates adorned with silver falcons 5 km (3 mi) outside Clones on the R183 Ballyhaise road. ✉ *Co. Monaghan* ☎ *047/56007* 🖷 *047/56033* ⊕ *www.hiltonpark.ie/* ⟿ *6 rooms with bath* ⚫ *Dining room, 9-hole golf course, lake, boating, fishing, croquet; no room phones, no room TVs, no kids under 8, no smoking* ⊟ *MC, V* ☽ *Closed Oct.–Mar.* ⧉⟩ *BP.*

Sports & the Outdoors

Clones Golf Club (✉ Hilton Park ☎ 047/56017) is a 9-hole course on limestone that's dry year-round.

THE WESTERN MIDLANDS

This section covers the area's western fringe, picking up in the town of Boyle in County Roscommon. It skirts Lough Key, Lough Ree, Lough Derg, and the River Shannon. Depending on how you travel south, you may journey through the hilly landscape of County Leitrim dappled with lakes and beloved of anglers for its fish-filled waters; this region is also almost uninhabited (though it has a liberal sprinkling of villages and is the home of one of Ireland's leading writers, John McGahern). Much of the land is bog. The towns are small and undistinguished, except Birr and Strokestown, both designed to complement the "big houses" that share their names. The route then takes you southward, to northern County Tipperary.

Boyle

🔟 *190 km (118 mi) northwest of Dublin.*

An old-fashioned town on the Boyle River midway between Lough Gara and Lough Key, Boyle makes a good starting point for visits to the nearby Curlew Mountains. **King House,** a massive edifice in the center of town, was built about 1730 by the local King family, who moved 50 years later to larger quarters at Rockingham in what is now Lough Key Forest Park; that house burned down in 1957. The King family originally came from Staffordshire, England, and aggressively worked to establish themselves as local nobility. Edward King, an ancestor of the Kings who settled here, drowned in the Irish Sea in 1636; he was the subject of Milton's poem "Lycidas." From 1788 to 1922 the house was owned by the British Army and used as a barracks for the Connaught Rangers, known as the fiercest regiment of the British Army (Wellington called them the "Devil's Own"). After extensive renovations, the house is now open to the public, with exhibits on the Connaught Rangers, the Kings of Connaught, and the history of the house. A coffee shop, popular with locals, serves traditional Irish breakfasts and hearty lunches, both with plenty of homemade baked goods on the menu. ☎ *079/ 63242* ⊕ *www.roscommoncoco.ie/kinghouse.htm* 🎫 *€4* ☽ *Apr.–mid-Oct., daily 10–6 (last tour at 5).*

The ruins of the **Cistercian abbey** reflect its long history. The church was founded in the late 12th century, when the Romanesque style still prevailed, but as construction went on, the then-hot Gothic style made it to Ireland, evident in arches on the north side. A 16th- to 17th-century gatehouse, through which you enter the abbey, has a small exhibition. ✉ *On N4* ☎ *079/62604* 🎫 *Free* ☽ *Apr.–Oct., daily 9:30–6:30.*

off the
beaten
path

LOUGH KEY FOREST PARK – Part of what was once the massive
Rockingham Estate, this park is now a popular base for campers,
backpackers, walkers, and anglers. It spans 840 acres on the shores of
the lake, and contains a bog garden, deer enclosure, and cypress grove.
Ruins from Rockingham days, including the remains of a stable block,
church, icehouse, and temple, are also here. Boats can be hired on the
lake, and there's also a restaurant. ⊠ *3 km (2 mi) northeast of Boyle
off N4* ☎ *079/62363* ⊠ *Parking €2.55* ⊙ *June–Sept., daily 9–dusk.*

Where to Stay

$ ⊞ **Royal Hotel.** The Royal has been at its town-center location for more
than 250 years. The chief reason to stay here, apart from good angling
nearby, is to experience the slower pace of life of an old-fashioned Irish
small town. Rooms vary in shape and size and are plainly but adequately
furnished and well equipped. The restaurant overlooks a pretty stretch
of river and serves both Chinese and Continental food. ⊠ *Bridge St.,
Co. Roscommon* ☎ *079/62016* ☎ *079/62016* ⇨ *16 rooms with bath*
⚬ *Restaurant, coffee shop, in-room data ports, cable TV, bar* ⊟ *AE,
DC, MC, V* ⚭ *BP.*

Sports & the Outdoors

Boyle is a good starting point for bicycling over the lake-dotted landscape that extends north into neighboring County Leitrim and west into
County Sligo. The 40-km (25-mi) scenic Arigna Drive from Boyle to Coote-
hall winds through unspoiled countryside on the shores of Lough Key
and Lough Arrow on narrow, quiet roads that are ideal for cycling. **Brendan Sheerin** (⊠ Main St. ☎ 079/62010) rents bicycles.

Strokestown

⑮ *28 km (17 mi) south of Boyle.*

Strokestown has the widest main street in Ireland—laid out to rival the
Ringstrasse in Vienna—and the curious, Anglo-Irish Strokestown Park
House. The town's main street leads to three Gothic arches that mark the
Fodor'sChoice entrance to the grounds of **Strokestown Park House,** occupied by the Pak-
★ enham Mahon family from 1660 to 1979. The house once sat on 27,000
acres and was the second-largest estate in County Roscommon, after the
King family's Rockingham. To some degree, the complicated architectural
history mirrors the histories of other Anglo-Irish houses. The oldest parts
of the house date from 1696; Palladian wings were added in the 1730s
to the original block; and the house was extended again in the early 19th
century. Its contents are a rich trove specific to the site, as they were never
liquidated in the auctions experienced by similar houses. The interior is
full of curiosities, such as the gallery above the kitchen, which allowed
the lady of the house to supervise domestic affairs from a safe distance.
Menus were dropped from the balcony on Monday mornings with instructions to the cook for the week's meals. The 4-acre walled pleasure
garden has the longest herbaceous border in Britain and Ireland. The **Irish
Famine Museum,** in the stable yards, documents in detail the disastrous
famine (1845–49) and the subsequent mass emigration. ☎ *078/33013*
⊕ *www.strokestownpark.ie* ⊠ *House €5; house, museum, and garden
€12* ⊙ *Apr.–Oct., daily 9:30–5:30; Nov.–Mar., groups by appointment.*

Roscommon

⑯ *19 km (12 mi) south of Strokestown.*

Sheep- and cattle-raising are the main occupations here in the capital
of County Roscommon, a pleasant little town with many solid stone

buildings, including the Bank of Ireland, in the former courthouse. The former county jail, a large stone building in the town center, has been transformed into a shopping mall—an unlikely venture that has to be seen to be believed. On the southern slopes of a hill in the lower part of town sit the remains of **Roscommon Abbey,** founded in the 12th century. In the abbey's principal ruin, a church, are eight sculpted figures that represent gallowglasses (medieval Irish professional soldiers) and stand at the base of the choir. The ruins are freely accessible. To the north of Roscommon town are the weathered remains of **Roscommon Castle,** a large Norman stronghold first built in the 13th century.

Athlone

⑰ *29 km (18 mi) southeast of Roscommon, 127 km (79 mi) west of Dublin, 121 km (75 mi) east of Limerick.*

This is the main shopping hub for the surrounding area and an important road and rail junction. The introduction of a bypass that has eased traffic congestion and a local initiative highlighting the attractions of Athlone's "Left Bank" (behind the castle), where many of the buildings date from at least 200 years ago, have combined to make Athlone a more attractive destination.

Athlone Castle, built in the 13th century, lies beside the River Shannon, at the southern end of Lough Ree. After their defeat at the Battle of the Boyne in 1691, the Irish retreated to Athlone and made the river their first line of defense. The castle, a fine example of a Norman stronghold, houses a small museum of artifacts relating to Athlone's eventful past. Admission includes access to an interpretive center depicting the siege of Athlone in 1691, the flora and fauna of the Shannon, and the life of the tenor John McCormack (1884–1945), an Athlone native and perhaps the finest lyric tenor Ireland has ever produced. ⊠ *Town Bridge* ☎ *0902/92912* ⊠ *€5* ⊙ *May–Sept., daily 10–5; Oct.–Apr. by appointment.*

Where to Stay & Eat

$$ ✕ **Le Château.** A former Presbyterian church in Athlone's colorful Old Quarter now houses this romantic restaurant. The furniture may be ecclesiastical, but the decoration strikes a nautical note appropriate to the quayside location. The raised floors of the upstairs section resemble the deck of a galleon; the church theme is present in the original windows. Candlelighted tables are set with fine old bone china. Owner-chef Stephen Linehan's menu may include medallions of veal with smoked bacon and garlic or roast peppered monkfish with fresh herb sauce. For dessert try the lemon tart or, in summer, fresh strawberry vol-au-vents with homemade ice cream. ⊠ *St. Peter's Port, The Docks* ☎ *0902/94517* ⊟ *AE, DC, MC, V* ⊙ *No lunch Mon.–Sat.*

$$$–$$$$ ✕▥ **Wineport Lodge.** Once a wooden boathouse, headquarters of FodorśChoice Lough Ree Yacht Club, this lakeside restaurant-with-rooms today ★ draws crowds for its imaginative cooking and warm welcome. The menu of new Irish cuisine changes every eight weeks, but roast organic venison served in a juniper marinade is popular year-round. Braised lamb shank with a spicy butterbean cassoulet might also appear on the menu. Bar food ($) is available from 4 to 6 PM. Ten guest rooms are in a striking, light-filled wood-and-glass building. Glasson lies 5 km (3 mi) north of town on the shores of Lough Ree. ⊠ *Glasson, Co. Westmeath* ☎ *0902/85466* ⊞ *0902/85471* ⊕ *www.wineport.ie* ↯ *10 rooms with bath* ⌂ *Restaurant, in-room data ports, fishing, bar* ⊟ *AE, DC, MC, V* ⊙▮ *BP.*

CloseUp

GOLDSMITH COUNTRY

SINCE THE EARLY 1990S, the Irish tourist board has made great efforts to promote the Northern Lakelands to the burgeoning literary tourism market as "Goldsmith Country." This is the region that gave birth to the writer Oliver Goldsmith (1730–44), celebrated for his poems and witty essays and plays. Among his most well-known works are the farcical drama She Stoops to Conquer and his classic novel The Vicar of Wakefield.

There is little to be found of Goldsmith in the area, and how much you actually get from visiting here will depend on your level of interest in the writer. Goldsmith himself left as a teenager and returned rarely, if at all. He is thought to have drawn on memories of his native Longford for his most renowned poem, "The Deserted Village." At Goldsmith's childhood home in Lissoy in County Longford, only the bare walls of the family house, a parsonage in Goldsmith's youth, remain standing. At Pallas, near Ballymahon in County Longford, his birthplace, there's a statue in his memory but little else of note.

The plot of She Stoops to Conquer involves a misunderstanding in which a traveler mistakes a private house for an inn. This actually happened to Goldsmith at Ardagh House, now a domestic science college, in the center of the village of Ardagh (just off N55) in County Longford. In the same play the character Tony Lumpkin sings a song about a pub called the Three Jolly Pigeons; today the pub of the same name, on the Ballymahon road (N55) north of Athlone, is the headquarters of the Oliver Goldsmith Summer School. Every year on the first weekend in June, leading academics from around the world speak on Goldsmith at this pub and other venues, and there are readings by the best of Ireland's contemporary poets. In the evening, there are lively traditional-music sessions in this tiny, atmospheric, traditional country pub. Call 0902/85162 for more information on the Goldsmith lectures or the pub itself.

★ $$$ ✕⊡ **Hodson Bay Hotel.** On the shores of Lough Ree, this four-story mansion—once an 18th-century family home—has its own marina and is adjacent to Athlone's golf course. All of the guest rooms are coordinated in deep pastel shades with art deco–style wooden furniture. L'Escale restaurant, a romantic, candlelighted room, overlooks the lake. The menu consists of imaginative Irish cooking with a French accent. To get to the hotel from Athlone (the hotel is 4 km [2½ mi]) outside of town), take the Athlone bypass–ring road to the N61 Roscommon road, from where the hotel is clearly signposted. ✉ *Roscommon Rd., Co. Westmeath* ☎ *0902/80500* 🖷 *0902/80520* ⊕ *www. hodsonbayhotel.com* ➯ *133 rooms with bath, 7 suites* ♨ *2 restaurants, cable TV, 18-hole golf course, 2 tennis courts, indoor pool, health club, massage, fishing, horseback riding, bar, meeting rooms* ▤ *AE, DC, MC, V* ⦿I *BP.*

Sports & the Outdoors

BICYCLING A combination of unfrequented back roads and lakeside scenery makes this attractive biking country. Rent bikes from **M. R. Hardiman** (✉ Irishtown ☎ 0902/78669).

BOATING A boat trip reveals the importance of Athlone's strategic location on the River Shannon as well as the beauty of the region. *The Viking* (✉ The Strand ☎ 0902/79277) is a riverboat that travels up the Shannon to nearby Lough Ree. The cost is €6.35; sailings take place daily from July through September at 11, 2:30, and 4.

A river cruiser for a floating holiday can be rented by the week from **Athlone Cruisers Ltd.** (✉ Jolly Mariner Marina ☎ 0902/72892).

GOLF **Athlone Golf Club** (✉ Hodson Bay ☎ 0902/92073) is a lakeside 18-hole parkland course. **Glasson Golf & Country Club** (✉ Glasson ☎ 0902/85120), an 18-hole parkland course, is bordered on three sides by Lough Ree and the River Shannon. **Mount Temple Golf Club** (✉ Campfield Lodge, Moate ☎ 0902/81545) is an 18-hole parkland course 8 km (5 mi) east of Athlone.

Clonmacnoise

❸ *20 km (12 mi) south of Athlone, 93 km (58 mi) east of Galway.*

Fodor'sChoice
★

Many ancient sites dot the River Shannon, but Clonmacnoise is early Christian Ireland's foremost monastic settlement and, like Chartres, a royal site. The monastery was founded by St. Ciaran between 543 and 549 at a location that was not as remote as it now appears to be: near the intersection of what were then two of Ireland's most vital routes—the Shannon River, running north–south, and the Eiscir Riada, running east–west. Like Glendalough, Celtic Ireland's other great monastic site, Clonmacnoise benefited from isolation; surrounded by bog, it is accessible only via one road or the Shannon.

The monastery was founded on an esker (natural gravel ridge) overlooking the Shannon and a marshy area known as the Callows, which today is protected habitat for the corncrake, a wading bird. Numerous buildings and ruins remain. The small **cathedral** dates as far back as the 10th century but has additions from the 15th century. It was the burial place of kings of Connaught and of Tara, and of Rory O'Conor, the last High King of Ireland, buried here in 1198. The two round towers include **O'Rourke's Tower,** which was struck by lightning and subsequently rebuilt in the 12th century. There are eight **smaller churches,** the littlest of which is thought to be the burial place of St. Ciaran. The only church not built within the monastery walls is Nun's Church, about 1 km (½ mi) to the east. The high crosses have been moved into the visitor center to protect them from the elements (copies stand in their original places); the best preserved of these is the Cross of the Scriptures, also known as Flann's Cross. Some of the treasures and manuscripts originating from Clonmacnoise are now housed in Dublin; most are at the National Museum, although the 12th-century *Book of the Dun Cow* is at the Royal Irish Academy Library.

Clonmacnoise survived raids by feuding Irish tribes, Vikings, and Normans for almost 1,000 years, until 1552, when the English garrison from Athlone reduced it to ruin. Since then it has remained a prestigious burial place. Among the ancient stones are many other graves of local people dating from the 17th to the mid-20th century, when a new graveyard was consecrated on adjoining land. ✉ *Near Shannonbridge* ☎ *0905/*

CloseUp

BORD NA MONA BOG RAIL TOUR

FROM A DISTANCE an Irish peat bog looks like a flat, treeless piece of waterlogged land. But a close-up view shows a much more exciting landscape. Bogs support an extraordinary amount of wildlife, including larks and snipe, pale-blue dragonflies, and Greenland white-fronted geese. Amid the pools and lakes of the peat bog, amazing jewellike wildflowers thrive, from purple bell heather to yellow bog asphodel, all alongside grasses, lichens, and mosses.

As you pass through the small town of Shannonbridge, 10 km (6 mi) south of Clonmacnoise, on either side of the road are vast stretches of chocolate-brown boglands and isolated industrial plants for processing this area's natural resource. Bord na Mona, the same government agency that makes commercial use of other boglands, has jurisdiction over the area. To take a closer look at the bog, join the **Bord na Mona Bog Rail Tour,** which leaves from Uisce Dubh. A small, green-and-yellow diesel locomotive pulls one coach across the bog while the driver provides commentary on a landscape unchanged for millennia. There are more than 1,200 km (745 mi) of narrow-gauge bog railway, and the section on the tour, known as the Clonmacnoise and South Offaly Railway, is the only part accessible to the public. ⊠ Uisce Dubh, near Shannonbridge ☎ 0905/74114 ⊕ www.bnm.ie ☎ €5.50 ⊙ Tour Apr.–Oct., daily on the hr 10–5.

74195 ⊕ *www.heritageireland.ie* ☎ *€4.40* ⊙ *Mid-June–Sept., daily 9–7; Oct.–May, daily 10–6 or dusk.*

Banagher

⑲ *31 km (19 mi) south of Clonmacnoise.*

A small but lively village on the shores of the River Shannon, Banagher has a marina that makes the town a popular base for water-sports fans. Anthony Trollope (1815–82), who came to Ireland as a post office surveyor in 1841, lived here while he wrote his first book, *The Macdermots of Ballycloran*. Charlotte Brontë (1816–55) spent her honeymoon here. **Flynn's** (⊠ Main St. ☎ 0509/51312), in the center of town, is worth visiting to appreciate its light and spacious Victorian-style design. The lunch menu includes generously filled sandwiches, salad platters, a roast meat of the day, and chicken, fish, or burgers with chips.

If you happen to be in Banagher on a Thursday or a Sunday in summer, consider taking a two-hour **Shannon cruise** on *The River Queen,* an enclosed launch that seats 54 passengers and has a full bar on board. *Silver Line Cruisers Ltd.* ⊠ *The Marina* ☎ *0509/51112* ☎ *€9* ⊙ *Cruises June–mid-Sept., Thurs. at 3, Sun. at 2:30 and 4:30, weather permitting.*

Birr

▶ **⑳** *12 km (7 mi) southeast of Banagher, 130 km (81 mi) west of Dublin.*

This heritage town is a quiet, sleepy place with tree-lined malls and modest Georgian houses. The settlement's roots go back to the 6th century, but it was much later, in the mid-18th century, that Birr was given its modern-day appearance, as a Georgian building boom took hold.

★ All roads in Birr lead to the gates of **Birr Castle Demesne,** a Gothic Revival castle (built around an earlier 17th-century castle that was damaged by fire in 1823) that is still the home of the earls of Rosse. It's not open to the public, but you can visit the surrounding 150 acres of gardens. The present earl and countess of Rosse continue the family tradition of making botanical expeditions for specimens of rare trees, plants, and shrubs from all over the world. The formal gardens contain the tallest (32 feet) box hedges in the world and vine-sheltered hornbeam allées. In spring, check out the wonderful display of flowering magnolias, cherries, crab apples, and naturalized narcissi; in autumn, the maples, chestnuts, and weeping beeches blaze red and gold. The grounds are laid out around a lake and along the banks of two adjacent rivers; above one of these stands the castle. The grounds also contain **Ireland's Historic Science Centre,** an exhibition on astronomy, photography, botany, and engineering housed in the stable block. The giant (72-inch) reflecting telescope, built in 1845, remained the largest in the world for the next 75 years. Allow at least two hours to see everything. ⊠ *Rosse Row* ☎ *0509/20336* ⊕ *www.birrcastleireland.com* ☑ €8 ☉ *Nov.–Mar., daily 10–4; Apr.–Oct., daily 9–6.*

Where to Stay & Eat

$–$$ ✕ **The Thatch Bar.** It's worth venturing 2 km (1 mi) south of Birr, just off the N62 Roscrea road, into this thatched country pub and restaurant, which together serve a good selection of imaginative, freshly cooked Irish food. Inexpensive meals are available at the bar at lunchtime and early evening (until 7:30), although in the evening the restaurant offers a choice of a five-course dinner menu or an à la carte menu. Local pigeon and rabbit terrines, sirloin steak with mushrooms in garlic, or roast loin of pork with a rhubarb compote might appear on the changing menu. ⊠ *Crinkle* ☎ *0509/20682* ▤ *DC, MC, V* ☉ *Closed Mon. Oct.–Apr. and Sun.–Tues. May–Sept.*

$$$$ ✕▤ **Kinnitty Castle.** Venture over to the foot of the Slieve Bloom Mountains, 16 km (10 mi) east of Birr, to this exuberant, turreted, Gothic Revival edifice, rebuilt in 1927 of ashlar granite. Everything is on a grand scale—large four-poster beds and intricately carved chairs fill the bedrooms, and heavy old beams are incorporated into the bathrooms in the old house. Accommodations in the new wing are smaller. The dining room has enormously tall windows and a dark wood floor. Typical main courses are panfried loin of lamb with its own sweetbreads or ragout of lobster, finished with sevruga caviar. ⊠ *Kinnitty, Co. Offaly* ☎ *0509/ 37318* 🖨 *0509/37284* ⊕ *www.kinnittycastle.com* ⇲ *37 rooms with bath* ⌂ *Restaurant, cable TV, tennis court, fishing, horseback riding, Ping-Pong, bar, meeting rooms* ▤ *AE, DC, MC, V* ⫧❘ *BP.*

$ ✕▤ **Dooly's.** Tucked away in a corner of Birr's central square is this 250-year-old, black-and-white coaching inn, where a log fire often burns in the Georgian-style front lobby. Floral drapes and bedspreads decorate the pastel rooms. The relaxed bar and coffee shop are busy all day; a more formal dining experience can be had in Emmet Restaurant ($–$$). The five-course table d'hôte dinner menu may include medallions of beef and onions flambéed in whiskey or fresh Corrib salmon steak poached in pink peppercorns and white wine. ⊠ *Emmet Sq., Co. Offaly* ☎ *0509/ 20032* 🖨 *0509/21332* ⊕ *www.doolyshotel.com* ⇲ *18 rooms with bath* ⌂ *Restaurant, coffee shop, cable TV, fishing, horseback riding, bar, meeting rooms* ▤ *AE, DC, MC, V* ⫧❘ *BP.*

¢ ✕▤ **The Maltings.** In a picturesque riverside spot near Birr Castle stands this beautiful cut-stone and brick malt house, a family-run accommodation. The spacious rooms have small windows, country pine furniture, and simple matching floral drapes and spreads. The cheerful, low-ceiling restaurant ($–$$) overlooks the river and serves good value in plain Irish cooking. ⊠ *Castle St., Co. Offaly* ☎☎ *0509/21345* ⇥ *13 rooms with bath* ⚲ *Restaurant* ☰ *MC, V* ⧦ *BP.*

Lough Derg

㉑ *16 km (10 mi) west of Birr on R489.*

Between Portland and Portumna the River Shannon widens into 32,000 acres of unpolluted water, known as Lough Derg, a popular center for water sports, including waterskiing, yachting, and motor cruising. Anglers flock here as well for pike and coarse fishing. Excellent woodland walks wind around the shore of the lake. (Be sure not to confuse this Lough Derg with the lake of the same name in County Donegal.) The well-signposted, scenic **Lough Derg Drive,** approximately 90 km (56 mi), encircles the lake, passing through a number of pretty waterside villages, from Portumna in the north to Killaloe in the south. **Terryglass,** on the eastern shore of Lough Derg and well signposted on R439 from Birr, is particularly popular with water-sports enthusiasts and anglers, as well as regular vacationers seeking an away-from-it-all destination; it's considered one of the prettiest villages in Ireland.

Where to Stay

⚲ $ ▦ **Kylenoe.** The Moeran family's 200-year-old stone house stands on 150 acres of farm and woodland close to Lough Derg. The farm breeds race-horses and is a natural wildlife haven. Relax in front of the log fire, explore the countryside on foot or horseback, or enjoy water sports. Rooms are spacious, with modest antique furniture and family heirlooms. Children are welcome. Virginia Moeran's breakfasts have won awards, and she also cooks dinner (for guests only), which must be booked by 2:30 PM, from fresh local produce. To get here follow the lakeside road from Terryglass in the Ballinderry direction. ⊠ *Terryglass, Nenagh, Co. Tipperary* ☎ *067/22015* ☐ *067/22275* ⇥ *4 rooms, 2 with bath* ⚲ *Dining room, some pets allowed; no room phones, no smoking* ☰ *MC, V* ⧦ *BP.*

Sports & the Outdoors

BOATING **Shannon Sailing** (⊠ New Marina Complex, Dromineer ☎ 067/24499) organizes cruises of scenic Lough Derg by water bus and also hires out cruisers and sailboards.

GOLF Discerning golfers love the 18-hole parkland course at **Birr Golf Club** (⊠ The Glens ☎ 0509/20082).

HIKING Birr is in the heart of an excellent hiking area. The Offaly Way and the Grand Canal Way are marked trails to the north of town; to the east is the 50-km (31-mi) Slieve Bloom Trail, a circular route that winds through some infrequently visited areas with spectacular views and rich plant and wildlife. Pick up brochures and maps locally, or consult the expert, **Christine Byrne** (⊠ Ardmore House, Kinnitty ☎ 0509/37009 ⊕ www.kinnitty.net), who organizes guided walks for all levels.

Roscrea

㉒ *19 km (12 mi) south of Birr.*

The main Dublin–Limerick road (N7) passes through Roscrea, a charming town steeped in religious history, cutting right through a 7th-century monastery founded by St. Cronan. It also passes the west facade of a 12th-century Romanesque church that now forms an entrance gate to a modern Catholic church. Above the structure's round-headed doorway is a hood molding enclosing the figure of a bishop, probably St. Cronan.

Damer House is a superb example of an early 18th-century town house on the grand scale. It was built in 1725 within the curtain walls of a Norman castle, at a time when homes were often constructed beside or attached to the strongholds they replaced. The house has a plain, symmetrical facade and a magnificent carved-pine staircase inside; on display are exhibits of local historical interest. The 13th-century stone castle is surrounded by a moat and consists of a gate tower, curtain walls, and two corner towers. To get here, start with your back to St. Cronan's monastery, turn left, and then right onto Castle Street. ⊠ *Castle St.* ☎ *0505/21850* ⊕ *www.heritageireland.ie* ☞ *€3.10* ☉ *May–Sept., daily 9:30–6; Oct.–Apr., weekends 10–5.*

Sports & the Outdoors

Three marked trails—measuring 9 km (5½ mi), 3 km (2 mi), and 1½ km (1 mi)—run through the 450-acre, organic **Fairymount Farm** (⊠ Ballingarry ☎ 067/2139 ⊕ www.fairymountfarm.com), with woodlands, horses, and sheep. Points of interest are explained in a booklet you can pick up here. The trails can also be followed on horseback (they'll help you arrange this), and you can fish for pike or perch in the farm's 25-acre lake. Access to the farm costs €5.

Nenagh

㉓ *35 km (22 mi) west of Roscrea, 35 km (22 mi) east of Limerick.*

Originally a Norman settlement, Nenagh grew into a market town in the 19th century. Standing right in the center of Nenagh, the **Castle Keep** is all that remains of the original town. Once one of five round towers linked by a curtain wall, and measuring 53 feet across the base, it rises to 100 feet, with 19th-century castellations at the top. The gatehouse and governor's house of Nenagh's old county jail now form the **Nenagh Heritage Centre,** which has permanent displays of rural life before mechanization, as well as temporary painting and photography exhibits. ⊠ *Kickham St.* ☎ *067/44587* ☞ *€3* ☉ *Easter–Oct., weekdays 9:30–5, Sun. 2:30–5; Nov.–Easter, weekdays 9:30–5.*

Where to Stay & Eat

$ ✕ **Country Choice.** Food lovers from all over Ireland seek out this well-stocked delicatessen or come to sample the home-cooked fare in the simple coffee shop at the back of the store. Owner Peter Ward is known as one of the best suppliers of Irish farmhouse cheese, and locally made cheese features on the menus of his wife, Mary. Specialties include a soup of broccoli and Cashel Blue (an Irish blue cheese), as well as slow-cooked meat dishes like lamb ragout or beef in Guinness casserole. Home-baked bread and pastries are made with local flour. ⊠ *25 Kenyon St.* ☎ *067/32596* ▤ *No credit cards* ☉ *Closed Sun. No dinner.*

$$ ✕▦ **Waterman's Lodge.** Escape to this lovely lodge, an ideal rural retreat perched on a hilltop with bay windows overlooking the Shannon and distant County Clare. Open fires, piles of books, high ceilings, and timber floors create a relaxing country-house mood. Rooms have brass or cast-iron beds and modest antiques. The Courtyard Restaurant is renowned for its imaginative treatment of seasonal local produce. Try the roast rack of lamb with a parsley crust and lamb jus. ⊠ *Ballina, Killaloe, 26 km (16 mi) north of Nenagh, Co. Clare* ☎ *061/376–333* ▤ *061/375–445* ⊕ *www.watermanslodge.ie* ⇲ *10 rooms with bath* ⚐ *Restaurant, in-room data ports, fishing, horseback riding* ▤ *AE, DC, MC, V* ☉ *Closed Christmas wk* ⦿ *BP.*

$ ▦ **Ashley Park House.** Experience informal country-house living in Margaret and P. J. Mounsey's 18th-century fishing lodge overlooking Lough Ourna. The large bedrooms have high ceilings, country views, and lots of antiques. Formal gardens and 76 acres of beech woodland surround the house, and from a rowboat on the lake you can observe abundant wildlife—herons, swans, dabchicks, moorhens, and tufted ducks and mallards nesting in reed banks. Dinners created from fresh local produce may include the trout you'll hopefully catch in the lake. ⊠ *Ardcroney, Co. Tipperary* 🕿🕿 *067/38223* ⌁ *5 rooms with bath* ⚓ *Boating, fishing; no room phones, no TV in some rooms* ⊟ *No credit cards* ⭤ *BP.*

THE MIDLANDS A TO Z

· *To research prices, get advice from other travelers, and book travel arrangements, visit www.fodors.com.*

AIRPORTS
Dublin Airport is the principal international airport that serves the Midlands; car-rental facilities are available here. Sligo Airport has daily flights from Dublin on Aer Lingus.

🛈 Airport Information **Aer Lingus** 🕿 01/844-4747. **Dublin Airport** 🕿 01/844-4900. **Sligo Airport** 🕿 071/68280.

BUS TRAVEL
Bus Éireann runs an express bus from Dublin to Mullingar in 1½ hours, with a round-trip fare of €12.05. Buses depart three times daily. A regular-speed bus, leaving twice daily, makes the trip in two hours. The express buses also make stops at Longford (2¼ hours), Carrick-on-Shannon (3 hours), Boyle (3¼ hours), and Sligo (4¼ hours). There's also a daily bus from Mullingar to Athlone and an express service connecting Galway, Athlone, Longford, Cavan, Clones, Monaghan, and Sligo. Details of all bus services are available from the Bus Éireann depots listed below.

🛈 Bus Information **Athlone Railway Station** 🕿 0902/72651. **Bus Éireann** 🕿 01/836-6111 in Dublin ⊕ www.buseireann.ie. **Cavan Bus Office** 🕿 049/433-1353. **Longford Railway Station** 🕿 043/45208. **Monaghan Bus Office** 🕿 047/82377. **Sligo Railway Station** 🕿 071/69888.

CAR RENTAL
🛈 Agencies **Gerry Mullin** ⊠ North Rd., Monaghan 🕿 047/81396. **Hamill's Rent-a-Car** ⊠ Dublin Rd., Mullingar 🕿 044/44500. **O'Reilly & Sons/Euromobil** ⊠ Dublin Rd., Longford 🕿 043/46496.

CAR TRAVEL
A car is necessary to really explore the region. Mullingar, Longford, and Boyle are on the main N4 route between Dublin and Sligo. It takes one hour to drive the 55 km (34 mi) from Dublin to Mullingar and two hours from Mullingar to Sligo (150 km [93 mi]). To get from Mullingar to southwestern Ireland, you can take N52 to Nenagh, where it meets N7, and follow that into Limerick. R390 from Mullingar leads you west to Athlone, where it connects with N6 to Galway. The 120-km (75-mi) drive takes about 2½ hours.

If you're driving in the north of Counties Cavan and Monaghan, be sure to avoid "unapproved" roads crossing the border into Northern Ireland. The approved routes into Northern Ireland connect the towns of Monaghan and Aughnacloy, Castlefinn and Castlederg, Swalinbar and Enniskillen, Clones and Newtownbutler, and Monaghan and Rosslea. If you're driving a rental car, make sure it has been cleared for cross-border journeys.

ROAD
CONDITIONS
Most of the winding roads in the Midlands are uncongested, although you may encounter an occasional animal or agricultural machine crossing the road. In Mullingar, the cattle-trading town, roads can become badly crowded, however.

EMERGENCIES

The general emergency number in the area is 999. For medical service, contact the General Hospital in Mullingar.

🔁 Emergency services **Ambulance, fire, police** ☎ 999. **General Hospital** ✉ Mullingar ☎ 044/40221.

🔁 Pharmacy **Weir's Chemist** ✉ Market Sq., Mullingar ☎ 044/48462.

TRAIN TRAVEL

A direct-rail service links Mullingar to Dublin (Connolly Station), with three trains every day making the 1½-hour journey. It costs €13 one-way and €18.50 round-trip. Contact Irish Rail for information. Trains from Mullingar, departing twice daily weekdays and Sunday, stop at Longford (35 minutes), Carrick-on-Shannon (1 hour), Boyle (1¼ hours), and Sligo (2 hours).

🔁 Train Information **Irish Rail** ☎ 01/836-6222 🌐 www.irishrail.ie.

VISITOR INFORMATION

Five Midlands Tourist Information Offices (TIOs) are open all year: Carrick-on-Shannon, Cavan, Monaghan, Mullingar, and Portlaoise. The Mullingar TIO has information on Counties Westmeath, Offaly, Monaghan, Cavan, and Laois.

Another six Midlands TIOs are open seasonally: Athlone (April–October), Birr (May–September), Clonmacnoise (April–October), Longford (June–September), Tipperary (May–October), and Tullamore (mid-June–mid-September). For inquiries about Boyle and Roscommon, consult the Sligo TIO. For off-season inquiries about Tipperary, contact the Waterford City TIO.

🔁 Tourist Information **Athlone** ✉ Church St., Co. Westmeath ☎ 0902/94630. **Birr** ✉ Rosse Row, Co. Offaly ☎ 0509/20110. **Carrick-on-Shannon** ✉ The Marina, Co. Leitrim ☎ 078/20170. **Cavan** ✉ Farnham St., Co. Cavan ☎ 049/433-1942 🌐 www.irelandnorthwest.travel.ie. **Clonmacnoise** ✉ near Clonmacnoise ruins, Co. Offaly ☎ 0905/74134. **Longford** ✉ Main St., Co. Longford ☎ 043/46566. **Monaghan** ✉ Market House, Co. Monaghan ☎ 047/81122 🌐 www.irelandnorthwest.travel.ie. **Mullingar** ✉ Dublin Rd., Co. Westmeath ☎ 044/48650 🖶 044/40413 🌐 www.ecoast-midlands.travel.ie. **Portlaoise** ✉ James Fintan Lawlor Ave., Co. Laois ☎ 0502/63989 🌐 www.laoistourism.ie. **Sligo Town TIO** ✉ Temple and Charles Sts., Co. Sligo ☎ 071/61201 🌐 www.irelandnorthwest.ie. **Tipperary** ✉ Excel Centre, Co. Tipperary ☎ 062/51451. **Tullamore** ✉ Bury Quay, Co. Offaly ☎ 0506/52617. **Waterford City TIO** ✉ 41 The Quay, Co. Waterford ☎ 051/875823 🌐 www.southeastireland.com.

THE SOUTHEAST

4

FODOR'S CHOICE

Ballyhack, *Waterford village*

Dunbrody Country House, *New Ross inn*

Jerpoint Abbey, *Thomastown*

Kilmore Quay, *Wexford village*

Mount Juliet, *Thomastown inn*

O'Gradys Restaurant, *Waterford City*

Rock of Cashel, *monastic ruins*

Waterford Treasures, *Waterford City museum*

Wine Vault, *Waterford City restaurant*

HIGHLY RECOMMENDED

RESTAURANTS   Chez Hans, *Cashel*

Dwyers of Mary Street, *Waterford City*

HOTELS   Ballyduff House, *Thomastown*

Butler House, *Kilkenny City*

Hanora's Cottage, *Ballymacarbry*

Kelly's, *Rosslare*

Waterside, *Graiguenamanagh*

SIGHTS   Irish National Heritage Park, *Ferrycarrig*

Kilkenny Castle, *Kilkenny City*

Kilmore Quay Maritime Museum, *Kilmore Quay*

Lismore Castle, *Lismore*

Round tower, *Ardmore*

SHOPPING   Nicholas Mosse Pottery, *Kilkenny City*

Updated by
Muriel Bolger
and Naomi
Coleman

THE IRISH LIKE TO PUT LABELS ON AREAS, and "Ireland's Sunny Southeast" is the tag they've taken to calling Counties Wexford, Carlow, Kilkenny, Tipperary, and Waterford. The moniker is by no means merely fanciful: the weather station on the coast at Rosslare reports that this region receives more hours of sunshine than anywhere else in the country. The southeast has the driest weather in Ireland, with as little as 40 inches of rainfall per year—compared to an average of 80 inches on parts of the west coast. This is saying something in a country where seldom do more than three days pass without a shower of rain, which can vary from the finest light drizzle (a soft day, thank goodness!) to a downpour. Little wonder the outdoors-loving Irish have made the southeast's coast a popular vacation area. The whole area is rich with natural beauty: not the rugged and wild wonders found to the north and west, but an inland landscape of fertile river valleys and lush, undulating pastureland, with a coast that alternates between long, sandy beaches and rocky bays backed by low cliffs. Although the region is blessed with idyllic country sights and small and charming fishing villages, you'll find you never have to travel that far to find the bright lights—the cities of Kilkenny, Waterford, and Wexford.

The landscape of the region is diverse, the appeal universal: white-sand beaches and fishing villages with thatched cottages along the coast, Kilkenny's Georgian cobbled streets and Tudor stone houses, Tipperary's verdant, picturesque Golden Vale. Anglers appreciate the variety of fishing and scenery along the Rivers Barrow, Nore, and Suir, and especially in the Blackwater Valley area. There are plenty of intrinsically Irish things to offer here as well—including Waterford's famed handcut crystal. The region doesn't lack for culture, either: fans flock to Wexford for the renowned Opera Festival, which draws top talent from around the world.

The southeast's coastal and inland areas both have a long, interesting history. The kings of Munster had their ceremonial center on the Rock of Cashel, a vast, cathedral-topped rock rising above the plain. Legend has it that St. Patrick converted the High King of Ireland to Christianity here. In the 7th century Cashel became an important monastic settlement and bishopric, and there were other thriving early Christian monasteries at Kilkenny, Ardmore, and Lismore. But the quiet life of early Christian Ireland was disrupted from the 9th century onward by a series of Viking invasions. The Vikings liked what they found here—a pleasant climate; rich, easily cultivated land; and a series of safe, sheltered harbors—so they stayed and founded the towns of Wexford and Waterford. (Waterford's name comes from the Norse Vadrefjord, Wexford's from Waesfjord.) Less than two centuries later, the same cities were conquered by Anglo-Norman barons and turned into walled strongholds. The Anglo-Normans and the Irish chieftains soon started to intermarry, but the process of integration came to a halt in 1366 with the Statutes of Kilkenny, based on English fears that if such intermingling continued they would lose whatever control over Ireland they had. The next great crisis was Oliver Cromwell's Irish campaign of 1650, which, in attempting to crush Catholic opposition to the English parliament, brought widespread woe.

History-rich Carlow Town, the cities of Kilkenny and Waterford, and Wexford Town have retained traces of their successive waves of invaders—Celt, Viking, and Norman. The most beautiful is Kilkenny City, an important ecclesiastic and political center up to the 17th century and now a lively market town. Its streets still hold remnants from medieval times, most notably St. Canice's Cathedral and a magnificent 12th-century castle that received a sumptuous Victorian makeover. Wexford's narrow streets are built on one side of a wide estuary, and it has a delightful maritime air. Waterford, although less immediately attractive than Wexford, is also built on the confluence of two of the region's rivers, the Suir and the Barrow. It offers a rich selection of Viking and Norman remains, some attractive Georgian buildings, and the world-renowned Waterford Glass Factory, which is open to visitors.

Deeper into the countryside rustic charms beckon. The road between Rosslare and Ballyhack passes through quiet, atypical, flat countryside dotted with thatched cottages. Beyond Tramore, level, sandy beaches give way to rocky Helvick Head and the foothills of the Knockmealdown Mountains at Dungarvan. Among the inland riverside towns, Carrick-on-Suir and Clonmel each have a quiet charm worth exploring. In the far southwest of County Waterford, near the Cork border, Ardmore presents early Christian remains on an exposed headland, while in the wooded splendor of the Blackwater Valley, the tiny cathedral town of Lismore has a hauntingly beautiful fairy-tale castle.

Exploring the Southeast

The southeast is geographically a large region, stretching from the town of Carlow near the border of County Wicklow in the north to Ardmore near the border of County Cork in the south. A car is essential for getting around here, but apart from June, July, and August, when the Irish head here for their own vacations, the region is relatively free of traffic, making it ideal for leisurely exploration. Wexford, Waterford, and Kilkenny all have compact town centers best explored on foot, and they also make good touring bases.

About the Restaurants

This region of Ireland holds some real dining treasures, often in the smallest and most informal places. Seafood—especially Wexford mussels, crab, and locally caught salmon—appears on most menus, along with local lamb, beef, and game in season. Food is usually prepared in a simple, country-house style, but be ready for some pleasant surprises, as there are a number of ambitious Irish chefs at work in the area in both restaurants and hotels.

About the Hotels

The coast is popular with Irish families during July and August, so if you are planning to come then, it is advisable to book in advance, especially at places right on the water.

WHAT IT COSTS In Euros				
$$$$	$$$	$$	$	¢
RESTAURANTS over €29	€22–€29	€15–€22	€8–€15	under €8
HOTELS over €230	€180–€230	€130–€180	€80–€130	under €80

Restaurant prices are per person for a main course at dinner. Hotel prices are for two people in a double room, including VAT and a service charge (often applied in larger hotels).

Timing

Off-season is a good time to visit the southeast. Most restaurants and accommodations stay open between November and March, months when many places in the more touristy western regions are closed. Avoid late December through at least mid-January, though, when many restaurateurs take their own holidays and some lodgings and restaurants refurbish for the following season. Drier weather in the southeast also makes

Numbers in the text corresp...
east, Kilkenny City, Wexfor...

If you have
3 days

Start by taking the main Cor... popular seaside resort and cl... **Ardmore** 41 . Stop in **Dungar**... to tour the gardens of the Duk... more drive north along the Ve... castle at ⊞ **Cahir** 43. On the ... ing the Rock of Cashel, in the ... . Drive via Urlingford on the main N8 to **Kilkenny City** 4–10, where you can wander the time-hallowed streets. Head to **Leighlinbridge** 2 for a salmon steak at the Lord Bagenal Inn, then down to the riverside village of ⊞ **Graigue-namanagh** 12 and its Duiske Abbey. On the following morning head for the coast again and have a look at **Wexford Town** 15–22. Drive on through the waterside villages of **Kilmore Quay** 24 and **Ballyhack** 25 and cross by car ferry to ⊞ **Waterford City** 26–36.

If you have
5 days

Start in the north of the region, approaching it through **Carlow Town** 1 ▶. Cross the River Barrow at **Leighlinbridge** 2 and drive down to **Graigue-namanagh** 12, a hilly riverside village with an abbey. Continue on through **Thomastown** 11, a stone-built village on the River Nore, to ⊞ **Kilkenny City** 4–10. Next morning you can explore the medieval city center with its castle and cathedral on foot. Drive on through Urlingford to the Rock of Cashel in **Cashel** 45. If you continue to ⊞ **Cahir** 43 at the foot of the Galtee Mountains, you can visit a Norman castle.

The next day drive up through the scenic Vee Gap and detour to visit Mount Melleray Abbey. Continue to **Lismore** 42, which has one of Ireland's prettiest castles. Then head for the coast and the main road south, which leads to **Ardmore** 41, where the early Christians built a cliff-top monastery. You can spend the night either in ⊞ **Dungarvan** 39—a cheerful little fishing town—or inland among the sparsely populated Knockmealdown Mountains in the ⊞ **Nire Valley** 40. The next day drive through the pretty market town **Clonmel** 46, and follow the River Suir through **Carrick-on-Suir** 47 to the port of **Waterford City** 26–36. If you follow the River Nore north, you will reach **New Ross** 13, a busy river port; signposts from here mark the way to the John F. Kennedy Arboretum, which is near the cottage at Dunganstown where the president's great-grandfather was born. Then you can pick up the main road to ⊞ **Wexford Town** 15–22.

On the next day, if you are heading north, take the N11 Dublin road via **Enniscorthy** 14, a historic town dominated by a Norman castle. If you are heading south with time to spare, take the small coastal road through **Kilmore Quay** 24, past thatched cottages and narrow lanes, to **Ballyhack** 25, where you can take a car ferry across the harbor back to Waterford and the road south.

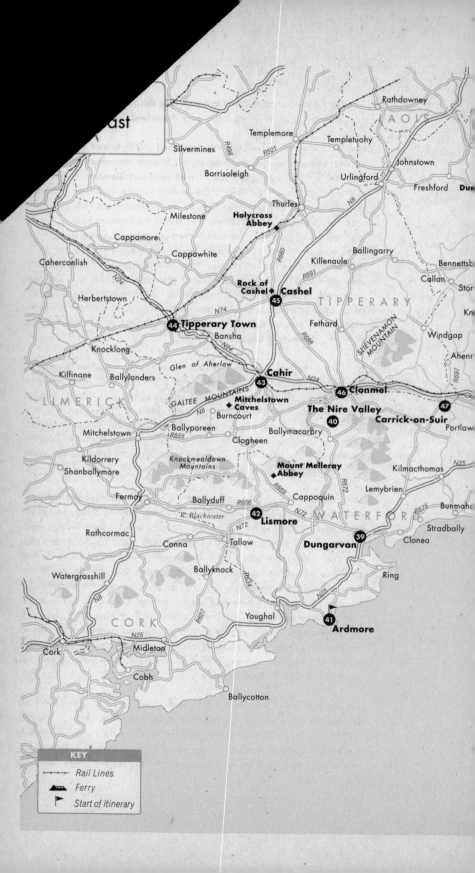

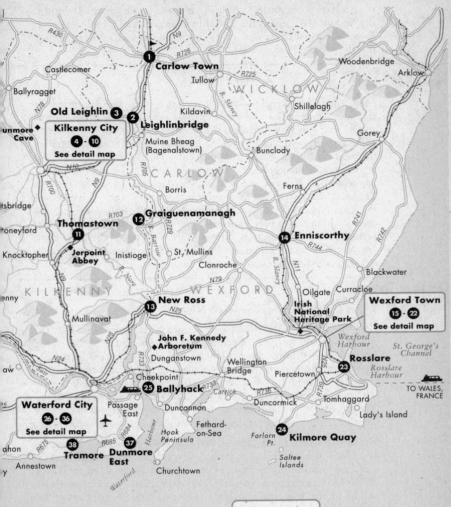

R430

N9

R726

Castlecomer

Carlow Town ①

Tullow

R725

Woodenbridge

Arklow

Ballyragget

N78

WICKLOW

Old Leighlin ③ ② **Leighlinbridge**

Kildavin

Shillelagh

unmore ◆
Cave

Kilkenny City
④ · ⑩
See detail map

Muine Bheag
(Bagenalstown)

Bunclody

Gorey

N10

C A R L O W

sbridge

R700

N9

R703

Borris

R706

Ferns

R741

oneyford

Thomastown
⑪

R729

⑫ **Graiguenamanagh**

R742

Knocktopher

◆ **Jerpoint
Abbey**

Inistioge

St. Mullins

⑭ **Enniscorthy**

R744

Clonroche

Blackwater

enny

K I L K E N N Y

N79

W E X F O R D

N11

Curracloe

Mullinavat

⑬ **New Ross**

N25

Oilgate

**Irish
National
Heritage Park**

Wexford Town
⑮ · ㉒
See detail map

St. George's
Channel

N24

R733

John F. Kennedy
◆ **Arboretum**
Dunganstown

Wellington
Bridge

Piercetown

Wexford
Harbour

㉓ **Rosslare**

Rosslare
Harbour

TO WALES,
FRANCE

aw

N24

R575

Waterford City
㉖ · ㊱
See detail map

Passage
East

Cheekpoint

Duncannon

㉕ **Ballyhack**

R733

Carrick

Duncormick

R736

Tomhaggard

Lady's Island

ahon

R675

R685

㊲ **Dunmore
East**

R684

Fethard-
on-Sea

Hook
Peninsula

Forlorn
Pt.

㉔ **Kilmore Quay**

㊳ **Tramore**

Annestown

Churchtown

Waterford

Saltee
Islands

Celtic Sea

NORTHERN
IRELAND

IRELAND

0   20 miles
0   30 km

it a good choice if you're visiting in the spring and autumn. Remember that in July and August, the Irish themselves descend on the coastal resorts, so if you plan to head for the beaches of the southeast in the summer, be prepared for crowds.

KILKENNY & WEXFORD

Many sights in this region—notably rich in historical and maritime attractions—make a visit here memorable. From Carlow Town's small county seat you travel through the farmlands of the Barrow Valley to Kilkenny City—which, from an architectural point of view, is among the most pleasing towns of inland Ireland. Thanks to the country gentry who made their headquarters here in the 18th century, the historic city center of Kilkenny is endowed with fine Georgian town houses. From Thomastown, just outside Kilkenny, another cross-country drive follows the River Nore to New Ross, where it meets the River Barrow and proceeds to John F. Kennedy's ancestral home and the arboretum planted in his memory. You can then journey to the old Viking port of Wexford Town, which hosts a celebrated opera festival that presents rare works in the restored 18th-century Theatre Royal.

Carlow Town

➊ *83 km (52 mi) south of Dublin on N9.*

Carlow Town was established on the banks of the River Barrow by the Anglo-Normans in the 12th century. Its position on the border of the English Pale—the area around Dublin that was dominated by the English from Elizabethan times on—made it an important strategic center and hence the scene of many bloody battles and sieges. Today Carlow is a lively market town about an hour and a half from central Dublin. The presence of the large Institute of Technology here gives the town a lively buzz. It also has a thriving indigenous arts-and-crafts community.

The Gothic-style, Roman Catholic **Cathedral of the Assumption**, completed in 1883, is notable for its stained-glass windows and a magnificently sculpted marble monument of its builder, Bishop James Doyle (1786–1834), a champion of Catholic emancipation. The monument was carved by the Irish sculptor John Hogan (1800–58). ⊠ *College St.* ☎ *0503/31227* ☜ *Free* ⊙ *Daily 7:30–7:30.*

The ruins of the 13th-century **Carlow Castle**, a strategically important fortification held by the English on the southeastern corner of the Pale, afford imposing views of the River Barrow. This castle withstood a siege by Cromwell's troops in 1650, only to be destroyed accidentally in 1814 when a Dr. Philip Middleton attempted to renovate the castle for use as a mental asylum. While setting off explosives to reduce the thickness of the walls, he managed to demolish all but the west-side curtain wall and its two flanking towers.

One of the most poignant sites in Carlow town is the **Croppies Grave** (⊠ 98 St. off Maryborough St.), a small memorial garden where the bodies of 640 United Irishmen—called "Croppies" because they cropped their hair to mark their allegiance to a free, independent Ireland—were buried in a mass grave, following the Battle of Carlow during the 1798 rebellion against English rule. Two trees planted by a widowed mother of three young men who died still stand; the third fell in a storm, and its two halves are inscribed with a testimonial to the courage of the Croppies.

The famous **Browne's Hill Dolmen**, a stone monument dating from 2500 BC with a capstone weighing in at 100 tons, is one of the largest in Europe. The Stone Age megalithic tomb is thought to mark the burial place of a local king. The dolmen is reached via a pathway from the parking lot. ⊠ *Hacketstown Rd., 3 km (2 mi) east of Carlow Town on R726* ⊠ *Free.*

Where to Stay

¢ ⌂ **Barrowville Town House.** Sensitively restored by its owners, Randal and Marie Dempsey, this elegant Regency-style house blends modern comforts with fine antique furnishings. The Irish breakfast, which includes smoked salmon and an Irish-cheese board, is served in a large conservatory overlooking the garden, under a grapevine that enjoys rude good health, despite the Irish weather. The guest house is minutes away from the center of Carlow Town. ⊠ *Kilkenny Rd., Co. Carlow* ☎ *0503/43324* 🖷 *0503/41953* ⊕ *www.barrowvillehouse.com* ⤳ *7 rooms with bath* ⌂ *Croquet* ☰ *AE, MC, V* ⎪⊙⎪ *BP.*

Nightlife & the Arts

Started in 1979 as a weekend event to bring together arts, literature, and the Irish language, **Éigse,** Carlow's annual festival, takes over the town in June for 10 days. Drama, classical and pop music, and street entertainment vie with impressive visual-arts exhibitions—including works by international artists—around the town. Irish music and dance play a prominent part in the celebrations. For information, contact the **Éigse Festival Office** (☎ *0503/40491*).

Sports & the Outdoors

GAELIC FOOTBALL & HURLING Gaelic football and hurling are played at **Dr. Cullen Park GAA** (GAA Association of Ireland ☎ 01/836–3222 in Dublin).

GOLF **Carlow Golf Club** (⊠ Deerpark ☎ 0503/31695), 3 km (2 mi) north of town on the Dublin road, is set in a wild deer park; the 18-hole course remains open all year.

Leighlinbridge

❷ *10 km (6 mi) south of Carlow Town on N9.*

In Leighlinbridge, the first bridge over the River Barrow was built in 1320 and is reputed to be one of the oldest functioning bridges in Europe. On the east bank of Leighlinbridge lie the ruins of **Black Castle,** built in 1181, one of the earliest Norman fortresses constructed in Ireland and the scene of countless battles and sieges over the centuries. A lone, ruined 400-year-old tower stands today.

Where to Eat

$$$$ ✕ **Lord Bagenal Inn.** This famous old family pub beside the River Barrow is full of cozy nooks and warm, open fires. It even has a small playroom for children (open until 8 PM). Besides being a wine buff, owner James Kehoe is something of an art connoisseur, as the contemporary Irish art collection that lines the walls of the inn testifies. The restaurant's seasonal prix-fixe menu is based on French country cooking and includes steak and poultry entrées, but it is renowned locally for its fresh seafood dishes. If you are interested in staying overnight in Leighlinbridge, inquire about the standard rooms ($). ⊠ *Main St.* ☎ *0503/21668* ⊕ *www.lordbagenal.com* ☰ *DC, V.*

Old Leighlin

❸ *5¾ km (3 mi) west of Leighlinbridge, signposted to the right off N9.*

The tiny village of Old Leighlin is the site of a monastery, founded in the 7th century by St. Laserian, that once accommodated 1,500 monks.

It hosted the church synod in AD 630 at which the Celtic Church initially accepted the Roman date for the celebration of Easter (the date was officially accepted at the Synod of Whitby in AD 664); this decision marked the beginning of a move away from old Brehon Law and the deliberalization of the Church. The old monastery was rebuilt in the 12th century as **St. Laserian's Cathedral** and enlarged in the 16th century. Guided tours are available. ☎ *0503/21411* ✉ *Free* ☉ *July–Aug., weekdays 10–5.*

Carey's, the village pub, has been in the same family since 1542.

Kilkenny City

24 km (15 mi) southwest of Leighlinbridge on N10, 121 km (75 mi) southwest of Dublin.

One of Ireland's most alluring destinations, Kilkenny City demands to be explored by foot or bicycle, thanks to its easily circumnavigable town center. It's a lovely place that's filled with Georgian streets and Tudor stone houses, and the great town castle is a bewitching marriage of Gothic and Victorian styles. The city (population 20,000) is an impressively preserved, 900-year-old Norman citadel attractively situated on the River Nore, which forms the moat of its magnificently restored castle. In the 6th century, St. Canice (a.k.a. "the builder of churches") established a large monastic school here. The town's name reflects Canice's central role: Kil Cainneach means "Church of Canice." Kilkenny did not take on its medieval look for another 400 years, when the Anglo-Normans fortified the city with a castle, gates, and a brawny wall.

Kilkenny holds a special place in the history of Anglo-Irish relations. The infamous 1366 Statutes of Kilkenny, intended to strengthen English authority in Ireland by keeping the heirs of the Anglo-Norman invaders from becoming absorbed into the Irish way of life, was an attempt at apartheid. Intermarriage became a crime punishable by death. Anglo-Norman settlers could lose their estates for speaking Irish, for giving their children Irish names, or for dressing in Irish clothes. The native Irish were forced to live outside town walls in shantytowns. Ironically, the process of Irish and Anglo-Norman assimilation was well under way when the statutes went into effect; perhaps if this intermingling had been allowed to evolve, Anglo-Irish relations in the 20th century might have been more harmonious.

By the early 17th century, the Irish Catholics had grown impatient with such repression; they tried to bring about reforms with the Confederation of Kilkenny, which governed Ireland from 1642 to 1648, with Kilkenny as the capital. Pope Innocent X sent money and arms. Cromwell responded in 1650 by overrunning the town and sacking the cathedral, which he then used to stable his horses.

The city center is small, and despite the large number of historic sights and picturesque streets—in particular, Butter Slip and High Street—it can easily be covered in less than three hours. One of the most pleasant cities south of Dublin (and one of the most popular in summer, when it can be swamped with visitors), Kilkenny City is a center for well-designed crafts, especially ceramics and sweaters; the premier venue is the Kilkenny Design Centre. The city also has more than 60 pubs, many of them on Parliament and High streets, which also support a lively music scene. Many of the town's pubs and shops have old-fashioned, highly individualized, brightly painted facades, created as part of the town's 1980s revival of this Victorian tradition.

4 In spite of Cromwell's defacements, **St. Canice's Cathedral** is still one of the finest cathedrals in Ireland, and it is the country's second-largest medieval church, after St. Patrick's Cathedral in Dublin. The bulk of the 13th-century structure (restored in 1866) was built in the early English style. Within the massive walls is an exuberant Gothic interior, given a somber grandeur by the extensive use of a locally quarried black marble. Many of the memorials and tombstone effigies represent distinguished descendants of the Normans, some depicted in full suits of armor. Look for a female effigy in the south aisle wearing the old Irish or Kinsale cloak; the 12th-century black-marble font at the southwest end of the nave; and St. Ciaran's Chair in the north transept, also made of black marble, with 13th-century sculptures on the arms.

The biggest attraction on the grounds is the 102-foot round tower, which was built in 847 and is all that remains of the monastic development reputedly begun in the 6th century, around which the town arose. If you have the energy, climb the tower's 167 steps: the 360-degree view from the top is tremendous. Next door is St. Canice's Library, containing some 3,000 16th- and 17th-century volumes. ⊠ *Dean St.* ☎ *056/64971* 🖪 *Cathedral €3 tower €2* ⊙ *Cathedral Easter–Sept., Mon.–Sat. 9–1 and 2–6, Sun. 2–6; Oct.–Easter, Mon.–Sat. 10–1 and 2–4, Sun. 2–4; tower access depends on weather.*

5 The 13th-century **Black Abbey** has been restored as a Dominican church by the order whose black capes gave the abbey its name. Nearby is the Black Freren Gate (14th century), the last remaining gateway to the medieval city. ⊠ *South of St. Canice's Cathedral* ☎ *056/21279* 🖪 *Free* ⊙ *Daily 9–1 and 2–6.*

6 **Rothe House** is an example of a typical middle-class house of the Tudor period. Built by John Rothe between 1594 and 1610, it is owned by the Kilkenny Archaeological Society and houses a motley collection of Bronze Age artifacts, ogham stones, and period costumes. There's also a genealogical research facility that can help you trace your ancestors. ⊠ *Parliament St.* ☎ *056/22893* 🖪 *€3* ⊙ *Mar.–Oct., Mon.–Sat. 10:30–5, Sun. 3–5; Nov.–Feb., Mon.–Sat. 1–5.*

7 **Kyteler's Inn,** the oldest in town, is notorious as the place where Dame Alice Kyteler, a member of a wealthy banking family and an alleged witch, was accused of poisoning her four husbands in 1324. The restaurant retains its medieval aura, thanks to its 14th-century stonework and exposed beams. Food and drink in this popular pub are as simple and plentiful as they would have been in Dame Alice's day—without her extra ingredients. ⊠ *Kieran St.* ☎ *056/21064.*

8 The **Tholsel,** or town hall, which was built in 1761 on Parliament Street, stands near the site of the medieval Market Cross. You can recognize it by its distinctive clock tower.

9 The **Tourist Information Office (TIO)** is housed in the Shee Alms House (off the east side of High Street). The building was founded in 1582 by Sir Richard Shee as a hospital for the poor and served in that capacity until 1895. ⊠ *Rose Inn St.* ☎ *056/51500* ⊕ *www.southeastireland.com* ⊙ *Apr.–Oct., Mon.–Sat. 9–6; Nov.–Mar., Mon.–Sat. 9–5.*

★ **10** Founded in 1172 and dominating the south end of town, **Kilkenny Castle** served for more than 500 years, beginning in 1391, as the seat of the Butler family—later designated earls and dukes of Ormonde—one of the more powerful clans in Irish history. In 1967 the sixth marquess of Ormonde handed over the present building, which dates largely from

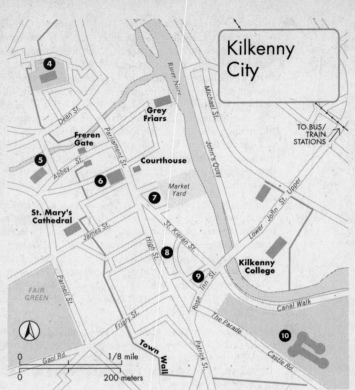

Kilkenny City

1820, to the state; since then it's been through a series of restorations. The gray-stone building, with two turreted wings and numerous chimneys poking over the battlements, stands amid rolling lawns beside the River Nore on 49 acres of landscaped parkland. Most impressive is the 150-foot-long, aptly named Long Gallery, a refined airy hall that contains a collection of family portraits, frayed tapestries, and a skylighted, decorated ceiling of carved oak beams adjoined with Celtic lacework and adorned with brilliantly painted animal heads. The Butler Gallery houses a collection of modern art and frequently changing exhibitions. ⊠ *The Parade* 🕾 *056/21450* ⊕ *www.heritageireland.ie* 🎫 *Castle tour €5, grounds and Butler Gallery free* ⊘ *Apr. and May, daily 10:30–5; June–Sept., daily 10–7; Oct.–Mar., Mon.–Sat. 10:30–12:45 and 2–5, Sun. 10:30–12:45 and 2–5.*

Where to Stay & Eat

$–$$$ ✕ **Ristorante Rinuccini.** Kilkenny City's premier Irish-Italian restaurant occupies the basement of a Georgian town house opposite Kilkenny Castle. Owner-chef Antonio Cavaliere is intensely involved in preparing the luscious pasta dishes—tortellini stuffed with ricotta cheese and spinach, served in a creamy Gorgonzola-cheese sauce—as well as specialties of the house, such as organic Irish veal, and fresh seafood from Kilmore Quay. A splendid all-Italian wine list complements the menu, and there's a host of delicious homemade desserts. ⊠ *1 The Parade* 🕾 *056/61575* ⊕ *www.rinuccini.com* ⚱ *Reservations essential* 🖃 *AE, DC, MC, V.*

$–$$ ✕ **Café Sol.** Everything at this small, cheerful spot is homemade, except the pasta and baguettes. All dishes, ranging from steak to pasta to fish of the day, are cooked with attention to detail. The roasted-pepper-and-parsnip soup is an excellent starter, followed by roasted organic goose with potato-and-apple stuffing, and date-and-orange cake. Oilcloths cover the tables during the day; dinner settings appear in the evenings. ✉ *William St.* ☎ *056/64987* ▤ *MC, V* ☺ *Closed Sun.*

$$ ✕▣ **Langton's.** The main building, two penthouses, tranquil gardens, and one of Ireland's most famous "eating pubs" make up this country-house hotel. It's a family-run establishment—a landmark since the 1940s—and a labyrinth of interconnected bars and restaurants. Most of the seating areas, with open fires, have different personalities—from the leather-upholstered gentlemen's club in the Horseshoe Bar to an attempt at art deco in the spacious dining room ($$–$$$). Creams and browns decorate the art deco–style rooms, which have king-size beds. Entrées include roast rack of lamb on eggplant and *capsicum frites* (fried peppers), traditional Irish stew, and a selection of steaks. ✉ *69 John St., Co. Kilkenny* ☎ *056/65133* 🖷 *056/63693* ➟ *28 rooms with bath, 2 suites* ▤ *AE, DC, MC, V* ⦿ *BP.*

★ $$ ▣ **Butler House.** This elegant Georgian house, with its magnificent plastered ceilings and marble fireplaces, is an integral part of the Kilkenny Castle complex and once belonged to the earls of Ormonde. All of the rooms are beautifully decorated; ask for one with a bay window overlooking the secluded gardens and Kilkenny Castle. ✉ *16 Patrick St., Co. Kilkenny* ☎ *056/65707* 🖷 *056/65626* ⊕ *www.butler.ie* ➟ *12 rooms with bath, 1 suite* ⧖ *Restaurant, meeting rooms* ▤ *AE, DC, MC, V* ⦿ *BP.*

Nightlife & the Arts

John Cleere's (✉ 22 Parliament St. ☎ 056/62573) is the best pub in town for a mix of live traditional music, poetry readings, and theatrical plays. **The Pumphouse** (✉ 26 Parliament St. ☎ 056/63924) has traditional music during the week and live rock and pop weekends. The **Widow McGraths** (✉ 29 Parliament St. ☎ 056/52520) celebrates the Fourth of July (yes, the Fourth of July) with a barbecue in its beer garden. It's also a good spot for live music.

Sports & the Outdoors

BICYCLING   Bikes for exploring the quiet countryside around Kilkenny can be rented through **J. J. Wall** (✉ 88 Maudlin St. ☎ 056/21236).

GAELIC FOOTBALL & HURLING   The 1366 Statutes of Kilkenny expressly forbade the ancient Irish game of hurling; today Kilkenny is considered one of the great hurling counties. Gaelic football and hurling matches are held at **Kilkenny GAA Grounds** (✉ Nowlan Park ☎ 056/70008).

GOLF   **Kilkenny Golf Club** (✉ Glendine ☎ 056/65400), 2 km (1 mi) northeast of town, is an 18-hole, par-71, mainly flat course.

GREYHOUND & HORSE RACING   At **Kilkenny Greyhound Racetrack** (✉ St. James's Park, Freshford Rd. ☎ 056/21214), evening meets are held each Wednesday and Friday where betting is the main attraction. **Gowran Park** (✉ Gowran, 15 km [9 mi] south of Kilkenny City ☎ 056/26126) holds horse races regularly.

Shopping

Kilkenny is a byword for attractive, original crafts that combine traditional arts with modern elements of design. You can see glass being blown at the **Jerpoint Glass Studio** (✉ Stoneyford ☎ 056/24350), where the glass is heavy, modern, uncut, and hand-finished. Their factory shop is a good place to pick up a bargain. The town's leading outlet, the **Kilkenny Design Centre** (✉ Kilkenny Castle ☎ 056/22118), in the old stable yard opposite the castle, sells ceramics, jewelry, sweaters, and handwoven textiles. **Murphy's Jewellers** (✉ 85 High St. ☎ 056/21127) specializes in heraldic jewelry.

★ At **Nicholas Mosse Pottery** (✉ Bennettsbridge ☎ 056/27505) you can buy attractive hand-crafted and -decorated pottery—and see it made. **Rudolf**

Heltzel (✉ 10 Patrick St. ☎ 056/21497) is known for its striking, modern designs of gold and silver jewelry. **Stoneware Jackson Pottery** (✉ Bennettsbridge ☎ 056/27175) makes distinctive, hand-thrown tableware and lamps. The **Sweater Shop** (✉ 81 High St. ☎ 056/63405) carries great sweaters.

Thomastown

⓫ *14½ km (9 mi) south of Kilkenny on R700 and N9.*

Thomastown, originally the seat of the kings of Ossory (an ancient Irish kingdom), is a pretty, stone-built village on the River Nore. It takes its name from Thomas FitzAnthony of Leinster, who circled the town with a wall in the 13th century. Fragments of this medieval wall remain to this day, as do the partly ruined 13th-century church of St. Mary and Mullins Castle, which stands adjacent to the town bridge.

Fodor'sChoice
★
Jerpoint Abbey, near Thomastown, is one of the most notable Cistercian ruins in Ireland, dating from about 1160. The church, tombs, and the restored cloisters—decorated with affecting human figures and fantastical mythical creatures—are a must for lovers of the Irish Romanesque. Guides are available from mid-June to mid-September. The last admission is 45 minutes before closing. ✉ *2 km (1 mi) south of Thomastown on N9* ☎ *056/24623* ⊕ *www.heritageireland.ie* ⊡ *€2.75* ☉ *Mar.–May and Oct.–mid-Nov., daily 10–5; June–Sept., daily 9:30–6:30.*

Where to Stay & Eat

$$$$
Fodor'sChoice
★
✕⌂ **Mount Juliet.** Within a walled 1,500-acre estate stands this imposing three-story Georgian mansion. Bedrooms are large and individually decorated, with super-king-size beds and original fireplaces. Rooms are also available in a separate building, the Hunters Yard, and there are 11 modern two-bedroom lodges. Major activities here include horseback riding on the extensive trails within the estate, clay shooting, and golfing on the Jack Nicklaus–designed course. The Lady Helen McAlmont Restaurant, its tables adorned with crystal, silverware, and fine linen, serves haute cuisine with contemporary Irish touches. ✉ *Co. Kilkenny* ☎ *056/73000* ⎙ *056/73009* ⊕ *www.mountjuliet.com* ⇗ *48 rooms with bath, 11 lodges* ♿ *2 restaurants, 18-hole golf course, tennis court, indoor pool, sauna, spa, fishing, archery, croquet, horseback riding, 3 bars* ⊟ *AE, DC, MC, V* ⊺⊙⊺ *EP.*

★ $
⌂ **Ballyduff House.** This picturesque 18th-century manor house, set in rolling countryside overlooking the River Nore, has been used as a film location on more than one occasion (including for the 1995 film *Circle of Friends*). Three large period bedrooms, decorated with Georgian furniture and ornate wallpaper, afford wonderful views of the river. You're welcome to walk around the gardens and partake in trout and salmon fishing. Mount Juliet Golf Course is less than a five-minute drive away. ✉ *Co. Kilkenny* ☎☎ *056/58488* ⇗ *3 rooms with bath* ♿ *Fishing* ⊟ *No credit cards* ⊺⊙⊺ *BP* ☉ *Closed Nov.–Feb.*

Sports & the Outdoors

GOLF   Visitors are welcome at the 18-hole **Mount Juliet Golf Course** (✉ Mount Juliet Estate ☎ 056/24455), a championship parkland course. The course was designed by Jack Nicklaus and includes practice greens and a driving range.

HORSEBACK RIDING   The excellent facilities at **Mount Juliet** (✉ Mount Juliet Estate ☎ 056/73000) are open to nonresidents.

Graiguenamanagh

12 *15 km (9 mi) northeast of Thomastown on R703.*

The village of Graiguenamanagh (pronounced *gray*-gun-a-manna) sits on the banks of the River Barrow at the foot of Brandon Hill. This is good walking country; ask for directions to the summit of **Brandon Hill** (1,694 feet), a 7-km (4½-mi) hike. In the 13th century the early English–style church of **Duiske Abbey** was the largest Cistercian church in Ireland. The choir, the transept, and a section of the nave of the original abbey church are now part of a Catholic church. Purists will be disappointed by the modernization, carried out between 1974 and 1980, although medieval building techniques were used. ☎ *0503/24238* ⏱ *Daily 9:30–7.*

Where to Stay & Eat

★ $ ✕⊞ **Waterside.** This beautifully restored 19th-century stone corn mill is on the River Barrow. The mill's original pitch-pine beams have been retained in the guest rooms, which are simply and brightly decorated with reds and yellows. The restaurant ($$), which occupies the ground floor of the old mill building, also has exposed beams and decorated windows; it serves Continental cuisine and has a good wine list. Waterside is popular with hikers and those who value the nearby riding and golf. ⊠ *The Quay, Co. Kilkenny* ☎ *0503/24246* 🖶 *0503/24733* ⊕ *www. watersideguesthouse.com* ↷ *10 rooms with bath* ♨ *Restaurant, fishing* ▭ *AE, MC, V* ⍟ *BP.*

New Ross

13 *17 km (11 mi) south of Graiguenamanagh on R705.*

New Ross is a busy inland port on the banks of the River Barrow. Even though it's one of the oldest towns in County Wexford, settled in the 13th century on an ancient monastic site, only the most dedicated history buffs will be tempted to stop and explore the steep, narrow streets above its unattractive docks. The major attraction in New Ross is a cruise up the River Barrow on the **Galley Cruising Restaurant** (☎ 051/421–723 ⊕ www.rivercruises.ie). You can take in the peaceful farmlands along the riverbank while sampling lunch, afternoon tea, or dinner. The emphasis is on fresh local produce and seafood. The restaurant is open Easter through October only.

The **John F. Kennedy Arboretum** has more than 600 acres of forest, nature trails, and gardens, plus an ornamental lake. The grounds contain some 4,500 species of trees and shrubs, and serve as a resource center for botanists and foresters. Go to the top of the park to get fine panoramic views. The arboretum is clearly signposted from New Ross on R733, which follows the banks of the Barrow southward for about 5 km (3 mi). The cottage where the president's great-grandfather was born is in Dunganstown; Kennedy relatives still live in the house. About 2 km (1 mi) down the road at Slieve Coillte you'll see the entrance to the arboretum. ⊠ *Dunganstown* ☎ *051/388–171* ⊕ *www.heritageireland.ie* 🎫 *€2.75* ⏱ *May–Aug., daily 10–8; Apr. and Sept., daily 10–6:30; Oct.–Mar., daily 10–5.*

Ballylane Farm, a 200-acre working farm, supplies maps and information sheets to guide you along a nature walk, where you can observe local wildlife, farm animals, and crops. A coffee shop–restaurant serves light meals when the nature walk is open to visitors. ✚ *Signposted about 1 km (½ mi) past the turn to the Kennedy Arboretum (from Graiguenamanagh) on N25 New Ross–Wexford Rd.* ☎ *051/425–666* 🎫 *€4.70* ⏱ *May–Oct., daily 10–6; or by appointment.*

Enniscorthy

⑭ *32 km (20 mi) northeast of New Ross on N79.*

Enniscorthy, on the sloping banks of the River Slaney and on the main road between Dublin and Wexford, to the south of the popular resort of Gorey, is a thriving market town, rich in history. The town is dominated by **Enniscorthy Castle**, built in the first quarter of the 13th century by the Prendergast family. The imposing Norman castle was the site of fierce battles against Oliver Cromwell in the 17th century and during the Uprising of 1798. Its square-towered keep now houses the County Wexford Museum, which contains thousands of historic items, including military memorabilia from the 1798 and 1916 uprisings. ⊠ *Castle Hill* ☎ *054/35926* ⌑ *€4.50* ⊙ *May–Sept., Mon.–Sat. 10–6, Sun. 2–5:30.*

The **National 1798 Center** tells the tale of the United Irishmen and the ill-fated 1798 rebellion. ⊠ *Arnold's Cross* ☎ *054/37596* ⌑ *€6* ⊙ *Mid-Mar.–Nov., Mon.–Sat. 9:30–5, Sun. 11–5; Dec.–mid-Mar., weekdays 9:30–4, weekends 11–4.*

St. Aidan's Cathedral stands on a commanding site overlooking the Slaney. This Gothic Revival structure was built in the mid-19th century under the direction of Augustus Welby Pugin, the architect of the Houses of Parliament in London. ⊠ *Cathedral St.* ☎ *054/35777* ⌑ *Free* ⊙ *Daily 10–6.*

Sports & the Outdoors

The **Showgrounds** (☎ 054/33172) have greyhound racing on Monday and Thursday at 8 PM, with bar and catering facilities available.

Shopping

Carley's Bridge Pottery (⊠ Carley's Bridge ☎ 054/33512), established in 1654, specializes in large terra-cotta pots. **Kiltrea Bridge Pottery** (⊠ Kiltrea, Caime ☎ 054/35107) stocks garden pots, plant pots, and country kitchen crocks.

Wexford Town

24 km (15 mi) south of Enniscorthy on N11, 142 km (88 mi) south of Dublin.

From its appearance today, you would barely realize that Wexford is an ancient place—in fact, it was defined on maps by the Greek cartographer Ptolemy as long ago as the 2nd century AD. Its Irish name is Loch Garman, but the Vikings called it Waesfjord—the harbor of the mud flats—which became Wexford in English. Wexford became an English garrison town after it was taken by Oliver Cromwell in 1649. (The Anglo-Norman conquest of Ireland began in County Wexford in 1169, so the British presence has deep roots, and Wexford has been an English-speaking county for centuries.)

The River Slaney empties into the sea at Wexford Town. The harbor has silted up since the days when the Viking longboats docked here; nowadays only a few small trawlers fish from here. Wexford Town's compact center is on the south bank of the Slaney. Running parallel to the quays on the riverfront is the main street (the name changes several times)—the major shopping street of the town, with a pleasant mix of old-fashioned bakeries, butcher shops, stylish boutiques, and a share of Wexford's many pubs. It can be explored on foot in an hour or two. Allow at least half a day in the area if you also intend to visit the Heritage Park at nearby Ferrycarrig, and a full day if you want to take in Johnstown Castle Gardens and its agricultural museum, or walk in the nature reserve at nearby Curracloe Beach. The town is at its best in late October and early November, when the Wexford Opera Festival creates a carnival atmosphere that permeates the town.

Rising above the town's rooftops are the graceful spires of two elegant examples of 19th-century Gothic architecture. These **twin churches** have identical exteriors, their foundation stones were laid on the same day, and their spires both reach a height of 230 feet. The **Church of the Assumption** is on Bride Street. The **Church of the Immaculate Conception** is on Rowe Street.

15 The **Tourist Information Office** (TIO; ⊠ Crescent Quay ☎ 053/23111) is a good place to start exploring Wexford Town on foot and to find out about guided walking tours organized by local historians.

16 Standing in the center of Crescent Quay, a large bronze **statue of Commodore John Barry** (1745–1803) commemorates the man who came to be known as the "Father of the American Navy." Born in 1745 in nearby Ballysampson, Barry settled in Philadelphia at age 15, became a brilliant naval fighter during the War of Independence (thus avenging his Irish ancestors), and trained many young naval officers who went on to achieve fame for themselves.

17 The **Franciscan Church** has a ceiling worth noting for its fine, locally crafted stuccowork. ⊠ *School St.* ☎ *053/22758* ☜ *Free* ⊘ *Daily 8:30–6:30.*

18 The **Wexford Bull Ring** (⊠ Quay St., back toward the quays) was once the scene of bullbaiting, a medieval sport that was popular among the Norman nobility. Also in this arena, in 1649, Cromwell's soldiers massacred 300 panic-stricken townspeople who had gathered here to pray as the army stormed their town.

19 The red sandstone **Westgate Tower** (⊠ Westgate) was the largest of five fortified gateways in the Norman and Viking town walls, and it is the only one remaining. The early-13th-century tower has been sensitively restored. Keep an eye out as you wander this part of town for other preserved segments of the old town walls.

20 The ruins of the 12th-century **Selskar Abbey** (⊠ Selskar St., south of Westgate Tower) still stand. Here the first treaty between the Irish and the Normans was signed in 1169.

21 The **Wexford Wildfowl Reserve,** on the north bank of the Slaney, is a short walk across the bridge from the main part of town. One-third of the world's Greenland white-fronted geese—as many as 10,000—spend their winters on the mud flats, known locally as slobs, which also draw ducks, swans, and other waterfowl. Hides are provided for bird-watchers, and an audiovisual show and exhibitions are available at the visitor center. ⊠ *North Slob, Wexford Harbor* ☎ *053/23129* ☜ *Free* ⊘ *Mid-Apr.–Sept., daily 9–6; Oct.–mid-Apr., daily 10–5.*

★ ☺ **22** The **Irish National Heritage Park,** a 35-acre, open-air living history museum beside the River Slaney, is one of Ireland's most successful and enjoyable family attractions. In about an hour and a half, a guide takes you through 9,000 years of Irish history—from the first evidence of humans on this island, at around 7000 BC, to the Norman settlements of the mid-12th century. Full-scale replicas of typical dwelling places illustrate the changes in beliefs and lifestyles. Highlights of the tour include a prehistoric homestead, a *crannóg* (lake dwelling), an early Christian *rath* (fortified farmstead), a Christian monastery, a horizontal water mill, a Viking longhouse, and a Norman castle. There are also examples of pre-Christian burial sites and a stone circle. Most of the exhibits are "in-

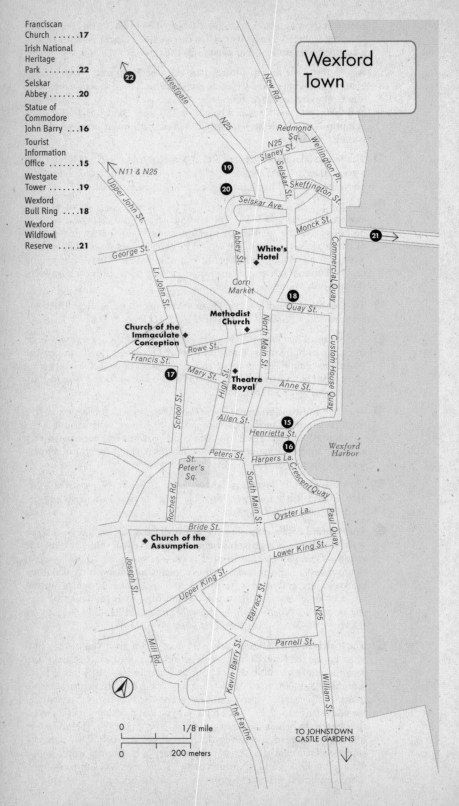

Wexford Town

habited" by students in appropriate dress who will answer questions. The riverside site includes several nature trails. ⊠ *Ferrycarrig, 5 km (3 mi) north of Wexford Town on N11* ☎ *053/20733* ⊕ *www.inhp.com* ☞ *Mar.–Oct. €7, Nov.–Feb. €5.50* ☉ *Mar.–Oct., daily 9:30–6:30; Nov.–Feb., daily 9:30–5:30.*

off the beaten path

CURRACLOE BEACH – This was the location used for the Normandy landing in Steven Spielberg's film *Saving Private Ryan*. It's a popular swimming place in summer and is home to many migratory birds in winter. It's 9 km (5½ mi) long, with a 1-km (½-mi) nature trail in the seashore sand dunes. ⊠ *11 km (7 mi) northeast of Wexford Town on R742.*

Where to Stay & Eat

$$ ✕ **La Riva.** Lots of people opt for two or three starters at this charming first-floor bistro, in order to try as many as possible of owner-chef Warren Gillen's unusual combos—such as panfried rabbit loin with Parma ham and goat-cheese ravioli, or the warm coffee-poached pear served with a chocolate brownie and Baileys custard. The extensive menu makes use of organic ingredients, and a wide selection of fresh seafood is available. The bistro, with a modern Mediterranean interior design and friendly staff, is right in the center of town, near the TIO. ⊠ *Henrietta St.* ☎ *053/24330* ▤ *MC, V.*

$–$$ ✕ **Heavens Above.** Chef Joel Warren cooks up a storm in this delightful evening restaurant and the pub—called the Sky and the Ground—below it. Main courses include wild venison noisettes panfried in a juniper berry and cognac sauce, and lamb cutlets enriched with mint and wild mushrooms. Complement your meal with one of more than 250 wines from owners John and Nuala Barron's adjoining wine shop. Traditional music is played in the pub Monday through Wednesday. ⊠ *112 S. Main St.* ☎ *053/21273* ▤ *MC, V.*

$–$$ ✕ **Oak Tavern.** The pub-restaurant in this family-run old-fashioned inn on the River Slaney is a good place to stop for a bite on your way into Wexford Town. In cold weather, you can warm yourself beside the log fires that blaze in the lounge; in fair weather, you can relax on the riverside terrace. The menu includes steaks, local salmon, and simple seafood. The tavern is about 2 km (1 mi) from town, and not far from the gates of the Irish National Heritage Park on the N11 Dublin road. ⊠ *Enniscorthy Rd., Ferrycarrig* ☎ *053/20922* ▤ *AE, MC, V.*

$$–$$$$ ✕▥ **Ferrycarrig.** Regular visitors to Wexford Town love this hotel, which overlooks the Slaney Estuary 3 km (2 mi) from town on the N11. Even with its very modern architecture, the hotel blends well into its peaceful, riverside location—for example, trees have been placed just offshore to encourage birds to perch there. All the bedrooms have wonderful views of the river, and some also have balconies. Choose between dining in the casual Boathouse Bistro or the more formal Tides Restaurant, which serves Continental cuisine. One of Ireland's not-so-numerous millionaires takes over the entire hotel for three weeks each year. ⊠ *Ferrycarrig Bridge, Co. Wexford* ☎ *053/20999* 🖶 *053/20982* ⊕ *www. griffingroup.ie* ⇔ *103 rooms with bath* ⚬ *2 restaurants, indoor pool, health club, fishing, bar* ▤ *AE, DC, MC, V* ◉❙ *BP.*

$$ ▥ **White's Hotel.** If you're looking for a friendly, convivial place in the heart of town, try this redbrick hotel, established in 1779 and fronted by a modern conservatory. The guest rooms are a hodgepodge of different styles, though each has an old-fashioned, comfortable charm. Forty additional executive bedrooms are in the reclaimed Abbey Street wing. There's live music in the Shelmalier Bar every Friday and Saturday. ⊠ *George's St., Co. Wexford* ☎ *053/22311* 🖶 *053/45000* ⇔ *82* rooms with bath ⟁ Restaurant, health club, 2 bars ⊟ AE, DC, MC, V ⫶◯⫶ BP.

$ ⊡ **McMenamin's Town House.** Early breakfast by arrangement and exceptional comfort—for the price range—make this four-story Victorian villa an ideal stopover en route to or from the Rosslare ferries. The bedrooms are spacious, warm, and immaculate, with large pieces of highly polished Victorian furniture and antique beds, including a mahogany half-tester. There are about eight choices at breakfast, including fresh fish of the day or porridge. Make sure you taste Kay and Seamus McMenamin's homemade whiskey marmalade. Book months in advance if you want a room here during the Opera Festival. ✉ *3 Auburn Terr., Redmond Rd., Co. Wexford* ☎☎ *053/46442* ⊕ *www.wexford-bedandbreakfast.com* ⇆ *5 rooms with bath* ⊟ *MC, V* ⫶◯⫶ *BP* ⊘ *Closed last 2 wks of Dec.*

Nightlife & the Arts

Touring companies and local productions can be seen in Wexford at the **Theatre Royal** (✉ 27 High St. ☎ 053/22400). The **Wexford Opera Festival** (☎ 053/22144 box office ⊕ www.wexfordopera.com), held during the last two weeks of October and the beginning of November, is the town's leading cultural event. The festival, which has been going strong for half a century, features seldom-performed operas with top talent from all over the world. Along with an ever-expanding fringe element, the festival supplies a feast of concerts and recitals that start at 11 AM and continue until midnight.

Centenary Stores (✉ Charlotte St. ☎ 053/24424) is a Victorian-style pub, popular with a young crowd. Lunch is available Monday through Saturday, and there's traditional music every Sunday morning. The **Sky and the Ground** (✉ 112 S. Main St. ☎ 053/21273) is one of the best pubs in town for good food (served daily) and fine traditional music sessions (Monday through Thursday). Dating to the 13th century, the **Thomas Moore Tavern** (✉ Cornmarket ☎ 053/24348) is Wexford's oldest pub, named after the renowned Irish poet whose parents once lived here. The pub still has its original medieval walls and fine old beams along the ceiling. It's the perfect place for a quiet drink by the fire.

Sports & the Outdoors

BICYCLING   If you'd like to explore the long, sandy coast of this area at a leisurely pace, rent bicycles at **Hayes Cycles** (✉ 108 S. Main St. ☎ 053/22462).

GAELIC FOOTBALL   Gaelic football and hurling can be seen at the **Wexford Park GAA**
& HURLING   (✉ Clonard Rd. ☎ 01/836–3222 for the GAA Association of Ireland in Dublin).

HORSE RACING   Horse races are held regularly (every few months) at the **Wexford Racecourse** (✉ Bettyville ☎ 053/42307) on N25 at the outskirts of Wexford Town.

HORSEBACK   **Curracloe House Equestrian Centre** (✉ Curracloe ☎ 053/37582) will take
RIDING   you cantering on the spectacular Curracloe Beach (although local authority regulations are presently trying to ban beach riding) or trekking through the Wexford Sloblands. Facilities include a 25-jump cross-country course. **Horetown Equestrian Centre** (✉ Horetown House, Foulksmills ☎ 051/565–786) specializes in residential riding holidays—cross-country riding across farmland—and will teach you how to play polo-crosse. **Shelmalier Riding Stables** (✉ Trinity, Forth Mountain, Taghmon ☎ 053/39251) has cross-country riding over 3,000 acres of forest and mountainous terrain.

Shopping

Barker's (⌧ 36 S. Main St. ☎ 053/23159) stocks Waterford crystal, local pottery, and crafts. **Martins Jewelers** (⌧ 14 S. Main St. ☎ 053/22635) sells handmade Celtic jewelry and Waterford crystal. **Simone Walsh** (⌧ 85 S. Main St. ☎ 053/23567) features Irish art and design and original paintings.

Westgate Design (⌧ 22 N. Main St. ☎ 053/23787) carries a good selection of Irish crafts, pottery, candles, and jewelry; there's also a restaurant here. **The Wool Shop** (⌧ 39–40 S. Main St. ☎ 053/22247) is a good place to buy souvenirs, knitting yarn, and Aran sweaters.

en route   The massive, Victorian-Gothic, gray-stone castle at **Johnstown Castle Gardens** is now an agricultural college, but the attractive and well-maintained grounds, with ornamental lakes and more than 200 different trees and shrubs, are open to the public. The main attraction is the **National Museum of Agriculture and Rural Life,** housed in the quadrangular stable yards, which shows what life was once like in rural Ireland. It also contains a 5,000-square-foot exhibition on the potato and the Great Famine (1845–49). You'll find the signpost for the gardens by following N25 from Wexford Town for 5 km (3 mi) toward Rosslare. ☎ *053/42888* ⌧ *Gardens May–Sept. €2, Oct.–Apr. free. Museum €5* ☉ *Gardens daily 9:30–5:30. Museum Apr., May, and Sept.–Nov., weekdays 9–12:30 and 1:30–5, weekends 2–5; June–Aug., weekdays 9–5, weekends 11–5; Dec.–Mar., weekdays 9–12:30 and 1:30–5.*

ALONG THE COAST TO WATERFORD

This journey takes you along mainly minor roads through the prettiest parts of the coast in Counties Wexford and Waterford, pausing midway to explore Waterford City on foot.

Rosslare

㉓   *16 km (10 mi) southeast of Wexford Town on R470.*

Sometimes called Ireland's sunniest spot, the village of Rosslare is a seaside resort with an attractive beach. Vacationers generally head here to hike, golf, sun, and swim. Rosslare Harbor, 8 km (5 mi) south of the village, is one of Ireland's busiest ports, and the terminus for car ferries from Fishguard and Pembroke in Wales and from Cherbourg and Roscoff in France.

Where to Stay & Eat

★ **$$**   ✕⊡ **Kelly's.** Comfortable, rustic furnishings fill the guest rooms at this traditional seaside resort owned and run by the Kelly family since 1895. Rooms facing the front have lovely sea views. Waterford-glass chandeliers hang in the Ivy Room restaurant, where the menu includes fresh local produce served in classic French style. You can also dine in La Marine, a casual, bistro-style restaurant that does a fine job of cooking up Mediterranean-style Irish produce. The resort has extensive recreational facilities. In July and August there's a one-week minimum stay. ⌧ *Co. Wexford* ☎ *053/32114* ⊟ *053/32222* ⊕ *www.kellys.ie* ⊅ *106 rooms with bath* ₰ *2 restaurants, 18-hole golf course, 4 tennis courts, indoor pool, wading pool, gym, hair salon, hot tub, outdoor hot tub, sauna, steam room, bicycles, badminton, croquet, Ping-Pong, squash, playground* ⊟ *AE, MC, V* ⍩⍥ *BP* ☉ *Closed Dec.–Feb.*

¢–$ ⊞ **Tuskar House Hotel.** For an ideal spot to unwind, book a room at this small, family-run hotel in a quiet area near the ferry port. The bright and comfortable rooms are decorated with functional, modern furniture. For the best views of the sea, try to get a room at the rear of the hotel, and, if possible, with a balcony. Public rooms have lots of polished pine, glass, and greenery. Seafood is a specialty at the restaurant. ✉ *St. Martin's Rd., Rosslare Harbor, Co. Wexford* ☎ *053/33363* 🖷 *053/33033* ⊕ *www.tuskarhousehotel.com* ➷ *30 rooms with bath* ⌂ *Restaurant, bar* ⊟ *AE, DC, MC, V* ¶◎¶ *BP.*

Nightlife & the Arts
Portholes bar (✉ Rosslare Harbor ☎ 053/33110), at the Hotel Rosslare, is a popular spot for live music weekends.

Sports & the Outdoors
Rosslare Golf Club (✉ Rosslare Strand ☎ 053/32203) is a 27-hole, par-72 championship links. A mixture of links and parkland can be found at the 27-hole **St. Helen's Bay** (✉ Kilrane ☎ 053/33234).

Kilmore Quay

㉔ *22 km (14 mi) south of Rosslare on R739.*

A quiet, old-fashioned seaside village of thatched and whitewashed cottages noted for its fishing industry, Kilmore Quay is also popular with recreational anglers and bird-watchers. From the harbor there is a pleasant view to the east over the flat coast that stretches for miles. **Kehoe's Pub** (✉ Kilmore Quay ☎ 053/29830) is the hub of village activity; its collection of maritime artifacts is as interesting as that of many museums. During two weeks in July (generally mid-July), the village hosts a lively **seafood festival** (☎ 053/29922) with a parade, seafood barbecues, and other events.

★ The **Kilmore Quay Maritime Museum** is on board the lightship *Guillemot*. The boat, built in 1923, is the last Irish lightship to be preserved complete with cabins and engine room, and it contains models and artifacts relating to the maritime history of the area. ✉ *Kilmore Quay* ☎ *053/ 21572* ◩ *€5* ☉ *June–Aug., daily noon–6; Sept. and Apr., weekends noon–6.*

☾ The **Saltee Islands,** Ireland's largest bird sanctuary, are a popular offshore day trip from Kilmore Quay. In late spring and early summer, several million seabirds nest among the dunes and on the rocky scarp on the south of the islands. Even if you are not an ornithologist, it's worth making the trip at these times to observe the sheer numbers of gulls, kittiwakes, puffins, guillemots, cormorants, and petrels. From mid-May to mid-September, look for boats at the village waterfront or on the marina to take you to the islands, weather permitting.

Where to Stay & Eat
$–$$ ✕ **Silver Fox.** Simplicity and freshness define the food at this busy family-run seafood restaurant. Chef and co-owner Nicky Cullen prepares up to a dozen seafood options, including a very popular grilled lemon sole, topped with a creamy sauce of fresh prawns, scallops, mushrooms, and onions—plus a sprinkling of cheese. He also cooks a few non-seafood options: stuffed garlic mushrooms and deep-fried St. Killian (a local Camembert-like) cheese. ✉ *Kilmore Quay* ☎ *053/29888* ⌕ *Reservations essential* ⊟ *AE, MC, V* ☉ *Closed mid-Jan.–mid-Feb. No lunch Mon–Sat.*

¢ ⊞ **Quay House.** From this whitewashed guest house—originally the village post office—it's only a 3-minute walk to the pier. The solid old house has been carefully refurbished with Douglas fir pine floors throughout and country pine bedroom furniture. Guests—generally outdoor types—are encouraged to socialize in the lounge and the dining room. A room for drying and storing diving equipment is available. ☒ *Kilmore Quay, Co. Wexford* ☎ *053/29988* 🖶 *053/29808* ⊕ *www.quayhouseguesthouse. com* ⇌ *10 rooms with bath* ⟁ *Restaurant, fishing* ☰ *AE, MC, V* ⟊ *BP.*

Shopping

Country Crafts (☒ Kilmore Quay ☎ 053/29885), which overlooks the harbor of Kilmore Quay, sells Irish-made crafts, antique pine furniture, and paintings by local artists.

| en route | On leaving Kilmore Quay, make your way north to R736, and then head west through Duncormick and on to Wellington Bridge. Past the bridge, head toward Fethard-on-Sea on the **Ring of Hook** drive. This is a strange and atypical part of Ireland, where the land is exceptionally flat and the narrow roads are straight. |

The Ring of Hook leads out to Hook Lighthouse and north again to **Duncannon**, a small, delightful resort with a sandy beach, on the north side of Waterford Harbor. Its history is marked by the visits of two kings: James II beat a hasty retreat out of Ireland through Duncannon port after his defeat at the Battle of the Boyne in 1690, and his successor, William III, also spent some days here before leaving for England. The imposing, star-shape stone Duncannon Fort was built in the 16th century on the site of an Iron Age fortification; it was placed on the water's edge as a defense against a feared attack by the Spanish Armada. ☒ *Duncannon* ☎ *051/389–454* ☒ €4 ⊙ *Easter–Sept., daily 10–5:30.*

Ballyhack

㉕ *34 km (21 mi) west of Kilmore Quay.*

Fodor'sChoice ★

On the upper reaches of Waterford Harbor, the pretty village of Ballyhack, with its square castle keep, wooden buildings, thatched cottages, and green, hilly background, is admired by painters and photographers. A small car ferry makes the five-minute crossing to Passage East and Waterford. The gray-stone keep of **Ballyhack Castle** dates from the 16th century. It was once owned by the Knights Templars of St. John of Jerusalem, who held the ferry rights by royal charter; traditionally, they were required to keep a boat at Ballyhack to transport injured knights to the King's Leper Hospital at Waterford. The first two floors have been renovated and house a number of local-history exhibits. Guided tours are available by appointment, and the last admission is 45 minutes before closing. ☎ *051/389–468* ⊕ *www.heritageireland.ie* ☒ €1.50 ⊙ *Mid-June–mid-Sept., weekdays 10–1 and 2–6, weekends 10–6.*

Where to Stay & Eat

$$$ ✕🏠 **Dunbrody Country House.** The seventh marquess of Donegall, Dermot Chichester, used to live at this stylish and pleasantly informal country retreat. Kevin and Catherine Dundon now own and run the sprawling two-story Georgian manor house. Kevin is a master chef with international experience, and Catherine oversees the restoration program. The spacious rooms, which are individually decorated and furnished with Georgian antiques, have peaceful country views. In the oak-floor dining room ($$$$), which overlooks a small sunken garden that's floodlighted at night, you can dine on excellent contemporary Continental cuisine. ☒ *Arthurstown, New Ross, Co. Wexford* ☎ *051/389–600*

Fodor'sChoice ★

🖃 *051/389–601* ⊕ *www.dunbrodyhouse.com* ⇆ *15 rooms with bath,*
7 suites ⚅ *Restaurant, horseback riding, bar* ⊟ *AE, DC, MC, V* ⏀ *BP.*

Waterford City

10 km (6 mi) west of Ballyhack by ferry and road (R683), 62 km (39
mi) southwest of Wexford Town, 158 km (98 mi) southwest of Dublin.

The largest town in the southeast and Ireland's oldest city, Waterford
was founded by the Vikings in the 9th century and was taken over by
Strongbow, the Norman invader, with much bloodshed in 1170. The
city resisted Cromwell's 1649 attacks—his phrase "by Hook or by
Crooke" refers to his two siege routes here, one via Hook Head, the
other via Crooke Village on the estuary—but fell the following year. It
did not prosper again until 1783, when George and William Penrose
set out to create "plain and cut flint glass, useful and ornamental," and
thereby set in motion a glass-manufacturing industry without equal.

Waterford has better-preserved city walls than anywhere else in Ireland
but Derry. Initially, the slightly run-down commercial center doesn't look
too promising. You'll need to park your car and proceed on foot to discover the heritage that the city has made admirable efforts over the past
decade to preserve. The compact town center can be visited in a couple
of hours. Allow at least another hour if you intend to take the Waterford Crystal factory tour.

The **city quays**—at the corner of Custom House Parade and Peter Street—
are a good place to begin a tour of Waterford City. (The TIO is also
down here, at the Granary on Merchant's Quay.) The city quays stretch
for nearly 2 km (1 mi) along the River Suir and were described in the
18th century as the best in Europe.

26 **Reginald's Tower,** a waterside circular tower on the east end of Waterford's
quays, marks the apex of a triangle containing the old walled city of Waterford. Built by the Vikings for the city's defense in 1003, it has 80-foot-
high, 10-foot-thick walls; an interior stairway leads to the top. The
tower served in turn as the residence for a succession of Anglo-Norman
kings (including Henry II, John, and Richard II), a mint for silver coins,
a prison, and an arsenal. It is said that Strongbow's marriage to Eva, the
daughter of Dermot MacMurrough, took place here in the late 12th century, thus uniting the Norman invaders with the native Irish. It has been
restored to its original medieval appearance and furnished with appropriate 11th- to 15th-century artifacts. ✉ *The Quay* ☎*051/304–220* 🖻€2
🕑 *Easter–Mar. and Oct., daily 9–5; Apr.–Sept., daily 9:30–6.*

27 One of Waterford's finer Georgian buildings, **City Hall,** on the Mall, dates
from 1783 and was designed by John Roberts, a native of the city. Nearby
are some good examples of domestic Georgian architecture—tall, well-
proportioned houses with typically Irish semicircular fanlights above the
doors. The arms of Waterford hang over City Hall's own entrance, which
leads into a spacious foyer that originally was a town meeting place and
merchants' exchange. The building contains two lovely theaters, an old
Waterford dinner service, and an enormous 1802 Waterford glass chandelier, which hangs in the Council Chamber (a copy of the chandelier
hangs in Independence Hall in Philadelphia). The Victorian horseshoe-
shape Theatre Royal is the venue for the annual Festival of Light Opera
in September. ✉ *The Mall* ☎ *051/309–900* 🖻 *Free* 🕑 *Weekdays 9–5.*

28 The **Bishop's Palace** is among the most imposing of the remaining Georgian town houses. Only the foyer is open to the public. ✉ *Alongside*
City Hall on the Mall 🖻 *Free* 🕑 *Weekdays 9–5.*

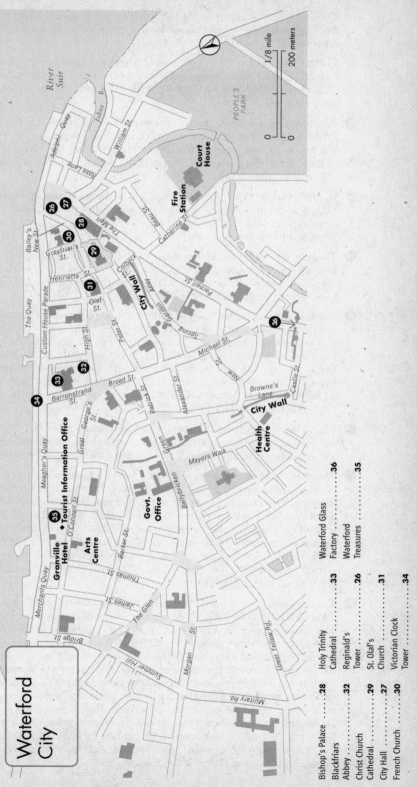

Waterford City

Off Colbeck Street along Spring Garden Alley, you'll see one of the remaining portions of the **old city wall**; there are sections all around the town center.

㉙ The late-18th-century Church of Ireland **Christ Church Cathedral**, designed by local architect John Roberts, is the only neoclassical Georgian Cathedral in Ireland. ⊠ *Henrietta St.* ☎ *051/858–958* ⊠ *€3* ☉ *Easter–Sept., daily 10–1 and 2–5.*

㉚ Roofless ruins are all that remain of **French Church** (⊠ Greyfriar's St.), a 13th-century Franciscan abbey. The church, also known as Greyfriars, was given to a group of Huguenot refugees (hence the "French") in 1695. A splendid east window remains amid the ruins. The key is available at Reginald's Tower.

㉛ **St. Olaf's Church** (⊠ St. Olaf's St.) was built, as the name implies, by the Vikings in the mid-11th century. All that remains of the old church is its original door, which has been incorporated into the wall of the existing building (a meeting hall).

㉜ The ruined tower of **Blackfriars Abbey** (⊠ High St.) belonged to a Dominican abbey founded in 1226 and returned to the crown in 1541 after the dissolution of the monasteries. It was used as a courthouse until Cromwellian forces destroyed it in the 17th century.

㉝ The Roman Catholic **Holy Trinity Cathedral** has a simple facade and a richly (some would say garishly) decorated interior with high, vaulted ceilings and ornate Corinthian pillars. It was designed in neoclassical style by John Roberts, who also designed Christ Church Cathedral and City Hall. Surprisingly, it was built in the late 18th century—when Catholicism was barely tolerated—on land granted by the Protestant city fathers. ⊠ *Barronstrand St. between High St. and the clock tower on the quays* ☎ *051/875–166* ⊠ *Free* ☉ *Daily 8:30–5:30.*

㉞ The **Victorian Clock Tower** (⊠ Merchant's Quay) was built in 1864 with public donations. Although it has no great architectural merit, it serves as a reminder of the days when Waterford was a thriving, bustling port.

㉟ **Waterford Treasures,** above the southeast's main TIO, uses interactive audiovisual technology to guide you through 1,000 years in the history of Waterford. Entertaining and educational, the exhibition displays Waterford's rich inheritance of rare and beautiful artifacts—from the Charter Roll 1372, a list of all charters granted to Waterford up to that time, written in Latin on vellum, to the sword of King Edward IV to 18th-century crystal. A restaurant and a shop are also on the premises. ⊠ *The Granary, Merchant's Quay* ☎ *051/304–500* ⊠ *€6* ☉ *Sept.–May, daily 10–5; June–Aug., daily 9:30–9.*

Fodor'sChoice
★

㊱ The city's most popular attraction is the **Waterford Glass Factory**, about 2 km (1 mi) from the TIO, where the world-famous crystal is created. The factory opened in 1783, crafting elegant and ornate stemware, chandeliers, and other pieces. Over the years, its clientele and product line diversified, and today the United States is the biggest market. The tour of the factory takes you through the specialized crafts of blowing, cutting, and polishing glass—all carried out against a noisy background of glowing furnaces and ceaseless bustle. An extensive selection of crystal is on view (and for sale) in the showroom. To reserve a place in a 60-minute tour, which includes an optional 18-minute audiovisual show, call the factory or the tourist office. To get here take the N25 Waterford–Cork road south from the quay, or ask at the tourist office about the regular bus service. ⊠ *Cork Rd., Kilbarry* ☎ *051/332–500* ⊕ *www.*

ROLLS-ROYCE OF CRYSTAL

WHEN THE WATERFORD GLASS FACTORY opened in 1783, it provided English royalty and nobility with a regular supply of ornate handcrafted stemware, chandeliers, and decorative knickknacks. Since then Waterford crystal has graced the tables of heads of states the world over, and Waterford's earlier pieces have become priceless heirlooms. The best Waterford glass was produced from the late 18th century to the early 19th century. This early work, examples of which can be found in museums and public buildings all over the country, is characterized by a unique, slightly opaque cast that is absent from the modern product.

From a humble but magical mix of silica sand, potash, and litharge comes the equally magical result—it reads like cold science, but something inexplicable happens when the craftspeople of Waterford produce arguably the finest crystal on the planet. Crystal glass is not cheap: each piece is individually fashioned by almost two dozen pairs of hands before it passes final inspection and receives the discreet Waterford trademark. If you're in Waterford, put a tour of the factory at the top of your itinerary. There you can see master craftspeople at work, fashioning the molten glass, blowing it into bulbous shapes, and then cutting and carving to give each piece those wonderful light-catching facets that cast multicolored reflections.

---

waterford.com ✉ €6.50 ☉ *Mar.–Oct., daily tours 8:30–4; Nov.–Feb., weekday tours 9:30–3:15.*

If the weather is favorable, consider taking a **cruise** along Waterford's harbor and the wide, picturesque estuary of the River Suir. You can enjoy lunch, afternoon tea, or dinner aboard a luxury river cruiser or simply take in the sights. The boat departs from the quay opposite the TIO, where you can purchase tickets. *Galley Cruises* ☎ 051/421–723 🖷 051/421–723 ⊕ *www.rivercruises.ie* ☉ *Cruises Apr.–Oct., daily at 12:30, 3, and 7, weather permitting.*

Where to Stay & Eat

$$–$$$$ ✕**Chez Ks Steak & Seafood Restaurant.** At this busy spot with bright walls, dark-wood furniture, colorful mosaic details, and an open kitchen, you can select a steak or seafood item from the chill cabinet, then entrust it to the theatrical chefs who will work their magic before your eyes. Grilled food is the specialty, and you can customize your meal with a choice of trimmings, sauces, and side dishes. House favorites include steak fillet with a pepper sauce, and Irish sea bass with a lemon beurre blanc. Portions are large, the service is good, and the food is an excellent value. ✉ *20–22 William St.* ☎ *051/844–180* ⚱ *Reservations essential* ▤ *DC, MC, V.*

★ $$–$$$ ✕**Dwyers of Mary Street.** Walls painted in shades of gray and wine, and beech dressers displaying both antique and modern glass soften and warm the interior of the old Royal Irish Constabulary barracks, which is where you'll find this French-influenced restaurant. The menu changes every four weeks; a typical meal might consist of a tartlet of Jerusalem artichokes and roast scallops, followed by a venison loin roast, carved on a bed of celeriac, and served with a port-and-orange sauce. ✉ *8 Mary*

St. ☎ *051/877–478* ⊕ *www.dwyersrestaurant.com* ⌔ *Reservations essential* ⊟ *AE, DC, MC, V* ۞ *Closed Sun. No lunch.*

$$–$$$
Fodor'sChoice
★
✕ **Wine Vault.** Yes, in the cellar of this Elizabethan town house, there really is a wine vault—and what a vault it is, with more than 350 labels. The ground floor houses a busy, informal bistro with polished wooden tables. Head chef Fergal Phelan uses traditional Irish ingredients to produce intriguing dishes. Glazed monkfish served on a ragout of butter beans and red peppers, and char-grilled balsamic chicken with lime and baby potatoes are favorites. ⊠ *High St.* ☎ *051/853–444* ⊟ *AE, MC, V* ۞ *Closed Sun.*

$$
✕ **Goose's Barbecue & Wine House.** The rustic dining room complements the ranch-style cooking that's served at this unusual restaurant in the historic quarter of the city. The exposed brick, robust furniture, and bright walls make convivial surroundings for a meat-heavy menu. Locals return again and again for the house specialties—saucy sausages, hickory-smoked spareribs, and Cajun chicken wings—which are cooked in an open kitchen. Balance your meal with a giant baked potato, healthy helping of greens from the self-service salad bar, and a bottle of wine from an interesting list. Efficient table service, good desserts, and hearty food guarantee a satisfying night out. ⊠ *19 Henrietta St.* ☎ *051/858–426* ⌔ *Reservations essential* ⊟ *MC, V* ۞ *Closed Sun. and Mon.*

$$$$
✕⌸ **Waterford Castle.** A magnificent 17th-century stone castle (with 19th-century additions) occupies its own 310-acre island in the River Suir. You can only reach the island, 3 km (2 mi) outside Waterford City, by car ferry. The Great Hall and the drawing room have fine oak paneling, ornate antique furniture, and tapestries. Guest rooms are luxuriously decorated and have four-poster beds. At the Munster Room restaurant, adorned with oak furniture and deep-burgundy Donegal carpet, the food tends to country-style dishes: poached salmon, asparagus served in puff pastry, and bread-and-butter pudding. ⊠ *The Island, Ballinakill, Co. Waterford* ☎ *051/878–203* ⊞ *051/879–316* ⊕ *www.waterfordcastle.com* ↩ *14 rooms with bath, 5 suites* ⌔ *Restaurant, 18-hole golf course, 2 tennis courts, fishing, croquet* ⊟ *AE, DC, MC, V* ⧨ *BP.*

$
Fodor'sChoice
★
✕⌸ **O'Gradys Restaurant & Guesthouse.** The modest exterior of O'-Gradys belies the first-class cooking that goes on inside. Low-key furnishings and a good art collection dominate the family-friendly restaurant ($–$$; reservations essential) run by welcoming husband-and-wife team Cornelius and Sue. The freshest local ingredients are given a modern Irish treatment, with seafood taking center stage. Expect staples like rock oysters gratiné, lobster in various tempting guises, and baked paupiettes of lemon sole with a lemongrass vinaigrette. There are nine simple, comfortable guest rooms and one apartment. ⊠ *Cork Rd., Co. Waterford* ☎ *051/878–851* ⊕ *www.ogradyshotel.com* ↩ *9 rooms with bath, 1 apartment* ⌔ *Restaurant* ⊟ *AE, DC, MC, V* ⧨ *BP.*

$$–$$$
⌸ **Dooleys Hotel.** Established in 1947, this family-run hotel has passed from mother to daughter for three generations and is now owned and managed by June Darrer and daughters Tina and Margaret. The rooms are simple and bright, and the service is excellent. The New Ship restaurant serves Continental dishes and has an early-bird menu. Waterford's main shopping, business, and cultural centers are just a few minutes' walk away. ⊠ *30 The Quay, Co. Waterford* ☎ *051/873–531* ⊞ *051/870–262* ⊕ *www.dooleys-hotel.ie* ↩ *115 rooms with bath* ⌔ *Restaurant, bar* ⊟ *AE, DC, MC, V* ⧨ *BP.*

$$–$$$
⌸ **Tower Hotel.** This three-story modern building overlooking the River Suir and a ten-minute walk from the TIO is one of the largest hotels in the southeast. It's touted as a family-friendly hotel, and there's a kid's club June through August with activities ranging from face painting to disco dancing to storytelling. Creams, beiges, and solid wood furniture

decorate the guest rooms. ⊠ *The Mall, Co. Waterford* ☎ *051/875–801* ⊜ *051/870–129* ⊕ *www.towerhotelwaterford.com* ⇨ *140 rooms with bath* ⚐ *2 restaurants, bar, indoor pool, gym, hot tub, sauna, children's programs (ages 2–7)* ▭ *AE, DC, MC, V.*

$ ⊞ **Foxmount Farm & Country House.** For a pleasant change of pace, you can stay on a working dairy farm in the peaceful countryside. This elegant 17th-century creeper-clad farmhouse on its own extensive grounds has an informal style, with welcoming log fires and intriguing antiques. It's about 5 km (3 mi) outside town on the road to the Passage East ferry. Your host, Margaret Kent, is renowned for her evening meals (for residents only). She uses the farm's produce, and fruit and herbs from her own garden. You're invited to bring your own wine and enjoy a glass or two around the hearth after dinner. ⊠ *Passage East Rd., Co. Waterford* ☎ *051/874–308* ⊜ *051/854–906* ⇨ *5 rooms with bath* ⚐ *Dining room, tennis court* ▭ *No credit cards* ⎇*BP* ⊙ *Closed Nov.–mid-Mar.*

Nightlife & the Arts

The **Spraoi Festival** (☎ 051/841–808 ⊕ www.spraoi.com) is billed as the "biggest street carnival in Ireland"—with street theater, live music, and fireworks. This free outdoor festival, which appeals to children and adults alike, takes place annually during the August bank-holiday weekend (the first weekend in August). The **Waterford International Festival of Light Opera** (☎ 051/874–402), the only competitive event of its kind, is a great draw for amateur musical societies from Ireland and Great Britain. The festival runs for 17 nights every September at the **Theatre Royal** (⊠ City Hall, The Mall ☎ 051/874–402). The **Waterford Show** tells the story of Waterford's culture and heritage through music, song, and dance. The show takes place at City Hall May through September at 9 PM on Tuesday, Thursday, and Saturday. The admission cost of €11 includes a preshow drink and a glass of wine during the show. Book at Waterford Glass Factory or the **Tourist Information Office** (☎ 051/875–788).

You can see a wide selection of work by contemporary artists at the **Dyehouse Gallery and Waterford Pottery** (⊠ Dyehouse La. ☎ 051/844–770). The **Forum** (⊠ The Glen ☎ 051/871–111 ⊕ www.forumwaterford. com) is a large entertainment venue that houses a 300-seat theater. Here you can watch local productions or those of traveling theater companies. Two separate music venues host big names as well as local acts performing all kinds of music. Culture buffs shouldn't miss the **Garter Lane Arts Centre** (⊠ 22A O'Connell St. ☎ 051/855–038), which hosts concerts, exhibits, and theater productions. The five-screen **Waterford Cineplex** (⊠ Patrick St. ☎ 051/874–595) shows current releases.

Geoffs (⊠ 9 John St. ☎ 051/874–787) is a dimly lighted pub frequented by students on weekends. A mixed crowd gathers during the week. Big flagstones cover the floors, and seating is on old wooden benches. A wide selection of food is served all day, every day. **Muldoons Bar** (⊠ 26–31 John St. ☎ 051/856–624) is a large, modern pub that serves until 2 AM weekends. A resident DJ plays most nights, and the dance club Merlins is next door. Housed in an 800-year-old building, the **Old Ground** (⊠ 10 The Glen ☎ 051/852–283) is a popular pub with locals. Lunch is served daily, and traditional-music sessions are held every Friday night. The circa-1700 **T & H Doolan's Bar** (⊠ 32 George's St. ☎ 051/872–764), reputed to be one of the oldest pubs in Ireland, hosts traditional Irish music most summer nights and Monday through Wednesday year-round.

Sports & the Outdoors

GAELIC FOOTBALL & HURLING   Gaelic football and hurling can be seen at the **Waterford GAA Grounds** (⊠ Walsh Park ☎ 01/836–3222 for the GAA Association of Ireland in Dublin).

GOLF **Faithlegg Golf Club** (✉ Faithlegg House, Checkpoint ☎ 051/382–241) is an 18-hole, par-72 course set in mature landscape on the banks of the River Suir. **Waterford Castle Golf Club** (✉ The Island, Ballinakill ☎ 051/871–633) is an 18-hole, par-72 course that claims to be Ireland's only true island course.

HORSEBACK Horses are available by the hour at **Kilotteran Equitation Centre** (✉ Kilo-
RIDING tteran ☎ 051/384–158).

Shopping

City Square Shopping Centre (✉ City Sq. ☎ 051/853–528) has more than 40 shops ranging from small Irish fashion boutiques to large international department stores. Fashion shows and other forms of entertainment take place on the stage area in the center of the mall. **Joseph Knox** (✉ 3 Barronstrand St. ☎ 051/875–307) displays the best selection of crystal in Waterford City. **Kellys** (✉ 75–76 The Quay ☎ 051/873–557) has excellent Irish souvenirs, including traditional musical instruments, dolls, Irish linen, jewelry, Waterford crystal, and CDs.

While in Waterford, definitely pay a visit to the world-famous **Waterford Glass Factory** (✉ Cork Rd., Kilbarry ☎ 051/332–500). The showroom displays an extensive selection of Waterford crystal and Wedgwood china.

Dunmore East

㊲ *16 km (10 mi) southeast of Waterford City via R683 and R684.*

Dunmore East is a quaint, one-street fishing village of thatched cottages and an attractive lighthouse at the head of Waterford Harbor. You'll find many colorful but noisy kittiwakes that nest in the steep cliffs overlooking the harbor. Plenty of small beaches and cliff walks are nearby, and you get a wonderful view of the estuary from the hill behind the village.

Where to Eat

$$–$$$ ✕ **Ship Restaurant.** Chef Billy Fitzpatrick emphasizes fresh, local seafood at this simply furnished restaurant on the ground floor of a 19th-century house overlooking the bay. The cuisine mixes French and Irish influences. Start with an arrangement of seafood with ratatouille enhanced by gazpacho sauce. Entrées include grilled or panfried black sole, and roulade of Dover sole filled with saffron mousse. ☎ 051/383–141 ▭ *AE, DC, MC, V.*

Tramore

㊳ *11 km (7 mi) south of Waterford City on R675, 4 km (2½ mi) west of Dunmore East.*

☞ Tramore's 5-km-long (3-mi-long) **beach** is a popular escape for families from Waterford and other parts of the southeast, as the many vacation homes and camper parks indicate. This is Ireland's biggest seaside resort and a dream-come-true for young children, but it's not to everybody's taste. A 50-acre amusement park, a miniature railway, and vacation-home developments overshadow part of the seafront. (The upper half of town is more quiet and reserved.) At the western end of the beach, the sand gives way to rocky cliffs guarded by the Metal Man, a giant cast-iron figure who stands atop a great pillar. It's said that if a young woman hops on one foot around the base of the pillar three times, she will be married within a year. This custom, which is still observed in a lighthearted way, can be traced back to a stone that stood on the spot centuries ago and was used in ancient Celtic fertility rites.

Where to Stay & Eat

$–$$ ✕ **Esquire.** Originally built in 1932 as a gentlemen's bar, the upstairs restaurant here retains the air of a gentleman's club. Patron and chef Paul Horan applies his skills to fresh local produce. A full à la carte menu includes such dishes as smoked salmon, Irish peppered steak with brandy, and vegetarian specials. A simpler—and faster—bar-food menu is also available. ⊠ *Cross Market St.* ☎ *051/381–324* ▤ *MC, V.*

$ ▦ **Annestown House.** Romantically perched above the sea, this large, white Victorian house has its own private path down to Annestown Cove, one of many secluded coves along this breathtakingly beautiful stretch of coast between Tramore and Dungarvan. The house has been in the family of John Galloway since 1820. John and his wife, Pippa, welcome guests into a home full of nooks and crannies, lots of books, and a large billiard table. Bedrooms are generally large and full of character, with wonderful sea views at the front of the house. Dinner is served at 7:45 PM; book by noon. ⊠ *Annestown, Co. Waterford* ☎ *051/396–160* ⊞ *051/396–474* ⊕ *www.annestown.com* ⤳ *5 rooms with bath* ☾ *Dining room, tennis court, billiards, croquet* ▤ *AE, MC, V* ⦿| *BP* ☯ *Closed Nov.–mid-Mar.*

Sports & the Outdoors

GOLF The Comeragh Mountains overlook the **Tramore Golf Club** (⊠ Newtown Hill ☎ 051/386–170), an 18-hole championship parkland course.

HORSE RACING Horse races are held regularly at **Tramore Racecourse** (✛ signposted on R675 from Waterford ☎ 051/381–425).

> **en route** West of Tramore on R675 is **Annestown,** a small, quiet resort town with a good, sandy beach. The former copper-mining center of **Bunmahon,** now a fishing village popular with vacationers, is 8 km (5 mi) past Annestown. A scenic footpath, signposted from Bunmahon, follows the Mahon River as it tumbles down from the Comeragh Mountains. This pleasant coastal drive offers views of unusual rock formations in the cliffs interspersed with sand dunes, as well as various rare flowers and birds. Attractive, easily accessible beaches are at **Stradbally** and **Clonea.**

Dungarvan

39 *42 km (26 mi) southwest of Tramore on R675.*

With their covering of soft grasses, the lowlands of Wexford and eastern Waterford gradually give way to heath and moorland; the wetter climate of the hillier western Waterford countryside creates and maintains the bog. The mountains responsible for this change in climate rise up behind Dungarvan, the largest coastal town in County Waterford. This bustling fishing and resort spot sits at the mouth of River Colligan, which empties into Dungarvan Bay here. It's a popular base for climbers and hikers.

> **off the beaten path** RING (AN RINNE) – In this Gaeltacht area on Dungarvan Bay, the Irish language is still in daily use—this is unusual in the south and east of the country. At Colaiste na Rinne, a language college, courses have been provided in Irish since 1909. ⊠ *7 km (4¼ mi) southeast of Dungarvan, off N674F.*

Where to Stay & Eat

$$–$$$ ✕ **The Tannery.** Mediterranean and Asian spices occasionally surface in the cooking of chef-owner Paul Flynn. The secret, he says, is knowing when to meddle in what is otherwise classic French cuisine. Quiet mainstream jazz provides sophisticated background music in the high-ceiling room with tall windows in an old waterside tannery. ⊠ *10 Quay St.* ☎ *058/45420* ⊟ *AE, DC, MC, V* ☉ *Closed Mon. and 1st wk of Sept. and 2 wks in Jan. No dinner Sun.*

$ ☷ **The Gold Coast Golf Hotel.** This hotel with great views of Dungarvan Bay is one of the newest parts of a family-run and family-friendly property, including 21 self-catering holiday cottages (built around the 37-bedroom hotel) and 10 golf villas on the edge of a woodland course on a links setting. Rooms are bright, comfortable, and spacious. If you stay here you can use the facilities of the Gold Coast's sister hotel, the Clonea Strand, just 2½ km (1½ mi) away; they include a games room, a leisure complex, and Clonea's 3-km (2-mi) sandy beach. ⊠ *Co. Waterford* ☎ *058/42249 or 058/42416* 🖷 *058/43378* ⊕ *www.clonea.com* ⟿ *37 rooms with bath, 21 cottages, 10 villas* ዋ *Restaurant, 18-hole golf course, tennis court, indoor pool, gym, fishing, bar, playground* ⊟ *AE, DC, MC, V* ⍥ *BP.*

Nightlife & the Arts

A *ceilí* (Irish dance) is held nightly in summer at **Colaiste na Rinne** (⊠ Ring ☎ 058/46104).

Sports & the Outdoors

GOLF   **West Waterford Golf Club** (⊠ Coolcormack ☎ 058/43216) is an 18-hole, par-72 parkland course open year-round.

GAELIC FOOTBALL Gaelic football and hurling are played at **Fraher Field GAA** (☎ 01/836–
& HURLING   3222 for the GAA Association of Ireland in Dublin), a seven-minute walk north of town on the ring road.

IN & AROUND COUNTY TIPPERARY

"It's a long way to Tipperary . . .": so run the words of that famed song sung all over the world since World War I. Actually, Tipperary is *not* so far to go, considering that, as Ireland's biggest inland county, it's within easy striking distance of Waterford and Cork. Moving in from the coastline, you can travel through some of Ireland's most lush pasturelands and to some of its most romantic sights, such as Lismore Castle. The Nire Valley, in the mountains between Dungarvan and Clonmel, is a popular area for hiking and pursuing other outdoor pleasures. The Blackwater Valley is renowned for its beauty, peacefulness, and excellent fishing. Some of the finest racehorses in the world are raised in the fields of Tipperary, which is also the county where you'll find the Rock of Cashel—the greatest group of monastic ruins in all Ireland.

The Nire Valley

40 . *29 km (18 mi) northwest of Dungarvan on R672.*

A visit to the Nire Valley is worthwhile only if you have time to take a walk in this remote but enchanting spot. The valley of the River Nire starts in the village of Ballymacarbry and runs along the base of the Comeragh Mountains. Both forest and mountain walks pass through quiet country where sheep far outnumber people. **Knocknagriffin,** the highest peak in the Comeraghs, at 2,476 feet, is easily accessible to a moderately fit walker. It affords views back to Waterford on the coast and inland to Tipperary Town.

Where to Stay & Eat

★ $$–$$$$ ✕☷ **Hanora's Cottage.** It's one of Ireland's premier bed-and-breakfasts, built in the heart of the Nire Valley in the late 19th century. Pretty chintz curtains and spreads decorate the sizable guest rooms (large by cottage standards), all of which have single or double hot tubs. This is especially nice if you take part in the main activities here—golf (nearby), riding, and walking. The less energetic simply unwind in front of the open fire and wait to be fed dishes such as fillet of salmon in prawn and Chablis sauce, or medaillons of steak with onions, mushrooms, and mustard. ⊠ *Ballymacarbry, Co. Waterford* ☎ *052/36134* 🖷 *052/36540* 🛏 *10 rooms with bath ⚲ Restaurant, hot tub ☰ MC, V ☉ Restaurant closed Sun.* ⚭ *BP.*

Sports & the Outdoors

Explore the Nire Valley on horseback by joining a guided hack from **Melody's Riding Stables** (⊠ Ballymacarbry ☎ 052/36147).

Ardmore

▶ **41** *24 km (15 mi) south of Dungarvan on N25.*

Ardmore is a delightful village, with ancient roots, on its own peninsula at the base of a tall cliff. In the 5th century, St. Declan is reputed to have disembarked here from Wales and founded a monastery, 30 years before St. Patrick arrived in Ireland. Ardmore's monastic remains are found on the top of the cliff. The ruined 12th-century **Cathedral of St. Declan** has some ogham stones inside and weathered but interesting biblical scenes carved on its west front. The saint is said to be buried in **St. Declan's Oratory**, a small early Christian church that has been partially reconstructed. On the grounds of the ruined cathedral, the 97-foot-high **round tower**, one of 70 round towers remaining in Ireland, is in exceptionally good condition. Round towers were built by the early Christian monks as watchtowers and belfries but came to be used as places of refuge for the monks and their valuables during Viking raids. This is the reason the doorway is 15 feet above ground level—once inside, the monks could pull the ladder into the tower with them.

Lismore

42 *40 km (25 mi) northwest of Ardmore on N72 and R671.*

Popular with both anglers and romantics, the enchanting little town of Lismore is built on the banks of the Blackwater, a river famous for its trout and salmon. From the 7th to the 12th century it was an important monastic center, founded by St. Carthac (or Carthage), and it had one of the most renowned universities of its time. The village has two cathedrals, a Roman Catholic one from the late 19th century and the Church of Ireland St. Carthage's, which dates from 1633 and incorporates fragments of an earlier church.

As you cross the bridge entering Lismore, take in the dramatic view of the magnificent **Lismore Castle**, a vast, turreted gray-stone building atop a rock that overhangs River Blackwater. There has been a castle here since the 12th century, but the present structure, built by the sixth duke of Devonshire, dates from the mid-19th century. The house is not open to the public, unlike the upper and lower gardens, which consist of woodland walks, including an unusual yew walk said to be more than 800 years old, and an impressive display of magnolias, camellias, and shrubs. ☎ *058/54424* 🎟 *€5 ☉ Apr., May, Sept., and Oct., daily 1:45–4:45; June–Aug., daily 11–4:45.*

Mount Melleray Abbey was the first post-Reformation monastery, founded in 1832 by the Cistercian Order in what was then a barren mountainside wilderness. Over the years the order has transformed the site into more than 600 acres of fertile farmland. The monks maintain strict vows of silence, but you are welcome to join in services throughout the day and are permitted into most areas of the abbey. It is also possible to stay in the guest lodge by prior arrangement. If you are heading into the Knockmealdown Mountains from Lismore, you can easily stop on the way at the abbey for a visit. ⊠ *Cappoquin, south of the Vee Gap, signposted off R669, 13 km (8 mi) from Lismore* ☎ *058/54404* ⊠ *Free* ⊙ *Daily 7:45 AM–8 PM.*

Leaving Lismore, heading east on N72 for 6½ km (4 mi) toward Cappoquin, a well-known coarse-angling center, you can pick up R669 north into the **Knockmealdown Mountains.** Your route is signposted as the Vee Gap road, the Vee Gap being its summit, from where you'll have superb views of the Tipperary plain, the Galtee Mountains in the northwest, and a peak called Slievenamon in the northeast. If the day is clear, you should be able to see the Rock of Cashel, ancient seat of the kings of Munster, some 32 km (20 mi) away. Just before you enter the Vee Gap, look for a 6-foot-high mound of stones on the left side of the road. It marks the grave of Colonel Grubb, a local landowner who liked the view so much that he arranged to be buried here standing up so that he could look out over the scene for all eternity.

Where to Stay & Eat

$$–$$$ ✕⊡ **Richmond House.** Deep in the countryside, just outside Cappoquin, stands this handsome three-story Georgian country house with an informal, unpretentious, and very relaxing environment—under the personal supervision of owners Claire and Paul Deevy. The public rooms, with log fires and traditional rust-and-cream decor, are reminiscent of a classic country hotel. In the restaurant ($$$$), Paul, a talented chef, uses local produce whenever possible to create such dishes as cassoulet of local seafood (scallops, monkfish, salmon, Dover sole, and prawns) with saffron cream sauce. ⊠ *Cappoquin, Co. Waterford* ☎ *058/54278* 🖶 *058/54988* ⊕ *www.richmondhouse.net* ↘ *9 rooms with bath* ⌂ *Restaurant, fishing, horseback riding, bar* ▤ *AE, DC, MC, V* ⊠*Ι BP* ⊙ *Closed late Dec.–mid-Jan.*

Cahir

🔁 *37 km (23 mi) north of Lismore, at crossroads of R668, N24, and N8.*

Cahir Castle, on a rocky island on the River Suir, in the middle of the town of Cahir, is one of Ireland's largest and best-preserved castles, retaining its dramatic keep, tower, and much of its original defensive structure. An audiovisual show and guided tour are available upon request. ☎ *052/41011* ⊕ *www.heritageireland.ie* ⊠ *€2.75* ⊙ *Mid-Mar.–mid-June and mid-Sept.–mid-Oct., daily 9:30–5:30; mid-June–mid-Sept., daily 9–7:30; mid-Oct.–mid-Mar., daily 9:30–4:30; last admission 45 mins before closing.*

Where to Stay

¢ ⊡ **Bansha Castle.** Venture into the heart of quiet, wooded country backed by the Glen of Aherlow, about 8 km (5 mi) from Cahir on the N24 Tipperary road, to this 18th-century stone house with a Norman-style round tower. Large rooms, all with great views, are simply furnished with plain carpets and mahogany reproduction pieces, but walls are decorated in strong, vibrant colors. Locally grown organic produce is used in the good home cooking. Outdoor activities, such as walking, golfing, salmon and trout fishing, and horseback riding, are nearby. ⊠ *Bansha, Co. Tipperary* ☎ *062/54187* 🖶 *062/54294* ↘ *6 rooms, 5 with bath* ⌂ *Dining room* ▤ *No credit cards* ⊠*Ι BP.*

Sports & the Outdoors

Explore the Galtee Mountains and the Glen of Aherlow on horseback with **Bansha House Stables** (⊠ Bansha ☎ 062/54194).

en route   To your left as you drive from Cahir to Tipperary Town on N24 is the **Glen of Aherlow**, a lovely 16-km-long (10-mi-long) wooded stretch skirting the River Aherlow and its tributaries between the Galtee Mountains to the south and the Slievenamuck Hills to the north. The highest summit in the Galtees is the 3,018-foot Galtymore Mountain.

Tipperary Town

44 *22 km (14 mi) northwest of Cahir on N24.*

Tipperary Town, a dairy-farming center at the head of a fertile plain known as the Golden Vale, is a good starting point for climbing and walking in the hills around the Glen of Aherlow, but the small country town, on the River Ara, is worth visiting in its own right, too. In New Tipperary, a neighborhood built by local tenants during Ireland's Land War (1890–91), old buildings, like Dalton's Heritage House, have been restored; you can visit the Heritage House by calling the offices of Clann na hEireann. You can also visit the old Butter Market on Dillon Street; the Churchwell at the junction of Church, Emmet, and Dillon streets; and the grave of the grandfather of Robert Emmett—one of the most famous Irish patriots—in the graveyard at St. Mary's Church. A statue of Charles Kickham, whose 19th-century novel *The Homes of Tipperary* chronicled the devastation of this county through forced emigration, has a place of honor in the center of town. Adjacent to Bridewell Jail on St. Michael's Street is St. Michael's Church, with its stained-glass window of a soldier killed during World War I. The **headquarters of Clann na hEireann** (⊠ 45 Main St. ☎ 062/33188) researches the origins and history of surnames throughout Ireland, and promotes clan gatherings.

Sports & the Outdoors

Tipperary Racecourse (⊠ Limerick Junction ☎ 062/51357), 5 km (3 mi) northwest of town, is used for horse racing.

Cashel

45 *17 km (11 mi) northeast of Tipperary Town on N74.*

Cashel is a market town on the busy Cork–Dublin road, with a lengthy history as a center of royal and religious power. From roughly AD 370 until 1101, it was the seat of the kings of Munster, and it was probably at one time a center of Druidic worship. Here, according to legend, St. Patrick arrived in about AD 432 and baptized King Aengus, who became Ireland's first Christian ruler. One of the many legends associated with this event is that St. Patrick plucked a shamrock to explain the mystery of the Trinity, thus giving a new emblem to Christian Ireland.

Fodor'sChoice   The awe-inspiring, oft-mist-shrouded **Rock of Cashel** is one of Ireland's
★   most visited sites. The rock itself, a short walk to the north of the town, rises as a giant, circular mound 200 feet above the surrounding plain; it's crowned by a tall cluster of gray monastic remains. Legend has it that St. Patrick baptized King Aengus here and that the devil, flying over Ireland in a hurry, took a bite out of the Slieve Bloom Mountains to clear his path (the gap, known as the Devil's Bit, can be seen to the north of the rock) and spat it out in the Golden Vale.

The shell of **St. Patrick's Cathedral** is the largest structure on the summit. The 13th-century cathedral was originally built in a flamboyant variation on Romanesque style, but it was destroyed by fire in 1495. The restored building was desecrated during the 16th century in an ugly incident in which hundreds of townspeople who had sought sanctuary in the cathedral were burned to death when Cromwell's forces surrounded the building with turf and set it afire. A series of sculptures in the north transept represents the apostles, other saints, and the Beasts of the Apocalypse. Look for the octagonal staircase turret that ascends beside the Central Tower to a series of defensive passages built into the thick walls. From the top of the Central Tower, you'll have a wonderful view of the surrounding plains and mountains. Another passage gives access to the round tower, a well-preserved, 92-foot-high building.

The entrance to **Cormac's Chapel,** the best-preserved building on top of the Rock, is behind the south transept of the cathedral. The chapel was built in 1127 by Cormac Macarthy, king of Desmond and bishop of Cashel (combination bishop-kings were not unusual in the early Irish church). Note the high corbeled roof, modeled on the traditional covering of early saints' cells (as at Glendalough and Dingle); the typically Romanesque, twisted columns around the altar; and the unique carvings around the south entrance.

The **museum** across from the entrance to the Rock provides a 15-minute audiovisual display, as well as enthusiastic young guides who will ensure that you don't miss the many interesting features of the buildings on top of the Rock of Cashel. The best approach to the rock is along the Bishop's Walk, a 10-minute hike that begins outside the drawing room of the Cashel Palace hotel on Main Street. ⊠ *Rock of Cashel* ☎ *062/61437* ⊕ *www.heritageireland.ie* ✇ *€5* ⊙ *Mid-Mar.–mid-June, daily 9–5:30; mid-June–mid-Sept., daily 9–7; mid-Sept.–mid-Mar., daily 9–4:30.*

In the same building as the TIO, the **Cashel of the Kings Heritage Center** explains the historic relationship between the town and the Rock and includes a scale model of Cashel as it looked during the 1600s. ⊠ *City Hall, Main St.* ☎ *062/62511* ✇ *Free* ⊙ *Daily 9:30–5:50.*

The **G. P. A. Bolton Library,** on the grounds of the St. John the Baptist Church of Ireland Cathedral, has a particularly fine collection of rare books, manuscripts, and maps, some of which date from the beginning of the age of printing in Europe. ⊠ *John St.* ☎ *062/61944* ✇ *€2* ⊙ *Daily 10–4.*

Where to Stay & Eat

★ **$$–$$$$**   ✕ **Chez Hans.** This small, converted Victorian church at the foot of the Rock of Cashel oozes old-world charm, with its dark wood and tapestries, which provide a wonderfully elegant background for the white-linen tables. The chef prepares contemporary cuisine with a hint of nouvelle and does wonders with fresh Irish ingredients—especially seafood. You can order salmon, hake, or mussels, served in a light chive velouté. Another specialty is diced lamb with ratatouille and couscous. ⊠ *Rockside* ☎ *062/61177* ⚷ *Reservations essential* ⊟ *MC, V* ⊙ *Closed Sun. and Mon. and late Jan.–early Feb. No lunch.*

$$$–$$$$ ✕⊡ **Cashel Palace.** Antiques fill the luxurious guest rooms on the first floor of the main house. Rooms on the second floor are cozier, though not small. The Bishop's Buttery restaurant ($$–$$$) relies on game in season, local lamb and beef, and fresh fish creatively prepared, and also serves simple, light meals all day. Don't miss the lovely gardens at the rear of the house, where you can see the descendants of the original hop plants used by Richard Guinis to brew the first "Wine of Ireland." Guinis went on, with his son, Arthur, to found the famous Guinness Brewery in Dublin. ⊠ *Main St., Co. Tipperary* ☎ *062/62707* 🖷 *062/61521* ⊕ *www.cashel-palace.ie* ⥷ *23 rooms with bath* ⚭ *2 restaurants, fishing, bar* ⊟ *AE, DC, MC, V* ⦿⧉ *BP.*

$$ ⛻ **Dundrum House Hotel.** Nestled beside the River Multeen, 12 km (7½ mi) outside busy Cashel, is this magnificent, four-story Georgian house. Sixteen high-ceiling bedrooms take up the main house; the rest are in a three-story wing built during the house's previous incarnation as a convent. All the older rooms have large pieces of early Victorian furniture and lovely views of the surrounding parkland. The old convent chapel, stained-glass windows intact, is now a cocktail bar. Elaborate plaster ceilings, attractive period furniture, and open fires make the spacious dining room and lounge inviting. ⊠ *Dundrum, Co. Tipperary* ☎ *062/ 71116* 🖷*062/71366* ⊕*www.dundrumhousehotel.com* ⥷*85 rooms with bath* ⚭ *2 restaurants, 18-hole golf course, pool, sauna, steam room, fishing, 3 bars* ⊟ *AE, DC, MC, V* ⦿⧉ *BP.*

Nightlife & the Arts

You can enjoy folksinging, storytelling, and dancing evenings from mid-June through September, Tuesday through Saturday, at the **Bru Boru Heritage Center** (☎ 062/61122) at the foot of the Rock of Cashel. Entertainment usually begins at 9 PM and costs €15, €40 with dinner.

Sports & the Outdoors

GAELIC FOOTBALL & HURLING
About 20 km (12 mi) north of Cashel, **Semple GAA Stadium** (⊠ Thurles ☎ 0504/22702) is where major hurling and football championships in the southeast take place, as well as many exciting minor contests.

GOLF
The natural features of the mature Georgian estate at Dundrum House Hotel have been incorporated into an 18-hole, par-72 course for the **County Tipperary Golf and Country Club** (⊠ Dundrum House Hotel, Dundrum ☎ 062/71717).

Clonmel

46 *24 km (15 mi) southeast of Cashel on R688.*

As the county seat of Tipperary, Clonmel is set on the prettiest part of the River Suir, with wooded islands and riverside walks. This is one of Ireland's largest and most prosperous inland towns. There has been a settlement here since Viking days; in the 14th century the town was walled and fortified as a stronghold of the Butler family. At one end of town is the West Gate, built in 1831 on the site of the medieval one. Among other notable buildings are the Main Guard, built in 1695 to house the courts of the Palatinate, a separate jurisdiction ruled by the Butlers, and the Franciscan friary and St. Mary's Church of Ireland, both of which incorporate remains of earlier churches and some interesting tombs and monuments.

Where to Stay & Eat

$–$$ ✕ **Mulcahy's of Clonmel.** In this superb series of interconnecting bars and restaurant areas you'll find a wide selection of food, from the East Lane Cafe's à la carte to the daily carvery lunch to the Kitchen Grill menu of good pub grub, like deep-fried scampi. Mulcahy's has 10 modern bedrooms over the pub. ⊠ *47 Gladstone St.* ☎ *052/22825* ⊟ *AE, DC, MC, V.*

$$–$$$ ✕⛻ **Hotel Minella.** This granite-face Georgian manor hotel is in a quiet neighborhood on the bank of the River Suir. The bedrooms, particularly those in the front and in the east wing, have fine views of the river. Three of the eight suites have four-poster beds and private steam rooms;

the remaining five have hot tubs. Comfortable Victorian furnishings fill the main house, and hunting prints line the walls. The oak-panel restaurant ($–$$$) has a good reputation for well-prepared traditional Irish cuisine. ⊠ *Coleville Rd., Co. Tipperary* ☎ *052/22388* 🖷 *052/24381* ⊕ *www.hotelminella.ie* ↩ *62 rooms with bath, 8 suites, 10 apartments* ⚘ *Restaurant, health club, fishing, bar* ☰ *AE, DC, MC, V* ⦿❘ *BP.*

Sports & the Outdoors

GAELIC FOOTBALL & HURLING
Gaelic football and hurling are played at the **Clonmel GAA Grounds** (⊠ Western Rd. ☎ 052/23873).

GOLF
Clonmel Golf Club (⊠ Lyreanearla ☎ 052/24050) is an 18-hole course on the slopes of the Comeragh Mountains, 5 km (3 mi) from Clonmel.

HORSE RACING
Horse races are held at **Clonmel Racecourse** (⊠ Powerstown Park ☎ 052/22611).

Carrick-on-Suir

❹⑦ *20 km (12 mi) east of Clonmel on N24.*

Carrick-on-Suir lies partly in County Tipperary and partly in County Waterford. The beautifully restored **Ormonde Castle** is the town's main attraction. The castle, dating from 1450, is fronted by the 16th-century Ormonde Manor House, an interesting and well-preserved Tudor mansion. The town is one of several claiming to be the birthplace of Anne Boleyn, and the house is said to have been built in order to entertain her daughter, Queen Elizabeth I, who never visited here. The castle contains some good early stuccowork, especially in the 100-foot Long Room, and many arms and busts of the English queen. ☎ *051/640–787* ⊕ *www.heritageireland.ie* ⊠ *€2.55* ⦿ *Mid-June–Sept., daily 9:30–6:30.*

Shopping

The **Tipperary Crystal Factory Shop** (⊠ Ballynoran ☎ 051/641–188), a factory outlet, has its showroom in a replica of a thatched cottage.

THE SOUTHEAST A TO Z

To research prices, get advice from other travelers, and book travel arrangements, visit www.fodors.com.

AIR TRAVEL

Aer Arann flies once daily in both directions between Waterford City and London's Luton Airport.

🖪 Carrier **Aer Arann** ☎ 1890/462–726 ⊕ www.aerarannexpress.ie.

AIRPORT

Waterford Regional Airport is on the Waterford–Ballymacaw road in Killowen. Waterford City is less than 10 km (6 mi) from the airport. A hackney cab from the airport into Waterford City costs approximately €15.

🖪 Airport Information **Waterford Regional Airport** ☎ 051/875–589.

BOAT & FERRY TRAVEL

The region's primary ferry terminal is just south of Wexford Town at Rosslare. Irish Ferries connects Rosslare to Pembroke, Wales, and France's Cherbourg and Roscoff. Stena Sealink sails directly between Rosslare Ferryport and Fishguard, Wales.

🖪 Boat & Ferry Information **Irish Ferries** ☎ 053/33158. **Stena Sealink** ☎ 053/33115.

BUS TRAVEL

Bus Éireann makes the Waterford–Dublin journey 10 times a day for about €10 one-way. There are six buses daily between Waterford City and Limerick, and four between Waterford City and Rosslare. The Cork–Waterford bus runs 13 times a day. In Waterford City, the terminal is Waterford Bus Station.

🔢 Bus Information **Bus Éireann** ☎ 01/836-6111 in Dublin, 051/879-000 in Waterford.

CAR RENTAL

The major car-rental companies have offices at Rosslare Ferryport, and in most large towns rental information is available through the local tourism office. Typical car-rental prices start at about €55 per day (€32 per day for seven days) with unlimited mileage, and they usually include insurance and all taxes. Budget has offices in Rosslare Harbor and at Waterford Airport. Hertz has offices in Rosslare Harbor.

🔢 Agencies **Budget** ✉ The Ferryport, Rosslare Harbor ☎ 053/33318 ✉ Waterford Airport ☎ 051/421-670. **Hertz** ✉ The Ferryport, Rosslare Harbor ☎ 053/33238.

CAR TRAVEL

Waterford City, the regional capital, is easily accessible from all parts of Ireland. From Dublin, take N7 southwest, change to N9 in Naas, and continue along this highway through Carlow Town and Thomastown until it terminates in Waterford. N25 travels east–west through Waterford City, connecting it with Cork in the west and Wexford Town in the east. From Limerick and Tipperary Town, N24 stretches southeast until it, too, ends in Waterford City.

ROAD CONDITIONS For the most part, the main roads in the southeast are of good quality and are free of congestion. Side roads are generally narrow and twisting, and you should keep an eye out for farm machinery and animals on country roads.

EMERGENCIES

🔢 Emergency Services **Ambulance, fire, police** ☎ 112 or 999.

🔢 Hospital **Waterford Regional Hospital** ✉ Ardkeen ☎ 051/848-000.

TOURS

Irish City Tours in Kilkenny operates open-top coach tours from the castle gate Easter through September, daily 10:30–5.

Burtchaell Tours in Waterford City leads a Waterford walk at noon and 2 PM daily from March through September. Tours depart from the Granville Hotel. Walking tours of Kilkenny are arranged by Tynan Tours from the Kilkenny TIO; tours take place daily April through October, and Tuesday through Saturday, November to March. Walking tours of historic Wexford Town can be prebooked for groups by contacting Seamus P. Molloy of Wexford Town Walking Tours.

🔢 Bus Tour **Irish City Tours** ☎ 01/458-0054.

🔢 Walking Tours **Burtchaell Tours** ☎ 051/873-711. **Tynan Tours** ☎ 087/265-1745. **Wexford Town Walking Tours** ☎ 053/22663.

TRAIN TRAVEL

Waterford City is linked by Irish Rail service to Dublin. Trains run from Plunkett Station in Waterford City to Dublin four times daily, making stops at Thomastown, Kilkenny, Bagenalstown, and Carlow Town. The daily train between Waterford City and Limerick makes stops at Carrick-on-Suir, Clonmel, Cahir, and Tipperary Town. The train between Rosslare and Waterford City runs twice daily.

🔢 Train Information **Irish Rail** ☎ 01/836-6222 in Dublin, 051/873-401 in Waterford ⊕ www.irishrail.ie.

VISITOR INFORMATION

Ten Tourist Information Offices (TIOs) in the southeast are open all year. They are Carlow Town, Carrick-on-Suir, Clonmel, Dungarvan, Enniscorthy, Gorey, Kilkenny, Lismore, Waterford City, and Wexford Town. Another seven TIOs are open seasonally: Ardmore (June–mid-September); Cahir (May–September); Cashel (April–September); New Ross (May–September); Rosslare (April–September); Tipperary Town (May–October); Tramore (June–August).

🚹 Tourist Information **Ardmore** ✉ Ardmore, Co. Waterford ☎ 024/94444. **Cahir** ✉ Castle Car Park, Co. Tipperary ☎ 052/41453. **Carlow Town** ✉ College St., Co. Carlow ☎ 0503/31554. **Carrick-on-Suir** ✉ Heritage Centre, Main St., Co. Tipperary ☎ 051/640-200. **Cashel** ✉ Cashel Heritage Centre, Co. Tipperary ☎ 062/62511. **Clonmel** ✉ Community Office, 8 Sarsfield St., Co. Tipperary ☎ 052/22960. **Dungarvan** ✉ The Courthouse, Co. Waterford ☎ 058/41741. **Enniscorthy** ✉ Wexford Museum, The Castle, Castle Hill, Co. Wexford ☎ 054/34699. **Gorey** ✉ Markethouse, Main St., Co. Wexford ☎ 055/21248. **Kilkenny** ✉ Shee Alms House, Rose Inn St., Co. Kilkenny ☎ 056/51500. **Lismore** ✉ Heritage Centre, Co. Waterford ☎ 058/54975. **New Ross** ✉ Harbour Centre, The Quay, Co. Wexford ☎ 051/421-857. **Rosslare** ✉ Rosslare Ferry Terminal, Kilrane, Rosslare Harbor, Co. Wexford ☎ 053/33232. **Tipperary Town** ✉ 3 Mitchel St., Co. Tipperary ☎ 062/51457. **Tramore** ✉ Town Centre, Co. Waterford ☎ 051/381-572. **Waterford City** ✉ 41 The Quay, Co. Waterford ☎ 051/875-823 ⊕ www.southeastireland.com. **Wexford Town** ✉ Crescent Quay, Co. Wexford ☎ 053/23111.

THE SOUTHWEST

5

FODOR'S CHOICE

Ballymakeigh House, *Killeagh hotel*
Ballymaloe House, *Shanagarry restaurant-inn*
Blasket Islands, *Dunquin*
Casino House, *Kilbrittain restaurant*
Longueville House, *Mallow hotel*
Park Hotel, *Kenmare hotel*
The Vintage, *Kinsale restaurant*

HIGHLY RECOMMENDED

RESTAURANTS
Chart House, *Dingle Town*
Crackpots, *Kinsale*
Hayfield Manor, *Cork City*
Old Presbytery, *Killarney*

HOTELS
Ard na Sidhe, *Glenbeigh*
Assolas Country House, *Kanturk*
Clarion Hotel, *Limerick City*
Mustard Seed at Echo Lodge, *Ballingarry*
Old Bank House, *Kinsale*
Sea View House, *Ballylickey*
Tahilla Cove Country House, *Sneem*

SIGHTS
Bunratty Castle & Folk Park, *Bunratty*
Charles Fort, *Kinsale*
English Market, *Cork City*
Gap of Dunloe, *Killarney*
Glin Castle, *Glin*

Updated by
Alannah
Hopkin

CORK, KERRY, LIMERICK, AND CLARE—the sound of these southwest Ireland county names has an undeniably evocative Irish lilt. Just as evocative is the scenery in each county: from Kinsale along the coast west to Mizen Head in the far southwest corner to the glorious mountains and lakes of Killarney. And the food! Thanks to its accomplished chefs and the bounty of farms, fields, lakes, and coast, County Cork has become a little paradise of fresh, rustic Irish cuisine. You'll also find a mild climate, Irish-speaking areas, and Ireland's second- and third-largest cities—Cork and Limerick. But the most notable attractions are rural: miles and miles of pretty country lanes meandering through rich but sparsely populated farmland. To be in a hurry here is to be ill-mannered. It was probably a Kerryman who first remarked that when God made time, he made plenty of it.

As you look over thick, fuchsia hedges at thriving dairy farms or stop at a wayside restaurant to sample seafood or locally raised meat, it's difficult to imagine that some 150 years ago this area was decimated by famine. Thousands perished in fields and workhouses, and thousands more took "coffin ships" from Cobh in Cork Harbour to the New World. Between 1845 and 1849 Ireland's population decreased by more than a million, or roughly 30% (according to the 1841 census, the Irish population was 8,175,124). Many small southwest villages were wiped out. The region was battered again in the War for Independence and the Civil War that was fought with intensity in and around "Rebel Cork" between 1919 and 1921. Economic recovery didn't pick up until the late 1960s, and tourist developments were low-key until the mid-1990s.

The Irish economic boom coincided with a marketing push to increase visitor numbers. The result has been a mixed blessing. The southwest's main routes are no longer traffic-free, but the roads themselves are better. There's a bigger choice of accommodations, with improved facilities, but many of the newer hotels and bed-and-breakfasts are bland. Even the traditional warm Irish welcome is less ubiquitous, given the increased pace of everyday life. Furthermore, all the development has threatened the environment. The southwest is, however, making a concerted effort to attract more visitors while keeping beaches and rivers clean and scenery unspoiled.

South of Cork City, the region's main business and shopping community, the resort town of Kinsale is the gateway to a rocky, attractive coastline containing Roaring Water Bay, with its main islands, and Bantry Bay, a magnificent natural harbor. The region's southwest coast is formed by three peninsulas: the Beara, the Iveragh, and the Dingle; the road known as the Ring of Kerry makes a complete circuit of the Iveragh Peninsula. Killarney's blue lakes and sandstone mountains, inland from the peninsulas, have a unique and romantic splendor, immortalized in the 19th century by the writings of William Thackeray and Sir Walter Scott. Around the Shannon Estuary you enter "castle country," an area littered with ruined castles and abbeys, the result of Elizabeth I's 16th-century attempt to subdue the old Irish province of Munster. Limerick City, too, bears the scars of history from a different confrontation with the English—the Siege of Limerick, which took place in 1691. Today, its other "scars"—described so memorably in Frank McCourt's best-seller *Angela's Ashes*—lure travelers.

Although the southwest has several sumptuous country-house hotels, it's basically an easygoing, unpretentious region, where informality and simplicity prevail. As in the rest of Ireland, social life revolves around the pub, and a visit to your "local" is the best way to find out what's going on.

GREAT ITIN

Numbers in the text correspond t...
west, Cork City, and Killarney a...

If you have 3 days

Base yourself in 🏠 **Killarney** 40 ... one day to explore Killarney's la... **of Dunloe** 47 on a tour and wal... gap itself, crossing the lake bey... head for the Ring of Kerry via ki... as well as the subtropical vegetation, which exists thanks to the Gulf Stream. On the third day, follow the Pass of Keimaneigh to **Bantry** 31. The cliff-top road between Bantry and Glengarriff affords sea views along the 24-km (15-mi) Bantry Bay inlet. The stretch between **Glengarriff** 32 and Killarney, known as the tunnel road, is a famous scenic route. It comes into Killarney past the **Ladies' View** 48, which has changed little since it impressed Queen Victoria's ladies-in-waiting.

If you have 5 days

For a gastronomic tour, begin in 🏠 **Cork City** 1 – 17 ☞ with a trip to the English Market. Stay overnight and sample the classic French cuisine at Fleming's. The next day head out to Ballymaloe House in 🏠 **Shanagarry** 21, where the emphasis is on local produce and fish from nearby Ballycotton. If you plan carefully, you may be able to fit in a one-day cooking class at the nearby Ballymaloe Cookery School and Gardens. Next drive northwest to 🏠 **Mallow** 24 and Longueville House. Proprietor William O'Callaghan's President's restaurant earns raves as one of the finest in Ireland. From here, head to 🏠 **Kenmare** 33, where the Park Hotel's terraced lawns sweep down to Kenmare Bay; stroll in the gardens before dinner. The following day drive back toward the waterfront village of 🏠 **Kinsale** 26, for a meal in one of its many acclaimed restaurants. Return to Cork City the next day.

If you have 7 days

Start at **Bunratty Castle and Folk Park** 61 ☞, the nearest attraction to Shannon Airport. Continue on to 🏠 **Limerick City** 60 to see King John's Castle or the Hunt Museum. The following day, head south to **Blarney** 18 to kiss the stone and shop for crafts. Proceed to 🏠 **Cork City** 1 – 17 for the night. The next day head east to Cobh, where the Queenstown Heritage Centre documents Irish emigration. Cross the harbor by ferry and visit 🏠 **Kinsale** 26, a historic and fashionable port town. The following day, drive through West Cork around Bantry Bay and into **Glengarriff** 32, where you can take a boat to the gardens on Ilnacullin. Continue on to 🏠 **Kenmare** 33 and 🏠 **Killarney** 40 via the Windy Gap. Spend the night here and make an early start the next day, either visiting the **Gap of Dunloe** 47 or touring **Muckross House** 43. In the afternoon, leave for the Ring of Kerry, driving past 🏠 **Sneem** 34 to 🏠 **Waterville** 35 or Caragh Lake. From Cahirciveen you can see the Dingle Peninsula and the stretch of road that takes you to 🏠 **Dingle Town** 50. Cliffs and early Christian remains are just a short ride outside town, beyond **Slea Head** 52. On the final day, drive across the Connor Pass and up to 🏠 **Tralee** 56. Return to Limerick City and Shannon Airport on the Adare road (N21) or take N69 to Tarbert and the ferry into County Clare to reach Galway.

outhwest

s chapter is organized into seven sections: Cork City, which includes side trip to Blarney Castle, home of the Blarney Stone; East Cork and the Blackwater Valley, covering Youghal and Ballymaloe; Kinsale to Glengarriff, including Mizen Head, Cape Clear, and other points in the far southwest); the Ring of Kerry; In and Around Killarney; the Dingle Peninsula; and North Kerry and Shannonside. The first section is Cork City, and there's an assumption that you'll approach from points east and make a clockwise sweep of the area. The chapter ends on the northern fringe, crossing over the border from County Kerry into County Limerick and then briefly dipping into the very southeastern reaches of County Clare in the area immediately around Shannon Airport. If you fly into Shannon, you can easily travel the entire sequence in reverse.

Among the southwest's most notable attractions are Killarney's lakes, which require a day or more; you simply must explore these wonders partly on foot to enjoy them fully. Killarney also makes a good base for discovering the Ring of Kerry and the Dingle Peninsula. The main cities in the area—Cork, Tralee, and Limerick—have quiet charm, but they can't compete with the magnificent scenery farther west. Kinsale is a favorite starting point for a leisurely drive through the coast west to Bantry, which can take one day or three, depending on your appetite for unscheduled stops and impromptu exploration. Two national parks, Glengarriff near the sea and Gougane Barra in the mountains, are also worth visiting.

About the Restaurants

The southwest, especially County Cork, rivals Dublin as Ireland's food-culture epicenter. Cork has astonishing resources: waters full of a wide array of fish, acre after acre of potato fields, cows galore, wild mushrooms and berries—not to mention inventive chefs who transform this bounty into feasts. In tiny Shanagarry, Darina Allen trains hundreds of chefs every year at the Ballymaloe Cookery School. Outstanding restaurants and the Festival of Fine Food in October draw crowds to Kinsale, where high quality cuisine is the order of the day. Whether trained at home or abroad, area chefs put a premium on fresh, local (often organically grown) produce.

If you want to dress for dinner, as some people do, feel free. By and large, however, informality rules. Restaurants outside main cities tend to be seasonal, and choices will be limited between November and mid-March. To sample the region's best cuisine, consult the gastronomic tour, below.

About the Hotels

The southwest has a number of sumptuous country-house hotels, and although some appear grand, their main aim is to provide a relaxed stay in beautiful surroundings. There are more modest establishments, too, and many are in spectacular seaside locations. A good pair of walking boots and a sensible raincoat are more useful here than a fancy wardrobe. Keep in mind that facilities may be minimal—only expensive hotels have fitness centers, for instance. The staffs at many places can, however, organize golf, deep-sea-fishing, freshwater-angling, and horseback-riding expeditions as well as recommend hiking routes.

Most B&Bs have introduced private bathrooms; rooms at such properties in larger towns may also have TVs and direct-dial phones. Accommodations in West Cork, Killarney, and Dingle are seasonal; between

November and March, many places close down, but outside these months—especially from July to mid-October—hotels are busy, so book well in advance.

WHAT IT COSTS In Euros				
	$$$$	**$$$**	**$$**	**$**	**¢**
RESTAURANTS	over €29	€22–€29	€15–€22	€8–€15	under €8
HOTELS	over €230	€180–€230	€130–€180	€80–€130	under €80

Restaurant prices are per person for a main course at dinner. Hotel prices are for two people in a double room, including VAT and a service charge (often applied in larger hotels).

Timing

The weather is most likely to be warm and sunny in July and August, though there's never really a guarantee against rain. July and August are the busiest months, with Irish, British, and Continental tourists heading for the area in large numbers. Visiting in high season means the bars and restaurants of the area will be lively but also crowded. The best time to visit is in the "shoulder seasons"—May through June and September through October, when the weather is still mild; most, if not quite all, accommodations and attractions are open; and crowds are scarce. You may feel chilled from the dampness and the rain, but it rarely gets truly cold. Regardless of when you visit, pack clothing that you can layer and a good windbreaker or rain slicker—preferably one that you can readily fold and put in a handbag or knapsack with your collapsible umbrella.

CORK CITY

▶ **①**–**⑰** *254 km (158 mi) south of Dublin, 105 km (65 mi) south of Limerick City.*

The major metropolis of the south, Cork is Ireland's second-largest city (population 175,000), but put this in perspective—roughly half of Ireland's 3.6 million people live in and around Dublin, a city 10 times the size. Though small relative to the capital, Cork is a spirited, lively place, with a formidable pub scene, a lively traditional music scene, a respected and progressive university, attractive art galleries, and offbeat cafés. Preparations are well under way for 2005, when Cork will be designated European City of Culture, and the buzz had already started, with a striking but controversial redesign of the city center (Patrick's Street and Grand Parade by Barcelona-based architect Beth Galli.

The city received its first charter in 1185 from Prince John of Norman England, and it takes its name from the Irish word *corcaigh,* meaning "marshy place." The original 6th-century settlement was spread over 13 small islands in the River Lee. Major development occurred during the 17th and 18th centuries with the expansion of the butter trade, and many attractive Georgian-design buildings with wide bowfront windows were constructed during this time. As late as 1770, Cork's present main streets—Grand Parade, Patrick Street, and the South Mall—were submerged under the Lee. Around 1800, when the Lee was partially dammed, the river divided into two streams that now flow through the city, leaving the main business and commercial center on an island, not unlike Paris's Ile de la Cité. As a result, the city features a number of bridges and quays, which, although initially confusing, add greatly to the port's unique character.

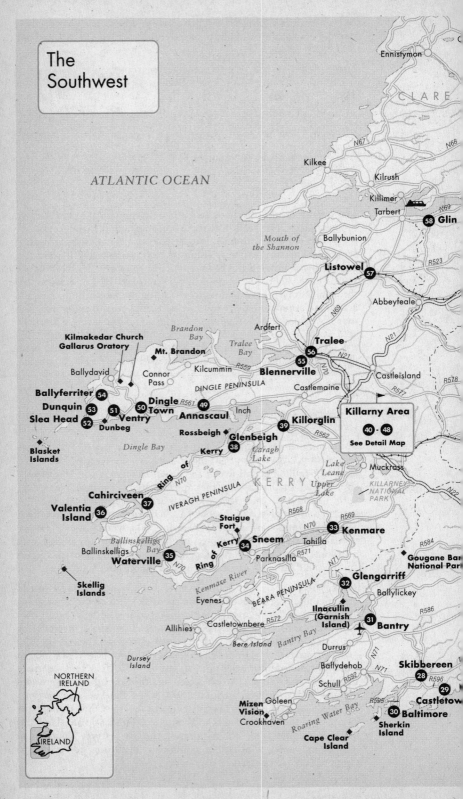

The
Southwest

ATLANTIC OCEAN

CLARE

Ennistymon

N67

N68

Kilkee

Kilrush

Killimer

Tarbert

N69

58 Glin

Mouth of
the Shannon

Ballybunion

R523

Listowel

57

Abbeyfeale

N69

N21

Ardfert

Brandon
Bay

Mt. Brandon

Tralee
Bay

Tralee

N21

**Kilmakedar Church
Gallarus Oratory**

Kilcummin

R559

56

Castleisland

R578

Ballydavid

Connor
Pass

DINGLE PENINSULA

Blennerville

55

Castlemaine

N70

R577

Ballyferriter 54

R561

**Dingle
Town**

49

Inch

Castlemaine

Dunquin 53

50

Annascaul

Slea Head

51

Ventry

39 Killorglin

52

Dunbeg

Rossbeigh

R562

Killarny Area

40 - 48

See Detail Map

Blasket
Islands

Dingle Bay

Glenbeigh

Kerry 38

Caragh
Lake

Lake
Leane

KERRY

Upper
Lake

Muckrass

KILLARNEY
NATIONAL
PARK

Ring

of

N70

Cahirciveen

37

IVERAGH PENINSULA

N22

**Valentia
Island 36**

Staigue
Fort

R568

R569

33 **Kenmare**

Ballinskelligs
Bay

Ring

34

Sneem

Tahilla

N70

R584

Ballinskelligs

35

of
Kerry

Parknasilla

R571

**Gougane Bar
National Park**

Waterville

N70

Kenmare River

BEARA PENINSULA

32

Glengarriff

Skellig
Islands

Eyenes

Ballylickey

R586

Allihies

Castletownbere

R572

Bere Island

**Ilnacullin
(Garnish
Island)**

31 **Bantry**

Bantry Bay

Durrus

N71

Dursey
Island

Ballydehob

Skibbereen

N71

Schull

R592

28 R596

29

**Mizen
Vision**

Goleen

Crookhaven

R595

Castletow

30 **Baltimore**

Roaring Water Bay

Sherkin
Island

**Cape Clear
Island**

NORTHERN
IRELAND

IRELAND

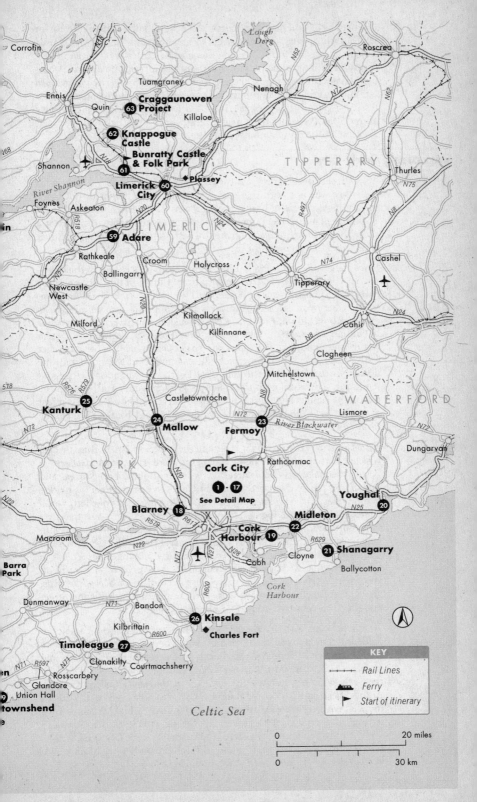

Corrofin

Tuamgraney

Ennis

Quin

63 **Craggaunowen Project**

Killaloe

Nenagh

Roscrea

Lough Derg

N52

N7

N62

TIPPERARY

Thurles

62 **Knappogue Castle**

Shannon

61 **Bunratty Castle & Folk Park**

Limerick City 60 • Plassey

N75

River Shannon

Foynes

Askeaton

59 **Adare**

Rathkeale

Croom

Holycross

Cashel

Newcastle West

Ballingarry

Tipperary

N74

Milford

Kilmallock

Kilfinnane

Cahir

Clogheen

N8

WATERFORD

25 **Kanturk**

Castletownroche

Mitchelstown

Lismore

24 **Mallow**

N72

23 **Fermoy**

River Blackwater

Dungarvan

N72

CORK

Rathcormac

Cork City

1 - 17

See Detail Map

Youghal 20

18 **Blarney**

N25

Midleton 22

Cork Harbour 19

21 **Shanagarry**

Cloyne

Ballycotton

Macroom

Cobh

Cork Harbour

Barra Park

Dunmanway

Bandon

26 **Kinsale**

Kilbrittain

♦ **Charles Fort**

Timoleague 27

Clonakilty

Courtmachsherry

Rosscarbery

Glandore

Union Hall

townshend

Celtic Sea

0   20 miles

0   30 km

"Rebel Cork" emerged as a center of the Nationalist Fenian movement in the 19th century. The city suffered great damage during the War of Independence in 1919–21, when much of its center was burned. Cork is now regaining some of its former glory as a result of sensitive commercial development and an ongoing program of inner-city renewal. In late summer and early autumn, the city hosts some of Ireland's premier festivals, including October's huge Cork Jazz Festival, which draws about 50,000 visitors from around the world; the Cork Film Festival, also in October; and a number of others.

Exploring Cork City

"Cork is the loveliest city in the world. Anyone who does not agree with me either was not born there or is prejudiced." Whether or not Cork merits this accolade of native poet and writer Robert Gibbings, the city does have plenty to recommend it, including several noteworthy historic sites. These, though spread out, are still best visited on foot. Patrick Street is the center city's main thoroughfare.

a good walk

Start your walk on Grand Parade, the geographical center of the city— where you find the Tourist Information Office (TIO). **Bishop Lucey Park** ❶ ▶, a green space opposite the TIO, leads to the **Triskel Arts Centre** ❷, where you can see exhibitions and films and find out about arts events around town. From here, take Washington Street to the corner of Grattan Street and the 19th-century **Court House** ❸. Backtrack to North Main Street and take it to the **Cork Vision Centre** ❹, in a once derelict 18th-century church; it has a helpful scale model of the city. Continue down North Main Street to the River Lee. Cross Shandon Bridge and make the serious hike up to **St. Mary's Pro-Cathedral**. Halfway up the hill on the right is Shandon, a maze of tiny terraced houses, in the midst of which is **St. Anne's Church** ❺, and Cork's old butter market, the Firkin Crane.

Take Upper Street back to the river and the modern Christy Ring Bridge, which leads to **Cork Opera House** ❻ and **Crawford Municipal Art Gallery** ❼. Beside the gallery is **Paul Street** ❽, with boutiques, bookstores, and cafés. Take one of the narrow left-hand lanes to **Patrick Street** ❾, Cork's main, pedestrian-only shopping street. Following it to your left, you'll come upon **Patrick's Bridge** ❿, from where you'll have a view of the city's steep north side. Take Winthrop Street, off Patrick Street, to Oliver Plunkett Street, and admire the neoclassic **General Post Office** ⓫; browse, if you wish, at the shops nearby. Return, via Oliver Plunkett Street, to the Grande Parade, with the **English Market** ⓬, a covered food bazaar, on your right. A left will take you to a pedestrian footbridge across the river; go right, following the quays westward, until you reach Bishop Street and the 19th-century Gothic **St. Finbarre's Cathedral** ⓭.

To extend your walk by about 3 km (2 mi), turn left upon leaving the cathedral and take the small road downhill on the right. Go left where it meets the river and cross the bridge to Lancaster Quay. Follow the street, which turns into Western Road, and make a left—you'll reach the architecturally noteworthy campus of **University College Cork** ⓮. Across Western Road is the **Mardyke** ⓯, a riverside walk that leads to the well-tended **Fitzgerald's Park** ⓰ and the Cork Public Museum. Turn left out of the museum and take Daly Bridge, which leads to Sunday's Well, a hilly residential area with the castlelike **Cork City Gaol** ⓱. Return to the city center along Sunday's Well Road and North Mall, where you'll pass several restored Georgian houses.

TIMING You could easily complete the first part of this walk, from the TIO to St. Finbarre's Cathedral, in a morning or an afternoon, depending on how much you plan to shop along the way. To really see everything, however, allow a full day, with a break for lunch at the Farmgate Café in the English Market. Also note that the Crawford Gallery and the English Market are closed on Sunday.

What to See

▶ **①** **Bishop Lucey Park.** This tiny green park in the heart of the city was opened in 1985 in celebration of the 800th anniversary of Cork's Norman charter. During its excavation, workers unearthed portions of the city's original fortified walls, now preserved just inside the arched entrance. Sculptures by contemporary Cork artists are scattered throughout the park. ⊠ *Grand Parade, Washington Village* 🖾 *Free.*

⑰ **Cork City Gaol.** This castlelike building contains an austere, 19th-century prison. Life-size figures occupy the cells, and sound effects illustrate the appalling conditions that prevailed here from the early 19th century through the founding of the Free State, after the 1916 Uprising. A Radio Museum in the Governor's House tells the history of broadcasting in Cork. ⊠ *Sunday's Well Rd., Sunday's Well* 🖀 *021/430–5022* ⊕ *www.cork-guide.ie/citygaol.htm* 🖾 *€5* ☽ *Oct.–Easter, daily 10–4; Easter–Sept., daily 9:30–5.*

⑥ **Cork Opera House.** It's an unattractive concrete hulk that went up in 1965 to replace an ornate and much-loved opera house that was ruined in a fire. Attempts to integrate the opera house with its neighbor, the Crawford Municipal Art Gallery, have softened the grim facade. The piazza outside has sidewalk cafés and street performers. ⊠ *Lavitt's Quay, City Center South* 🖀 *021/427–0022* ⊕ *www.corkoperahouse.ie.*

④ **Cork Vision Centre.** The center, which is in an area that was once the bustling heart of medieval Cork, provides an excellent introduction to the city's geography and history. The highlight is a detailed 1:500 scale model of Cork, showing how it has grown and changed over the ages. ⊠ *N. Main St., Washington Village* 🖀 *021/427–9925* ⊕ *www.corkvisioncentre. com* 🖾 *Suggested donation. Guided tours of city model on request €1.50* ☽ *Tues.–Sat. 10–5.*

③ **Court House.** A landmark in the very center of Cork, this magnificent classical building has an imposing Corinthian portico and is still used as the district's main court house. The exterior has been cleaned and fully restored and looks every bit as good as when it was built in 1835. ⊠ *Washington St., Washington Village* 🖀 *021/427–2706* ☽ *Weekdays 9–5.*

⑦ **Crawford Municipal Art Gallery.** The large redbrick building was built in 1724 as the customs house and is now home to Ireland's leading provincial art gallery. An imaginative expansion added an extra 10,000 square feet of gallery space—for visiting exhibitions and adventurous shows of modern Irish artists. The permanent collection includes landscape paintings depicting Cork in the 18th and 19th centuries. Take special note of works by Irish painters William Leech (1881–1968), Daniel Maclise (1806–70), James Barry (1741–1806), and Nathaniel Grogan (1740–1807). The café, run by the Allen family of Ballymaloe, is a good place for a light lunch or a homemade sweet. ⊠ *Emmet Pl., City Center South* 🖀 *021/427–3377* ⊕ *www.synergy.ie/crawford* 🖾 *Free* ☽ *Weekdays 9–5, Sat. 9–1.*

★ **⑫** **English Market.** Food lovers: head for one of the misleadingly small entrances to this large market in an elaborate, brick and cast-iron Victo-

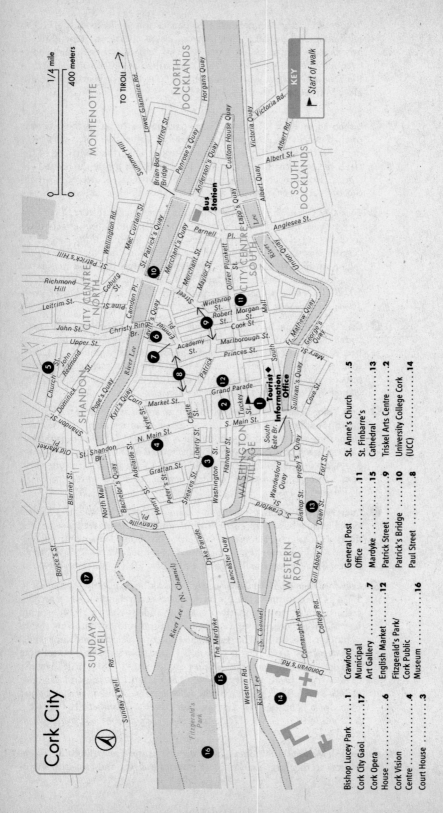

Cork City

1/4 mile

400 meters

KEY

▲ Start of walk

rian building. (Its official name is the Princes Street Market, and it's also known locally as the Covered Market.) Among the 140 stalls, keep an eye out for the Alternative Bread Co., which produces more than 40 varieties of handmade bread every day. Iago, Sean Calder-Potts's deli, has fresh pasta, lots of cheeses, and charcuterie. The Olive Stall sells olive oil, olive-oil soap, and olives from Greece, Spain, France, and Italy. Kay O'Connell's Fish Stall, in the legendary fresh-fish alley, purveys local smoked salmon. O'Reilly's Tripe and Drisheen is the last existing retailer of a Cork specialty, tripe (cow's stomach), and *drisheen* (blood sausage). Upstairs is the Farmgate, an excellent café. ⊠ *Entrances on Grand Parade and Princes St., City Center South* ⊕ *www.corkcity.ie* ⊘ *Mon.–Sat. 9–5:30.*

⑯ Fitzgerald's Park. This small, well-tended park is beside the River Lee's north channel in the west of the city. The park contains the **Cork Public Museum,** a Georgian mansion that houses a well-planned exhibit of Cork's history from ancient times to the present, with a strong emphasis on the city's Republican history. ⊠ *Western Rd., Western Road* ☎ *021/427–0679* ⊕ *www.corkcity.ie* 🖃 *Free* ⊘ *Museum: weekdays 11–1 and 2:15–5, Sun. 3–5.*

⑪ General Post Office. This neoclassical building with an elegant colonnaded facade was once Cork's Opera House. It dominates a street otherwise occupied by boutiques, jewelry stores, and antiques shops. ⊠ *Oliver Plunkett St., City Center South* ☎ *021/427–2000* ⊘ *Weekdays 9–5:30, Sat. 9–5.*

The friendly, old **Long Valley** (⊠ Winthrop St., City Center South ☎ 021/427–2144), popular with artists, writers, students, and eccentrics, serves tea, coffee, pints, and oversize sandwiches.

⑮ Mardyke. This popular riverside walk links the city center with Fitzgerald's Park. Beside it is a field where cricket, very much a minority sport in Ireland, is played on summer weekends. ⊠ *Western Rd., Western Road.*

⑨ Patrick Street. Extending from Grand Parade in the south to Patrick's Bridge in the north, Panna (as it's known locally) is Cork's main shopping thoroughfare. It was redesigned in 2003 as a pedestrian-only area with wide walks and landmark, tilted lamp standards. A mainstream mix of department stores, boutiques, pharmacies, and bookshops line the way. If you look above some of the plate-glass storefronts, you'll see examples of the bowfront Georgian windows that are emblematic of old Cork. The street saw some of the city's worst fighting in the years 1919–21, during the War of Independence. ⊠ *City Center South.*

⑩ Patrick's Bridge. From here you can look along the curve of Patrick Street and north across the River Lee to St. Patrick's Hill, with its tall Georgian houses. The hill is so steep that steps are cut into the pavement. Tall ships that once served the butter trade used to load up beside the bridge at Merchant's Quay before heading downstream to the open sea. The design of the large, redbrick shopping center on the site today evokes the warehouses of old. ⊠ *Patrick St., City Center South* ⊕ *www.corkcity.ie.*

⑧ Paul Street. A narrow street between the River Lee and Patrick Street and parallel to both, Paul Street is the backbone of the trendy shopping area that now occupies Cork's old French Quarter. The area was first settled by Huguenots fleeing religious persecution in France. Musicians and other street performers often entertain passersby in the Paul Street Piazza. The shops here offer the best in modern Irish design—from

CloseUp

REBEL CITY IN A REBEL COUNTY

F COUNTY CORK IS THE *"Rebel County"*—a label it wears proudly— Cork City can claim to be the heart of that tradition of stout resistance. Since its formation the city has gallantly resisted domination, in turn defying the Vikings, Oliver Cromwell, and King Billy's Protestant army. In more recent times Cork was a beehive of IRA activity (Michael Collins, the IRA's greatest tactician and leader, was a Corkman) and a constant thorn in the side of the crown forces. In the 1920s the infamous Black and Tans were unleashed with great ferocity on troublesome Cork City. They quickly murdered Thomas MacCurtain, the mayor. His successor, Terence MacSwiney, was arrested and died on hunger strike with his comrade Joseph Murphy in Brixton prison, London. The two men refused food for 76 days, one of the longest strikes in history, and their names have become myths in the Republican cause, especially in the southwest. In the bloody civil war that followed victory in the War of Independence, Cork remained staunch IRA country and in general opposed the new State and its army. Michael Collins was killed by a sniper as he drove through Béal na mBlath (pronounced aale-na-blah), not far from the city.

local fashions to handblown glass—and antiques, particularly in the alley north of the piazza. ⊠ *City Center South.*

⑤ St. Anne's Church. The church's pepper-pot Shandon steeple, which has a four-sided clock and is topped with a golden, salmon-shape weather vane, is visible from throughout the city and is the chief reason why St. Anne's is so frequently visited. The Bells of Shandon were immortalized in an atrocious but popular 19th-century ballad of that name. Your reward for climbing the 120-foot tower is the chance to ring the bells, with the assistance of sheet tune cards, out over Cork. Beside the church, Firkin Crane, Cork's 18th-century butter market, houses two small performing spaces. Adjacent is the Shandon Craft Market. ⊠ *Church St., Shandon* ⊕ *www.corkcity.ie* ⊠ *€1.50 church, €2 church and bell tower* ⊗ *May–Oct., Mon.–Sat. 9:30–5; Nov.–Apr., Mon.–Sat. 10–3:30.*

| off the beaten path | **ST. MARY'S PRO-CATHEDRAL –** It's worth hiking up to St. Mary's, which dates from 1808, only if you're interested in tracing your Cork ancestors. Its presbytery has records of births and marriages dating from 1784. ⊠ *Cathedral Walk, Shandon* ⊕ *www.corkcathedral.com* ⊠ *Free* ⊗ *Daily 9–6.* |

⑬ St. Finbarre's Cathedral. This was once the entrance to medieval Cork. According to tradition, St. Finbarre established a monastery on this site around AD 650 and is credited as the founder of Cork. The present, compact, three-spire Gothic cathedral, which was completed in 1879, belongs to the Church of Ireland and houses a 3,000-pipe organ. ⊠ *Bishop St., Washington Village* ☎ *021/496–3387* ⊕ *www.cathedral.cork. anglican.org* ⊠ *Free* ⊗ *Oct.–Mar., Mon.–Sat. 10–12:45 and 2–5; Apr.–Sept., Mon.–Sat. 10–5:30.*

❷ **Triskel Arts Centre.** A converted pair of town houses displays contemporary arts and crafts. They're also home to a coffee shop and a small auditorium that hosts films and plays. The center really is a good place to get the pulse of artsy goings-on. ⊠ *Tobin St., Washington Village* ☎ *021/ 427–2022* ✉ *Free* ⊙ *Weekdays 11–6, Sat. 11–5.*

⓮ **University College Cork.** The Doric, porticoed gates of UCC stand about 2 km (1 mi) from the center of the city. The college, which has a student body of roughly 10,000, is a constituent of the National University of Ireland. The main quadrangle is a fine example of 19th-century university architecture in the Tudor-Gothic style, reminiscent of many Oxford and Cambridge colleges. Several ancient ogham stones are on display, as are occasional exhibitions of archival material from the old library. The Honan Collegiate Chapel, to the east of the quadrangle, was built in 1916 and modeled on the 12th-century, Hiberno-Romanesque style, which is best exemplified by the remains of Cormac's Chapel at Cashel. Its stained-glass windows, as well as its collection of arts and crafts, altar furnishings, and textiles in the Celtic Revival style, are noteworthy. Three large modern buildings have been successfully integrated with the old, including the Boole Library, named for mathematician George Boole (1815–64), a past alumnus, whose Boolean algebra laid the foundation for modern computing. Both indoors and out the campus is enhanced by works from its outstanding collection of contemporary Irish art. At this writing a dedicated art gallery was in the works. ⊠ *Western Road* ☎ *021/490–3000* ⊕ *www.ucc.ie* ✉ *Free* ⊙ *Weekdays 9–5, but call to confirm Easter wk, July–Aug., and mid-Dec.–mid-Jan.*

Where to Eat

$$$–$$$$ ✕ **Ivory Tower.** Seamus O'Connell, the adventurous young owner-chef, describes his approach as "trans-ethnic fusion." He has cooked in Mexico and Japan, so his accomplished menu has such brilliantly eclectic dishes as wild duck with vanilla, sherry, and jalapeños; pheasant tamale; and salmon smoked to order over oak. There are bare wooden floors, stick-back chairs, and original artwork in the first-floor Georgian dining room. ⊠ *35 Princes St., Washington Village* ☎ *021/427–4665* 🖃 *AE, DC, MC, V* ⊙ *Closed Mon. and Tues.*

$$–$$$$ ✕ **Lovett's.** Since 1977 the Lovett family has been setting high culinary standards in the formal, portrait-lined dining room of a Georgian house 5 km (3 km) south of Cork City. The extensive wine list emphasizes vineyards whose owners have Irish roots as they left Ireland for Bordeaux and other wine-making regions in the 18th-century. Try the hot black-and-white pudding terrine with onion and raisin confit, followed, perhaps, by black sole on the bone with citrus butter. The brasserie is less formal. ⊠ *Churchyard La., off Well Rd., Douglas* ☎ *021/429–4909* 🖃 *AE, DC, MC, V* ⊙ *Closed Sun., Mon., first wk in Aug., and 1 wk at Christmas. No lunch.*

$$–$$$ ✕ **Café Paradiso.** The Mediterranean-style food is so tasty that even dedicated meat eaters forget that it's vegetarian. Chef Denis Cotter garners raves for his risottos with seasonal vegetables, his *gougère-choux* pastries with savory fillings, and his homemade desserts. The dining room is basic, with assorted tables and spindly chairs, daily specials chalked up on a board, and enormous platters of food. The restaurant is near the university and across from Jurys Hotel. ⊠ *16 Lancaster Quay, Western Road* ☎ *021/427–7939* 🖃 *MC, V* ⊙ *Closed Sun., Mon., and last 2 wks in Aug.*

$–$$$ ✕ **Jacobs on the Mall.** Mercy Fenton's imaginative cooking is one attraction; the other is the location—an erstwhile Victorian-style Turkish bath. The dining room has a high ceiling, an enormous skylight, cast-iron pillars, modern art, and a tall banquette room divider. Starters include duck liver parfait with plum chutney and oysters with ginger and lime relish. For a main course, try steamed brill with crisp vegetable parcels or roast rump of lamb with mash (mashed potatoes), vegetables, and a thyme jus. Look for such desserts as date and butterscotch pudding with bourbon cream. ⊠ *30A South Mall, City Center South* ☎ *021/425–1530* ⊟ *AE, DC, MC, V* ☉ *Closed Sun.*

$–$$ ╳ **Isaac's.** Cross Patrick's Bridge to the River Lee's north side and turn right to reach this popular brasserie in a converted warehouse. Modern art, jazz, high ceilings, and well-spaced tables covered in oilcloth set an eclectic tone. The East-meets-Mediterranean menu includes many tempting dishes—warm salads with Clonakilty black pudding, and king prawns in spicy tomato sauce. ⊠ *MacCurtain St., City Center North* ☎ *021/450–3805* ⊟ *AE, MC, V* ☉ *No lunch Sun.*

$–$$ ╳ **Proby's Bistro.** The menu at this riverside bistro is mainly rustic Italian—bruschetta, polenta, risotto, mixed-leaf salads with flavored oils. It's in a striking modern building, with patio tables and sun umbrellas optimistically placed on the terrace and an interior dining room that has an open fire and bold Mediterranean furnishings that suit the light, flavorful food. A pianist plays in the evening. ⊠ *Proby's Quay, Crosses Green, Washington Village* ☎ *021/431–6531* ⊟ *AE, MC, V* ☉ *Closed Sun.*

$ ╳ **Café Bar Deli.** The portions are generous, and the ingredients are fresh. Share a selection of freshly baked breads with olive oil while you choose from the tempting, imaginative salads, pizzas, and pasta dishes. This minimalist café is a smaller, more intimate annex of the fashionable Bodega Bar—a stylish, noisy establishment that serves the same menu. ⊠ *Cornmarket St., City Center South* ☎ *021/427–2878* ⊟ *AE, MC, V* ☉ *Closed Mon. and Tues. No lunch.*

$ ╳ **Farmgate Café.** One of the best lunch spots in town is on a terrace above the fountain at the Princes Street entrance to the English Market. One side of the terrace opens onto the market and is self-service; the other side is glassed in and has table service (reservations advised). Tripe and drisheen are always on the menu; daily specials include less challenging but no less traditional dishes, such as corned beef with *colcannon* (potatoes and cabbage mashed with butter and seasonings) and loin of smoked bacon with *champ* (potato mashed with scallions or leeks). ⊠ *English Market, City Center South* ☎ *021/427–8134* ⊟ *AE, DC, MC, V* ☉ *Closed Sun. No dinner.*

Where to Stay

$$$$ ▥ **Jurys Cork Hotel.** Beside the River Lee, a five-minute walk from the city center, you'll find a modern low-rise made of smoked glass and steel. Its plain but spacious guest rooms have quilted spreads, small sofas, and floor-to-ceiling windows. The most desirable rooms overlook the interior patio garden and pool. Cork's Bar is popular among locals at lunch and in the early evening. The Glandore restaurant serves an à la carte international menu. ⊠ *Western Rd., Western Road, Co. Cork* ☎ *021/427–6622* ▤ *021/427–4477* ⊕ *www.jurysdoyle.com* ⇖ *185 rooms with bath* ♿ *Restaurant, cable TV, 2 tennis courts, indoor-outdoor pool, health club, squash, 2 bars, meeting rooms* ⊟ *AE, DC, MC, V* ⍻ *BP.*

★ **$$$–$$$$** ▥ **Hayfield Manor.** The Manor, a surprisingly successful pastiche of the country-house style, is beside the UCC campus, five minutes' drive from the city center. A splendid, carved-wood double staircase dominates the marble-floor lobby, and a wood-paneled library overlooks a walled patio and garden. Rooms are spacious and furnished in a vaguely Louis

XV way. The Victorian-style bar serves lunch, and then bar food until 7 PM, when the Manor Room restaurant opens for dinner. ✉ *College Rd., Western Road, Co. Cork* ☎ *021/431–5900* 🖷 *021/431–6839* ⊕ *www.hayfieldmanor.ie* 🖘 *53 rooms with bath* ⚴ *Restaurant, in-room data ports, cable TV, indoor pool, health club, bar, meeting rooms* 🖃 *AE, DC, MC, V* ⦿ *BP.*

$$$–$$$$ 🏨 **Kingsley Hotel.** Just a 10-minute walk from city center, the Kingsley overlooks a rowing club on a pretty section of the River Lee. The lobby and lounge evoke an old-style gentleman's club, with dark woods and velvet armchairs. Guest rooms have large bathrooms, super-king-size beds, mahogany furniture, workstations, and CD players. Otters Brasserie serves imaginative local seafood and seasonal game dishes. The health center has a 20-meter pool and an outdoor hot tub. ✉ *Victoria Cross, Western Road, Co. Cork* ☎ *021/480–0500* 🖷 *021/480–0527* ⊕ *www.kingsleyhotel.com* 🖘 *69 rooms with bath* ⚴ *Restaurant, in-room data ports, in-room fax, cable TV, indoor pool, health club, bar* 🖃 *AE, DC, MC, V* ⦿ *BP.*

$$–$$$ 🏨 **Comfort Inn & Suites.** This urban riverside hotel, a two-minute walk from Patrick Street, has regular rooms as well as spacious, modern, one- and two-bedroom suites with kitchens. All quarters have light-oak furniture and half the rooms have river views. Four penthouses have terrace views of both the city and the river. Polished marble floors and terra-cotta-color walls lend the Mall bar-restaurant warmth and style. Choose from pasta, seafood, and steak dishes. ✉ *Morrison's Quay, City Center South, Co. Cork* ☎ *021/427–5858* 🖷 *021/427–5833* ⊕ *www.choicehotelscork.com* 🖘 *26 suites, 30 rooms with bath* ⚴ *Restaurant, in-room data ports, in-room fax, some kitchenettes, cable TV, bar* 🖃 *AE, DC, MC, V* ⦿ *BP.*

$–$$$ 🏨 **Hotel Isaac's.** A stylish renovation transformed an old, city center warehouse into a busy restaurant and hotel complex. Rooms are bright and cheerful, with polished wood floors and rustic pine furniture. The restaurant and some of the rooms overlook a tiny courtyard garden with a waterfall cascading down one side. The dining room also operates as Greene's restaurant, where they serve seafood—king prawns with chili sauce, oysters poached in Guinness, brill, swordfish, and hake—as well as other intriguing concoctions using fresh produce. Think veal with apricot stuffing, Asian vegetables, and ginger soufflé. ✉ *48 MacCurtain St., City Center North, Co. Cork* ☎ *021/450–0011* 🖷 *021/450–6355* ⊕ *www.isaacs.ie* 🖘 *36 rooms with bath* ⚴ *Restaurant, cafeteria, in-room data ports, cable TV, Ping-Pong* 🖃 *AE, MC, V* ⦿ *BP.*

$–$$$ 🏨 **Rochestown Park.** On 7 lovely acres of mature gardens in the fashionable suburb of Douglas, 5 km (3 mi) south of the city, this stylish hotel was built around a Victorian manor house once used as a convent. Rooms are modern with cotton spreads, wool carpets, and light-oak fixtures. Good access to the city's four-lane ring road includes a view of same from some rooms, which is compensated for by the river estuary beyond. The large health center specializes in thalassotherapy—seaweed wraps and baths. ✉ *Rochestown Rd., Douglas, Co. Cork* ☎ *021/489–0800* 🖷 *021/489–2178* ⊕ *www.rochestownpark.com* 🖘 *162 rooms with bath* ⚴ *Restaurant, cable TV, indoor pool, health club, bar, meeting rooms* 🖃 *AE, DC, MC, V* ⦿ *BP.*

$$ 🏨 **Lancaster Lodge.** Free city center parking, a great location next to the lively Jurys Hotel, and value for money are the main reasons to stay at this modern, four-story inn. Rooms look out over the car park or the busy main road, which is across a narrow branch of the River Lee, but in compensation they're spacious and have well-designed bathrooms. A hearty breakfast from an extensive menu—served in your room or in the bright, contemporary dining room—is another plus. ✉ *Lancaster*

Quay, Western Road, Co. Cork ☎ 021/425–1125 🖷 021/425–1126 ⊕ www.lancasterlodge.com 📎 2 suites, 37 rooms with bath ⚒ Dining room, in-room data ports, cable TV, free parking ⊟ AE, DC, MC, V ⊞ BP.

$ ⊡ **Flemings.** The quiet, commodious guest rooms in this elegant Georgian house have brocade fabrics. The large dining room is adorned with plush Louis XV–style chairs, gilt-framed portraits, and crystal chandeliers. Owner-chef Michael Fleming applies French techniques to local meat and seafood, which is served with seasonal vegetables that often come from the on-site garden. Ask about the special-value "dine and stay" package. ⊠ Silver Grange House, Tivoli, Co. Cork ☎ 021/482–1621 🖷 021/482–1178 📎 4 rooms with bath ⚒ Restaurant, cable TV, bar ⊟ AE, DC, MC, V ⊞ BP.

$ ⊡ **Jurys Cork Inn.** The bright, airy rooms at this modern budget hotel sleep two or three adults and two children. All are well appointed for the price range, with light-wood trim and matching drapes and spreads. Beside a busy bridge over the River Lee, the inn is a short walk from the city center and bus and rail stations. ⊠ Anderson's Quay, City Center South, Co. Cork ☎ 021/427–6444 🖷 021/427–6144 ⊕ www.jurysdoyle.com 📎 133 rooms with bath ⚒ Restaurant, cable TV, bar ⊟ AE, DC, MC, V ⊞ BP.

$ ⊡ **Seven North Mall.** Discerning visitors favor Angela Hegarty's home, a substantial, 250-year-old, terraced house on a tree-lined mall overlooking the River Lee. Common area furnishings are quietly elegant, and modest antiques are used to good advantage in the guest rooms. From here it's only a short walk to theaters, art galleries, shops, and restaurants. A limited amount of off-road parking is available. ⊠ 7 North Mall, Shandon, Co. Cork ☎ 021/439–7191 🖷 021/430–0811 ⊕ www.sevennorthmall.com 📎 5 rooms with bath ⚒ Cable TV ⊟ MC, V ⊞ BP ☉ Closed 2 wks at Christmas.

Nightlife & the Arts

See the *Examiner* or the *Evening Echo* for details about movies, theater, and live music performances.

Galleries

The **Fenton Gallery** (⊠ Wandesford Quay, Washington Village ☎ 021/431–5294 ⊕ www.artireland.net) shows work by important Irish artists. The **Lavit Gallery** (⊠ 5 Father Mathew St., off South Mall, City Center South ☎ 021/427–7749 ⊕ www.the lavitgallery.com) sells work by members of the Cork Arts Society and other Irish artists. Offbeat exhibits can be found at the **Triskel Arts Centre** (⊠ Tobin St., off S. Main St., Washington Village ☎ 021/427–2022). The **Vangard Gallery** (⊠ Carey's La., Paul St., City Center South ☎ 021/427–8718) exhibits leading contemporary Irish artists.

Performing Arts & Film

Cork Opera House (⊠ Lavitt's Quay, City Center South ☎ 021/427–0022) is the city's major hall for touring productions and variety acts. Smaller theatrical productions are staged at the **Everyman Palace** (⊠ MacCurtain St., City Center North ☎ 021/450–1673), which has an ornate Victorian interior. **The Kino** (⊠ Washington St., Washington Village ☎ 021/427–1571) is Cork's only art-house cinema. Three films are usually showing, from 2:30 onward.

Pubs & Nightclubs

La Bodega (⊠ Cornmarket St., City Center South ☎ 021/427–2878), a converted wine warehouse, is the hip meeting spot for Cork's thirtysomethings. Traditional music sessions can happen anytime at **An Bodhrán** (✉ 42 Oliver Plunkett St., City Center South ☎ 021/437–1392). You'll hear Cajun, folk, or Irish music from Sunday to Wednesday at the **Corner House** (✉ 7 Coburg St., City Center North ☎ 021/450–0655). Night owls will appreciate **Half Moon** (✉ Half Moon St., City Center South ☎ 021/427–0022), the Cork Opera House's late-night music club. It showcases local, up-and-coming jazz and blues bands most weekends starting at 11 PM.

Loafers (✉26 Douglas St., South Docklands ☎021/431–1612) is a friendly gay bar with a beer garden. **The Lobby** (✉ Union Quay, South Docklands ☎ 021/431–1113) has nightly music sessions: traditional and acoustic in the bar, folk and rock upstairs. **Long Valley** (✉ Winthrop St., South City Center ☎ 021/427–2144) is a Cork institution, famous for its doorstep sandwiches (made with very thick slices of bread and lots of fillings) that are impossible to eat tidily and its conversation, which is always lively. The bar at the **Metropole Hotel** (✉ MacCurtain St., City Center North ☎ 021/450–8122) is one of Cork's best jazz spots. The **Pavilion** (✉ Carey's La., City Center South ☎ 021/427–6228) has late-night disco every night but Tuesday.

Shopping

Department Stores
Brown Thomas (✉ 18 Patrick St., City Center South ☎ 021/427–6771), Ireland's high-end department store, carries items by Irish and international designers. The ground floor has an excellent cosmetics hall and a good selection of menswear and Irish crystal. Refuel at the coffee shop, which sells healthful open sandwiches and homemade soups. **Dunne Stores** (✉ Merchant's Quay, City Center South ☎ 021/427–4200) began in Cork as a family-owned drapery store and became the place where all of Ireland buys its socks, underwear, and much more. Given the chain's roots, the Cork branch is obviously the flagship store.

The British retail giant **Marks and Spencer** (✉ 6–8 Patrick St., Merchant's Quay, City Center South ☎ 021/427–5555) is as popular for its foods (great for picnics) and housewares as for its clothing basics. For inexpensive rain gear, T-shirts, underwear, and any other garments you forgot to pack, head for **Penney's** (✉27 Patrick St., City Center South ☎ 021/427–1935). **Roches Stores** (✉ Patrick St., City Center South ☎ 021/427–7727), Cork's largest department store, is a family-owned business that occupies a beautiful landmark building with a central glass dome.

Mall
The **Merchant's Quay Shopping Centre** (✉ Merchant's Quay, City Center South ☎ 021/427–5466) is a large downtown mall.

Specialty Shops
ANTIQUES **Irene's** (✉ 22 Marlboro St., City Center South ☎ 021/427–0642) sells antique jewelry. **Mills Antiques** (✉ 3 Paul's La., City Center South ☎ 021/427–3528) carries Irish, English, and European paintings, printings, silver, porcelain, and small furniture. **Pinnacle** (✉ 44A MacCurtain St., City Center North ☎ 021/450–1319) stocks antique glass, porcelain, paintings, and prints. **Victoria's** (✉ 2 Oliver Plunkett St., City Center South ☎ 021/427–2752) carries interesting jewelry and Victoriana.

BOOKS **Connolly's Bookshop** (✉ Paul Street Piazza, City Center South ☎ 021/427–5366) has an extensive stock of new and secondhand books, with a good selection of Irish interest titles.

Mainly Murder Bookstore is a must for lovers of crime fiction (✉ 2A Paul St., City Center South ☎ 021/427–2413). **Mercier Bookshop** (✉ 18 Academy St., City Center South ☎ 021/427–5040), off Patrick Street, sells new books and publishes its own list of Irish and local-interest titles.

Vibes & Scribes (✉ 3 Bridge St., City Center North ☎ 021/450–5370 ⊕ www.vibesandscribes.com) attracts a loyal following of avid readers, with three floors of new, secondhand, and discount books as well as CDs and videos. **Waterstones** (✉ Patrick St., City Center South ☎ 021/427–6522) is the biggest bookshop in town, with a great choice of new fiction and nonfiction as well as a wide selection of locally published books.

CLOTHING **Cocoon** (✉ 6 Emmet Pl., City Center South ☎ 021/427–3393), a little shop in a hexagonal tower, has a ravishing selection of sexy Italian boots and shoes alongside unusual jewelry and accessories. Fashion lovers will find a choice of evening business attire at the **Dressing Room** (✉ 8 Emmet Pl., City Center South ☎ 021/427–0117), a tiny but tony boutique opposite the entrance to the Cork Opera House. For funky, retro styles and vintage clothes check out **Hale Bopp** (✉ 22 Paul St., City Center South ☎ 021/425–4876).

Monica John (✉ French Church St., City Center South ☎ 021/427–1399) sells locally designed high-fashion ladies' wear as well as some imported lines. **Quills** (✉ 107 Patrick St., City Center South ☎ 021/427–1717) has a good selection of Irish-made apparel for both women and men. **Samui** (✉ 17 Drawbridge St., City Center South ☎ 021/427–8080) stocks dramatic—often quirky, but always flattering—clothes from Ireland, France, Germany, and the UK. For casual weatherproof clothing, try the **Tack Room** (✉ Unit 3, Academy St., City Center South ☎ 021/427–2704).

JEWELRY **Marlboro Gold Arts Ltd.** (✉ 33 Marlboro St., City Center South ☎ 021/427–7052) has a selection of imaginative, modern jewelry.

MUSIC **HMV** (✉ Patrick St. ☎ 021/427–4433) the first floor of this international chain has a good selection of Irish traditional music in the classical and jazz section. The best place for Irish music is **Living Tradition** (✉ 40 Mac-Curtain St., City Center North ☎ 021/450–2040). **Vibes & Scribes** (✉ 3 Bridge St., City Center North ☎ 021/450–5370) has a good selection of bargain and secondhand tapes, CDs, DVDs, and videos. The **Vinyl Room** (✉ 79 Grand Parade, City Center South ☎ 021/427–3379) specializes in dance, house, and hip-hop. Chart hits are the main business of the **Virgin Megastore** (✉ Queen's Old Catle, City Center South ☎ 021/427–9299), but you'll find some traditional Irish music for sale in the small classical, country, and jazz section.

SPORTING GOODS The **Golf Addict** (✉ 6 Emmet Pl., City Center South ☎ 021/427–3393) stocks everything the serious golfer could need, as well as nonessential golf paraphernalia and gifts. The **Great Outdoors** (✉ 23 Paul St., City Center South ☎ 021/427–6382) caters to most outdoor sports needs. **Matthews** (✉ Academy St., City Center South ☎ 021/427–7633) has a wide selection of sporting gear.

Side Trips From Cork City

Blarney, northwest of Cork City on R617, and Cork Harbour, east of the city on N25 (follow signposts to Waterford), make perfect day trips. Blarney's attractions are Blarney Castle and the famous Blarney Stone. Cork Harbour's draws include Fota Island, with an arboretum, a wildlife park, and Fota House—a renovated hunting lodge and estate—and the fishing port of Cobh.

Blarney

⑱ *10 km (6 mi) northwest of Cork City.*

"On Galway sands they kiss your hands, they kiss your lips at Carney, but by the Lee they drink strong tea, and kiss the stone at Blarney." This famous rhyme celebrates one of Ireland's most noted icons—the Blarney Stone, which is the main reason most people journey to this small community built around a village green.

In the center of Blarney is **Blarney Castle,** or what remains of it: the ruined central keep is all that's left of this mid-15th-century stronghold. The castle contains the famed Blarney Stone; kissing the stone, it's said, endows the kisser with the fabled "gift of gab." It's 127 steep steps to the battlements. To kiss the stone, you must lie down on the battlements, hold on to a guardrail, and lean your head way back. It's good fun and not at all dangerous. Expect a line from mid-June to early September; while you wait, you can admire the views of the wooded River Lee valley and chuckle over how the word "blarney" came to mean what it does. As the story goes, Queen Elizabeth I wanted Cormac MacCarthy, Lord of Blarney, to will his castle to the crown, but he refused her requests with eloquent excuses and soothing compliments. Exhausted by his comments, the queen reportedly exclaimed, "This is all Blarney. What he says he rarely means."

You can take pleasant walks around the castle grounds; Rock Close contains oddly shaped limestone rocks landscaped in the 18th century and a grove of ancient yew trees that is said to have been the center of Druid worship. Two hundred yards from the castle is Blarney Castle House, which was built in 1784 in the style of a Scottish baronial mansion. The three-story, gray-stone building has picture-book turrets and fancy, stepped gables. Inside are Elizabethan and Victorian antiques, a fine stairwell, and family portraits. ☎ *021/438–5252* ⊕ *www.blarneycastle.ie* ✉ *Blarney Castle: €7. Blarney Castle House: €5* ☉ *Blarney Castle: May and Sept., Mon.–Sat. 9–6:30, Sun. 9–5:30; June–Aug., Mon.–Sat. 9–7, Sun. 9–5:30; Oct.–Apr., Mon.–Sat. 9–sundown, Sun. 9–5:30. Blarney Castle House: June–mid-Sept., Mon.–Sat. noon–5.*

WHERE TO STAY &
EAT
$–$$

✗ **Blair's Inn.** Surrounded by woods just five minutes from Blarney, Blair's Inn—noted for its exuberant window-box displays—is the perfect retreat from Blarney's tour-bus crowds. In summer, enjoy the beer garden; in winter warm wood fires flicker in the cozy interior. Freshly prepared local produce is served in generous portions: favorites include Irish stew with lamb, carrots, and potatoes, as well as corned beef. There's live entertainment every Sunday at 9 PM as well as on Monday from May to October. ✉ *Cloghroe* ☎ *021/438–1470* ▭ *MC, V.*

¢–$

▦ **Maranatha Country House.** The guest rooms in this family home, a substantial Victorian manor on 27 woodland acres, are individually decorated and full of antiques. The Regal Suite has a four-poster bed as well as a sunken bath with a hot tub. Breakfast is served in the conservatory, which looks over rolling lawns and majestic trees. The inn is a handy base for trips to Killarney and West Cork. To get here drive through Blarney village on the R617 for 3 km (2 mi) to the town of Tower. ✉ *Tower* ☎ *021/438–5102* ⤴ *6 rooms with bath* ♿ *No smoking* ▭ *MC, V* ⊚ *BP* ☉ *Closed Dec.–mid-Mar.*

SHOPPING

Blarney has loads of crafts shops south and west of the village green, a two-minute walk from the castle. **Blarney Woolen Mills** (☎ 021/438–5280 ⊕ www.blarney.ie) has the largest stock and the highest turnover of all of Blarney's crafts shops. It sells everything from Irish-made high fashion to Aran hand-knit items to leprechaun key rings.

Cork Harbour

⑲ *16 km (10 mi) east of Cork City.*

☙ The 70-acre **Fota Island Wildlife Park** is 12 km (7 mi) east of Cork via N25, R624, and the main Cobh road. It's an important breeding center for cheetahs and wallabies that also has monkeys, zebras, giraffes, ostriches, flamingos, emus, and kangaroos. ☎ *021/481–2678 ⊕ www. fotawildlife.ie ⌦ €8 ☉ Mid-Mar.–Oct., Mon.–Sat. 10–6, Sun. 11–6; Nov.–St. Patrick's Day, Sat. 10–3, Sun. 11–3.*

Next to the Fota Island Wildlife Park is **Fota House,** an 18th-century hunting lodge with a magnificent garden and arboretum. The lodge was built in the mid-18th century for the powerful Smith Barry family, which owned vast tracts of land in South Cork, including the whole of Fota Island. The next generation of Smith Barrys employed the renowned architects Richard and William Vitruvius Morrison to convert the structure into an impressive, Classical Regency–style house that has been painstakingly restored. The symmetrical facade is relatively unadorned and stands in contrast to the gilded plasterwork of the formal reception rooms. The servant's quarters are almost as big as the house proper. You can relax over cake and scones in the tearoom after shopping in the crafts store. ☎ *021/481–5543 ⊕ www.fotahouse.com ⌦ €5 ☉ Mon.–Sat. 10–6, Sun. 11–6.*

Many of the people who left Ireland on immigrant ships for the New World departed from **Cobh,** a pretty fishing port and seaside resort, 24 km (15 mi) southeast of Cork City on R624. The **Queenstown Heritage Center,** in the old Cobh railway station, re-creates the experience of the million emigrants who left the town between 1750 and the mid-20th century. It also tells the stories of great transatlantic liners, including the *Titanic,* whose last port of call was Cobh, and the *Lusitania,* which was sunk by a German submarine off this coast on May 7, 1915. Many of the *Lusitania's* 1,198 victims are buried in Cobh, which has a memorial to them on the local quay. ☎ *021/481–3591 ⊕ www.cobhheritage.com ⌦ €5 ☉ Oct.–Apr., daily 10–5; May–Sept., daily 10–6.*

The best view of Cobh is from **St. Colman's Cathedral,** an exuberant neo-Gothic granite church designed by Pugin in 1868. Inside, granite niches portray scenes of the Roman Catholic Church's history in Ireland, beginning with the arrival of St. Patrick. ☎ *021/481–3222 ⊕ www. cloyne.irl.com ⌦ Free.*

SPORTS & THE OUTDOORS Explore the sheltered, island-studded waters of Cork Harbour by renting a sailing dinghy from **International Sailing Center** (⌂ 5 E. Beach, Cobh ☎ 021/481–1237).

EAST CORK & THE BLACKWATER VALLEY

Although most visitors to Cork head west out of the city for the coastal areas between Cork and Glengarriff, the east and the north of the county are also worth exploring. East Cork, Youghal in particular, is popular with Irish tourists, who love the long sandy beaches here. North Cork's main attraction is the Blackwater River, which crosses the county from east to west. It's famous for its trout and salmon fishing and its scenery.

Youghal

20 *48 km (30 mi) east of Cork City on N25, 74 km (46 mi) south of Waterford.*

Youghal (pronounced yawl), an ancient walled seaport with a fine natural harbor, has a long sandy beach, making it popular with summertime day-trippers. The town is at the mouth of the Blackwater River, on the border between Counties Cork and Waterford. It was included in a 40,000-acre land grant given to Sir Walter Raleigh by Elizabeth I in the late 16th century. According to local legend, Sir Walter Raleigh planted the first potatoes in Ireland here, a claim disputed by several other locations (and by all accounts he spent little time here). The town is in the throes of some major investment, aimed at updating its appeal. Rising above it all is Main Street's clock tower, which dates from 1776 and was originally built as a jail. Steps beside the tower lead to a well-preserved stretch of the old town walls. From here there's a magnificent panorama of town and the estuary.

The **Youghal Heritage Centre** relates the town's history through an audiovisual presentation. If this whets your appetite, trained guides are available to show you the town; a walking tour takes about 90 minutes. ⊠ *Market Sq.* ☎ *024/20170* ⊕ *www.youghal.ie* ☎ *€1.50, tour €3.50* ⊗ *June–mid-Sept., daily 9:30–7; mid-Sept.–May, weekdays 9:30–5:30.*

The **Moby Dick Lounge Bar** (⊠ Market Sq. ☎ 024/92756) contains memorabilia of the filming here of John Huston's version of Melville's *Moby-Dick,* in which Youghal masqueraded as New Bedford, Massachusetts.

St. Mary's Collegiate Church dates from the 13th century and contains many interesting monuments, including the tomb of Richard Boyle (1566–1643), who succeeded Sir Walter Raleigh as Mayor of Youghal and became the first earl of Cork. The brightly painted monument commemorates his three wives and 16 children and is similar to the monument in St. Patrick's Cathedral in Dublin, which Sir Richard ordered because he was not sure whether he would die in Dublin or Youghal. ⊠ *Emmet Pl.* ☎ *024/92350* ☎ *Free* ⊗ *Key available from adjacent lodge.*

Where to Stay & Eat

$$–$$$ ✕☒ **Aherne's.** In the Fitzgibbon family since 1923, Aherne's has a highly regarded seafood restaurant-bar ($–$$$$) with a magnetic appeal—it even draws food lovers from Cork City (it's less than an hour's drive). Popular main courses include hot buttered lobster, grilled salmon with fresh fennel, and plaice (flounder) stuffed with oysters in a red-wine sauce. The inexpensive bar food includes seafood pie topped with mashed potatoes. The 12 bedrooms, which occupy their own modern wing, are furnished with Victorian and Georgian antiques. ⊠ *163 N. Main St., Co. Cork* ☎ *024/92424* 🖶 *024/93633* ⊕ *www.ahernes.com* 🛏 *13 rooms with bath* ⟋ *Restaurant, cable TV, fishing, bar* 🖃 *AE, DC, MC, V* ⏐◯⏐ *BP.*

¢–$ ☒ **Ballymakeigh House.** Consider this the Irish farmhouse of your dreams, the kind of place where you can easily end up staying a day or two longer than planned. From the conservatory behind the creeper-clad house—with its cozy, impeccably kept guest rooms—you can breakfast on one of Margaret Browne's fresh strawberry muffins while watching the cows. Reserve by 5 PM for her legendary six-course dinners, often made with herbs and edible flowers straight from the garden. The house is signposted off N25, 9½ km (6 mi) west of Youghal. ⊠ *Killeagh, Co. Cork* ☎ *024/95184* 🖶 *024/95370* 🛏 *6 rooms with bath* ⟋ *Cable TV, tennis court, bicycles, Ping-Pong* 🖃 *MC, V* ⏐◯⏐ *BP* ⊗ *Closed Nov.–Mar.*

FodorsChoice
★

Shanagarry

㉑ *27 km (17 mi) southwest of Youghal via N25 and R632.*

There are two reasons to come to Shanagarry, a farming village known chiefly for its Quaker connections: Ballymaloe House, one of Ireland's first country-house hotels, and Ballymaloe Cookery School and Gardens, a top destination for chefs-in-training.

The most famous Shanagarry Quaker was William Penn (1644–1718), the founder of the Pennsylvania colony, who grew up in **Shanagarry House,** still a private residence in the center of the village. The entry gates are across from Shanagarry Castle, now owned and being restored by the potter and entrepreneur Stephen Pearce. The house's most famous tenant since William Penn was Marlon Brando, who stayed here in the summer of 1995 while filming *Divine Rapture* in nearby Ballycotton.

☙ **Ballymaloe Cookery School and Gardens,** run by Darina Allen, one of Ireland's best-known chefs, attracts culinary arts students from all over Ireland and, increasingly, points beyond. Its cooking classes and programs range from one day to 12 weeks, and you'll find graduates in the kitchens of many Irish restaurants. Darina tends formal herb, fruit, and vegetable gardens as well as a knee-high Celtic maze. The property's free range hens delight children. A meal or a snack at the Garden Café, serving the famous Ballymaloe-style food as well as pizzas from a wood-burning oven, will add greatly to your visit. ⊠ *Kinoith House* ☎ *021/464–6785* ⊕ *www.cookingisfun.ie* ☞ *Gardens €5* ⊙ *May–Sept., daily 9–6.*

off the beaten path

BALLYCOTTON – Five kilometers (3 mi) beyond Shanagarry on R629, this pretty fishing village is built on the top of a cliff overlooking an island where large colonies of seabirds breed. Pleasant cliff walks and a beach are nearby.

Where to Stay & Eat

$$$–$$$$
Fodor'sChoice
★

✕🏠 **Ballymaloe House.** Originally a farmhouse and family home, albeit on a grand scale, Ballymaloe is one of Ireland's best known country houses. It still functions partly as a working farm, and is surrounded by pleasant, fertile countryside. Each guest room is elegantly, if simply, decorated. Myrtle Allen, the doyenne of Irish cooking, presides over the dining room ($$$$), which houses the family's notable Irish art collection. Chef Rory O'Connell presents a six-course, haute Irish menu that relies on fresh fish from nearby Ballycotton, local lamb and beef, and homegrown herbs and vegetables—testament to Myrtle's practice of supporting small, local food purveyors. ⊠ *Co. Cork* ☎ *021/465–2531* 🖷 *021/465–2021* ⊕ *www.ballymaloe.ie* ☞ *32 rooms with bath* ⚘ *Restaurant, tennis court, pool, bar, some pets allowed; no TV in some rooms* ▤ *AE, DC, MC, V* ⦿ *BP.*

$–$$
✕🏠 **Barnabrow House.** Owners John and Geraldine O'Brien stylishly combined the old and the new when they renovated the interior of this rambling 17th-century house. Specially made modern wood furniture sits beside Victorian antiques and against intensely colored walls. It's romantic, relaxed, and practical. Main house rooms have high ceilings and canopy beds; courtyard rooms are cozier and have low, beamed ceilings. The Trinity Rooms restaurant ($–$$$) serves imaginative dishes made with local produce. ⊠ *Cloyne* ☎ *021/465–2534* ⊕ *www.barnabrowhouse.com* ☞ *21 rooms with bath* ⚘ *Restaurant, bar, some pets allowed; no room TVs, no smoking* ▤ *MC, V* ⦿ *BP.*

Shopping

The ceramicist Stephen Pearce makes tableware and bowls in four signature styles that are available in many Irish crafts shops. He sells a wide selection at his own **Stephen Pearce Emporium** (✉ near Cloyne ☎ 021/464–6262), where he also stocks an interesting range of Irish-made crafts.

Midleton

② *15 km (9 mi) northwest of Shanagarry on R629, 12 km (8 mi) east of Cork City on N25.*

Midleton is famous for its school, Midleton College, founded in 1696, and its distillery, founded in 1825 and modernized in 1975, which manufactures spirits—including Irish whiskey—for distribution worldwide. It's also a pleasant market town at the head of the Owenacurra estuary, near the northeast corner of Cork Harbour. Its gray-stone buildings date mainly from the early 19th century.

The **Jameson Heritage Centre** has tours of the Old Midleton Distillery, to show you how Irish whiskey—*uisce beatha* (pronounced ooshka baa-her), "the water of life"—was made in the old days. The old stone buildings are excellent examples of 19th-century industrial architecture, the impressively large old waterwheel still operates, and the pot still—a copper dome that can hold 32,000 imperial gallons of whiskey—is the world's largest. Early in the tour, requests are made for a volunteer "whiskey taster"—so be alert if this option appeals. The tours end with a complimentary glass of Jameson's Irish whiskey (or a soft drink). A crafts center and café are also on the premises. ☎ 021/461–3594 ⊕ *www.whiskeytours.ie* ✉ €7 ⊙ *Mar.–Oct., daily 9–4:30; Nov.–Feb., tours only, weekdays at 12:30 and 3, weekends at 2 and 4.*

Fermoy

㉓ *35 km (22 mi) north of Cork City on N8, 43 km (27 mi) west of Youghal on R634 (Tallow Rd.), which adjoins N72.*

An army town dating mainly from the mid-19th century, Fermoy is a major crossroads on the Dublin–Cork road (N8); the east–west road that passes through town (N72) is an attractive 98-km (61-mi) alternative route to Killarney. The bridge that spans the Blackwater is flanked by two weirs dating from 1689.

Where to Stay & Eat

$$ ✕⌧ **Ballyvolane House.** Although this 1728 stone mansion looks imposing, life here unfolds with country-house informality. The rooms are exceptionally large, sitting areas are generous, and furnishings consist of a rich assortment of antiques and heirlooms. Outside are extensive gardens and a 100-acre dairy farm. Dinner is served at a large table in the elegant dining room ($$$$) family silver is set on white linens. (Both dinner and rooms must be booked at least 24 hours in advance). The village of Castlelyons is signposted off N8 in Rathcormac, just south of Fermoy. ✉ *Castlelyons, Co. Cork* ☎ *025/36349* 🖶 *025/36781* ⊕ *www. ballyvolanehouse.ie* ⇝ *6 rooms with bath* ⟁ *Dining room, fishing; no room phones, no room TVs, no smoking* ⊟ *AE, MC, V* ⎜⎜⎜ *BP.*

Mallow

㉔ *30 km (18 mi) west of Fermoy on N72.*

Mallow, an angling center and market town, was, in the 18th century, a popular spa—often mentioned in the same breath as Bath. Mallow lies at the intersection of the Cork–Limerick and Waterford–Killarney roads, within an hour's drive of all four towns. At the bottom of Mallow's Main Street, you'll find the **Clock House**, a half-timber building dating from 1855. It shares the site with the Rakes of Mallow Club, the headquarters of the notorious 18th-century gamblers, drinkers, and fortune hunters remembered in the song "The Rakes of Mallow." Not much remains today of Mallow's glory, but the old **Spa Well** can still be seen in the town center, and there are several interesting facades with overhanging bay windows on Main Street, dating from the 18th and early 19th centuries. The English novelist Anthony Trollope lived at No. 139 for a time, and he rode with the Duhallow Hunt, enhancing the fame of the local pack. The ruins of the late-16th-century **Mallow Castle** are at the bottom of the main street, freely accessible behind ornamental gates. The castle was burned by the Jacobites in 1689, and its stables were later converted into a house, which is still in use as a private home. From here you can view the white fallow deer that are unique to Mallow and were originally presented by Elizabeth I.

off the beaten path

ANNE'S GROVE GARDENS – These gardens were inspired by the ideas of William Robinson, a 19th-century gardener who favored naturalistic planting. Exotic foliage borders paths winding down to the Blackwater; magnificent spring magnolias and primulas and summer hydrangeas are among the plants on view in the rolling countryside. ⊠ *Castletownroche, 12 km (7 mi) east of Mallow* ☎ *022/26145* ☜ *€5* ☽ *Mid-Mar.–Sept., Mon.–Sat. 10–5, Sun. 1–6.*

Where to Stay & Eat

$$$-$$$$
Fodor's Choice
★

✕☐ **Longueville House.** Limestone quoins frame the facade of this imposing Georgian mansion, which is on a tranquil 500-acre estate that rolls down to the river. A Victorian-era glass-and-iron conservatory graces the house's eastern end, and the comfortable bedrooms are furnished with fine antiques. At the Presidents' Restaurant ($$$$), chef William O'Callaghan, son of founding proprietors Michael and Jane O'Callaghan, serves an outstanding and elegant Irish-French–style menu prepared largely using produce from the houses's own farm, garden, and river. ⊠ *Co. Cork* ☎ *022/47156* ☎ *022/47459* ⊕ *www.longuevillehouse. ie* ☞ *20 rooms with bath* ☼ *Restaurant, cable TV, fishing, bar, meeting rooms* ☐ *AE, DC, MC, V* ☜☐ *BP* ☽ *Closed late Dec.–Mar.*

Sports & the Outdoors
Mallow Golf Club (⊠ Ballyellis, Co. Cork ☎ 022/21145) is an 18-hole, par-72 parkland course with excellent views of the Blackwater Valley.

Kanturk

㉕ *15 km (9 mi) west of Mallow on N72 and R579.*

Kanturk is at the confluence of two rivers, the Allow and the Dalua. It's more of a village than a town, but its interesting Victorian shop fronts bear witness to its past importance as a market town. The freely accessible **Kanturk Castle** (⊠ 2 km [1 mi] outside town on the R579 Banteer road) was built by a local MacCarthy chieftain in 1601, but its completion was prevented by English neighbors who complained that it was too large for an Irishman. Ornate stone fireplaces and mullioned windows in the five-story shell give some idea of the scope of MacCarthy's ambitions.

Where to Stay & Eat

★ **$$$-$$$$**
✕☐ **Assolas Country House.** Hosts Joe and Hazel Bourke have furnished the public areas and guest rooms of this 17th-century, ivy-covered manor with period antiques. Dinner ($$$$) begins in front of the blazing log

fire in the drawing room, where you peruse the night's menu over aperitifs. Family silver is on the tables in the red Queen Anne dining room. Hazel's refined culinary skills, as well as the well-manicured gardens, are renowned. ✉ *Co. Cork* ☎ *029/50015* ⊟ *029/50795* ⊕ *www. assolas.com* ⮑ *9 rooms with bath* ⚭ *Restaurant, tennis court, boating, fishing; no room TVs* ▤ *MC, V* ⦿❘ *BP* ⊘ *Closed Nov.–mid-Mar.*

KINSALE TO GLENGARRIFF

The historic old port—and now booming seaside town—of Kinsale is the perfect place to begin the 136-km (85-mi) trip, via Bantry Bay and through a variety of seascapes, to the lush vegetation of Glengarriff. If you tackle this scenic West Cork coastal route nonstop, the drive takes less than two hours, but the whole point of this journey is to linger in places that tickle your fancy.

Kinsale

❷❻ *29 km (18 mi) southwest of Cork City on R600.*

Foodies flock to Kinsale—long considered Ireland's culinary capital—for its annual Festival of Fine Food each fall. In the town center, at the tip of the wide, fjordlike harbor that opens out from the River Bandon, upscale shops and eateries with pastel facades line small streets. Still other narrow streets climb the slopes of Compass Hill.

Houses with slate roofs and unusual slate fronts have Spanish influences that can be traced back to the Battle of Kinsale in 1601, when the Irish and Spanish joined forces to fight the English—and lost. The defeat was a serious one for the Irish aristocracy, and they soon took off for Europe, leaving their lands to English settlers. Kinsale went on to become an important fishing port as well as a British army and naval base.

Kinsale has two yacht marinas, and skippers with deep-sea angling boats offer day charters. The Kinsale Yacht Club hosts racing and cruising events during the sailing season, which runs from March to October for hardy souls and from June to August for everyone else. This town is also where you'll find Ireland's only bareboat charter company.

The **Desmond Castle and the International Museum of Wine** are in a 15th-century fortified town house—originally the custom house—that has a dark history. It was used as a prison for French and American seamen in the 1700s, and was subsequently a jail and then a workhouse. Now it contains displays that tell the story of Ireland's long involvement with the wine trade. Many Irish emigrants became involved in the wine trade in France, America, Australia, and New Zealand. ✉ *Cork St.* ☎ *021/ 477–4855* ⊕ *www.heritageireland.ie* 🎟 *€2.50* ⊘ *Mid–Apr. to mid–June, Tues.–Sun. 10–6; mid–June–mid–Oct., daily 10–6.*

Memorabilia from the wreck of the *Lusitania* are among the best artifacts in the **Kinsale Museum,** which is in the 17th-century, Dutch-style courthouse. The 1915 inquest into that ship's sinking took place in the courtroom, briefly making it the focus of the world's attention; it has been preserved as a memorial. As the staff consists of volunteers, it's best to call ahead to confirm opening times. ✉ *Old Courthouse, Market Pl.* ☎ *021/477–2044* 🎟 *€2.50* ⊘ *Mon.–Sat. 11–5, Sun. 3–5.*

★ The British built **Charles Fort** on the east side of the Bandon River estuary in the late 17th century, after their defeat of the Spanish and Irish forces. One of Europe's best-preserved "star forts" encloses some 12 clifftop acres and is similar to Fort Ticonderoga in New York State. If the sun is shining, take the footpath signposted Scilly Walk; it winds along the harbor's edge under tall trees and then through the village of Summer Cove. ⊠ *3 km (2 mi) east of town* ☎ *021/477–2263* ⊕ *www. heritageireland.ie* 🎫 *€3.10* ⏱ *Mid-Mar.–Oct., daily 10–6; Nov.–mid-Mar., weekends 10–5.*

The **Spaniard Inn** (⊠ Scilly ☎ 021/477–2436) looks over the town and harbor from a hairpin bend on the road to Charles Fort. Inside, sawdust-covered floors and a big open fire make this onetime fishermen's bar a cozy spot in winter. In summer, you can take a pint to the veranda and watch the world go by on land and sea.

Where to Stay & Eat

$$$–$$$$

FodorsChoice

★ ✕ **The Vintage.** The cozy, beamed interior of this informal, cottage-style restaurant is enhanced by Swiss owner Raoul de Gendre's art collection. Tables are beautifully set, with specially designed glassware and white linen cloths. European dishes with Irish influences fill the à la carte menu; consider trying the whole lobster with a mustard-whiskey sauce. Appetizers include caviar and fresh duck foie gras. The wine list has more than 150 wines, primarily from Europe. ⊠ *50 Main St.* ☎ *021/477–2502* ⊟ *AE, DC, MC, V* ⏱ *Closed Jan.–mid-Feb. No lunch.*

$$–$$$ ✕ **Man Friday.** The name refers to Kinsale's alleged connection with the original Robinson Crusoe, Alexander Selkirk (the town was reputedly his last port of call before shipwreck). Man Friday occupies a series of interconnected rooms and has a terrace for drinks in fine weather. Steaks and seafood, prepared in an unpretentious Continental style, are the main business here. The generous portions make it the sort of place that garners repeat customers. It's about 1 km (½ mi) outside town, on a hilltop overlooking the harbor. ⊠ *Scilly* ☎ *021/477–2260* ⊟ *AE, DC, MC, V* ⏱ *Closed Sun. No lunch.*

★ $–$$$ ✕ **Crackpots.** A grocery shop was transformed into Carole Norman's "ceramic café," a simple but elegant eatery with warm yellow walls and cozy dining areas. Behind the restaurant is Carole's pottery workshop; if you like your dinner plate, you can buy it. The eclectic menu won't put you in the poorhouse. Choices range from Moroccan meatballs with couscous to Thai-style prawns with fragrant rice; there also always a steak option. ⊠ *3 Cork St.* ☎ *021/477–2847* ⊟ *MC, V* ⏱ *Closed Mon.–Wed. Nov.–Mar.*

$–$$$ ✕ **Fishy Fishy Café.** Behind an impressive display of fresh seafood, chef Martin Shanahan's team concocts the specials that make this a place of pilgrimage for fish-lovers. People stand in line for a table at peak times (1–2:30). Martin, who learned his craft in San Francisco, brings California pizzazz to his dishes. Look for langoustines with lemon, garlic and sweet chilli sauce; a fresh crab open sandwich; and seafood salad with a tangy herb dressing. ⊠ *Guardwell (opposite St. Multose Church)* ☎ *021/477–4453* ⌘ *Reservations not accepted* ⊟ *No credit cards* ⏱ *Closed Sun. Oct.–Mar. No dinner.*

$–$$$ ✕ **Max's Wine Bar.** Low, beamed ceilings and polished antique tables of different shapes and sizes lend this town house considerable charm. Lunches are light; it's a good place if you're keen on salads. At dinner, owner-chef Olivier Queva's classical French background is evident in his treatment of the daily catch and in his clever ways with such unusual cuts of meat as oxtail and pig's trotters. The wine list is long and includes a good selection of French and New World wines, ranging in price from €15 to €76. ⊠ *Main St.* ☎ *021/477–2443* ⊟ *MC, V* ⏱ *Closed Nov.–mid-Mar.*

$–$$ ✕ **The Bulman.** Kinsale has other pub-restaurants, but none with such an idyllic waterside location. At lunchtime simple pub grub—mussels steamed in white wine or a meaty burger and chips—is served at the bar. In the evening the first-floor restaurant has tables with splendid views of the sun setting over the harbor. The menu includes steaks, freshly made pasta, Thai chicken curry, and local salmon with lemon-herb butter sauce. ⊠ *Summercove* ☎ *021/477–2131* ▤ *MC, V* ◷ *No lunch Sun.*

$$$–$$$$ ⊞ **Innishannon House.** The house that contains this small, romantic hotel was built in 1720 in the Petit Château style on the banks of the Bandon. Rooms vary greatly in shape and size, but all are full of antiques and character. The hotel is surrounded by woods and is just off N7, about 6 km (4 mi) from Kinsale; it's perfect both as a retreat and as base for touring the area. ⊠ *Innishannon, Co. Cork* ☎ *021/477–5121* ▤ *021/477–5609* ⊕ *www.innishannon-hotel.ie* ⤻ *13 rooms with bath* ⚲ *Restaurant, cable TV, boating, fishing, bar, meeting rooms* ▤ *AE, DC, MC, V* ⏐○⏐ *BP.*

$$$–$$$$ ⊞ **Perryville House.** This pink, 19th-century house with a wrought-iron balcony overlooks the inner harbor. Public areas are well appointed and give you the impression of being in a private home. Front bedrooms have sea views, but rooms at the rear are quieter—key in July and August, when the town gets busy. All rooms are imaginatively furnished with Victorian antiques and have large beds and such extras as robes and fresh flowers. The lodging has a wine license, so you can buy by the glass or the bottle. ⊠ *Long Quay, Co. Cork* ☎ *021/477–2731* ▤ *021/477–2298* ⊕ *www.perryvillehouse.com* ⤻ *27 rooms with bath* ⚲ *Cable TV; no kids under 13, no smoking* ▤ *AE, DC, MC, V* ⏐○⏐ *BP* ◷ *Closed Nov.–Mar.*

★ **$$–$$$$** ⊞ **Old Bank House.** Owners Michael and Marie Riese manage this Georgian town house with flair. The large, high-ceilinged rooms have dried-flower arrangements, modern prints, and tall double-glazed windows. Michael was previously chef-owner of Vintage restaurant, and his breakfasts are memorable. ⊠ *Pearse St., Co. Cork* ☎ *021/477–4075* ▤ *021/477–4296* ⊕ *www.oldbankhousekinsale.com* ⤻ *17 rooms with bath.* ⚲ *Cable TV* ▤ *AE, MC, V* ⏐○⏐ *BP.*

$$$ ⊞ **Blue Haven.** A restaurant and small hotel occupy this attractive, yellow-stucco, blue-trim town house. Rooms in the main house, though small, are cheerful and have paintings by local artists; newer rooms in an adjacent building have dark-oak furniture, antique canopy beds, and spacious baths. Inexpensive bar food is served until 9:30 PM in the lounge, the patio, and the conservatory, all of which have swagged curtains and nautical brass. The quiet, pastel-color seafood restaurant overlooks a garden and fountain. ⊠ *3 Pearse St., Co. Cork* ☎ *021/477–2209* ▤ *021/477–4268* ⊕ *www.bluehavenkinsale.com* ⤻ *17 rooms with bath* ⚲ *Restaurant, cable TV, fishing, bar* ▤ *AE, DC, MC, V* ⏐○⏐ *BP.*

$$ ⊞ **Sovereign House.** Built in 1708 as the home of the Sovereign (Lord Mayor) of Kinsale, this imposing Queen Anne town house has a symmetrical stone facade and a quiet, central location. The baronial interior is furnished with heavy antiques and has flagstone floors and several fireplaces. Rooms are large and luxurious, with such original features as massive exposed beams; bathrooms are Victorian in style. The lodging has a wine license. ⊠ *Newman's Mall, Co. Cork* ☎ *021/477–2850* ▤ *021/477–4723* ⤻ *4 rooms with bath* ⚲ *Cable TV, billiards; no smoking* ▤ *MC, V* ⏐○⏐ *BP* ◷ *Closed Nov.–Feb.*

$–$$ ⊞ **The White House.** One of Kinsale's oldest inns has maintained the tradition of a warm Irish welcome. Bedrooms vary in size, but all have fully tiled, good-size bathrooms and pastel color schemes. A bar menu is served both in the bar and in the quieter Chelsea's Bistro; the boiled bacon and cabbage—served with enormous potatoes—and the fish of the day are good bets. Ask about the two- and three-day dinner-and-lodging specials. ⊠ *Pearse St. and the Glen, Co. Cork* ☎ *021/477–2125* ▤ *021/477–2045* ⊕ *www.whitehouse-kinsale.ie* ⤻ *12 rooms with bath* ⚲ *Restaurant, cable TV, bar* ▤ *AE, DC, MC, V* ⏐○⏐ *BP.*

¢ 🏠 **Guardwell Lodge.** Rooms at the rear of this modern, five-story block in the town center look out over a 13th-century church, but that's as romantic as it gets. The area is noisy at night—especially on weekends and in July and August—and rooms, though clean and bright, have few frills. Make your own breakfast in the communal kitchen, or head to one of the nearby cafés. ✉ *Guardwell, Co. Cork* ☎ *021/477-4686* 🖷 *021/477-4684* ⊕ *www.guardwelllodge.com* ➔ *23 double rooms with bath, 9 single rooms with bath, 40 bunk beds in dorm rooms* ♿ *No TV or direct dial phones in rooms* ▭ *MC, V* ⊙ *EP.*

¢ 🏠 **Kilcaw House.** Low room rates and off-street parking make this guest house a good choice. On busy weekends, when the town buzz continues into the small hours, Kilcaw's location—2 km (1 mi) outside town on the Cork side of the R600—guarantees peace and quiet. An open fire in the lobby, polished pine floors, and striking colors add character to the farmhouse-style building. Rooms are well equipped, spacious, and uncluttered, with country pine furniture and throw rugs on wooden floors. ✉ *Pewter Hole Cross (on R600) Co. Cork* ☎ *021/477-4155* 🖷 *021/477-4755* ⊕ *www.kilcawhouse.com* ➔ *7 rooms with bath* ♿ *Cable TV* ▭ *AE, MC, V* ⊙ *BP.*

Nightlife

The **Boom Boom Room** (✉ Guardwell ☎ 021/477-2382) has late-night dancing for the over-25s. The **Shanakee** (✉ Market St. ☎ 021/477-4472) is renowned for live music—both rock and Irish traditional. Check out the **Spaniard Inn** (✉ Scilly ☎ 021/477-2436) for rock and folk groups.

Sports & the Outdoors

BICYCLES · Rent a bike from **D&C Cycles** (✉ 18 Main St., Co. Cork ☎ 021/477-4884) to explore the picturesque hinterland of Kinsale.

FISHING For deep-sea angling off the Old Head of Kinsale contact **William Van Dyk** (☎ 021/477-8944) or **Arthur Long** (☎ 021/477-8969), both of whom operate out of **Castlepark Marina** (✉ Castlepark, Co. Cork). For bare-boat charters or skippered cruises—of a day or longer—contact **Sail Ireland Charters** (✉ Trident Hotel, Kinsale, Co. Cork ☎ 021/477-2927 ⊕ www.sailireland.com).

WATER SPORTS & TENNIS The **Oysterhaven Holiday and Activity Center** (✉ Oysterhaven, sign-posted off R600 ☎ 021/477-0738), in a sheltered inlet 16 km (10 mi) east of Kinsale, rents sailboarding equipment and wet suits for €25 per hour. Topaz dinghies rent for €30 per hour. If Irish weather permits, you can also book a tennis court here for €10 an hour.

Shopping

Boland's (✉ Pearse St. ☎ 021/477-2161) sells some unusual items, including sweaters, designer rain gear, and linen shirts exclusive to this shop only. **Giles Norman Photography Gallery** (✉ 44 Main St. ☎ 021/477-4373) sells black-and-white photographs of Irish scenes. **Granny's Bottom Drawer** (✉ 53 Main St. ☎ 021/477-4839) has a selection of fine linen and lace in classic and contemporary styles. The **Keane on Ceramics** (✉ Pier Rd. ☎ 021/477-2085) gallery represents the best of Ireland's ceramics artists. **Kingfisher Crafts** (✉ 41 Main St. ☎ 021/477-4434) sells unusual, Irish-made decorative items,

You can spend quite a bit of time browsing through the excellent selection of Irish poetry and books on local history at the **Kinsale Bookshop** (✉ 8 Main St. ☎ 021/477-4244 ⊕ www.kinsalebookshop.ie). **Kinsale Crystal** (✉ Market St. ☎ 021/477-4463) is a studio that sells 100% Irish, handblown, hand-cut crystal. Ceramics artist **Sara Flynn** (✉ 42 Main St. ☎ 021/477-7201 ⊕ www.saraflynnceramics.com) has a studio and gallery in a cleverly converted old town house. Her porcelain forms are simultaneously simple and elegant. The **Trading House** (⌧ 54 Main St. ☎ 021/477–7497) has exclusive housewares from France, Spain, and Scandinavia alongside Irish and French antiques. **Victoria Murphy** (⌧ Market Quay ☎ 021/477–4317) sells a selection of small antiques and antique jewelry.

| en route | Leave Kinsale through its center, and follow the quays, driving west along the Bandon River toward the bridge on R600. This takes you through **Garretstown Woods** (signposts for Clonakilty on R600), carpeted with wild bluebells in April. You'll then travel past the edge of Courtmacsherry Bay, alongside a wide, saltwater inlet that teems with curlew, plover, and other waders. |

Timoleague

㉗ *19 km (12 mi) west of Kinsale on R600.*

The romantic silhouette of its ruined abbey dominates the view when you're approaching Timoleague, a village of multicolored houses on the Argideen River estuary. The town marks the eastern end of the Seven Heads Peninsula, which stretches around to Clonakilty. A mid-13th-century **Franciscan abbey** at the water's edge is Timoleague's most striking monument. (Walk around the back to find the entrance gate.) It was sacked by the English in 1642 but, like many other ruins of its kind, was used as a burial place until the late 20th century. A tower and walls with Gothic-arched windows still stand, and you can trace the ground plan of the old friary—chapel, refectory, cloisters, and wine cellar (at one time the friars were well-known wine importers).

The **Timoleague Castle Gardens** are right in the village. Although the castle is now a ruin adjoining a modest early-20th-century gray-stone house, the original gardens have survived. Palm trees and other frost-tender plants flourish in the mature shrubbery. There are two large, old-fashioned walled gardens, one for flowers and one for fruits and vegetables. ☎ 023/46116 ⌧ €3 ☉ *Easter weekend and June–Aug., daily noon–6.*

You can glimpse the village of **Courtmacsherry** and its colorful cottages and sandy beaches, across the water. To reach it follow the signposts from Timoleague.

Many storefronts in **Clonakilty**, a small market town 9½ km (6 mi) west of Timoleague on R600/N71, have charmingly traditional, hand-painted signs and wooden facades. **Inchydoney**, 3 km (2 mi) outside Clonakilty, is one of the area's finest sandy beaches. It's a great place for shell collectors.

| off the beaten path | **BIRTHPLACE OF MICHAEL COLLINS –** The birthplace of Michael Collins (1890–1922) is signposted 9 km (6 mi) west of Timoleague off N71 (past the village of Lissavaird). You can see the ground plan of the simple homestead where the controversial founder of the modern Irish Army was born. There's also a bronze memorial (freely accessible), and another memorial in the nearest village, Woodfield, opposite the pub where Collins is said to have had his last drink on the day he was shot in an ambush. |

Where to Stay & Eat

$$–$$$
FodorsChoice
★

✕ **Casino House.** Stop midway between Kinsale and Timoleague, on coastal route R600, for a meal at this farmhouse, which has been converted to an informal restaurant. The two small dining rooms—one blue

BACK OF THE BEYOND

Rustic, seafaring charm and cheerful fishing villages abound in a tiny, remote corner of the world just west of Timoleague. From Timoleague, take the N71 road, which briefly joins the sea at Rosscarbery, and turn left at the signpost for lovely Glandore at the end of the causeway. Glandore and Union Hall are twin fishing villages on either side of the landlocked Glandore Harbour. With its steep hill, pretty church, and emerald harbor, Glandore is a popular destination for people coming from the United Kingdom and Germany and is locally nicknamed "Millionaire's Row." The influx of affluent visitors and expensive yachts is less obvious in Union Hall, where fishing trawlers still tie up at the quay.

and one green—have private sitting rooms for predinner drinks next to an open fire. Menu highlights from talented Croatian owner-chef Michael Relja include starters of garlic prawn salad and lobster risotto; main courses include roast loin of lamb served with Roman gnocchi. Summer fruits with sabayon are one of the fine seasonal desserts. ☒ *Coolmaine, Kilbrittain* ☎ *023/49944* ▤ *MC, V* ☉ *Closed Wed. mid-Jan.–mid-Mar.; Easter–Oct.; and Mon.–Thurs. Nov.–early Jan.*

$$$$ 🏠 **The Lodge & Spa at Inchydoney Island.** With its dream location above a long beach, this modern hotel is a refuge for overworked city folk. Although the island is connected to the mainland by a causeway, it still feels remote. Earthtones, plump sofas, and terrific natural light—reflected off the Atlantic—are soothing. Public area palettes continue in the guest rooms, which have plush robes, soft slippers, and posh soaps. Although staffers are pleasant, service can be laid back. If this causes you stress, unwind in the thalassotherapy spa, where treatments draw on the benefits of seawater, or head out on a golf, fishing, or horseback-riding excursion. ☒ *Inchydoney Island, 5 km (3 mi) south of Clonakilty* ☎ *023/ 33143* 🖷 *023/35229* ⊕ *www.inchydoneyisland.com* ▰ *64 rooms with bath, 3 suites* ♨ *Restaurant, room service, IDD phones, in-room data ports, in-room safes, minibars, cable TV, indoor saltwater pool, fitness classes, health club, hot tub, massage, sauna, spa, steam room, beach, Ping-Pong, bar* ▤ *AE, DC, MC, V* ⌖ *BP.*

Shopping

The hand-crafted gifts and housewares at **Clonakilty Craft Centre** (☒ Strand Rd., Clonakilty ☎ 023/35802) showcase contemporary Irish design. **Delaney's** (☒ Clonakilty ☎ 023/48361) is full of small antiques as well as antiquarian and secondhand books. **Edward Twomey** (☒ 16 Pearse St., Clonakilty ☎ 023/33365) is a traditional butcher's shop famed for its Clonakilty Black Pudding, a breakfast product that features prominently on the shop's nifty T-shirts—-the ultimate West Cork souvenirs. **Spiller's Lane Gallery** (☒ Spiller's La., Clonakilty ☎ 023/38416), in a converted grain store at a pretty mews, sells Irish-made jewelry, cutlery, pottery, and paintings.

Skibbereen

28 *35 km (22 mi) west of Timoleague.*

Skibbereen is the main market town in this neck of southwest Cork, and a good base for nearby sights. The Wednesday cattle market, the Friday country market, and the plethora of pubs punctuated by bustling shops and coffeehouses all keep the place jumping year-round.

A thoughtful renovation of a stone gas works building has created an attractive, architecturally appropriate home for the **Skibbereen Heritage Center.** An elaborate audiovisual exhibit on the Great Famine presents dramatized firsthand accounts of what it was like to live in this community when it was hard hit by hunger. Other attractions include displays on area marine life, walking tours, access to local census information, and a varying schedule of special programs. ✉ *Upper Bridge St., Skibbereen* ☎ *028/40900.* ✉ *€4* ☉ *Mid-Mar.–late May and mid-Sept.–mid-Oct., Tues.–Sat. 10–6; late May–mid-Sept., daily 10–6; mid-Oct.–mid-Mar. by appointment.*

The **Mizen Vision Visitor Centre,** which occupies a lighthouse at the tip of the Mizen Head (follow the R591 through Goleen to the end of the road), is the Irish mainland's most southerly point. The lighthouse itself is on a rock at the tip of the headland; to reach it, you must cross a dramatic 99-step suspension footbridge. The lighthouse was completed in 1910; the Engine Room and Keepers' House have been restored by the local community. The exhilaration of massive Atlantic seas swirling 164 feet below the footbridge, and the great coastal views, guarantee a memorable outing. ✉ *Harbour Rd., Goleen* ☎ *028/35115* ⊕ *www. mizenhead.net* ✉ *€4.50* ☉ *Mid-Mar.–May and Oct., daily 10:30–5; June–Sept., daily 10–6; Nov.–mid-Mar., weekends 11–4.*

Where to Stay & Eat

$$$$ ✕ **Island Cottage.** This unlikely venture is a pilgrimage spot for food lovers, who praise the high standard of cooking and the location. Hosts John Desmond and Ellmary Fenton prepare set five-course meals using local produce, some of it picked in the wild on the island. Expect good, honest, unfussily prepared food. Cape Clear turbot with sea spinach is typical; for dessert, try the terrine of vanilla ice cream with meringue in blackberry sauce. Advance booking is necessary; call 24 hours ahead of time for details about the four-minute nightly ferry ride to the island from Cunnamore, which is about 15 km (9 mi) west of Skibbereen (follow signs on the road to Ballydehob). ✉ *Heir Island* ☎ *028/38102* ▭ *No credit cards* ☉ *Closed mid-Sept.–mid-May and Mon.–Tues. June–Sept. No lunch.*

$$$ ✕ **Annie's.** A meal at this mildly eccentric cottage, in an offbeat village 16 km (10 mi) west of Skibbereen, is an essential West Cork experience. Annie Barrie and her chef husband, Dano, have been running the place for over 20 years. When you arrive, chances are that Annie will send you across the road to Levi's Pub, where you'll wait for your table, peruse the menu, and eventually give Annie your order. Dano's simple, well-judged cooking lends the restaurant considerable magic. Dishes are made from outstanding farmhouse cheeses, locally reared meats, and the freshest seafood. ✉ *Main St., Ballydehob* ☎ *028/37292* ▭ *MC, V* ☉ *Closed Sun. and Mon. and Oct. and Nov.*

$–$$ ✕▦ **West Cork Hotel.** This family-run hotel in a large Victorian building on the River Ilen is an excellent value. Rooms are comfortable, and a good value for the price range. Ask about midweek packages. The restaurant ($–$$$), famous for its steaks, serves such trendy dishes as Louisiana crab cakes alongside traditional favorites. ✉ *Bridge St., Co. Cork* ☎ *028/21277* 🖶 *028/22333* ⊕ *www.westcorkhotel.com* ⇌ *36 rooms with bath* ↺ *Restaurant, cable TV, fishing, bar* ▭ *AE, DC, MC, V* ⊙ *BP.*

¢ ✕▦ **Heron's Cove.** Expect to see herons outside your window at Sue Hill's harborside retreat. The modern house, on the edge of a secluded inlet, is only minutes by foot from Goleen's village center. The well-equipped rooms, furnished in part with antiques, have excellent views from every window. In summer, fresh local seafood stars on the menu ($$–$$$), which also includes lamb, duck, and steak. Fresh herb sauces and home-made mayonnaise make subtle accompaniments, and there's a terrific wine list. Off-season (November–March), evening meals are prepared for guests only. ⊠ *The Harbour, Goleen, Co. Cork* ☎ *028/35225* 🖷 *028/35422* ⊕ *www.heronscove.com* ⇨ *5 rooms with bath* ⅃ *Restaurant, cable TV, fishing; no room phones, no smoking* ⊟ *AE, DC, MC, V* ❘◎❘ *BP.*

The Arts

The **West Cork Arts Center** (⊠ North St. Skibbereen ☎ 028/22090) has regular exhibits of work by local artists and an on-site crafts shop.

Castletownshend

㉙ *8 km (5 mi) southeast of Skibbereen.*

This town has an unusual number of large, gracious stone houses, most of them dating from the mid-18th century, when it was an important trading center. The main street runs steeply downhill to the 17th-century castle (built by the Townshends) and the sea. The sleepy town awakens in July and August, when its sheltered harbor bustles. Sparkling views await from cliff-top St. Barrahane's Church, which has a medieval oak altarpiece and three stained-glass windows by early-20th-century Irish artist Harry Clarke.

Where to Eat

$$–$$$$ ✕ **Mary Ann's.** Writer Edna O'Brien is among the many fans of the pub, which is one of Ireland's oldest. Owner-manager Fergus O'Mahoney often mingles with patrons in the low-beamed front bar room, the quieter back room, or the large garden beyond. Upstairs the 28-seat restaurant nearly always buzzes; reservations are a good idea. Try the trademark baked avocado stuffed with crab meat, the massively generous seafood platter, or the succulent T-bone steak. ⊠ *Main St.* ☎ *028/36146* ⊟ *MC, V* ☉ *Nov.–Mar. closed on Mon.*

Baltimore

㉚ *13 km (8 mi) southwest of Skibbereen on R595.*

The beautiful, crescent-shape fishing village of Baltimore is a popular sailing center and attracts its share of vacationing families from Ireland and abroad, especially in summer. The village was sacked in 1631 by a band of Algerian sailors; as a result, watchtowers were installed at the harbor mouth.

Sherkin Island (☎ 028/20125 for ferry information) is 1 km (½ mi) off the coast, only a 10-minute ferry ride away. On the island, you'll find the ruins of Dún Na Long Castle and Sherkin Abbey, both built around 1470 by the O'Driscolls, a seafaring clan known as the "scourge of the Irish seas." The island's population today is 90, and there are several safe, sandy beaches and abundant wildlife. Simply walking on Sherkin's almost-traffic-free roads and taking in the scenery is memorable.

The rugged, dramatic **Cape Clear Island** (☎ 028/39119 for ferry information ⊕ www.oilean-chleire.ie) is part of the West Cork Gaeltacht, or Irish-speaking area. The ferry to the 2- by 5-km (1- by 3-mi) island, which is 6 km (4 mi) offshore, takes about an hour from Baltimore. It's exciting to watch the skipper thread his way through the rocks and islets of Roaring Water Bay. You'll get excellent views of the Fastnet Rock Lighthouse, which is the focus of a biennial yachting race. Sparsely populated (about 150 residents), the island has little road traffic, a few bars, a youth hostel, and a few simple B&Bs. Bird-watchers will relish their time here—Cape Clear is the southernmost point of Irish territory, and its observatory, the country's oldest, has racked up all kinds of sightings of rare songbird migrants. Whales, dolphins, and large flocks of oceangoing birds can be seen offshore in the summer. In late August, the island hosts the International Story-telling Festival, a long weekend of simple entertainment for adults and kids; beware, it gets packed.

Where to Stay & Eat

¢ ✕ Rolf's Holiday Hostel. More like a Continental pension than a true hostel, this family-run establishment is just outside the village, surrounded by wild gorse and above Roaring Water Bay. The communal kitchen and unpretentious, cheery rooms are in stone structures that were originally farmyard outbuildings. Views are pastoral. Cafe Art, the contemporary yet rustic restaurant ($–$$), offers simply prepared local produce, steaks, and seafood. ⊠ *Baltimore Hill* ☎ *028/20289* 🖷 *028/ 20289* ⊕ *www.rolfsholidays.com* ⇆ *8 doubles with bath; 4 family rooms with bath; 1 12-bed dorm room* ⚭ *Restaurant, laundry, self-catering kitchen* ▭ *MC, V* ⦿ *EP.*

$ ⊡ Islander's Rest. Overnighting on an island—even one that's just off-shore—is a romantic idea. This island hotel, with its farmhouse-style gables and dormers, overlooks the sea. It's only a short walk from the pier, but proprietor Mark Murphy can arrange for you to be met by a minibus. Rooms are simple with bright, checked fabrics and cottage-style pine furniture; most quarters have ocean views. The bar here is lively; the island's only other bar-restaurant is just across the road. ⊠ *Sherkin Island* ☎ *028/20116* 🖷 *028/20360* ⊕ *www.islandersrest.ie* ⇆ *21 rooms with bath* ⚭ *Restaurant, bar* ▭ *MC, V* ⦿ *BP.*

Sports & the Outdoors

Sailing dinghies and sailboards can be rented by the hour or the day from **Baltimore Sailing School** (⊠ The Pier ☎ 028/20141).

Bantry

㉛ *25 km (16 mi) northwest of Skibbereen on N71.*

This unprepossessing town at the head of Bantry Bay is known for its manor, Bantry House; its large market square; and its long plaza, which attracts artisans, craftspeople, and musicians in summer.

As you enter Bantry, on the right-hand side of the road you'll see the porticoed entrance to **Bantry House.** One of Ireland's most magnificent manors (closed to tours) was built in the early 1700s and then subsequently altered and expanded later that century. The house as it looks today is largely the vision of Richard White, the second earl of Bantry, who also created the Italianate gardens that surround it. The long climb to the top of the rear garden pays off with what has been called "one of the great views in Ireland"—overlooking the sea. Next to Bantry House is the **Bantry 1796 French Armada Exhibition Center,** a small but worth-while museum illustrating the abortive attempt by Irish Nationalist Wolfe Tone and his French ally General Hoche to land 14,000 troops in Bantry Bay to effect an uprising. ☎ *027/50047* ⊕ *www.corkkerry. ie* ⊠ *Museum and gardens €4* ⊙ *Mar.–Oct., daily 9–6.*

Where to Stay & Eat

$$-$$$ ✕⊡ Blair's Cove House. In the converted stables of a Georgian mansion, gleaming silverware, pink tablecloths, and a large crystal chandelier are set off against stone walls and exposed beams. A covered, heated terrace overlooks a fountain and a rose-filled courtyard. As the owners are

French, the cuisine ($$$$) is a mixture of French and Irish. Stone out-buildings have been converted into well-equipped rooms furnished with country antiques. The morning views of Dunmanus Bay are breathtaking. ⊠ *Blair's Cove, Durrus* ☎ *027/61041* ⟆ *3 rooms with bath* ⚭ *Cable TV, some pets allowed* ⊟ *DC, MC, V* ⦿l *BP* ⊙ *Restaurant closed Sun., July, Aug., and Sun.–Mon. Sept.–June.*

★ **$$$** ⊡ **Sea View House.** Among private, wooded grounds overlooking Bantry Bay, you'll find a large, three-story, 19th-century country house. Owner-manager Kathleen O'Sullivan keeps an eagle eye on what was, until 1980, her private home. Antique furniture, polished brass, and ornate curtains speak of elegance. Some bedrooms have sea views and small sofas in bay windows; others have views of the wooded gardens. In the dining room, polished tables are set with crocheted mats and linen napkins; service is friendly and informal. ⊠ *Ballylickey, Co. Cork* ☎ *027/50073* ⊞ *027/51555* ⟆ *16 rooms with bath* ⚭ *Restaurant, cable TV, fishing, bar* ⊟ *AE, DC, MC, V* ⦿l *BP* ⊙ *Closed mid-Nov.–mid-Mar.*

Sports & the Outdoors

Bantry Park Golf Club (⊠ Donemark, Co. Cork ☎ 027/50579) is an 18-hole, par-71 course that overlooks Bantry Bay.

Shopping

One of the southwest's larger independents, **Bantry Bookstore** (⊠ New St. ☎ 027/50064) has six rooms full of new, antiquarian, and second-hand books. **Manning's Emporium** (⊠ Ballylickey ☎ 027/51049) is a showcase for locally made farmhouse cheeses, pâtés, and salamis—an excellent place to put together a picnic or just to browse.

Glengarriff

❸❷ *14 km (8 mi) northwest of Bantry on N71, 21 km (13 mi) south of Kenmare.*

One of the jewels of Bantry Bay is Glengarriff, the "rugged glen" much loved by Thackeray and Sir Walter Scott. The descent into wooded, sheltered Glengarriff reveals yet another landscape: thanks to the Gulf Stream, it's mild enough down here for subtropical plants to thrive. Trails along the shore are covered with rhododendrons and offer beautiful views of the nearby inlets, loughs, and lounging seals. You're very much on the beaten path, however, with crafts shops, tour buses, and boatmen soliciting your business by the roadside.

☾ On **Ilnacullin** (also known as Garnish Island), about 10 minutes offshore from Glengariff and beyond islets populated by comical-looking basking seals, you'll find formal Italian gardens; subtropical plants; and excellent views from a Grecian temple. From the island's martello tower, built at the end of the 18th century, the British watched for attempted landings by Napoleonic forces. ☎ 027/63040 ⊕ *www.heritageireland.ie* ⊠ *Gardens: €3.50. Boat ride: €7.50 round-trip* ⊙ *July and Aug., Mon.–Sat. 9:30–6:30, Sun. 11–7; Apr.–June and Sept., Mon.–Sat. 10–6:30, Sun. 1–7; Mar. and Oct., Mon.–Sat. 10–4:30, Sun. 1–5.*

Glengarriff is the gateway to the **Ring of Beara**, a 137-km (85-mi) scenic drive that circles the Beara Peninsula on R572. The least famous of the southwest's three peninsulas is also the least frequented—and, some would say, the most ruggedly beautiful. One of the main attractions is the Beara Way, a 196-km (120-mi), marked, walking route that visits many prehistoric archaeological sites. Just beyond the busy fishing port of Castletownbere are the freely accessible ruins of Dunboy Castle and House. Dursey Island, at the peninsula's tip, is a bird-watcher's paradise that you reach by cable car. From Dursey Island, head for tiny Allihies, the former site of a huge copper mine, which now houses studios (open May–September) for some of Ireland's leading artists. This is also great hiking country—known for some of the most scenic stretches of the Beara Way. Continue along a breathtaking coastal road to Eyeries—a village overlooking Coulagh Bay—and then up the south side of the Kenmare River to Kenmare.

If you have time left over after exploring the Ring of Beara, you might want to backtrack to R584 and visit **Gougane Barra National Park** (⊕ www.coillte.ie/tourism_and_recreation/guagan.htm), where the hermit St. Finbarr had his mountain retreat. It's the source of the River Lee, and it has nature trails.

Where to Stay

¢ ▦ **Old Presbytery.** This waterside house, amid 4 acres of gardens, used to be the home of the parish priest. It's about 1 km (½ mi) from the busy fishing port of Castletownbere, on a narrow peninsula. Rooms are comfortable and individually furnished, with pleasant sea views. Breakfast is served in the conservatory, which overlooks a private cove. This is an excellent base for touring Beara. Hosts David and Mary Wrigley will arrange dinner at one of the restaurants nearby, most of which specialize in seafood. ⊠ *Brandy Hall, Castletownbere* ☎ *027/70424* 🖷 *027/70420* ⊕ *www.midnet.ie/oldpresbytery/index.htm* ⤤ *5 rooms with bath* ⅃ *Cable TV* ▤ *MC, V* ⅃◎⅃ *BP* ⊙ *Closed Oct.–Mar.*

THE RING OF KERRY

Along the perimeter of the Iveragh Peninsula, the dramatic Ring of Kerry is probably Ireland's single most popular tourist route. Stunning mountain and coastal views are around almost every turn. The only drawback: on a sunny day, it seems like half the nation's visitors are traveling along this two-lane road, packed into buses, riding bikes, or backpacking. The route is narrow and curvy, and the local sheep think nothing of using it for a nap; take it slowly.

Tour buses tend to start in Killarney and ply the Ring counterclockwise, so consider jumping ahead and starting in Killorglin or following the route clockwise, starting in Kenmare. Either way, bear in mind that most of the buses leave Killarney between 9 and 10 AM. The trip covers 176 km (110 mi) on N70 (and briefly R562) if you start and finish in Killarney; the journey will be 40 km (25 mi) shorter if you only venture between Kenmare and Killorglin. Allow at least one full day to circumnavigate the Ring. And because rain blocks views across the water to the Beara Peninsula in the east and the Dingle Peninsula in the west, hope for sunshine. It makes all the difference.

Kenmare

🅣 *21 km (13 mi) north of Glengarriff on N71, 34 km (21 mi) south of Killarney.*

A lively touring base, this market town at the head of the sheltered Kenmare River estuary has lots of restaurants and accommodations for such a small place. The town was founded in 1670 by Sir William Petty (Oliver Cromwell's surveyor general, a multitasking entrepreneur), and most of its buildings date from the 19th century, when it was part of the enormous Lansdowne Estate—itself assembled by Petty. The **Kenmare Heritage Centre** explains the town's history and supplies a walking route pointing out places of interest. ⊠ *The Square* ☎ *064/41233* ☞ *Free* ⊙ *Easter–Sept., Mon.–Sat. 9:30–5:30.*

Where to Stay & Eat

$$ ✕ **Lime Tree.** An open fire, stone walls, and a minstrel's gallery on a large balcony above the main room lend considerable character to this restaurant in a former schoolhouse. Try one of the imaginative vegetarian options—millefeuille of goat's cheese with spicy crumble—or go for local free-range duck or Kerry lamb oven roasted with sweet mint pesto. Leave room for a warm dessert, such as blackberry and pear fruit crumble. ✉ *Shelburne St.* ☎ *064/41839* ⊟ *MC, V* ☽ *Closed Nov.–Mar.*

$–$$ ✕ **An Leath Phingin.** The name means "The Half Penny." It's a stylish little place with stone walls and modern pine tables, and it specializes, oddly enough, in northern Italian cuisine. The explanation lies in owner-chef Con Guerin's links with Bologna, where he learned the art of making fresh pasta. The combination of Irish and Italian dishes is reflected in a starter of baked aubergine with olive oil, tomato, local goat's cheese, and basil, or a 12-inch *quattro formaggi* pizza with four Irish cheeses—Milleens, Cashel Blue, local goat's, and Gubeen. ✉ *35 Main St.* ☎ *064/41559* ⊟ *MC, V* ☽ *Closed mid-Nov.–mid-Dec. No lunch.*

$–$$ ✕ **Packies.** Owner-chef Maura O'Connell Foley established Kenmare's original first-class restaurant, the Lime Tree, but has since opted for a quieter life at Packies. The small room has a flagstone floor, a stone fireplace, and paintings by local artists. The Mediterranean-cum-Irish dishes include wild smoked salmon with red onion and caper salsa and rack of lamb with rosemary and garlic sauce. ✉ *Henry St.* ☎ *064/41508* ⊟ *AE, MC, V* ☽ *Closed Sun. and Mon. and Nov.–mid-Mar. No lunch.*

$$$$
Fodor'sChoice
★
✕⊡ **Park Hotel.** One of Ireland's premier country-house hotels, this 1897 stone château has spectacular views of the Caha Mountains. Its 11 acres include terraced lawns that sweep down to the bay. A marble fireplace and a tall grandfather clock preside over the thickly carpeted lobby. Each of the spacious bedrooms is unique, though most have late-Victorian pieces; suites have walnut or mahogany beds, wardrobes, and chests of drawers. Be sure to eat at the restaurant ($$$–$$$$), which serves justly famed modern Irish cuisine. ✉ *Shelburne Rd., Co. Kerry* ☎ *064/41200* 🖷 *064/41402* ⊕ *www.parkkenmare.com* ↪ *40 rooms with bath, 9 suites* ⚘ *Restaurant, cable TV, 18-hole golf course, tennis court, fishing, bicycles, croquet, Ping-Pong, bar, library, some pets allowed* ⊟ *AE, DC, MC, V* ⊠ *BP* ☽ *Closed Jan. 2–mid-Apr.*

$$$$ ✕⊡ **Sheen Falls Lodge.** The magnificence of the setting—300 secluded acres of lawns, gardens, and forest between Kenmare Bay and the falls of the River Sheen—is matched by that of the bright-yellow, slate-roof manor. Public rooms, painted in orange tones, include a mahogany-paneled library with more than 1,000 books, mainly on Ireland, and a billiards room. Bedrooms have bay or river views. La Cascade restaurant ($$$$) overlooks the falls and has modern Irish cuisine. Oscar's Bistro ($–$$$) serves Mediterranean fare. You can hire one of the hotel's vintage cars, which include a Bentley and a Rolls, for picnics, trips into town, and other excursions. ✉ *Sheen Falls, Co. Kerry* ☎ *064/41600* 🖷 *064/41386* ⊕ *www.sheenfallslodge.ie* ↪ *58 rooms with bath, 8 suites* ⚘ *2 restaurants, cable TV, tennis court, indoor pool, health club, sauna, steam room, fishing, bicycles, billiards, croquet, horseback riding, 2 bars, library, meeting rooms* ⊟ *AE, DC, MC, V* ⊠ *EP* ☽ *Closed 1st 2 wks of Dec. and Jan.*

$$ ⊡ **Sallyport House.** Across the bridge on the way into Kenmare, this 1932 family home has been enlarged to serve as a comfortable B&B. The spotless rooms, all with harbor or mountain views, are furnished with a variety of Victorian and Edwardian antiques. Owner Janey Arthur has placed family heirlooms everywhere; if you're interested in old Irish furniture, ask for a tour. ✉ *Glengarriff Rd., Co. Kerry* ☎ *064/42066* 🖷 *064/42067*

⊕ *www.sallyporthouse.com* ⬦ *5 rooms with bath* ⚬ *Cable TV* ⊟ *No credit cards* ⊺⊙⫿ *BP* ⊘ *Closed Nov.–Mar.*

$ ⊞ **Sea Shore Farm.** Mary Patricia O'Sullivan offers a warm but professional welcome to her spacious farmhouse on Kenmare Bay. Weather permitting, there are views across the sea to the hills on the Beara Peninsula, and although the place is very close to Kenmare, it's also within walking distance of deserted seashore. Rooms are furnished with ornate heirlooms and have good-size bathrooms and placid views. Breakfast includes a choice of pancakes, kippers, or smoked salmon as well as the usual fry. ⊠ *Tubrid, Co. Kerry* 🕾🕾 *064/41270* ⬦ *6 rooms with bath* ⚬ *No smoking* ⊟ *MC, V* ⊺⊙⫿ *BP* ⊘ *Closed mid Nov.–Feb.*

Nightlife

Try **O Donnabhain** (⊠ Henry St. 🕾 064/41361) for traditional music.

Sports & the Outdoors

Seafari (⊠ Kenmare Pier 🕾 064/83171 ⊕ www.seafariireland.com) has two-hour, nature and seal-watching cruises and also runs the Marine Activities Centre (May–October, weather permitting), which offers sea fishing, sailboat day trips, sailboarding, canoeing, waterskiing, and tube rides.

Shopping

Avoca Handweavers (⊠ Moll's Gap 🕾 064/34720) sells wool clothing and mohair rugs and throws in remarkable palettes and a variety of weaves. **Black Abbey Crafts** (⊠ 28 Main St. 🕾 064/42115) specializes in fine Irish-made crafts. **Brenmar Jon** (⊠ 25 Henry St. 🕾 064/41138 ⊕ www.brenmar-jon.com) sells sophisticated knitwear. **Cleo's** (⊠ 2 Shelbourne St. 🕾 064/41410) stocks Irish-made woolens and linens that have striking designs, often drawn from Ireland's past.

Jam (⊠ 6 Henry St. 🕾 064/41591 ⊕ www.jam-kenmare.com) is a busy café that sells deli items and baked goods. **Kenmare Art Gallery** (⊠ Bridge St. 🕾 064/42999 ⊕ www.kenmareartgallery.com) has a good selection of works by contemporary artists, all of whom live locally but show internationally. **Noel & Holland** (⊠ 3 Bridge St. 🕾 064/42464) stocks secondhand books, including Irish-interest and children's titles. At **PFK**, Paul Kelly makes striking, modern jewelry in gold and silver.

Sneem

34 *27 km (17 mi) southwest of Kenmare on N70.*

The pretty village of Sneem (from the Irish for "knot") is settled around an English-style green on the Ardsheelaun River estuary, and its streets are filled with houses washed in different colors. Beside the parish church are the "pyramids," as they're known locally. These 12-foot-tall, traditional stone structures with stained-glass insets look as though they've been here forever. In fact, the sculpture park was completed in 1990 to the design of the Kerry-born artist James Scanlon, who has won international awards for his work in stained glass.

The approximately 2,500-year-old, stone **Staigue Fort,** signposted 4 km (2 mi) inland at Castlecove, is almost circular and about 75 feet in diameter with a single south-side entrance. From the Iron Age (from 500 BC to the 5th century AD) and early Christian times (6th century AD), such "forts" were, in fact, the fortified homesteads for several families of one clan and their cattle. The walls at Staigue Fort are almost 13 feet wide at the base and 7 feet wide at the top; they still stand at 18 feet on the north and west sides. Within them stairs lead to narrow platforms on which the lookouts stood. (Private land must be crossed to reach the fort, and a nominal "compensation for trespass" of €1 is often requested by the landowner.)

Where to Stay

$$$$ ▥ **Parknasilla Great Southern.** A porter in a frock coat and striped gray pants typifies the grand, slightly stuffy, early-20th-century sensibility of this hotel. General de Gaulle and Princess Grace stayed here, and it's where George Bernard Shaw wrote much of *Saint Joan*. Although some rooms are a bit plain, all are tasteful in soft pinks and blues. Continental cuisine is served in the Pygmalion restaurant. The sheltered coastal location—3 km (2 mi) south of Sneem—and excellent sporting facilities make this hotel an ideal retreat. ⊠ *Parknasilla, Co. Kerry* ☎ *064/ 45122* 🖷 *064/45323* ⊕ *www.gshotels.com* ➥ *84 rooms with bath, 1 suite* ♺ *Restaurant, cable TV, 9-hole golf course, tennis court, indoor pool, sauna, windsurfing, boating, fishing, horseback riding, bar, meeting rooms, some pets allowed* ☰ *AE, DC, MC, V* ❏◯❙ *BP.*

★ **$** ▥ **Tahilla Cove Country House.** An idyllic location—with its own stone jetty in a sheltered private cove—gives this place its particular charm. The house itself is modern and much-added-to over the years. No doubt it won't be difficult to enjoy the plump chintz armchairs and open log fire in the large sitting room, or to laze on the terrace overlooking 14 acres of subtropical gardens and the cove. Rooms vary in size and are comfortably furnished, and all but two have sea views. ⊠ *Tahilla Cove, Co. Kerry* ☎ *064/45204* 🖷 *064/45104* ⊕ *www.tahillacove.com* ➥ *9 rooms with bath* ♺ *Restaurant, cable TV, fishing, bar, some pets allowed* ☰ *AE, DC, MC, V* ❏◯❙ *BP* ❍ *Closed mid-Oct.–Mar.*

en route **Derrynane House** was once the home of Daniel O'Connell (1775–1847), "The Liberator," who campaigned for Catholic Emancipation (the granting of full rights of citizenship for Catholics), which became a reality in 1828. The house with its lovely garden and 320-acre estate now forms Derrynane National Park. The south and east wings of the house (which O'Connell himself remodeled) are open to visitors and contain much of the original furniture and other items associated with O'Connell. ⊠ *Near Caherdaniel, 30 km (18 mi) west of Sneem off N70* ☎ *066/947–5113* 🎟 *€2.50* ❍ *Nov.–Mar., weekends 1–5; Apr. and Oct., Tues.–Sun. 1–5; May–Sept., Mon.–Sat. 9–6, Sun. 11–7.*

Waterville

㉟ *35 km (22 mi) west of Sneem.*

Waterville is famous for its game-fishing, its 18-hole championship golf course (adopted as a warm-up spot for the British Open by Tiger Woods, who was a big hit with the locals), and for the fact that Charlie Chaplin and Charles de Gaulle once spent their summers here. Besides all that, the village, like many others on the Ring of Kerry, has a few restaurants and pubs, but little else. There's excellent salmon and trout fishing at nearby Lough Currane.

Outside Waterville and 1 km (½ mi) before Ballinskelligs, an Irish-speaking fishing village, is the **Cill Rialaig,** an artistic retreat. Here, a cluster of derelict old stone cottages in a deserted village were given new life as ceramics, metal-working, jewelry-making, and other arts or crafts studios. Cill Rialaig attracts both Irish and international artists for residencies, and their works are exhibited and sold at the store. There's also a coffee shop. ⊠ *R566* ☎ *066/947–9277* 🎟 *Free* ❍ *Daily 11–5.*

Where to Stay & Eat

$ ✕🏠 **Smuggler's Inn.** Lucille and Harry Hunt's small cliff-top pub is on a 2-km-long (1-mi-long) sandy beach, and has an immensely popular restaurant with fine, fresh seafood. It's an ideal spot for a leisurely dinner ($$–$$$$) or a quick pint and sandwich. Bedrooms are individually decorated with chintz spreads and curtains; in seven of them expect great sea views. ⊠ *Cliff Rd., Co. Kerry* ☎ *066/947–4330* 🖷 *066/947– 4422* ➭ *17 rooms with bath* ⚴ *Cable TV, fishing* 🖃 *AE, DC, MC, V* 🍴 *BP* ⊘ *Closed Nov.–Feb.*

$$$$ 🏠 **Butler Arms.** Charlie Chaplin loved it here. The building—with white, castellated corner towers—is a familiar landmark on the Ring. It has been in the same family for three generations, and the clientele return year after year for the excellent fishing and golf facilities nearby. Accommodations are neither smart nor chic, but the rambling old lounges with open turf fires are comfortable places to relax and converse. ⊠ *Waterville, Co. Kerry* ☎ *066/947–4144* 🖷 *066/947–4520* ⊕ *www. butlerarms.com* ➭ *30 rooms with bath* ⚴ *Restaurant, in-room data ports, cable TV, tennis court, fishing, horseback riding* 🖃 *AE, DC, MC, V* 🍴 *BP* ⊘ *Closed Nov.–Mar.*

Nightlife

Head to the **Inny Tavern** (⊠ Inny Bridge, Waterville ☎ 066/947–4512) for live Irish music.

Sports & the Outdoors

Waterville Golf Links (⊠ Co. Kerry ☎ 066/947–4102), an 18-hole, par-72 course, is one of the toughest and most scenic in Ireland or Britain.

Valentia Island

㊱ *21 km (13 mi) northwest of Waterville.*

In the far northwestern corner of the Ring, Valentia Island lies across Portmagee Channel. Some of the romance of visiting an island has been lost since Valentia was connected to the mainland by a bridge in 1971.

★ **Skelligs**—Little Skellig, Great Skellig, and the Washerwoman's Rock— are distinctive conical-shape rock islands visible from Valentia Island on a clear day. The largest rock, the Great Skellig, or Skellig Michael, rises 700 feet from the Atlantic. It has the remains of a settlement of early Christian monks, reached by climbing 600 increasingly precipitous steps. In spite of 1,000 years of battering by Atlantic storms, the church, oratory, and beehive-shape living cells are surprisingly well preserved.

The **Skellig Experience,** where the bridge joins Valentia Island, contains exhibits on local bird life, the history of the lighthouse and keepers, and the life and work of the early Christian monks. There's also a 15-minute audiovisual show that allows you to "tour" the monastery on Skellig Michael without leaving dry land. If, however, you'd like to see the Skelligs up close (landing is prohibited without a special permit), you can take a 1½-hour guided cruise. Little Skellig is the breeding ground of more than 22,000 pairs of gannets, and Puffin Island to the north has a large population of shearwaters, storm petrel, and puffins. Note that the waters are choppy at the best of times, and trips are made when the weather permits; call ahead for information. ⊠ *Valentia Island* ☎ *066/947–6306* 🖾 *Museum: €6. Cruise: €32 (includes admission to museum)* ⊘ *Apr.–June and Sept., daily 9:30–5; July and Aug., daily 9:30–7.*

Cahirciveen

③⑦ *18 km (11 mi) north of Waterville on N70.*

Cahirciveen (pronounced cah-her-sigh-*veen*) is the gateway to the western side of the Ring of Kerry, and the main market town for southern Kerry, at the foot of Bentee Mountain. Following the tradition in this part of the world, the modest, terraced houses are painted in different colors—the brighter the better.

The **O'Connell Memorial Church,** a large, elaborate, neo-Gothic church that dominates the main street, was built in 1888 of Newry granite and black limestone to honor the local hero, Daniel O'Connell. It's the only church in Ireland named after a layman.

The **Cahirciveen Heritage Centre** is in the converted former barracks of the Royal Irish Constabulary, an imposing, castlelike structure built after the Fenian Rising of 1867 to suppress any further revolts. The center has well-designed displays depicting scenes from times of famine in the locality, the life of Daniel O'Connell, and the restoration of this fine building from a blackened ruin. ⊠ *Barracks* ☎ *066/947–2777* ⊕ *www. kerry-insight.com* ⊉ *€3.50* ⊗ *June–Sept., Mon.–Sat. 10–6, Sun. 2–6; Mar.–May and Oct., weekdays 9:30–5:30.*

en route The road from Cahirciveen to Glenbeigh is one of the Ring's highlights. To the north is Dingle Bay and the jagged peaks of the Dingle Peninsula, which will, in all probability, be shrouded in mist. If they aren't, the gods have indeed blessed your journey. The road runs close to the water here, and beyond the small village of Kells, it climbs high above the bay, hugging the steep side of Drung Hill before descending to Glenbeigh. Note how different the stark character of this stretch of the Ring is from the gentle, woody Kenmare Bay side.

Glenbeigh

③⑧ *27 km (17 mi) northeast of Cahirciveen on N70.*

On a boggy plateau by the sea, the block-long town of Glenbeigh is a popular holiday base, with excellent hiking in the Glenbeigh Horseshoe, as the surrounding mountains are known, and exceptionally good trout fishing in Lough Coomasaharn.

The area south of Glenbeigh and west of Carrantouhill Mountain, around the shores of the Caragh River and the village of Glencar, is known as the Kerry Highlands. The scenery is wild and rough but still strangely appealing. A series of circular walks have been way marked, and parts of the Kerry Way pass through here. The area attracts serious climbers who intend to scale Carrantouhill, Ireland's highest peak (3,408 feet).

Worth a quick look, the **Kerry Bog Village Museum** is a cluster of reconstructed, fully furnished cottages that vividly portray the daily life of the region's working class in the early 1800s. ⊠ *Beside Red Fox Bar* ☎ *066/976–9184* ⊉ *€3.50* ⊗ *Mar.–Nov., daily 8:30–7; Jan. and Feb. by request.*

A signpost to the right outside Glenbeigh points to **Caragh Lake,** a tempting excursion south to a beautiful expanse of water set among gorse- and heather-covered hills and majestic mountains. The road hugs the shoreline much of the way.

North of Glenbeigh, the beach at **Rossbeigh** consists of about 3 km (2 mi) of soft, sandy coast backed by high dunes. It faces Inch Strand, a similar formation across the water on the Dingle Peninsula.

Where to Stay & Eat

$$$–$$$$ ✕⌨ **Caragh Lodge.** Seven acres of gardens filled with azaleas, camellias, and magnolias surround this mid-19th-century fishing lodge by Caragh Lake. Two large rooms in the main house are furnished with Victorian and Georgian antiques, rooms in the courtyard and the garden annexes are smaller; another block has six larger rooms and one suite. Comfortable sitting rooms overlook the lake, as does the dining room. Owner Mary Gaunt supervises the four-course, set dinners ($$–$$$: nonguests should book in advance). The food is Irish, with produce from the gardens, homemade bread, and local meats and seafood. ⌧ *Caragh Lake, Killorglin, Co. Kerry* ☎ *066/976–9115* 🖷 *066/976–9316* ⊕ *www.caraghlodge.com* ⇔ *14 rooms with bath, 1 suite ⌂ Restaurant, tennis court, sauna, boating, fishing; no room TVs* ▭ *AE, DC, MC, V* ⭘| *BP* ⊘ *Closed mid-Oct.–mid-Apr. No lunch.*

★ $$$$ ⌨ **Ard na Sidhe.** "Sidhe" (pronounced sheen) means "Hill of the Fairies," and this secluded, gabled Edwardian mansion certainly looks like it belongs in a fairy tale. Its ivy-covered stone walls are punctuated by casement windows set in stone mullions. Attractive, large rooms have coordinated carpets and spreads, and floral drapes on bay windows; rooms in the main building are the nicest. Antiques and fireplaces fill the traditionally furnished lobby and lounges. The hotel also has lakeside gardens. ⌧ *Caragh Lake, Co. Kerry* ☎ *066/976–9105* 🖷 *066/976–9282* ⇔ *20 rooms with bath ⌂ Restaurant, boating, fishing, bar* ▭ *AE, DC, MC, V* ⭘| *BP* ⊘ *Closed Oct.–3rd wk in Apr.*

$–$$ ⌨ **Glencar House.** A hunting lodge—built in 1670 by the Earl of Lansdowne—on the Caragh River is now an unpretentious guest house with huge elk antlers over its fireplace and taxidermy hung at every turn. The large rooms have country pine furniture and breathtaking views of Killarney's famous mountains, MacGillicuddy's Reeks. The house is a 20-minute drive from Killarney and a 10-minute drive from Killorglin. (From Killarney, turn off the N72 Killorglin road for Beaufort, and follow signs for Glencar.) ⌧ *Glencar, Co. Kerry* ☎ *066/976–0102* 🖷 *066/976–0167* ⊕ *www.glencarhouse.com* ⇔ *18 rooms with bath ⌂ Restaurant, tennis court, fishing, Ping-Pong, bar* ▭ *AE, MC, V* ⭘| *BP.*

¢ ⌨ **Blackstones House.** Padraig and Breda Breen's farmhouse is a rambling old building on Caragh River in Lickeen Wood, where a gentle stretch of rapids leads to a salmon pool. With four golf courses within 15 minutes' drive, and fishing and hiking on the doorstep, the conversion to guest house was a good move. All rooms have a river view and are simply furnished with country pine bedsteads and pink, blue, and yellow floral drapes and spreads against plain walls and carpets. Breda provides a simple evening meal on request. ⌧ *Glencar* ☎ *066/976–0164* 🖷 *066/976–0164* ⊕ *www.iol.ie/~blstones* ⇔ *9 rooms with bath ⌂ Dining room, fishing, bicycles; no room phones, no TV in some rooms* ▭ *MC, V* ⭘| *BP* ⊘ *Closed Nov.–Mar.*

Sports & the Outdoors

Dooks Golf Club (☎ 066/976–8205) is a challenging traditional links on the shore of Dingle Bay. **Burke's Horse Trekking Centre** (⌧ Rossbeigh Rd. ☎ 087/237–9110) has horses and ponies to suit all levels of riders.

Killorglin

39 *14 km (9 mi) east of Glenbeigh, 22 km (14 mi) west of Killarney.*

The hilltop town of Killorglin is the scene of the Puck Fair, three days of merrymaking during the second weekend in August. A large billy goat with beribboned horns, installed on a high pedestal, presides over the fair. The origins of the tradition of King Puck are lost in time. Though some horse, sheep, and cattle dealing still occurs at the fair, the main attractions these days are free outdoor concerts and extended drinking hours. The crowd is predominantly young and invariably noisy, so avoid Killorglin at fair time if you've come for peace and quiet. On the other hand, if you intend to join in the festivities, be sure to book accommodations well in advance.

Where to Eat

$–$$$$ ✕ **Nick's Seafood and Steak.** Owner Nick Foley comes from the family that established Killarney's famous eatery, Foley's, and has made a name for himself as a chef. The old stone town house has a bar–cum–dining room at street level and a quieter dining room on the floor above. Foley is known for his generous portions, his wide choice of local seafood, and his steaks. In winter, sample the haunch of Kerry venison in red-wine and juniper sauce. ✉ *Main St.* ☎ *066/976–1219* ▤ *AE, DC, MC, V* ✪ *Closed Nov. and Mon.–Tues. Dec.–Easter.*

IN & AROUND KILLARNEY

One of southwest Ireland's most attractive locales, Killarney is also the most heavily visited city in the region (its proximity to the Ring of Kerry and to Shannon Airport helps to ensure this). Light rain is typical of the area, but because of the topography, it seldom lasts long. And the clouds' approach over the lakes, and the subsequent showers, can actually add to the spectacle of the scenery. The rain is often followed within minutes by brilliant sunshine and, yes, even a rainbow.

Exploring Killarney & Environs

▶ **40–48** *Killarney: 87 km (54 mi) west of Cork City on N22, 19 km (12 mi) south-east of Killorglin, 24 km (15 mi) north of Glengarriff.*

Such great writers as Sir Walter Scott and William Thackeray struggled to find the superlatives to describe Killarney's heather-clad peaks, subtropical vegetation, and deep-blue waters dotted with wooded isles. Indeed, the lakes and the mountains have left a lasting impression on a long stream of people, beginning in the 18th century with the English travelers Arthur Young and Bishop Berkeley. Visitors in search of the natural beauty so beloved by the Romantic movement began to flock to the southwest. By the mid-19th century, Killarney's scenery was considered as exhilarating and awe-inspiring as anything in Switzerland. The influx of affluent visitors that followed the 1854 arrival of the railway transformed the lives of Kerry's impoverished natives and set in motion the commercialization that continues today.

The air here smells of damp woods and heather moors. The red fruits of the Mediterranean strawberry tree (*Arbutus unedo*) are at their height in October and November, which is also about the time when the bracken turns rust, contrasting with the evergreens. In late April and early May, the purple flowers of the rhododendron *ponticum* put on a spectacular display. This Turkish import has adapted so well to the climate that its vigorous growth threatens native oak woods, and many of the purple plants are being dug up by volunteers in an effort to control their spread.

Much of the area is part of Killarney National Park, which has more than 24,000 acres and is famous for such native habitats and species as oak holly woods, yew woods, and red deer. Signposted self-guiding trails within the park introduce these habitats. At the park's heart is Muckross Demesne; the entrance is 4 km (2½ mi) from Killarney on N71. The National Park Visitor Centre is at Muckross House. Cars aren't allowed in Muckross Demesne; you can either walk, hire a bicycle, or take a traditional jaunting car—that is, a pony and a trap.

40 You may want to limit time spent in **Killarney** itself if discos, Irish cabarets, and singing pubs—the last a local specialty with a strong Irish-American flavor—aren't your thing. The nightlife is at its liveliest from May to September; the Irish and Europeans pack the town in July and August. Peak season for Americans follows in September and October. At other times of the year, particularly from November to mid-March, when many of the hotels are closed, the town is quiet to the point of being eerie. Given the choice, go to Killarney in April, May, or early October.

41 **Aghadoe** (✉ 5 km [3 mi] west of Killarney on the R562 Beaufort–Killorglin road) is an outstanding place to get a feel for what Killarney is all about: lake and mountain scenery. Stand beside Aghadoe's 12th-century ruined church and round tower, and watch the shadows creep gloriously across Lower Lake, with Innisfallen Island in the distance and the Gap of Dunloe to the west.

42 You reach **Torc Waterfall** (✉ Killarney National Park, N71 [Muckross Rd.], 8 km [5 mi] south of Killarney) by a footpath that begins in the parking lot outside the gates of the Muckross Demesne. After your first view of the roaring cascade, which will appear after about 10 minutes' walk, it's worth the climb up a long flight of stone steps to the second, less-frequented clearing.

43 **Muckross House,** a 19th-century, Elizabethan-style manor, now houses the Kerry Folklife Centre, where bookbinders, potters, and weavers demonstrate their crafts. Upstairs elegantly furnished rooms portray the lifestyle of the landed gentry in the 1800s; downstairs in the basement you can experience the conditions of servants employed in the house. Inside you'll also find the Killarney National Park Visitor Centre. The informal grounds are noted for their rhododendrons and azaleas, the water garden, and the outstanding limestone rock garden. In the park beside the house, the Muckross Traditional Farms comprise reconstructed farm buildings and outhouses, a blacksmith's forge, a carpenter's workshop, and a selection of farm animals. It's a reminder of the way things were done on the farm before the electricity and the mechanization of farming. Meet and chat with the farmers and their wives as they go about their work. The visitor center has a shop and a restaurant. ✉ *Killarney National Park, Muckross Demesne, Muckross Rd. (N71), 6½ km (4 mi) south of Killarney* ☎ *064/31440* ⊕ *www.muckrosshouse.ie/* ☞ *Visitor center free, farms or house €5, farms and house €8* ⊙ *House Sept.–June, daily 9–5:30. Visitor center Nov.–mid-Mar., on request; mid-Mar.–June, Sept., and Oct., daily 9–6; July and Aug., daily 9–7. Farms mid-Mar.–Apr., weekends 2–6; May, daily 1–6; June–Sept., daily 10–7; Oct., daily 2–6.*

44 The 15th-century Franciscan **Muckross Friary** is amazingly complete, although roofless. The monks were driven out by Oliver Cromwell's army in 1652. An ancient yew tree rises above the cloisters and breaks out over the abbey walls. Three flights of stone steps allow access to the

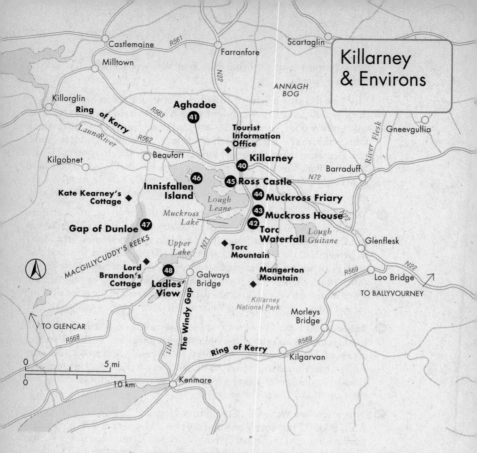

upper floors and living quarters, where you can visit the cloisters and what was once the dormitory, kitchen, and refectory. ⊠ *Killarney National Park, Muckross Demesne, Muckross Rd. (N71), 4 km (2½ mi) south of Killarney* ☎ *Free* ⊙ *Mid-June–early Sept., daily 10–5.*

45 **Ross Castle,** a fully restored 14th-century stronghold, was the last place in the province of Munster to fall to Oliver Cromwell's forces in 1652. A later dwelling has 16th- and 17th-century furniture. ⊠ *Knockreer Estate, off Muckross Rd. (N71), 2 km (1 mi) south of Killarney* ☎ *064/ 35851* ☎ *€3.80* ⊙ *Apr. and Oct., daily 10–5; May and Sept., daily 9–6; June–Aug., daily 9–6:30.*

46 The romantic ruins on **Innisfallen Island** date from the 6th or 7th century. Between 950 and 1350 the *Annals of Innisfallen* were compiled here by monks. (The book survives in the Bodleian Library in Oxford.) To get to the island, which is on Lough Leane, you can rent a rowboat at Ross Castle (€4 per hour), or you can join a cruise (€8) in a covered, heated launch.

★ **47** Massive, glacial rocks form the side of the **Gap of Dunloe,** a narrow mountain pass that stretches for 6½ km (4 mi) between MacGillicuddy's Reeks and the Purple Mountains. The rocks create strange echoes: give a shout to test it out. Five small lakes are strung out beside the road. Cars are banned from the gap, but in summer the first 3 km (2 mi) are busy with horse and foot traffic, much of which turns back at the halfway point.

At the entrance to the Gap of Dunloe, **Kate Kearney's Cottage** (⊠ 19 km [12 mi] west of Killarney ☎ 064/44116) is a good place to rent a jaunting car or pony. Kate was a famous beauty who sold illegal *poteen* (moonshine) from her home, contributing greatly, one suspects, to their enthusiasm for the scenery. Appropriately enough, it's now a pub and a good place to pause for an Irish coffee.

The gap's southern end is marked by **Lord Brandon's Cottage,** a tea shop serving soup and sandwiches. From here, a path leads to the edge of Upper Lake, where you can journey onward by rowboat. It's an old tradition for the boatman to carry a bugle and illustrate the echoes. The boat passes under Brickeen Bridge and into Middle Lake, where 30 islands are steeped in legends, many of which your boatman is likely to recount. Look out for caves on the left-hand side on this narrow stretch of water. ⊠ *7 km (4½ mi) west of Killarney* ☉ *Easter–Sept., 10 AM–dusk.*

If the weather is fine, head southwest 19 km (12 mi) out of Killarney ➍➑ on N71 to **Ladies' View,** a panorama of the three lakes and the surrounding mountains. The name goes back to 1905, when Queen Victoria was a guest at Muckross House. Upon seeing the view, her ladies-in-waiting were said to have been dumbfounded by its beauty.

Where to Stay & Eat

$$$–$$$$ ✕ **Gaby's Seafood.** Expect the best seafood in Killarney from Belgian owner-chef Gert Maes. Inside the rustic exterior is a little bar beside an open fire; steps lead up to the main dining area. Try the seafood platter (seven or eight kinds of fish in a cream-and-wine sauce) or lobster Gaby (shelled, simmered in a cream-and-cognac sauce, and served back in the shell). ⊠ *27 High St.* ☎ *064/32519* ▤ *AE, DC, MC, V* ☉ *Closed Sun. and mid-Feb.–mid-Mar. No lunch.*

★ $$–$$$ ✕ **Old Presbytery.** This beautiful Georgian house is across the road from Killarney's cathedral and was once a residence for the clergy. Its interior has been transformed into a spacious, two-floor restaurant. Proceed past the bar area, with its open fire and leather sofas, into a room with wooden floors, brocade-upholstered chairs, and candlelit tables. Chef Simon Regan's imaginative menu is served by a friendly, efficient staff. Try the baked monkfish with aubergine caviar and sauce Provençale or the grilled beef fillet with horseradish and red onion soufflé. ⊠ *Cathedral Pl.* ☎ *064/30555* ▤ *AE, DC, MC, V* ☉ *Closed Tues. and Jan. 7–Feb. 1. No lunch.*

¢–$ ✕ **Panis Angelicus.** Daylight streams in through the large plate-glass shop windows of this stylish, contemporary café, and mellow jazz plays softly in the background. Add black-tile floors, original art on dark red walls, and the smell of freshly ground coffee, and you have the ideal place to take a break. There are home-baked breads and cakes as well as a good selection of sandwiches, and the hot Irish potato cake with garlic butter and green salad is delicious. Dinner menus feature pasta specials, seafood salad, and other light bites. ⊠ *15 New St.* ☎ *064/39648* ▤ *MC, V* ☉ *No dinner Oct.–Apr.*

$$$$ ✕▥ **Aghadoe Heights.** The lake views from here are unforgettable, and the 8 acres of grounds ensure absolute peace. The interior is an agreeable combination of antique and modern styles. Most bedrooms have mountain vistas, and all are large, with good-size bathrooms, floral fabrics, lace-covered cushions, and natural wood furniture. Fredericks, the rooftop restaurant ($$$$; jacket and tie required), is romantic with silver candelabras, white linen, and upholstered chairs. Chef Robin Suter prepares a seasonal, French menu. Main courses include both classics— black sole grilled or meunière—and more unusual dishes, such as medallions of veal with crab soufflé. ⊠ *Aghadoe Heights, 4 km (2½ mi) outside Killarney (on the Tralee side, signposted off N22), Co. Kerry* ☎ *064/31766* 🖨 *064/31345* ⊕ *www.aghadoeheights.com* ⊅ *66 rooms with bath, 3 suites* ⚭ *Restaurant, in-room data ports, cable TV, tennis*

court, indoor pool, health club, sauna, fishing, bar, meeting rooms ⊟ *AE, DC, MC, V* ⏐◯⏐ *BP.*

$$$$ ✕⊡ **Killarney Park.** The building that houses this family-run hotel is modern, but the lobby is done in a Victorian country-house style that's complemented by a sweeping staircase. Sofas and armchairs are invitingly grouped around open fires, and there's a fine library in which to lounge. Guest rooms are spacious, with soothing color schemes and well-chosen antiques. The staff's warmth and commitment are key to the experience here. The large, opulent restaurant ($$$–$$$$) serves classic Continental cuisine with Irish influences. Simpler meals are served in the Garden Bar. ⊠ *Kenmare Pl., Co. Kerry* ☎ *064/35555* 📠 *064/35266* ⊕ *www.killarneyparkhotel.ie* ⮌ *30 rooms with bath, 23 suites* ♣ *Restaurant, in-room safes, cable TV, indoor pool, health club, hot tub, outdoor hot tub, bicycles, billiards, bar, library, meeting rooms* ⊟ *AE, DC, MC, V* ⏐◯⏐ *BP* ⊘ *Closed Dec. 9–26.*

$ ✕⊡ **Foley's Townhouse and Restaurant.** Rooms in this 19th-century former coaching inn have Victorian antiques and rustic, pine furniture. Windows are double-glazed, so the rooms are quieter than you would expect for a hotel right in the center of Killarney. In the restaurant ($$–$$$$) chef-owner Carol Hartnett makes use of local ingredients, including superior Irish cream and butter. Roulade of trout stuffed with prawn mousse and grilled T-bone steak with garlic butter are typical. The wine list has more than 200 selections, and a pianist entertains in summer. ⊠ *23 High St., Co. Kerry* ☎ *064/31217* 📠 *064/34683* ⊕ *www.foleystownhouse.com* ⮌ *32 rooms with bath* ♣ *Restaurant, cable TV* ⊟ *AE, DC, MC, V* ⏐◯⏐ *BP* ⊘ *Closed mid-Nov.–Feb.*

$ ✕⊡ **Mills Inn.** If you wince at tour-bus crowds, consider this coaching inn in Ballyvourney, a village 15 minutes outside Killarney and on the main Cork–Killarney road. The inn is beside the rapid-flowing River Sullane, and its grounds have old castle ruins as well as a stable yard and gardens. Its bar, established in 1755, is popular with Irish-speaking locals and has music on Wednesday and Sunday nights. Rooms are well insulated from bar and traffic noise and have cottage-style furnishings. The restaurant ($$–$$$) serves generous portions of local beef and seafood; at the bar you'll get simple fare, such as Irish stew. ⊠ *Ballyvourney, Macroom, Co. Cork* ☎ *026/45237* 📠 *026/45454* ⊕ *www.millsinn.ie* ⮌ *12 rooms with bath* ♣ *Restaurant, cable TV, 2 bars* ⊟ *MC, V* ⏐◯⏐ *BP.*

$$–$$$ ⊡ **Europe.** A secluded lakeside location (a five-minute drive from Killarney) and a luxurious but unfussy style give this modern, five-story hotel the edge over its competitors. Most bedrooms have solid-pine details, a lake view, and a private balcony. The spacious lounges and lobbies have picture windows overlooking the lake and mountains, an imaginative display of old carved timber, and antiques. The sports facilities, including an Olympic-size pool, are among the area's most up-to-date. ⊠ *Killorglin Rd., Fossa, Co. Kerry* ☎ *064/31900* 📠 *064/32118* ⊕ *www.iol.ie/khl* ⮌ *205 rooms with bath* ♣ *2 restaurants, in-room data ports, cable TV, tennis court, indoor pool, health club, sauna, fishing, bicycles, horseback riding, 2 bars* ⊟ *AE, DC, MC, V* ⏐◯⏐ *BP* ⊘ *Closed Nov.–mid-Mar.*

$–$$ ⊡ **Arbutus.** Run by the Buckley family since it was built more than 60 years ago, Arbutus is a good choice in Killarney's town center—a short step from the bus and train stations and a three-minute walk from the main shopping and dining areas. There's an open fire in the lobby, and a quiet, oak-paneled bar that's popular with locals. Ask for one of the spacious rooms—with updated furnishings—on the second floor. ⊠ *College St., Co. Kerry* ☎ *064/31037* 📠 *064/34033* ⊕ *www.arbutuskillarney.com* ⮌ *36 rooms with bath* ♣ *Restaurant, bar* ⊟ *AE, DC, MC, V* ⏐◯⏐ *BP.*

$–$$ ⌾ **Earls Court House.** In a quiet suburb within walking distance of Killarney's center, this comfortable guest house is furnished with interesting antiques collected by Emer Moynihan, who likes to greet her guests with tea or coffee and scones. Bedrooms are spacious, with large bathrooms and a mix of antique and reproduction Victorian furniture. Breakfast is served at mahogany tables in a large, sunny, wooden-floored room; menu choices include pancakes and kippers. The house has a wine license. ✉ *Woodlawn Junction, Muckross Rd. (N71), Co. Kerry* ☎ *064/34009* ⎙ *064/34366* ⊕ *www.killarney-earlscourt.ie* ⤳ *11 rooms with bath* ⌕ *Dining room, in-room data ports* ▭ *MC, V* ⟋⊙⟍ *BP* ☾ *Closed Dec.–Feb.*

¢ ⌾ **Lime Court.** On the Muckross Road between Killarney and the national park—yet only a five-minute walk from the town center—this modern hotel has two large bay windows in front. Rooms are in an extension at the back and away from the road. Antiques and large potted plants decorate the reception area; a baby grand piano anchors the spacious lounge. Although guest rooms are plain, they're comfortable and light; all overlook green fields and have small sitting areas. ✉ *Muckross Rd. (N71), Co. Kerry* ☎ *064/34547* ⎙ *064/34121* ⊕ *www.lime-court.com* ⤳ *16 rooms with bath* ⌕ *Cable TV* ▭ *MC, V* ⟋⊙⟍ *BP.*

Nightlife & the Arts

Bars where a professional leads the songs and encourages audience participation and solos are popular in Killarney. Try the **Laurels** (✉ Main St. ☎ 064/31149). **Buckley's Bar** (✉ College St. ☎ 064/31037) in the Arbutus Hotel has traditional entertainment nightly from June to September. **Gleneagles** (✉ Muckross Rd. ☎ 064/31870) is the place for big-name cabaret—from Sharon Shannon to the Wolfe Tones. It also has a late-night disco. **McSorleys Nite Club** (✉ College St. ☎ 064/39770) is a lively late-night venue for the over-23s.

Sports & the Outdoors

BICYCLING   A bicycle is the perfect way to enjoy Killarney's mild air, whether within the confines of Muckross Park or farther afield in the Kerry Highlands. Rent by the day or week from **O'Sullivan's Cycles** (✉ Bishop's La., off New St. ☎ 064/31282).

FISHING   Salmon and brown trout populate Killarney's lakes and rivers. To improve your technique contact **Angler's Paradise** (✉ Loreto Rd., Muckross ☎ 064/33818), where the Michael O'Brien International Fishing School organizes game, coarse, and deep-sea fishing trips by day or by night. **O'Neill's** (✉ Plunkett St. ☎ 064/31970) provides fishing tackle, bait, and licenses.

GOLF   **Beaufort Golf Course** (✉ Churchtown, Beaufort ☎ 064/44440) has an 18-hole, par-71 course surrounded by magnificent scenery, and unlike most other Irish golf clubs, it has buggy-, trolley-, and club-rental facilities. For many, the two courses at the legendary **Killarney Golf and Fishing Club** (✉ Mahony's Point ☎ 064/31034) are the chief reason for coming to Killarney.

HIKING   The **Kerry Way,** a long-distance walking route, passes through the Killarney National Park on its way to Glenbeigh. You can get a detailed leaflet about the route from the tourist information office. For the less adventurous, four safe and well-signposted nature trails of varying lengths are in the national park. Try the 4-km (2½-mi) Arthur Young's Walk, which passes through old yew and oak woods frequented by Sika deer. You can reach the **Mangerton walking trail,** a small tarred road leading to a scenic trail that circles Mangerton Lake, by turning left off N71 midway between Muckross Friary and Muckross House (follow the signposts). The summit of **Mangerton Mountain** (2,756 feet) can be reached on foot in about two hours—less if you rent a pony. It's perfect if you want a fine, long hike with good views of woodland scenery. **Torc Mountain** (1,764 feet) can be reached off Route N71; it's a satisfying 1½-hour climb, with lake views. Don't attempt mountain climbing in the area in misty weather; visibility can quickly drop to zero.

HORSEBACK RIDING **Killarney Riding Stables Ltd.** (⊠ Ballydowney ☎ 064/31686) organizes four- and seven-day treks in Killarney National Park, with accommodation. Riding by the hour or half day along wooded paths and mountain tracks is also available.

Shopping

Bricín Craft Shop (⊠ 26 High St. ☎ 064/34902) has interesting handicrafts, including candles, ceramics, and woolens. **Christy's Design Store** (⊠ 3 New St. ☎ 064/35406) stocks contemporary Irish pottery, ironwork, woodwork, crystal, and jewelry. Visit the **Frank Lewis Gallery** (⊠ 6 Bridewell La., beside General Post Office ☎ 064/34843) for original paintings and sculptures. If you have Irish roots, you can learn all about your name and buy an item with its heraldic crest—from key rings to crystal to sweaters—at **House of Names** (⊠ Kenmare Pl. ☎ 064/ 36320 ⊕ www.iol.ie/shopping/house of names/).

The **Killarney Bookshop** (⊠ 32 Main St. ☎ 064/34108) has local-interest books as well as fiction, biography, and travel titles. **MacBee's** (⊠ New St. ☎ 064/33622) is a modern boutique stocking the best of Irish high fashion. **Quills Woollen Market** (⊠ Market Cross ☎ 064/32277) has the town's biggest selection of Irish knitwear. It also carries tweeds, linens, and Celtic jewelry. **The Woodpotters** (⊠ 24 High St. ☎ 064/31217) sells unusual gifts and such housewares as picture frames, potpourri, and wicker trays.

THE DINGLE PENINSULA

The brazenly scenic Dingle Peninsula stretches for some 48 km (30 mi) between Tralee (pronounced tra-*lee*) in the east and Slea Head in the west. Rugged mountains and cliffs are interspersed with softly molded glacial valleys and lakes. Long sandy beaches and Atlantic-pounded cliffs unravel along the coast. Drystone walls enclose small, irregular fields, and exceptional prehistoric and early Christian remains dot the countryside.

Dingle is notorious for its heavy rainfall and impenetrable sea mists, which can strike at any time of year. If they do, sit them out in Dingle Town or the village of Dunquin and enjoy the friendly bars, cafés, and crafts shops. West of Dingle Town, the peninsula, like parts of County Kerry, is Gaeltacht: Irish is still spoken, and English is considered a second language.

You can cover the peninsula in a long day trip of about 160 km (99 mi). If mist or continuous rain is forecast, postpone your trip until visibility improves. From Killarney, Killorglin, or Tralee, head for Castlemaine, and take the coast road (R561 and R559) to Dingle Town. You'll pass through the sheltered seaside resort of Inch, 19 km (12 mi) west of Castlemaine and 45 km (28 mi) northwest of Killarney, where the head of Dingle Bay is cut off by two sand spits that enclose Castlemaine Harbour. Inch has a 6½-km (4-mi) beach backed by dunes that are home to a large colony of natterjack toads.

Annascaul

49 *7 km (4½ mi) west of Inch.*

An important livestock center until the 1930s, this village—near the junction of the Castlemaine and Tralee—has a wide road as cattle trading was once carried out in the streets. The town also has a lot of pubs. Photographers will be tempted to snap **Dan Foley's** (☎ 066/915–7252) flamboyantly painted pub. Wander in for a pint; the legendary Dan Foley, who was a magician, a farmer, and an expert on local history, is no longer with us, but tales about him are still told in Annascaul.

Dingle Town

50 *18 km (11 mi) west of Annascaul, 67 km (42 mi) west of Killarney, 45 km (28 mi) west of Killorglin on R561.*

Backed by mountains and facing a sheltered harbor, Dingle, the chief town of its eponymous peninsula, has a year-round population of 1,400 that more than doubles in summer. Although many expect Dingle to be a quaint and undeveloped Gaeltacht village, it in fact has lots of crafts shops, seafood restaurants, and pubs. Still, you can explore its main thoroughfares—the Mall, Main and Strand streets, and the Wood—in less than an hour. Celebrity hawks, take note: off-season Dingle is favored as a hideaway by several celebrities, including Julia Roberts, Paul Simon, and Dolly Parton. These and others have their visits commemorated on Green Street's "path of stars."

Dingle's pubs are well known for their music, but among them **O'Flaherty's** (✉ Bridge St., at the entrance to town ☎ 066/915–1983), a simple, stone-floored bar, is something special and a hot spot for traditional musicians. Spontaneous sessions occur most nights in July and August, less frequently at other times. Even without music, this pub is a good place to compare notes with fellow travelers.

Since 1985 Dingle's central attraction, apart from its music scene, has been a winsome bottle-nosed dolphin who has taken up residence in the harbor. The Dingle dolphin, or **Fungie,** as he has been named, will play for hours with swimmers (a wet suit is essential) and scuba divers, and he follows local boats in and out of the harbor. It is impossible to predict whether he will stay, but boatmen have become so confident of a sighting that they offer trippers their money back if Fungie does not appear. Boat trips (€8) leave the pier hourly in July and August between 11 and 6, weather permitting. At other times, call **Jimmy Flannery Sr.** (☎ 066/915–1163).

Where to Stay & Eat

$$–$$$ ✕**Beginish.** Unlike many other Dingle restaurants, which have cottage-style interiors, Beginish has high ceilings and a conservatory overlooking a tiny, floodlit garden. The chef imaginatively interprets French nouvelle cuisine: specialties include Glenbeigh oysters, Dingle Bay lobster Thermidor, and honey glazed duck breast with apple and Calvados sauce. The wine list, with about 100 choices, includes a good selection of half-bottles. ✉ *Green St.* ☎ *066/915–1588* ▭ *MC, V* ☉ *Closed Mon. and mid-Dec.–mid-Feb. No lunch.*

★ **$$** ✕**Chart House.** Nautical artifacts, including an antique compass, complement the rusty-red walls and the harbor views. Owner-chef Jim McCarthy and his team give local produce a light, imaginative, Mediterranean-influenced treatment. Roast guinea fowl is served with a simple but perfectly judged port-wine jus. Filet of beef is a perennial favorite, seared and served on a bed of bubble and squeak (fried cabbage and potato) with a peppercorn sauce. ⊠ *The Mall* ☎ *066/915–2255* ⊟ *MC, V* ⊘ *Closed Tues. and Jan.–mid-Feb. No lunch.*

$–$$ ✕ **Fenton's.** Step beyond the yellow door of this town house to find a cozy, cottage-style restaurant with quarry-tile floors and local art for sale on the walls. The candlelit tables are covered in oilcloth, but the napkins are linen. The bistro-style menu is unfussy, allowing for a quick turnover during Dingle's hectic high season. Some dishes, such as the cassoulet of mussels in a garlic cream sauce, are available in starter or main-course portions. Sirloin steak is served with caramelized onions and a red-wine sauce. ⊠ *Green St.* ☎ *066/915–1209* ⊟ *AE, DC, MC, V* ⊘ *Closed mid-Nov.–mid-Mar.*

$$$$ ✕🏨 **Dingle Skellig.** This imaginatively designed building has a beehive-like shape that's intended to echo local *clocháns* (prehistoric beehive huts). The light-wood-framed, octagonal reception area has contemporary stained-glass doors and original paintings. Modern, pale-wood furniture and bold fabrics adorn the spacious rooms, more than half of which have sea views. Floor-to-ceiling windows in the Coastguard restaurant look out over Dingle Bay. As you'd expect, the specialty is seafood. ⊠ *Co. Kerry* ☎ *066/915–0200* 🖨 *066/915–1501* ⊕ *www. dingleskellig.com* ↝ *112 rooms with bath* ⅃ *Restaurant, cable TV, indoor pool, gym, health club, hot tub, spa, steam room, bar, meeting rooms* ⊟ *AE, DC, MC, V* ⏐◯⏐ *BP.*

$ 🏨 **Alpine House.** The landmark Alpine is neither spanking new nor old-world. One of Dingle's original guest houses—dating from 1963—is a plain, family-run, three-story establishment that has many fans; book well in advance. Pine pieces furnish bright, cheerful, well-equipped rooms. The location, at the entrance to town with views over Dingle Bay, is superb: it's quiet, yet the harbor, pubs, and restaurants are only a two-minute walk away. ⊠ *Mail Rd., Co. Kerry* ☎ *066/915–1250* 🖨 *066/915–1966* ⊕ *www.alpineguesthouse.com* ↝ *10 rooms with bath* ⅃ *Cable TV, free parking* ⊟ *AE, MC, V* ⏐◯⏐ *BP.*

$ 🏨 **Greenmount House.** Wonderful views of the town and harbor await at this modern B&B, a short walk uphill from the town center (turn right at the traffic circle at the entrance to Dingle and right again when you come to the first T-junction). A modern bungalow has six suites, each with a sitting room and balcony. Rooms in the original house, though smaller, are impeccable and comfortable, with pine beds and floral fabrics. An outstanding breakfast is served in the conservatory, which connects the two buildings. ⊠ *Upper John St., Co. Kerry* ☎ *066/915–1414* 🖨 *066/915–1974* ⊕ *www.greenmounthouse.com* ↝ *9 rooms with bath* ⅃ *Cable TV, lobby lounge* ⊟ *MC, V* ⏐◯⏐ *BP* ⊘ *Closed Dec. 10–27.*

$ 🏨 **Pax House.** You can stand on the outdoor terrace of this modern bungalow and watch the boats return with their catch while the sun sets slowly in the west. Rooms are simple but well equipped. Breakfast is a generous affair, with fresh seafood on the menu and a selection of Irish cheeses on the buffet. Pax House is 1 km (½ mi) from the town center. ⊠ *Upper John St., Co. Kerry* ☎ *066/915–1518* 🖨 *066/915–2461* ⊕ *www.pax-house.com* ↝ *12 rooms with bath* ⅃ *Cable TV, lobby lounge* ⊟ *MC, V* ⏐◯⏐ *BP* ⊘ *Closed Jan.*

Nightlife

Nearly every bar on the Dingle Peninsula, particularly in the town of Dingle, offers music nightly in July and August. **O'Flaherty's** (⊠ Bridge St., at the entrance to town ☎ 066/915–1983) is a gathering place for traditional musicians—you can hear impromptu music sessions most nights in July and August. For sing-along and dance, try **An Reált—The Star Bar** (⊠ The Pier ☎ No phone).

Sports & the Outdoors

You're likely to remember a bike ride around Slea Head for a long time to come. You can rent bicycles at **Dingle Bicycle Hire** (⊠ The Tracks ☎ 066/ 915–2166).

Shopping

Don't miss Dingle's café-bookshop, **An Cafe Liteartha** (⊠ Bothar An Dadhgaide ☎ 066/915–2204), which locals insist is one of the world's first (it has been here since the '70s). Regardless, you'll find friendly conversation as well as new and secondhand books. You can watch **Brian de Staic** (⊠ Green St. ☎ 066/915–1298 ⊕ www.briandestaic.com) and his team make modern, Celtic-inspired jewelry in the this studio, which is also a shop.

At **Leác a Ré** (⊠ Strand St. ☎ 066/915–1138) sells handmade Irish crafts. Lisbeth Mulcahy at the **Weaver's Shop** (⊠ Green St. ☎ 066/915– 1688) sells outstanding handwoven, vegetable-dyed woolen wraps, mufflers, and fabric for making skirts.

Ventry

⑤ *8 km (5 mi) west of Dingle Town on R561.*

The next town after Dingle along the coast, Ventry has a small outcrop of pubs and small grocery stores (useful, since west of Dingle Town you'll find few shops of any kind), and a long sandy beach with safe swim and ponies for rent. Between Ventry and Dunquin there are several interesting archaeological sites on the spectacular cliff-top road along Slea Head.

en route   **Dunbeg,** an Iron Age promontory fort, can be seen on the left below the road, after you pass between two tall hedges of fuchsia bushes about 6 km (4 mi) west of Ventry (follow the signposts across fields). A fortified stone wall cuts off the promontory, and the landward side is protected by a system of earthworks and trenches. Within the enclosure is a ruined circular building. This wasn't a homestead but probably a refuge in times of danger.

Continuing west along the coast road beyond Dunbeg, you'll see signs for PREHISTORIC BEEHIVE HUTS, called clocháns (pronounced clock-awns) in Irish. Built of drystone on the southern slopes of Mt. Eagle, these cells were used by hermit monks in the early Christian period; some 414 exist between Slea Head and Dunquin. Some local farmers, on whose land these monuments stand, charge a "trespass fee" of €1 to €2.

Slea Head

㊿ *16 km (10 mi) west of Dingle Town on R561, 8 km (5 mi) west of Ventry.*

From the top of the towering cliffs of Slea Head at the southwest extremity of the Dingle peninsula the view of the Blasket Islands and the Atlantic Ocean is guaranteed to stop you in your tracks. Alas, Slea Head has become so popular that tour buses, barely able to negotiate the narrow road, are causing traffic jams, particularly in July and August. Coumenole, the long sandy strand below, looks beautiful and sheltered, but swimming here is dangerous. This treacherous stretch of coast has claimed many lives in shipwrecks—most recently in 1982, when a large cargo boat, the *Ranga,* foundered on the rocks and sank. In 1588, four ships of the Spanish Armada were driven through the Blasket Sound; two made it to shelter, and two sank. One of these, the *Santa Maria de la Rosa* is currently being excavated by divers during the summer months.

The largest of the **Blasket Islands** visible from Slea Head, the Great Blasket was inhabited until 1953. The Blasket islanders were great storytellers and were encouraged by Irish linguists to write their memoirs. *The Islandman*, by Tomás O Crohán, gives a vivid picture of a hard way of life. "Their likes will not be seen again," O Crohán poignantly observed. The Blasket Centre explains the heritage of these islanders and celebrates their use of the Irish language with videos and exhibitions. ✉ *Dunquin* ☎ *066/915-6371* ⊕ *www.heritageireland.ie* 🎟 *€3.10* ⊙ *Easter–June and Sept., daily 10–6; July and Aug., daily 10–7.*

Dunquin

53 *13 km (8 mi) west of Ventry on R559, 5 km (3 mi) north of Slea Head.*

Once the mainland harbor for the Blasket islanders, Dunquin is at the center of the Gaeltacht, and attracts many students of Irish language and folklore. David Lean shot *Ryan's Daughter* hereabouts in 1969. The movie gave the area its first major boost in tourism, though it was lambasted by critics—"Gush made respectable by millions of dollars tastefully wasted," lamented Pauline Kael—sending Lean into a dry spell he didn't come out of until 1984's *A Passage to India*. **Kruger's Pub** (☎ 066/915-6127), Dunquin's social center, has long been frequented by artists and writers, including Brendan Behan; it's also the only eatery for miles.

Dunquin's **pier** (signposted from the main road) is surrounded by cliffs of colored Silurian rock, more than 400 million years old and rich in fossils. Down at the pier you'll see *curraghs* (open fishing boats traditionally made of animal hide stretched over wooden laths and tarred) stored upside down, usually covered in canvas. Three or four men walk the curraghs out to the sea, holding them aloft over their heads. Similar boats are used in the Aran Islands, and, when properly handled, they're extraordinarily seaworthy. In good weather **Blasket Island Boatmen** (✉ Dunquin Pier ☎ 066/915-6455 ⊕ www.greatblasketisland.com) vessels ferry you from Dunquin Pier to the Great Blasket Island, a 20-minute trip. Landing is by transfer to rubber dinghy, and the island is steep and rocky, so you need to be fit and agile. Still, the unique experience offered by the deserted village and old cliff paths of the island makes it well worth the effort. The cost of the boat ride is €20 round-trip. Boats run from 10 to 4, weather permitting, between Easter and September.

en route **Clogher Strand,** a dramatic, windswept stretch of rocks and sand, is not a safe spot to swim, but a good place to watch the ocean dramatically pound the rocks when a storm is approaching or a gale is blowing. Overlooking the beach is **Louis Mulcahy's pottery studio.** One of Ireland's leading ceramic artists, Mulcahy produces large pots and urns that are both decorative and functional. You can watch the work in progress and buy items at workshop prices. ✉ *Clogher Strand* ☎ *066/915-6229* ⊙ *Daily 9:30–6.*

Ballyferriter

54 *5 km (3 mi) northeast of Dunquin, 14 km (9 mi) west of Dingle on R559.*

Like the other towns at this end of the Dingle Peninsula, Ballyferriter is a Gaeltacht village and mainly a spot for vacationers with RVs, many of them German or Dutch. The area around here is great for walking.

One of Ireland's best-preserved, early Christian churches, **Gallarus Oratory** dates from the 7th or 8th century and ingeniously makes use of corbeling—successive levels of stone projecting inward from both side walls until they meet at the top to form an unmortared roof. The structure is still watertight after more than 1,000 years. ⊠ *8 km (5 mi) northeast of Ballyferriter on R559* ◩ €2.50.

Kilmakedar Church is one of the finest surviving examples of Romanesque architecture. Although the Christian settlement dates from the 7th century, the present structure was built in the 12th century. Native builders integrated foreign influences with their own local traditions, keeping the blank arcades and round-headed windows but using stone roofs, sloping doorway jambs, and weirdly sculpted heads. Ogham stones and other interestingly carved, possibly pre-Christian stones are on display in the churchyard. ⊠ *8 km (5 mi) northeast of Ballyferriter on R559* ◩ *Free.*

off the beaten path

CONNOR PASS – This mountain route, which passes from south to north over the center of the peninsula, offers magnificent views of Brandon Bay, Tralee Bay, and the beaches of North Kerry. The road is narrow, and the drops on the hairpin bends are precipitous; be sure to nominate a confident driver who isn't scared of heights—such a soul is especially important in misty weather. It was from Brandon Bay that Brendan the Navigator (AD 487–577) is believed to have set off on his famous voyages in a specially constructed curragh. On his third trip he may have reached Newfoundland or Labrador, then Florida. Brendan was the inspiration for many voyagers, including Christopher Columbus.

The summit of Mt. Brandon (3,127 feet) is on the left as you cross the Connor Pass (from south to north). It's accessible only to hikers. Don't attempt the climb in misty weather. The easiest way to make the trek is to follow the old pilgrims' path, Saint's Road; it starts at Kilmakedar Church and rises to the summit from Ballybrack, which is the end of the road for cars. At the summit, you'll reach the ruins of an early Christian settlement. You can also approach the top from a path that starts just beyond Cloghane (signposted left on descending the Connor Pass); the latter climb is longer and more strenuous.

Blennerville

⑤⑤ *60 km (37 mi) east of Ballyferriter, 5 km (3 mi) west of Tralee on R560.*

The five-story **windmill** with black and white sails is the main attraction in Blennerville, a village on the western edge of Tralee. The surrounding buildings have been turned into a visitor center, with crafts workshops and an exhibition recalling the town's past as County Kerry's main point of emigration during the Great Famine (1845–49). ☎ *066/712–1064* ◩ *€4* ◷ *Apr.–Oct., daily 9–6.*

A very popular **steam railway** shuttles back and forth along the 3 km (1½ mi) of tracks between Blennerville and Tralee, with departures from each terminus every half hour from May through September. ☎ *066/712–7444* ◩ *€4.*

Tralee

⑤⑥ *5 km (3 mi) northeast of Blennerville, 50 km (31 mi) northeast of Dingle on R559.*

County Kerry's capital and its largest town, Tralee (population 21,000) has long been associated with the popular Irish song "The Rose of

Tralee," the inspiration for the annual Rose of Tralee International Festival. The last week of August, Irish communities worldwide send young women to join native Irish competitors; one of them is chosen as the "Rose of Tralee." Visitors, musicians, and entertainers pack the town then. A two-day horse race meeting—with seven races a day—runs at the same time, which contributes to the crowds. Tralee is also the home of Siamsa Tíre—the National Folk Theatre of Ireland, which stages dances and plays based on Irish folklore.

Kerry the Kingdom, Tralee's major cultural attraction, traces the history of Kerry's people from 5000 BC to the present, using dioramas and an entertaining audiovisual show. There's also a streetcar ride through a life-size reconstruction of Tralee in the Middle Ages. ⊠ *Ashe Memorial Hall, Denny St.* ☎ *066/712–7777* ⊕ *www.kerrycountymuseum.com* ⊠ *€7* ⊗ *Sept.–July, Mon.–Sat. 10–6; Aug., Mon.–Sat. 10–8.*

Ⓒ Ireland's biggest water complex, **AquaDome,** includes sky-high water slides, a wave pool, raging rapids, water cannons, and other thrills. Adults can seek refuge in the Sauna Dome. ⊠ *Dingle Rd.* ☎ *066/712–8899* ⊕ *www. discoverkerry.com/aquadome* ⊠ *€7* ⊗ *Mid-May–Aug., daily 10–10; Sept.–mid-May, weekdays 2–10, weekends 11–8.*

Where to Stay

$$$ ▦ **Brandon.** Although it's not especially exciting, this modern five-story hotel in the center of town is the only hotel with a pool and fitness center. The decent-size rooms are furnished plainly with chunky pine furniture and have uninspiring urban views. The restaurant is reputable. Rates shoot up during the Rose of Tralee Festival (late August) and the Listowel races (third week in September). ⊠ *Princes St., Co. Kerry* ☎ *066/712–3333* ☖ *066/712–5019* ⊕ *www.brandonhotel.ie* ➥ *182 rooms with bath* ⚘ *Restaurant, cable TV, indoor pool, health club, fishing, 2 bars, meeting rooms* ☰ *AE, DC, MC, V* ⫮ *BP.*

$–$$$ ▦ **Barrow Country House.** Its location—on Barrow Harbour and next to the Arnold Palmer–designed Tralee Golf Club—makes this period house popular with golfers. The breakfast room looks across water to the mountains of the Dingle peninsula. Rooms are spacious and well equipped, more like those in a hotel than a B&B. A helicopter service is provided for golfers keen to sample Killarney, Ballybunion, and Waterville. (Leave Tralee on R551, turning left on the R558 after Oyster Tavern. Follow signs to Churchill.) ⊠ *West Barrow, Ardfert* ☎ *066/ 713–6437* ☖ *066/713–6402* ⊕ *www.barrowhouse.com* ➥ *16 rooms with bath* ⚘ *Fishing, helipad* ☰ *AE, MC, V* ⫮ *BP* ⊗ *Closed Dec. 20–Feb. 14.*

$$ ▦ **Abbeygate.** Built on the site of Tralee's old marketplace, in a quiet spot behind the main shopping street, Abbeygate is an attractive modern hotel. Rooms have country-style wood furniture and large, tiled bathrooms. The Old Market Place Pub, a rambling, imaginatively designed bar, seats 500 people and is built in the traditional style, with wooden floors and open fireplaces. There's bar food at lunchtime and music and dancing nightly from June to September and at least three nights a week at other times. ⊠ *Maine St., Co. Kerry* ☎ *066/712–9888* ☖ *066/712– 9821* ⊕ *www.abbeygate-hotel.com* ➥ *100 rooms with bath* ⚘ *Restaurant, cable TV, 2 bars, meeting rooms* ☰ *AE, DC, MC, V* ⫮ *BP.*

Nightlife & the Arts

Ballad sessions are more popular here than traditional Irish music. **Horan's Hotel** (⊠ Clash St. ☎ 066/712–1933) has dance music and cabaret acts nightly during July and August and on weekends only during the off-season.

Try to catch the **National Folk Theater of Ireland** (Siamsa Tíre). Language is no barrier to this colorful entertainment, which re-creates traditional rural life through music, mime, and dance. ⊠ *Godfrey Pl.* ☎ *066/712–3055* ⊘ *Shows July and Aug., Mon.–Sat. at 8:30 PM; May, June, and Sept., Tues. and Thurs. at 8:30 PM.*

Sports & the Outdoors

BICYCLES You can rent bicycles from **Tralee Bicycle Supplies** (⊠ Strand St. ☎ 066/712–2018).

GOLF Tralee is the heart of great golfing country. The **Ballybunion Golf Club (Old Course)** (⊠ Ballybunion ☎ 068/27146) is universally regarded as one of golf's holiest grounds. The **Tralee Golf Club** (⊠ West Barrow, Ardfert ☎ 066/713–6379) is a seaside links, designed by Arnold Palmer, with cliffs, craters, and dunes.

HORSEBACK **El Rancho Farmhouse and Riding Stables** (⊠ Ballyard ☎ 066/712–1840)
RIDING specializes in treks on the Dingle trail between Tralee and the Dingle Peninsula.

off the beaten path

BALLYBUNION – A detour 41 km (25 mi) northwest of Tralee on N69 and R553 will take you to this seaside resort, famous for its long sandy beach and championship golf course. A large bronze statue of former president Clinton commemorates a round he played in 1998.

NORTH KERRY & SHANNONSIDE

Until several decades ago, Shannon meant little more to most people—if it meant anything at all—than the name of the longest river in Ireland and Great Britain, running for 273 km (170 mi) from County Cavan to Limerick City in County Clare. But mention Shannon nowadays and people think immediately of the airport, which has become western Ireland's principal gateway. In turn, what also comes to mind are many of the glorious sights of North Kerry and Shannonside: a slew of castles, including Bunratty, Glin, and Knappogue; Adare, sometimes called "Ireland's Prettiest Village," and the neighboring Adare Manor, a grand country-house hotel; and Limerick City, which attracts visitors tracing the memories so movingly captured in Frank McCourt's international bestseller *Angela's Ashes*.

You could begin a tour of the area in Listowel, in northwest County Kerry, and then jump across the Kerry–Limerick border to Glin, on the south side of the Shannon River estuary. Limerick City and those parts of County Clare on the north side of the Shannon round out the tour.

Listowel

57 *27 km (16 mi) northeast of Tralee on N69.*

The small, sleepy market town of Listowel comes alive for its annual horse race during the third week of September. You reach the town from the west by driving along a plain at the base of Stack's Mountain.

Where to Stay & Eat

$ ✕▨ **Allo's Bar and Bistro.** Just off Listowel's main square, this rustic bar, which dates from 1859, serves the best local foods. Chef Armel Whyte and his partner, Helen Mullane, prepare local beef, lamb, and seafood and are known for their imaginative combinations of traditional and contemporary Irish cooking ($–$$$). The spacious bedrooms are furnished with stylish antiques and four-poster beds and have large, Connemara marble bathrooms. ⊠ *41 Church St.* ☎☎ *068/22880* ⊸ *3* *rooms with bath* ⟨ *Restaurant, bar* ▤ *AE, MC, V* ⦿ *BP* ⊘ *Bar and bistro closed Sun.*

en route   From Listowel, head north on N69 18 km (11 mi) to Tarbert, the terminus for the ferry to Killimer in west Clare, a convenient 20-minute shortcut if you're heading for the west of Ireland. The Shannon is 273 km (170 mi) long, and its magnificent estuary stretches westward for another 96 km (60 mi) before reaching the sea.

Glin

 6½ km (4 mi) east of Tarbert on N69, 51 km (32 mi) north of Tralee on N69.

★   The Fitzgerald family has held the title of Knight of Glin since the 14th century. Although the family has built numerous structures in the area, the present **Glin Castle**, on the banks of the Shannon, dates only from 1785. Between 1820 and 1836 the 25th knight added crenellations and Gothic details to make the house look more like an ancestral home. A delicate plasterwork ceiling, painted in the original red and green, graces the neoclassic hall, which opens onto a splendid "flying" staircase. The present Knight of Glin (the 29th), Desmond Fitzgerald, a Harvard-educated art historian, is an expert on Irish decorative arts and an outspoken arts advocate, so it's fitting that the house has an exceptional collection of Irish 18th-century mahogany and walnut furniture. ☎ 068/34173 ⊕ *www.glincastle.com* ▤ €5.50 ⊘ *May and June, daily 10–noon and 2–4; other times by appointment.*

off the beaten path   FLYING BOAT MUSEUM – Nine kilometers (5½ mi) east of Glin on N69, Foynes was the landing place for transatlantic air traffic in the 1930s and 1940s. This museum in the terminal of the original Shannon Airport celebrates Foynes's aviation history; it's a must for aviation buffs. ☎ 069/65416 ▤ €4 ⊘ *Apr.–Oct., daily 10–5.*

Where to Stay & Eat

$$$$ ✕▦ **Glin Castle.** Experience Irish castle living at the Fitzgerald family home, which has 500 acres of formal gardens and parkland and a dairy farm. The large elegant rooms showcase Glin's famous collection of Irish furniture, yet are quite comfortable. Country-house cuisine is served in the dining room ($$$$), beneath portraits of Fitzgerald ancestors. On the menu you'll find locally produced meat and poultry, freshly caught fish, and produce from the walled garden. Nonresidents are welcome for dinner but must reserve in advance. ⊠ Co. Limerick ☎ 068/34112 ▤ 068/34364 ⊕ *www.glincastle.com* ⇌ *15 rooms with bath* ⟨ *Dining room, cable TV, tennis court, boating, fishing, croquet, horseback riding, meeting rooms, some pets allowed; no kids under 10* ▤ *AE, DC, MC, V* ⦿ *BP* ⊘ *Closed Mar.–Nov.*

Adare

19 km (12 mi) southwest of Limerick City on N21, 82 km (51 mi) northeast of Tralee on N21, 40 km (25 mi) east of Glin.

A picture-book village with several thatched cottages amid wooded surroundings on the banks of the River Maigue, Adare is rich in ruins. On foot, you can find the remains of two 13th-century abbeys, a 15th-century friary, and the keep of a 13th-century Desmond castle. Providing that once-upon-a-time allure that has helped make Adare famous as one of Ireland's prettiest villages, the many stone-built cottages, often adorned with colorful, flower-filled window boxes, have a centuries-old look; they were, in fact, built in the mid-19th century by the third Earl of Dunraven, a popular landlord, for the tenants on his estate. Nowadays they house boutiques selling Irish crafts and antiques and also a gourmet restaurant called Wild Geese. Adare Manor, an imposing Tudor–Gothic Revival mansion, which was once the grand house of the Dunraven peerage, is now a celebrated hotel.

Adare Heritage Center has an exhibit with a 15-minute audiovisual display that details the history of the village from 1223 to the present. There's also a restaurant and three retail outlets: one sells sweaters, another crafts, and the third heraldry items. Guided walking tours (€5) of the village are offered from July to September. ✉ *Main St.* ☎ *061/396666* 🖃 *€5* ✆ *Jan.–Mar., daily 10–5; Apr. and May, daily 9:30–5:30; June–Sept., daily 9–6:30; Dec., daily 9:30–4:30.*

Where to Stay & Eat

$$$–$$$$ ✕ **Wild Geese.** In a series of small dining rooms of a low-ceiling thatched cottage, co-owner and chef David Foley uses the best local produce to create imaginative and seriously good dishes. Try roast rack of lamb with tempura vegetables or roast breast of duck on creamed leeks with deep-fried mushroom wontons. Lobster is a popular summer option. The house dessert platter for two lets you sample all desserts, including the fantastic homemade ice cream. The restaurant is opposite the Dunraven Arms. ✉ *Rose Cottage* ☎ *061/396451* 🖃 *AE, DC, MC, V* ✆ *Closed Sun., Mon. and 3 wks in Jan.*

$$$$ ✕🖾 **Dunraven Arms.** Adare's landmark inn, established in 1792, oozes charm. It makes a popular first port of call if you're arriving at Shannon Airport, 40 km (25 mi) northwest. (Charles Lindbergh stayed in Room 6 while he advised on the airport's design.) Paintings and prints of horseback riders decorate the dark walls of the cozy bar and lounges. The comfortable bedrooms are tastefully furnished with antiques. Junior suites in the newer wing have antique four-poster beds. The elegant Maigue restaurant ($$–$$$$) specializes in modern Irish cuisine; you can dine informally in the pretty bar. ✉ *Main St., Co. Limerick* ☎ *061/396633* 🖃 *061/396541* ⊕ *www.dunravenhotel.com* ⬅ *76 rooms with bath, 6 executive suites, 14 junior suites* ⚹ *Restaurant, in-room data ports, cable TV, indoor pool, health club, fishing, horseback riding, bar, meeting rooms* ▭ *AE, DC, MC, V* ¶◎¶ *BP.*

★ $$ ✕🖾 **Mustard Seed at Echo Lodge.** Dan Mullane's spacious Victorian country-house hotel and restaurant ($$$$) has themed guest rooms— black-and-white, carnival, Chinese, and so on—and looks out over the countryside. Chef Tony Schwartz uses only the best local produce, plus herbs and vegetables from his organic garden. Shark is an unusual seafood option in summer; more typical is the honey-glazed lamb shank with a cassoulet of beans and homegrown baby vegetables. Fruits from the garden are used in such desserts as hot crunchy apple-and-black-currant crumble with Calvados, cream, and caramel sauce. The hotel is 13 km (8 mi) southwest of Adare in Ballingarry. ✉ *Ballingarry, Co. Limerick* ☎ *069/68508* 🖃 *069/68511* ⊕ *www.mustardseed.ie* ⬅ *17 rooms with bath, 3 suites* ⚹ *Restaurant, bar, library; no kids* ▭ *AE, MC, V* ¶◎¶ *BP.*

$–$$ ✕🖾 **Fitzgeralds Woodlands House Hotel and Spa.** In the energetic, capable hands of the Fitzgerald family, what was once a small B&B has evolved into a thriving modern hotel. It's on 44 acres of landscaped grounds, at the Limerick side of the village. Rooms are spacious, individually decorated in various modern styles, and well maintained. Expect to see locals in Timmy Mac's bar. The Brennan Rooms ($$) serves a traditional Irish table d'hôte menu: lamb, pork, and beef. More adventurous cooking takes place in the bistro-style restaurant in Timmy Mac's ($), which serves locally grown organic food. ⊠ *Knockanes, Co. Limerick* ☎ *061/ 605100* 🖷 *061/396073* ⊕ *www.woodlands-hotel.ie* ➶ *84 rooms with bath, 8 suites & 2 restaurants, cable TV, indoor pool, health club, massage, spa, fishing, horseback riding, bar, meeting rooms* ⊟ *AE, DC, MC, V* ⊺◉⊺ *BP.*

$$$$ 🖼 **Adare Manor.** Play king or queen for a day at this grand (and, interestingly, American-owned) Victorian Gothic mansion—once the abode of the earls of Dunraven. There are vast stone arches, heavy wood carvings, and a decorated ceiling in the baronial central hall. But the glorious 36-foot-high, 100-foot-long gallery, wainscoted in oak, is the highlight. The eight "staterooms" in the original house are the most sumptuous, with huge marble bathrooms and stone-mullioned windows. Most rooms have super-king-size beds; all have heavy drapes and carpets and overlook the 840 acres of grounds. Adare's golf course, designed by Robert Trent Jones, Sr., is one of Ireland's best. (Note that breakfast is a hefty €23 extra here; plan accordingly.) ⊠ *Co. Limerick* ☎ *061/ 396566* 🖷 *061/396124* ⊕ *www.adaremanor.ie* ➶ *63 rooms with bath & Restaurant, cable TV, 18-hole golf course, indoor pool, sauna, fishing, horseback riding, 2 bars, meeting rooms* ⊟ *AE, DC, MC, V* ⊺◉⊺ *EP.*

Sports & the Outdoors

GOLF **Adare Manor Golf Course** (☎ 061/396204) is an 18-hole, par-69 parkland course.

HORSEBACK The **Clonshire Equestrian Center** (☎ 061/396770) has all-weather riding
RIDING facilities, a superb selection of top-quality Irish sport horses, and a variety of organized outings.

Shopping

Adare Gallery (⊠ Main St. ☎ 061/396898) sells Irish-made jewelry, porcelain, and woodwork, as well as original paintings. **Carol's Antiques** (⊠ Main St. ☎ 061/396977) has antique furniture, silver, china, and art objects from one of Adare's tiny cottages. At **George Stacpoole** (⊠ Main St. ☎ 061/396409) you'll find antiques and books.

Limerick City

🌀 *19 km (12 mi) northeast of Adare, 198 km (123 mi) southwest of Dublin.*

Before you ask, there's *no* direct connection between Limerick City and the facetious five-line verse form known as a limerick, which was first popularized by the English writer Edward Lear in his 1846 *Book of Nonsense.* The city, at the head of the Shannon estuary and at the intersection of a number of major crossroads, is an industrial port and the republic's fourth-largest city (population 75,000). If you fly into or out of Shannon Airport, and have a few hours to spare, do take a look around. The area around the cathedral and the castle is dominated by mid-18th-century buildings with fine Georgian proportions. What's more, the city has undergone considerable revitalization since the days recounted in Frank McCourt's childhood memoir, *Angela's Ashes.*

Limerick was originally a 9th-century Danish settlement; Richard I granted the city's charter in 1197. In 1691, after the Battle of the Boyne, the Irish retreated to the walled city, where they were besieged by William of Orange, who made three unsuccessful attempts to storm the city but then raised the siege and marched away. A year later, another of William's armies overtook Limerick for two months, and the Irish opened negotiations. The resulting Treaty of Limerick—which guaranteed religious tolerance—was never ratified, and 11,000 men of the Lim-

RISEN FROM THE ASHES

THE ALCOHOLIC PA. *The starving, shivering brood of children. The sheep's head for Christmas. The rags for diapers. The little white coffin. And the long-suffering, abused ma.* These are some of the elements that rivet the reader of Angela's Ashes (1996, Scribners), Frank McCourt's memoir of his impoverished childhood in Limerick—a rags-to-riches story, with the riches always being more spiritual than material. Called by Newsweek "the publishing event of the decade," and compared by some to the Grapes of Wrath in its power, pain, and joy, Angela's Ashes has sold a few million hardcover copies, won the Pulitzer, and gone Hollywood. The book seems to speak to the Irish in everyone's soul if best-seller lists, from Japan to Germany, are any indication. Not surprisingly, the city of Limerick—the rain-sodden setting of this 1930–40s hard-luck saga—has become a pilgrimage place for readers eager to partake of the tearfulness of it all. Busloads of McCarthys and O'Dwyers now clamber over the sites described in the book, ending up at South's pub to raise a pint in Frank's honor and to count their blessings.

In the memoir narrated from a child's perspective, Limerick looms as "a gray place with a river that kills." Many children, including McCourt's twin brothers, succumb to tuberculosis, with the rest to run an obstacle course—in shoes with flapping soles—of flea-ridden bedcovers, cane-wielding teachers, doomsday-spouting priests, and fathers who drink their paycheck, beat their wives, and tell their sons to search the skies for the Angel of the Seventh Step, bringer of new babies. Yes, Limerick has its historic sights—King John's Castle, St. Mary's Cathedral, and other landmarks of the town's medieval district—but now the down-and-out addresses of McCourt's childhood draw as much attention from visitors.

As it turns out, the slums described so unflinchingly in the book have long been torn down; in fact, Limerick today is flush with new money, renovated 19th-century Georgian row houses, prosperous shopping malls, and restaurants with fancy names. A special exhibit featuring a replica of the rooms where the McCourt family lived and memorabilia of the film has been built in the coach house behind 2 Pery Square, a refurbished Georgian row house overlooking the People's Park.

Even the dread River Shannon has undergone a makeover—swans, not refuse, now navigate its flowing stream, and a high-rise hotel has transformed the skyline. Nevertheless, plenty of Angela's Ashes sites remain: Leamy's National School on Hartstonge Street, where "Hoppy" O'Halloran and other schoolmasters used to beat any charges who couldn't add 19 to 47; the St. Vincent de Paul Society, where Angela once went begging for furniture and other assistance; People's Park, where Frank once took his younger brothers to make them forget their empty stomachs; plus many other emotional landmarks.

Like the Irish shanachie—storyteller—still spouting tales at many a local pub, Frank McCourt has dug deep into the communal wellspring of Irish memory. The fact that his story has nothing to do with leprechauns and Celtic queens and everything to do with a family history that most families would wish to hide, let alone hang out in the sun to dry, says a good deal about the new Ireland and its people's wish for closure. McCourt's childhood experiences may not have been the happiest, but they are surely worth reading about, remembering, and revisiting, as so many travelers are now making a point of doing.

erick garrison joined the French Army rather than fight in a Protestant "Irish" army.

In the Old Customs House on the banks of the Shannon in the city center, the **Hunt Museum** has the finest collection of Celtic and medieval treasures outside the National Museum in Dublin. Ancient Irish metalwork, European objets d'art, and a selection of 20th-century European and Irish paintings—including works by Jack B. Yeats—are on view. A café overlooks the river. ⊠ *Rutland St.* ☎ *061/312833* ⊕ *www.huntmuseum. com* ⊠ *€6* ☉ *Mon.–Sat. 10–5, Sun. 2–5.*

Limerick is a predominantly Catholic city, but the Protestant **St. Mary's Cathedral** is the city's oldest religious building. Once a 12th-century palace—pilasters and a rounded Romanesque entrance were part of the original structure—it dates mostly from the 15th century (the black-oak carvings on misericords in the choir stalls are from this period). ⊠ *Bridge St.* ☎ *061/416238* ☉ *Daily 9–5.*

The office of the **Limerick Regional Archives** (⊠ Michael St. ☎ 061/ 415125 ⊕ www.limerickancestry.com) is in the granary, built in 1774 for grain storage. For a small fee, the archives provides a genealogical research service.

First built by the Normans in the early 1200s, **King John's Castle** still bears traces on its north side of the 1691 bombardment. If you climb the drum towers (the oldest section), you'll have a good view of the town and the Shannon. Inside, a 22-minute audiovisual show illustrates the history of Limerick and Ireland; an archaeology center has three excavated, pre-Norman houses; and two exhibition centers display models of Limerick's history from its founding in AD 922. ⊠ *Castle St.* ☎ *061/411201* ⊕ *www.shannonheritage.com/KingJohnsCastle/* ⊠ *€6.15* ☉ *Apr.–Sept., daily 9:30–5; Oct.–Mar., weekends 9:30–5.*

The **Georgian House and Garden** will show you how people lived in Limerick's Georgian heyday. A tall, narrow, row house has been meticulously restored and filled with furnishings from the period, and the garden has been planted in a manner true to the time. The coach house at the rear of the house leads on to a Limerick lane and contains displays relating to the filming of *Angela's Ashes,* including a life-size reconstruction of the McCourt family home. ⊠ *Tontine Buildings, 2 Pery Sq.* ☎ *061/ 314130* ⊠ *€5* ☉ *Weekdays 10–4:30; weekends by appointment.*

On **O'Connell Street,** you'll find the main shopping area, which mainly consists of modest chain stores. However, the street lies one block inland from (east of) the Arthur's Quay Shopping Centre, a mall, which, along with the futuristic tourist information center, is one of the first fruits of a civic campaign to develop the Shannonside quays. **Cruises Street,** an inviting pedestrian thoroughfare, has chic shops and occasional street entertainers. It's on the opposite side of O'Connell Street from the Arthur's Quay Shopping Centre.

Plassey, 5–10 minutes from Limerick on the ring road (signposted Dublin N7), is the setting for the University of Limerick, which has a small, but very attractive, campus notable for its rolling lawns and several striking architectural features.

Where to Stay & Eat

$$–$$$ ✕ **Brulées Restaurant.** The dining rooms in this redbrick Georgian town house, on a corner just a block from the River Shannon, are classical. Chef and co-owner Teresa Murphy uses only the finest local ingredients, and gives a contemporary touch to Irish fare. Try the beef fillet with black-pudding mash or the grilled liver and bacon with grain mustard and mushroom cream. And, yes, the menu does include a classic crème brûlée among the tempting desserts. ✉ *8 Lower Mallow St.* ☎*061/319931* ⊟*AE, DC, MC, V* ☉ *Closed Sun. No lunch Mon. and Sat.*

$$–$$$ ✕ **Freddy's Bistro.** On a quiet lane between busy O'Connell and Henry streets, this informal two-story restaurant fills a charming 18th-century coach house. Old brick walls are complemented by a warm color scheme that glows in candlelight. Steak with a brandy, bacon, and mushroom sauce and monkfish with a basil and lemon pesto are popular main courses. For dessert try the hot, sticky, toffee pudding. ✉ *Theatre La., off Lower Glentworth St.* ☎ *061/418749* ⊟ *MC, V* ☉ *No lunch. Closed Sun. and Mon.*

$$ ✕ **Green Onion Café.** The Irish–French chef team of Marie Munnelly and Geoff Gloux produces a witty, stylish menu at this hip eatery across from the Hunt Museum. The large room, which used to be the town hall, is split into two levels, which are, in turn, divided into intimate spaces through a judicious use of booths. Typical dishes include smoked Irish cheese (Gubbeen) and spinach tartlet, pork fillet coated in pistachio nuts with herb butter, jerk chicken with jalapeño salsa, and salmon with basil beurre blanc. For dessert, try the prune and toffee pudding with roasted nutty butterscotch. ✉ *Old Town Hall Building, Rutland St.* ☎ *061/ 400710* ⊟ *AE, DC, MC, V* ☉ *Closed Sun.*

¢–$ ✕ **Mortell's.** For fish-and-chips, this is *the* place. It's a simple café, but it serves only the freshest local seafood. You can also get full Irish breakfasts and baked goods. Mortell's has been in the family for more than 40 years, and everything, from the doughnuts to the brown bread to the mayo, is made on the premises. It's in the main shopping area. ✉ *49 Roches St.* ☎ *061/415457* ⊟ *AE, DC, MC, V* ☉ *Closed Sun. No dinner.*

★ $$$ ⊞ **Clarion Hotel.** A dramatic, 17-story, boat-shape building is the focal point of Limerick's dock redevelopment. The interior is a triumph of modern design—from the cutlery to the carpets—with simple geometric lines and earthy color schemes. Rooms are spacious and restful with white Egyptian-cotton comforters, large windows, and views of the twinkling cityscape upriver or the wide estuary downriver. The Kudos bar offers Thai food, and the boldly minimalist Sinergie restaurant serves imaginative Continental cuisine. ✉ *Steamboat Quay, Co. Limerick* ☎ *061/444100* ⊟ *061/444101* ⊕ *www.clarionhotellimerick.com* ⇦ *93 rooms with bath* ⌂ *Restaurant, in-room data ports, cable TV, indoor pool, health club, bar, meeting rooms* ⊟ *AE, DC, MC, V* ﭏ *BP.*

$$–$$$ ⊞ **Castletroy Park.** This large, redbrick-and-stone hotel, which grandly crowns a hill on the outskirts of town, has splendid views of the university campus. The lobby, with its polished woods and Asian rugs, leads to a conservatory–cum–coffee shop overlooking an Italian-style courtyard. Guest rooms, scented with potpourri, have solid wood furniture, muted floral drapes and spreads, and rag-rolled walls. The fitness center is one of the best around. You can mix with the locals in the Merry Pedlar Pub and Bistro or enjoy a formal meal in MacLaughlin's restaurant. ✉ *Dublin Rd., Co. Limerick* ☎ *061/335566* ⊟ *061/331117* ⊕ *www.castletroy-park.ie* ⇦ *101 rooms with bath, 6 suites* ⌂ *2 restaurants, in-room data ports, cable TV, indoor pool, health club, bar, meeting rooms* ⊟ *AE, DC, MC, V* ﭏ *BP.*

$$ ⊞ **Greenhills.** This friendly, family-run low-rise is in a quiet suburban area, 20 minutes from Shannon and 5 minutes from Limerick's city center. The best rooms are in a quiet wing above the fitness center and are big enough to have a small couch, tables, and chairs. All the rooms are color coordinated and have dark-wood furniture and tiled bathrooms. Children will love the pool, and in high season they can take part in the children's club. ✉ *Ennis Rd., Co. Limerick* ☎ *061/453033* ⊟ *061/453307*

⊕ *www.greenhillsgroup.com* ↩ *55 rooms with bath* ♿ *3 restaurants, coffee shop, cable TV, tennis court, indoor pool, sauna, steam room, bar, children's programs (ages 4–12), meeting rooms* ⊟ *AE, DC, MC, V* ⦿ *BP.*

$ 🏨 **Jurys Inn.** Clean, airy, and in good shape, unlike some of Limerick's other budget spots, this hotel is part of the Jurys chain. Rooms are a good size and have light-wood furnishings. The hotel overlooks an urban stretch of the Shannon being converted from industrial to leisure use and is a short step from the main shopping and business district. ⊠ *Lower Mallow St., Mount Kennett Pl., Co. Limerick* ☎ *061/207000* 🖷 *061/400966* ⊕ *www.jurysdoyle.com* ↩ *151 rooms with bath* ♿ *Restaurant, cable TV, bar* ⊟ *AE, DC, MC, V* ⦿ *BP.*

$ 🏨 **Sarsfield Bridge Hotel.** This modern budget accommodation has a great location beside the Sarsfield Bridge, midway between old Limerick and the shopping area. The popular, ground-floor Pier One bar-restaurant has leather sofas overlooking the river. Rooms above are built in a square around an enclosed courtyard; those on the inside have no views but are really quiet. Red velvet armchairs are the only touches of luxury in otherwise plain, small rooms, but overall, the hotel offers good value for the money. ⊠ *Sarsfield Bridge* ☎ *061/317179* 🖷 *061/317182* ⊕ *www.tsbh.ie* ↩ *55 rooms with bath* ♿ *Restaurant, cable TV,* ⊟ *AE, MC, V* ⦿ *EP.*

Nightlife & the Arts

ART GALLERIES The **Belltable Arts Center** (⊠ 69 O'Connell St. ☎ 061/319866) has exhibition space and a small auditorium for touring productions. The **Limerick City Gallery** (⊠ Pery Sq. ☎ 061/310633) owns a small permanent collection of Irish art and mounts exhibits of contemporary art.

PUBS, CABARET **Dolan's Pub** (⊠ 3–4 Dock Rd. ☎ 061/314483) is a lively waterfront spot
& DISCOS with traditional Irish music every night, and dancing classes from September to May. Dolan's Warehouse, under the same management and in the same location, is a live music venue with top national and international acts. **Hogan's** (⊠ 20–24 Old Clare St. ☎ 061/411279) has a traditional music session every Monday, Wednesday, and Saturday year-round. The riverside **Locke Bar** (⊠ 3 George's Quay ☎ 061/413733) is one of Limerick's oldest bars, dating from 1724, and has Irish music Sunday, Monday, and Tuesday nights. It's also a great place for outdoor drinking in summer. There's traditional music at **Nancy Blake's Pub** (⊠ 19 Denmark St. ☎ 061/416443) year-round Sunday–Wednesday from 9 PM. **William G. South's Pub** (⊠ The Crescent ☎ 061/318850) is an old-fashioned pub that's typical of the age of Frank McCourt's *Angela's Ashes*. There's no music, but do drop by for bar food (1:30 to 3, Mon.–Sat.) or a drink.

Sports & the Outdoors

FISHING **Bonds Fishing Tackle** (⊠ 40 Wickham St. ☎ 061/316809) has fly-fishing gear and rod repair. You can arrange fishing tackle, bait, and licenses at **Steve's Fishing and Shooting Store** (⊠ 7 Denmark St. ☎ 061/413484).

GOLF **Castletroy Golf Club** (⊠ Golf Links Rd., Castletroy ☎ 061/335753) is a challenging 18-hole, par-71 parkland course in the suburbs. **Limerick County Golf and Country Club** (⊠ Ballyneety ☎ 061/351881) is a championship, 18-hole, par-72 parkland course that welcomes visitors.

HORSEBACK **Clarina Riding Center** (⊠ Clarina, near Limerick City ☎ 061/353087) has
RIDING riding by the hour and can also organize post-to-post trail riding with baggage transfer along quiet scenic routes.

Shopping

DEPARTMENT STORES   Limerick has a branch of **Brown Thomas** (✉ O'Connell St. ☎ 061/472222), Ireland's upscale department store. **Dunnes Stores** (✉ 130 Sarsfield St. ☎ 061/412666) is, perhaps, Ireland's favorite department store chain. **Penneys** (✉ 137 O'Connell St. ☎ 061/227244) sells inexpensive clothing; it's a great place for low-price rain gear. **Roches Stores** (✉ O'Connell St. ☎ 061/415622) is a large, mid-range department store.

MALLS   The shops in **Arthur's Quay Shopping Centre** (✉ Arthur's Quay ☎ 061/419888) mainly sell clothing and accessories. The **Crescent Shipping Center** (✉ Dooradoyle ☎ 061/228560), Limerick's biggest, swankiest mall, is a 5-minute bus or car ride from the city center.

SPECIALTY SHOPS   The **Celtic Bookshop** (✉ 2 Rutland St. ☎ 061/401155) specializes in books of Irish interest. **Davern & Bell** (✉ 22 Thomas St. ☎ 061/481967) is a gallery of contemporary Irish crafts, mainly ceramics. **Deoidín** (✉ 6 Sarsfield St. ☎ 061/318011) has an interesting selection of crafts, jewelry, and gifts. **Lane Antiques** (✉ 45 Catherine St. ☎ 061/339307) sells collectibles, antiquarian books, prints, and paintings.

Bunratty Castle & Folk Park

★ ☺ ▶ ❻   *18 km (10 mi) west of Limerick City on N18 (road to Shannon Airport).*

Bunratty Castle and Folk Park are two of those rare attractions that appeal to all ages and manage to be both educational and fun. The castle, built in 1460, has been fully restored and decorated with 15th- to 17th-century furniture and furnishings. It gives wonderful insight into the life of those times. As you pass under the walls of Bunratty, look for the three "murder holes" that allowed defenders to pour boiling oil on attackers below.

The castle is the site of medieval banquets, which are held nightly at 5:45 and 8:45; the cost is €47.50. You're welcomed by Irish colleens in 15th-century dress, who bear the traditional bread of friendship. Then you're led off to a reception, where you'll quaff mead made from fermented honey, apple juice, clover, and heather. Before sitting down at long tables in the candlelit great hall, you don a bib. You'll need it, because you eat the four-course meal medieval-style—with your fingers. Serving "wenches" take time out to sing a few ballads or pluck harp strings. The banquets may not be authentic, but they're fun; they're also popular, so book as far in advance as possible.

On the castle grounds the quaint Bunratty Folk Park re-creates a 19th-century village street and has examples of the traditional rural housing. Exhibits include a working blacksmith's forge; demonstrations of flour milling, bread making, candle making, thatching, and other skills; and a variety of farm animals. An adjacent museum of agricultural machinery can't compete with the furry and feathered live exhibits. If you can't get a reservation for the medieval banquet at the castle, a *ceilí* (traditional music session; held nightly May to September at 5:45 and 9 for €40) at the folk park is the next-best thing. The program features traditional Irish dance and song and a meal of Irish stew, soda bread, and apple pie. No visit to Bunratty is complete without a drink in **Durty Nelly's** (☎ 061/364072), an old-world (but touristy) pub beside the folk park entrance. Its fanciful decor has inspired imitations around the world.

☎ *061/361511* ⊕ *www.shannonheritage.com* ▣ *€10* ⊙ *Sept.–May, daily 9:30–5:30 (last entry 4:15); June–Aug., daily 9:30–7 (last entry 6).*

Knappogue Castle

62 *21 km (13 mi) north of Bunratty.*

A 15th-century MacNamara stronghold, Knappogue Castle has been extensively restored and furnished in 15th-century style. Its name means the "hill of the kiss," and, like Bunratty, it's a venue for medieval-style banquets. The castle looks spectacular at night when floodlit. ✉ *5 km (3 mi) southeast of Quin on R649* ☎ *061/368103* ⊕ *www.shannonheritage.com* ⌨ *€7* ⊙ *May–Sept., daily 9:30–4:30.*

Craggaunowen Project

63 *6 km (4 mi) northeast of Knappogue Castle.*

The **Craggaunowen Project** includes Craggaunowen Castle, a 16th-century tower house restored with furnishings from the period. Particularly worth seeing are the two replicas of early Celtic-style dwellings that have been constructed on the castle grounds. On an island in the lake, reached by a narrow footbridge, is a clay-and-wattle *crannóg*, a fortified lake dwelling; it resembles what might have been built in the 6th or 7th century when Celtic influence still predominated in Ireland. The reconstruction of a small ring fort shows how an ordinary farmer would have lived in the 5th or 6th century, at the time Christianity was being established. Characters from the past explain their Iron Age (500 BC–AD 450) lifestyle; show you around their small holding, stocked with animals; and demonstrate crafts skills from bygone ages. It's a strange experience to walk across the little wooden bridge above reeds rippling in the lake into Ireland's Celtic past as a jumbo jet passes overhead on its way into Shannon Airport—1,500 years of history compressed into an instant. ✉ *Kilmurry, Sixmilebridge, signposted off road to Sixmilebridge about 10 km (6 mi) east of Quin* ☎ *061/367178* ⊕ *www.shannonheritage.com* ⌨ *€7* ⊙ *May–Oct., daily 10–6.*

THE SOUTHWEST A TO Z

To research prices, get advice from other travelers, and book travel arrangements, visit www.fodors.com.

AIR TRAVEL

AIRPORTS The southwest has two international airports: Cork on the southwest coast, and Shannon in the west. Cork Airport, 5 km (3 mi) south of Cork City on the Kinsale road, is used primarily for flights to and from the United Kingdom. Regular 30-minute internal flights are scheduled between Shannon and Dublin, Shannon and Cork, and Cork and Dublin. Shannon Airport, 26 km (16 mi) west of Limerick City, is the point of arrival for many transatlantic flights; it also serves some flights from the United Kingdom and Europe. Kerry County Airport at Farranfore, 16 km (10 mi) from Killarney, mainly services small planes but is gradually increasing its commercial traffic with at least one daily flight from London.

🔒 Airport Information **Cork Airport** ☎ 021/431-3131. **Kerry County Airport** ☎ 066/976-4644. **Shannon Airport** ☎ 061/471444.

TRANSFERS Bus service runs between Cork Airport and the Cork City Bus Terminal every 30 minutes, on the hour and the half hour. The ride takes about 10 minutes and costs about €3. Bus Éireann runs a regular bus service from Shannon Airport to Limerick City between 8 AM and midnight. The ride takes about 40 minutes and costs about €5.

You'll find taxis outside the main terminal building at Shannon and Cork airports. The ride from Shannon Airport to Limerick City costs about €28; from Cork Airport to Cork City costs about €8.

🚌 Shuttles **Bus Éireann** ☎ 061/474311. **Cork City Bus Terminal** ✉ Parnell Pl. ☎ 021/450-6066.

BOAT & FERRY TRAVEL

From the United Kingdom, the southwest has two ports of entry: Rosslare (in County Wexford) and Cork City. Stena Sealink sails directly between Rosslare Ferryport and Fishguard, Wales. Pembroke, Wales, and France's Cherbourg and Roscoff can be reached on Irish Ferries. Swansea–Cork Ferries, which can also be accessed from the United Kingdom, operates a 10-hour crossing between the two ports on a comfortable, well-equipped boat. Supabus will get you to the Swansea ferry from anywhere in the United Kingdom.

🚢 Boat & Ferry Information **Irish Ferries** ☎ 053/33158. **Stena Sealink** ☎ 053/33115. **Swansea–Cork Ferries** ☎ 1792/456116.

BUS TRAVEL

Bus Éireann operates express services from Dublin to Limerick City, Cork City, and Tralee. Most towns in the region are served by the provincial Bus Éireann network. The main bus terminals in the region are at Cork, Limerick, and Tralee. An Irish company, Slattery's, runs a bus service from London to Cork and Tralee. The journey to Cork via Rosslare is by bus and ferry, and, at about 14 hours, arduous.

FARES & SCHEDULES The provincial bus service, cheaper and more flexible than the train, covers all the region's main centers. Express services are available between Cork City and Limerick City (twice a day); Cork and Tralee (once a day, high season only); and Killarney, Tralee, Limerick, and Shannon (once a day, twice in peak season).

If you plan to travel extensively by bus, a copy of the Bus Éireann timetable (€1.30 from bus terminals) is essential. As a general rule, the smaller the town, and the more remote, the less frequent its bus service. For example, Kinsale, a well-developed resort 29 km (18 mi) from Cork, is served by at least five buses a day, both arriving and departing; Castlegregory, a small village on the remote Dingle Peninsula, has bus service only on Friday.

🚌 Bus Information **Bus Éireann** ☎ 01/836-6111 in Dublin; 061/313333 in Limerick; 021/450-8188 in Cork; 066/712-3566 in Tralee. **Cork Station** ✉ Parnell Pl. ☎ 021/450-8188. **Limerick Station** ✉ Colbert Station ☎ 061/313333. **Slattery's** ✉ London ☎ 020/7482-1604 add the prefix 00-44 if dialing from Ireland. **Tralee Station** ✉ Casement Station ☎ 066/712-3566.

CAR RENTAL

All the major car-rental companies have desks at Shannon and Cork airports.

🚗 Agencies **Alamo** ✉ Cork Airport ☎ 021/431-8638. **Avis** ✉ Cork Airport ☎ 021/428-1111 ⊕ www.avis.com ✉ Killarney ☎ 064/36655 ✉ Shannon Airport ☎ 061/471094. **Budget** ✉ Cork Airport ☎ 021/431-4000 ⊕ www.budget.ie ✉ Killarney ☎ 064/34341 ✉ Shannon Airport ☎ 061/471361. **Dan Dooley** ✉ Shannon Airport ☎ 061/471098 ⊕ www.dan-dooley.com. **Enterprise** ✉ Cork Airport ☎ 021/497-5133. **Hertz** ✉ Cork Airport ☎ 021/496-5849 ✉ Shannon Airport ☎ 061/471369. **Murray's Europcar** ✉ Cork Airport ☎ 021/491-7300 ⊕ www.europcar.ie ✉ Shannon Airport ☎ 061/701200. **Sixt Irish Car Rentals** ✉ Shannon Airport ☎ 061/328328 ⊕ www.irishcarrentals.ie ✉ Ennis Rd., Limerick ☎ 061/206000.

CAR TRAVEL

The main driving access route from Dublin is N7, which goes 192 km (120 mi) directly to Limerick City; from Dublin, pick up N8 in Portlaoise and drive 257 km (160 mi) to Cork City. The journey time between Dublin and Limerick runs just under 3 hours; between Dublin and Cork it takes about 3½ hours. From Rosslare Harbour by car, take N25 208 km (129 mi) to Cork; allow 3½ hours for the journey. You can pick up N24 in Waterford for the 211-km (131-mi) drive to Limerick City, which also takes about 3½ hours.

A car is the ideal way to explore this region, packed as it is with scenic routes, attractive but remote towns, and a host of out-of-the-way restaurants and hotels that deserve a detour. Getting around the southwest is every bit as enjoyable as arriving, provided you set out in the right frame of mind—a relaxed one. There's no point in imposing a rigid timetable on your journey when you're visiting one of the last places in western Europe where you are as likely to be held up by a donkey cart, a herd of cows, or a flock of sheep as by road construction or heavy trucks.

ROAD CONDITIONS — Roads are generally small, with two lanes (one in each direction). You will find a few miles of two-lane highway on the outskirts of Cork City, Limerick City, and Killarney, but much of your time will be spent on roads so narrow and twisty that it is not advisable to exceed 64 kph (40 mph).

EMERGENCIES

🔲 **Ambulance, fire, police** ☎ 999. **Mid-Western Health Board** ✉ 31–33 Catherine St., Limerick ☎ 061/316655. **Southern Health Board** ✉ Dennehy's Cross, Cork ☎ 021/454-5011.

🔲 Pharmacies **Phelan's** ✉ 9 Patrick St., Cork ☎ 021/427-2511. **P. O'Donoghue** ✉ Main St., Killarney ☎ 064/31813. **Roberts** ✉ 105 O'Connell St., Limerick City ☎ 061/414414.

TOURS

BOAT TOURS — Cork Harbour opens to the sea some 8 km (5 mi) from Cobh at Roches Point. One-hour harbor tours from Marine Transport are a splendid way to take in Cobh's glorious watery environs. They're conducted daily from May to September at 10, 11, noon, 1:30, and 2:30; the cost is €4.45.
🔲 **Marine Transport** ✉ Kennedy Pier ☎ 021/481-1485.

BUS TOURS — Bus Éireann, part of the state-run public-transport network, offers a range of day and half-day guided tours from June to September. You can book them at the bus stations in Cork or Limerick or at any tourist office. A full-day tour costs €17.50, half-day €10. Bus Éireann also offers open-top bus tours of Cork City on Tuesday and Saturday in July and August for €5.10.

Dero's Tours, Corcoran's Tours, and Killarney & Kerry Tours will organize full-day and half-day trips by coach or taxi around Killarney and the Ring of Kerry.
🔲 Fees & Schedules **Corcoran's Tours** ✉ 10 College St., Killarney, Co. Kerry ☎ 064/36666. **Dero's Tours** ✉ 22 Main St., Killarney, Co. Kerry ☎ 064/31251 ⊕ www.derostours.com. **Killarney & Kerry Tours** ✉ Innisfallen, 15 Main St., Killarney, Co. Kerry ☎ 064/33880.

SPECIAL-INTEREST TOURS — Gerry Coughlan of Arrangements Unlimited can prearrange special-interest group tours of the region. Half-day and full-day tours are individually planned for groups of 10 or more to satisfy each visitor's needs. Country House Tours organizes self-driven or chauffeur-driven group tours with accommodations in private country houses and castles. It also conducts special-interest tours, including gardens, architecture, ghosts, and golf. Into the Wilderness organizes guided walking, climbing, and cycling tours in the Kerry Highlands and Killarney National Park.

Shannon Castle Tours will escort you to an "Irish Night" in Bunratty Folk Park or take you to a medieval banquet at Bunratty or Knappogue Castle; although the banquets aren't authentic, they are boisterous occasions and full of goodwill.

Destination Killarney is the foremost Killarney tour operator. Besides offering full-day and half-day tours of Killarney and Kerry by coach or taxi, the group will prearrange your visit, lining up accommodations, entertainment, special-interest tours, and sporting activities in one package. A full-day (10:30–5) tour costs from €15 to €18 per person, excluding lunch and refreshments. The Killarney Local Circuit tour is an excellent half-day 10:30–12:30 orientation. The memorable Gap of Dunloe tour at €20 includes a coach and boat trip. Add €15 for a horseback ride through the gap. More conventional day trips can also be made to the Ring of Kerry, the Loo Valley, and Glengarriff; the city of Cork and Blarney Castle; Dingle and Slea Head; and Caragh Lake and Rossbeigh.

Jaunting cars (pony and trap) that carry up to four people can be rented at a stand outside the Killarney tourist office. They can also be found at the entrance to Muckross Estate and at the Gap of Dunloe. A ride costs between €16 and €32, negotiable with the driver, depending on duration (one to two hours) and route. Tangney Tours is the leading jaunting-car company and will also organize tours by coach or water bus, as well as entertainment.

🔒 Fees & Schedules **Arrangements Unlimited** ✉ 1 Woolhara Park, Douglas, Cork City, Co. Cork ☎ 021/429-3873 🖷 021/429-2488 ⊕ www.arrangements.ie. **Country House Tours** ✉ 71 Waterloo Rd., Dublin 4 ☎ 01/668-6463 🖷 01/668-6578 ⊕ www. tourismresources.ie. **Destination Killarney** ✉ Scott's Gardens, Killarney, Co. Kerry 🖷☎ 064/32638 ⊕ www.gleneagle-hotel.com. **Shannon Castle Tours** ✉ Bunratty Folk Park, Bunratty, Co. Clare ☎ 061/360788 ⊕ www.shannonheritage.ie. **Tangney Tours** ✉ Kinvara House, Muckross Rd., Killarney, Co. Kerry ☎ 064/33358.

WALKING TOURS   **South**West Walks Ireland has a variety of packages for all levels of walkers. Trips include accommodation, baggage transfer, and evening meals for self-guided or escorted groups. Go Ireland specializes in active vacations, included walking and cycling excursions along the Kerry Way or the Dingle Peninsula. Michael Martin's Titanic Trail, a 90-minute guided walking tour of Cobh, takes its name from the *Titanic,* but in fact covers the whole of Cobh's fascinating history, ranging from coffin ships to ocean liners via naval fire power and Tall Ships. Trips are held daily at 11 AM starting from outside the Commodore Hotel; the cost is €7.50. Martin can also customize a walk or tour by minibus.

Richard Clancy, an expert on the legends and history of Killarney, offers a two-hour guided walk in Killarney National Park daily at 11 AM (other times by arrangement). Trips leave from the Shell gas station on Lower New Street. The cost is €7. Limerick City Tours provides inexpensive walking tours of Limerick from June to September (and by arrangement other months). St. Mary's Action Centre has walking tours of Limerick's historic centers and of locations highlighted in Frank McCourt's *Angela's Ashes*. They're conducted daily at 11 and 2:30.

🔒 **Go Ireland** ✉ Killorglin, Co. Kerry ☎ 066/976-2094 ⊕ www.goactivities.com. **Limerick City Tours** ✉ Noel Curtin, Rhebogue, Co. Limerick ☎ 061/311935. **Richard Clancy** ☎ 064/33471 ⊕ www.kerrygems.ie/killarneywalks. **St. Mary's Action Centre** ✉ 44 Nicholas St., Limerick, Co. Limerick ☎ 061/318106 ⊕ www.iol.ie/~smidp/. **SouthWest Walks Ireland** ✉ 6 Church St., Tralee, Co. Kerry ☎ 066/712-8733 ⊕ www.southwestwalksireland. com. **Titanic Trail** ✉ Cobh ☎ 021/481-5211 ⊕ www.titanic-trail.com.

TRAIN TRAVEL

From Dublin Heuston Station, the region is served by three direct rail links to Limerick City, Tralee, and Cork City. Journey time from Dublin to Limerick is 2½ hours; to Cork, 2¾; to Tralee, 3¾.

The rail network, which covers only the inner ring of the region, is mainly useful for moving from one touring base to another. Except during the peak season of July and August, only four trains a day run between Cork (or Limerick) and Tralee. More frequent service is offered between Cork City and Limerick City, but the ride involves changing at Limerick Junction—as does the journey from Limerick to Tralee—to wait for a connecting train. Be sure to ascertain the delay involved in the connection. The journey from Cork to Tralee takes about 2 hours; from Cork to Limerick, about 1¼ hours; from Limerick to Tralee, about 3 hours.

A suburban rail service from Kent Station has stops at Fota Island and Cobh and offers better Cork Harbour views than the road.

🚊 Train Information **Dublin Heuston Station** ☎ 01/836-6222. Inquiries ☎ 061/315555 in Limerick; 021/450-6766 in Cork; 066/712-3522 in Tralee. **Kent Station** ☎ 021/450-6766 for timetable.

VISITOR INFORMATION

Bord Fáilte provides a free information service; its tourist information offices (TIOs) also sell a selection of tourist literature. For a small fee it will book accommodations anywhere in Ireland.

Seasonal TIOs in Bantry, Cahirciveen, and Clonakilty are open from May to October; offices in Dingle and Kinsale are open from March to November; the TIO in Kenmare is open April to October, and the one in Youghal is open May to mid-September. All of the seasonal TIOs are generally open Monday–Saturday 9–6; in July and August they are also open Sunday 9–6. Year-round TIOs can be found in Blarney, Clonakilty, Cork City, Dingle, Killarney, Limerick, Shannon, Skibbereen, and Tralee and are open Monday–Saturday 9–6; in July and August they are also open Sunday 9–6.

🚊 Tourist Information **Adare** ✉ Heritage Centre ☎ 061-396255 ⊕ www.shannondev.ie. **Bantry** ✉ Co. Cork ☎ 027/50229 ⊕ www.corkkerry.ie. **Blarney** ✉ Co. Cork ☎ 021/438-1624 ⊕ www.corkkerry.ie. **Cahirciveen** ✉ The Old Barracks, Co. Kerry ☎ 066/947-2589 ⊕ www.corkkerry.ie. **Clonakilty** ✉ Co. Cork ☎ 023/33226 ⊕ www.corkkerry.ie. **Cork City** ✉ Grand Parade, Co. Cork ☎ 021/425-5100 🖷 021/425-5199 ⊕ www.corkkerry.ie. **Dingle** ✉ The Quay, Co. Kerry ☎ 066/915-1188. **Kenmare** ✉ Co. Kerry ☎ 064/41233. **Killarney** ✉ Aras Fáilte, Beech Rd., Co. Kerry ☎ 064/31633 🖷 064/34506 ⊕ www.corkkerry.ie. **Kinsale** ✉ Pier Rd., Co. Cork ☎ 021/477-2234; 021/477-4417 offseason 🖷 021/477-4438. **Limerick** ✉ Arthur's Quay, Co. Limerick ☎ 061/317522 ⊕ www.shannon-dev.ie. **Shannon Airport** ✉ Co. Clare ☎ 061/471664 ⊕ www.shannon-dev.ie. **Skibbereen** ✉ North St., Co. Cork ☎ 028/21766. **Tralee** ✉ Ashe Memorial Hall, Denny St., Co. Kerry ☎ 066/712-1288 ⊕ www.shannon-dev.ie. **Youghal** ✉ Co. Cork ☎ 024/92390.

THE WEST

FODOR'S CHOICE

Ballynahinch Castle, *Recess inn*

Delphi Lodge, *Leenane lodge*

Erriseask House, *Ballyconneely restaurant-inn*

Kenny's Bookshop, *Galway City*

Killary Harbour, *Kylemore Valley fjord*

Kylemore Abbey, *Kylemore Valley*

Monk's Pub, *Ballyvaughan*

Moy House, *Lahinch inn*

Museum of Country Life, *Turlough*

Norman Villa, *Galway City hotel*

Tíg Neáchtain, *Galway City pub*

HIGHLY RECOMMENDED

SIGHTS The Burren, *County Clare*

Céide Fields, *near Ballycastle*

Clifden, *Connemara*

Cliffs of Moher

Inishmore Island

Salmon Weir Bridge, *Galway City*

Westport, *County Mayo*

SHOPPING Design Concourse Ireland, *Galway City*

Doolin Crafts Gallery, *Doolin*

Many other great hotels and restaurants enliven this area. For other favorites, look for the black stars as you read this chapter.

Updated by
Alannah
Hopkin

WHILE MOST OF IRELAND CHARGES HEADFIRST into the 21st century, the west retains an unspoiled and rugged way of life. With the most westerly seaboard in Europe, the region remains a place apart, where nature's magnificence awaits: the majestic Cliffs of Moher, the eerie expanse of the Burren, the "hidden kingdom" of Connemara, and the Aran Islands, which do constant battle with the stormy Atlantic. But there are also grand baronial houses to visit—Ashford Castle and Kylemore Abbey—and Galway, the city that loves to celebrate.

Within Ireland, the west refers to the region that lies west of the River Shannon; most of this area falls within the old Irish province of Connaught. The coast of this region lies at the far western extremity of Europe, facing its nearest neighbors in North America across 3,200 km (2,000 mi) of Atlantic ocean. Although the east, the southwest, and the north were influenced by either Norman, Scots, or English settlers, the west escaped systematic resettlement and, with the exception of the walled town of Galway, remained purely Irish in language, social organization, and general outlook far longer than the rest of the country. The land in the west, predominantly mountains and bogs, did not immediately tempt the conquering barons. Oliver Cromwell was among those who found the place thoroughly unattractive, and he gave the Irish chieftains who would not conform to English rule the choice of going "to Hell or Connaught."

It wasn't until the late 18th century, when better transport improved communication, that the west started to experience the so-called foreign influences that had already Europeanized the rest of the country. The west was, in effect, propelled from the 16th century into the 19th. Virtually every significant building in the region dates either from before the 17th century or from the late 18th century onward. As in the southwest, the population of the west was decimated by the Great Famine (1845–49) and by the waves of mass emigration that persisted until the 1950s. Towns were unknown in pre-Christian Irish society, and even today, more than 150 years after the famine, many residents still live on small farms rather than in towns and villages. Especially during the wet, wintry months, you can still walk out of your country house, hotel, or bed-and-breakfast in the morning and smell the nearby turf fires.

Today, the west is, for many, the most typically Irish part of the country. Particularly in western County Galway, the region has the highest concentration of Gaeltacht (Irish-speaking communities) in all of Ireland, with roughly 40,000 native Irish speakers making their homes here. The country's first Irish-language TV station broadcasts from the tiny village of Spiddle, on the north shore of Galway Bay in the heart of the Gaeltacht. Throughout this area, you'll see plenty of signs that are in Irish only. Who would suspect that Gaillimh is Irish for Galway? But wherever you go in the west, you'll not only see, but more importantly *hear,* the most vital way in which traditional Irish culture survives here—musicians play in pubs all over the west, and they are recognized as being the best in the Republic.

A major factor in the region's economic development has been the lure of its spectacular scenery to visitors. So far, the development that has come with the cultivation of tourism in the west has been mercifully low-key. Yes, residents of the west have encouraged the revival of such cottage industries as knitting, weaving, and woodworking. But they have become strong environmentalists as well, lobbying on behalf of land preservation. This is perhaps the result of having witnessed much of the bogland in Connemara and County Mayo being overfarmed for its peat, leaving behind bereft swaths of land. The 5,000-acre Connemara

Numbers in the text correspond to numbers in the margin and on the West and Galway City maps.

If you have
5 days

If you're arriving in the west via Shannon Airport or by crossing into County Clare via the Killimer–Tarbert ferry, head west for the beach town of **Kilkee** ④ ☞ or Milltown Malbay. If not, head right for the **Cliffs of Moher** ⑥. Next stop should be the heart of **the Burren** ⑨. Both **Doolin** ⑦ and ⊡ **Lisdoonvarna** ⑧ are within the Burren and famous for their traditional music. Spend the night in Lisdoonvarna, or in ⊡ **Kinvara** ⑭ or ⊡ **Ballyvaughan** ⑩, both on Galway Bay. On your second day, head for ⊡ **Galway City** ⑮–㉘. Spend the morning exploring on foot. In the afternoon, take a cruise up the River Corrib or drive along the north shore of Galway Bay to Salthill and beyond into the Gaeltacht.

On your third day, you can kick around Galway, take the ferry out to the **Aran Islands** ㉙–㉛ for the day, or make the quick trip south to **Coole Park** ⑫ and **Thoor Ballylee** ⑬. Spend the night in Galway or at one of the country houses outside town. Another option for your third day is to head out through the moorlands of Connemara through **Oughterard** ㉜ to **Bally-nahinch** ㉟ or Roundstone for lunch. Then go on to the Alpine-like coastal village of ⊡ **Clifden** ㊱. Spend the night here or in a country house, hotel, or B&B in or around ⊡ **Cashel** ㉞ or ⊡ **Letterfrack** ㊲.

If you've spent your third night in Galway, or if you have stayed the night in or near Clifden, follow the alternative day-three itinerary above, but don't linger too long in Clifden. Push on, first to Connemara National Park and then to Kylemore Abbey in the **Kylemore Valley** ㊳. Continue through **Leenane** ㊴ to ⊡ **Westport** ㊵, the prettiest village in County Mayo and a good place to spend the night. On the way, you won't be able to miss the distinctive conical shape of Croagh Patrick. On your fifth day, walk up Croagh Patrick or stroll around Clew Bay and see how many islands you can count. If the weather cooperates, venture out to **Achill Island** ㊶. At the end of the day, continue north to Sligo or head for a Midlands destination.

If you have
7 days

The five-day itinerary can easily be expanded into a seven-day trip, with the following modifications: spend a full two days exploring western County Clare, staying one night in the seaside town of ⊡ **Lahinch** ⑤ ☞ and another in any of the towns noted above. Depending on how much time you want to spend in Galway, you might want to make it to **Coole Park** ⑫ and **Thoor Ballylee** ⑬ on one of your first two days in the west, rather than taking a bite out of the time you have for Galway and the Aran Islands. Begin your third (rather than your second) day by heading to ⊡ **Galway City** ⑮–㉘. Spend two days in Galway itself and one visiting the **Aran Islands** ㉙–㉛. On your sixth day, travel through Connemara and end up either in ⊡ **Cashel** ㉞, ⊡ **Clifden** ㊱, or ⊡ **Letterfrack** ㊲ for the night.

National Park is the result of a successful lobby for peatland protection, and is among the few protected places in one of Ireland's most important bogland areas. With increasing investment in the west, time will tell how long this part of the country will remain undeveloped. Residents are already being faced with the difficult task of striking a balance between conservation and economic prosperity.

There may be no better example of the way the west is balancing change with tradition than its thatched cottages, which have become popular as holiday homes. Some of the traditional whitewashed cottages are truly old, while others have been built to resemble the old.

It's nothing new that the west's greatest virtue for visitors—apart from its glorious scenery and high-flying capital city—is its people. No matter how many times you get out of the car for a photo-op (and you should expect to *fly* through rolls of film here), the stories that you'll most likely tell when you show your friends and family those pictures are going to be about the *seisún,* or sessions (informal performance of traditional music), you stumbled upon in a small pub; the tiny, far-from-the-madding-crowds lake near Connemara that you made your own; and the great *craic* ("crack," or good conversation and fun) you're likely to discover wherever you go.

Exploring the West

This chapter is organized into five parts, covering the territory from south to north. The first section, the Burren and Beyond—West Clare to South Galway, picks up minutes from Shannon Airport and is not far from Ennis, the gateway to coastal County Clare. The second section shows you the very best of buzzing, bustling Galway City, and the third takes you out to the three Aran Islands, standing guard at the mouth of Galway Bay. The fourth section, covering Connemara and County Mayo, brings you north of Galway Bay and west of Galway City into the fabled "hidden kingdom" of Connemara and beyond to the highlights of County Mayo: monumental Croagh Patrick, the pretty town of Westport, and the breathtaking Achill Island. The fifth section gives a brief overview of some of the highlights along the North Mayo Coast. Allow at least four days for exploring the region, seven days if you aim to visit the Aran Islands and Achill Island. Although distances between sights are not great, you may want to take scenic—and slower—national secondary routes. Covering 80 km to 112 km (50 mi to 70 mi) per day on these roads is a comfortable target.

About the Restaurants

Because the west has a brief high season—from mid-June to early September—and a quiet off-season, it doesn't have as broad a choice of small, owner-operated restaurants as do other parts of Ireland. Often the best place to eat is a local hotel—Sheedy's Restaurant and Country Inn in Lisdoonvarna, for example, which has one of the best chefs in County Clare, or Rosleague Manor in Letterfrack. The dominant style of cuisine in the west might be called "country-house cooking"—classic, dinner-party fare, such as homemade pâté, a seafood cocktail, tournedos or salmon hollandaise, and chocolate mousse. A handful of restaurants in Galway and Clifden, including Kirwan's Lane Creative Cuisine and K. C. Blake's in Galway, and Erriseask House in Clifden, showcase adventurous contemporary Irish cooking.

About the Hotels

Some of Ireland's finest country-house and castle hotels, distinguished old hotels, and inexpensive B&Bs are in the west. Ashford and Dro-

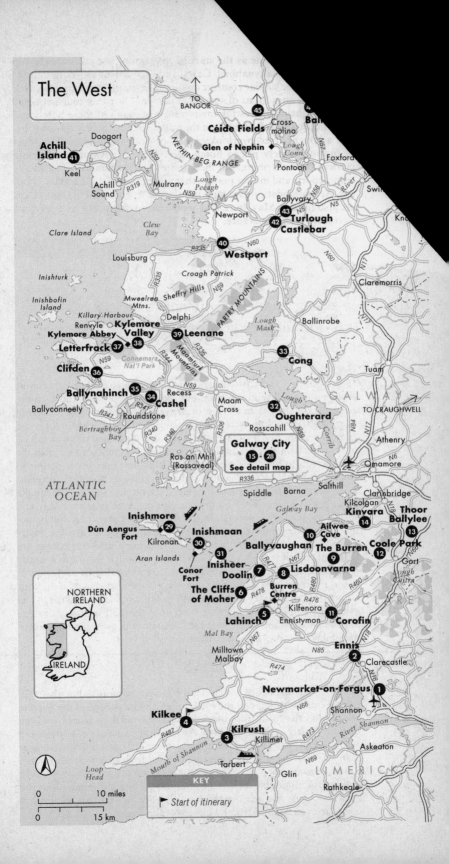

The West

TO BANGOR

45

Céide Fields
Cross-
molina

Bal

**Achill
Island** 41
Doogort

Keel

Achill
Sound

R319 Mulrany

Louigh
Peeagh

N59

NEPHIN BEG RANGE

Glen of Nephin ◆

Lough
Conn

Foxford

Pontoon

Ballyvary

N5

43 **Turlough**
42 **Castlebar**

N5

Kno

Swii

MAYO

N58

River

Claremorris

N17

Clew
Bay

Clare Island

Newport

N60

40 **Westport**

Louisburg

R335

Croagh Patrick

N59

Croagh Patrick

Inishturk

Mweelrea
Mtns.

Sheffry Hills

PARTRY MOUNTAINS

Lough
Mask

Ballinrobe

N17

Inishbofin
Island

Killary Harbour

Renvyle

Delphi

R335

Maamturk
Mountains

**Kylemore
Abbey** 37
**Kylemore
Valley** 38

39 **Leenane**

Connemara
Nat'l Park

33 **Cong**

Tuam

Letterfrack

Clifden 36

N59

R344

R336

Maam
Cross

Ballynahinch 35
34 **Cashel**

Ballyconneely

R341

Recess

N59

Lough

GALWAY

TO CRAUGHWELL

Roundstone

R341

R340

R336

Rosscahill

32 **Oughterard**

Corrib

N84

Athenry

N6

Bertraghboy
Bay

Ros an Mhil
(Rossaveal)

Galway City
15 - 28
See detail map

R336

N59

Spiddle

Barna

Salthill

N18

Oranmore

ATLANTIC
OCEAN

Inishmore

29

**Dún Aengus
Fort** ◆

Kilronan

Aran Islands

30

31

Inishmaan

**Conor
Fort** ◆

Inisheer
Doolin

Galway Bay

Kilcolgan

Clarinbridge

Kinvara
14

**Thoor
Ballylee**

13

Ballyvaughan

10

**Ailwee
Cave**

The Burren

9

Coole Park

12

Gort

7

8 **Lisdoonvarna**

R480

R460

Lough
Cuirra

CLARE

**The Cliffs
of Moher** 6

R478

**Burren
Centre**

Kilfenora

R476

Corofin

11

R471

N67

R478

5

Lahinch

Ennistymon

Ennis

2

Clarecastle

Mal Bay

R474

Milltown
Malbay

N67

N85

Newmarket-on-Fergus

1

Shannon

N68

Kilkee

4

R487

Kilrush

3

Killimer

Killimer

N18

River Shannon

Askeaton

Loop
Head

Mouth of Shannon

Tarbert

N69

Glin

LIMERICK

Rathkeale

NORTHERN
IRELAND

IRELAND

KEY

▶ *Start of itinerary*

0   10 miles

0   15 km

rs of the region, but less over-the-top
stle and Cashel House—both in Con-
n a smaller, more intimate scale. One
g in the west, however much you pay
onment of many of these hotels and
e middle of a large private estate be-
the sea or distant mountains. Most
are relatively new, and thus more
newer hotels often have facilities—
at are scarce at B&Bs and older holy and August, and the best places
tember, particularly on weekends,

	$$$$	$$$	$$	$	¢
RESTAURANTS	over €29	€22–€29	€15–€22	€8–€15	under €8
HOTELS	over €230	€180–€230	€130–€180	€80–€130	under €80

Restaurant prices are per person for a main course at dinner. Hotel prices are for
two people in a double room, including VAT and a service charge (often applied
in larger hotels).

Timing

"Soft weather," as the Irish call on-again, off-again rainy days, is almost
always a possibility in the west, but the months of May and October
are generally drier than the rest of the year. The Burren is at its best in
May, when the wildflowers are in season. April, May, and October are
good times for an off-peak visit. In July and August, expect to rub el-
bows with Irish families taking their holidays here; these are also the
best months to hear traditional music. It doesn't take many people to
overwhelm Galway City's narrow streets, so if you don't love crowds,
steer clear in late July, when the Arts Festival and Galway Race take
place back-to-back. The best time to visit the Aran Islands is May and
early June while the unusual, Burren-like flora is at its best and before
the bulk of the approximately 200,000 annual visitors arrives. Many
restaurants and accommodations in Connemara and the Burren are
seasonal and close from October to Easter, although thanks to a steady
rise in demand, the season is definitely extending slightly each year. If
you do choose to visit the west between November and March, your
choice of places to stay and to eat will be limited, but you do get to feel
as though you have the place to yourself. A word of warning, though:
in winter, the weather in the west can be harsh, with gales and rain sweeping in day after day from the Atlantic.

THE BURREN & BEYOND

County Clare claims two of Ireland's unique natural sights: the awesome Cliffs of Moher and the stark, mournful landscape of the Burren,
which hugs the coast from Black Head in the north to Doolin and the
Cliffs of Moher in the south. Yet western County Clare is widely beloved
among native Irish for a natural phenomenon significantly less unique
than these: its beaches. Though just another Irish beach town to some,
Kilkee, to name just one, is a favorite summer getaway. So whether you're
looking for inimitable scenery or just a lovely beach to plunk down on
for a few hours and relax in the sun (if you're lucky!), this section will
introduce you to the natural wonders of the west.

This journey begins at Newmarket-on-Fergus, within minutes of Shannon Airport, and it makes a good jumping-off point for a trip through the west if you've just arrived in Ireland and are planning to head for Galway. It also follows directly from the end of Chapter 5, which concludes 10 km (6 mi) down the road, at Bunratty Castle and Folk Park (and the Knappogue Castle and Craggaunowen Project, also nearby), so be sure to take a moment to glance at those sights to decide whether to include them as you get under way. This area is also the connecting link between County Limerick (and other points in the southwest) and Galway City. If you're approaching it from the southwest and you're not going into Limerick City itself, it's easy to begin exploring the region from Killimer, reached via the ferry from Tarbert.

Newmarket-on-Fergus

① *13 km (8 mi) north of Shannon Airport on N18.*

A small town in County Clare, Newmarket-on-Fergus is chiefly remarkable nowadays as the town nearest to Dromoland Castle, formerly the home of Lord Inchiquin, chief of the O'Brien clan.

Where to Stay & Eat

★ **$$$$** ⨯⊡ **Dromoland Castle.** This massive, turreted, neo-Gothic castle—the ancestral home of the O'Briens, the descendants of Brian Boru, High King of Ireland—looks the part. It stands beside a lake, surrounded by formal gardens and a golf course. Dating from the 19th century (it replaced its 16th-century predecessor), the castle has plushly carpeted rooms with ancestral portraits, crystal chandeliers, and oak paneling. Bedrooms furnished in Regency style overlook the old Queen Anne stable yard. The vast suites have ruched drapes on the tall windows and Irish-Georgian antiques. Expect outstanding Continental cuisine in the formal, oak-wainscoted Earl of Thomond Restaurant; the Fig Tree restaurant is casual. ⊠ *Co. Clare* ☎ *061/368–144* 📠 *061/363–355* ⊕ *www.dromoland.ie* ⇝ *100 rooms with bath* ⟡ *2 restaurants, 18-hole golf course, 2 tennis courts, spa, fishing, bicycles, bar* ⊟ *AE, DC, MC, V* ⊣⊙⊢ *EP.*

$ ⨯⊡ **Hunter's Lodge.** A comfortable, unpretentious village pub, the lodge makes an ideal first or last stop if you're traveling to or from the west via Shannon Airport, 12 km (7 mi) down the road. The pub has an old-world style, with an open fire and a quiet local trade. Select pieces of old oak furniture fill the attractive, well-equipped guest rooms, and scatter rugs decorate the timber floors. The restaurant ($–$$), known for its cheerful service and simply prepared surf and turf, is a good value. ⊠ *The Square, Co. Clare* ☎ *061/368–577* 📠 *061/368–057* ⇝ *6 rooms with bath* ⟡ *Restaurant, bar, free parking* ⊟ *AE, DC, MC, V* ⊣⊙⊢ *BP.*

Sports & the Outdoors

Dromoland Golf Course (☎ 061/368–144) is one of the most scenic in the country, set in a 700-acre estate of rich woodland on the grounds of Dromoland Castle. The 18-hole, par-71 course has a natural lake that leaves little room for error on a number of holes.

Ennis

② *9½ km (6 mi) north of Newmarket-on-Fergus on N18, 37 km (23 mi) northwest of Limerick, 142 km (88 mi) north of Tralee.*

A major crossroads and a convenient stop between the west and the southwest, Ennis is the main town of County Clare, a pleasant market town with an attractively renovated, pedestrian-friendly center. Ennis has always fostered traditional arts, especially fiddle playing and step-dancing (a kind of square dance). The **Fleadh Nua** (pronounced fla-*nooa*) festival at the end of May attracts both performers and students of Irish music and serves as the venue for the National Dancing Championships.

Two **statues** in Ennis bear witness to the role its citizens have played in Irish democracy. On a tall limestone column above a massive pediment in the town center stands a **statue of Daniel O'Connell** (1775–1847), "The Liberator," who was a member of Parliament for County Clare between 1828 and 1831 and instrumental in bringing about Catholic Emancipation. Outside the courthouse (in the town park, beside the River Fergus, on the west side of Ennis) stands a larger-than-life bronze **statue of Eamon De Valera** (1882–1975), who successfully contested the election here in 1917, thus launching a long political career. He was the dominant figure in Irish politics during the 20th century, serving as prime minister for most of the years from 1937 until 1959, when he resigned as leader of Fianna Fáil, the party he founded, and went on to serve as president of Ireland until 1973. Although De Valera was born in the United States, his maternal forebears were from County Clare.

Where to Stay & Eat

$$ ✕⊡ **Lynch West County.** Catering successfully to both leisure and business travelers is this popular stopping point on the Limerick–Galway road (N18), a lively modern hostelry affiliated with Best Western. It's also just a five-minute walk from Ennis's town center. Rooms are ample; most overlook the car park but at least are quiet. Service is helpful and friendly despite the hotel's relatively large size. In July and August there's nightly Irish cabaret-style entertainment at the bar. Boru's Porterhouse ($–$$) serves traditional Irish fare, including local steak and seafood. ⊠ *Clare Rd., Co. Clare* ☎ *065/682–3000* 🖷 *065/682–3759* ⊕ *www.lynchotels.com* 🛏 *152 rooms with bath* ⌂ *Restaurant, 3 indoor pools, health club, fishing* ⊟ *AE, DC, MC, V* ⥾⦶ *BP.*

$$ ⊡ **Temple Gate.** Before its conversion, this lodging was a Gothic-style convent, and remnants of its previous existence (including the chapel, which is now a banquet hall) give character to this bright, modern hotel in the town center. Coordinated drapes and bedspreads in warm, earthy colors decorate the compact, well-equipped rooms, which have views of Ennis's historic center. Preacher's Bar is popular with locals, although the guest lounge is a country-house-style library. The entrance is via a cobblestoned courtyard adorned with Victorian street lamps. ⊠ *The Square, Co. Clare* ☎ *065/682–3300* 🖷 *065/692–3322* ⊕ *www.templegatehotel.com* 🛏 *70 rooms with bath* ⌂ *Restaurant, in-room data ports, bar, library* ⊟ *AE, DC, MC, V* ⥾⦶ *BP.*

Nightlife & the Arts

Although Ennis is not as fashionable as, say, Galway, it is one of the west's traditional-music hot spots. You're likely to hear sessions at the following pubs, but keep in mind that sessions don't necessarily take place every night and that the scene is constantly changing. Phone ahead to check whether a session is happening.

Cruise's (⊠ Abbey St. ☎ 065/684–1800). **Fawl's** (⊠ The Railway Bar, 69 O'Connell St. ☎ 065/682–4463). **Kerins'** (⊠ Lifford ☎ 065/682–0582). **Knox's** (⊠ Abbey St. ☎ 065/682–9264). **Poet's Corner Bar** (⊠ Old Ground Hotel, Main St. ☎ 065/682–8155). **Preachers** (⊠ The Temple Gate Hotel, The Square ☎ 065/682–3300).

Sports & the Outdoors

BICYCLING You can follow the scenic Burren Cycleway (69 km [43 mi]) to the famous Cliffs of Moher on a bike rented from **Tierney Cycles & Fishing** (⊠ 17 Abbey St. ☎ 065/682–9433 ⊕ www.ennisrentabike.com).

HORSEBACK
RIDING

Clare Equestrian Center (⊠ Doora, Clarecastle ☎ 065/684–0136) offers horseback riding by the hour on 60 acres of private land and adjacent quiet roads. You can also take a lesson in the indoor arena, and test your skill afterward on a cross-country course.

Shopping

Stop in at the **Antique Loft** (⊠ Clarecastle ☎ 065/684–1969) for collectibles and pine and mahogany antiques. The **Belleek Shop** (⊠ 36 Abbey St. ☎ 065/682–9607) carries Belleek china, Waterford crystal, and Donegal Parian china, as well as Lladró, Hummel, and other collectible china. **Carraig Donn** (⊠ 29 O'Connell St. ☎ 065/682–8188) sells its own line of knitwear.

Clare Craft and Design (⊠ 20 Parnell St. ☎ 065/684–4723) exhibits and sells art, pottery, and crafts produced by local artists. **The Rock Shop** (⊠ 2 O'Connell St. ☎ 065/682–2636) displays polished gemstones, fossils, and other rocks alongside jewelry and small sculptures in stone and marble. At the factory outlet **Shannon Crystal** (⊠ Sandfield Center, Galway Rd. ☎ 065/682–1250), craftspeople display the art of hand-cutting lead crystal.

Kilrush

❸ *43 km (27 mi) southwest of Ennis on N68.*

Like most other mid-19th-century towns in West Clare, Kilrush was laid out as a large central square radiating out into the town's main streets. The widest of these leads to the harbor and the docks. This plan makes the small market town (population 3,000) seem bigger than it actually is.

Scattery Island Ferries runs a 20-minute boat trip to **Scattery Island**, a picturesque destination that has a ruined 6th-century monastic settlement complete with round tower. Weather permitting, ferries depart up to four times daily in July and August and two times daily May through June and September. From May to early September, two-hour dolphin-watching trips run out to the Shannon Estuary, where a school of 40 or so bottle-nosed dolphins regularly plays. Call for departure times and to reserve a space. ⊠ *Kilrush Marina* ☎ *065/905–1327* ⌂ *Ferry to Scattery Island €10 round-trip, dolphin-watching cruise €16.*

Where to Stay

¢   🏠 **Bruach Na Coille.** Michael and Mary Clarke's two-story Georgian-style house, a family-run B&B, is across from the Kilrush woods, five minutes from the Killimer–Tarbert Ferry. Upon arrival, you're greeted with coffee, tea, and fresh-baked cakes. Bedrooms in the back of the house overlook Loop Head and the Shannon estuary; those in front have views of the countryside. Floral bedspreads and drapes and built-in wardrobes decorate the pastel guest rooms. After sampling the eggs, puddings, and soda bread of the complimentary Irish breakfast, you may want to skip lunch. The Kilrush woods are perfect for an after-dinner stroll. ⊠ *Killimer Rd., Co. Clare* ☎ *065/905–2250* 🖷 *065/905–2250* ⊕ *www.clarkekilrush.com* 🛏 *4 rooms, 2 with bath* 🖃 *No credit cards* ☾ *Closed Christmas wk* ⫧ *BP.*

Sports & the Outdoors

Kilrush Golf & Sports Club (⊠ Parknamoney, Ennis Rd. ☎ 065/905–1138) is an 18-hole, par-70 course with superb views of the Shannon estuary.

Kilkee

4 *12 km (7 mi) west of Kilrush on N68.*

Kilkee is one of the most beloved west-coast beach resorts among the Irish, many of whom have summered here for generations. Its major draw is its safe bathing—both in the waters along the magnificent, long, sandy beach and in deep rock pools known as Pollock holes, which remain full at low tide (they attract scuba divers as well as swimmers). From Kilkee, you can take an excursion to **Loop Head Lighthouse** on R487, about a 38-km (24-mi) round-trip. Loop Head is the westernmost point of County Clare—at the northern tip of the mouth of the Shannon, the very end of its long estuary.

Where to Stay

$ ⊞ **Thomond Guesthouse and Thalassotherapy Centre.** These facilities by the sea in Kilkee town center provide a rejuvenating break in the form of spa treatments. Among the treatments are seaweed baths, algae body wraps, and facials using products made of marine extracts. The guest rooms are small but comfortable. Most people who stay here come for a spa weekend, but rooms are also available even if you don't wish to partake in thalassotherapy. You may still, of course, feel tempted to get a massage or use the sauna. ⊠ *Grattan St., Co. Clare* ☎ *065/905–6742* 📠*065/905–6762* ⊕*www.kilkeethalasso.com* 🛏*5 rooms with bath* ⛄*In-room data ports, hair salon, sauna, spa, fishing; no kids under 16* ▭ *MC, V* ⊘ *Closed late Dec.–mid-Jan.* ⟦◯⟧ *BP.*

Sports & the Outdoors

The 18-hole, par-72 **Kilkee Golf and Country Club** (⊠ East End ☎ 065/ 905–6048), founded in 1896, overlooks the sea and has spectacular cliff-edge holes.

> **en route**   The main route heads north up the coast on N67. Sandy beaches and more Pollock holes can be found by taking a left off the main road at any sign that indicates STRAND and traveling for about 2½ km (1½ mi). One of the seaside towns worth visiting along this route is **Milltown Malbay,** an important center of traditional music and dancing, which take place informally in pubs and in the parish hall.

Lahinch

5 *47 km (30 mi) north of Kilkee on N67, 30 km (18 mi) west of Ennis on N85.*

Lahinch, a busy resort village beside a long, sandy beach backed by dunes, is best known for its links golf courses and—believe it or not—its surfing. In 1972, the European Surfing Finals were held here, putting Lahinch on the world surfing map, where it has stayed ever since. Tom and Rosemary Buckley's **Lahinch Surf Shop** (⊠ The Promenade ☎ 065/ 708–1543) is ground zero for County Clare surfers.

Where to Stay & Eat

$$ ✕⊞ **Burke's Armada Hotel.** The Armada majestically crowns the seaside cliffs near Spanish Point, just south of Lahinch, where the Spanish Armada was defeated in the 17th century. Storytellers and lovers of folklore use this event to explain the dark hair and eyes of so many inhabitants of the west. Bright, modern furnishings fill the large guest rooms, most of which have a double or two twin beds. The Cape Restaurant ($$–$$$), which serves fresh fish, is only 20 feet from land's end. The Flagship bar hosts a week of *ceilís* (Irish dancing and songs) in July. Ask about

holiday packages. ⊠ *Spanish Point, Milltown Malbay, Co. Clare* ☎ *065/ 708–4110* 🖷 *065/708–4632* ⊕ *www.burkesarmadahotel.com* ⇆ *61 rooms with bath* ♿ *Restaurant, bar* ⊟ *MC, V* ⊠⧉ *BP.*

$$$
Fodor'sChoice
★

🏠 **Moy House.** This 18th-century Italianate-style lodge sits amid 15 private acres on a cliff top that's a three-minute drive from Lahinch. It's a world away from the bustling seaside resort—a peaceful haven, with the air of a country house. Some rooms have open fires, six have stunning sea views, and two overlook the sheltered garden. Brocade curtains and Oriental rugs complement the guest rooms' Georgian and Victorian antiques in polished mahogany. The spacious, elegant drawing room has an "honesty bar"—help yourself and write it down. The cozy dining room (residents only) serves an imaginative four-course dinner of contemporary cuisine. ⊠ *Milltown Malbay Rd., Co. Clare* ☎ *065/ 708–2800* 🖷 *065/708–2500* ⊕ *www.moyhouse.com* ⇆ *9 rooms with bath* ♿ *Dining room, in-room data ports* ⊟ *AE, MC, V* ⊗ *Closed 1st 2 wks in Jan.* ⊠⧉ *BP.*

$$

🏠 **The Greenbrier Inn.** Location is everything. The Greenbrier Inn is a striking modern house 250 yards from the beach, town center, and championship golf course. Simple white linens and old-fashioned pine furnishings decorate the guest rooms, which, along with the bright, airy lounge, overlook the famous golf links and the Atlantic Ocean. The property is just a 30-minute drive to the Doonbeg golf course just south of Lahinch, which was designed by Greg Norman. ⊠ *Ennistymon Rd., Co. Clare* ☎ *065/708–1242* 🖷 *065/708–1247* ⊕ *www.greenbrierinn.com* ⇆ *14 rooms with bath* ⊟ *MC, V* ⊗ *Closed early Jan.–early Mar.* ⊠⧉ *BP.*

Nightlife & the Arts

For traditional music try the **19th Bar** (⊠ Main St. ☎ 065/708–1440). **O'Looney's** (⊠ The Promenade ☎ 065/708–1414) is known as Lahinch's surfers' pub; there's music every night in summer and Saturday nights in winter.

Sports & the Outdoors

Doonbeg Golf Club (⊠ Doonbeg, on main N67 between Lahinch and Ballybunion ☎ 065/905–5246), an 18-hole links course designed by Greg Norman, winds along 2½ km (1½ mi) of crescent-shape beach; the ocean is visible from almost every hole. The 6,613-yard, 18-hole, par-72 championship course at **Lahinch Golf Club** (⊠ The Seafront ☎ 065/ 708–1003), which opened in 1892, has challenging links that follow the natural contours of the dunes. The 18-hole, par-72 **Castle Course** (⊠ The Seafront ☎ 065/708–1003) is ideal for a carefree round of seaside golf, with shorter holes than the championship course at Lahinch Golf Club.

Shopping

The small **Design Lodge** (⊠ Main St. ☎ 065/708–1744) carries Irish-made goods, including sweaters, linen, tweed, and other gift items.

The Cliffs of Moher

★ ❻ *10 km (6 mi) northwest of Lahinch on R478.*

One of Ireland's most breathtaking natural sights, the majestic Cliffs of Moher rise vertically out of the sea in a wall that stretches over a long, 8-km (5-mi) swath and as high as 710 feet. Stratified deposits of five different rock layers are visible in the cliff face. Numerous seabirds, including a large colony of puffins, make their home in the shelves of rock on the cliffs. On a clear day you can see the Aran Islands and the mountains of Connemara to the north, as well as the lighthouse on Loop Head and the mountains of Kerry to the south. **O'Brien's Tower** is a defiant, broody sentinel built at the cliffs' highest point. The parking area is a favorite spot of performers; in the high season, there's likely to be free entertainment—step dancers, fiddle players, or even a one-man band. The **Visitor Centre**, a good refuge from passing rain squalls, has a gift shop and tearoom. ☎ 065/708–1565 ⊕ *www.shannonheritage.com* ✉ *Free, parking €2.50* ⊘ *Cliffs daily, 24 hrs; Visitor Centre daily 9:30–5:30; O'Brien's Tower Mar.–Oct., daily 9:30–5:30, weather permitting.*

Doolin

❼ *6 km (4 mi) north of the Cliffs of Moher on R479.*

A tiny village consisting almost entirely of B&Bs, hostels, pubs, and restaurants, Doolin is widely said to have three of the best pubs in Ireland for traditional music. But with the worldwide surge of interest in Irish music during the last decade, the village is more of a magnet for European musicians than it is for young, or even established, Irish artists. On **Doolin Pier**, about 1½ km (1 mi) outside the village, local fisherfolk sell their catch fresh off the boat—lobster, crayfish, salmon, and mackerel. From spring until early fall (weather permitting), a regular ferry service makes the 30-minute trip to Inisheer, the smallest of the Aran Islands.

Where to Stay & Eat

Because Doolin is known as a center of traditional music, it gets quite crowded with foreign visitors. If you're having trouble finding a room or you want to stay somewhere other than a B&B, you may want to follow the lead of many Irish vacationers, who tend to stay in nearby Lisdoonvarna, which is just 5 km (3 mi) away and has a wider selection of lodgings.

★ **$–$$$** ✕▦ **Ballinalacken Castle.** One hundred acres of wildflower meadows surround this Victorian lodge beside the 16th-century ruins of an O'Brien stronghold, about 1 km (½ mi) outside Doolin on the Lisdoonvarna road. Through the bay windows you can take in fine panoramic views of the Atlantic, the Aran Islands, and the Connemara hills. Some guest rooms have marble fireplaces and high ceilings. The public rooms are a mix of hand-me-downs and lovely old Irish oak. Local chef Frank Sheedy, who has cooked in some of Ireland's best restaurants, serves an imaginative and sophisticated Continental menu ($$$$) using local seafood, lamb, and beef. ✉ *Coast Rd., Co. Clare* ☎ *065/707–4025* 🖨 *065/707–4025* ⊕ *www.ballinalackencastle.com* ⇆ *12 rooms with bath* ♿ *Restaurant, bar* ▭ *AE, DC, MC, V* ⊘ *Closed early Oct.–mid-Apr.* ⍏◎ *BP.*

$–$$ ✕▦ **Aran View House.** Expect nothing less than magnificent views of the Aran Islands to the west, Doolin Pier and the Cliffs of Moher to the south, and the gray limestone rocks of the Burren to the north. The 1736 house on 100 acres of farmland is decorated with lovely antique touches, such as four-poster beds and Georgian reproduction furniture. You can savor the view from the restaurant's bay windows while enjoying the Continental cuisine ($$–$$$$), Regency chairs, and dusky pink napery. It's on the coast road in the Fanore direction, about a 10-minute walk from Doolin village. ✉ *Coast Rd., Co. Clare* ☎ *065/707–4061* 🖨 *065/707–4540* ⊕ *www.aranview.com* ⇆ *19 rooms with bath* ♿ *Restaurant, fishing, bar* ▭ *AE, DC, MC, V* ⊘ *Closed Nov.–mid-Apr.* ⍏◎ *BP.*

★ **$** ✕▦ **Cullinan's Seafood Restaurant and Guesthouse.** The small restaurant ($$–$$$) here, in the back of a traditional farmhouse, is famed for its fresh, simply prepared seafood, but vegetarian and meat dishes are also served. Local ingredients—Inagh goat cheese, Burren smoked salmon, Doolin crabmeat, and Aran scallops—form the basis of a light, imaginative menu. A €25 early-bird set menu is served from 6 to 7. The floor-to-ceiling windows on two sides of the restaurant overlook the Aille River. The cottage-style rooms have simple pine furniture, fresh cotton-covered comforters, and pleasant country views. Room televisions are available upon request. ✉ *Coast Rd., Co. Clare* ☎ *065/707–4183* 🖷 *065/707–4239* ⊕ *www.cullinansdoolin.com* ↩ *6 rooms with bath* ⚫ *Restaurant* 🖃 *MC, V* ⊘ *Guesthouse closed Christmas wk, restaurant closed Oct.–Easter* ⦿ *BP.*

Nightlife & the Arts

Doolin's three pubs are famous for their traditional-music sessions. They all serve simple bar food from midday until 9 (Irish stew is a good bet) and are designed to hold big crowds, which means you should expect minimal comfort: hard benches or bar stools if you're lucky, and "spit 'n' sawdust" flooring. The theory is that the music will be so good, you won't notice anything else. Interesting music-related memorabilia hangs on the walls. **Gus O'Connor's** (✉ Fisher St. ☎ 065/707–4168) sits midway between the village center and the pier and has tables outside near a stream. **McDermott's** (✉ Lisdoonvarna Rd. ☎ 065/707–4700) is popular with locals. Autumn through spring it's sometimes closed during the daytime. **McGann's** (✉ Lisdoonvarna Rd. ☎ 065/707–4133), across the road from McDermott's, is the smallest of Doolin's three famous pubs and has been run by the same family for 70 years.

Sports & the Outdoors

Cycle along the coast on a bike rented from **Patrick Moloney, Doolin Hostel** (✉ Coast Rd. ☎ 065/707–4006).

Shopping

★ **Doolin Crafts Gallery** (✉ Coast Rd. ☎ 065/707–4309), beside the cemetery and the church, carries only Irish-made goods: sweaters, modern lead crystal, linen, lace, and tweed. A jeweler's workshop and a resident batik maker are also on the premises. Don't miss the 1-acre garden, which has more than 600 plants from all over the world. The garden and the Flagship Restaurant are open daily Easter through September.

Lisdoonvarna

❽ *5 km (3 mi) east of Doolin on R478.*

One of only three spa towns in Ireland (the others are Enniscrone, in western County Sligo, and Ballybunion, in County Kerry), Lisdoonvarna has several sulfurous and iron-bearing springs with radioactive properties, all containing iodine. In the late 19th century the town grew to accommodate visitors who wanted to "take the waters." The buildings reflect a mishmash of mock architectural styles: Scottish baronial, Swiss chalet, Spanish hacienda, and American motel. Depending on your taste, it's either lovably kitschy or just plain tacky.

In July and August, Lisdoonvarna is a favorite getaway for Irish under-30s. It's also the traditional vacationing spot for the west's bachelor farmers, who used to congregate here at harvest time in late September with the vague intention of finding wives. (Irish farmers are notoriously shy with women and reluctant to marry, often postponing the event until their mid- or late fifties, if ever.) This tradition is now formalized in the Matchmaking Festival, held during late September. Middle-aged singles dance to the strains of country-and-western bands, and a talent contest is held to name the most eligible bachelor.

If you're curious about health cures, the **Lisdoonvarna Spa and Bath House** is worth a visit. Iron and magnesia elements make the drinking water taste terrible (as does most spa water), but the bathing water is pleasant, if enervating. Electric sulfur baths, massage, wax baths, a sauna, and a solarium are available at the spa complex, which is on the edge of town in an attractive parkland setting. ⊠ *Town Park* ☎ *065/707–4023* 🎟 *Complex free, sulfur baths €6.50 (book in advance)* ⊘ *Early June–early Oct., daily 10–6.*

Where to Stay & Eat

★ **$–$$** ✕🖪 **Sheedy's Restaurant and Country Inn.** A 17th-century farmhouse just a short walk from the town center and the spa wells has been converted into this small, friendly hotel. It's been in the hands of the Sheedy family since 1855. Proprietor John Sheedy, who was chef de cuisine at Ashford Castle until moving back home, makes creative use of local produce in contemporary French-Irish fare ($$–$$$). The informal Seafood Bar in the foyer serves simple dishes: crab claws in garlic butter, local smoked salmon, and seafood platters. The simple but stylish guest rooms have restful views of the surrounding countryside. ⊠ *Spa Rd., Co. Clare* ☎ *065/707–4026* 🖨 *065/707–4555* ⊕ *www.sheedyscountryhouse.com* 🖙 *11 rooms with bath* 🖒 *Restaurant, bar* ⊟ *MC, V* ⊘ *Closed Oct.–mid-Mar.* ❑| *BP.*

$ ✕🖪 **Carrigann.** Hikers, who come for the guided walks and independent exploration, love this small, friendly hotel, ensconced in trim, pretty gardens, and just a 2-minute walk from the village center. Hosts Mary and Gerard Howard keep a library of special-interest books on the Burren beside the turf fire in the sitting room; their maps and notes are also available. Rooms are modestly furnished but well equipped for the price range. Gerard also runs his own butcher shop, guaranteeing top-quality meat on the hotel's Continental menu ($$–$$$). Meals are supplemented by herbs from the garden and fresh local fish. ⊠ *Carrigann Rd., Co. Clare* ☎ *065/707–4036* 🖨 *065/707–4567* ⊕ *www.gateway-to-the-burren.com* 🖙 *20 rooms with bath* 🖒 *Restaurant, fishing* ⊟ *MC, V* ⊘ *Closed Nov.–Feb.* ❑| *BP.*

Nightlife & the Arts

Country music and ballad singing are popular in the bars of Lisdoonvarna. For traditional music try the **Roadside Tavern** (⊠ Doolin Rd. ☎ 065/707–4084).

Shopping

To see an audiovisual presentation on smoking Atlantic salmon, plus live demonstrations of the oak-smoking process, visit the **Burren Smokehouse Ltd.** (⊠ Ballyvaughan Rd. ☎ 065/707–4432). Neatly packaged whole sides of salmon, organic treats, and unusual crafts are for sale.

The Burren

★ ❾ *Extending throughout western County Clare from the Cliffs of Moher in the south to Black Head in the north, as far southeast as Corofin.*

As you travel north toward Ballyvaughan, the landscape becomes rockier and stranger. Instead of the seemingly ubiquitous Irish green, gray becomes the prevailing color. You're now in the heart of the Burren, a 300-square-km (116-square-mi) expanse that is one of Ireland's fiercest landscapes. The Burren is aptly named: it's an Anglicization of the Irish word *bhoireann* (a rocky place). Stretching off in all directions, as far as the eye can see, are vast, irregular slabs of fissured limestone, known as karst, with deep cracks between them. From a distance, it looks like a lunar landscape, so dry that nothing could possibly grow on it. But in the spring (especially from mid-May to mid-June), the Burren becomes a wild rock garden as an astonishing variety of wildflowers blooms between the cracks in the rocks, among them at least 23 native species of orchid. The Burren also supports an incredible diversity of wildlife, including frogs, newts, lizards, badgers, stoats, sparrow hawks, kestrels, and dozens of other birds and animals.

The wildflowers and other plants are given life from the spectacular caves, streams, and potholes that lie beneath the rough, scarred pavements. With the advent of spring, *turloughs* (seasonal lakes that disappear in dry weather) appear on the plateau's surface. Botanists are particularly intrigued by the cohabitation of Arctic and Mediterranean plants, many so tiny (and rare, so please do not pick any) you can't see them from your car window; make a point of exploring some of this rocky terrain on foot. Numerous signposted walks run through both coastal and inland areas. For a private guided tour, contact Mary Angela Keane (☎ 065/707–4003; €31.70 per hour), or Shane Connolly of Burren Hill Walks (☎ 065/707–7168; €12.70 per person). May and June are peak months for flora, but a tour is worthwhile at any time of year.

The tiny **Burren Centre** has a modest audiovisual display and other exhibits that explain the Burren's geology, flora, and archaeology. Also here are a café and a crafts shop with good maps and locally published guides. ⊠ *Kilfenora, 8 km (5 mi) southeast of Lisdoonvarna on R476* ☎ *065/708–8030* ⊕ *www.theburrencentre.ie* ☜ *€5* ☉ *Mid-Mar.–May, Sept., and Oct., daily 10–5; June–Aug., daily 9:30–6.*

Beside the Burren Centre in Kilfenora, the ruins of a small 12th-century church, once the **Cathedral of St. Fachtna,** have been partially restored as a parish church. There are some interesting carvings in the roofless choir, including an unusual, life-size human skeleton. In a field about 165 feet west of the ruins is an elaborately sculpted high cross that is worth examining, even though parts of it are badly weathered.

Nightlife & the Arts

Vaughan's Pub (⊠ Main St., Kilfenora ☎ 065/708–8004) is known for its traditional-music sessions.

Ballyvaughan

⑩ *16 km (10 mi) north of Lisdoonvarna on N67.*

A pretty little waterside village and a good base for exploring the Burren, Ballyvaughan attracts walkers and artists who enjoy the views of Galway Bay and access to the Burren. **Aillwee Cave** is the only such chamber in the region accessible to those who aren't spelunkers. This vast 2-million-year-old cave is illuminated for about 3,300 feet and contains an underground river and waterfall. ⊠ *5 km (3 mi) south of Ballyvaughan on R480* ☎ *065/707–7036* ⊕ *www.aillweecave.ie* ☜ *€8* ☉ *Jan.–June and Sept.–Dec., daily 10–6 (last tour at 5:30); July and Aug., daily 10–7 (last tour at 6:30).*

Where to Stay & Eat

★ **$$–$$$** ✕🏠 **Gregan's Castle Hotel.** The Haden family runs this quiet, meticulous, large Victorian country house at the base of the aptly named Corkscrew Hill (on N67, midway between Ballyvaughan and Lisdoonvarna). The house is surrounded by gardens and overlooks Galway Bay and the gray mountains of the Burren. Georgian and Victorian antiques fill the individually decorated bedrooms lined with wallpaper based on William Morris designs. The spacious rooms on the ground floor have private patio gardens but lack the splendid views of the rooms upstairs. Ask about special deals for three-day stays. The restaurant ($$$–$$$$; jacket and tie required) serves updated French cuisine. ⊠ *Base of Corkscrew Hill, Co. Clare* ☎ *065/707–7005* 🖶 *065/707–7111* ⊕ *www.*

gregans.ie 🛏 *18 rooms with bath, 4 suites* ♨ *Restaurant, fishing, bicycles, croquet, bar; no room TVs* 🗖 *AE, MC, V* ⊘ *Closed Nov.–Mar.* ¶◎¶ *BP.*

$ ✕🖬 **Hyland's Hotel.** A turf fire greets you in the lobby of the hotel, which is considered an artist's haven. This family-run, yellow-and-red coaching inn, in the heart of the Burren, dates from the early 18th century. Rooms vary in size and shape, but all have pine furniture and color-coordinated drapes and spreads. Ask for a room overlooking the Burren. The restaurant ($$), cheerfully decorated with country pine and red tablecloths, specializes in simply prepared local produce. The bar hosts live music most nights from June to mid-September, and Irish storytelling once a week. Ask about special weekend rates. ⊠ *Main St., Co. Clare* ☎ *065/707–7037* 🖷 *065/707–7131* 🛏 *30 rooms with bath* ♨ *Restaurant, bar* 🗖 *AE, DC, MC, V* ¶◎¶ *BP.*

¢ ✕🖬 **Admiral's Rest.** You can guess from the nautical bric-a-brac that this place belongs to a retired naval man—John Macnamara, an expert on the Burren's wildlife. In a modernized cottage on the coast road between Lisdoonvarna and Ballyvaughan, the restaurant ($–$$$) is across the street from the sea, which is visible through the large windows. Varnished stone floors, stone-topped tables, *súgán* (rope-seated) chairs, and an open wood-and-turf fire make up the rugged furnishings. Seafood is the mainstay here, including lobster, and there is also a Thai menu. The bungalow next door holds nine B&B rooms with shared baths. ⊠ *Coast Rd. Fanore, Co. Clare* ☎ *065/707–6105* 🖷 *065/707–6161* 🛏 *9 rooms* 🗖 *AE, MC, V* ¶◎¶ *BP* ⊘ *Closed Nov.–Easter.*

Nightlife & the Arts

Fodor'sChoice ★ The friendly **Monk's Pub** (⊠ *Main St.* ☎ *065/707–7059*), near the waterfront, hosts great sessions of traditional and folk music. The bar food is excellent.

> **en route** From Ballyvaughan, it's a 48-km (30-mi) trip circumnavigating Galway Bay to Galway City. If you're eager to get there, skip the next two towns and head there directly, first passing through Kinvara. If you're on a more leisurely pace, head back south through the Burren on R480 and R476 to Corofin.

Corofin

⓫ *23 km (14 mi) south of Ballyvaughan, 16 km (10 mi) east of Kilfenora on R476.*

Corofin's **Clare Heritage and Geneaogical Center** has a genealogical service and advice for do-it-yourselfers searching for their Irish roots. Displays on the history of the west of Ireland in the 19th century cover culture, traditions, emigration, and famine, and also expose some grim statistics. In 1841, for example, the population of County Clare was 286,394. Fifty years later, famine and emigration had reduced this number to 112,334, and the population continued to decline, reaching an all-time low of 73,597 in 1956. (It is now heading back to the 90,000 mark.) ⊠ *Main St.* ☎ *065/683–7955* 🌐 *www.clareroots.com* 🎫 *€3* ⊘ *Apr.–Oct., weekdays 9:30–5:30; Nov.–Mar. by appointment.*

A 15th-century castle on the edge of Corofin houses the **Clare Archaeology Centre,** which has an exhibition on the antiquities of the Burren. Twenty-five monuments stand within a 1½-km (1-mi) radius of the castle; these date from the Bronze Age to the 19th century, and all are described at the center. ⊠ *Dysert O'Dea Castle* ☎ *065/683–7722* 🎫 *€4* ⊘ *Daily 10–6.*

Coole Park

🔞 *24 km (15 mi) northeast of Corofin on N18.*

Coole Park, on the left side north of the little town of Gort, was once the home of Lady Augusta Gregory (1859–1932), patron of W. B. Yeats (1865–1939) and cofounder with the poet of Dublin's Abbey Theatre. Yeats visited here often, as did almost all the other writers who contributed to the Irish literary revival in the first half of the 20th century, including George Bernard Shaw (1856–1950) and Sean O'Casey (1880–1964). Douglas Hyde (1860–1949), the first president of Ireland, was also a visitor. The house fell derelict after Lady Gregory's death and was demolished in 1941; the grounds are now a national forest and wildlife park. Picnic tables make this a lovely alfresco lunch spot. The only reminder of its literary past is the Autograph Tree, a copper beech on which many of Lady Gregory's famous guests carved their initials. There's also a visitor center with displays on Lady Gregory and Yeats. ⊠ *Galway Rd.* ☎ *091/631–804* ✉ *Park free, visitor center €2.75* ☉ *Park daily 10–dusk; visitor center Apr.–mid-June, Tues.–Sun. 10–5; mid-June–Aug., daily 9:30–6:30; Sept., daily 10–5.*

Thoor Ballylee

🔞 *5 km (3 mi) north of Coole Park, signposted from N66.*

Thoor Ballylee is a sight Yeats fans won't want to miss. (It's one of the few major Yeats-affiliated sights in the west that's not in County Sligo.) In his fifties and newly married, Yeats bought this 14th-century Norman tower as a ruin in 1916 for £35 (about €44). The tower stands beside a whitewashed, thatched-roof cottage, with a tranquil stream running alongside it. Its proximity to Lady Gregory's house at Coole Park made this a desirable location, though it required significant work on Yeats's part to make the ruin livable. He stayed here intermittently until 1929 and penned some of his more mystical works here, including *The Tower* and *The Winding Stair*. It's now fully restored with his original furnishings. The audiovisual display is a useful introduction to the poet and his times. ⊠ *N66 3 mi outside of Gort* ☎ *091/631–436* ✉ *€5* ☉ *Easter–Sept., Mon.–Sat. 10–6.*

Kinvara

🔞 *13½ km (8 mi) east of Ballyvaughan, 15 km (9 mi) northwest of Gort on N67, 25 km (15½ mi) south of Galway City.*

The picture-perfect village of Kinvara is a growing holiday base, thanks to its gorgeous bayside locale, great walking and sea angling, and numerous pubs. It's well worth a visit, whether you're coming from Ballyvaughan or from Gort. Kinvara is best known for its long-standing early August sailing event, Cruinniú na mBád (Festival of the Gathering of the Boats), in which traditional brown-sailed Galway hookers laden with turf race across the bay. Hookers were used until the early part of this century to carry turf, provisions, and cattle across Galway Bay and out to the Aran Islands. A sculpture in Galway's Eyre Square honors their local significance.

On a rock to the north of Kinvara Bay, the 16th-century **Dunguaire Castle** commands all the approaches from Galway Bay. It is said to stand on the site of a 7th-century castle built by the King of Connaught. One of its previous owners, Oliver St. John Gogarty, was a surgeon, man of letters, and model for James Joyce's Buck Mulligan, a character in *Ulysses*. Today Dunguaire is used for a medieval-style banquet that honors local writers and others with ties to the west, including Lady Gregory, W. B. Yeats, Sean O'Casey, and Pádraic O'Conaire. ⊠ *West Village* ☎ *091/637–108* ⊞ *Castle €5, banquet €47.50* ⊙ *May–Sept., daily 9:30–5; banquet at 5:30 and 8:30.*

Where to Stay & Eat

$–$$$ ✕ **Moran's Oyster Cottage.** Signposted off the main road on the south side of Clarinbridge, this waterside thatched cottage, the home of the Moran family since 1760, houses a simply furnished restaurant at the back that serves only seafood. It's *the* place to stop to sample the local oysters, grown on a bed in front of the restaurant. ⊠ *The Weir, Kilcolgan* ☎ *091/796–113* 🖷 *091/796–503* ⊟ *AE, MC, V.*

$ ✕⌨ **Merriman Inn.** Don't let its traditional looks deceive you: this white-washed, thatched inn on the shores of Galway Bay is in fact a midsize hotel, decorated with locally made, well-designed furniture, and original crafts, paintings, and sculpture. The relaxed, friendly bar and lounge both have open fires. Guest rooms are quiet and well equipped. The Quilty Room is a large, airy restaurant ($–$$$). The French-influenced menu highlights local seafood—such as tournedos of salmon pan-seared with a confit of fennel and a sharp, spicy jus—but you can also try succulent local lamb. ⊠ *Main St., Co. Galway* ☎ *091/638–222* 🖷 *091/637–686* ⊕ *www.merrimanhotel.com* 🛏 *32 rooms with bath* ⚭ *Restaurant, bar, meeting room* ⊟ *AE, DC, MC, V* ⊙ *Closed Jan.–mid-Mar.* ⑩ *BP.*

¢–$ ⌨ **Burren View Farm.** A million-dollar view awaits you at this yellow, two-story B&B on the edge of Galway Bay, 5 km (3 mi) west of Kinvara. Set on a working sheep and cattle farm, the B&B is relatively isolated amid stone-walled fields dotted with sheep. The breakfast room, sun lounge, and front bedrooms look out across a wide sea inlet to the gray expanse of the Burren. Rooms are plain and homey but clean and well maintained. Wholesome evening meals, Irish or Continental style, are cooked on request, and food is also available in the local pub, a 5-minute walk away. ⊠ *Doorus, Co. Galway* ☎ *091/637–142* 🖷 *091/ 638–131* 🛏 *5 rooms, 2 with bath* ⚭ *Dining room, tennis court, fishing* ⊟ *AE, DC, MC, V* ⊙ *Closed Nov.–Mar.* ⑩ *BP.*

Nightlife & the Arts

The first weekend in May, Kinvara hosts the annual **Cuckoo Fleadh** (⊠ Main St. ☎ 091/637–145), a traditional-music festival. Traditional music is played most nights at the **Winkles Hotel bar** (⊠ The Square ☎ 91/ 637–137), where Sharon Shannon got her start in the music business.

GALWAY CITY

25 km (15½ mi) north of Kinvara, 219 km (136 mi) west of Dublin, 105 km (65 mi) north of Limerick.

Galway is often said to be a state of mind as much as it is a specific place. The largest city in the west today (population 60,000) and the ancient capital of the province of Connaught, Galway is also one of the fastest-growing cities in Europe. It's an astonishing fact, and you have to wonder where this city can possibly grow. For despite Galway's size, its heart is *tiny*—a warren of streets so compact that if you spend more than a few hours here, you'll soon be strolling along with the sort of easy familiarity you'd feel in your hometown.

For many Irish people, Galway is a favorite weekend getaway, the liveliest place in the Republic, and the city of festivals. It's also a university town: University College Galway (or UCG as it's locally known) is a center for Gaelic culture (Galway marks the eastern gateway to the west's large Gaeltacht). A fair share of UCG's 9,000 students pursue their studies in the Irish language. Galway is, in fact, permeated by youth culture. On festival weekends, you'll see as many pierced and tattooed teenagers and twentysomethings here as you'd find at a rock concert.

But its students aren't its only avant-garde, as Galway has long attracted writers, artists, and musicians. The last keep the traditional-music pubs lively year-round. And the city's two small but internationally acclaimed theater companies draw a steady stream of theater people.

Although you're not conscious of it when you're in the center of town, Galway is spectacularly situated, on the north shore of Galway Bay, where the River Corrib flows from Lough Corrib out into the sea. The seaside suburb of Salthill, on the south-facing shore of Galway Bay, has spectacular vistas across the vividly blue bay to Black Head on the opposite shore.

Galway's founders were Anglo-Normans who arrived in the mid-13th century and fortified their settlement against "the native Irish," as local chieftains were called. Galway became known as "the City of the Tribes" because of the dominant role in public and commercial life of the 14 families that founded it. Their names are still common in Galway and elsewhere in Ireland: Athy, Blake, Bodkin, Browne, D'Arcy, Dean, Font, French, Kirwan, Joyce, Lynch, Morris, Martin, and Skerret. The city's medieval heritage, a fusion of Gaelic and Norman influences, is apparent in the intimate two- and three-story stucco buildings, the winding streets, the narrow passageways, and the cobblestones underfoot.

Galway's growth and popularity mean that at its busiest moments, pedestrians jam-pack its narrow, one-way streets, while cars are gridlocked. If there's a city that doesn't sleep in Ireland, this is it. In fact, if you want to be guaranteed a quiet night's sleep, either ask for a room in the back of your center-city hotel or simply stay outside of town.

Exploring Galway City

Most of the city's sights, aside from the cathedral and the university campus, can be found in a narrow sector of the medieval town center that runs from Eyre Square in a southwesterly direction to the River Corrib. Eyre Square is easily recognizable, as it is the only green space in central Galway. It only takes five minutes to walk straight down Galway's main shopping street, the continuation of the north side of Eyre Square, to the River Corrib, where it ends (note that the name of this street changes several times). Not only is the city center compact, it is also largely pedestrianized, so the best way to explore it is on foot. Even the farthest point, the university campus, is less than a 15-minute walk from Eyre Square. A walk to Galway's seaside suburb, Salthill, 3 km (2 mi) west of Galway, and its long seaside promenade, is a favorite local occupation, traditionally undertaken on a Sunday afternoon; for this excursion you may prefer to take the car.

a good walk

Orient yourself at **Eyre Square** ⑮ ☞, part of which is occupied by Kennedy Park. Before you really get going, you may want to stop in at the **Tourist Information Office** ⑯ off the northeast corner of the square. At the top (north side) of Eyre Square, turn left down Williamsgate Street. This is the spine of old Galway. Its name changes four times before the street reaches the River Corrib: It's successively called William Street, Shop Street, High Street, and Quay Street. If you have any postcards to mail, you may want to stop at the General Post Office, on the left side of Eglinton Street, the first right off Williamsgate Street. At the corner of William and Shop streets, **Lynch's Castle** ⑰ is one of Galway's oldest buildings. Continue down Shop Street to the pedestrian way just beyond Abbeygate Street; here **Lynch Memorial Window** ⑱ and **Collegiate Church of St. Nicholas** ⑲ are adjacent to one another. James Joyce fans might want to make a brief detour across Lombard and Market streets to Bowling Green, site of the **Nora Barnacle House** ⑳.

It's a minute's walk from the church to **Tiġ Neaćhtain** ㉑ (Naughton's in English, pronounced *knock*-tons), a pub popular with locals, that stands at the corner of Cross Street and Quay/High Street. This corner is the very heart of old Galway's main historic and commercial district: Nearly all the city's best restaurants, bars, boutiques, art galleries, crafts shops, antiques stores, and bookstores line the narrow, winding streets and alleys in this vicinity. Nothing is more than a 5-minute walk from anything else. If this area is bursting at the seams, you may want to head one block to the east of Shop/High Street, between Abbeygate and Cross streets, to the quieter Middle Street, which has a number of worthwhile stores and restaurants, as well as the national Irish-language theater.

The **Spanish Arch** ㉒ and the **Galway City Museum** ㉓ are adjacent, right on the river's east bank, across from the Jurys Galway Inn parking lot. Just beyond Jurys but before crossing the Wolfe Tone Bridge, turn right onto the pedestrian path that parallels the river. Follow it past the William O'Brien Bridge to the **Salmon Weir Bridge** ㉔ (you'll need to jog off the path onto Abbeygate Street just short of the bridge to gain access to it). As you cross the bridge, look ahead to the **Cathedral of Our Lady Assumed into Heaven and St. Nicholas** ㉕, known locally simply as "the cathedral." A 5-minute walk northwest along University Road brings you to **University College Galway** ㉖. For a pretty stroll back to the center of town, turn right onto Canal Road and follow it back to the intersection of Dominick Street, Fairhill, and Raven Terrace. From here it's a brief stroll to Claddagh Quay, which will take you out to the **Claddagh** ㉗ district. If you've come this far, you may want to continue on to **Salthill** ㉘; otherwise, head back to the center of town.

TIMING You could easily complete this walk in a morning or afternoon (minus the walk out to Salthill), although if you browse in stores, chat with locals, or stop off for a pint or a cup of tea, you could stretch it out into a *very* leisurely all-day excursion. You may want to plan your day so you hit only what most interests you, leaving time to explore along the bay, get out to Salthill, or take a bay cruise.

What to See

㉕ **Cathedral of Our Lady Assumed into Heaven and St. Nicholas.** On Nun's Island, an island forming the west bank of the River Corrib beside the Salmon Weir Bridge, stands Galway's largest Catholic church, dedicated by Cardinal Cushing of Boston in 1965. The cathedral was built on the site of the old Galway jail; a white cross embedded into the pavement of the adjacent parking lot marks the site of the cemetery that stood beside the prison. ⌧ *Free* ☉ *Freely accessible.*

㉗ **Claddagh.** On the west bank of the Corrib estuary, this district was once an Irish-speaking fishing village outside the walls of the old town. The name is an Anglicization of the Irish *cladach,* which means "marshy ground." It retained a strong, separate identity until the 1930s, when its traditional thatched cottages were replaced by a conventional housing plan and its unique character and traditions were largely lost. One thing has survived: the Claddagh ring, composed of two hands clasped around a heart with a crown above it (symbolizing love, friendship, and loyalty), is still used by many Irish people as a wedding ring. Traditionally, the ring, which is often passed down from mother to daughter, is worn with the heart facing into you if you're married or otherwise unavail-

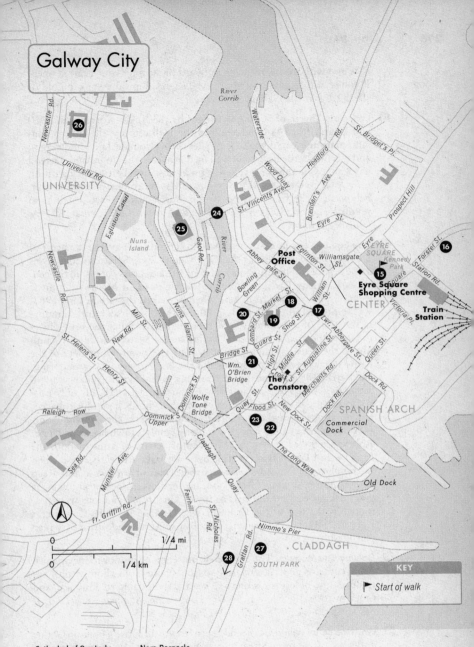

Galway City

River Corrib

Newcastle Rd.

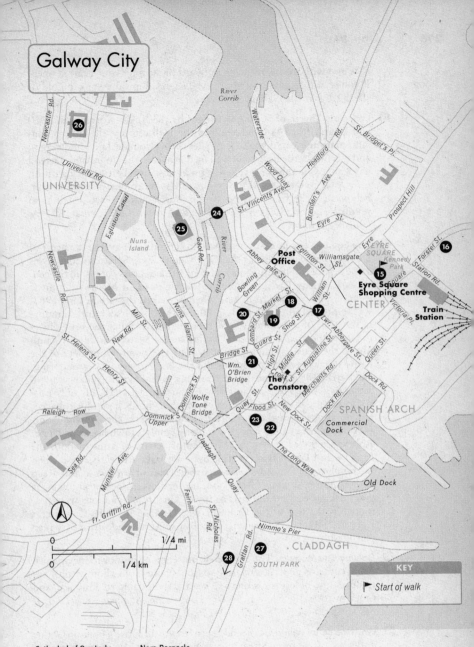

26

University Rd.

UNIVERSITY

Eglinton Canal

Nuns Island

Newcastle Rd.

Waterside

Wood Quay

St. Vincents Ave.

Headford Rd.

St. Bridget's Pl.

Prospect Hill

Forster St.

St. Bridget's Pl.

16

24 Salmon Weir Bridge

25

Gaol Rd.

River Corrib

Abbeygate St.

Bowling Green

Post Office

Eglinton St.

Williamsgate St.

Eyre St.

EYRE SQUARE

Kennedy Park

Eyre Square

15

Eyre Square Shopping Centre

CENTER

Victoria Pl.

Queen St.

Forster St.

Station Rd.

Train Station

Mill St.

New Rd.

Nuns Island St.

20

Lombard St.

Market St.

Shop St.

William St.

18

19

17

St. Helens St.

Henry St.

Bridge St.

Dominick St.

Guard St.

High St.

Middle St.

Cross St.

St. Augustine St.

Lwr. Abbeygate St.

Dock Rd.

Dock Rd.

Wm. O'Brien Bridge

21

Wolfe Tone Bridge

The Cornstore

Merchants Rd.

SPANISH ARCH

Commercial Dock

Raleigh Row

Dominick St. Upper

Sea Rd.

Munster Ave.

Claddagh

Quay

Flood St.

New Dock St.

23

22

The Long Walk

Old Dock

Fairhill

St. Nicholas Rd.

Fr. Griffin Rd.

0   1/4 mi

0   1/4 km

Grattan Rd.

Nimmo's Pier

28

27

CLADDAGH

SOUTH PARK

KEY
▶ *Start of walk*

able and with the heart facing outward (indicating your heart is open) if you're still looking for Mr. or Ms. Right. Reproductions in gold or silver are favorite Galway souvenirs.

⑲ Collegiate Church of St. Nicholas. Built by the Anglo-Normans in 1320 and enlarged in 1486 and again in the 16th century, the church contains many fine carvings and gargoyles dating from the late Middle Ages, and it is one of the best-preserved medieval churches in Ireland. Legend has it that Columbus prayed here on his last stop before setting off on his voyage to the New World. On Saturday mornings, a street market, held in the pedestrian way beside the church, attracts two dozen or so vendors and hundreds of shoppers. ⊠ *Lombard St., Center* ☎ *Free* ☉ *Daily 8–dusk.*

▶ ⑮ Eyre Square. The largest open space in central Galway and the heart of the city, on the east side of the River Corrib, Eyre Square encompasses a hodgepodge of monuments and concrete and grassy areas. In the center is **Kennedy Park,** a patch of lawn named in honor of John F. Kennedy, who spoke from here when he visited the city in June 1963. At the north end of the park, a 20-foot-high steel sculpture standing in the pool of a fountain represents the brown sails seen on Galway hookers, the area's traditional sailing boats. Seated beside this sculpture is the genial stone figure of Pádraic O'Conaire, a pioneer of the Irish-language revival at the turn of the last century who was born in Galway in 1882 (his birthplace fronting on the docks is marked with a plaque). When he died in a Dublin hospital in 1928, his only possessions were his pipe (a replica of which he holds here), his tobacco, and an apple. Now the entrance to Kennedy Park, the **Browne Doorway** was taken in 1905 from the Browne family's town house on Upper Abbeygate Street; it has the 17th-century coats of arms of both the Browne and Lynch families, called a "marriage stone" because when the families were joined in marriage their coats of arms were, too. Keep an eye out for similar if less elaborate versions of the entranceway as you walk around the old part of town. The **bronze cannons** were presented at the end of the Crimean War (1853–56) to the Connaught Rangers, a legendary regiment of the British Army made up of Irish men recruited from the west of Ireland.

㉓ Galway City Museum. The city's civic museum, next door to the Spanish Arch, contains materials relating to local history: old photographs, antiquities (the oldest is a stone axe head carbon-dated to 3500 BC), and other historical gewgaws. ⊠ *The Long Walk, Spanish Arch* ☎ *091/ 567–641* ☎ *€1.50* ☉ *Daily 10–1 and 2:15–5:15.*

⑱ Lynch Memorial Window. Embedded in a stone wall above a built-up Gothic doorway off Market Street, the window marks the spot where, according to legend, James Lynch FitzStephen, mayor of Galway in the early 16th century, condemned his son to death after he confessed to murdering a Spanish sailor who had stolen his girlfriend. When no one could be found to carry out the execution, Judge Lynch hanged his son himself, ensuring that justice prevailed, before retiring into seclusion. ⊠ *Market St., Center.*

⑰ Lynch's Castle. Now a branch of the Allied Irish Banks, this is the finest remaining example in Galway of a 16th-century fortified house—fortified because neighboring Irish tribes persistently raided the village, whose commercial life excluded them. Decorative details on its stone lintels are usually found only in southern Spain. Like the Spanish Arch, it serves as a reminder of the close trading links that once existed between Galway and Spain. ⊠ *Shop St., Center.*

LITTLE EYE-OPENERS

WHILE GALWAY *contains many grandiose monuments, it also holds many obscure yet fascinating relics— things that are only glimpsed on foot by visitors whose eyes aren't too fogged after the previous night's late session.*

Footscrapers: *In the 18th century, many areas of the city were unpaved and very mucky in wet weather. Gadgets called footscrapers became popular outside the front doors of prosperous houses, enabling guests to divest themselves of the street ooze before entering. The best examples of these cast-iron contraptions are on either side of the main door of the Great Southern Hotel in Eyre Square.* **Jostle stones:** *These small conical stones were placed at corners of narrow lanes and gateways to prevent carriage drivers from cutting corners too closely and breaking their wheels. One still remains outside*

Eason's bookshop on Church Lane. **Mermaids:** *Galway has more carvings of these sea nymphs than anywhere else in Ireland, and some fine examples can be seen in the windows of Collegiate Church of St. Nicholas on Lombard Street. Local historian Jim Higgins's book* Irish Mermaids *documents the many myths surrounding these creatures, including one that dubbed the sighting of a mermaid as a warning of a crime committed and a portent of severe bad luck.* **Marriage stones:** *Over many doorways are stone plaques bearing two interlinked coats of arms. The plaques commemorate marriages between the leading Galway families.* **Water troughs:** *One flower-filled example of these stone creations remains at the entrance to the Fairgreen car park in Forster Street.*

㉒ Nora Barnacle House. On June 16, 1904, James Joyce (1882–1941) had his first date with Nora Barnacle, who would later become his wife. He subsequently chose to set *Ulysses* on this day, now known universally as Bloomsday—"a recognition of the determining effect upon his life of his attachment to her," as Joyce's biographer Richard Ellman has said. Nora, the daughter of a poor baker, was born here. Today it has a modest collection of photographs, letters, and memorabilia, and a small gift shop. ⊠ *4 Bowling Green, Center* ☎ *091/564–743* ☒ *€1.30* ☉ *Mid-May–mid-Sept., Mon.–Sat. 10–5; mid-Sept.–mid-May by appointment.*

★ **㉔ Salmon Weir Bridge.** The bridge itself is nothing special, but in season— from mid-April to early July—shoals of salmon are visible from its deck as they lie in the clear river water before making their way upstream to the spawning grounds of Lough Corrib. ⊠ *West end of St. Vincent's Ave., Center.*

㉘ Salthill. This village 3 km (2 mi) west of Galway is a lively, hugely popular seaside resort with its own fun palace. Its promenade is the traditional place "to sit and watch the moon rise over Claddagh, and see the sun go down on Galway Bay"—as Bing Crosby used to croon in the city's most famous song.

㉒ Spanish Arch. Built in 1584 to protect the quays where Spanish ships unloaded cargoes of wines and brandies, the arch now stands in the parking lot opposite Jurys Galway Inn. It's easily (and often) mistaken for a pile of weathered stones, yet it's another reminder of Galway's—and Ireland's—past links with Spain. ⊠ *The Long Walk, Spanish Arch.*

㉑ Tig Neachtain (Naughton's Pub). You can hear traditional music every night at this popular pub, which stands at a busy little crossroads in the heart of the old town. Grab a spot at one of its old-fashioned partitioned snugs

Fodor'sChoice
★

at lunchtime for an inexpensive selection of imaginative bar food. It's a good place to mingle with local actors, writers, artists, musicians, and students, although it can get sardine-can crowded. ⊠ *17 Cross St., Spanish Arch* ☎ *091/566–172.*

⑯ Tourist Information Office (TIO). Just off Eyre Square, east of the bus and train station and the Great Southern Hotel, this is the place to make reservations and find out about the latest happenings around town. ⊠ *Forster Pl., Center* ☎ *091/537–700* ⊕ *www.irelandwest.ie* ☉ *Weekdays 9–6, Sat. 9–1.*

㉖ University College Galway (UCG). Opened in 1846 to promote the development of local industry and agriculture, the UCG today is a center for Irish-language and Celtic studies. The Tudor-Gothic-style quadrangle, completed in 1848, is worth a visit, though much of the rest of the campus is architecturally undistinguished. Its library has an important archive of Celtic-language materials, and in July and August, it also hosts courses in Irish studies for overseas students. The campus is across the River Corrib, in the northwestern corner of the city. ⊠ *Newcastle Rd., University.*

Where to Stay & Eat

★ **$–$$$$** ✕ **McDonagh's Seafood House.** This town landmark is partly a fish-and-chips bar and partly a "real" fish restaurant. If you haven't yet tried fish-and-chips, this is the place to start: cod, whiting, mackerel, haddock, or hake is deep-fried in a light batter while you watch. The fish is served with a heap of freshly cooked chips (french fries). Or try Galway oysters au naturel or a bowl of mussels steamed in wine and garlic. The McDonaghs are one of Galway's most entrepreneurial families, in charge of several hotels in addition to this spot. ⊠ *22 Quay St., Spanish Arch* ☎ *091/565–001* ▭ *DC, MC, V* ☉ *No lunch Sun. Oct.–Apr.*

$$–$$$ ✕ **Kirwan's Lane Creative Cuisine.** Look for Mike O'Grady's stylish modern restaurant in a revamped alley at the river end of Quay Street. Blue-stained wooden tables, narrow floor-to-ceiling windows, and a quarry-tile floor set the stage for a sophisticated contemporary menu. Fresh prawn cocktail is served with sauce Marie-Rose and a passion-fruit mayonnaise confit of duck leg comes with braised red cabbage, star anise, and balsamic oil. Main courses have similarly unpredictable twists—rack of lamb is accompanied by sweet potato mash, basil oil, and apricots, and monkfish tails are dressed with a simple lemon and coriander dressing. ⊠ *Kirwan's La., Spanish Arch* ☎ *091/562–353* ▭ *AE, DC, MC, V* ☉ *Closed Sun.*

$$–$$$ ✕ **Malt House.** Hidden away in an alley off High Street in the center of old Galway, Barry and Therese Cunningham's bustling pub-restaurant has long been popular with both locals and visitors for good food served in informal surroundings. You can either eat in the bar itself or just off the bar in the fancier main room with beamed ceilings, chintz curtains, and white, rough-cast walls. Fresh prawns panfried in garlic butter are popular; the sirloin steak with green-peppercorn sauce and the rack of lamb with a parsley crust should please landlubbers. ⊠ *Old Malte Arcade, High St., Center* ☎ *091/563–993* ▭ *AE, DC, MC, V* ☉ *Closed Sun. Oct.–Apr.*

$$–$$$ ✕ **Nimmo's.** Swiss chef Stephan Zeltner, who established himself on the Galway scene with a small restaurant above Naughton's Pub, now cooks at this riverside location, in an old stone building with a separately run wine bar downstairs. The long, spacious second-floor room has original paintings on the walls and well-spaced tables set with white linen. Zeltner prepares robust Continental food, exemplified by panfried chicken breast with duck foie gras or noisettes of venison with apple and Calvados. ⊠ *The Long Walk, Spanish Arch* ☎ *091/563–565* ▤ *AE, DC, MC, V* ☉ *Closed Sun. No lunch.*

$–$$ ✕ **K. C. Blake's.** K. C. stands for Casey, as in owner-chef John Casey, who turned a medieval stone town house once associated with the Blake family—one of the families that founded Galway—into a dark, ultramodern eatery. Dishes range from traditional beef-and-Guinness stew to funky combinations like black pudding croquettes with pear and cranberry sauce. ⊠ *10 Quay St., Spanish Arch* ☎ *091/561–826* ▤ *AE, MC, V.*

¢–$ ✕ **Bridge Mills.** Renovations have altered this 400-year-old former grain mill beside the River Corrib into a restaurant and mini-mall. You can even sit outdoors beside a bubbling stream and watch local fisherfolk pulling salmon out of the river. Lunch fare includes fresh salads, sandwiches, and hot specials. The dinner menu is more substantial, with large steaks and vegetarian choices, such as spinach and ricotta cannelloni. ⊠ *O'Brien's Bridge, Center* ☎ *091/566–231* ▤ *AE, MC, V* ☉ *No dinner Oct.–mid-May.*

$$$–$$$$ ✕▦ **St. Cleran's.** A gorgeous Georgian mansion that was once the home of director John Huston, St. Cleran's has been dramatically restored by its present owner, entertainer Merv Griffin. Subtle it is not, and some people are overwhelmed by the deep-pile carpets and ubiquitous crystal chandeliers; others find the luxurious furnishings delightful. Rooms are decorated with top-quality antiques. You can expect superb views of the rolling countryside, and excellent opportunities for country sports. The elegant, formal restaurant (reservations essential) serves such specialties as sea scallops and noisette of venison. It's 35 km (22 mi) east of Galway on the N6 Dublin road. ⊠ *Craughwell, Loughrea, Co. Galway* ☎ *091/846–555* ▤ *091/846–600* ⊕ *www.merv.com* ⇨ *12 rooms with bath* ⚇ *Restaurant, miniature golf, fishing, horseback riding, bar* ▤ *AE, MC, V* ⼮ *BP.*

$$–$$$$ ✕▦ **Glenlo Abbey.** Despite the name, this was never a monastery at all, but a private home, built in 1740. The lobby resembles a gentlemen's club, with parquet floors, chesterfield sofas, and leather-bound books. Georgian-style furniture and king-size beds fill the spacious bedrooms, in a newer wing. Bathrooms have marble walls; some have whirlpool baths. The Pullman Restaurant ($–$$), two *Orient Express* carriages installed in the grounds, offers a novel dining experience. Informal bar food is served in the Oak Cellar Bar. The hotel is surrounded by its own golf course, and is only five minutes outside the city on the N59 Clifden road. ⊠ *Bushy Park, Co. Galway* ☎ *091/526–666* ▤ *091/527–800* ⊕ *www.glenlo.com* ⇨ *38 rooms with bath, 6 suites* ⚇ *2 restaurants, in-room data ports, cable TV, 9-hole golf course, tennis court, sauna, fishing, bar* ▤ *AE, DC, MC, V* ⼮ *EP.*

$$–$$$$ ▦ **Galway Great Southern.** Built in 1845 right on Eyre Square to coincide with the arrival of the railway, this is still the best address in town, and a popular gathering spot. Tastefully muted, color-coordinated schemes and Georgian-style tables and chairs decorate all the guest rooms. The deluxe rooms in the original building have tall ceilings and windows and are particularly elegant, though those at the front directly above the bar can be noisy late into the night. Rooms in the back, on the fifth floor, have views of Galway Bay. French-Irish cuisine is served at the formal Oyster Room. ⊠ *Eyre Square, Center, Co. Galway* ☎ *091/564–041* ▤ *091/566–704* ⊕ *www.gsh.ie* ⇨ *112 rooms with bath, 3 suites* ⚇ *Restaurant, indoor pool, sauna, 2 bars* ▤ *AE, DC, MC, V* ⼮ *BP.*

$$$ ▦ **Galway Bay.** It's big and modern, but it's also restful and comfortable, with a panoramic view of Galway Bay. The facade of this giant at the quiet end of Salthill is divided into small-scale sections with peaked gables. The beach and the 1-km (½-mi) promenade, popular with joggers, are right across the road. More than two-thirds of the rooms have a sea view; the rest overlook a quiet residential area. The spacious color-coordinated rooms have large windows and all-modern facilities, from minibars to in-room data ports. Advantages of staying 3 km (2 mi) outside town include hassle-free parking and quiet nights. ⊠ *The Promenade, Salthill, Co. Galway* ☎ *091/520–520* 🖶 *091/520–530* ⊕ *www. galwaybayhotel.net* ↩ *148 rooms with bath, 2 suites* ⚐ *Restaurant, coffee shop, in-room data ports, cable TV, indoor pool, health club, sauna, steam room, fishing, bar* 🖃 *AE, DC, MC, V* ❚◯❚ *BP.*

★ **$$–$$$** 🏠 **Ardilaun House.** This lovely 19th-century house sits at the end of a tree-lined avenue in a quiet suburb, midway between the city center and the Salthill promenade. Open fires, fresh flower arrangements, and Regency-style furniture characterize the quiet public rooms overlooking the gardens. The individually designed bedrooms have pastel schemes and Irish-made mahogany furniture with brass trim. For views of the bay, book an even-numbered room on the top floor. Other rooms, which are just as pleasant, overlook the flower garden and a fountain. ⊠ *Taylor's Hill, Salthill, Co. Galway* ☎ *091/521–433* 🖶 *091/521–546* ⊕ *www.ardilaunhousehotel.ie* ↩ *81 rooms with bath, 7 suites* ⚐ *Restaurant, in-room data ports, indoor pool, health club, 2 bars* 🖃 *AE, DC, MC, V* ❚◯❚ *BP.*

$$ 🏠 **Cregg Castle.** Despite its grand interior, this 17th-century castle on a 165-acre wildlife preserve is pleasantly informal, thanks to the warm and laid-back welcome you receive from your hosts. The Brodericks, the owners, all play instruments; traditional sessions often take place around the huge log-and-turf fire in the Great Hall. Bedrooms, which vary in shape and size, are decorated mainly with sturdy Victorian bygones. Breakfast is served until noon around an antique dining table that seats 18 people. It's about 15 km (9 mi) north of Galway on N17 (turn left for Corrandulla just beyond Claregalway). ⊠ *Tuam Rd., Corrandulla, Co. Galway* ☎🖶 *091/791–434* ⊕ *indigo.ie/~creggcas/* ↩ *8 rooms, 7 with bath* 🖃 *AE, MC, V* ☉ *Closed Nov.–Feb.* ❚◯❚ *BP.*

¢–$$ 🏠 **Jurys Galway Inn.** Expect good-quality budget accommodation at this four-story hotel. Each room is big enough for three adults, or two adults and two children, and the fixed-price policy applies to all of them. The light, airy rooms have modern pine fittings, plain carpets and walls, double-glazed windows, and fully equipped bathrooms. Those overlooking the river are quieter than those in front. The atmosphere runs toward anonymous-international, but the inn is central—at the foot of Galway's busy Quay Street, right on the bank of the Corrib—and the level of comfort is high for the price range. ⊠ *Quay St., Spanish Arch, Co. Galway* ☎ *091/566–444* 🖶 *091/568–415* ⊕ *www.jurysdoyle.com* ↩ *128 rooms with bath* ⚐ *Restaurant, bar, parking (fee)* 🖃 *AE, DC, MC, V* ❚◯❚ *EP.*

$ 🏠 **Adare Guest House.** Just a 5-minute walk from the city center, this family-run guest house, now managed by the son of the original owners, makes a handy base for exploring Galway. There's ample space to park your car, and there's none of the nighttime noise of the city center. Rooms are relatively spacious for the price, extremely well equipped, and plainly decorated in browns and creams. The multichoice breakfast is served in a sunny room, with country pine furniture and floors, that overlooks a flower-filled patio. ⊠ *9 Father Griffin Pl., Spanish Arch, Co. Galway* ☎ *091/582–638* 🖶 *091/583–693* ⊕ *www. adarebedandbreakfast.com* ↩ *11 rooms with bath.* ⚐ *Dining room* 🖃 *AE, MC, V* ❚◯❚ *BP.*

¢–$ 🏠 **Norman Villa.** Dee and Mark Keogh's Victorian town house is away from the bustle but within easy walking distance of both the city center and the seaside promenade of Salthill. Brightly painted walls, Victorian brass beds with Irish-linen sheets, varnished floorboards, wooden shutters, and fun, offbeat paintings and artifacts characterize this lively, pleasant B&B. ⊠ *86 Lower Salthill, Salthill, Co. Galway* ☎☎ *091/521–131* ☎ *5 rooms with bath* ⚲ *Free parking* ☰ *MC, V* ☉ *Closed last 2 wks in Jan.* ⧉ *BP.*

Nightlife & the Arts

Because of its small size and concentration of pubs and restaurants, Galway can seem even livelier at 11 PM than it does at 11 AM. On weekends, when there are lots of students and other revelers in town, Eyre Square and environs can be rowdy late at night after pub-closing time. On the plus side, if you've been staying out in the countryside and you're ready for a little nightlife, you're certain to find plenty of it here.

Pubs & Other Nightspots

The best spot for traditional music is the area between Eyre Square and the Spanish Arch. There's a big post-nightclub (open 'til 1 or 2) scene here—there are some clubs in town, but most everyone heads to Salthill, the small suburban community 3 km (2 mi) west of Galway. The main road, Upper Salthill, is lined with clubs. **Aras na Gael** (⊠ 45 Lower Dominick St., Spanish Arch ☎ 091/526–509) is one of the few pubs in the city center where Irish is spoken. Up-and-coming young musicians play at the cozy **Cottage Bar** (⊠ 76 Lower Salthill, Salthill ☎ 091/526–754), which has good acoustics. Master of the tin whistle Seán Ryan plays every Sunday at **Crane's** (⊠ 2 Sea Rd. ☎ 091/587–419). You will usually find a session after about 9 PM at **King's Head** (⊠ 15 High St., Center ☎ 091/566–630). **Paddy's** (⊠ Prospect Hill, Center ☎ 091/567–843) is a good place for a pint near the bus and train station. **Taaffe's** (⊠ 19 Shop St., Center ☎ 091/564–066), in the midst of the shopping district, is very busy on afternoons. **Tig Neachtain** (⊠ 17 Cross St., Spanish Arch ☎ 091/568–820) is *the* place for traditional music in Galway City, and each visit will be an experience. **McSwiggan's** (⊠ 3 Eyre St., Wood Quay, Center ☎ 091/568–917) is a huge place with everything from church pews to ancient carriage lamps contributing to its eclectic character. **Roisin Dubh** (⊠ Dominick St., Spanish Arch ☎ 091/586–540) is a serious venue for emerging rock and traditional bands; it often showcases big, if still-struggling, talents. For late-night sounds heard from the comfort of your own table, try **Sevn'th Heav'n Restaurant** (⊠ Courthouse La., off Quay St., Spanish Arch ☎ 091/563–838), where blues and folk sounds pour forth from 11:30 PM onward.

Cuba (⊠ Prospect Hill, Center ☎ 091/565–991), on three floors, draws diners and salsa lovers for Cuban cocktails and cigars to the beat of Latin music from DJs and live bands. Busy with students from the university, **GPO** (⊠ Eglinton St., Center ☎ 091/563–073) is perhaps the most popular dance club in Galway City. Try **Liquid** (⊠ The Promenade, Salthill ☎ 091/722–715) for nightly independent and techno music. **Warwick** (⊠ O'Connor's Warwick Hotel, Lower Salthill, Salthill ☎ 091/521–244) plays '70s, '80s, and independent music, except for Sunday, when the dance-hall days return. Admission is €4 to €10.

Theater

An Taibhdhearc (⊠ Middle St., Center ☎ 091/562–024), pronounced awn *tie*-vark, was founded in 1928 by Hilton Edwards and Micháel Macliammóir as the national Irish-language theater. It continues to produce first-class shows, mainly of Irish works in both the English and the Irish languages.

The **Druid Theatre company** (⊠ Chapel La., Center ☎ 091/568–617) is esteemed for its adventurous and accomplished productions, mainly of

CloseUp

A YEAR-ROUND FLEADH

DUBLIN MAY BE THE POLITICAL capital of Ireland, but Galway is the center of its traditional-music universe, a place where you can hear this music all through the year, whether or not there's a fleadh, or traditional-music festival, going on. Galway City and its environs have given birth to some of the most durable names in Irish music: De Danann, Arcady, singers Dolores and Seán Keane, and the mercurial accordion genius Mairtín O'Connor. Seán Ryan, acknowledged master of the tin whistle, has been playing every Sunday at **Crane's** since the 1980s. The hottest sessions these days take place at the **Cottage Bar** in Lower Salthill, where up-and-coming young musicians are drawn by the cozy surroundings and the fine acoustics. In the city itself, there's still plenty of music to be found at old reliables such as **Tig Neaćhtain, Taaffe's,** and **Aras na Gael.**

South of Galway the fishing village of Kinvara hosts the annual **Cuckoo Fleadh,** a small but growing festival that takes place in May. Resident musicians like De Danann alumni Jackie Daly and Charlie Piggott play regularly at **Winkles Hotel,** where, in 1989, a very young and relatively unknown accordion player got together with a few friends for a casual recording session. The resulting album, Sharon Shannon, went platinum virtually overnight, becoming the most successful traditional-music recording ever released.

Today, Shannon, who grew up on a farm outside Corofin, County Clare, and played her first accordion when she was 11, is one of Ireland's leading traditional Irish musicians.

Down the road, the lively market town of Ennis (where Shannon took lessons from local maestro Frank Custy) has come into its own, attracting a growing cadre of musicians: the Custys, Siobhán and Tommy Peoples, Josephine Marsh, P. J. King, flute player Kevin Crawford, and accordion whiz kid Murt Ryan, from Tipperary. Sessions take place at an ever-changing roster of pubs, including **Knox's** and, most notably, **Cruise's.** This last pub has an adjacent concert venue where a group of local musicians recorded a lovely live album in the mid-1990s, The Sanctuary Sessions. Still available through stores specializing in traditional music, the album is an excellent introduction to Irish music, with the featured artists including most of the above-mentioned musicians as well as banjo player Mary Shannon and the wonderful Galway singer Seán Tyrrell. In May, Ennis hosts the **Fleadh Nua** festival—with concerts, competitions, workshops, and ceilis (Irish dancing and song).

20th-century Irish and European plays. The players perform at the Royal Court's small stage in London. When they're home, they usually appear at the Town Hall, and they host many productions during the Galway Arts Festival in late July.

Macnas (⊠ Fisheries Field, Salmon Weir Bridge, Center ☎ 091/561–462) is an internationally renowned, Galway-based troupe of performance artists who have raised street theater to new levels. Their participation in the Galway Arts Festival's annual parade is always much anticipated.

Visual Arts & Galleries

Art Euro Gallery (⊠ The Bridge Mills, O'Brien's Bridge, Spanish Arch ☎ 091/562–884) has a collection of free-blown glass and unusual hand-made ceramics by Irish and other European artists. High-quality paintings and sculpture by local artists can be found at **Kenny's Bookshop**

(⊠ High St., Center ☎ 091/562–739). The art gallery at **University College Galway** (⊠ Newcastle Rd., University ☎ 091/524–411) has a number of exhibits each year.

Sports & the Outdoors

Bicycling

Set off to explore the Galway area, especially its coast, by renting a bike from **Mountain Trail Bike Shop** (⊠ The Cornstore, Middle St., Center ☎ 091/569–888).

Fishing

Galway City is the gateway to Connemara, and Connemara is the place to fish. You can get fishing licenses, tackle, and bait and arrange to hire a traditional fly-fishing guide or book a sea-angling trip at **Freeny's Sports** (⊠ 19–23 High St., Center ☎ 091/562–609). **Murt's** (⊠ 7 Daly's Pl., Woodquay ☎ 091/561–018) can handle your fishing needs.

Golf

Galway Bay Golf and Country Club (⊠ Renville, Oranmore ☎ 091/790–500) is an 18-hole, par-72 parkland course, designed by Christy O'Connor, Jr., on the shores of Galway Bay. The **Galway Golf Club** (⊠ Blackrock, Salthill ☎ 091/522–033) is an 18-hole, par-71 course with excellent views of Galway Bay, the Burren, and the Aran Islands. Some of the fairways run close to the ocean.

River Cruising

A **Corrib Cruise** (☎ 091/592–447) from Wood Quay, behind the Town Hall Theatre at the Rowing Club, is a lovely way to spend a fine afternoon; it lasts 1½ hours and travels 8 km (5 mi) up the River Corrib and about 6 km (4 mi) around Lough Corrib. The trip costs €8, and boats depart daily at 2:30 and 4:30 from May through September, with an additional departure at 12:30 July through August. You can also rent the boat for an evening.

Tennis

There are nine courts at the **Galway Lawn Tennis Club** (⊠ Threadneedle St., Salthill ☎ 091/522–353), available to nonmembers at €5.10 per hour.

Water Sports

Bow Waves (⊠ 11 Ashleigh Grove, Knockacarra ☎ 091/591–481) schedules individually tailored trips around Galway Bay on high-performance inflatables. Life jackets and wet gear are included in the price. Ride the waves for thrills, or take it easy on a seal and dolphin watch. **Galway Bay Sailing Club** (⊠ Renville, Oranmore ☎ 091/794–527) arranges dinghy sailing and windsurfing on Lough Corrib or on coastal waters. Instruction is also available.

Shopping

Bookstores

Charlie Byrne's Bookshop (⊠ The Cornstore, Middle St., Center ☎ 091/561–766) sells a large, varied selection of used books and remainders.
Fodor'sChoice **Kenny's Bookshop** (⊠ High St., Center ☎ 091/562–739) has five floors
★ of books on Irish topics, mainly secondhand and antiquarian, as well as prints, maps, and a small art gallery.

Clothing, Crafts, & Gifts

★ Don't miss **Design Concourse Ireland** (⊠ Kirwan's La., Center ☎ 091/566–016), a spectacular one-stop shop for the best in Irish handcrafted design. **Design Ireland Plus** (⊠ The Cornstore, Middle St., Center ☎ 091/567–716 ⊠ The Grainstore, Lower Abbeygate St., Center ☎ 091/566–

620) carries an excellent range of contemporary Irish-made crafts and clothing. **Faller's Sweater Shop** (✉ 25 High St., Center ☎ 091/564–833 ✉ 35 Eyre Sq., Center ☎ 091/561–255) has the choicest selection of Irish-made sweaters, competitively priced. **Galway Irish Crystal** (✉ Dublin Rd., Merlin Park ☎ 091/757–311 ⊕ www.galwaycrystal.ie), a factory outlet on the city's ring road, has hand-cut Irish glass, an informative heritage center on Galway lore, a crystal workshop you can visit, and a restaurant with a view of Galway Bay.

Meadows & Byrne (✉ Castle St., Center ☎ 091/567–776) sells the best in modern household items. **O'Máille's** (✉ 16 High St., Center ☎ 091/562–696) carries Aran sweaters, handwoven tweeds, and classically tailored clothing. Browse in **Treasure Chest** (✉ William St., Center ☎ 091/563–862) for china, crystal, gifts, and classic clothing.

Jewelry

Dating from 1750, **Thomas Dillon's** (✉ 1 Quay St., Spanish Arch ☎ 091/566–365 ⊕ www.claddaghring.ie) claims to be the original maker of Galway's famous Claddagh ring. In the back of the shop there's a small but interesting display of antique Claddagh rings and old Galway memorabilia.

Malls

Slightly off the beaten path, the **Cornstore** (✉ Middle St., Center) has some stylish shops selling contemporary goods; the shops tend to be less crowded than their competitors on the main streets. On the southwest side of Eyre Square and imaginatively designed to incorporate parts of the old town walls, the **Eyre Square Shopping Centre** is a good spot to pick up moderately priced clothing and household goods.

Music

Back2Music (✉ 30 Upper Abbeygate St., Center ☎ 091/565–272) specializes in traditional Irish musical instruments, including the handheld drum, the *bodhrán* (pronounced bau-rawn). **Mulligan** (✉ 5 Middle St. Court, Center ☎ 091/564–961) carries more than 6,000 CDs, records, and cassettes, with a large collection of traditional Irish music.

Vintage Goods

Twice as Nice (✉ 5 Quay St., Spanish Arch ☎ 091/566–332) sells a mix of new and vintage men's and women's clothing, linens, lace, and jewelry at reasonable prices.

THE ARAN ISLANDS

The Aran Islands—Inishmore, Inishmaan, and Inisheer—are remote western outposts of the ancient province of Connaught (though they are not the country's westernmost points; that honor belongs to the Blasket Islands). These three islands were once as barren as the limestone pavements of the Burren, of which they are a continuation. Today, the land is parceled into small, human-made fields surrounded by stone walls. The views from here are spectacular: the uninterrupted expanse of the Atlantic on the western horizon; the Connemara coast and its Twelve Bens to the northeast and County Clare's Burren and the Cliffs of Moher to the southeast.

The islands have been populated for thousands of years. Nowadays the Irish-speaking inhabitants enjoy a daily air service to Galway (subsidized by the government), motorized curraghs, multichannel TVs, and all the usual modern home conveniences. Yet they have retained a distinctness from mainlanders, preferring simple home decor, very plain food, and tightly knit communities, like the hardy fisher and farming folk from whom they are descended. Crime is virtually unknown in these parts; at your B&B, you'll likely find no locks on the guest-room doors, and the front-door latch will be left open.

Many islanders have sampled life in Dublin or cities abroad but have returned to raise families, keeping the population stable at around 1,500. Through the years, the islands have also attracted writers and artists, including J. M. Synge (1871–1909), who learned Irish on Inishmaan and wrote about its people in his play *Riders to the Sea*. The film *Man of Aran*, made on Inishmore in 1932 by the American director Robert Flaherty, is a classic documentary recording the islanders' dramatic battles with sea and storm. (The film is shown in the Community Hall in Kilronan, Inishmore, every afternoon during July, August, and early September.)

The only hotel on the islands is on Inisheer, but there's no shortage of B&Bs, mostly in simple family homes. The best way to book is through the Galway City TIO. Each island has at least one wine-licensed restaurant serving plain home cooking. Most B&Bs will provide a packed lunch and an evening meal (called high tea) on request.

Inishmore

★ ➋➒ *24 km (15 mi) south of Rós an Mhil (Rossaveal), 48 km (30 mi) west of Galway Docks.*

With a population of 900, Inishmore (Inis Mór) is the largest of the islands and the closest to the Connemara coast. It's also the most commercialized, its appeal slightly diminished by road traffic. In the summer, ferries arriving at Kilronan, Inishmore's main village and port, are met by minibuses and pony and cart drivers, all eager to show visitors "the sights." More than 8 km (5 mi) long and about 3 km (2 mi) wide at most points, with an area of 7,640 acres, the island is just a little too large to explore comfortably on foot in a day. The best way to see it is really by bicycle; bring your own or rent one from one of the vendors right near the quay. The **Aran Heritage Centre** explains the history and culture of the islanders, who for many years lived in virtual isolation from the mainland. ⊠ *Kilronan* ☎ *099/61355* ☒ *€3* ☉ *Apr.–Oct., daily 10–7.*

The main attraction on Inishmore is **Dún Aengus,** one of the finest prehistoric monuments in Europe, dating from about 2000 BC. Spectacularly set on the edge of a 300-foot cliff overlooking a sheer drop, the fort has defenses consisting of three rows of concentric circles. Whom the builders were defending themselves against is a matter of conjecture. From the innermost rampart there's a great view of the island and the Connemara coast. In order to protect this fragile monument from erosion, you should approach it only through the visitor center, which gives access to a 1-km (½-mi) uphill walk over uneven terrain, so wear sturdy footwear. ⊠ *Kilmurvey, 7 km (4 mi) west of Kilronan* ☎ *099/61010* ⊕ *www.heritageireland.ie* ☒ *€1.25* ☉ *Mar.–Oct., daily 10–6; Nov.–Feb., daily 11:30–3:30.*

Where to Stay

¢–$ ⊞ **Kilmurvey House.** This rambling 200-year-old stone farmhouse is the first choice of many visitors to the island—about 60% of them American. It's at the foot of Dún Aengus fort, about 6½ km (4 mi) from the quay and the airport (accessible by minibus). ⊠ *Kilronan, Co. Galway* ☎ *099/61218* 🖷 *099/61397* ⊕ *www.kilmurveyhouse.com* ↩ *12 rooms with bath* ⚘ *Dining room; no room TVs* ▭ *MC, V* ☉ *Closed Nov.–Mar.* ⏹ *BP.*

¢ ⊡ **Ard Einne Guesthouse.** Almost every window at this B&B on Inishmore looks out to the sea, making it the perfect place to de-stress. Because of its proximity to the beach and small town, it's a perfect base for exploring the Aran Islands. It's also considered a refuge for writers and artists. The public rooms and guest rooms are relaxed, with light-color linens and walls paneled with blond wood. Evening meals are available, and the dining room has a wine license. ⊠ *Kilronan, Co. Galway* ☏ *099/61126* 🖷 *099/61388* ⊕ *www.galway.net/pages/ardeinne/* ⤶ *14 rooms with bath* ⚘ *Dining room, fishing; no room phones, no room TVs* ▭ *MC, V* ☉ *Closed mid-Dec.–Jan.* ⦿| *BP.*

Nightlife

The place to go for traditional music is the **American Bar** (⊠ Kilronan ☏ 099/61130). **Joe Mac's** (⊠ Kilronan ☏ 099/61248), right off the pier, is a good place for a pint while waiting for the ferry home. **Joe Watty's** (⊠ Main Rd., Kilronan ☏ 099/61155) is a good bet for traditional music virtually every night in summer.

Sports & the Outdoors

Bicycles can be rented from May through October for €10 per day from **Aran Bike Hire** (☏ 099/61132), at the ferry landing at Inishmore Pier.

Inishmaan

㉚ *3 km (2 mi) east of Inishmore.*

The middle island in both size and location, Inishmaan (Inis Meáin) has a population of about 300 and can be comfortably explored on foot. In fact, you have no alternative if you want to reach the island's major antiquities: **Conor Fort,** a smaller version of Dún Aengus; the ruins of two **early Christian churches**; and a chamber tomb known as the **Bed of Diarmuid and Grainne,** dating from about 2000 BC. You can also take wonderful cliff walks above secluded coves. It's on Inishmaan that the traditional Aran lifestyle is most evident. Until the mid-1930s or so, Aran women dressed in thick, red-woolen skirts to keep out the Atlantic gales, while the men wore collarless jackets, baggy trousers made of home-spun tweed with *pampooties* (hide shoes without heels, suitable for walking on rocks), and a wide, hand-plaited belt called a *críos* (pronounced krish). Most islanders still don hand-knitted Aran sweaters, though nowadays they wear them with jeans and sneakers.

Shopping

Inis Meáin Knitting Co. Ltd. (⊠ Carrown Lisheen ☏ 099/73009) is a young company producing quality knitwear in luxury fibers for the international market—including Liberty of London, Barneys New York, and Bergdorf Goodman—while providing much-needed local employment. The factory showroom has an extensive selection of garments at discount prices. To get here from the pier, walk five minutes due west.

Inisheer

㉛ *4 km (2½ mi) east of Inishmaan, 8 km (5 mi) northwest of Doolin.*

The smallest and flattest of the islands, Inisheer (Inis Oirr) can be explored on foot in an afternoon, though if the weather is fine you may be tempted to linger on the long, sandy beach between the quay and the airfield. Only one stretch of road, about 500 yards long, links the airfield and the sole village. In the summer, Inisheer's population of 300 is augmented by high school students from all over Ireland attending the Gaeltacht, or Irish-language, school.

It's worth making a circuit of the island to get a sense of its utter tranquility. A maze of footpaths runs between the high stone walls that divide the fields, which are so small that they can support only one cow each, or two to three sheep. Those that are not cultivated or grazed turn into natural wildflower meadows between June and August, overrun with harebells, scabious, red clover, oxeye daisies, saxifrage, and tall grasses. It seems almost a crime to walk here—but how can you resist taking a rest in the corner of a sweet-smelling meadow on a sunny afternoon, sheltered by high stone walls with no sound but the larks above and the wind as it sifts through the stones? "The back of the island," as Inisheer's uninhabited side facing the Atlantic is called, has no beaches, but people still swim off the rocks.

The **Church of Kevin,** signposted to the southeast of the quay, is a small, early Christian church that gets buried in sand by storms every winter. Every year the islanders dig it out of the sand for the celebration of St. Kevin's Day on June 14. A pleasant walk through the village takes you up to **O'Brien's Castle,** a ruined 15th-century tower on top of a rocky hill—the only hill on the island.

Where to Stay

¢ ☒ **Hotel Inisheer.** A pleasant, modern low-rise in the middle of the island's only village, a few minutes' walk from the quay and the airstrip, this simple, whitewashed building with a slate roof and half-slated walls has bright, plainly furnished rooms. The five newer rooms are slightly larger than the other 10. The restaurant (open to nonguests) is the best bet on the island, although much of the food is imported frozen. ☒ *Lurgan Village, Co. Galway* ☎ *099/75020* 🖶 *099/75099* 🛏 *15 rooms, 12 with bath* ⟨ *Restaurant, bicycles, bar; no room phones, no room TVs* ⊟ *AE, DC, MC, V* ☉ *Closed Oct.–Mar.* ℐ◯ℐ *BP.*

CONNEMARA & COUNTY MAYO

Bordered by the long expanse of Lough Corrib on the east and the jagged coast of the Atlantic on the west is the rugged, desolate region of western County Galway, known as Connemara. Like the American West, it's an area of spectacular, almost myth-making geography—of glacial lakes; gorgeous, silent mountains; lonely roads; and hushed, uninhabited boglands. The Twelve Bens, "the central glory of Connemara," as author Brendan Lehane has called them, together with the Maamturk Mountains to their north, lord proudly over the area's sepia boglands. More surprisingly, stands of Scotch pine, Norwegian spruce, Douglas fir, and Japanese Sitka grow in Connemara's valleys and up hillsides—the result of a concerted national project that has so far reforested 9% of Ireland. In the midst of this wilderness, there are few people, for Connemara's population is sparse even by Irish standards. Especially in the off-season, you're far more likely to come across sheep strolling its roads than another car.

Two main routes—one inland, the other coastal—lead through Connemara. To take the inland route described below, leave Galway City on the well-signposted outer-ring road and follow signs for N59—Moycullen, Oughterard, and Clifden. If you choose to go the coastal route, you'll travel due west from Galway City to Rossaveal on R336 through Salthill, Barna, and Spiddle—all in the heart of the west's strong Gaeltacht, home to roughly 40,000 Irish speakers. Although this is one of the most impressive and unspoiled coastal roads in Ireland, it has been scarred by modern one-story concrete homes—a sort of faux–Spanish hacienda style favored by locals. (Most of the traditional thatched houses in the west are now used as vacation homes.) You can continue north on R336 from Rossaveal to Maam Cross and then head for coastal points west, or pick up R340 and putter along the coast.

Oughterard

32 *27 km (17 mi) northwest of Galway City on N59.*

Bustling Oughterard (pronounced *ook*-ter-ard) is the main village on the western shores of Lough Corrib and one of Ireland's leading angling resorts. The prettiest part of the village is on the far (Clifden) side, beyond the busy commercial center, beside a wooded section of the River Corrib. The lough is signposted to the right in the village center, less than 1½ km (1 mi) up the road. From mid-June to early September, local boatmen offer trips on the lough, which has several islands. It's also possible to take a boat trip to the village of Cong, at the north shore of the lough. Midway between Oughterard and Cong, Inchagoill Island (the Island of the Stranger), a popular destination for a half-day trip, has several early Christian church remains. The cost of boat rides is negotiable; expect to pay about €10 per person.

Where to Stay

$$–$$$$ 🏨 **Ross Lake House.** Well off the beaten path, this low-key country hideaway sits near a stream and is surrounded by five acres of colorful gardens. The Georgian house, managed by the enthusiastic Henry and Elaine Reid, has a comfortably furnished interior, with Victorian antiques and welcoming open fires. Guest rooms in the converted stables are simpler and a little smaller than those in the house, but all have peaceful garden views. A table d'hôte dinner menu offers good-quality, plain country-house cooking. The house is 5 km (3 mi) from Oughterard. ⊠ *Rosscahill, Co. Galway* 🕿🕿 *091/550–109* ⊕ *www.rosslakehotel.com* ⇱ *13 rooms with bath* ☍ *Restaurant, tennis court, fishing, horseback riding, bar* ⊟ *AE, DC, MC, V* ☯ *Closed Nov.–mid-Mar.* ❑ *BP.*

$$$ 🏨 **Connemara Gateway.** This modern low-rise with traditional, gray-slate roofs above whitewashed walls combines the best of the old and the new. With a nod to the classic Irish cottage, the lobby and bar are decorated with wooden and cast-iron artifacts and chintz sofas. Guest rooms have modern furniture and floral wall panels with matching drapes. All have sitting areas beside the large teak-framed windows, which overlook the gardens and the distant hills. There's a strong tour-bus trade, but it doesn't spoil the charm. Ask about weekend specials. ⊠ *On N59, 1 km (½ mi) before village on the Galway side, Co. Galway* 🕿 *091/552–328* 🖷 *091/552–332* ⊕ *www.sinnotthotels.com* ⇱ *62 rooms with bath* ☍ *Restaurant, tennis court, indoor pool, sauna, fishing, bar* ⊟ *AE, DC, MC, V* ❑ *BP.*

Nightlife

For good traditional music try **Faherty's** (⊠ Main St. 🕿 091/552–194).

<table>
<tr><td>en route</td><td>As you continue northwest from Oughterard on N59, you'll soon pass a string of small lakes on your left; their shining blue waters reflecting the blue sky are a typical Connemara sight on a sunny day. About 16 km (10 mi) northwest of Oughterard, the continuation of the coast road (R336) meets N59 at Maam Cross in the shadow of Leckavrea Mountain. Once an important meeting place for the people of north and south Connemara, it's still the location of a large monthly cattle fair. Walkers will find wonderful views of Connemara</td></tr>
</table>

by heading for any of the local peaks visible from the road. Beyond Maam Cross, some of the best scenery in Connemara awaits on the road to Recess, 16 km (10 mi) west of Maam Cross on N59. At many points on this drive, a short walk away from either side of the main road will lead you to the shores of one of the area's many small loughs. Stop and linger if the sun is out—even intermittently—for the light filtering through the clouds gives splendor to the distant, dark-gray mountains and creates patterns on the brown-green moorland below. In June and July, it stays light until 11 PM or so, and it's worth taking a late-evening stroll to see the sun's reluctance to set. In Recess, **Joyce's** (☎ 095/34604) carries a good selection of contemporary ceramics, handwoven shawls, books of Irish interest, original paintings, and small sculptures.

Cong

③ *23 km (14 mi) northeast of Maam Cross on N59.*

On a narrow isthmus between Lough Corrib and Lough Mask on the County Mayo border, the pretty, old-fashioned village of Cong, near Maam Cross, is dotted with ivy-covered thatched cottages and dilapidated farmhouses. Cong is surrounded by many stone circles and burial mounds, but its most notable ruins are those of the **Augustine Abbey** (⊠ Abbey St.), dating from the early 13th century and still exhibiting some finely carved details. It can be seen overlooking a river near fabulous Ashford Castle, now a hotel.

Cong's 15 minutes of fame came in 1952, when John Ford filmed *The Quiet Man,* one of his most popular films, here; John Wayne plays a prizefighter who goes home to Ireland to court the fiery Maureen O'Hara. (Film critic Pauline Kael called the film "fearfully Irish and green and hearty.") The **Quiet Man Heritage Cottage,** in the village center, is an exact replica of the cottage used in the film, with reproductions of the furniture and costumes, a few original artifacts, and pictures of actors Barry Fitzgerald and Maureen O'Hara on location. ⊠ *Cong Village Center* ☎ *092/46089* 🖼 *€3.50* ⊙ *Mar.–Nov., daily 10–6.*

Where to Stay

★ **$$$** 🏨 **Ashford Castle.** Built in 1870 for the Guinness family in a mock-Gothic baronial style, this massive, flamboyantly turreted and crenellated castle incorporates an earlier 1228 structure built by the De Burgos family. Now American owned, Ashford is one of Ireland's most luxurious castle-hotels. Large paintings in gilt frames hang from the castle's carved stone walls above polished-wood paneling, illuminated by crystal chandeliers. Deluxe rooms have generous sitting areas, heavily carved antique furniture, and extra-large bathrooms. The suites are vast, furnished with Georgian antiques, and blissfully comfortable. ⊠ *Co. Mayo* ☎ *092/46003* 🖶 *092/46260* 🌐 *www.ashford.ie* 🛏 *72 rooms with bath, 11 suites* 🍴 *2 restaurants, in-room data ports, cable TV, 9-hole golf course, 2 tennis courts, health club, boating, fishing, bicycles, horseback riding, 2 bars* 🖃 *AE, DC, MC, V* 🍽 *EP.*

Cashel

③ *8 km (5 mi) south of Recess on R340, 49½ km (31 mi) west of Cong.*

Cashel is a quiet, extremely sheltered angling center at the head of Bertraghboy Bay. General de Gaulle is among the many people who have sought seclusion here. A word of caution: stray sheep, bolting Connemara ponies, cyclists, and reckless local drivers are all regular hazards on the narrow mountain roads hereabouts.

Where to Stay & Eat

★ $$$$ ✕⌂ **Cashel House.** Forty acres of woodlands at the head of Cashel Bay—with exotic shrubs flowering and Connemara ponies grazing out back—seclude this luxurious country house. Cashel House may well have more antiques and curios than any other hotel in Ireland. Intricately carved tables, Biedermeier bureaus, gilt mirrors, Georgian bookcases, and or-molu clocks are scattered around the public rooms; more antiques turn up in the bedrooms, which have king-size beds (canopied in the 13 mini-suites). Front rooms have views of the sea. The table d'hôte menu in the dining room lists more choices than most country houses and is strong on fresh local seafood. ⊠ *Cashel Bay, Co. Galway* ☎ *095/31001* 📠 *095/31077* ⊕ *www.cashel-house-hotel.com* ⇆ *19 rooms with bath, 13 suites* ⚘ *Restaurant, tennis court, beach, boating, fishing, bicycles, horseback riding* ▭ *AE, DC, MC, V* ⊗ *Closed mid-Jan.–mid-Feb.* ⦿ *BP.*

$$$ ⌂ **Zetland Country House.** Built for the Earl of Zetland on a hill over-looking secluded Cashel Bay, John and Mona Prendergast's mid-Victo-rian hunting lodge offers an unforgettable experience. Large old trees, wooded grounds, and flowering shrubs set the scene. A dining room with massive antique sideboards adorned with family silver overlooks the bay, as does the large and blissfully serene sitting room. Bedrooms are large, and many have sea views, but those with garden views are also attrac-tive. Elegant Georgian and Victorian antiques of polished mahogany dec-orate the comfortable quarters. ⊠ *Cashel Bay, Co. Galway* ☎ *095/31111* 📠 *095/31117* ⊕ *www.zetland.com* ⇆ *19 rooms with bath* ⚘ *Restau-rant, tennis court, fishing, bar* ▭ *AE, DC, MC, V* ⊗ *Closed Nov.–mid-Apr.* ⦿ *BP.*

Sports & the Outdoors

Cashel Equestrian Center (⊠ Cashel House, Cashel Bay ☎ 095/31001) offers scenic treks and the chance to ride a Connemara pony on its home ground.

Ballynahinch

㉟ *10 km (6 mi) west of Cashel on R341.*

Forested country runs along the shores of Ballynahinch Lake. Wood-land in this part of Ireland indicates the proximity of a "big house" whose owner can afford to plant trees for pleasure and prevent their being cut down for fuel.

Where to Stay

$$–$$$$ ⌂ **Ballynahinch Castle.** Built in the late 18th century on the Owenmore
Fodor'sChoice River amid 40 walkable wooded acres, this was once the home of
★ Richard Martin (1754–1834), known as "Humanity Dick," the founder of the Royal Society for the Prevention of Cruelty to Animals. The tiled lobby with Persian rugs has two inviting leather chesterfields in front of an open fire. The biggest bedrooms, in the ground-floor wing, have four-poster beds and floor-to-ceiling windows overlooking the river. Rooms in the old house are equally comfortable and quiet. The castle is signposted off N59 between Recess and Clifden. ⊠ *Ballynahinch, Re-cess, Co. Galway* ☎ *095/31006* 📠 *095/31085* ⊕ *www.ballynahinch-castle.com* ⇆ *30 rooms with bath, 10 suites* ⚘ *Restaurant, tennis court, fishing, bar* ▭ *AE, DC, MC, V* ⊗ *Closed last wk of Dec. and Feb.* ⦿ *BP.*

ROUNDSTONE MUSICAL INSTRUMENTS – From Ballynahinch, take N59 to the small seaside town of Roundstone, where you'll find this delightful music shop and museum. Artisans here have been handcrafting bodhráns (Irish drums) here for years. The workshop is an old Franciscan monastery with a beautiful bell tower. Besides the bodhráns, you can buy traditional CDs, books, and coffee—and you can also expect a good chat. If you wish, you can have your drum hand-painted with your family crest, a Celtic design, or your initials while you wait. ⊠ *I.D.A. Craftcenter, Roundstone* ☎ *095/35808* ⊕ *www.bodhran.com* ⊗ *May, June, Sept., and Oct., daily 9:30–6; July and Aug., daily 9–7; Nov.–Apr., Mon.–Sat. 9:30–6.*

Clifden

★ ➌➏ *23 km (14 mi) west of Recess, 79 km (49 mi) northwest of Galway City on N59.*

With roughly 1,100 residents, Clifden would be called a village by most, but in these parts it's looked on as something of a metropolis. It is far and away the prettiest town in Connemara, as well as its unrivaled "capital." Clifden's first attraction is its location—perched high above Clifden Bay on a forested plateau, its back to the spectacular Twelve Ben Mountains. The tapering spires of the town's two churches add to its alpine feel. A selection of small restaurants, lively bars with music most summer nights, pleasant accommodations, and excellent walks make the town a popular base. It's quiet out of season, but in July and August crowds flock here, especially for August's world-famous Connemara Pony Show. Horse breeders come from around the world to check out Ireland's finest yearlings and stallions. Clifden's popularity, which has led to a chaotic one-way traffic system and loud techno music blasting out of certain bars, means that if you're over 25 and value your peace and quiet, you'd best choose a base outside town.

A 2-km (1-mi) walk along the beach road through the grounds of the ruined **Clifden Castle** is the best way to explore the seashore. The castle was built in 1815 by John D'Arcy, the town's founder, who laid out the town's wide main street on a long ridge with a parallel street below it. D'Arcy was High Sheriff of Galway, and his greatest wish was to establish a center of law and order in what he saw as the lawless wilderness of Connemara. Before the founding of Clifden, the interior of Connemara was largely uninhabited, with most of its population clinging to the seashore. Take the aptly named **Sky Road** to really appreciate Clifden's breathtaking scenery. Signposted at the west end of town, this high, narrow circuit of about 5 km (3 mi) heads west to Kingstown, skirting Clifden Bay's precipitous shores.

Where to Stay & Eat

$$–$$$ ✕ **Mitchell's Seafood.** A town-center shop has been cleverly converted into a stylish, two-story eatery. On the first floor, beyond the plate-glass windows, there's a welcoming open fire, and you can eat at the bar or at one of the polished wood tables. Exposed stone walls and wooden floors also feature on the quieter second level. Braised whole sea bass with fennel butter typifies the simple treatment given to seafood. There are also several meat options, including traditional Irish stew of Connemara lamb and fresh vegetables. ⊠ *Market St.* ☎ *095/21867* ☰ *MC, V* ⊗ *Closed Nov.–Feb.*

$$–$$$ ✕ **O'Grady's Seafood.** A Clifden institution, this intimate, town-center restaurant serves fresh local ingredients, primarily seafood, in a style that's more modish than you might expect in the wilds of Connemara. Typi-

cal main courses might include a duo of monkfish and blackened scallops on cilantro duxelles with two sauces, or crisp breast of duckling with sweet caramelized onions. The small main room, once a shop, is decorated in dark pinks and reds with wrought-iron dividers between the tables. ⊠ *Market St.* ☎ *095/21450* ▤ *MC, V* ⊗ *Closed Sun. and Nov.–Apr.*

★ **$$$** ✕⬚ **Rock Glen Manor House.** Riding boots and tennis rackets in the hall make John and Evangeline Roche's beautifully converted 1815 shooting lodge feel more like a private home than a top-class hotel. A turf fire warms the large, sunny drawing room, with plump white armchairs, magazines, books, and board games. Fluffy mohair or chintz spreads cover the beds in the nicely furnished guest rooms. In the Victorian-style restaurant ($$–$$$), you can expect such dishes as roasted rack of lamb with an herb crust and mushroom duxelles. To get here from Clifden, cross the bridge at the west end of town and walk less than 1 km (½ mi) down the R341 Roundstone road. ⊠ *Co. Galway* ☎ *095/21035* 🖷 *095/21737* ⊕ *www.connemara.net/rockglen-hotel* 🛏 *26 rooms with bath* ⚅ *Restaurant, tennis court, fishing, horseback riding, bar* ▤ *AE, MC, V* ⊗ *Closed Nov.–mid-Feb. No lunch* ⎮⊙⎮ *BP.*

$$ ✕⬚ **Erriseask House.** This rambling, two-story modern house has its own

Fodor'sChoice
★ private beach along the rocky shore of Mannin Bay. Warm wooden floors, well-crafted furniture, and an admirable lack of clutter create a restful and very comfortable interior. Chef Fabrice Galand's cooking ($$$) is planned daily according to market availability, but often makes use of local seafood, including scallops, mussels, crab, and prawns. Freshly turf-smoked fillet of beef is a house specialty. ⊠ *R341 Ballyconneely, Co. Galway* ☎ *095/23553* 🖷 *095/23639* ⊕ *www.erriseask.connemara-ireland.com* 🛏 *12 rooms with bath* ⚅ *Restaurant, beach* ▤ *AE, DC, MC, V* ⊗ *Closed early Jan.–mid-Feb.* ⎮⊙⎮ *BP.*

$$ ⬚ **Quay House.** A roaring turf fire in the sitting room greets you at this three-story Georgian house, Clifden's oldest building (1820). It's a short walk from the busy town center, and an oasis of calm beside the harbor quay. Rooms are unusually spacious, and those in the main house are imaginatively decorated with deep-color walls and witty bygones; all but one have sea views. There are also seven studio rooms with balconies overlooking the harbor. Proprietors Julia and Patrick Foyle tucked in homey touches, such as books and model boats. ⊠ *The Quay, Connemara, Co. Galway* ☎ *095/21369* 🖷 *095/21608* ⊕ *www.thequayhouse. com* 🛏 *14 rooms with bath* ⚅ *Some kitchenettes, fishing* ▤ *MC, V* ⊗ *Closed Nov.–mid-Mar., except by arrangement* ⎮⊙⎮ *EP.*

¢–$ ⬚ **Abbeyglen Castle Hotel.** Amid gardens with waterfalls and streams, the hotel sits at the foot of the Twelve Bens. Abbeyglen was built in 1832 by John D'Arcy, who also built Clifden Castle. Each guest room is uniquely decorated with heavy, ornate, dark-wood furniture and rich colors befitting a castle. Although it's in a very quiet and seemingly remote location, the hotel becomes busy during afternoon tea, which is complimentary, and has a busy nightlife scene, with live traditional music in its bar and big-name touring acts in its function room. ⊠ *Sky Rd., Co. Galway* ☎ *095/22832* 🖷 *095/21797* ⊕ *www.abbeyglen.ie* 🛏 *38 rooms with bath* ⚅ *Restaurant, tennis court, pool, sauna, fishing, bar* ▤ *AE, DC, MC, V* ⊗ *Closed last 3 wks Jan.* ⎮⊙⎮ *BP.*

Nightlife

Abbeyglen Castle Hotel (⊠ Sky Rd. ☎ 095/21201) hosts musical sessions in the bar most nights from June to September and occasional visits by big-name acts.

Sports & the Outdoors

BICYCLING   Explore Connemara by renting a bike from **John Mannion & Son** (⊠ Railway View ☎ 095/21160).

GOLF   On a dramatic stretch of Atlantic coastline, the 18-hole, par-72 course at the **Connemara Golf Club** (⊠ Ballyconneely, south of Clifden ☎ 095/23502) measures 7,174 yards.

HORSEBACK   The **Errislannan Manor Connemara Pony Stud and Riding Center** (⊠ Errislannan ☎ 095/21134), which is signposted off the R341 Roundstone
RIDING   road 3 km (2 mi) outside Clifden, has scenic treks on the famous locally bred Connemara pony, instruction, and courses for children.

Shopping

The Connemara Hamper (⊠ Market St. ☎ 095/21054), a small but well-stocked specialist food shop, is an ideal place to pick up picnic fare, with its excellent Irish farmhouse cheeses, pâtés, smoked Connemara salmon, and Irish handmade chocolates. **Millar's Connemara Tweeds** (⊠ Main St. ☎ 095/21038), an arts-and-crafts gallery, carries a good selection of traditional tweeds and hand knits. The **Station House Courtyard** (⊠ Old Railway Station, Bridge St. ☎ 095/21699) is a cobbled courtyard with crafts studios and designer-wear outlets.

en route   As you drive north on N59 toward Letterfrack you'll pass through the **Inagh Valley**, which is flanked by two impressive mountain ranges with distinctive, conical-shape peaks, rising almost directly—without any foothills—to more than 1,968 feet.

Letterfrack

❸ *14 km (9 mi) north of Clifden on N59.*

The 5,000-acre **Connemara National Park** lies southeast of the village of Letterfrack. Its visitor center covers the area's history and ecology, particularly the origins and growth of peat—and presents the depressing statistic that more than 80% of Ireland's peat, 5,000 years in the making, has been destroyed in the last 90 years. You can also get details on the many excellent walks and beaches in the area. ☎ 095/41054 ⊠ *Park free, visitor center €2.50* ☉ *Park freely accessible; visitor center Apr., May, and Sept.–mid-Oct., daily 10–5:30; June, daily 10–6:30; July and Aug., daily 9:30–6:30.*

Where to Stay & Eat

$$$ ✕🏨 **Renvyle House.** A lake at its front door, the Atlantic Ocean at its back door, and the mountains of Connemara as a backdrop form the enthralling setting for this hotel 8 km (5 mi) north of Letterfrack. Once the retreat of the man of letters Oliver St. John Gogarty of Dublin, Renvyle's is rustic and informal; it has exposed beams and brickwork, and numerous open turf fires. All the comfortable guest rooms, elegantly decorated in a floral style, have breathtaking views. The softly lighted restaurant's table d'hôte menu is based on traditional Irish fare ($$$$). Ask about midweek specials. ⊠ *Renvyle, Co. Galway* ☎ *095/43511* 🖷 *095/43515* 🌐 *www.renvyle.com* 🛏 *65 rooms with bath* ⚒ *Restaurant, 9-hole golf course, 2 tennis courts, pool, fishing, horseback riding, bar* ⊟ *AE, DC, MC, V* ☉ *Closed Jan.–mid-Feb.* 🍴 *BP.*

★ $$$ ✕🏨 **Rosleague Manor.** Anne and Patrick Foyle's pink, creeper-clad, two-story Georgian house occupies 30 lovely acres overlooking Ballinakill Bay and the mountains of Connemara. Inside, the clutter of walking and shooting sticks beneath the grandfather clock in the hall sets the informal tone. Well-used antiques, four-poster or large brass bedsteads, and drapes that match the William Morris wallpaper decorate the solidly comfortable bedrooms. The best rooms are at the front on the first floor, overlooking the bay. At dinner in the superb restaurant ($$–$$$$), baked monkfish with crispy capers and balsamic vinegar is a typical entrée. ⊠ *Rosleague Bay, Co. Galway* ☎ *095/41101* 🖷 *095/41168* ⊕*www.rosleague.com* ↰*16 rooms with bath* ⚘ *Restaurant, tennis court, sauna, horseback riding, bar* ▭ *AE, MC, V* ⊘ *Closed Nov.–mid-Mar.* ⫧*◯ BP.*

Nightlife

For traditional music, try the **Bards' Den** (⊠ Main St. ☎ 095/41042).

Sports & the Outdoors

Little Killary Adventure Center (⊠ Salruck, Renvyle ☎ 095/43411) provides sailing and windsurfing instruction on sheltered, coastal waters.

Shopping

Connemara Handcrafts (⊠ village center ☎ 095/41058), on the N59, carries an extensive selection of crafts and women's fashions made by the stellar Avoca Handweavers; there's also a quaint coffee shop.

Kylemore Valley

㉚ *Runs for 6½ km (4 mi) between Letterfrack and the intersection of N59 and R344.*

One of the more conventionally beautiful stretches of road in Connemara passes through Kylemore Valley, which is between the Twelve Bens to the south and the naturally forested Dorruagh Mountains to the north. Kylemore (the name is derived from Coill Mór, Irish for "big wood") looks "as though some colossal giant had slashed it out with a couple of strokes from his mammoth sword," as artist and author John Fitz-Maurice Mills has written. **Kylemore Abbey,** one of the most photographed castles in all of Ireland, is visible across a reedy lake with a backdrop of wooded hillside. The vast Gothic Revival, turreted, graystone castle was built as a private home between 1861 and 1868 by Mitchell Henry, a member of Parliament for County Galway, and his wife, Margaret, who had fallen in love with the spot during a carriage ride while on their honeymoon. The Henrys spared no expense—the final bill for their house is said to have come to £1.5 million—and employed mostly local laborers, thereby abetting the famine relief effort (this area was among the worst hit in all of Ireland). In 1920, nuns from the Irish Abbey of the Nuns of St. Benedict, fleeing their abbey in Belgium during World War I, eventually sought refuge in Kylemore, which had been through a number of owners and decades of decline after the Henrys. Still in residence today, the Benedictine nuns now run a girls' boarding school here. Three reception rooms and the main hall are open to the public, as are a crafts center and simple cafeteria. There's also a 6-acre walled Victorian garden; a shuttle bus from the abbey departs every 15 minutes for the garden. An exhibition and video explaining the history of the house can be viewed year-round at the abbey, and the grounds are freely accessible most of the year. Ask at the excellent crafts shop for directions to the **Gothic Chapel** (a 5-minute walk from the abbey), a tiny replica of Norwich Cathedral built by the Henrys. (Norwich was built by the English Benedictines, in a felicitous anticipation of Kylemore's fate.) ⊠ *About ¾ km (½ mi) back from the Kylemore Valley road* ☎ *095/41146* ⊕ *www.kylemoreabbey.com* 🖷 *Chapel and grounds free; exhibition and garden €7, including shuttle bus to garden* ⊘ *Crafts shop, grounds, and cafeteria mid-Mar.–Nov., daily 10–6 exhibition and garden Easter–Nov., daily 9–5:30.*

Fodor'sChoice
★

Fodor'sChoice
★
Beyond Kylemore, N59 travels for some miles alongside **Killary Harbour,** a narrow fjord (the only one in Ireland) that runs for 16 km (10 mi) between County Mayo's Mweelrea Mountains to the north and County Galway's Dorruagh Mountains to the south. The dark, deep water of the fjord reflects the magnificent steep-sided hills that border it, creating a haunting scene of natural grandeur. The harbor has an extremely safe anchorage, 13 fathoms (78 feet) deep for almost its entire length and sheltered from storms by mountain walls. The rafts floating in Killary Harbour belong to fish-farming consortia that artificially raise salmon and trout in cages beneath the water. This is a matter of some controversy all over the west. Although some people welcome the employment opportunities, others bemoan the visual blight of the rafts. From mid-April through mid-October **Sea Cruise Connemara** (✉ Nancy's Point, 2 km [1 mi] west of Leenane on the N59 Clifden road ☎ 091/566–736) runs 1½-hour trips around Killary Harbour in an enclosed catamaran launch with seating for 120 passengers, plus a bar and restaurant.

Leenane

39 *18 km (11 mi) east of Letterfrack on N59.*

Nestled idyllically at the foot of the Maamturk Mountains and overlooking the tranquil waters of Killary Harbour, Leenane is a tiny village noted for its role as the setting for the film *The Field*, which starred Richard Harris. Its name appears in Martin McDonagh's *Leenane Trilogy*, an unflattering view of rural Irish life featuring a cast of tragicomic grotesques. Although the play was an international hit for Galway's Druid Theatre Company, it brought a renown that the people of Leenane presumably could have done without. Leenane's **Cultural Centre,** in the center of the small town, focuses on the traditional industry of North Connemara and West Mayo. More than 20 breeds of sheep graze around the house, and there are live demonstrations of carding, spinning, weaving, and the dyeing of wool with natural plant dyes. ☎ 095/42323 ⊕ *www.leenane-connemara.com* ✉ €3 ☉ *Apr.–June, Sept., and Oct., daily 9:30–7; July and Aug., daily 9–7.*

Where to Stay

$$$
Fodor'sChoice
★
🏠 **Delphi Lodge.** In the heart of what is arguably Mayo's most spectacular mountain and lake scenery, 5 km (3 mi) east of Leenane off N59, this attractive Georgian sporting lodge heavily stocked with fishing paraphernalia has a lovely lakeside setting. Owners Peter and Jane Mantle are gracious hosts and valuable storehouses of information and stories. Pine furniture, floral curtains, and wonderfully comfortable beds fill the bright, spacious bedrooms, some with lake views. Guests dine together; there's an excellent wine list and a self-service bar. There are also cottages, which require a three-day minimum stay. ✉ *Co. Mayo* ☎ *095/42222* 🖶 *095/42296* ⊕ *www.delphilodge.ie* ⇆ *12 rooms with bath, 5 cottages* ⚘ *Dining room, fishing, billiards, lounge, library* ⊟ *AE, MC, V* ☉ *Closed mid-Dec.–mid-Jan.* ⧆ *BP.*

en route You have two options for traveling onward to Westport. The first is to take the direct route on N59. The second is to detour through the **Doolough Valley** between the Mweelrea Mountains (to the west) and the Sheeffry Hills (to the east) and on to Westport via Louisburgh (on the southern shore of Clew Bay). This latter route adds about 24 km (15 mi) to the trip, but devotees of this part of the west claim that it will take you through the region's most impressive, unspoiled stretch of scenery. If you opt for the longer route, turn left onto R335 1½ km (1 mi) beyond Leenane. Just after this turn, you'll hear the powerful rush of the Aasleagh Falls. You can park over the bridge, stroll along the river's shore, and soak in the splendor of the surrounding mountains.

Look out as you travel north for the great bulk of 2,500-foot **Croagh Patrick**; its size and conical shape make it one of the west's most distinctive landmarks. On clear days a small white building is visible at its summit (it stands on a ½-acre plateau), as is the wide path that ascends to it. The latter is the Pilgrim's Path. Each year about 25,000 people, many of them barefoot, follow the path to pray to St. Patrick in the oratory on its peak. St. Patrick spent the 40 days and nights of Lent here during the period in which he was converting Ireland to Christianity. The traditional date for the pilgrimage is the last Sunday in July; in the past, the walk was made at night, with pilgrims carrying burning torches, but that practice has been discontinued. The climb can be made in about three hours (round-trip) on any fine day and is well worth the effort for the magnificent views of the islands of Clew Bay, the Sheeffry Hills to the south (with the Bens visible behind them), and the peaks of Mayo to the north. The climb starts at Murrisk, a village about 8 km (5 mi) before Westport on the R335 Louisburgh road.

Westport

★ **40** *32 km (20 mi) north of Leenane on R335.*

By far the most attractive town in County Mayo, Westport is on an inlet of Clew Bay, a wide expanse of sea dotted with islands and framed by mountain ranges. The town is a popular fishing center and has several good beaches close by. The architect James Wyatt planned the town in the late 18th century when he was employed to finish nearby Westport House. Westport's streets radiate from its central **Octagon**, where an old-fashioned farmers' market is held on Thursday mornings; look for work clothes, harnesses, tools, and children's toys for sale. Traditional shops—ironmongers, drapers, and the like—dot the streets that lead to the Octagon, while a riverside mall is lined with tall lime trees.

At Westport's Quay, about 2 km (1 mi) outside town, a large warehouse has been attractively restored as holiday apartments, and there are some good bars and decent restaurants; its central attraction, however, is **Westport House and Country Park,** a stately home built on the site of an earlier castle (believed to have been the home of the 16th-century warrior queen, Grace O'Malley). The house was begun in 1730 to the designs of Richard Castle, added to in 1778, and completed in 1788 by architect James Wyatt for the marquess of Sligo. The rectangular, three-story house is furnished with late-Georgian and Victorian pieces. Family portraits by Opie and Reynolds, old Irish silver, and a collection of old Waterford glass are all on display. The home is superbly situated beside a lake with a small formal garden. A word of caution: Westport isn't your usual staid country house. The old dungeons, which belonged to the earlier castle, now house video games, and the grounds have given way to a small amusement park for children and a children's zoo. If these elements don't sound like a draw, arrive early when it's less likely to be busy. The Farmyard area has garden-plant sales, an indoor soft play area, a gift shop, and a coffee shop. ⊠ *Off N59 south of Westport turnoff, clearly signposted from the Octagon* ☎ *098/25430* ⌂ *House €10, family day ticket for all attractions €38* ☉ *House May and Sept., weekends 2–5. Grounds and house June and Aug. 22–31, daily 2–6; July–Aug. 21, Mon.–Sat. 11:30–6, Sun. 2–6.*

Clew Bay is said to have 365 islands, one for every day of the year. The biggest and most interesting to visit is **Clare Island,** at the mouth of the bay. In fine weather the rocky, hilly island, which is 8 km (5 mi) long and 5 km (3 mi) wide, affords beautiful views south toward Connemara, east across Clew Bay, and north to Achill Island. About 150 people live on the island today, but before the 1845-47 famine it had a population of about 1,700. A 15th-century tower overlooking the harbor was once the stronghold of Granuaile, the pirate queen, who ruled the area until her death in 1603. She is buried on the island in its 12th-century Cistercian Abbey. Today most people seek out the island for its unusual peace and quiet, golden beaches, and unspoiled landscape. Ferries depart from Roonagh Pier, near Louisburgh, a scenic 19-km (12-mi) drive from Westport on R335 past several long sandy beaches. The crossing takes about 15 minutes. Dolphins often accompany the boats on the trip, and there are large populations of seals under the island's cliffs. Birdwatchers, hikers, cyclists, and sea anglers may want to stay for longer than a day trip; enquire at the Westport TIO or call the **Clare Island Development Office** (☎ 098/25087) for information about accommodations on the island. ☎ 098/25045 O'Malley's Ferries, 098/25212 *the Pirate Queen boat* 🚢 *Ferry €15 round-trip* ⊙ *Sailings usually twice daily, May–mid-Sept., weather permitting.*

Where to Stay & Eat

★ **$$–$$$** ✕ **Quay Cottage.** Fishing nets, glass floats, lobster pots, and greenery hang from the high-pitched, exposed-beam roof of this tiny waterside cottage at the entrance to Westport House. It is both an informal wine bar and a shellfish restaurant. Rush-seated chairs, polished-oak tables, and an open fire in the evenings add to the comfortable, none-too-formal atmosphere. Try the chowder special (a thick vegetable and mussel soup), garlic-butter crab claws, or a half-pound steak fillet, and be sure to sample the homemade brown bread and ice cream. The restaurant serves wine only. ⊠ *The Quay* ☎ 098/26412 ☰ *AE, MC, V* ⊙ *Closed Jan.*

★ **$$** ✕▣ **Olde Railway Hotel.** When the English novelist William Makepeace Thackeray stayed here in 1842, he called it "one of the prettiest, comfortablist inns in Ireland." You can understand why. Fishing trophies, Victorian plates, framed prints, and watercolors brighten up the lobby and lounge of this unusual, family-run inn. A fascinating mix of Victorian and older antiques decorates the sunny bedrooms, which have double-glazed Georgian sash windows. The rooms overlook either the river or the pretty gardens. The Conservatory Restaurant ($$$$) serves fresh local produce and game specialties, although the bar has an excellent, good-value menu. Ask about weekend specials. ⊠ *The Mall, Co. Mayo* ☎ 098/25166 🖷 098/25090 ⊕ *www.anu.ie/railwayhotel* 🛏 *25 rooms with bath* ♲ *Restaurant, cable TV, fishing, bar* ☰ *AE, MC, V* ⅧⅡ *BP.*

¢ ✕▣ **Newport House.** This handsome, riverside Georgian house dominates the village of Newport, 12 km (7 mi) north of Westport on N59. Kieran and Thelma Thompson's grand and elegant private home has spacious public rooms furnished with gilt-framed family portraits, Regency mirrors and chairs, handwoven Donegal carpeting, and crystal chandeliers. A sweeping staircase leads to the bedrooms, which are decorated with pretty chintz drapes and a mix of Victorian antiques and old furniture. Most bedrooms have sitting areas and good views of the gardens. Oysters, smoked salmon, and roast breast of duck are served in the restaurant ($–$$), along with homemade ice creams. ⊠ *Newport, Co. Mayo* ☎ 098/41222 🖷 098/41613 ⊕ *www.newporthouse.ie* 🛏 *19 rooms with bath* ♲ *Restaurant, fishing, bar* ☰ *AE, DC, MC, V* ⊙ *Closed Oct.–mid-Mar.* ⅧⅡ *BP.*

$$$ 🏨 **Atlantic Coast Hotel.** The stone exterior of this hotel converted from an old warehouse may be old-fashioned, but the interior is entirely modern. Most guest rooms have two beds and are sparsely decorated in contemporary light-wood furniture and, strangely, orange-and-black print curtains and bedspreads. Rooms have a water view plus all the conveniences of a 21st-century hotel. There's a nice fireplace in the lobby, and breakfast is served in the rooftop restaurant, which has beautiful views of the bay. The hotel is in the busy, fashionable quay area about a mile outside town. ✉ *The Quay, Westport, Co. Mayo* ☎ *098/29000* 🖨 *098/29111* ⇌ *85 rooms with bath* ⚅ *Restaurant, in-room data ports, cable TV, indoor pool, gym, fishing, bar* ⊟ *AE, MC, V* ⊠ *BP.*

Nightlife

A good spot to try for traditional music and good pub grub is the **Towers Pub and Restaurant** (✉ The Quay ☎ 098/26534). In the summer, there are outdoor tables set up here beside the bay. In Westport's town center try **Matt Molloy's** (✉ Bridge St. ☎ 098/26655); Matt Malloy is not only the owner but also a member of the musical group the Chieftains. Traditional music is, naturally, the main attraction.

Sports & the Outdoors

BICYCLING   Enjoy the spectacular scenery of Clew Bay at a leisurely pace on a rented bike from **J. P. Breheny & Sons** (✉ Castlebar St. ☎ 098/25020).

FISHING   Fishing tackle, bait, and licenses can be obtained at **Hewetson Bros.** (✉ Bridge St. ☎ 098/26018).

To book a place for the day on a deep-sea-fishing boat operating out of Westport's Clew Bay, contact **Francis Clarke or Austin Gill** (☎ 098/25481).

GOLF   The Fred Hawtree–designed **Westport Golf Club** (✉ Carrowholly ☎ 098/28262), beneath Croagh Patrick, overlooks Clew Bay. The 18-hole, par-73 course has twice been the venue for the Irish Amateur Championship.

HORSEBACK   **Drummindoo Stud and Equitation Center** (✉ Castlebar Rd. ☎ 098/25616)
RIDING   will take you on the Clew Bay Trail, a three-day trek that entails riding on the superb beaches around Clew Bay and staying in farmhouses along the route. Alternatively, you can rent a horse by the hour.

Shopping

Carraig Donn (✉ Bridge St. ☎ 098/26287) carries its own line of knitwear and a good selection of crystal, jewelry, and ceramics. **McCormack's** (✉ Bridge St. ☎ 098/25619) has a traditional butcher shop downstairs, but upstairs it's an attractive gallery and café with work by local artists for sale. **O'Reilly/Turpin** (✉ Bridge St. ☎ 098/28151) sells the best of contemporary Irish design in knitwear, ceramics, and other decorative items.

Satch Kiely (✉ Westport Quay ☎ 098/25775) carries fine antique furniture and decorative pieces. **Treasure Trove** (✉ Bridge St. ☎ 098/25118) has a good stock of antiques and curios, including linen and local memorabilia. **Westport Crystal** (✉ The Quay ☎ 098/27780) is a factory outlet that sells exclusive stemware and giftware.

Achill Island

41 *16 km (10 mi) west of Mulrany, 58 km (36 mi) northwest of Westport.*

Heaven on earth in good weather, when its splendid scenery can be fully appreciated, Achill Island is a destination you'll probably want to head for—but only if you're able to *see* its cliff walks and sandy beaches. At 147 square km (57 square mi) and only 20 feet away from the mainland, this mass of bogs and wild heather is the largest island off Ireland's coast. A short causeway leads from the mainland to Achill Sound, the first village on the island. The main road runs through rhododendron plantations to Keel, which has a 3-km (2-mi) beach with spectacular cathedral-like rock formations in the cliffs at its east end. There's a longer scenic route signposted ATLANTIC DRIVE. Dugoort, on the north shore of the island, is a small village with a beautiful golden strand. Nearby is the cottage used by Heinrich Böll, the German writer and Nobel Prize winner whose *Irish Diary*, written in the 1950s, has introduced many people to this part of Ireland. The cottage today is part of a center for German-Irish cultural exchanges. On Achill's north coast above Dugoort, 2,204-foot Slievemore is the island's highest summit. Until just a few years ago, the people of Achill made a very poor living. Tourism has improved things, as has the establishment of cottage industries (mainly knitting) and shark fishing, which is popular from April through July. Alas, Achill's popularity has led to a rash of new, not always appropriate, development, most noticeably clusters (or "villages") of bleak concrete vacation cottages that stand empty for 10 months out of 12.

Where to Stay

$ 🖾 **Ostan Gob A'Choire.** In the first village you approach arriving from the mainland is this small, waterside, two-story town house (its name means "Achill Sound Hotel") with a brick-and-plate-glass bedroom extension. All bedrooms have sea views, but the nicer ones, with tweed curtains and reproductions of Georgian furniture, are in the old building. 🖾 *Achill Sound, Co. Mayo* ☎ *098/45245* 📠 *098/45621* ↘ *36 rooms with bath* ♿ *Restaurant, bicycles, bar* 🖃 *MC, V* ☯ *Closed Nov.–Mar.* ⏏ *BP.*

Sports & the Outdoors

Tour the cliffs of Achill on a bike from **O'Malley's Island Sports** (🖾 Keel ☎ 098/43125).

en route   The shortest route to Ballina (N59 via Bangor and Crossmolina) runs for about 24 km (15 mi) across desolate, almost uninhabited bog, some of which has had its turf cut down to rock level by successive generations searching for fuel. If you intend to visit the Mullet peninsula, take this route. If you are heading directly for Ballina, take the longer but more interesting route by backtracking to Newport and continuing through Castlebar, Pontoon, and Foxford.

Castlebar

42 *40 km (26 mi) east of Achill Island, 18 km (11 mi) east of Westport on N5.*

The administrative capital of Mayo, Castlebar is a tidy little town with an attractive, tree-bordered green. Hatred of landlords ran high in the area, due to the ruthless, battering-ram evictions ordered by the earl of Lucan during the mid-19th-century famine. The disappearance in the 1960s of his high-living successor, the seventh earl, after the violent death in London of his children's nanny, is said to have given today's tenants a perfect pretext for withholding their rents. In 1879 Michael Davitt founded the Land League, which fought for land reform, here, in the **Imperial Hotel** (🖾 The Green ☎ 094/21961); it's worth a visit to check out the Gothic-style dining room, which serves simply prepared country food. At the **Linen Hall Arts Centre** (🖾 Linenhall St. ☎ 094/23733), exhibitions and performances are often scheduled.

Turlough

43 *6½ km (4 mi) east of Castlebar on N5.*

Before the opening of the Museum of Country Life, Turlough was chiefly visited for its round tower, which marks the site of an early monastery, traditionally associated with Saint Patrick, and the nearby ruins of a 17th-century church. Nowadays, it is one of many Irish villages whose empty streets bear witness to dramatic changes in the rural way of life. Once a thriving hub, with a village school, two pubs, and a busy shop, Turlough now has a population of about 300, one pub with a small shop attached, and no school. Rather than working on the land, most of the locals commute to jobs in nearby Castlebar.

Fodor'sChoice ★

To understand the forces that have led to such dramatic changes in Turlough, pay a visit to the **Museum of Country Life**, which focuses on life in rural Ireland between 1860 and 1960—a way of life that remained unchanged for many years, then suddenly came to an end within living memory. At this highly acclaimed museum, the only branch of the National Museum of Ireland outside Dublin, you're invited to imagine yourself back in a vanished world, before the internal combustion engine, rural electrification, indoor plumbing, television, and increased education transformed people's lives and expectations. For many, this is a journey into a strange place, where water had to be carried from the well, turf brought home from the bog, fires lighted daily for heat and cooking, and clothes made painstakingly by hand in the long winter evenings. Among the displayed items are authentic furniture and utensils; hunting, fishing, and agricultural implements; clothing; and objects relating to games, pastimes, religion, and education.

The museum experience starts in Turlough Park House, built in the Gothic Revival style in 1865 and set in pretty lakeside gardens. Just three rooms have been restored to illustrate the way the landowners lived. A sensational four-story, curved building houses the main exhibit. Cleverly placed windows take in panoramic views of both the surrounding park and the distant round tower, allowing you to reflect on the reality beyond the museum's walls. The shop sells museum-branded and handcrafted gift items as well as a good selection of books on related topics. A café with indoor and outdoor tables is in the stable yard, and you can take scenic lakeside walks in the park. Craft demonstrations and workshops take place on Wednesday and Sunday afternoons. ⊠ *Turlough Park* ☎ *01/648–6453 in Dublin* ⊕ *www.museum.ie* ✉ *Free* ☉ *Tues.–Sat. 10–5, Sun. 2–5.*

en route

As you travel from Turlough northeast to Ballina, you have a choice of two routes. The longer and more scenic is via the tiny, wooded village of Pontoon, skirting the western shore of Lough Conn and passing through the rough bogland of the Glen of Nephin, beneath the dramatic heather-clad slopes of Nephin Mountain (2,653 feet). The shorter route follows N5 and N58 to Foxford, a pretty village with several crafts and antiques shops. A good place for a break is the **Foxford Woollen Mills Visitor Center**, where you can explore the crafts shop and grab a bite at the restaurant. The "Foxford Experience" tells the story of the wool mill, famous for its tweeds and blankets, from the time of the famine in the mid-19th century—when it was founded by the Sisters of Charity to combat poverty—to the present day. ⊠ *Lower Main St., Foxford* ☎ *094/56756* ✉ *€8* ☉ *Nov.–Apr., Mon.–Sat. 10–6, Sun. 2–6; May–Oct., Mon.–Sat. 10–6, Sun. noon–6; tour every 20 mins.*

Ballina

44 *34 km (22 mi) northeast of Turlough.*

Ballina's chief attraction is fishing for salmon and trout in the River Moy and nearby Lough Conn. With a population of 7,500, this is the largest town in County Mayo. To some eyes, Ballina's town center may appear run-down, but its unspoiled, old-fashioned shops and pubs contain many treasures. Try the bar food at **Gaughan's** (⊠ O'Rahilly St. ☎ 096/21151), where the classic wooden interior dates from the mid-19th century.

Where to Stay & Eat

$$ ✕⊞ **Enniscoe House.** Colorful corridors, fishing motifs, and quirky, crooked stairways make this pink, Georgian mansion on the shores of Lough Conn an appealing spot. Its 150 acres are crisscrossed with walks and have more than 3 km (2 mi) of peaceful lakeshore. Owner Susan Kellett converted many of the farm buildings into offices, which now house independent organizations, including a Mayo genealogy center, an antiques shop, and a tearoom. Meals ($$$$; reserve ahead) include fruits and vegetables grown in the organic garden. The hotel lies 4½ km (3 mi) south of Crossmolina and 20 km (12½ mi) west of Ballina. ⊠ *Castlehill, Co. Mayo* ☎ *096/31112* ⧉ *096/31773* ⊕ *www.enniscoe.com* ⇌ *6 rooms with bath* ⟂ *Restaurant, fishing* ⊟ *AE, MC, V* ☉ *Closed mid-Oct.–Mar.* ⦿ *BP.*

$$ ⊞ **Downhill House Hotel.** Anglers and outdoorsy types flock to this hotel on 40 wooded acres beside a gushing tributary of the River Moy (just off the N59 Sligo road). The late-Victorian main house feels a little gloomy downstairs, but it's comfortable. Georgian-style furniture and tastefully coordinated quilts and drapes decorate the rooms here. The rooms in the newer wing tend to be smaller than those in the main house, but the former have good views of the river across the garden. There's music in the bar on weekends and midweek in July and August. Ask about weekend specials. ⊠ *Downhill Rd., Co. Mayo* ☎ *096/21033* ⧉ *096/21338* ⊕ *www.downhillhotel.ie* ⇌ *50 rooms with bath* ⟂ *Restaurant, 3 tennis courts, indoor pool, gym, hot tub, sauna, steam room, fishing, squash, 2 bars, convention center* ⊟ *AE, DC, MC, V* ⦿ *BP.*

Sports & the Outdoors

BICYCLING Head for the coast north of Ballina on a bike from **Gerry's Cycle Center** (⊠ 6 Lord Edward St. ☎ 096/70455).

FISHING Fishing bait, tackle, and licenses can be obtained from **John Walkin** (⊠ Tone St. ☎ 096/22442).

GOLF **Ballina Golf Club** (⊠ Bonniconlon Rd. ☎ 096/21718) is an 18-hole parkland course, built in 1924, 1½ km (1 mi) from the town center; you can rent golf clubs here. The 18-hole **Carne Golf Links** (⊠ Belmullet ☎ 097/82292), at Belmullet Golf Club, 72 km (45 mi) west of Ballina, is one of Ireland's renowned links courses.

Shopping

McGrath's Foodland Delicatessen (⊠ O'Rahilly St. ☎ 096/21198) is an old-fashioned grocery, handy for picnic ingredients.

The North Mayo Coast

Starts 12 km (7½ mi north of Ballina at Killala.

The north Mayo coast, a dramatic, windswept stretch of cliffs, runs from Killala, the gateway to the coast, to Erris Head on the Mullet peninsula in the far west of the county. The sparsely inhabited landscape beneath an ever-changing sky consists of small farms and open moorland. The small roads and stunning views are attractive to cyclists, but be warned: the wind howls in across the Atlantic directly from Iceland, the nearest landmass. Although there are no signposted trails on this coast, there are plenty of cliff footpaths and small roads for walkers to explore. Don't miss the blowholes on Downpatrick Head—great gaps in the rocks through which plumes of water spew in rough weather.

Killala, 12 km (7½ mi) north of Ballina, is a pleasant little seaside town overlooking Killala Bay. This was the scene of the unsuccessful French invasion of Ireland, led by Wolfe Tone in 1798. The history of this tiny bishopric goes back much further, though, as evidenced by its round, 12th-century tower.

★ 45 Nowadays, the chief reason for visiting this coast is to see the **Céide Fields.** Widely recognized as one of Europe's most significant megalithic sites, the fields consist of rows and patterns of stones that have been preserved under a 5,000-year-old bog. These stones are the remnants of dwelling places and stone-walled fields built by a peaceful, well-organized farming community. A striking glass-and-steel pyramid houses the visitor center, where displays and an audiovisual show bring this strange landscape to life. Admission includes an optional guided walk through an excavated section of the stones; wet-weather gear is provided when necessary. ⊠ *R314, 5 km (3 mi) west of Ballycastle* ☎ *096/43325* ⊕ *www. heritageireland.ie* ⚲ *€3.50* ⊙ *Mid-Mar.–May and Oct., daily 10–5; June–Sept., daily 9:30–6:30; Nov., daily 10–4:30; Dec.–mid-Mar. by advance booking only.*

Shopping
Hackett & Turpin (⊠ Carrowteige, Ballina ☎ 097/88925) is a factory outlet for Irish sweaters. From R314 beyond the Céide Fields, follow signs for Benwee Head.

THE WEST A TO Z

To research prices, get advice from other travelers, and book travel arrangements, visit www.fodors.com.

AIR TRAVEL
Aer Lingus has daily flights from London's Heathrow Airport to Galway and Knock via Dublin; the trip takes about two hours. Ryanair flies to Knock twice daily from London's Stanstead Airport; flying time is 80 minutes. Aer Arann flies to Knock from Manchester daily.

Aer Arann has four flights daily on weekdays and two flights on weekends to the Aran Islands from Connemara Airport in Inverin. During July and August planes leave every half hour. The flights call at all three of the Aran Islands. The journey takes about six minutes and costs about €44 round-trip, or about €69 including one night's B&B. For about €32 you can fly one-way and travel one-way by boat from Rossaveal. Ask about other special offers at the time of booking.
🛈 Carriers **Aer Arann** ☎ 091/593-034. **Aer Lingus** ☎ 01/844-4747. **Ryanair** ☎ 01/ 844-4411.

AIRPORTS
The west's most convenient international airport is Shannon, 25 km (16 mi) east of Ennis in the southwest. Galway Airport, near Galway City, is used mainly for internal flights, with steadily increasing U.K. traffic. Knock International Airport, at Charlestown—near Knock, in County Mayo—is also used for internal flights and has direct daily services to London's Stansted, and Manchester. A small airport for internal traffic

only is at Knockrowen, Castlebar, in County Mayo. Flying time from Dublin is 25 to 30 minutes to all airports. No scheduled flights run from the United States to Galway or Knock; use Shannon Airport. Connemara Airport at Inverin, which is 29 km (18 mi) west of Galway on R336, services the Aran Islands.

🛪 Airport Information **Connemara Airport** ☎ 091/593-034. **Galway Airport** ☎ 091/752-874. **Knock International Airport** ☎ 094/67222. **Knockrowen Airport** ☎ 094/22853. **Shannon Airport** ☎ 061/471-444.

TRANSFERS From Shannon Airport you can pick up a rental car to drive into the west, or you can take a bus to Limerick, from which there are bus connections into the west.

Galway Airport is 6½ km (4 mi) from Galway City. No regular bus service is available from the airport to Galway, but most flight arrivals are taken to Galway Rail Station in the city center by an airline courtesy coach. Inquire when you book. A taxi from the airport to the city center costs about €10.

If you're flying to Knock International Airport, you can pick up your rental car at the airport. Otherwise, inquire at the time of booking about transport to your final destination. No regular bus service is available from the airport. Connemara Airport is accessible by shuttle bus.

BOAT & FERRY TRAVEL

A ferry leaves Tarbert for Killimer every hour on the half hour and takes 20 minutes. The ferry runs every day of the year except Christmas and costs €13 one-way, €20 round-trip. (Ferries return from Killimer every hour on the hour.)

There are several options for traveling to the Aran Islands. Aran Ferries runs a boat to the Aran Islands from Rossaveal, 32 km (20 mi) west of Galway City, which makes the crossing in 20 minutes and costs about €28 round-trip, including the shuttle bus from Galway. If you are heading for Inisheer, the smallest island, the shortest crossing is from Doolin in County Clare. A ferry, operated by Aran Ferries, leaves from Doolin Pier, with up to 12 sailings daily, from June through the end of September. The crossing takes about 20 minutes and costs €20 round-trip.

Island Ferries, which has a booking office in the TIO in Galway City, has a one-hour crossing from Rossaveal for €25 round-trip, with up to five sailings a day in summer, weather permitting. Bicycles are transported free off-season, but there may be a charge in July and August: inquire when booking. Discounts are available for families, students, and groups of four or more. If you stay a night or two on the islands, ask about accommodations when booking your ferry, as there are some very competitive deals. Between June and September, O'Brien Ferries sails for the Aran Islands from Galway Docks, a five-minute walk from Eyre Square. The ferries run three times a week in June and September (usually Tuesday, Thursday, and Saturday), daily in July and August. The crossing takes 90 minutes and costs €20 round-trip.

For travel between the Aran Islands, frequent inter-island ferries (run by Aran Ferries, Island Ferries, and O'Brien Ferries) are available in summer, but tickets are nontransferable, so ask the captain of your ferry about the inter-island schedule if you plan to visit more than one island; otherwise, your trip can become expensive. You can purchase your ferry tickets on the island or at the TIO in Galway.

🛥 Boat & Ferry Information **Aran Ferries** ✉ TIO, Forster St., Eyre Sq., Galway City ☎ 091/568-903 or 091/537-700. **Island Ferries** ☎ 091/565-352. **O'Brien Ferries** ✉ New Docks, Galway City ☎ 091/567-676. **Tarbert–Killimer Ferry** ☎ 065/905-3124.

BUS TRAVEL

Bus Éireann runs several expressway buses into the region from Dublin, Cork City, and Limerick City to Ennis, Galway City, Westport, and Ballina, the principal depots in the region. Expect bus rides to last about one hour longer than the time it would take you to travel the distance by car.

In July and August, the provincial bus service is augmented by daily services to most resort towns. Outside these months, many coastal towns receive only one or two buses per week. Bus routes are often slow and circuitous, and service can be erratic. A copy of the Bus Éireann timetable (€0.95 from any station) is essential.

Citylink operates frequent buses, with up to 14 departures daily, between Galway City and Dublin and Dublin Airport. The trip costs €10 one-way, €15 round-trip.

🚌 Bus Depots **Ballina Station** ☎ 096/71800. **Ennis Station** ☎ 065/682-4177. **Galway City Station (Ceannt Station)** ☎ 091/562-000. **Westport Station** ☎ 098/25711.
🚌 Bus Lines **Bus Éireann** ☎ 01/836-6111 in Dublin; 061/313-333 in Limerick; 021/508-188 in Cork ⊕ www.buseireann.ie. **Citylink** ✉ Unit 1, Forster Court, Galway City ☎ 091/564-163 ⊕ www.citylink.ie.

CAR RENTAL

If you haven't already picked up a rental car at Shannon Airport, try the following rental agencies.

🚗 Agencies **Avis** ✉ Galway City ☎ 091/568-886. **Budget** ✉ Galway City ☎ 091/566-376. **Casey's Auto Rentals** ✉ Turlough Rd., Castlebar ☎ 094/24618. **Diplomat Rent A Car** ✉ Knock International Airport, Charlestown ☎ 094/67252. **Enterprise** ✉ Galway City ☎ 091/771-200. **Euro Mobil** ✉ Galway City ☎ 091/753-037. **Hertz Rent A Car** ✉ Galway Airport ☎ 091/752-502. **Johnson & Perrot** ✉ Galway City ☎ 091/568-886. **National** ✉ Galway City ☎ 091/771-929.

CAR TRAVEL

A car is the best means of traveling within the west. The 219-km (136-mi) Dublin–Galway trip takes about three hours. From Cork City take N20 through Mallow and N21 to Limerick City, picking up the N18 Ennis–Galway road in Limerick. The 209-km (130-mi) drive from Cork to Galway takes about three hours. From Killarney the shortest and most pleasant route to cover the 193 km (120 mi) to Galway (three hours) is to take N22 to Tralee, then N69 through Listowel to Tarbert and the ferry across the Shannon Estuary to Killimer in County Clare from there, join N68 in Kilrush, and then pick up N18 in Ennis.

ROAD CONDITIONS The west has good, wide main roads (National Primary Routes) and better-than-average local roads (National Secondary Routes), both known as "N" routes. If you stray off the beaten track on the smaller Regional ("R") or unnumbered routes, particularly in Connemara and County Mayo, you may encounter some hazardous mountain roads. Narrow, steep, and twisty, they are also frequented by untended sheep, cows, and ponies grazing "the long acre" (as the strip of grass beside the road is called) or simply straying in search of greener pastures. If you find a sheep in your path, just sound the horn, and it should scramble away. A good maxim for these roads is: "you never know what's around the next corner." Bear this in mind, and adjust your speed accordingly. Hikers and cyclists constitute an additional hazard on narrow roads in the summer.

Within the Connemara Irish-speaking area, signs are in Irish only. The main signs to recognize are Gaillimh (Galway), Ros an Mhil (Rossaveal), An Teach Doite (Maam Cross), and Sraith Salach (Recess).

ROAD MAPS A good map, available through newsagents and TIOs, gives Irish and English names where needed.

EMERGENCIES

For a doctor or dentist in County Clare, contact the Mid-Western Health Board (in County Limerick) in Counties Galway and Mayo, contact the Western Health Board.

🔽 Doctors & Dentists **Mid-Western Health Board** ⊠ Catherine St., Limerick ☎ 061/316-655. **Western Health Board** ⊠ Merlin Park, Galway City ☎ 091/751-131.
🔽 Emergency Services **Ambulance, fire, police** ☎ 999.
🔽 Pharmacies **Matt O'Flaherty** ⊠ 39 Eyre Sq., Galway City ☎ 091/562-927. **O'Donnell's** ⊠ Bridge St., Westport ☎ 098/25163.

TOURS

Galway City's TIO has details of walking tours of Galway, which are organized by request. All TIOs in the west provide lists of suggested cycle tours.

The only full- and half-day guided bus tours in the region start from Galway. Bus Éireann coordinates two full-day tours, one covering Connemara and the other the Burren (each €15.25). Tours run from early June to mid-October only, with the widest choice available between mid-July and mid-August. Book in advance at the Galway City TIO, Ceannt Railway Station on Eyre Square, or the Salthill TIO, which also serve as departure points.

Lally Tours runs a day tour through Connemara and County Mayo and another to the Burren. It also operates a vintage double-decker bus, departing from Eyre Square, which runs hourly tours of Galway City from 10:30 AM until 4:30 PM from mid-March to October; tickets cost €10.

O'Neachtain Day Tours operates full-day tours of Connemara and the Burren. Tickets, €16.50 each, can be purchased from the Galway City TIO; tours depart across the street.

🔽 Bus Tours **Bus Éireann** ☎ 091/562-000. **Ceannt Railway Station** ☎ 091/562-000. **Lally Tours** ☎ 091/562-905. **O'Neachtain Day Tours** ☎ 091/553-188 ⊕ www.oneachtaintours.com. **Salthill TIO** ☎ 091/520-500.

TRAIN TRAVEL

Galway City, Westport, and Ballina are the main rail stations in the region. For County Clare, travel from Cork City, Killarney, or Dublin's Heuston Station to Limerick City and continue the journey by bus. Trains for Galway, Westport, and Ballina leave from Dublin's Heuston Station. The journey time to Galway is three hours; to Ballina, 3¾ hours; and to Westport, 3½ hours.

Rail service within the region is limited. The major destinations of Galway City and Westport/Ballina are on different branch lines. Connections can only be made between Galway and the other two cities by traveling inland for about an hour to Athlone.

🔽 Train Information **Ballina Station** ☎ 096/71818. **Galway Station** ☎ 091/564-222. **Heuston Station** ☎ 01/836-6222. **Limerick City Station** ☎ 061/315-555. **Westport Station** ☎ 098/25253.

TRANSPORTATION AROUND THE WEST

A car is essential in the west, especially from September through June. Although the main cities of the area are easily reached from the rest of Ireland by rail or bus, transport within the region is sparse and badly coordinated. If a rental car is out of the question, your best option is to make Galway your base and take day tours (available mid-June through

September) west to Connemara and south to the Burren, and a day or overnight trip to the Aran Islands. It *is* possible to explore the region by local and intercity bus services, but you will need plenty of time.

VISITOR INFORMATION

Bord Fáilte provides free information service, tourist literature, and an accommodations booking service at its TIOs. The following offices are open all year, generally weekdays 9–6, daily during the high season: Aran Islands (Inishmore), Ennis, Galway City, Oughterard, and Westport.

Other TIOs, which are open seasonally, generally weekdays 9–6 and Saturday 9–1, are as follows: Achill (June–August), Ballina (April–October), Castlebar (May–mid-September), Clifden (March–October), Cliffs of Moher (April–October), Kilkee (May–August), Kilrush (June–August), Salthill (May–September), Thoor Ballylee (April–mid-October).

🚩 Tourist Information **Achill** ⊠ Co. Mayo ☎ 098/45384. **Aran Islands (Inishmore)** ⊠ Co. Galway ☎ 099/61263 🖷 099/61420. **Ballina** ⊠ Cathedral Rd., Co. Mayo ☎ 096/70848. **Castlebar** ⊠ Linenhall St., Co. Mayo ☎ 094/21207. **Clifden** ⊠ Galway Rd., Co. Galway ☎ 095/21163. **Cliffs of Moher** ⊠ Co. Clare ☎ 065/708-1171. **Ennis** ⊠ Arthur's Row, Town Center, Co. Clare ☎ 065/682-8366 ⊕ www.shannon-dev.ie/tourism. **Galway City** ⊠ Forster St., Eyre Sq., Co. Galway ☎ 091/537-700 ⊕ www.irelandwest.ie. **Kilkee** ⊠ O'Connell Sq., Co. Clare ☎ 065/905-6112. **Kilrush** ⊠ The Square, Co. Clare ☎ 065/905-1577. **Oughterard** ⊠ Main St., Co. Galway ☎ 091/552-808. **Salthill** ⊠ The Promenade, Co. Galway ☎ 091/520-500. **Thoor Ballylee** ⊠ Near Gort, Co. Clare ☎ 091/631-436. **Westport** ⊠ The Mall, Co. Mayo ☎ 098/25711 🖷 098/26709.

THE NORTHWEST

7

FODOR'S CHOICE
Corncrake Restaurant, *Carndonagh*
Cromleach Lodge, *Castlebaldwin hotel*
Glenveagh National Park, *Church Hill*
St. Ernan's House, *Donegal Town hotel*
Green Gate, *Ardvally B&B*

HIGHLY RECOMMENDED

HOTELS
Coopershill, *Riverstown*
Rathmullan House, *Rathmullan*
St. John's Country House and Restaurant, *Fahan*
Woodhill House, *Ardara*

RESTAURANTS
L'Atlantique Restaurant, *Ardara*
Blueberry Tea Room, *Donegal Town*
Castle Murray House Hotel Restaurant, *Dunkineely*
Glebe House, *Collooney*

SIGHTS
Ardara, *County Donegal town*
Grianan Fort, *near Letterkenny*
Horn Head, *Dunfanaghy*
Lough Gill, *lake near Sligo Town*
Sligo Town

Updated by
Anneliese Paull

GLANCE AT A MAP OF IRELAND THAT HAS scenic roads marked in green, and chances are your eye is quickly drawn to the far-flung peninsulas of northwest Ireland. At virtually every bend in the roads of Counties Donegal, Leitrim, and Sligo there's something to justify all those green ribbons. On an island where there's no shortage of majestic scenery, the northwest claims at least its fair share. Cool, clean waters from the roaring Atlantic Ocean shape the terrain into long peninsulas—a raw, sensual landscape that makes it seem as if Earth is still under construction.

But what you see *now* may not be what it looks like an hour from now. Clouds and rain linger over mountains, glens, cliffs, beaches, and bogs, to be chased minutes later by sunshine and rainbows. The air, the light, and the colors of the countryside change as though with a turn of a kaleidoscope. The fickle skies brighten and darken, tempting a spectrum of subtle reds and purples from the unkempt gorse and heather, then washing the grassy meadows greener than any green you've ever seen. The writer William Butler Yeats and his brother Jack Butler Yeats, a painter, immortalized this land in their work. Walk in their footsteps through the splendidly lush and rugged countryside.

Northwest Ireland covers the most northerly part of Ireland's Atlantic coastline, running from Sligo in the south along Donegal's remote, windswept peninsulas to Malin Head in the far north. These maritime landscapes are said to have given their colors to the most famous local product, handwoven tweed, which reflects the browns of the peaty heathland and the purples of the heather. Donegal, a sparsely populated rural county of small farms and fishing boats, shares its inland border with Northern Ireland; the border is partly formed by the River Foyle. Inland from Sligo is Leitrim, a county best known for its numerous lakes and loughs, some of which join up with the River Shannon, on the easterly border of this region.

County Donegal was part of the near-indomitable ancient kingdom of Ulster, which was not conquered by the English until the 17th century. By the time the English withdrew in the 1920s, they had still not eradicated rural Donegal's Celtic inheritance. It thus shouldn't come as a surprise that County Donegal contains Ireland's largest Gaeltacht (Irish-speaking) area. Driving in this part of the country, you may either be frustrated or amused whenever you come to a crossroads. Signposts show only the Irish place-names, often so unlike the English versions as to be completely unrecognizable. All is not lost, however, as maps generally give both the Irish and the English names, and locals are usually more than happy to help out with directions (in English)—usually with a yarn thrown in. So if you're in a hurry, first of all you're in the wrong place, and second, you should have started earlier.

Tucked into the folds of the hills, modest little market towns and unpretentious villages with muddy streets go about their business quietly. In the squelchy peat bogs, cutters working with long shovels pause to watch and wave as you drive past. Remember to drive slowly along the country lanes, for around any corner you may find a whitewashed thatched cottage with children playing outside its scarlet door, a shepherd leading his flock, a wayward sheep or two looking philosophical about having strayed from their field, or a farmer wobbling along in the middle of the road on his old faithful sit-up-and-beg bicycle.

The area is overwhelmingly rural and underpopulated. That's not to say there isn't a bit of action here. Sligo Town, has gone through a major renaissance. On a typical weekday, the little winding streets are as busy as those of Galway, and it seems to be giving Dublin's Temple Bar a run

Numbers in the text correspond to numbers in the margin and on the Yeats Country, Sligo Town, and the Northern Peninsulas maps.

7

If you have 2 days

Start in **Sligo Town** ❶–❼, and look at the Yeats memorabilia in the **Model Arts Centre and Niland Gallery** ❷. Take along a volume of W. B.'s poetry (or at the least his poem "The Lake Isle of Innisfree"), as you follow the Yeats Trail around woody **Lough Gill** ❾. After the road north passes W. B.'s grave in **Drumcliff** ⓭ churchyard, detour to **Lissadell House** ⓮, where he was a frequent visitor, and then head to Creevykeel, a tomb dating from 3000 BC. Drive through **Ballyshannon** ⓱ and on to ⌂ **Donegal Town** ⓲. The next day head for the port of **Killybegs** ⓴, beyond which the views of Donegal Bay improve as the road twists and descends into Kilcar, a village known for its tweeds. The road then passes through moorland and reaches **Glencolumbkille** ㉑, a hamlet around the rocky harbor of Glen Bay. On the far side of the Glengesh Pass, the village of **Ardara** ㉒ is the center of the region's tweed heritage and also a good spot to hear traditional music. Return from here southward to Donegal Town and either to Dublin via Ballyshannon or to Galway via Sligo.

If you have 5 days

Stretch the first day of the itinerary above into two days. You may want to push on at the end of your second day to ⌂ **Ardara** ㉒ and visit the tweed heritage center there rather than stopping at ⌂ **Donegal Town** ⓲. On your third day, follow the coast road from Ardara up to Dungloe. North of here is a large Irish-speaking parish known as **The Rosses** ㉜. Working northward around this peninsula brings you to Benbeg. From here you can follow another route through the **Gweedore Headland** ㉛, with its bleak terrain, to Bloody Foreland Head. Meenlaragh, east along the same headland, is the departure point for **Tory Island** ㉚, a rocky, inaccessible place that has nevertheless been inhabited since prehistoric times.

The town of ⌂ **Dunfanaghy** ㉙ is on the shores of Sheephaven Bay and within easy reach of **Ards Forest Park** ㉘, which has trails leading to prehistoric sites. Explore Doe Castle, near **Creeslough** ㉗. **Carrigart** ㉖, a village with old-fashioned pubs, gives access to a signposted Atlantic Drive around the Rosguill Peninsula. From here either head south through sleepy Milford to **Ramelton** ㉔, a hilly town on the edge of Lough Swilly, one of the loveliest of Donegal's big fjordlike inlets, and on to ⌂ **Letterkenny** ㉓, a convenient base for exploring the rest of the county; or head north to ⌂ **Rathmullan** ㉕, where a number of hotels are right on the shores of Lough Swilly. The next day head for the Glebe House and Gallery, on the northwest shore of **Gartan Lough** ㉟, which exhibits works by major Impressionists, Picasso, Jack B. Yeats, and Tory Islanders. Alternatively, you can head northwest to **Glenveagh National Park** ㉞ or drive east to **Grianan Fort** ㊱, with its panorama of Donegal, Derry, and the Inishowen Peninsula. From Letterkenny head northeast across the border into Northern Ireland and the city of Derry or south for Sligo Town and Galway.

for its money when it comes to stylish restaurants and trendy people—an amazing feat for a town of only 19,000 souls. Sligo Town pulses not only in the present but with the charge of history, for it was the childhood home of W. B. and Jack B. Yeats, the place that, more than any other, gave rise to their particular geniuses—or, as Jack B. put it: "Sligo was my school and the sky above it." There are more bright lights in Letterkenny, which has to its credit the longest main street of any town in Ireland. Glenveagh National Park exemplifies the surprising alliance between nature and culture in northwest Ireland: perched on the edge of a glorious lake in the midst of 24,000 acres of some of Ireland's most thrilling wilderness, sits a fairy-tale castle. The castle reflects the life and times of the man who owned it for 50 years: Henry McIlhenny, the millionaire American philanthropist and art collector whose Impressionist paintings now hang in the Philadelphia Museum of Art.

Keep in mind, though, that the whole region—and County Donegal in particular—attracts droves of tourists during July and August; this is a favorite weekend vacation area for people who live in neighboring Northern Ireland. A few places, frankly, are quite spoiled by popularity with tourists, careless development, and uninspired architecture—particularly the ugly bungalows that have replaced thatched cottages and Georgian farmhouses as typical Irish rural homes. The Rosses Peninsula on Donegal's west coast, still sometimes described as beautiful, is marred by too much building. Bundoran, on the coast between Sligo Town and Donegal Town, a cheap and cheerful family beach resort full of so-called "Irish gift shops" and "amusement arcades," is another place to pass through rather than visit. On the whole, though, northwest Ireland is big enough, untamed enough, and grand enough to be able to absorb all of its summer (and weekend) tourists without too much harm.

Exploring the Northwest

This chapter outlines three autonomous routes through northwest Ireland. These routes can easily be linked if you want to poke around the area over five or so days. The first journey begins in Sligo Town and covers its immediate environs—all the major sights within a roughly 24-km (15-mi) radius, many of which have strong associations with the Yeatses. The second trip skirts the entirety of Donegal Bay, from Mullaghmore in the south to Glencolumbkille to the far north and west, before heading inland as far as Ardara. The last route begins at the other end of Donegal, in Letterkenny, and covers the far northwest corner of County Donegal before swinging you back around to the Inishowen Peninsula, the tip-top of Ireland, delicately balanced between the Republic and Northern Ireland. If you decide to explore this chapter from back to front (this makes sense if you're arriving from Northern Ireland), begin with the last itinerary, in Letterkenny; skip the trip to the Inishowen Peninsula; and pick up the middle tour from either Gratan Lough or Burtonport.

About the Restaurants

Although northwest Ireland has not been considered a great gastronomic center, in the last few years Sligo Town has established itself as a sort of last stop for food lovers, with a number of food-related shops worth visiting. On the dining front, here and there, newcomers are serving up well-above-average food in memorable settings, though overall, the majority of restaurants serve plain and simple fare such as traditional Irish lamb stew or bacon and cabbage served with generous helpings of potatoes (often prepared in at least two ways on the same plate), washed down with creamy, lip-smacking pints of Guinness. You're likely to find

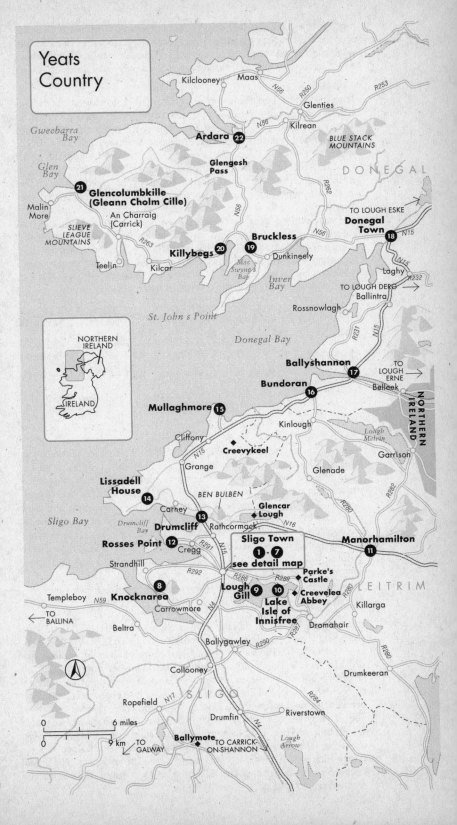

Yeats
Country

NORTHERN
IRELAND

IRELAND

Kilclooney
Maas
N56
R250
R253
Glenties
N56
Kilrean
Gweebarra
Bay
BLUE STACK
MOUNTAINS
Ardara 22
DONEGAL
Glen
Bay
**Glengesh
Pass**
R262
21 **Glencolumbkille
(Gleann Cholm Cille)**
TO LOUGH ESKE
Malin
More
An Charraig
(Carrick)
N56
**Donegal
Town** 18 N15
SLIEVE
LEAGUE
MOUNTAINS
R263
Bruckless
19
Laghy
R232
Teelin
Kilcar
Killybegs 20
Dunkineely
TO LOUGH DERG
Ballintra
Mac
Swyne's
Bay
Inver
Bay
Ballintra
Rossnowlagh
N15
St. John's Point
Donegal Bay
R231
Ballyshannon
17
TO
LOUGH
ERNE
Bundoran
16
Belleek
Mullaghmore 15
Kinlough
Lough
Melvin
NORTHERN
IRELAND
Cliffony
N15
Garrison
Creevykeel
R282
Grange
Glenade
BEN BULBEN
**Lissadell
House**
14
Carney
**Glencar
Lough**
N16
R280
Sligo Bay
Drumcliff
Bay
13
Drumcliff
Rathcormack
Manorhamilton
11
Rosses Point 12
R291
Cregg
Sligo Town
1 · 7
see detail map
Strandhill
R292
R286
R288
**Parke's
Castle**
LEITRIM
8
Knocknarea
**Lough
Gill**
9
10
**Creevelea
Abbey**
Killarga
Templeboy
N59
Carrowmore
**Lake Isle of
Innisfree**
Dromahair
Beltra
N4
Ballygawley
R290
R281
Drumkeeran
R280
Colooney
Drumin
Drumkeeran
TO
BALLINA
SLIGO
R284
Ropefield
N17
0   6 miles
0   9 km
TO
GALWAY
Ballymote
TO CARRICK-
ON-SHANNON
Drumfin
N4
Riverstown
Lough
Arrow

the finest food at the higher-quality country houses, where chefs elegantly prepare local meat, fish, and produce in a hybrid Irish-French haute cuisine. Another trend: several of the area's more successful restaurants have added accommodations, making them good overnight destinations.

About the Hotels

True, it's the farthest-flung corner of Ireland, but northwest Ireland has a steady stream of arrivals—especially in July and August. Thanks to the area's popularity as a weekend getaway for residents of Northern Ireland, good bed-and-breakfasts and small hotels are prevalent. In the two major towns—Sligo Town and Donegal Town—and the small coastal resorts in between, traditional provincial hotels have been modernized (albeit not always elegantly). Yet they retain some of the charm that comes with older buildings and personalized service. Away from these areas, your best overnight choice is usually a modest guest house that includes bed, breakfast, and an evening meal, though you can find a number of first-class country-house hotels with a gracious professionalism comparable to properties elsewhere in Ireland. Consider staying in an Irish-speaking home to get to know members of the area's Gaeltacht population; the local Tourist Information Office (TIO) can be helpful in making a booking with an Irish-speaking family.

WHAT IT COSTS in euros					
	$$$$	**$$$**	**$$**	**$**	**¢**
RESTAURANTS	over €29	€22–€29	€15–€22	€8–€15	under €8
HOTELS	over €230	€180–€230	€130–€180	€80–€130	under €80

Restaurant prices are per person for a main course at dinner. Hotel prices are for two people in a double room, including VAT and a service charge (often applied in larger hotels).

Timing

In July and August, the region is busy with families from Northern Ireland, Dublin, and Great Britain. Musicians play most nights at village pubs, and the weather may be warm enough for hardy folk to swim in the sea, but accommodations may be hard to come by. Between November and February, in contrast, the area is empty of tourists, and with good reason—gales bring cold, lashing rain in from the Atlantic, shrouding the wild, lonely scenery that is the northwest Ireland's greatest asset. What's more, because so many of the area's hotels are seasonal, you have a limited choice. The best months to visit are April through June, September, and October.

YEATS COUNTRY

Just as James Joyce made Dublin his own through his novels and stories, Sligo and environs are bound to the work of W. B. Yeats (1865–1939), Ireland's first of four Nobel laureates, and, no less, his brother, Jack B. (1871–1957), one of Ireland's most important 20th-century painters, whose expressionistic landscapes and portraits are as emotionally fraught as his brother's poems are lyrical and plangent. The brothers intimately knew and eloquently celebrated in their art not only Sligo Town itself but the surrounding countryside with its lakes, farms, woodland, and dramatic mountains that rise up not far from the center of town. Often on this route, you have glimpses of Ben Bulben Mountain, which looms over the western end of the Dartry range. The areas covered here are the most accessible parts of northwest Ireland, easily reached from Galway.

Sligo Town

★ *60 km (37 mi) northeast of Ballina, 138 km (86 mi) northeast of Galway, 217 km (135 mi) northwest of Dublin.*

Sligo (population 19,000), the only sizable town in the whole of northwest Ireland, is the best place to begin a tour of Yeats Country. It retains all the charm of smaller, sleepier villages, all the while in the throes of an economic boom. Europe's largest videotape factory is just outside of town, it's the center of Ireland's plastics industry, and for the past three years the streets have been ringing with the bite of buzz saws as apartments, shopping malls, and cinema complexes have been tastefully erected behind traditional facades. By day Sligo is as lively and crowded as Galway, its considerably larger neighbor to the southwest. Locals, students from the town's college, and tourists bustle past its historic buildings and along its narrow sidewalks and winding streets and crowd its one-of-a-kind shops, restaurants, and traditional pubs. More than any other town in northwest Ireland, Sligo has a buzz and energy that come as a surprise to anyone who hasn't been there in the last few years.

Squeezed onto a patch of land between Sligo Bay and Lough Gill, Sligo is clustered on the south shore between two bridges that span the River Garavogue, just east of where the river opens into the bay. The pedestrian zone along the south shore of the river between the two bridges means that you can enjoy vistas of the river right in the center of town. Along High Street and Church and Charles streets, Sligo has churches of all denominations. Presbyterians, Methodists, and even Plymouth Brethren are represented, as well as Anglicans (Church of Ireland) and, of course, Roman Catholics. According to the Irish writer Sean O'Faolain, "The best Protestant stock in all Ireland is in Sligo." The Yeats family was part of that stock.

Sligo was often a battleground in its earlier days. It was attacked by Viking invaders in 807 and, later, by a succession of rival Irish and Anglo-Norman conquerors. In 1642, the British soldiers of Sir Frederick Hamilton fell upon Sligo, killing every visible inhabitant, burning the town, and destroying the interior of the beautiful medieval abbey. Then, between 1845 and 1849, more than a million inhabitants died in the potato famine or fled to escape it—an event poignantly captured in the words of a letter from local father Owen Larkin to his son in America in 1850, inscribed on a brass plaque down by the river: "I am now I may say alone in the world all my brothers and sisters are dead and children but yourself. We are all ejected out of Lord Ardilaun's ground, the times was so bad and all Ireland in such a state of poverty that no person could pay rent. My only hope now rests with you, as I am without one shilling and I must either beg or go to the poorhouse." Stand there a moment by the river, then turn again to the bustling heart of Sligo today, and marvel at humanity's capacity to reinvent itself.

❶ The Sligo Art Gallery in the **Yeats Memorial Building** shows rotating exhibits of contemporary art; call ahead to see if there's an exhibition during your visit. The Yeats International Summer School is conducted here every August. Across the street is Rohan Gillespie's innovative sculpture of the poet, draped in a flowing coat overlaid with excerpts from his work. It was unveiled in 1989 by Michael Yeats, W. B.'s son, in commemoration of the 50th anniversary of his father's death. ⊠ *Hyde Bridge* ☎ *Gallery 071/914–5847; summer school 074/42693* 🖶 *071/ 914–7426* ⊕ *www.sligoartgallery.com* ✉ *Free* ⊙ *Mon.–Sat. 10–5:30.*

▶ ❷ The **Model Arts Centre and Niland Gallery,** beautifully housed in a 19th-century school, has one of Ireland's largest collections of works by 20th-century artists from Ireland and abroad. The gallery displays works by Jack B. Yeats, who once said, "I never did a painting without putting a thought of Sligo in it." (Beckett once wrote that Yeats painted "desperately immediate images.") Paintings by John Yeats (father of Jack B. and W. B.), who had a considerable reputation as a portraitist, also hang here, as do those by Sean Keating, and Paul Henry. The center has performance and workshop spaces and hosts various literature, music, and film programs. There's also The Atrium café. ⊠ *The Mall* ☎ *071/ 914–1405* ⊕ *www.modelartes.ie* 🎟 *Free* ☉ *Tues.–Sat. 10–5:30 and during performances.*

❸ Maurice FitzGerald built the **Sligo Abbey,** the town's only existing relic of the Middle Ages, for the Dominicans in 1253. After a fire in 1414, it was extensively rebuilt, only to be destroyed again by Cromwell's Puritans under the command of Sir Frederick Hamilton in 1642. Today the abbey consists of a ruined nave, aisle, transept, and tower. Some fine stonework remains, especially in the 15th-century cloisters. The visitor center is the base for guided tours, which are included with admission. The site is accessible to the disabled, though some parts of the grounds are quite rocky. ⊠ *Abbey St.* ☎ *071/914–6406* ⊕ *www.heritageireland. ie* 🎟 *€2* ☉ *Apr.–Oct., daily 10–6; Nov.–Jan., Fri.–Sun. 9:30–4:30.*

❹ The **Courthouse,** built in 1878 in the Victorian Gothic style, has a flamboyant, turreted sandstone exterior. Unfortunately it's not open to tourists. After it was built, the structure became a symbol for English power. The Courthouse takes its inspiration from the much larger Law Courts in London. Just north of the Courthouse on the east side of Teeling Street, look for the window designating the law firm Argue and Phibbs, one of Sligo's most popular photo-ops. ⊠ *Teeling St.* ☉ *Closed to public.*

❺ Designed in 1730 by Richard Castle, who designed Powerscourt and Russborough houses in County Wicklow, little **St. John's Cathedral** (Church of Ireland) has a handsome square tower and fortifications. In the north transept is a memorial to Susan Mary Yeats, mother of W. B. and Jack B. Next door is the larger and newer Roman Catholic Cathedral of the Immaculate Conception (with an entrance on Temple Street), consecrated in 1874. ⊠ *John St.*

❻ Sligo's most famous pub, **Hargadon's,** is a dark, old-style public house with cozy, private, wood-paneled snugs (cubicles); stone and wood floors; rust-red interior walls; and a handsome golden-oak and green-painted facade. It's a good place for a bowl of stew and a creamy pint of Guinness. ⊠ *4 O'Connell St.* ☎ *071/917–0933.*

❼ The main items of interest at the **Sligo County Museum** are first editions by W. B. Yeats and memorabilia such as the author's personal letters and the Irish tricolor (flag) that draped his coffin when he was buried at nearby Drumcliff. The museum also has small sections on local society, history, and archaeology. Some works by Jack B. Yeats hang in the adjoining church. ⊠ *Stephen St.* ☎ *071/914–2212* 🎟 *Free* ☉ *June–Sept., Tues.–Sat. 10–5; Oct.–May, Tues.–Sat. 2–4:50.*

Where to Stay & Eat

$–$$ ✕ **Bistro Bianconi.** With blond-wood furniture and white-tile floors, Bianconi lives up to its name in the dining room's design, but it serves Italian food full of color. Peruse the long list of fancy pizzas baked in a wood-burning oven. Cannelloni and ravioli are also popular. ⊠ *44 O'-Connell St.* ☎ *071/914–1744* 🖃 *MC, V* ☉ *Closed Sun.*

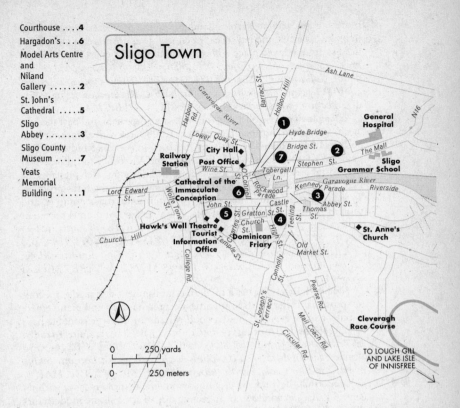

$$$$ ✕🏠 **Cromleach Lodge.** Comfort is paramount at this small hotel with fan-
Fodor'sChoice   tastic views out over Lough Arrow. Spacious country bedrooms are dec-
★   orated in pastel shades. The restaurant ($$–$$$; reservations required)
is notable; all the tables have panoramic views. Two typical—and delicious—entrées are a fillet of turbot on a julienne of fennel with Pernod
cream, and a warm salad of marinaded lamb fillet with organic lentils.
The staff leads walks in the area—from 20-minutes to 2-hours long. ⚓ *27
km (17 mi) east of Sligo, 8 km (5 mi) east of Ballymote ⊠ Off N4 at
Castlebaldwin, Lough Arrow, Co. Sligo* ☎ *071/916–5155* 🖶 *071/916–
5455* ⊕ *www.cromleach.com* ⇥ *11 rooms with bath* ⚐ *Restaurant, golf
privileges, hiking, bar, Internet, meeting room* ▤ *AE, DC, MC, V*
🍽️ *BP, MAP* ⏺ *Closed Nov.–Jan.*

$$$ ✕🏠 **Markree Castle.** The 350-year ancestral home of Charles Cooper—
who now owns and manages it with his wife, Mary—Markree is Sligo's
oldest (1640) inhabited castle. The facade is fortresslike but the 1,000-
acre grounds with gardens soften the effect. Enter into an oak-panel hall
with a grand staircase and stained-glass window. Bedrooms are a mix
of traditional styles (somewhat haphazardly furnished); bathrooms are
modern. A skylit gallery doubles as the bar, and the restaurant dining
room has ornate Louis XIV plasterwork. Ask about the three-course table
d'hôte menu (€38) occasionally served. Sunday lunch attracts a family
crowd. ⚓ *11 km (7 mi) south of Sligo Town ⊠ Off N4, Collooney, Co.
Sligo* ☎ *071/916–7800* 🖶 *071/916–7840* ⊕ *www.markreecastle.com*
⇥ *30 rooms with bath* ⚐ *Restaurant, horseback riding, bar* ▤ *AE, MC,
V* 🍽️ *BP, MAP.*

★ **$**   ✕🏠 **Glebe House.** Dorothy and Jeremy Bird run a Georgian guest house
and a restaurant ($$$$) with an emphasis on local produce. You might
choose from roast rack of Sligo lamb in an herb crust or wild Owen-

more salmon with an herb hollandaise on the prix-fixe menu. Indulge in pink grapefruit and gin sorbet or chocolate and Amaretto mousse for dessert. It's a relaxed place with simple but pleasant guest rooms. ⊹ *12 km (7 mi) south of Sligo Town* ⊠ *Coolaney Rd., off N4 at second round-about, Collooney, Co. Sligo* ☎ *071/916–7787* ⊕ *www.glebehousesligo. com* ⇆ *1 room with bath, 3 without bath* ⟲ *Restaurant, fishing, hiking, meeting rooms; no room TVs* ▤ *MC, V* ⦿ *BP, MAP.*

$ ╳⌂ **Temple House.** Stroll along formal terraced gardens and past the lake at this Georgian mansion on more than 1,000 acres with a working farm and organic garden. The property has been in owners Sandy and Deb Perceval's family since 1665. Georgian and Victorian furniture—mahogany tables and original rugs—adorn the bedrooms. Deb prepares the prix fixe evening meal ($$$$; book by noon) using the farm produce. Typical entrées include herbed leg of lamb with roast potatoes and tomato fondue with glazed carrots. High tea for children is served at 6:30 PM; they are not allowed at dinner. ⊹ *19 km (12 mi) south of Sligo* ⊠ *Off N17, Ballymote, Co. Sligo* ☎ *071/918–3329* 🖷 *071/918–3808* ⊕ *www.templehouse.ie* ⇆ *6 rooms with bath* ⟲ *Restaurant, boating, fishing; no room phones, no room TVs* ▤ *AE, MC, V* ⦿ *BP* ⊘ *Closed Dec.–Mar.*

$$ ⌂ **Sligo Park Hotel.** Expect a modern establishment designed for a contemporary traveler: a first-rate fitness center, dancing and piano entertainment some evenings, and a good restaurant. It's a reasonable base of operations for touring Yeats Country. The staff is quite friendly. ⊠ *Pearse Rd., off N4, Co. Sligo* ☎ *071/916–0291* 🖷 *071/916–9556* ⊕ *www.leehotels.ie* ⇆ *110 rooms with bath* ⟲ *Restaurant, tennis court, 2 indoor pools, health club, bar* ▤ *AE, MC, V* ⦿ *BP, MAP.*

★ $–$$ ⌂ **Coopershill.** Beyond the elegant, symmetrical stone facade, with its central Palladian window, an appealing mix of antique and modern furniture fills the large public spaces. Spacious, beautifully furnished guest rooms have floral wallpaper, and most have four-poster or canopy beds. Dine by candlelight on meals made with fresh Irish ingredients, and a wide choice of wines, served from a grand sideboard set with family silver and crystal. Nonguests are invited only when the lodging is not full. Seven generations of the O'Hara family have lived in this three-story Georgian farmhouse since it was built in 1774. ⊠ *Off N4, 17 km (11 mi) southeast of Sligo, Riverstown, Co. Sligo* ☎ *071/916–5108* 🖷 *071/ 916–5466* ⊕ *www.coopershill.com* ⇆ *8 rooms with bath* ⟲ *Dining room, tennis court, fishing, billiards; no room TVs* ▤ *AE, DC, MC, V* ⦿ *BP* ⊘ *Closed Nov.–Mar.*

$ ⌂ **Silver Swan Hotel.** In the center of Sligo Town on the Hyde Bridge is a comfortable and inexpensive hotel with a wonderful view of the Garavogue River rushing beneath the bridge. The 1960s exterior may put off the stylish, but the interior is clean and rooms have more recent furnishings. Noise can be a problem on Saturday night when the hotel is hosting live music sessions, so ask for a room away from the bar below. ⊠ *Hyde Bridge, Co. Sligo* ☎ *071/914–3231* 🖷 *071/914–2232* ⊕ *www. yangonow.com/swan/* ⇆ *29 rooms with bath* ⟲ *Restaurant, bar* ▤ *AE, MC, V* ⦿ *BP, MAP.*

Nightlife & the Arts

PUBS A few miles south of town, a popular spot with the locals, the **Thatch pub** (⊠ Thatch, Ballysodare ☎ 071/916–7288), has traditional music sessions from Thursday to Sunday. A sizeable dance floor at **Toffs** (⊠ Kennedy Parade ☎ 071/916–1250) teems with Sligo's younger set moving to a mix of contemporary dance music and older favorites. It's open later than most places.

THEATER **Hawk's Well Theatre** hosts amateur and professional companies from all over Ireland (and occasionally from Britain) in an eclectic mix of shows. ⊠ *Temple St.* ☎ *071/916–1526* ⊠ *€8–€15* ☉ *Box office weekdays 10–6, Sat. 2–6.*

Sports & the Outdoors

For riding in the countryside around Sligo, contact the **Sligo Riding Centre** (⊠ 3 km [2 mi] from Sligo Town, Carramore ☎ 071/916–1253 ⊕ www.irelandonhorseback.com).

Shopping

Sligo Town has northwest Ireland's most thriving shopping scene, with lots of food-related, craft, and hand-knits shops. In addition to stylish sweaters, **Carraig Donn** (⊠ 41 O'Connell St. ☎ 071/914–4158 ⊕ www. carraigdonn.com) carries pottery, glassware, linens, and children's Aran knits. The **Cat & the Moon** (⊠ 4 Castle St. ☎ 071/914–3686 ⊕ www.thecatandthemoon.com) specializes in eclectic and stylish Irish-made crafts, jewelry, pottery, ironwork, and scarves. The upscale deli **Cosgrove and Son** (⊠ 32 Market St. ☎ 071/914–2809) sells everything from Parma ham to Carageen moss boiled in milk (a local cure for upset stomachs). Stock up here for a picnic. **Cross Sections** (⊠ 2 Grattan St. ☎ 071/914–2265) sells lovely tableware, glassware, and kitchenware. **Tír na nóg** (⊠ Grattan St. ☎ 071/916–2752), Irish for "Land of the Ever-young," sells organic foods, including local cheeses and honeys, and other health-oriented items. A sister store across the street sells cards and posters.

Knocknarea

❽ *8 km (5 mi) southwest of Sligo Town on R292 (Strandhill Rd.)*

Knocknarea—the "cairn-heaped grassy hill," as W. B. Yeats called it—rises 1,083 feet to the southwest of Sligo Town on a promontory that juts into Sligo Bay. The mountain is also memorably depicted in brother Jack B.'s painting *Knocknarea and the Flowing Tide.* A car park on R292 gives pedestrian access (a 45-minute walk) to the summit, where there's a tremendous view of the mountains of Counties Donegal and Sligo. At the summit, and visible from a distance, sits a huge cairn—a heaped-stone monument made with 40,000 tons of rock. The cairn is traditionally associated with Maeve, the 1st-century AD Celtic queen of Connaught who went to war with the men of Ulster in a bid to win the mighty Bull of Cuailgne, and who was subsequently killed while bathing in a lake. The story is told in the *Táin,* the greatest of all the Irish heroic legends. Romantics like to think that Maeve is buried in this massive cairn, although archaeologists suspect that it more likely covers a 3,000-year-old grave. Either way, it's a pleasant climb on a summer day, and nature has installed a handy stream for washing your boots as you take the lane back down.

Strandhill, a seaside resort with a touch of charm, is 3 km (2 mi) northwest of Knocknarea, off R292. It has a fine, sandy beach and rolling waves favored by surfers. The **Perfect Day Surf Club** (⊠ Strandhill ☎ 071/916–8464) caters to surfing novices and aficionados alike and is approved by the European Surf Federation and Irish Surfing Association. Two hours of instruction plus equipment is €25. **Celtic Seaweed Baths** (⊠ Strandhill ☎ 071/916–8686 ⊕ www.celticseaweedbaths.com) has a one-hour steam and seaweed bath treatment for €16.

en route | **Carrowmore,** the largest group of megalithic tombs in all of the British Isles, is a short drive southeast of Knocknarea (on the minor road back to Sligo Town). The oldest of the 60 tombs, dolmens, and other ruins here predate those at Newgrange by roughly 700 years; most are communal tombs dating from 4800 BC, though unfortunately more than 100 have been badly damaged, leaving around 40. A restored cottage houses a small exhibition about the tombs. ⊠ *Carrowmore* ☎ *071/916–1534* ⊠ *€2* ⊙ *May–Oct., daily 10–6.*

Lough Gill

★ ❾ *17½ km (11 mi) east of Knocknarea, 1½ km (1 mi) east of Sligo Town on R286.*

Beautiful, gentle Lough Gill means simply "Lake Beauty" in Irish. When the soldiers of Sir Frederick Hamilton sacked Sligo in 1642, legend has it that they flung the silver bell of the abbey into the depths of Lough Gill, where today it's said that only the "pure" can hear it ring. In fine weather the river-fed lough and its surroundings are serenity itself: sunlight on the meadows all around, loughside cottages, the gentle sound of water, salmon leaping, a yacht sailing by. To get to the Lough from Sligo Town, take Stephen Street, which turns into N16 (signposted to Manorhamilton and Enniskillen). Turn right almost at once onto R286. Within minutes you can see gorgeous views of the lake so adored by the young W. B. Yeats.

An English Planter (a Protestant colonist settling on Irish lands confiscated from Catholic owners) built the fortified house, **Parke's Castle,** in the 17th century on the eastern shore of Lough Gill. He needed the strong fortifications to defend himself against a hostile populace. His relations with the people were made worse by the fact that he obtained his building materials mainly by dismantling a historic fortress on the site that had belonged to the clan leaders the O'Rourkes of Breffni (once the name of the district). The entrance fee includes a short video show on the castle and local history and a guided tour. In the summer, boat tours of the lough leave from here. There's also a snack bar. ⊠ *R288, Fivemile Bourne, Co. Leitrim* ☎ *071/916–4149; 087/270–4032 for appointment* ⊠ *€3* ⊙ *Mid-Apr.–Oct., 10–6 (last admission at 5:15); Nov.–mid-Apr., by appointment.*

A few minutes' walk along a footpath south of Parke's Castle lie the handsome ruins of **Creevelea Abbey.** In fact not an abbey but a friary, Creevelea was founded for the Franciscans in 1508 by a later generation of O'Rourkes. It was the last Franciscan community to be founded before the suppression of the monasteries by England's King Henry VIII. Like many other decrepit abbeys, the place still holds religious significance for locals—who revere it. One curiosity here is the especially large south transept; notice, too, its endearing little cloisters, with well-executed carvings on the pillars of St. Francis of Assisi. ⊠ *R288, Dromahair, Co. Leitrim.*

Where to Stay & Eat

¢ ✕ ▣ **Stanford Village Inn.** This stone-front inn is one of the few stops for sustenance near Lough Gill. A hearty meal of traditional homey food ($–$$), an open fire, and, if your timing is good, an impromptu session of traditional Irish music await you. It has six newly refurbished, country rooms. ✛ *7 km (5 mi) from Parke's Castle, 19 km (12 mi) from Sligo Town* ⊠ *Off R288, Dromahair, Co. Leitrim* ☎ *071/916–4140* 🖷 *071/ 916–4770* ⌖ *6 rooms with bath* ↻ *Restaurant, bar* ▤ *MC, V* ¶⊙¶ *BP.*

Lake Isle of Innisfree

⑩ *15 km (9 mi) south of Sligo Town via Dromahair on N4 and R287.*

In 1890 W. B. Yeats was walking through the West End of London when, seeing in a shop window a ball dancing on a jet of water, he was suddenly overcome with nostalgia for the lakes of his Sligo home. It was the moment, and the feeling, that shaped itself into his most famous poem, "The Lake Isle of Innisfree":

I will arise and go now, and go to Innisfree,
And a small cabin build there, of clay and wattles made:
Nine bean-rows will I have there, a hive for the honey-bee,
And live alone in the bee-loud glade.

Though there is nothing visually exceptional about Innisfree (pronounced *innish*-free), the "Lake Isle" is a must-see if you're a W. B. Yeats fan. To reach Innisfree from Dromahair, take R287, the minor road that heads back along the south side of Lough Gill, toward Sligo Town. Turn right at a small crossroads, after 4 or 5 km (2 or 3 mi), where signposts point to Innisfree. A little road leads another couple of miles down to the lakeside, where you can see the island just offshore.

Manorhamilton

⑪ *16 km (10 mi) northeast of Dromahair on R280, 25 km (15 mi) east of Sligo Town on N16.*

The small rural town of Manorhamilton was built in the 17th century for the Scottish Planter Sir Frederick Hamilton, who had been given the local manor house by Charles I of England (hence the town's name). The manor itself is now an ivy-covered ruin, and there's not much to see here. The surrounding scenery, however, is spectacular.

en route On your way to Manorhamilton, stop at **Glencar Lough** (✉ N16, 9 km [5 mi] east of Sligo Town), where there are several waterfalls; a footpath veering off from a parking lot leads to one of the highest. The lake is fed by the River Drumcliff and streams at the foot of the Dartry Mountains: "Where the wandering water gushes/From the hills above Glencar/In pools among the rushes/That scarce could bathe a star," as W. B. Yeats put it in his poem "The Stolen Child."

Rosses Point

⑫ *38½ km (24 mi) west of Manorhamilton, 8 km (5 mi) northwest of Sligo Town on R291.*

It's obvious why W. B. and Jack B. Yeats often stayed at Rosses Point during their summer vacations: glorious pink and gold summer sunsets over a seemingly endless stretch of sandy beach. Coney Island lies just off Rosses Point. Local lore has it that the captain of the ship *Arathusa* christened Brooklyn's Coney Island after this island, but there's probably more legend than truth to this, as it's widely agreed that New York's Coney Island was named after the Dutch word *konijn* (wild rabbits); they abounded there during the 17th century.

The popular **County Sligo Golf Club** (✉ Rosses Point ☎ 071/917–7186 ⊕ www.countysligogolfclub.ie) is one of Ireland's grand old venues, as it's more than a century old, and has hosted most of the country's major championships. It has magnificent views of the sea and Ben Bulben. The **Sligo Yacht Club** (✉ Rosses Point ☎ 071/917–7168 ⊕ www.

rossespoint.com/sligoyc), with a fleet of some 25 boats, has sailing and social programs, and regularly hosts races.

Drumcliff

⓭ *15 km (9 mi) northeast of Rosses Point, 7 km (4½ mi) north of Sligo Town on N15.*

W. B. Yeats lies buried with his wife, Georgie, in an unpretentious grave in the cemetery of Drumcliff's simple Protestant church, where his grandfather was rector for many years. W. B. actually died on the French Riviera in 1939; it took almost a full decade for his body to be brought back here—to the place that more than any other might be called his soul-land. In the poem "Under Ben Bulben," he spelled out not only where he was to be buried but also what should be written on the tombstone: "Cast a cold eye/On life, on death./Horseman, pass by!" It is easy to see why the majestic Ben Bulben (1,730 feet), with its sawed-off peak (not unlike Yosemite's Half-Dome), made such an impression on the poet: the mountain gazes calmly down upon the small church, as it does on all of the surrounding landscape—and at the same time stands as a sentinel facing the mighty Atlantic.

Drumcliff is where St. Columba, a recluse and missionary who established Christian churches and religious communities in northwest Ireland, is thought to have founded a monastic settlement around AD 575. The monastery that he founded before sailing off to the Scottish isle of Iona flourished for many centuries, but all that is left of it now is the base of a round tower and a carved high cross (both across N15 from the church) dating from around AD 1000, with scenes from the Old and New Testaments, including Adam and Eve with the serpent and Cain slaying Abel.

Drumcliff Visitors' Centre is a good place to buy local crafts, books of W. B. Yeats poetry, and books about the poet's life. You can also get a snack here. ✉ *Next to the Protestant church, Co. Sligo* ☎ *071/914–4956* ☼ *Mon.–Sat. 9–6, Sun. 1–6.*

Lissadell House

⓮ *3 km (2 mi) west of Drumcliff, 15 km (9 mi) northwest of Sligo Town off N15.*

Beside the Atlantic waters of Drumcliff Bay, on the peninsula that juts out between Donegal and Sligo bays, Lissadell—"That old Georgian mansion," as W. B. Yeats called it—is an austere but classic residence built in 1834 by Sir Robert Gore-Booth. An enlightened landlord, he mortgaged the house to help his poverty-stricken tenants during the famine years. His descendants still own Lissadell, which is filled with all manner of artifacts brought back from every corner of the globe by the family, who were great travelers. W. B. became good friends of the family. On a visit to the house in 1894, he met the two Gore-Booth daughters, Eva and Constance, and subsequently recalled their meeting in verse: "The light of evening, Lissadell,/Great windows open to the south,/Two girls in silk kimonos." Eva became a poet, while sister Constance Markievicz led a dramatic political life as a fiery Irish nationalist, taking a leading role in the 1916 Easter Uprising against the British. She survived the uprising, going on to become the first woman member of the Dáil (Irish Parliament).

Lissadell was designed by the London architect Francis Goodwin. Its two most notable features are a dramatic 33-foot-high gallery, with 24-

foot-tall Doric columns, clerestory windows, and skylights; and the dining room, where Constance's husband, Count Markievicz, painted portraits of members of the family and household employees on the pilasters. A copy of W. B.'s poem, "In Memory of Eva Gore-Booth and Con Markievicz," is displayed in the house. A guided tour lasts 45 minutes. The woods of the Lissadell estate have become a forestry and wildlife reserve; they house Ireland's largest colony of barnacle geese, along with several other species of wildfowl. It's a fine place for bird-watchers. ☎071/916-3150 ☒ €6 ⊙ June–mid-Sept., Mon.–Sat. 10:30–1 and 2–5.

AROUND DONEGAL BAY

As you drive north to Donegal Town, the glens of the Dartry Mountains (to which Ben Bulben belongs) gloriously roll by to the east. Look across coastal fields for views of the waters of Donegal Bay to the west. In the distant horizon the Donegal hills beckon. This stretch, dotted with numerous prehistoric sites, has become northwest Ireland's most popular vacation area. There are a few small and unremarkable seashore resorts, and in some places you may find that haphazard and fairly tasteless construction detracts from the scenery. In between these minor resort developments wide-open spaces are free of traffic. The most intriguing area lies on the north side of the bay—all that rocky indented coastline due west of Donegal Town. Here you enter the heart of away-from-it-all: County Donegal.

Mullaghmore

🅖 *20 km (13 mi) northeast of Lissadell House, 37 km (24 mi) north of Sligo Town off N15.*

In July and August, the picturesque, sleepy fishing village of Mullaghmore gets congested with tourists. Its main attractions: a 3-km-long (2-mi-long) sandy beach; and the turreted, fairy-tale Classie Bawn—the late Lord Louis Mountbatten's home (he, his grandson, and a local boy were killed when the IRA blew up his boat in the bay in 1979). A short drive along the headland is punctuated by unobstructed views beyond the rocky coastline out over Donegal Bay. When the weather is fair, you can see all the way across to St. John's Point and Drumanoo Head in Donegal.

Creevykeel is one of Ireland's best megalithic court-tombs. There's a burial area and an enclosed open-air court where rituals were performed around 3000 BC. Bronze artifacts found here are now in the National Museum in Dublin. The site (signposted from N15) lies off the road, just beyond the edge of the village of Cliffony. ⊕ *3 km (2 mi) southeast of Mullaghmore off N15.*

Where to Stay & Eat

$ ✕🏨 **Beach Hotel.** If there's a chill in the air, you can warm up at the roaring fires in the restaurant ($–$$$) and residents' lounge of this large harborside Victorian hotel. The dramatic red building is decorated in a nautical theme to commemorate the loss of three galleons of the Spanish Armada in the bay in September 1588. Enjoy wonderful views of the pier and the bay from the hotel bars, or tuck into the de'Cuellar Restaurant's acclaimed seafood menu. Try the favorites: hot crab claws, lobster, and the house seafood platter. Save room for the homemade apple and rhubarb crumble. ⊠ *The Harbour, Co. Sligo* ☎ *071/916–6103* 🖷 *071/916–6448* ⊕ *www.beachhotelmullaghmore.com* ⊷ *29 rooms with bath* ⚹ *Restaurant, indoor pool, gym, hot tub, sauna, steam room, beauty salon, massages, 2 bars* ⊟ *AE, MC, V* ⧈ *BP, MAP.*

Bundoran

⑯ *17 km (11 mi) northeast of Mullaghmore, 35 km (22 mi) northeast of Sligo Town on N15.*

Resting on the south coast of County Donegal, Bundoran is one of Ireland's most popular seaside resorts, a favorite haunt of the Irish from both the north and the south. To avoid souvenir shops and amusement arcades, head north of the center to the handsome beach at **Tullan Strand,** washed by good surfing waves. Between the main beach and Tullan, the Atlantic has sculpted cliff-side rock formations that the locals have christened with whimsical names such as the Fairy Bridges, the Wishing Chair, and the Puffing Hole (this last one blows wind and water from the waves pounding below).

Sports & the Outdoors

Good fishing is 6 km (4 mi) from Bundoran at **Lough Melvin.** Ask locally at **Pat Barrett's Tackle Shop** (⊠ Main St.) for bait, tackle, and local information.

Bundoran Golf Club (⊠ Headland ☎ 071/984–1302) is an 18-hole, par-70 course on the cliffs above Bundoran beach.

Ballyshannon

⑰ *6 km (4 mi) north of Bundoran, 42 km (26 mi) northeast of Sligo Town on N15.*

The former garrison town of Ballyshannon rises gently from the banks of the River Erne and has good views of Donegal Bay and the surrounding mountains. Come in early August, when this quiet village springs to life with a grand festival of folk and traditional music. The town is a hodgepodge of shops, arcades, and hotels. Its triangular central area has several bars and places to grab a snack. The town was also the birthplace of the prolific Irish poet William Allingham.

A few kilometers down the road are several factories where eggshell-thin Irish porcelainware has been made by master craftsmen for generations. It's said that if a newlywed couple receives a piece of this china, their marriage will be blessed with everlasting happiness. The name Belleek has become synonymous with much of Ireland's delicate ivory porcelain figurines and woven baskets (sometimes painted with shamrocks); **Belleek Pottery Ltd.** is the best known of the producers, in operation since 1857. Watch the introductory film, take the 30-minute tour, stop by for refreshment in the tearoom, or just head to the on-site shop. A cup-and-saucer set starts at UK£16, a typical basket UK£69, and head skyward from there. The factory-museum-store is near the border with Northern Ireland. Company products can also be found in the shops of Donegal and Sligo. ⊠ *6 km (4 mi) east of Ballyshannon, Belleek, Northern Ireland* ☎ *028/6865–8501 in Northern Ireland* ⊕ *www.belleek.ie* ▣ *UK£4* ⊙ *Apr.–June, Sept., and Oct., weekdays 9–5:30, Sat. 10–5:30, Sun. 2–6; July and Aug., weekdays 9–8, Sat. 10–6, Sun. 11–6; Nov.–Mar., weekdays 10–5:30.*

The fourth generation (since 1866) of the Daly family hand crafts and paints the elaborate floral and basket-weave designs at **Celtic Weave China.** Because it's a small, personal operation, they can make a single piece of china to your specifications. Prices start at €7, and most pieces cost less than €125. ✛ *5 km (3 mi) east of Ballyshanon* ⊠ *R230, Cloghore* ☎ *071/985–1844* ⊕ *www.celticweavechina.ie* ▣ *Free* ⊙ *Mon.–Sat. 9–6.*

Donegal Irish Parian China Factory is the Republic's largest manufacturer of Parian china (so named because it resembles the clear white marble statuary from the Greek island of Paros)—the cream-color pottery crafted by traditional methods, to a large degree by hand. There's a 15-minute tour, a 10-minute video, a showroom, a shop, and a tearoom. The factory sells its wares at lower prices here than in retail stores. The least expensive items (spoons or thimbles) cost around €8. A full tea set starts at about €250. ⊠ *N15 just south of town* ☎ *071/985–1826* ⊕ *www.donegalchina.ie* ☞ *Free* ⊙ *June–Aug., daily 9–5:30; Sept.–May, weekdays 9–5:30.*

off the beaten path

LOUGH DERG – From Whitsunday to the Feast of the Assumption (June to mid-August), tens of thousands beat a path to this lake, ringed by heather-clad slopes. In the center of the lough, Station Island—known as St. Patrick's Purgatory—is one of Ireland's most popular pilgrimage sites. It's also the most rigorous and austere of such sites in the country. Pilgrims stay on the island for three days without sleeping, and eat only black tea and dry toast. They walk barefoot around the island, on its flinty stones, to pray at a succession of shrines. The pilgrimage has been followed since time immemorial; during the Middle Ages, devotees from foreign lands flocked here. Nonpilgrims may not visit the island from June to mid-August. To find out how to become a pilgrim, write to the Reverend Prior. To reach the shores of Lough Derg, turn off the main N15 Sligo–Donegal road in the village of Laghy onto the minor R232 Pettigo road, which hauls itself over the Black Gap and descends sharply into the border village of Pettigo, about 21 km (13 mi) from N15. From here, take the Lough Derg access road for 8 km (5 mi). ⊠ *Station Island, Lough Derg, Pettigo, Co. Donegal.*

Where to Stay & Eat

$$$$ ✕🏨 **Sandhouse Hotel.** Behind the mock manor-house exterior of this 19th-century former fishing lodge lies a large modern hotel. On Donegal Bay, this makes a peaceful, well-positioned base for sightseeing along the coast. The hotel has access to 3 km (2 mi) of beach. Renovated, well-kept bedrooms are decorated with antiques and overlook either the sea or the Donegal hills. Fresh seafood, including Donegal Bay oysters and mussels, is the specialty of the restaurant, which caters to hearty appetites. ✣ *8 km (5 mi) northwest of Ballyshannon* ⊠ *Off R231, Rossnowlagh, Co. Donegal* ☎ *071/985–1777* ☒ *071/985–2100* ⊕ *www.sandhouse-hotel.ie* ☞ *64 rooms with bath* ⅋ *Restaurant, golf privileges, tennis court, fishing, horseback riding, spa, bar, Internet, meeting rooms, helipad* ⊟ *AE, DC, MC, V* ⅋◯❙ *BP, MAP* ⊙ *Closed Dec. and Jan.*

Nightlife

The biggest and most popular pub, **Seán Óg's** (⊠ Market St. ☎ 071/985–8964), has live music on Friday, Saturday, and Sunday evenings.

Donegal Town

⓲ *21 km (13 mi) north of Ballyshannon, 66 km (41 mi) northeast of Sligo Town on N15.*

The town of Donegal was previously known in Irish as Dun na nGall, "Fort of the Foreigners." The foreigners were Vikings, who set up camp here in the 9th century to facilitate their pillaging and looting. They were driven out by the powerful O'Donnell clan (originally Cinel Conaill), who made it the capital of Tyrconnail, their extensive Ulster territories. Donegal was rebuilt in the early 17th century, during the Plantation period, when Protestant colonists were planted on Irish property confiscated from their Catholic owners. The **Diamond**, like that of many other Irish villages, dates from this period. Once a marketplace, it has a 20-foot obelisk monument to the Four Masters.

With a population of about 3,000, Donegal is northwest Ireland's largest small village—marking the entry into the back-of-the-beyond of the wilds of County Donegal. The town is centered on the triangular Diamond, where three roads converge (N56 to the west, N15 to the south and the northeast) and the mouth of the River Eske pours gently into Donegal Bay. You should have your bearings in five minutes, and seeing the historical sights takes less than an hour; if you stick around any longer, it'll probably be to do some shopping—arguably Donegal's top attraction.

Donegal Castle was built by clan leader Hugh O'Donnell in the 1470s. More than a century later, this structure was the home of his descendant Hugh Roe O'Donnell, who faced the might of the invading English and was the last clan chief of Tyrconail. In 1602 he died on a trip to Spain while trying to rally reinforcements from his allies. In 1610, its new English owner, Sir Basil Brooke, reconstructed the little castle, adding the fine Jacobean fortified mansion with towers and turrets that can still be seen today (he was responsible for the Diamond, as well). Inside, there are only a few rooms to see, including the garderobe (the rest room) and a great hall with an exceptional vaulted wood-beam roof. The small enclosed grounds are pleasant. ⊠ *Tirchonaill St., near north corner of the Diamond* ☎ *074/972–2405* ⊠ *€4* ☉ *Easter–Oct., daily 10–5:30.*

The ruins of the **Franciscan Abbey,** founded in 1474 by Hugh O'Donnell, are a 5-minute walk south of town at a spectacular site perched above the Eske River, where it begins to open up into Donegal Bay. The complex was burned to the ground in 1593, razed by the English in 1601, and ransacked again in 1607; the ruins include the choir, south transept, and two sides of the cloisters, between which lie hundreds of graves dating back to the 18th century. The abbey was probably where the *Annals of the Four Masters,* which chronicles the whole of Celtic history and mythology of Ireland from earliest times up to the year 1618, was written from 1632 to 1636. The Four Masters were four monks who believed (correctly, as it turned out) that Celtic culture was doomed after the English conquest, and they wanted to preserve as much of it as they could. At the National Library in Dublin, you can see copies of the monks' work; the original is kept under lock and key. ⊠ *Off N15, behind Hyland Central Hotel* ⊠ *Free* ☉ *Freely accessible.*

Where to Stay & Eat

★ ¢   ✕ **Blueberry Tea Room.** Proprietors Brian and Ruperta Gallagher serve breakfast, lunch, afternoon tea, and a light evening meal—always using home-grown herbs. Daily specials—Irish lamb stew, pasta dishes, and quiche—are served from 8 AM to 8 PM. Soups, sandwiches, salads, and fruit are on the regular menu, along with homemade desserts, breads, scones, and jams. Upstairs is an Internet café. It's across the street from Donegal Castle. ⊠ *Castle St.* ☎ *074/972–2933* ▤ *V* ☉ *Closed Sun.*

$$$$ ✕🏠 **St. Ernan's House.** A spectacularly situated country house, St. Ernan's
Fodor'sChoice   sits on its own wooded tidal island in Donegal Bay. The two-story
★   house was built by a nephew of the Duke of Wellington in 1826. Owner-managers Brian and Carmel O'Dowd have created a relaxed, serene lodging. Guest rooms are elegant, with antiques, fine fabrics, and bay views. Dinner, from a light meal to a leisurely five-course event, is served in

the intimate dining room ($$$). Menu choices are based on fresh local foodstuffs: homemade tagliatelle with smoked salmon is a typical starter; crispy breast of duckling or wild salmon might follow. ⚓ *3 km (2 mi) south of Donegal Town* ✉ *Off R267, St. Ernan's, Co. Donegal* ☎ *074/ 972–1065* 🖷 *074/972–2098* ⊕ *www.sainternans.com* ⬎ *10 rooms with bath, 2 suites* ⚭ *Restaurant* ▭ *MC, V* ꙮ *BP* ☉ *Closed Nov.–mid-Apr.*

$$$ ✕🏨 **Harvey's Point.** Complimentary decanters of brandy and sherry await you in spacious, crisp-white rooms with cherrywood beds. The Swiss-owned hotel has spirit-lifting views of Lough Eske at the foot of the Blue Stack Mountains. The dining room ($$$$), facing the lake, serves a four-course dinner with a choice of roast Donegal lamb with crispy sweetbreads, monkfish, hake, and other fresh Irish fare served with a French twist. ⚓ *6 km (4 mi) northwest of Donegal Town* ✉ *Off N15, Lough Eske, Co. Donegal* ☎ *074/972–2208* 🖷 *074/972–2352* ⊕ *www. harveyspoint.com* ⬎ *33 rooms with bath* ⚭ *Restaurant, bicycles, bar, meeting rooms* ▭ *AE, DC, MC, V* ꙮ *MAP.*

$ 🏨 **Central Hotel.** This family-run hotel on Donegal's central square is affiliated with Best Western. Huge picture windows in the back reveal lovely views of Donegal Bay. The efficient staff serves good, filling food in the large dining room. ✉ *The Diamond, Co. Donegal* ☎ *074/972–1027* 🖷 *074/972–2295* ⊕ *www.bestwestern.com* ⬎ *212 rooms with bath* ⚭ *Restaurant, in-room data ports, cable TV, indoor pool, health club, bar, no-smoking rooms* ▭ *AE, DC, MC, V* ꙮ *BP, MAP.*

Nightlife

The **Abbey Hotel** (✉ The Diamond ☎ 073/21014 ⊕ www.whites-hotelsireland.com) has music every night in July and August and a disco every Saturday and Sunday night throughout the year. During the summer, people pack **McGroarty's Bar** (✉ The Diamond ☎ 074/972–1049) to hear traditional music Thursday nights and contemporary music on weekends. It's also a good place to stop for a casual bite to eat.

Sports & the Outdoors

Donegal Golf Club (⚓ 8 km [5 mi] from Donegal Town ✉ Murvagh, Laghy ☎ 074/973–4054 ⊕ www.donegalgolfclub.ie) is one of Ireland's great championship courses.

Shopping

Long the principal marketplace for the region's wool products, Donegal Town has several smaller shops with local hand weaving, knits, and crafts.

Browse a While (✉ Main St. ☎ 074/22783) is a good place to stop off if you're in the mood for some light reading. The shop is stocked with tons of magazines and a small selection of pulp fiction. Explore **Donegal Craft Village** (✉ N15, 1½ km [1 mi] south of town ☎ No phone), a complex of workshops where you can buy pottery, handwoven goods, and ceramics from local young craftspeople. You can even watch the items being made Monday to Saturday 9–6, and Sunday 11–6.

The main hand weaving store in town, **Magee's** (✉ The Diamond ☎ 074/972–2660 ⊕ www.mageeshop.com), carries renowned private-label tweeds for both men and women (jackets, hats, scarves, suits, and more), as well as pottery, linen, and crystal. **Simple Simon's** (✉ The Diamond ☎ 074/972–2687), the only fresh food shop here, sells organic vegetables, essential oils, and other whole-earth items, as well as breads and cakes from the kitchen on the premises. They also stock a lot of local Irish cheeses.

en route

As you travel west on N56, which runs slightly inland from a magnificent shoreline of rocky inlets with great sea views, it's worthwhile turning off the road from time to time to catch a better view of the coast. About 6 km (4 mi) out of Donegal Town, N56 skirts Mountcharles, a bleak hillside village that looks back across the bay.

Bruckless

19 *19 km (12 mi) west of Donegal Town on N56.*

Don't be fooled by the round tower in the churchyard at Bruckless—it's 19th-century, not medieval. Soon after Bruckless, N56 turns inland across the bogs toward Ardara. The road now becomes R263, which runs through attractive heathland and wooded hills down to Killybegs.

Where to Stay & Eat

★ $ ✕⚑ **Castle Murray House Hotel.** Panoramas of distant mountains, the sapphire-blue waters of MacSwyne's Bay, and the long, narrow peninsula, punctuated at its tip by a lighthouse, await you at this hotel 1½ km (1 mi) out on the 10-km-long (6-mi-long) St. John's Point Peninsula. The original house has been extended and modernized; rooms are basic and contemporary with individual color schemes. Natives trek here for the white-tablecloth restaurant overlooking the bay ($$$$). Prix fixe selections might include glazed duck breast with confit of sweet ginger or steamed black sole with brandy cream. Lobster is a specialty. ✛ *3 km (2 mi) southeast of Bruckless, 1½ km (1 mi) from Dunkineely* ✉ *Off N56, Dunkineely, Co. Donegal* ☎ *074/973–7022* 📠 *074/973–7330* ⊕ *www.castlemurray.com* 🛏 *10 rooms with bath* ⚘ *Restaurant, bar* ▭ *MC, V* ⅋⊙� *BP* ⊗ *Hotel closed mid-Jan.–mid-Feb.; restaurant closed Mon. and Tues., Jan.–Mar.*

$ ⚑ **Bruckless House.** A two-story, 18th-century farmhouse on the north side of Donegal Bay, this B&B occupies 19 acres, including woods, gardens, and a meadow where Irish draft horses and Connemara ponies roam. Public rooms in the main building have a fine view of Bruckless Bay. The Asian-inspired interior reflects the years the owners, Clive and Joan Evans, spent in Hong Kong. Upstairs, bedrooms are conventional but comfortable. A separate two-bedroom self-catering gate cottage, the former servants quarters, is at the entrance to the estate. Wholesome breakfasts are prepared with fruit from the Evanses' garden and freshly laid eggs from their hens. ✉ *N56, Co. Donegal* ☎ *074/973–7071* 📠 *074/973–7070* 🛏 *4 rooms, 2 with bath; 1 cottage* ⚘ *Dining room, Internet; no room phones, no room TVs* ▭ *MC* ⅋⊙ *BP* ⊗ *Closed Oct.–Mar.*

Killybegs

20 *6 km (4 mi) west of Bruckless on R263, 28 km (17 mi) west of Donegal Town.*

Trawlers from Spain and France are moored in the harbor at Killybegs, one of Ireland's busiest fishing ports. Though it's one of the most industrialized places along this coast, it's not without some charm, thanks to its waterfront location. Killybegs once served as a center for the manufacture of Donegal hand-tufted carpets, examples of which are in the White House and the Vatican.

en route

The narrows, climbs, and twists of R263 afford terrific views of Donegal Bay before descending into pretty Kilcar, a traditional center of tweed making. Signposted by its Irish name, the next village, An Charraig (Carrick), clings to the foot of the Slieve League Mountains, whose dramatic, color-streaked ocean cliffs are, at 2,000 feet, the highest in Ireland and among the most spectacular. To see the cliffs, take the little road to the Irish-speaking village of Teelin, 1½ km (1 mi) south from Carrick. Then take the narrow lane (signposted to Bunglass) that climbs steeply to the top of the cliffs. For an even more thrilling perspective—presuming you're hardy—walk on the difficult coastal path from Teelin.

Where to Stay & Eat

$ ✕⌂ **Bay View Hotel.** Across from Killybegs's harbor, the Bay View is the town's most bustling spot. The hotel lobby, in light wood, has a modern take on classic designs, and the functional bedrooms are decorated pale colors. The Irish table d'hôte menu changes daily, with Bruckless mussels in a white wine and garlic sauce and braised young duckling served with market vegetables and an orange and cherry coulis, as potential options ($$$$). The hotel is well placed for seeing the glorious north shore of Donegal Bay. Special rates include golf greens fees for Portnoo (outside Ardara) and Murvagh (outside Donegal). ✉ *Main St., Co. Donegal* ☎ *074/973–1950* 🖷 *074/973–1856* ⊕ *www.bayviewhotel.ie* 🛏 *40 rooms with bath* ⚭ *Restaurant, indoor pool, health club, bar* 🚭 *AE, MC, V* ⏐❍⏐ *BP, MAP.*

Shopping

The **Harbour Store** (✉ Main St. ☎ 074/973–2122), right on the wharf, has plenty to make both fisherfolk and landlubbers happy, including boots and rain gear, competitively priced sweaters, and unusual bright yellow or orange fiberglass-covered gloves (made in Taiwan).

Glencolumbkille

㉑ *27 km (17 mi) west of Killybegs on R263, 54 km (27 mi) west of Donegal Town.*

At the far end of a stretch of barren moorland, the tiny hamlet of Glencolumbkille (pronounced glen-colm-*kill*) clings dramatically to the rockbound harbor of Glen Bay. Because it's at the heart of County Donegal's shrinking Gaeltacht, or Irish-speaking region, it has a strong rural Irish flavor, as do its pubs and brightly painted row houses. The name means St. Columba's Glen (or, alternatively, Columba's Glen Church); the legend goes that St. Columba, the Christian missionary, lived here during the 6th century with a group of followers. Some 40 prehistoric cairns, scattered around the village, have become connected locally with the St. Columba myths.

The **House of St. Columba,** on the cliff top rising north of the village, is a small oratory said to have been used by the saint himself. Inside, stone constructions are thought to have been his bed and chair. Every year on June 9, starting at midnight, local people make a 3-km (2-mi) barefoot procession called "An Turas" (the journey) around 15 medieval crosses and ancient cairns, collectively called the stations of the cross.

Walk through the **Folk Village Museum** to explore rural life. The complex, which was built after local priest Father McDyer started a cooperative to help combat rural depopulation, includes an interpretive center, 1881 schoolhouse, nature walk, tea shop, and crafts shop selling local handmade products, including, intriguingly, wines made from fuchsias and bluebells. Three small cottages, with bare-earth floors, represent the very basic living conditions of the 1720s, 1820s, and 1920s. ✛ *Near the beach* ☎ *074/973–0017* ✒ *€3* ◷ *Easter–Sept., Mon.–Sat. 10–6, Sun. noon–6.*

Ardara

★ ❷   *28 km (17 mi) northeast of Glencolumbkille, 40 km (25 mi) northwest of Donegal Town on N56.*

At the head of a lovely ocean inlet, the unpretentious, old-fashioned hamlet of Ardara—is built around the L-shape intersection of its two main streets. (If you come from Glencolumbkille, expect a scenic drive full of hairpin curves and steep hills as you cross over Glengesh Pass.) For centuries great cloth fairs were once held on the first of every month, and today cottage workers in the surrounding countryside still provide Ardara (and County Donegal) with high-quality, handwoven cloths and hand knits. Aran sweaters—an area specialty—are durable, soft, and often weatherproof, made of undyed wool knit in distinct crisscross patterns. Ardara has several stores to choose among.

Where to Stay & Eat

★ $–$$$ ✕ **L'Atlantique Restaurant.** French couple Laure and Cyrille Troesch cook up excellent seafood in this relaxed little restaurant. Lobster, their specialty, drives the top price of main courses up, but the three-course prix fixe menu €18 is an excellent value. At this writing, the Troeschs were opening a pizzeria around the corner, which may well be worth a look. ⊠ *Main St.* ☎ *074/954–1707* 🖃 *MC, V* ◷ *Closed Tues. and Wed. Nov.–Jan. No dinner Sun.*

★ $ ✕🖾 **Woodhill House.** The cream-color exterior of John and Nancy Yates's spacious manor house is Victorian, but parts of the interior and the coach house date from the 17th century; there's even a small agricultural museum. High ceilings, marble fireplaces, and stained-glass are part of the public spaces. Bedrooms have superb views of the Donegal highlands. The 40-seat restaurant uses local ingredients in dishes on its French-Irish table d'hôte menus: roast duckling with cherry and orange sauce, rack of lamb with herbs picked from the 18th-century walled garden, elaborate homemade desserts. Frequent Irish folk music sessions take place in the bar. ✛ *Just outside Ardara* ⊠ *Donegal Rd., Co. Donegal* ☎ *074/ 954–1112* 🖷 *074/954–1516* ⊕ *www.woodhillhouse.com* ⌁ *9 rooms with bath* ↺ *Restaurant, fishing, horseback riding, bar* 🖃 *AE, DC, MC, V* ⦿ *BP* ◷ *Closed Christmas wk.*

¢   🖾 **Green Gate.** For an alternative to country estates and village hotels, try Frenchman Paul Chatenoud's remote cottage B&B overlooking Ardara, the Atlantic, and spectacular Donegal scenery—it's one of Ireland's most beautiful little guest houses. The four spare rooms are in a converted stone outbuilding with a thatched roof. Chatenoud, as charming as his hideaway, eagerly directs you to Donegal's best-kept secrets. To reach the hotel from Ardara, follow the sign for Donegal and turn right after 200 yards. ⊠ *Ardvally, Co. Donegal* ☎ *074/954–1546* ⌁ *4 rooms with bath* 🖃 *No credit cards* ⦿ *BP.*

FodorsChoice
★

Nightlife

For a small, old-fashioned village, Ardara has a surprising number of pubs, many of which have traditional music in the evenings. The **Central Bar** (⊠ *Main St.* ☎ *074/954–1311*) has music almost every night July and August and on weekends the rest of the year. One of the smallest bars in the Republic, **Nancy's Pub** (⊠ *Front St.* ☎ *074/954–1187*) makes you wonder if you've wandered into the owner's sitting room, but it occasionally finds space for a folk group. The long-established

Nesbitt Arms (✉ Main St. ☎ 074/954–1103) is a good place for a reasonably priced drink and snack. It can get very crowded during July and August.

Shopping

Many handwoven and locally made knitwear items are on sale in Ardara; some stores commission goods directly from knitters, and prices are about as low as anywhere. Handsome, chunky Aran hand-knit sweaters (€76–€127), cardigans (similar prices), and scarves (€20) are all widely available. Stores such as **Campbells Tweed Shop** (✉ Front St. ☎ 074/954–1128) carry ready-to-wear tweeds—sports jackets can run up to €100. **C. Bonner & Son** (✉ Front St. ☎ 074/954–1303) stocks factory knitwear from €29 to €100, as well as pottery, tweeds, jewelry, and gifts. **E. Doherty (Ardara) Ltd.** (✉ Front St. ☎ 074/954–1304) sells handwoven tweeds, from scarves for €25 to capes for €189, as well as traditional Irish products, such as glassware and linen, from Ardara and other parts of the country.

NORTHERN DONEGAL

Traveling on northern County Donegal's country roads, you've escaped at last from the world's hurry and hassle. There's almost nothing up here but scenery, and plenty of it: broad, island-studded loughs of deep, dark tranquility; unkempt, windswept, sheep-grazed grasses on mountain slopes; ribbons of luminous greenery following sparkling streams; and the mellow hues of wide bog lands, all under shifting and changing cloudscapes. This trip—apart from Inishowen Peninsula, which is included as a separate excursion at the end—could take anywhere from one day to a week, depending on how low a gear you slip into after a few breaths of Donegal air. It begins in Letterkenny, the largest town in the county (population 6,500), but if you want to pick up the journey from Ardara, follow the itinerary in reverse. If you choose to abbreviate the trip, try at least to catch the rewarding Fanad and Rosguill peninsulas and the drive around Sheephaven Bay. Just one word of warning—don't be a bit surprised if you find a sheep standing in the middle of a mountain road looking as though you, rather than it, are in the wrong place.

Letterkenny

㉓ *55 km (34 mi) northeast of Ardara, 51 km (32 mi) northeast of Donegal Town, 35 km (21 mi) west of Derry.*

One of the fastest-growing towns in all of Ireland, Letterkenny, like Donegal to the south, is at the gateway to the far northwest; you're likely to come through here if you're driving west out of Northern Ireland. Letterkenny's claim to fame has been that it has the longest main street in the whole country. Also distinctive is its towering neo-Gothic Victorian St. Eunan's Cathedral. None of Letterkenny's shops or pubs are particularly special, but lots of locals bustling around make it an interesting place to get a feel for what it's like to live in a modest-size Irish town.

Where to Stay & Eat

$$ ✕⊞ **Mount Errigal Hotel.** One of County Donegal's smartest and most modern hotels, although not at all posh, Mount Errigal Hotel appeals to both business and family travelers. Service is friendly and professional. The clean and comfortable bedrooms are efficiently arranged with light-colored wood furnishings. The Glengesh, the hotel's popular and softly-lit restaurant, decorated in the Roman style, serves contemporary Irish food ($$). The bar buzzes with locals seeking a relaxed night out, and

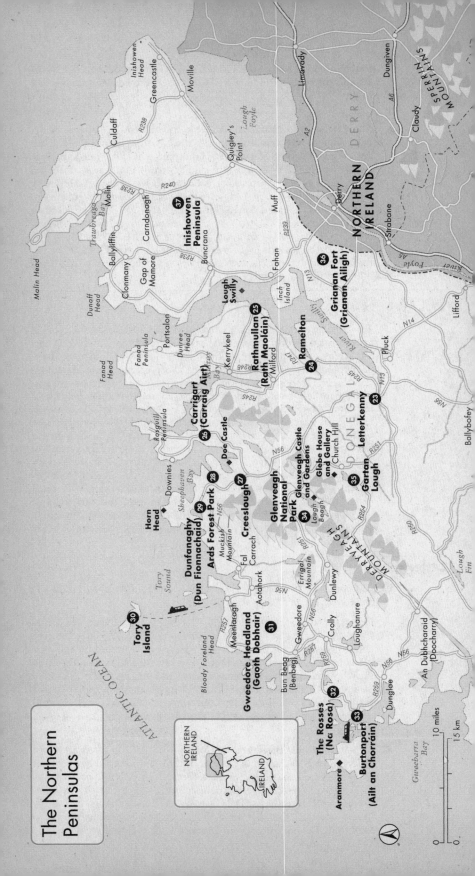

folk music, jazz, or dancing is frequently scheduled on weekends. ⊠ *Bal-lyraine, Co. Donegal* ☎ *074/22700* 🖶 *074/25085* ⊕ *www.amssligo.com/mterrigal/* ⇥ *103 rooms with bath, 2 suites* ⚲ *Restaurant, indoor pool, gym, health club, 2 bars, Internet, meeting rooms* ⊟ *AE, DC, MC, V* ⍥ *BP, MAP.*

Ramelton

㉔ *13 km (8 mi) northeast of Letterkenny on R245.*

A small, handsome former Plantation town built by the prosperous Stewart family, Ramelton (or Rathmelton, though the pronunciation is the same) climbs uphill from a river harbor close to Lough Swilly, one of the loveliest of Donegal's big, fjordlike ocean inlets. The village was the birthplace of Francis Makemie (1658–1708), who preached here before emigrating and founding the American Presbyterian church. In the 18th century it was an important port that exported salmon, butter, grain, linen, and iodine (made from the local seaweed). Houses of wealthy merchants of the time lined the Mall, but the coming of the railway to nearby Letterkenny heralded the end of Ramelton's prosperity. However, Lough Swilly continued to play its part in history, sheltering vast fleets of British ships during the First World War, when Ireland was still part of the Empire.

Nightlife

The **Bridge Bar** (⊠ Bridge End ☎ 074/51119), consistently named among the top 100 pubs in Ireland, has long been favored by locals and summertime visitors as a place to meet for a drink. Enjoy a good hearty meal (dinners are served upstairs, away from the bar), and take in the bands that regularly pack the place at night.

Rathmullan

㉕ *11 km (7 mi) northeast of Ramelton on R247.*

An ancient harbor village set among green fields, Rathmullan (Rath Maoláin, its Irish name, means "ring fort of Maoláin") looks across the broad expanse of Lough Swilly to the Inishowen hills on the eastern shore. Holiday homes have sprung up near Lough Swilly's sandy shores, bringing with them vacationers who swell the town's ordinarily tiny population and make for a livelier summer scene.

Rathmullan's modest harbor was where English naval officers, posing as ordinary merchant seamen, captured Red Hugh O'Donnell in 1587. They invited him aboard to taste some of their "cargo of foreign wines," and the sociable clan leader fell for it. Once on board, he was shipped to imprisonment in Dublin Castle. After six years he escaped and returned to Donegal with added determination to defend his homeland—but to no avail. In 1607, Rathmullan's harbor was the scene of the Flight of the Earls, the great exodus of Ulster nobility, which brought to an end the 13-year war with the English.

The **Flight of the Earls Heritage Centre** commemorates when the million-acre Ulster territories became part of the English domain. Two years later the Plantation era began: English and Scots Protestant colonists were "planted" here, and with them were sown the seeds of the Troubles that still dominate the affairs of Northern Ireland across the border. ☎ 074/58178 🖾 €3 ⊙ Limited hours vary.

Where to Stay & Eat

★ **$$$–$$$$** ✕⌂ **Rathmullan House.** Behind the rambling white facade of this two-story mansion awaits a place that's graceful *and* relaxed. Fine antiques and oil paintings fill the public rooms, including the bright-yellow drawing room. Bedrooms vary from old-fashion basic to grand, but all have antiques, elegant wallpaper, and lovely fabrics. Those in the front overlook Lough Swilly and its deserted beach, steps away. There's a speedboat available for a spin, and deep-sea angling. The restaurant ($$$$) serves freshly caught fish and Donegal lamb as choices on the changing prix-fixe menu. Breakfast is a feast. ⊠ *Lough Swilly, Rathmullan, Co. Donegal* ☎ *074/58188* ⬛ *074/58200* ⊕ *www.rathmullanhouse.com* ⤳ *25 rooms with bath* ⚬ *Restaurant, 2 tennis courts, indoor pool, massage, steam room, spa, beach, boating, fishing, croquet, bar, lounge, library, Internet, meeting rooms* ⊟ *AE, DC, MC, V* ⦿| *BP, MAP* ⊘ *Closed Nov.–mid-Feb.*

$$ 🏨 **Fort Royal Hotel.** Tim Fletcher's spacious hotel attracts a regular clientele that enjoys its relaxed professionalism and marvelous location on 18 acres of verdant grounds beside Lough Swilly. Once an aristocratic private home, this is a decent alternative to the Rathmullan House. Patterned wallpapers—pinstripes and florals—and gilt frames set the traditional tone for the guest rooms. Children under 10 dine at 6, not with the adults at the prix-fixe evening meal. ⊠ *Lough Swilly, Rathmullan, Co. Donegal* ☎ *074/58100* ⬛ *074/58103* ⊕ *www.fortroyalhotel.com* ⤳ *15 rooms with bath* ⚬ *Restaurant, 9-hole golf course, tennis court, beach, bar* ⊟ *AE, DC, MC, V* ⦿| *BP, MAP* ⊘ *Closed Nov.–Mar.*

en route | Extending north from Rathmullan is the barren and rock-strewn Fanad Peninsula. The signposted Fanad Scenic Drive takes you 27 km (17 mi) up along the west shore of Lough Swilly to low-lying Fanad Head at its northern tip, then down again through the tiny resort village of Kerrykeel, with views of long, narrow Mulroy Bay twisting and turning to your right. If you want to cut the journey short, you can take the back road directly from Rathmullan to Kerrykeel for 10 km (6 mi).

Carrigart

❷❻ *14 km (9 mi) north of Ramelton on R245.*

A small village with a lot of charm and many old-fashioned pubs, Carrigart (or Carraig Airt in Irish) is at the base of a slender isthmus. This is the neck of the extremely beautiful Rosguill Peninsula, which has a rocky heart and a fringe of sand dunes and beaches and is encircled by the signposted 15-km (9-mi) Atlantic Drive. It's not as far off the beaten track as you might think; there are several RV sites and housekeeping cottages, popular with people from Northern Ireland. The little resort town of **Downings** (Na Dúnaibh), near Carrigart, has a long, sandy beach and good fishing. Tweeds can be bought from **McNutts of Downings** (⊠ *Downings* ☎ *074/55314*).

Sports & the Outdoors

Horses for riding on the Rosguill Peninsula can be rented at **Carrigart Riding School** (⊠ *Co. Donegal* ☎ *087/227–6926*) for €15 an hour.

Creeslough

❷❼ *16 km (10 mi) southwest of Carraig Airt on N56.*

To the southwest of the Rosguill Peninsula and across Sheephaven Bay lies this small town at the foot of Muckish Mountain. On the southern end of Sheephaven Bay, stands **Doe Castle,** protected on three sides by the sea and by a moat on its fourth side. The tall, weather-beaten tower is at the center of a complex structure enclosed within sturdy defenses.

Described by attacking English forces in 1587 as "the strongest fortress in all the province," the edifice dates from at least 1440, when it became the home of MacSweeney Doe, one of the "gallowglasses" (from the Irish *gall o glach*)—foreign mercenaries employed by the O'Donnell clan. Despite the castle's present poor condition, it was occupied by his descendants until 1890. MacSweeney Doe's curiously carved tombstone is fixed to the southwest tower of the outer wall. It's usually open; if it's locked, inquire at the caretaker's cottage on approach path. ✛ *5 km (3 mi) northeast of Creeslough* ⊠ *Off N56* ☎ *No phone* 🖃 *Free* ⊙ *Freely accessible.*

Ards Forest Park

28 *8 km (5 mi) north of Creeslough on N56.*

Clinging to Sheephaven Bay's southwest shore, the 1,188-acre Ards Forest Park (reached by passing through adjacent Creeslough [pronounced *creesh*-la]) is the former wooded estate of a Capuchin friary. The friary itself is still occupied by the Capuchins. Four prehistoric, fortified sites and one dolmen lie within the grounds, which have some of the most varied landscape of any of Ireland's national forest parks, including rivers, loughs, salt marshes, valleys, and, of course, the bay. If the weather is fine, the park's forest trails and picnic sites are great places to enjoy the scrubbed sea air. ☎ *074/21139* 🖃 *Free* ⊙ *Apr.–Sept., daily 10–9; Oct.–Mar., daily 10–4:30.*

Dunfanaghy

29 *8 km (5 mi) northwest of Ards Forest Park on N56.*

On the edge of Sheephaven Bay, Dunfanaghy (Dun Fionnachaid) is a tidy, former Plantation village. If you're ready for a short break, the hotel serves decent, unpretentious local grub.

When the tide goes out, the vast sand flats of **Killyhoey Beach** are uncovered and the sea recedes into the far distance, but as it rises again, the sands are submerged in double-quick time. On the west side of Dunfanaghy, the signpost to **McSwyne's Gun** (McSwyne is the old spelling of MacSweeney) leads to a huge natural blowhole that gives out a deafening bang when the tide rushes in during rough weather.

The Workhouse exhibits illustrate the harsh life of a workhouse, where people turned when the famine forced them to accept hard labor for a roof and food. Following the story of "Wee Hannah" from her farmhouse upbringing through famine to an eventual peaceful old age. The center has a café and an Irish handicrafts shop. ⊠ *N56, just west of town* ☎ *074/36540* ⊕ *www.theirishfamine.com* 🖃 *€4* ⊙ *Mar.–Oct., daily 10–5.*

★ A little back road runs from Dunfanaghy up to **Horn Head**, the most spectacular of County Donegal's Atlantic headlands. From its sheer 600-foot cliffs, the views along the coast to the other headlands ranged one behind the other are inimitable. Bird-watchers should note that the cliffs are packed with hundreds of seabirds, including puffins and guillemots.

Where to Stay & Eat

$-$$ ✕🛏 **Arnold's Hotel.** This friendly hotel has been run by three generations of the Arnold family and is a favorite with Irish vacationers. Rooms are unassuming, with floral bedspreads, curtains, or wallpaper. Ask for one overlooking the landscaped garden. You can eat generous, traditional Irish meals in the dining room or in the more casual Gallery Bistro ($$-$$$). Special-interest classes, such as photography, writing, bridge, painting, and wine-tasting, are available on the weekends. ✉ *Main St., Dunfanaghy, Co. Donegal* ☎ *074/36208* 🖷 *074/36352* 🌐 *www. arnoldshotel.com* 🖛 *30 rooms with bath* ⬧ *Restaurant, café, tennis court, horseback riding, bar, baby-sitting* ▭ *AE, DC, MC, V* ⦿ *BP, MAP* ⊙ *Closed Nov.–mid-Mar.*

en route

West of Dunfanaghy the terrain is rougher, wilder, and rockier; you're also likely to hear the Irish language being spoken. The N56 reaches round 11 km (7 mi) to Fal Carrach (Falcarragh), the site of an Irish-language college. Another 13 km (8 mi) around the rugged seashore, in good weather, you can catch a ferry from Meenlaragh (near Gortahork) to Tory Island.

Tory Island

30 *15 km (9 mi) offshore from Meenlaragh.*

Harsh weather and difficult currents make Tory Island fairly inaccessible. (The boat trip lasts more than an hour on seas that are rough even on the best days. Be prepared to get soaked.) Despite being rocky, ocean-battered, and barren (not even a single tree), the island has been inhabited since prehistoric times. Islanders speak their own dialect and refer to the mainland as "Ireland." Prehistoric and medieval relics are scattered about the landscape. Poised on the cliffs is the partly ruined, pink-granite **round tower** with its conical cap still intact. At Tory Island's eastern end, the prehistoric ruin, **Balor's Fort**, was purportedly the residence of Balor, the terrifying, one-eyed Celtic god of night and darkness. At the northeastern tip, the **Wishing Stone** has the power, it is said, to destroy enemies. Still talked about is the time (1884) when the stone's powers were invoked against the British gunboat *Wasp*, whose passengers (mainly policemen) had come to collect taxes—something the islanders were unaccustomed to paying. The ship sank, and all but six of the crew were lost.

Most of the islanders live the simple life of fisherfolk, though quite a few have unexpected sidelines as artists. In 1968, the well-known Irish painter Derek Hill met islander James Dixon, who believed that he could do a better job of painting than Hill. Many other Tory Island residents thought they could, too, and today the Tory Island artists, depicting their own life and landscape in naive style using nothing more than standard house paints, are widely acclaimed and have exhibited elsewhere in Ireland, including Glebe House and Gallery in Gartan Lough and abroad. **Dixon's Gallery** sells the work of the Tory Islanders; prices range from €63 to €254. The owner of the Tory Island Hotel watches over the gallery.

Where to Stay & Eat

$ ✕⊞ **Tory Island Hotel (Ostan Thoraig).** After living and working in England for 10 years, native islander Pat Doohan returned with his wife, Berney, to build and run the Tory Island Hotel. (He also watches over the nearby Dixon's Gallery.) The comfortable guest rooms are large and sunny, decorated in a peach, blue, and green palette, with matching curtains and bedspreads. A fireplace warms the Peoples Bar, which is a popular local hangout. Traditional music sessions and *ceilí* traditional dancing regularly liven things up. The Lobster Room restaurant ($–$$) both overlooks the sea and serves dishes from it. ✉ *Main St., Co. Donegal* ☎ *074/35920* 🖷 *074/35613* 🌐 *www.toryhotel.com* 🖛 *12 rooms with bath* ⬧ *Restaurant, bar* ▭ *AE, MC, V* ⦿ *BP, MAP* ⊙ *Closed Nov.–Mar.*

Gweedore Headland

③ *27 km (17 mi) east of Meenlaragh on R257.*

When you return from Tory Island to Meenlaragh, you're on the edge of the Gweedore Headland (Gaoth Dobhair), which can be circumnavigated on the coast road (R257). Gweedore is rocky, sparsely covered with heather and gorse, and low-lying until you reach its northernmost point, **Bloody Foreland Head.** This dramatic name for once does not recall the slaughter of some historic battle, describing instead the vivid red hues of the gaunt rock face when illuminated at sunset.

The Rosses

㉜ *13 km (8 mi) south of Bloody Foreland Head on R259.*

The next distinctive headland south of Gweedore (on the road south after you pass through Bun Beag [Benbeg] and Croithli [Crolly]) are the Rosses (Na Rosa, meaning "the headlands in Irish")—even more beautiful than Gweedore. The bleak but dramatic terrain here, as at Gweedore, has not benefited from a liberal sprinkling of modern bungalows. The coast road (R259) struggles over the inhospitable, stony landscape, crisscrossed with water channels and strewn with more than 100 lakes. Yet quite a number of people manage to survive here, many of them Irish speakers (this is the heart of the Donegal Gaeltacht). The decline of population and living standards was reversed by Patrick Gallagher (1873–1964), who became known as Paddy the Cope. Son of a poor local family, he left school at 10, went to Scotland as a farmhand, and saved enough money to return home in the 1950s and buy a small holding of his own. Gallagher, affectionately remembered throughout the area, persuaded the citizens around the Rosses to set up cooperatives to bring in new farming methods and machinery, as well as cooperatively owned stores to keep prices down.

Burtonport

㉝ *16 km (10 mi) southwest of Crolly on R259.*

The village of Burtonport (Ailt an Chorráin in Irish), which claims to land more salmon and lobster than any other fishing port in Ireland, is the departure point for a trip over to **Aranmore,** 6 km (4 mi) offshore. Aranmore means "big island," and it is indeed the largest and most populous of County Donegal's rocky offshore fragments. The ride out takes 25 minutes (€9 round-trip), but although it's fairly accessible (seven crossings daily), the island still feels remote and ungoverned. It has been inhabited for thousands of years (about 1,000 people live on it today). A prehistoric fort sits on its south side. There's good fishing as well as striking cliff scenery and views back onto the Rosses. ✉ *Burtonport* ☎ *074/ 952–0532.*

en route Follow the coast from Burtonport southeast 6 km (4 mi) to An Clochan Liath (Dungloe), a pleasant little fishing town regarded as the capital of the Rosses, though there's little to do or see here. Travel north on N56, go a couple of miles beyond Gaoth Dobhair (Gweedore) village, on the little River Clady, and take R251 to skirt the south side of Errigal Mountain to the village of Dunlewy, 26 km (16 mi) east of Dungloe. This whole drive passes through some of the best scenery in all of County Donegal. Serene Errigal looks especially grand from Dunlewy. On the edge of Dunlewy Lough, the **Dunlewy Centre** is an interesting place to pause for a look at a reconstructed

19th-century weaver's home. Watch a demonstration of old-style weaving and an audiovisual show, then have a guided tour of the cottage. Half-hour boat trips on the lake leave from here and include storytelling and a history of the area. A café and crafts shop are also on the premises. ✉ *R251, Dunlewy* ☎ *074/953–1699* ✉ *Center €5; boat trip €5* ☉ *Mid-Mar.–Nov., Mon.–Sat. 10:30–6, Sun. 11–6.*

Glenveagh National Park

34 *45 km (28 mi) east of Burtonport on R251.*

Fodor's Choice
★

Bordered by the Derryveagh Mountains (Derryveagh means "forest of oak and birch"), Glenveagh National Park encompasses 24,000 acres of wilderness—mountain, moorland, lakes, and woods—that has been called the largest and most dramatic tract in the wildest part of Donegal. Within its borders, a thick carpet of russet-color heath and dense woodland rolls down the Derryveagh slopes into the broad open valley of the River Veagh (or Owenbeagh), which opens out into Glenveagh's spine: long and narrow, dark and clear Lough Beagh.

The Glenveagh lands have long been recognized as a remote and beautiful region. Between 1857 and 1859, John George Adair, a ruthless gentleman farmer, assembled the estate that now makes up the park. In 1861, he evicted the estate's hundreds of poor tenants without compensation and destroyed their cottages. Nine years later, Adair began to build Glenveagh Castle on the eastern shore of Lough Veagh, but he soon departed for Texas. He died in 1885 without returning to Ireland, but his widow, Cornelia, moved back to make Glenveagh her home. She created the four different gardens covering 27 acres, planted the luxuriant rhododendrons here, and began the job of making this turret-and-battlement laden, 19th-century folly livable.

The gardens and castle as they appear today are almost entirely an American invention—the product of the loving attentions of Glenveagh's last owner. U.S. millionaire Henry P. McIlhenny bought the estate in 1937 and, beginning in 1947, lived here for part of every year for almost 40 years. An avid art collector and philanthropist, McIlhenny decorated every inch of the house himself and entertained lavishly. The house has been maintained just as it was on his last occupancy in 1983; later that year, he made a gift of the house to the nation. He had sold the government the surrounding land in 1975, which it opened to the public in 1984 as Ireland's third national park.

Beyond the castle, footpaths lead into more remote sections of the park, including the Derrylahan Nature Trail, a 1½-km (1-mi) signposted trail where you may suddenly catch sight of a soaring falcon or chance upon a shy red deer. The park is the home of one of Ireland's two largest herds; the other is at Killarney. Guided walks are held May through October. The visitor center at the park's entrance has a permanent exhibition on the local way of life and on the influence of climate on the park's flora and fauna. Skip the sleep-inducing audiovisual and instead have a bite to eat in the cafeteria. A bus runs from the visitor center to the castle. ✉ *R251, Church Hill* ☎ *074/37090* ✉ *Bus €2 round-trip, castle tour and gardens €3* ☉ *Mid-Mar.–Oct., daily 10–6:30.*

Gartan Lough

35 *13 km (8 mi) southeast of Glenveagh National Park on R251.*

Gartan Lough and the surrounding mountainous country are astonishingly beautiful. St. Columba was supposedly born here in AD 521, and the legendary event is marked by a huge cross at the beginning of a footpath into Glenveagh National Park. (Close to Church Hill village, Gartan Lough is technically within the national park and is administered partly by the park authorities.) Nearby are other dubious "relics" of the saint, which are popularly believed to possess magical powers: the Natal Stone, where the saint is thought to have first opened his eyes, and the Stone of Loneliness, where he is said to have slept. However, the superstitions do rub off—the soil of Gartan was carried by soldiers from the area to the trenches of the First World War as a protective relic.

On the northwest shore of Gartan Lough, just off R251 is **Glebe House and Gallery,** a fine Regency manor with 25 acres of gardens. For 30 years, Glebe House was the home of the distinguished landscape and portrait artist Derek Hill, who furnished the house in a mix of styles with art from around the world; in 1981 he gave the house and its contents, including his outstanding art collection, to the nation. Highlights include paintings by Renoir and Bonnard, lithographs by Kokoschka, ceramics and etchings by Picasso, and the paintings *Whippet Racing* and *The Ferry, Early Morning* by Jack B. Yeats, as well as Donegal folk art produced by the Tory Islanders. The decoration and furnishings of the house, including original William Morris wallpaper, are also worth a look. ⊠ *Church Hill* ☎ *074/37071* ⌨ *€3* ☉ *Sat.–Thurs. 11–6:30.*

At the **Colmcille Heritage Centre** you can learn more about St. Columba and his times. The exhibition and interpretation center has medieval manuscripts, stained glass, and displays tracing the decline of the Celtic religion and the rise of Irish Christianity. Audiovisual displays and interactive computer presentations enhance the historical journey. The staff can show you walks in the area. ⊠ *R254, Church Hill* ☎ *074/37306* ⌨ *€2* ☉ *Mid-Apr.–Sept., Mon.–Sat. 10:30–6:30, Sun. 1–6:30.*

Grianan Fort

★ ㊱ *29 km (18 mi) northeast of Letterkenny on N13.*

A circular stone Celtic fort, the Grianan Fort (Grianan Ailigh) definitely merits a visit, although it is, like the Inishowen Peninsula, northeast of Letterkenny and thus closer to Northern Ireland than the majority of Donegal sites covered here. The fortress crowns an 810-foot hill. On a fine day, the panorama of the rolling Donegal and Derry landscape is breathtaking. To the north lies the River Swilly, flowing around Inch Island into Lough Swilly. On either side rise the hills of the Fanad and Inishowen peninsulas, though they're often partly veiled by mists. The fort is a 76-foot diameter circular stone enclosure, which you can enter through a gate. Inside, earth ramparts and concentric defenses punctured by passages surround a sturdy central structure. No one knows when Grianan Fort was built, but it was probably an Iron Age fortress. Its position was accurately recorded in the 2nd century AD by Ptolemy of Alexandria. In the 5th century it became the seat of Ulster's O'Neill chieftains and remained so until the 12th century, despite serious attempts by their enemies to destroy it, especially in the year 674 and again in 1101. The present-day fortress, however, owes a good deal to overzealous "restoration" in the 1870s by Dr. Walter Bernard, a Derry historian; before that, it was in ruins. If you're traveling north on N13, look for signs to Buncrana, because the easy-to-miss sign for the fort is opposite. Instead of turning to Buncrana, take the narrow lane that climbs and turns for more than 2 km (1 mi) to the top of the hill. The fort is freely accessible.

Inishowen Peninsula

37 *6 km (4 mi) north of Grianan Ailigh on R238.*

The most northerly point in all of Ireland, the huge Inishowen Peninsula is a grandly green, wild piece of land with a solid, mountainous interior. It's flanked by Lough Swilly on one side and Lough Foyle on the other, and the battering Atlantic thrashes to the north. Despite a string of small and untempting coastal resorts, the peninsula remains unspoiled and less traveled than most other parts of the country. If you decide to make the Inishowen circuit from Fahan to Muff via Malin Head (known as the "Inishowen 100," for its length in miles) plus the 64-km (40-mi) round-trip to reach it from Letterkenny, you need to allow at least one whole day, though it's possible to make an abbreviated visit in less time.

Just off R238, as you head toward Buncrana, is **Fahan** (pronounced fawn), which has monastic ruins that include the early Christian St. Mura cross slab. A popular, downscale beach resort favored by Derry denizens, **Buncrana** has a 14th-century O'Doherty tower that gradually became part of an 18th-century mansion. Shortly after you pass Buncrana, turn left at the fork in the road away from R238 onto the coast road, which takes you past the 19th-century fort on Dunree Head, up and over the spectacular viewpoint of the **Gap of Mamore**, where the 1,250-foot Croaghcarragh rises up on one side and the 1,361-foot Mamore Hill echoes it on the other. The road heads north toward Dunaff Head, where Lough Swilly opens into the ocean. Rejoin R238 at Clonmany and take it through Ballyliffin, a small resort town with an O'Doherty tower on the beach, and a convenient place for a snack or meal.

By the junction of R238 and R240 is a church with a curious remnant of early Christianity against one wall—the decorated, 7th-century **Donagh Cross**, accompanied by a couple of pillar stones. The strange carvings on the stones clearly date from a pre-Christian period. Around the corner from the Donagh Cross, **Carndonagh**, the area's main market town, has several more medieval monastic remains. Slieve Snaght, Inishowen's highest peak at 2,019 feet, lies just southwest of town. As Slieve Snaght runs up beside Trawbreaga Bay, R238 turns into R242 shortly before the picturesque village of **Malin**; it's another 16 km (10 mi) up to Malin Head, the most northerly point in all of Ireland and an important spot for birds migrating south in autumn. Although it has good views, Malin Head is not as dramatic a spot as some of the other headlands.

From Malin Head, take the signposted route across Inishowen peninsula to Moville, a sleepy waterside resort on the Lough Foyle side. From here, it's 8 km (5 mi) to **Inishowen Head**, the peninsula's rocky eastern tip. On the way to the head, at Greencastle, you can see the fortifications of foreigners who tried to control the nine counties of Ulster: a 14th-century Anglo-Norman fortress and an English fort built five centuries later to defend against French support for the Irish. The drive along the lough shore toward Derry, though attractive, is punctuated by small, uninteresting villages whose modernized pubs cater to visitors from Derry. If you want to turn away from Derry toward Letterkenny before reaching the border, take R239 from Muff to **Bridge End**, where there's one of the most attractive of Ireland's many new Catholic churches.

Where to Stay & Eat

$–$$ ✕ **Corncrake Restaurant.** Bríd McCartney and Noreen Lynch gave up the
Fodor'sChoice Dublin rat race to open the most stylish restaurant between Derry and
★ New York. They grow all their own herbs and specialize in seafood and

lamb. Try the cod, prawn, and fennel chowder followed, perhaps, by the sea bass fillet drizzled with lemon sauce and served with spinach. The two also run excellent weekend cooking courses during November and March for €330, which includes all meals, instruction, and accommodation at the nearby Rossaor House. ⊠ *Malin St., Carndonagh* ☎ *077/74534* 🗎 *No credit cards.*

★ $–$$$ ✕🏠 **St. John's Country House and Restaurant.** Intimate rooms graced with Victorian- and Georgian-era furnishings characterize this small lakeside country house. The experience here is enhanced by the exceptional hospitality of host Reggie Ryan. Homemade bread is baked daily—to serve with the fresh garden soups and pâtés. The five-course table d'hôte menu changes monthly ($$$$). Appetizers may include seafood salad or roast peppers with balsamic dressing. Cardamom and lime crepes stuffed with vegetables, and Irish beef sirloin with mushroom and Armagnach sauce, are typical main courses. Desserts include homemade ice creams and carrageen moss with fruit coulis. ⊠ *Off R238, Fahan, Co. Donegal* ☎ *077/60289* 🖷 *077/60612* ⊕ *http://homepage.tinet. ie/~stjohnscountryhouse/* 🛏 *4 rooms with bath, 1 suite* ♻ *No room phones, no room TVs* 🗎 *AE, DC, MC, V* 🍴 *BP* ✆ *Closed mid-Feb.–mid-Mar.*

Sports & the Outdoors

For horseback riding at €25 for an hour and a half on the Inishowen Peninsula contact **Lenamore Stables** (⊠ R239, Muff ☎ 077/84022). It also has a B&B package with riding included.

Shopping

National Knitting Centre and Cranaknits Sweater Shop (⊠ St. Oran's Rd., Buncrana ☎ 077/62355) sells hand-knit goods and gives classes in traditional Irish knitting.

THE NORTHWEST A TO Z

To research prices, get advice from other travelers, and book travel arrangements, visit www.fodors.com.

AIR TRAVEL

CARRIERS Aer Arann has direct flights between Dublin and Knock International, Donegal, and Sligo Airports. British Airways City Express flies to Eglinton (Derry) Airport from Manchester and Glasgow. Ryanair has flights to Knock Airport from London Stansted daily.

🛫 Airlines & Contacts **Aer Arann** ☎ 081/821-0210 or 0800/587-2324 ⊕ www.aerarann. ie. **British Airways City Express** ☎ 0845/773-3377 ⊕ www.britishairways.com. **Ryanair** ☎ 181/21212 ⊕ www.ryanair.com.

AIRPORTS

The principal international air-arrival point to northwest Ireland is the tiny airport at Charlestown, Knock International Airport, 55 km (34 mi) south of Sligo Town. City of Derry Airport, a few miles over the border, receives flights from Manchester and Glasgow. City of Derry (also called Eglinton) is a particularly convenient airport for reaching northern County Donegal. Donegal Airport, in Carrickfinn, is not far from Dungloe and typically receives flights from Dublin. Sligo Airport at Strandhill, 8 km (5 mi) west of Sligo Town, is the other area airport.

🛫 Airport Information **City of Derry Airport** ☎ 028/7181-0784. **Donegal Airport** ☎ 075/48232. **Knock International Airport** ☎ 094/67222. **Sligo Airport** ☎ 071/916-8280 or 071/916-8318.

TRANSFERS If you aren't driving, Knock Airport becomes less attractive, there are no easy public transportation links, except the once-a-day (in season) local bus to Charlestown, 11 km (7 mi) away. Nor can you rely on catching a bus at the smaller airports, except at Sligo Airport, where buses run from Sligo Town to meet all flights.

You can get taxis—both cars and minibuses—right outside Knock Airport. The average rate is €1.27 per mile. However, if you're not flying into Knock, you may have to phone a taxi company. Phone numbers of taxi companies are available from airport information desks and are also displayed beside pay phones inside the airport terminals.

🚕 Taxi Companies **Castle Cabs** ☎ 087/638-8588. **OK Cabs** ☎ 087/639-6666. **Tom Cronnolly** ☎ 087/244-0597.

BUS TRAVEL

Bus Éireann can get you from Dublin to Sligo Town in four hours for €14 one-way, €23 round-trip. Four buses a day from Dublin are available. Another bus route, five times a day from Dublin (six on Friday), goes to Letterkenny, in the heart of County Donegal, in 4¼ hours, via a short trip across the Northern Ireland border; it's €15 one-way, €23 round-trip. Other Bus Éireann services connect Sligo Town to towns all over Ireland. Bus Éireann also operates out of Sligo Town and Letterkenny to destinations all over the region, as well as to other parts of Ireland. From Sligo Town, you can reach almost any point in the region for less than €15. McGeehans is one of several local bus companies linking towns and villages in northwest Ireland.

🚌 Bus Information **Bus Éireann** ☎ 01/836-6111 in Dublin; 071/916-0066 in Sligo Town; 074/21309 in Letterkenny. **McGeehans** ☎ 074/954-6150.

CAR RENTAL

You can rent a car in Sligo Town from Euro Mobil. Murray's Europcar rents cars from Knock Airport. A medium-size four-door costs around €65 per day with unlimited mileage (inclusive of insurance and taxes) or around €300 per week. If you're planning to tour mostly northern County Donegal, you may find it more convenient to rent a car in Derry from Ford. If you're planning to drive a rental car across the border to Northern Ireland, inform the company in advance and check the insurance policy.

🚗 Agencies **Euro Mobil** ☎ 071/916-7291. **Ford** ☎ 028/7181-2222. **Murray's Europcar** ☎ 094/67221 at Knock Airport; 01/614-2800 for reservations.

CAR TRAVEL

Sligo, the largest town in the northwest Ireland, is relatively accessible on the main routes. The N4 travels the 224 km (140 mi) directly from Dublin to Sligo. Allow at least four hours for this journey. The N15 continues from Sligo Town to Donegal Town and proceeds from Donegal Town to Derry City, just over the border in Northern Ireland. The fastest approach for anyone driving up from the west and the southwest is on N17, connecting Sligo to Galway, though the landscape is undistinguished.

ROAD CONDITIONS Roads are not congested, but in some places they are in a poor state of repair (French bus drivers refused to take their buses into County Donegal some summers back, as a gesture of protest about the state of the roads). In the Irish-speaking areas, signposts are written only in the Irish (Gaelic) language, which can be confusing. Make sure that your map lists both English and Irish place names.

EMERGENCIES

🚑 **Ambulance, fire, police** ☎ 999. **Letterkenny General Hospital** ✉ High Rd., Letterkenny, Co. Donegal ☎ 074/25888. **Sligo General Hospital** ✉ The Mall, Sligo Town, Co. Sligo ☎ 071/917-1111.

TOURS

Bus Éireann has budget-priced, guided, one-day bus tours of the Donegal Highlands and to Glenveagh National Park, which start from Bundoran, Sligo Town, Ballyshannon, and Donegal Town. For a friendly, relaxed minibus tour of the area in July and August, call John Houze. He's a knowledgeable guide who leads popular tours (€14 each) to the Lake Isle of Innisfree, the Holy Well, Parke's Castle; and north of Sligo Town to W. B. Yeats's grave, Lissadell House, and Glencar lake and waterfall.

Walking tours of Sligo Town may be arranged in advance for groups, and last about 1½ hours. Depending on the number of people, the charge is approximately €4.

🔹 Bus Tours **Bus Éireann** ☎ 01/836-6111 ⊕ www.buseireann.ie. **John Houze** ☎ 071/914-2747 or 086/193-5045.

🔹 Walking Tours **Sligo Path Guided Walking Tours** ☎ 071/915-0920.

TRAIN TRAVEL

Sligo Town is the northernmost direct rail link to Dublin. From Dublin three trains a day make the 3 hour and 20 minute journey for €18 one-way, €27 round-trip. If you want to get to Sligo Town by rail from other provincial towns, you're forced to make some inconvenient connections and take roundabout routes. The rest of the region has no railway services.

🔹 Train Information **Irish Rail** ☎ 01/836-6222 ⊕ www.irishrail.ie.

VISITOR INFORMATION

The Tourist Information Office (TIO) in Sligo Town provides a walking map of Sligo, information about bus tours of Yeats Country, and details of boat tours of Lough Gill. It's also the main visitor information center for northwest Ireland. Open hours are September to mid-March, weekdays 9–5; mid-March to August, weekdays 9–6, Saturday 10–2, and Sunday 11–3. If you are traveling in County Donegal in the north, try the TIO at Letterkenny about 1½ km (1 mi) south of town. It's open September to May, weekdays 9–5; June to August, Monday–Saturday 9–6 and Sunday 12–3. The offices at Bundoran and Dungloe are open only during the summer months (usually the first week in June to the second week in September).

🔹 Tourist Information **Bundoran TIO** ✉ Main St., Bundoran, Co. Donegal ☎ 071/984-1350. **Co. Donegal TIO** ✉ N13, Derry Rd., Letterkenny, Co. Donegal ☎ 074/21160. **Co. Sligo TIO** ✉ Temple and Charles Sts., Sligo Town, Co. Donegal ☎ 071/916-1201. **Donegal Town TIO** ✉ Quay St., Donegal Town, Co. Donegal ☎ 074/972-1148. **Dungloe TIO** ✉ Village Center, Dungloe, Co. Donegal ☎ 074/952-1297.

NORTHERN IRELAND

8

FODOR'S CHOICE

Ardtara House, *Upperlands hotel*

Ash-Rowan Guest House, *Belfast*

Crown Liquor Saloon, *Belfast sight*

Giant's Causeway, *Co. Antrim sight*

Deane's, *Belfast restaurant*

Shanks, *Bangor restaurant*

Ulster Folk & Transport Museum, *northeast of Belfast*

HIGHLY RECOMMENDED

RESTAURANTS Aldens, *Belfast*

Café Rankin, *Belfast*

Grace Neill's, *Donaghadee*

Long's, *Belfast*

Ramore Wine Bar, *Portrush*

Wysner's, *Ballycastle*

HOTELS Dufferin Arms Coaching Inn, *Killyleagh*

Londonderry Arms, *Carnlough*

Merchant's House, *Derry*

The Old Inn, *outside Belfast in Crawfordsburn*

Portaferry Hotel, *Portaferry*

TENsq, *Belfast*

SIGHTS Botanic Gardens, *Belfast*

Castle Coole, *Co. Fermanagh (near Enniskillen)*

City Hall, *Belfast*

Dunluce Castle, *Portrush*

Grand Opera House, *Belfast*

High Street, *Belfast*

Glens of Antrim, *Co. Antrim*

Updated by
Anneliese Paull

LEGEND HAS IT THAT WELL OVER A MILLENNIUM ago a marauding chieftain caught sight of the shores of Northern Ireland from the deck of his boat and offered this green and fertile land to whichever of his two sons could first lay hand on it. As the two rival sons rowed for the shore in their separate boats, one began to draw ahead—whereupon the other drew his sword, cut off his own hand, and threw it onto the beach— and so, by blood and sacrifice, won this province. To this day the arms of Northern Ireland has this same severed limb: the celebrated "Red Hand of Ulster."

From this bardic tale to the most recent Troubles of 1969 to 1994, Northern Ireland has had a long and often ferocious history. But come here and thoughts of violence vanish in the face of the country's outstanding natural beauty; its magnificent, stately houses; and the genuine, open hospitality of its inhabitants. The Six Counties, or Ulster (as Northern Ireland is often called), cover less than 14,245 square km (5,500 square mi) in all. Within these boundaries is some of the most unspoiled scenery you could hope to find—the granite Mountains of Mourne; the Giant's Causeway, made of extraordinary volcanic rock; more than 320 km (200 mi) of coastline beaches and hidden coves; and rivers and leaf-sheltered lakes that provide fabled fishing grounds, including the largest freshwater lake in Europe, Lough Neagh. Ancient castles and Palladian-perfect 18th-century houses are as numerous here as almost anywhere else in Europe, and each has its own tale of heroic deeds, dastardly treachery, and lovelorn ghosts. Northern Ireland not only houses this great heritage in stone, but has also given the world an even greater legacy— its celebrated descendants. Nearly one in six of the more than 4½ million Irish who made the fateful journey across the Atlantic to seek their fortune in the New World was from Ulster, and of this group (and from their family stock), more than a few left their mark in America: Davy Crockett, President Andrew Jackson, General Ulysses S. Grant, President Woodrow Wilson, General Stonewall Jackson, financier Thomas Mellon, merchant Paul Getty, writers Edgar Allan Poe and Mark Twain, and astronaut Neil Armstrong.

Present-day Northern Ireland, a province under the rule of the United Kingdom, includes six of the old Ulster's nine counties and retains its sense of separation, both in the vernacular of the landscape and (some say) in the character of the people. The hardheaded and industrious Scots-Presbyterians, imported to make Ulster a bulwark against Ireland's Catholicism, have had a profound and ineradicable effect on the place. The north has more factories, neater-looking farms, better roads, and— in its cities—more of the two-story redbrick houses typical of Great Britain than does the Republic. For all that, the border between north and south is of little consequence if you're just here to see the country.

Ireland's ancient history truly began in the north, when settlers came to the banks of the River Bann 9,000 years ago. Five thousand years later Bronze Age settlers built the great stone circles idiomatic to Counties Down and Tyrone, and later the Iron Age brought the Celts. St. Patrick, son of a Roman official and once a slave in County Antrim, returned to spread Christianity in the 5th century. But from the first Norman incursions in the 12th century onward, the English made greater and greater inroads into Ireland, endeavoring to subdue what they believed was a potential enemy. Ulster proved the hardest part to conquer, but in 1607 Ulster's beaten Irish nobility fled their homeland forever, many of them going to France and Spain, in the great exodus known as the Flight of the Earls. Their abandoned lands were distributed by the English to "the Planters"—staunch Protestants from England and Scotland.

After three centuries of smoldering tensions and religious strife, 1916 saw the Easter Uprising and then, in the parliamentary elections of 1918, an overwhelming Nationalist vote across Ireland for Sinn Féin ("Ourselves Alone"), the party that believed in independence for all of Ireland. In the five northeastern counties of Ulster, however, only seven seats went to the Nationalists, and 22 to the Unionists, who wanted to remain an integral part of the United Kingdom. At 2:10 AM on December 6, 1921, in the British prime minister's residence at 10 Downing Street, Michael Collins—the Republican leader and controversial hero—signed the Anglo-Irish Treaty. This designated a six-county north to remain in British hands in exchange for complete independence for Ireland's 26 counties as the Irish Free State.

Fast-forward to 1968, when, in the spirit of the student protesters in Paris and Washington, and after 40 years of living with an apparently permanent and sectarian Unionist majority, students in Belfast's Queen's University launched a civil rights movement, claiming equal rights in jobs, housing, and opportunity. The brutality with which these marches were suppressed in front of the world's press led to worldwide revulsion, riots, and counter-riots. The Irish Republican Army (IRA), which had lain dormant for decades, took over what was left of the shattered civil rights movement, which once had a smattering of Protestant students among its ranks. Armed British troops who had at first been welcomed by many in the Catholic ghettos as protectors from Protestant paramilitaries now found themselves welcomed by neither side. Britain imposed Direct Rule. No one was happy, and the decades of guerrilla conflict that ensued between the IRA, the UDA/UVF (Protestant/Loyalist paramilitaries), and the British government continued in a mix of lulls and terrors—apart from the IRA's annual Christmas "truce"—until the summer of 1994, when the "Provos," as they are colloquially known, called an ongoing cease-fire, confirmed in July 1997.

Belfast reveled in its peace. New hotels, shopping malls, and restaurants came off dusty drawing boards. People who had not seen the city's center for a quarter of a century gazed at its bright lights. Today, the IRA and Loyalist cease-fires are still in place, but major divisions remain. The various shades of Unionism are closely identified with the "planted" Protestant population, and Nationalists are inextricably associated with the "native" Irish community, which traces its genetic inheritance back to the Iron Age Celtic invaders and which is almost entirely Catholic. Today, in blue-collar Protestant areas curbstones and lampposts are painted in the British colors of red, white, and blue; entwined British and Red Hand Ulster flags fluttering from tall poles raised in pocket-handkerchief front yards; and countless signs and crests declaring proud devotion to Ulster and the Queen. By contrast, in Nationalist Catholic districts, note the green, white, and gold of the Irish Republic's Tricolor flickering in the breeze.

Don't worry if this all seems impossibly complex. Even locals say wryly, "If you understand Northern Ireland politics, you're missing the point." In any case, the province's turbulent history cannot mask the fact that it is a region incredibly rich in natural beauty and artistic treasures. For overseas travelers, Northern Ireland remains one of the increasingly rare forgotten spots of Europe.

Exploring Northern Ireland

The city of Belfast is Northern Ireland's main gateway. A naturally lively, friendly city, Belfast has plenty of distinguished hotels and restaurants, fascinating museums, Victorian architecture, and strong mar-

Numbers in the text correspond to numbers in the margin and on the Northern Ireland and Belfast maps.

If you have 2 days

The first day tour bustling Victorian industrial metropolis and environs of **Belfast** ❶–⑱. In the morning start north through the breathtaking **Glens of Antrim** ⑳ to the remarkable natural formations of the **Giant's Causeway** ㉒ and the teetering cliff-top remains of **Dunluce Castle** ㉔. Spend the night in ⌗ **Coleraine** ㉕, ⌗ Ballymena, or if you wish to return the way you came, you could stay in one of the coastal towns before Belfast.

If you have 4 days

Follow the 2-day itinerary but continue on to spend the second night in the dramatically rejuvenated city of ⌗ **Derry** ㉘–㉟. In the morning drive south to the tranquil beauty of **Lower Lough Erne** ㊳. You may want to go on a boat ride, take a pottery tour in **Belleek** ㊴, visit the historic town of **Enniskillen** ㊵, or the exquisite neoclassic beauty of **Castle Coole** ㊶. The next day follow the road through leafy **Armagh** ㊷, Ireland's ecclesiastical capital, then southeast on B133 to the magnificent **Mountains of Mourne** ㊸. Spend the night in one of the towns in or near the mountains and work your way up the coast the next day past Strongford Lough back to Belfast.

If you have 7 days

Spend two nights in Belfast, then head north on A2. Take your time exploring the **Glens of Antrim** ⑳ with a look at the characteristic twin towns of rugged Cushendall and pretty Cushendun, and **Ballycastle** ㉑. Stop along the coast for the night before driving to **Giant's Causeway** ㉒ the next day. Stop for a tour and a sip if whiskey at **Bushmills** ㉓ before visiting **Dunluce Castle** ㉔. Continue on that evening to ⌗ **Derry** ㉘–㉟, where you spend that night. On Day 5 drive south and visit **Ulster-American Folk Park** ㊱ or the reconstructed dwellings of the **Ulster History Park** ㊲ before continuing on to **Lower Lough Erne** ㊳. The famous pottery-making town of **Belleek** ㊴ is at the east end of the lake. At the west end is the historic town of **Enniskillen** ㊵, which is near **Castle Coole** ㊶: take your pick. Day 6 is on to the **Mountains of Mourne** ㊸ with their trails and overlooks. You can choose among several towns in which to spend the night from Kilkeel to ⌗ **Portaferry** ㊺: The last day make your way to Belfast along the shores of Strangford Lough to the fairy-tale gardens of **Mount Stewart** ㊻ before returning to Belfast.

---

itime connections. It's testimony to the spirit of Belfast that the long years of sectarian violence have not dimmed its vivacity. Northern Ireland's second city, Derry, is also looking to the future and has an appealing personality all its own—beautiful rows of Georgian houses are being restored. Museums and crafts shops have opened in the small city center, which is still enclosed by its medieval walls and one of Europe's best-preserved examples of a fortified town.

Along the shores of Northern Ireland's coasts and lakes, green, gentle slopes descend majestically into hazy, dark-blue water against a background of more slopes, more water, and huge, cloud-scattered skies. The Antrim Coast is among the most scenic in all of Ireland: Dunluce Castle, the Giant's Causeway, and the small towns along the east coast give the traveler a choice of stops along excellent roads. Enniskillen, in

Northern
Ireland

Tory
Island

Horn
Head

Creeslough

Fanad
Head

Malin Head

Malin

Culdaff

Carndonagh

Inishowen
Head

Cau
Dunlu
Cast

Moville

Ports

25 C

Rathmullan

Milford

Ramelton

Carrowkeel

Muff

Lough
Foyle

Blackhill

Aghadowey

A2

27 Limavady

B66

Letterkenny

Derry
28 - 35
See detail map

Campsie

A6

Dungiven

B190

Gar

K

Claudy

A6

L

Lifford

B48

SPERRIN MOUNTAINS

DERRY

Tobermore

Be

Stranorlar

Castlefin

Strabane

Sion Mills

Ballybofey

A5 Newtownstewart

BLUE STACK MOUNTAINS

Ulster-American Folk Park 36

37 Ulster History Park

A505 Cookstown

Donegal Town

Omagh

B46

Pomeroy

TYRONE

A29

Dungannon

A4

Linen Green

Lower
Lough
Erne 38

B4

A32

White
Island

Dromore

Fintona

Castle Archdale
Country Park

B80

B192

Clogher

Augher

Bollygawley

Aughnacloy

A28

39

Belleek A46

FERMANAGH

Devenish
Island

Irvingstown

Ballinamallard

A4

Fivemiletown

Lough
Melvin

Enniskillen 40 41 Castle Coole

Lisbellaw

Florence
Court

A32

Upper
Lough
Erne

Lisnaskea

Rosslea

Ked

Newtown
Butler

Kintyre
(Scotland)

NORTHERN
IRELAND

IRELAND

♦Rathlin
Island

To Campbeltown, Scotland

Giant's
Causeway
22

Carrick
-a-Rede

Bruce
Castle
24

A2

B15

Fair Head

23

Bushmills

21

Ballycastle

ortstewart

Armoy

Cushendun

Coleraine

Ballymoney

A26

Cushendall

Red Bay

Glenariff

A2

North Channel

20

**Glens of
Antrim**

arvagh

R. Bann

A26

Kilrea

A29

ANTRIM

Carnlough Bay

Carnlough

MOUNTAINS

A42

Carnlough Bay

To Cairnryan, Scotland

26 **Upperlands**

Maghera

Ballymena

A43

Ballygally

Larne

A36

A8

To Stranraer

**Bellaghy
Bawn**

Bellaghy

A6

Ballyclare

Whitehead

To Heysham

Toome

Randalstown

Eden

To Isle of Man

Magherafelt

Antrim

19 **Carrickfergus**

To Liverpool

Newtownabbey

A2

Belfast Lough

Bangor

Lough
Neagh

A52

Crawfordsborn

Donaghadee

Ardboe

Crumlin

**Belfast
Castle** **16**

18 **Ulster Folk &
Transport Museum**

Stewartstown

A26

Holywood

Newtownards

**Belfast
1 - 15
See detail map**

A20

Mount Stewart
46

Lisburn

Comber

Greyabbey

Ardglass

en

Craigavon

Lurgan

17 **Irish Linen Centre
& Lisburn Museum**

Ards
Peninsula

Portadown

A3

Hillsborough

A1

A24

Saintfield

Strangford
Lough

A20

A29

Ballynahinch

Killyleagh

45 **Portaferry**

42

Armagh

D O W N

Banbridge

A25

44 **Downpatrick**

Strangford

Car Ferry

Markethill

Castlewellan

Dundrum

Ardglass

ARMAGH

R. Bann

A25

Keady

B133

Dundrum Bay

Bessbrook

Newry

Newcastle

Camlough

43

**The Mountains
of Mourne**

Slieve Donard
Mountain

Warrenpoint

A2

0   10 miles

Kilkeel

0   15 km

County Fermanagh, is bright and bustling, and the surrounding Lough Erne has magnificent lake views, as well as one of Ireland's round towers, on Devenish Island. On the other side of Enniskillen stand Castle Coole and Florence Court, two graceful mansions of the 18th-century Anglo-Irish nobility.

About the Restaurants

Belfast has witnessed an influx of international influences with restaurants, bistros, wine bars, and—as in Dublin—European-style café-bars where you can get good food *and* linger over a drink.

By and large, though, hearty, unpretentious cooking predominates, with good-quality, fresh local fish and meat simply prepared. You're virtually guaranteed to find certain traditional dishes on menus here, such as Guinness and beef pie; champ (creamy, buttery mashed potatoes with scallions); oysters from Strangford Lough; Ardglass herring; mussels from Dundrum; and smoked salmon from Glenarm. A widespread favorite is the Ulster fry, an inexpensive pub plate of bacon, black pudding, mushrooms, sausages, tomatoes, and eggs, served with potato or soda bread—one of the reasons Northern Ireland has a high rate of heart disease. The delights of ethnic restaurants, including Chinese, Japanese, Indian, Persian, and Thai, are available in Belfast, and even beyond.

Casual dress is acceptable at most establishments, though jeans are discouraged. As for the cost of a meal here, by the standards of the Republic or the United States, or even the rest of the United Kingdom, restaurant prices are surprisingly moderate. A service charge of 10% may be indicated on the bill; it's customary to pay this, unless the service was bad.

About the Hotels

Major hotel chains both in the Republic and abroad have invested in Northern Ireland's cities. In Belfast's environs you can also choose from the humblest terraced town houses or farm cottages to the grandest country houses. Dining rooms of country-house lodgings frequently reach the standard of top-quality restaurants. All accommodations in the province are inspected and categorized by the Northern Ireland Tourist Board Information Centre, which publishes all names, addresses, and ratings in the free guidebooks *Hotel and Guest House Guide* and *Bed & Breakfast Guide,* also available online. Hundreds of excellent-value specials become available in the low season from October to March— single nights to weekend deals, the most intimate bed-and-breakfasts to Belfast's finest hotels.

WHAT IT COSTS in pounds sterling				
$$$$	**$$$**	**$$**	**$**	**¢**
RESTAURANTS over £22	£18–£22	£13–£18	£7–£13	under £7
HOTELS over £160	£115–£160	£80–£115	£50–£80	under £50

Restaurant prices are for a main course at dinner. Hotel prices are for two people in a standard double room in high season, including VAT and a service charge (often applied in larger hotels), but with no meals (EP) or, if indicated, CP (with Continental breakfast), BP (Breakfast Plan, with full breakfast), or MAP (Modified American Plan, with breakfast and dinner).

Timing

The best time to visit the area is from May to September, when the weather is mild and a little friendlier to travelers, especially in coastal and lake areas. Apart from holiday weekends there should be no trouble getting accommodation anywhere outside Belfast. If heading for Belfast, book in advance. Most of the city's cultural events—except early August's lively West Belfast Festival—take place in the autumn.

BELFAST

Belfast was a great Victorian success story, an industrial boomtown whose prosperity was built on trade—especially linen and shipbuilding (the *Titanic* was built here, giving Belfast the nickname "Titanic Town"). The key word here, of course, is *was*—linen is no longer a major industry, and shipbuilding has severely suffered. For two decades, news about Belfast was news about the Troubles—until the 1994 cease-fire. Since then, Northern Ireland's capital city has benefited from major hotel investment, gentrified quaysides, or strands, a heralded performing arts center, and heartfelt efforts on the part of the tourist board to claim its share of the visitors pouring into the Emerald Isle. Although the 1996 bombing of offices at the Canary Wharf in London disrupted the 1994 peace agreement, cease-fire was officially reestablished on July 20, 1997, and this embattled city began its quest for a newfound identity. This is a fascinating place in the throes of a major historical transition, a city with some of the warmest, wryest people in all of Ireland—all with a palpable will to move forward.

Before English and Scottish settlers arrived in the 1600s, Belfast was a tiny village called Béal Feirste ("sandbank ford") belonging to Ulster's ancient O'Neill clan. With the advent of the Plantation period (when settlers arrived in the 1600s), Sir Arthur Chichester, from Devon in southwest England, received the city, and his son was made Earl of Donegall. Protestant French Huguenots fleeing persecution settled near here, bringing their valuable linen-work skills. In the 18th century, Belfast underwent a phenomenal expansion—its population doubled in size every 10 years, despite an ever-present sectarian divide. Although the Anglican gentry despised the Presbyterian artisans—who, in turn, distrusted native Catholics—Belfast's growth continued at a dizzying speed. Having laid the foundation stone of the city's university in 1845, Queen Victoria returned to Belfast in 1849 (she is recalled in the names of buildings, streets, bars, monuments, and other places around the city), and in the same year, the university opened and took the name Queen's College. Nearly 40 years later, in 1888, Victoria granted Belfast its city charter. Today its population is 300,000—one-quarter of all Northern Ireland's citizens.

Belfast is a fairly compact city, 167 km (104 mi) north of Dublin. The city center is made up of roughly three contiguous areas that are easy to navigate on foot; from the south end to the north it's about an hour's leisurely walk.

Golden Mile

This arrowhead-shape area extending from Howard Street in the north to Shaftesbury Square at the southern tip, bordered on the west by Great Victoria Street and on the east by Bedford Street and Dublin Road, is a great area to begin an exploration of Belfast. Although it doesn't quite glow the way the name suggests, bustling Golden Mile and its immediate environs harbor some of Belfast's most noteworthy historic buildings. In addition, the area is filled with hotels, major civic and office buildings, as well as some restaurants, cafés, and stores. Even if you don't end up staying here, you're likely to pass through it often.

a good
walk

Begin your stroll at the central **Europa Hotel** ❶ ▶ and the **Grand Opera House** ❷ next door. Even if you're just starting out, at least poke your head in the glorious **Crown Liquor Saloon** ❸, a restored Victorian gin palace across the street from the Europa. From the Crown, turn right along Great Victoria Street and then right again onto Howard Street to reach Belfast's Donegall Square, dominated by the columned and domed **City Hall** ❹. Walk away from Donegall Square and up May Street, taking an almost immediate right onto Alfred Street. When you come to the junction with Clarence Street, the Tudor-Gothic **St. Malachy's Church** ❺ is on the left. Stop in to gaze awhile at the beautiful fan-vault ceiling. From here, walk to the end of Clarence Street, and turn right onto Bedford Street into the Golden Mile proper, where you will come upon **Ulster Hall** ❻.

TIMING   You need about 1½ hours to enjoy this route—you can extend this time depending on how long you would like to spend soaking up the atmosphere of places like the Crown Liquor Saloon on your way.

What to See

★ ❹ **City Hall.** The massive, exuberant Renaissance Revival City Hall dominates Donegall Square. Built between 1898 and 1906 and modeled on St. Paul's Cathedral in London, it was designed by Brumwell Thomas, who was knighted but had to sue to get his fee. Before you enter, take a stroll around Donegall Square, to see statues of Queen Victoria; a monument commemorating the *Titanic* (built in Belfast); and a column honoring the U.S. Expeditionary Force, which landed in the city on January 26, 1942—the first contingent of the U.S. Army to land in Europe. Head inside under the porte cochere at the front of the building. From the entrance hall (the base of which is a whispering gallery), the view up to the heights of the 173-foot Great Dome is a feast for the eyes. With its complicated series of arches and openings, stained-glass windows, Italian marble inlays, decorative plasterwork, and paintings, this is Belfast's most ornate public space—homage to the might of the British empire. The guided tour gives access to the Council Chamber, Great Hall, and Reception Room, all upstairs. ⊠ *Donegall Sq., Central District* ☎ *028/ 9032–0202* ⊕ *www.belfastcity.gov.uk* ⊡ *Free* ☉ *Mon.–Thurs. 9–5, Fri. 9–4.30; guided tours June–Sept., weekdays at 11, 2, and 3, Sat. at 2:30; Oct.–May, weekdays at 11 and 2:30, Sat. at 2:30.*

❸ **Crown Liquor Saloon.** Opposite the Europa Hotel on Great Victoria Street and now owned by the National Trust (the United Kingdom's official conservation organization), the Crown is one of Belfast's glories. Built in 1894, the bar has richly carved woodwork around cozy snugs (cubicles), leather seats, colored tile work, and abundant mirrors. It has been kept immaculate and is still lit by gas. Most importantly it's a perfect place for a pint of Guinness and a plate of oysters. When you settle in your snug, note the little gunmetal plates used by the Victorians for lighting their matches. ⊠ *46 Great Victoria St., Golden Mile* ☎ *028/ 9027–9901* ☉ *Mon.–Sat. 11:30 AM–midnight, Sun. 11:30–10.*

FodorsChoice ★

▶ ❶ **Europa Hotel.** A landmark in Belfast, the Europa is a monument to the resilience of the city in the face of the Troubles. The most bombed hotel in western Europe, it was targeted 11 times by the IRA since the early 1970s and was refurbished every time. Today it's owned by affable Ulster millionaire hotel magnate Billy Hastings, it shows no signs of its explosive history. ⊠ *Great Victoria St. at Glengall St., Golden Mile* ☎ *028/ 9027–1066* ⊕ *www.hastingshotels.com.*

★ ❷ **Grand Opera House.** The Grand Opera House exemplifies the Victorian age fascination with ornamentation, opulent gilt moldings, and intricate plasterwork. The renowned theater architect Frank Matcham beautifully designed the building in 1894, and restoration was completed in the 1970s. Contemporary Irish artist Cherith McKinstry painted an exquisite angel-and-cherub-laden fresco on the ceiling. You can take a tour, but by far the best way to see and enjoy the place is to attend a show. The theater regularly stages musicals, operas, plays, and concerts. ⊠ *Great Victoria St., Central District* ☎ *028/9024–1919* ⊕ *www.goh. co.uk/menu.htm* ✉ *£3* ⊘ *Tours Sat., hrs vary.*

❺ St. Malachy's Church. Just inside the doors to St. Malachy's Cathedral is a memorial to its chief benefactor, Captain Thomas Griffiths. The church, designed by Thomas Jackson, was built in 1844, and its interior is well worth a viewing. Pay particular attention to its fan-vaulted ceiling. Although many of the original fixtures and fitting have succumbed to the ravages of time, this swirling masterpiece of plasterwork survives intact. Inspiration for the design was taken from the chapel of Henry VII at Westminster Abbey in London. Note the 150-year-old church organ. ⊠ *Alfred St., Golden Mile* ☎ *028/9032–1713* ✉ *Free.*

❻ Ulster Hall. The home of the Ulster Orchestra, and host to occasional rock concerts (one of the most famous being Led Zeppelin's world stage debut of the song "Stairway to Heaven" in March 1971), Ulster Hall was originally built as a ballroom in 1862. The hall was the venue for the political rallying of Nationalist politicians, such as Charles Stewart Parnell (1846–91) and Patrick Henry Pearse (1879–1916), before the Irish Republic was formed in 1921. There's also a splendid Mulholland Organ, a Victorian instrument of considerable size. It's free to look around when shows are not going on. ⊠ *Bedford St., Golden Mile* ☎ *028/9032–3900* ⊕ *www.ulsterhall.co.uk.*

Central District

Belfast's Central District, which is immediately north of the Golden Mile, extends from Donegall Square north to St. Anne's Cathedral. It's not geographically the center of the city, but it's the old heart of Belfast. Shoppers note: it also has the highest concentration of retail outlets in town. It's a frenetic place—the equivalent of Dublin's Grafton and Henry streets in one—where both locals *and* visitors shop. Cafés, pubs, offices, and stores of all kinds, from department stores to the Gap and Waterstone's (there's even a Disney store), occupy the redbrick and white-Portland-stone and modern buildings that line its narrow streets. Many of the streets are pedestrian-only, so it's a good place to take a leisurely stroll, browse, and see some sights to boot.

a good walk

Begin at the **Linen Hall Library ❼ ▶**, the gray building on Donegall Square's northwest corner. North on Donegall Place, Belfast's main shopping street, is the Northern Ireland Tourist Board Information Centre. Continue down Donegall Place as it becomes Royal Avenue, and turn right onto Church Street, at the end of which is **St. Anne's Cathedral ❽**. Take Donegall Street to North Street and go east down **High Street** to busy Victoria Street and the leaning **Albert Memorial Clock Tower ❾**. From here, walk up Queen's Square to the river and Donegall Quay. You can see parts of Belfast's historic shipyards and two of the world's largest cranes in the Harland and Wolff shipyard, which built the *Titanic*. Veer left at the river to the **Lagan Lookout Visitor Centre ❿**. Perched on the river, the center is opposite the back of the **Custom House ⓫**. Walk south along Oxford Street to Waterfront Hall on the river at the end of the street. From here, you can return to the city center via busy Chichester Street. Or instead wander north behind St. Anne's to the Cathedral Quarter, a maze of cobbled streets that the city fathers plan to

BELFAST'S WALL MURALS

N NORTHERN IRELAND they say the Protestants make the money and the Catholics make the art, and as with all clichés, there is some truth in it.

It is a truth that will become clear as you look up at the gable walls of blue-collar areas of Belfast on which the two communities have expressed themselves in colorful murals that have given rise to one of the more quirky tours of the city. Although the wildly romantic Catholic murals can often aspire to the levels of Sistine Chapel–lite, those in Protestant areas (like the tough, no-nonsense Shankill and the Newtownards Road) are more workmanlike efforts that sometimes resemble war comics without the humor.

It was not always this way. In Protestant areas, murals were once painted by skilled coachbuilders to mark the 12th of July celebrations of the defeat of the Catholic king James by King William at the Battle of the Boyne. As such, they typically depicted William resplendent in freshly laundered scarlet tunic and plumed cap, sitting on a white stallion that has mastered the art of walking on water. On the banks of the Boyne sits a mildly disheveled James, the expression on his face making him look as if he has just eaten an overdose of anchovies.

Other popular themes in Protestant areas are the Red Hand of Ulster, symbolizing the founding of the province, and, on Carnmore Street, the 13 Protestant apprentice boys shutting the gates of Derry against King James in 1688, leading to the famous siege. More recently, though, Protestant murals have taken on a grimmer air, and typical subjects include wall-eyed paramilitaries perpetually standing firm against increasing liberalism, nationalism, and all the other-isms that Protestants see eroding their stern, Bible-driven way of life.

Nationalist murals, on the other hand, first sprang up in areas like the Falls Road in 1981, when IRA inmates of the Maze prison began a hunger strike in an unsuccessful bid to be recognized by the British government as political prisoners rather than common criminals. Ten died,

and the face of the most famous, Bobby Sands, looks down now from a gable wall on the Falls Road alongside the words: "Our revenge will be the laughter of our children."

Since then, themes of freedom from oppression and a rising Nationalist confidence have expressed themselves in murals that romantically and surreally mix and match images from the Book of Kells, the Celtic Mist mock-heroic posters of Irish artist Jim Fitzpatrick, assorted phoenixes rising from ashes, and revolutionaries clad in splendidly idiosyncratic sombreros and bandannas from other ideological battlegrounds in Mexico and South America. Irish Gaelic words and phrases that you will see springing up regularly include the much-used slogan "Tiocfaidh çr lç" (pronounced chucky-ar-la and meaning) "Our day will come" and the simple cry "Saoirse" (pronounced seer-she) meaning "Freedom".

Less political are two fascinating community projects. The first, at Springhill Community Park, is the largest art project of its kind in Ireland, made up of traditional Celtic symbols such as birds, dogs, spirals, and knots, mingled with the art of several other mythologies by designer Gerard Kelly, who started it in 1998 with the aid of local children and finally completed it two years later. The other project, in the Upper Springfield area of Ballymurphy, was created by local people who used murals and mosaics to express their particular view of myths, legends, history, and their own family stories.

The murals in both Protestant and Catholic areas are safe to view in daylight and outside the sensitive week of the 12th of July marches by Protestant Orangemen. However, the most sensible way would be to take a guided tour with Citybus.

transform over the next few years into a funky combination of Temple Bar in Dublin and the Left Bank in Paris.

TIMING It's easy to get waylaid shopping and investigating sights along the river when taking this walk, so give yourself at least two hours to cover the area comfortably.

What to See

⑨ Albert Memorial Clock Tower. Tilting a little to one side, not unlike Pisa's more notorious leaning landmark, is the clock tower that was named for Queen Victoria's husband, Prince Albert. The dilapidated square on which it stands has undergone a face-lift. The tower itself is not open to the public. ⊠ *Victoria Sq., Central District.*

⑪ Custom House. The 19th-century architect Charles Lanyon designed the Custom House. This building, along with many others in Belfast, including the main building of Queen's University and the unusual Sinclair Seaman's Church, bear the hallmarks of his skill. It's not open to the public, but it's worth circling the house to view the lofty pediment of Brittania, Mercury, and Neptune on the front, carved by acclaimed stonemason Thomas Fitzpatrick. ⊠ *Donegall Quay, Central District.*

★ High Street. Off High Street, especially down to Ann Street (parallel to the south), run narrow lanes and alleyways called entries. Though mostly cleaned up and turned into chic shopping lanes, they still hang on to something of their former raffish character, and have distinctive pubs with little-altered Victorian interiors. Among the most notable are the Morning Star (Pottinger's Entry off High Street), with its large windows and fine curving bar; White's Tavern (entry off High Street), Belfast's oldest pub, founded in 1630, which, although considerably updated, is still warm and comfortable, with plush seats and a big, open fire; Magennis's Whiskey Café (on May Street) in splendid counterpoint to the Waterfront Hall's space-age style; and McHugh's (in Queen's Square), in what is reckoned to be the city's oldest extant building, dating from 1710.

Lagan Boat Company. Take a guided 75-minute river tour from Lagan Boat Company that departs from the dock by the Lagan Lookout Visitor Centre, travels down to Stranmillis and back with commentary on the history of the city. A one-hour Titanic tour takes in the shipyard where the famous liner was built and harbor sights related to the ship. Each tours costs £5. ⊠ *48 St. John's Close, at Laganbank Rd., Central District* ☎ *028/9033–0844* ⊕ *www.laganboatcompany.com.*

⑩ Lagan Lookout Visitor Centre. At the edge of Lagan Weir, the center delves into the history of the River Lagan and the weir by means of interactive exhibits. It's a good way for children to learn about the river's history and surroundings. At night, the exterior of the building is flooded with blue light, adding to the feel that the riverside developments in Belfast have been inspired by the Southbank in London. The shipyard cranes visible beyond—Samson and Goliath—are two of the world's largest. ⊠ *Lagan Weir, Donegall Quay, Central District* ☎ *028/9031–5444* ⊕ *www.laganside.com* ⊠ *£2* ☉ *Apr.–Sept., weekdays 11–5, Sat. noon–5, Sun. 2–5; Oct.–Mar., Tues.–Fri. 11–3:30, Sat. 1–4:30, Sun. 2–4:30.*

⑦ Linen Hall Library. This gray building on Donegall Square's northwest corner is in fact a comfortable private library, founded in 1788 and designed by Charles Lanyon. The library has an unparalleled collection of 80,000 documents relating to the Troubles. One early librarian, Thomas Russell, was hanged in 1803 for supporting an Irish uprising. On the walls are paintings and prints depicting Belfast views and landmarks. Much of this artwork is for sale. It's an ideal hideaway for relaxing with a newspaper and enjoying the library's café. ✉ *17 Donegall Sq. N, Central District* ☎ *028/9032–1707* ⊕ *www.linenhall.com* ☞ *Free* ⊙ *Weekdays 9:30–5:30, Sat. 9:30–4.*

⑧ St. Anne's Cathedral. A somber heaviness and deep rounded arches are the hallmarks of the Irish neo-Romanesque style, and both elements dominate this large edifice, which is basilica in plan and was built at the turn of the 20th century. Lord Carson (1854–1935), who was largely responsible for keeping the six counties inside the United Kingdom, is buried here beneath a suitably austere gray slab. New landscaping around the Anglican cathedral provides a place to rest your legs in good weather. The guides on duty show you around for no charge. ✉ *Donegall St., Central District* ☎ *028/9032–8332* ⊕ *www.belfastcathedral.com* ☞ *Free* ⊙ *Daily 10–4.*

> **need a break?** At the start of Royal Avenue, turn left onto Bank Street to find **Kelly's Cellars** (✉ 30–32 Bank St., Central District ☎ 028/9032–4835), a circa 1720 pub with loads of character. Try the two specialties: Ulster fry or champ and sausages. Two centuries ago, Kelly's Cellars was the regular meeting place of a militant Nationalist group, the Society of United Irishmen, whose leader, Wolfe Tone (who was a Protestant), is remembered as the founder of Irish Republicanism.

W5: Whowhatwherewhywhen. Part of the Odyssey complex in Belfast's docks, this science discovery center takes a high-tech, hands-on approach to interpreting science, engineering, and technology for adults and children. Video displays and flashing lights provide a modernistic feel, and you can do everything from explore the weather to build bridges and robots. ✉ *2 Queen's Quay, Central District* ☎ *028/9046–7700* ⊕ *www.w5online.co.uk* ☞ *£6* ⊙ *Mon.–Sat. 10–6, Sun. noon–6; last admission at 5.*

University Area

At Belfast's southern end, this part of the city around Queen's University is dotted with parks, botanical gardens, and leafy streets with fine, intact two- and three-story 19th-century buildings. The area evokes an older, more leisurely pace of life. The many pubs and excellent restaurants make this the center of the city's nightlife.

> **a good walk** From the southern tip of Shaftesbury Square, head south down Botanic Avenue and watch the cityscape quickly transform into a peaceful and residential university area. Take note of the Lower Crescent, with its bars and restaurants, on your right. Continue, crossing University Street, and you come to the **Union Theological College** ⑫ ☞ on your left. To your right, is **Queen's University** ⑬. Walk around the campus via University Square and University Road to Stranmillis Road. To the left are the **Botanic Gardens** ⑭, and next to the gardens is the **Ulster Museum** ⑮.

TIMING Allow a leisurely morning or afternoon to visit the sights, taking your time at the Botanic Gardens and Ulster Museum.

What to See

★ ⑭ Botanic Gardens. In the Victorian heyday, it was not unusual to find 10,000 of Belfast's citizens strolling on a Saturday afternoon. These gardens are a glorious haven of grass, trees, flowers, curving walks, and wrought-iron benches laid out in 1827 on land that slopes down to the River Lagan. The curved-iron and glass Palm House is a conservatory marvel designed by Charles Lanyon in 1839. The Tropical Ravine House, though not architecturally distinguished, has an outstanding collection of tropical

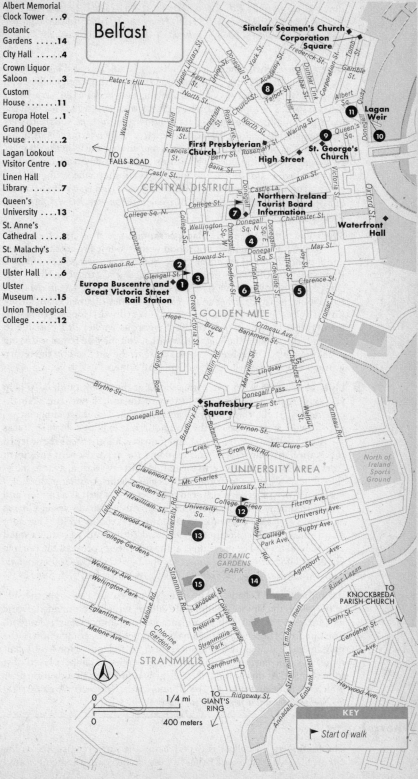

Belfast

flora. ⊠ *Stranmillis Rd., University Area* ☎ *028/9032–4902* ☜ *Free* ☉ *Gardens daily dawn–dusk; Palm House and Tropical Ravine House Apr.–Aug., weekdays 10–5, weekends 1–5; Sept.–Mar., weekdays 10–4, weekends 2–4.*

⓭ **Queen's University.** Dominating University Road is Queen's University itself. The main buildings, modeled on Oxford's Magdalen College and designed by the ubiquitous Charles Lanyon, were built in 1849 in a Tudor Revival style. The long, handsome redbrick-and-sandstone facade of the main building has large lead-glass windows, with three square towers and crenellations galore. University Square, really a terrace, is from the same era. The Seamus Heaney library is named after the Ulster-born 1997 Nobel prize–winning poet. The visitor center displays university artifacts and hosts exhibitions, and there's a small shop where you can buy gifts and university souvenirs. ⊠ *University Rd., University Area* ☎ *028/ 9033–5252* ⊕ *www.qub.ac.uk* ☉ *May–Sept., Mon.–Sat. 10–4; Oct.–Apr., weekdays 10–4.*

Stranmillis. Once its own village, Stranmillis is now an off-campus quarter—an appealing neighborhood with tree-lined residential streets and a wide choice of ethnic eateries. You can get here via Stranmillis Road (near the Ulster Museum). The "Little Paris" stretch of shops and cafés extends down to the riverside towpath along the Lagan. Malone Road joins the river farther south, close to the out-of-town Giant's Ring (off Ballyleeson Road), a large, Neolithic earthwork focused on a dolmen. To get this far, unless you're a vigorous walker (it's possible to come all the way on the Lagan towpath), you may be happier driving or taking a bus. Ulsterbus 13 passes close to the site, and on the return journey it will take you back to Donegall Square.

⓯ **Ulster Museum.** Pick up a free guidebook at the reception desk to help you explore the history and prehistory of Ireland, in particular Northern Ireland, at the three-story Ulster Museum. The most imaginative, user-friendly sections are on the first floor: one exhibit colorfully traces the rise of Belfast's crafts, trade, and industry; another tells the story of the Nationalist movement and explains the separation of the north from the rest of the country. In the natural history section, a large skeleton of the now extinct Irish giant deer is a highlight. Another major holding is the trove of jewelry and gold ornaments—as well as a cannon and other armaments—recovered from the Spanish Armada vessel *Girona* and two sister galleons sunk off the Antrim coast in 1588. There are also a considerable collection of 19th- and 20th-century art and a small café on level three. The museum is at the southwest corner of the Botanic Gardens. ⊠ *Stranmillis Rd., University Area* ☎ *028/9038–3000* ⊕ *www. ulstermuseum.org.uk* ☜ *Free* ☉ *Weekdays 10–5, Sat. 1–5, Sun. 2–5.*

▶ ⓬ **Union Theological College.** Like Queen's University on the opposite side of the street, the Union Theological College, with its colonnaded, Doric facade, owes the charm of its appearance to architect Charles Lanyon. The building's other claim to fame is that, before the completion of the parliament buildings at Stormont, Northern Ireland's House of Commons was convened in the library, and the college's chapel played host to the Senate. At this writing, the college was finishing a renovation after which it will begin tours. ⊠ *108 Botanic Ave., University Area* ☎ *028/ 9020–5080* ⊕ *www.union.ac.uk* ☜ *Free.*

Where to Eat

The food scene in Belfast is experiencing the same renaissance as the city itself. Two or three of Belfast's best kitchens are a match for any-

CHURCHES AROUND THE CITY

BELFAST HAS SO MANY CHURCHES you could visit a different one nearly every day of the year and still not make it to all of them. The oldest house of worship is the Church of Ireland **Knockbreda Parish Church** (✉ Church Rd. off A24 on the south side of the city). This dark, sturdy, and atmospheric structure was built in 1737 by Richard Cassels, who designed many of Ireland's finest mansions. It quickly became the place to be buried—witness the vast 18th-century tombs in the churchyard. Closer to the city center, the **First Presbyterian Church** (✉ Rosemary St.) dates from 1783 and has an interesting elliptical interior. It also hosts lunchtime concerts. The Church of Ireland's **St. George's** (✉ High St.), built in 1816, has a tremendous Georgian portico and pretty box pews. By the riverfront is one of the most appealing churches, Presbyterian **Sinclair Seamen's Church** (✉ Corporation Sq. off Donegall Quay). It was designed by Charles Lanyon, the architect of Queen's University, and has served the seafaring community since 1857. A maritime theme pervades the building: the pulpit is shaped like a ship's prow; the bell is from HMS Hood, sunk in 1916; and even the collection plates are shaped like lifeboats.

thing else in Ireland. The best chefs—Michael Deane, the Rankins, and Robbie Millar—have brought back to Ireland, from their work abroad, a sophisticated, internationalist approach to cooking. Beyond the top-tier places, there are plenty of other restaurants with fresh local fish and delectable meat dishes prepared simply but with style.

$$$ ✕ **Shanks.** Like many of Ireland's best young chefs, Robbie Millar stud-
Fodor'sChoice ied under Cayenne's Paul Rankin, and he spares nothing to produce won-
★ derful fish and game dishes. How demanding is he? A scuba diver hand picks his scallops from the Irish Sea (they're more tender than those dredged by a trawler). Start with grilled tuna and eggplant chutney, then indulge in a standout main course—peppered loin of venison with red cabbage. A three-course set menu is £38. The restaurant is on a 3,000-acre golf estate; to get here you can take a train from Belfast to Bangor and then a taxi. ⊹ *Right on Crawfordsburn Rd., 19 km (12 mi) from Belfast ✉ Blackwood Golf Centre, Bangor ☎ 028/9185–3313 ⌾ Reservations essential ▤ AE, MC, V ⊙ Closed 3 wks in July, Sun. and Mon. No lunch Sat.*

★ **$–$$$** ✕ **Aldens.** East Belfast was a gastronomic wilderness until this cool modernist restaurant opened with chef Cath Gradwell at the helm. Now city-center folk regularly make the pilgrimage to take advantage of an opulent menu and wine list at comparably reasonable prices. The set dinner menus Monday to Thursday are particularly good value—£16 for three courses. Dublin Bay prawns stand out as a starter. Try grilled quails with wild cranberry compote and baked polenta, and beef sausages with red wine sauce and mashed potato as entrées. The mood here is relaxed, and the staff perpetually friendly. ✉ *229 Upper Newtownards Rd., East Belfast ☎ 028/9065–0079 ▤ AE, DC, MC, V ⊙ No lunch weekends, no dinner Sun.*

$–$$ ✕ **Cayenne.** Celebrity TV chefs Paul and Jeanne Rankin, innovative cooks who travel widely, run this Golden Mile spot. Cayenne serves fusion cuisine with an Asian twist—coconut-crusted cod, breast of duck with wild rice pancakes and Donegal wild salmon with hazelnut beurre blanc. Tempting desserts include chocolate ginger tart and rice pudding crème brûlée. Cayenne takes orders until 11:15 on Friday and Saturday evenings, so it's great if you want a meal after a concert in Waterfront Hall. ⊠ *Shaftesbury Sq., at Great Victoria St., Golden Mile* ☎ *028/ 9033–1532* ▤ *AE, DC, MC, V* ⊘ *No lunch Sat.*

$–$$ ✕ **Deane's.** Chef Michael Deane has long been a chef-celebrity in the Belfast area. His tastes are eclectic—he has worked in Bangkok, and the influence of Thai cooking is revealed in his especially subtle way with spices. Squab is a specialty, served as a kedgeree with cucumber and quail eggs for a starter. As a main dish he serves French squab with local rabbit, roast potato and parsnip with Madeira. Ravioli of lobster is excellent as well. A nine-course menu is £55, and a two-course option £31. The brasserie is downstairs, and the more formal restaurant up. ⊠ *34–40 Howard St., Golden Mile* ☎ *028/9033–1134 restaurant; 028/9056–0000 brasserie* ▤ *AE, MC, V* ⊘ *Restaurant closed Sun.–Tues., brasserie closed Sun.*

Fodor'sChoice ★

$–$$ ✕ **Nick's Warehouse.** A cool, cozy wine bar and adjacent restaurant, Nick Price has created one of Belfast's most relaxing watering holes. At the busy bar you can get warm salads with a choice of nut oils and tasty casseroles. In the slightly more formal restaurant favorites include duck with red cabbage and apple compote, and halibut with langoustine and sweet peppers. Finish off your meal with a sampling of the cheese selection. The wine and imported beer lists are impressive. Nick's is on a narrow cobbled street in an increasingly fashionable area. ⊠ *35 Hill St., Central District* ☎ *028/9043–9690* ⌂ *Reservations essential (restaurant)* ▤ *AE, MC, V* ⊘ *Closed Sun. No lunch Sat. No dinner Mon.*

¢–$ ✕ **The Morning Star.** Halfway down a narrow lane is the 19th-century Morning Star, one of the city's most historic pubs. There's a traditional bar downstairs and a cozy velvet and wood-panel restaurant upstairs. Head chef Seamus McAlister, far from resting on the pub's laurels, is constantly experimenting—he's known for his quirky takes on fresh local ingredients. You might find venison and game in winter, lamb in spring, and in summer grilled haddock with dark rum or roast Antrim pork. Also notable is the steak menu; you'd be hard-pressed to find a larger assortment of aged beef cuts. ⊠ *17–19 Pottingers Entry, Central District* ☎ *028/9023–5986* ▤ *MC, V* ⊘ *Closed Sun.*

¢–$ ✕ **The Northern Whig.** The latest addition to Belfast entrepreneur Jas Mooney's stable of designer pubs, The Northern Whig is housed in an elegant former newspaper building. Three 30-foot-high statues of Soviet heroes that once topped Communist Party headquarters in Prague dominate the spacious and stylish wood and leather interior. In the evenings, one wall slides away so you can watch classic movies, a jazz band, or a DJ playing laid-back blues, soul, or retro. The food is brasserie-style—good, not astonishing. It's the environment, the thoughtful wine list, and the cocktail bar, which specializes in rare vodkas, that are the main draw. ⊠ *2 Bridge St., Central District* ☎ *028/9050–9888* ▤ *MC, V.*

¢–$ ✕ **Raj Put.** You won't leave this Indian restaurant feeling as if you've been kissing a flame-thrower: in even the Raj Put's hottest dishes, nuanced flavors shine through. Aromatic spices, nuts, and herbs mingle in the piquant chicken masala. The sauce that makes the lamb tikka so red it will be immediately attracted to any item of light-colored clothing within five feet. (Just red, not red-hot, so don't worry.) For side dishes, favorites include a tasty *saag aloo* (spicy potatoes and spinach). Wash it all down with cold Indian lager. ⊠ *461 Lisburn Rd., University Area* ☎ *028/9066–2168* ⊟ *AE, MC, V.*

★ ¢ ✕ **Café Rankin.** This city-center bakery-café is a good choice if you want to enjoy the culinary delights of chefs Paul and Jeanne Rankin (of Cayenne) without breaking the bank. Roscoff's has a Parisian sensibility to it, especially if the weather is fine and you're sitting outside. Try the walnut bread, sun-dried tomato bread, focaccia, and the delicious soups and desserts. ⊠ *27–29 Fountain St., Central District* ☎ *028/9031–5090* ⊟ *AE, MC, V* ☉ *Closed Sun.*

★ ¢ ✕ **Long's.** Long's has been serving fish-and-chips in its tiny, completely basic Athol Street premises for more than 80 years. Garbage collectors, millionaires, and everyone in between flock here for the secret-batter-recipe fish, and chips, served with bread, butter, and a mug of tea. Demand is so intense they've opened another shop in Donegall Pass, a one-minute walk from Shaftesbury Square. Slightly larger but not much less basic than the original, it also serves haddock, smoked fish, Dover sole, or skate with your chips. ⊠ *39 Athol St., Golden Mile* ☎ *028/9032–1848* ⊟ *No credit cards* ☉ *Closed Sun.* ⊠ *15 Donegall Pass, Golden Mile* ☎ *028/9024–1644* ⊟ *No credit cards* ☉ *Closed Sun.*

Where to Stay

Airport & Environs

$$$ ⊞ **Dunadry Hotel and Country Club.** This spacious, whitewashed former mill on 10 acres of land is a hotel of considerable charm. Renovations made use of large wooden components from the old mill's massive linen beetling (polishing) engines in the stairwell and a gallery over the bar. Bedrooms are large; the best open onto the inner courtyard. The restaurant is a popular spot for local weddings, so you may find yourself in the midst of a real Irish celebration. ✛ *10 mins from Belfast Airport on M2* ⊠ *2 Islandreagh Dr., Dunadry, Co. Antrim BT41 2HA* ☎ *028/9443–4343* ☐ *028/9443–3389* ⊕ *www.mooneyhotelgroup.com* ⇋ *83 rooms with bath* ⚘ *Restaurant, indoor pool, gym, croquet, bar, meeting rooms* ⊟ *AE, DC, MC, V.*

$$$ ⊞ **Hilton Templepatrick.** Modern amenities and golf are why you come to this hotel ensconced in 220 acres of wooded park with its own 18-hole championship course. Rooms are generously equipped, with satellite TV and full bathroom. The location is particularly good if you're planning a brief visit to the province and don't want to stay in the city. ✛ *6 km (4 mi) from Belfast Airport on A57* ⊠ *Castle Upton Estate, Templepatrick, Co. Antrim BT39 0DD* ☎ *028/9443–5500* ☐ *028/9443–5511* ⊕ *www.hilton.com* ⇋ *129 rooms with bath, 1 suite* ⚘ *Restaurant, coffee shop, driving range, putting green, 18-hole golf course, 2 tennis courts, indoor pool, gym, hair salon, sauna, bar, Internet, business services, meeting rooms, no-smoking rooms* ⊟ *AE, DC, MC, V.*

Central District

$$$ ⊞ **McCausland Hotel.** Clean, simple lines, a feeling of light and space—a sumptuous minimalism pervades this luxury establishment. Two 1867 grain warehouses house the hotel and the original cast-iron pillars and beams have been retained throughout. The well-equipped bedrooms, with entertainment centers that include VCRs and CD players, are tastefully color-coordinated. Dining, under the capable, inspired hands of chef Alexander Plumb, takes place in the Marco Polo bar-bistro or the more formal Merchants Brasserie. On the edge of the blossoming Laganside area, the hotel is a 5-minute walk from the heart of the city center. ⊠ *34–38 Victoria St., Central District BT1 3GH* ☎ *028/9022–0200* ☐ *028/9022–0220* ⊕ *www.slh.com* ⇋ *61 rooms with bath, 15 suites* ⚘ *Restaurant, bar, meeting rooms* ⊟ *AE, DC, MC, V* ⭐ *BP, MAP.*

$–$$$ ▢ **Belfast Hilton.** This riverside hotel should be able to cater to your every whim with its excellent business and leisure facilities. Earth colors and bold stripes decorate the guest room beds and windows. Ask for a suite or a room with a view of the river. The restaurant serves contemporary cuisine; along with some of the suites, it has good views of the river and across the city. The hotel is beside Waterfront Hall, in an area undergoing urban renewal. ⊠ *4 Lanyon Pl., Central District BT1 3LP* ☏ *028/9027–7000* 📠 *028/9027–7277* ⊕ *www.hilton.com* 🛏 *181 rooms with bath, 14 suites* ♨ *Restaurant, in-room data ports, minibars, cable TV, indoor pool, hair salon, sauna, bar, business services, meeting rooms, no-smoking floors* 🖃 *AE, DC, MC, V* ⦿ *BP.*

Golden Mile

★ $$$ ▢ **TENsq.** You don't get much more downtown or contemporary than this fashionable boutique hotel right behind City Hall. The neoclassical facade of this former post office hides a serene interior that also houses Red, a popular and fashionable urban bar, the cool yet cozy Wine Café, and the Restaurant Porcelain, where European dishes get a Japanese touch. The bedrooms are minimalist-Asian in style but still welcoming—with big, low-lying beds topped with white duvets, soft armchairs to sink into, and fresh flowers brought daily. There are ISDN lines for computers in all rooms, and a DVD and CD library at the hotel. ⊠ *10 Donegall Sq. S, Golden Mile BT1 5JD* ☏ *028/9024–1001* 📠 *028/9024–3210* ⊕ *www.ten-sq.com* 🛏 *23 rooms with bath* ♨ *Restaurant, café, in-room data ports, 2 bars, concierge, free parking* 🖃 *AE, MC, V* ⦿ *BP, MAP.*

$$–$$$ ▢ **Holiday Inn Belfast.** Expect outstanding facilities at a reasonable price. Furnishings are modernist blond wood and leather, and rooms are best described as Japan-meets-Sweden: strong, simple colors and sliding wooden screens (a lovely touch) instead of curtains. The Holiday Inn has a superb location—a 10-minute walk from the city center and only five minutes from the Golden Mile. ⊠ *22 Ormeau Ave., Golden Mile BT2 8HS* ☏ *870/0400–9005* 📠 *028/9062–6546* ⊕ *www.holiday-inn.co.uk* 🛏 *170 rooms with bath* ♨ *Restaurant, indoor pool, health club, hot tub, massage, sauna, steam room, bar* 🖃 *AE, DC, MC, V* ⦿ *BP, MAP.*

$ ▢ **Benedict's of Belfast.** Friendly, lively, and convenient, Benedict's stands out on Shaftsbury Square. Rooms on the second floor are bright and colorful, and have wooden floors; rooms on the third floor are darker, with an Asian influence—dark wood and light walls, simple but comfortable. If you don't feel like straying too far from home for some nightlife, Benedict's has a buzzing bar and restaurant serving finely done Continental food. ⊠ *7–21 Bradbury Pl., Golden Mile BT7 1RQ* ☏ *028/9059–1999* 📠 *028/9059–1990* ⊕ *www.benedictshotel.co.uk* 🛏 *32 rooms with bath* ♨ *Restaurant, in-room data ports, cable TV, bar, meeting rooms* 🖃 *AE, MC, V* ⦿ *BP.*

$ ▢ **Jurys Inn Belfast.** The first Jurys north of the border brings the chain's flat-rate pricing formula—one price for up to three adults or two adults and two children—to the Golden Mile. Once you get past the forbidding warehouselike exterior, a spacious, marble-tile foyer with warm green and salmon hues awaits. Room decor is pretty standard. Some rooms overlook College Square, the cricket lawn of the 1814 Royal Belfast Academical Institution. The Arches restaurant serves well-prepared hotel food. Tartan fabrics and dark wood decorate the Inn Pub, which serves pub-grub all day. ⊠ *Fisherwick Pl. at Great Victoria St., Golden Mile BT2 7AP* ☏ *028/9053–3500* 📠 *028/9053–3511* ⊕ *www.jurysdoyle.com* 🛏 *190 rooms with bath* ♨ *Restaurant, in-room data ports, bar, meeting rooms, no-smoking floors* 🖃 *AE, DC, MC, V* ⦿ *CP.*

Outside the City Center

$$$$ ⊞ **Culloden Hotel.** Hotelier Billy Hasting's flagship five-star hotel is a former 19th-century Scottish baronial mansion with 12 lovely acres of grounds. Public areas have ornate woodwork, Louis XV chandeliers, decorative plasterwork, and stained glass. Antiques and silk and velvet fabrics grace guest rooms both in the original section and in a newer wing. All have fine views. At mealtime choose from the Mitre restaurant—elegant and French—and the Cultra Inn, which serves both snacks and full meals. The hotel is close to the Ulster Folk and Transport Museum. ⊹ *8 km (5 mi) east of Belfast on A2* ⊠ *142 Bangor Rd., Holywood, Co. Down BT18 0EX* ☎ *028/9042–1066* 🖷 *028/9042–6777* ⊕ *www.hastingshotels.com* ⬎ *79 rooms with bath, 10 suites* ◊ *2 restaurants, tennis court, indoor pool, hair salon, sauna, spa, croquet, squash, bar, laundry service, Internet, meeting rooms, no-smoking rooms* ⊟ *AE, DC, MC, V* ⦿ *BP, MAP.*

★ **$–$$** ⊞ **The Old Inn.** A 1614 coach inn, reputedly Ireland's oldest, looks the part: It's pure 17th-century England, with a sculpted thatched roof, half doors, and leaded-glass windows. Inside there are roaring open fires in winter. Some of the bedrooms have four-poster beds and sitting rooms. The Churn Bistro's menu is solidly Irish, the staff jovial, and the locals inquisitive. Past guests have included Peter the Great, the legendary highwayman Dick Turpin, and the 41st U.S. president, George H. W. Bush. ⊹ *16 km (10 mi) east of Belfast on A2* ⊠ *15 Main St., Crawfordsburn, Co. Down BT19 1JH* ☎ *028/9185–3255* 🖷 *028/9185–2775* ⊕ *www.theoldinn.com* ⬎ *32 rooms with bath* ◊ *Restaurant, 2 bars, Internet* ⊟ *AE, MC, V* ⦿ *BP.*

$–$$ ⊞ **Rayanne House.** Famous both for its food and for its hospitality, this country house run by the devoted Bernadette McClelland is in leafy Holywood, 10 km (6 mi) from Belfast city center. Rooms are airy, each with individual, country furnishings and garden views. Breakfast includes an Irish grill and such specialties as prune soufflé on a purée of green figs and hot Rayanne baked cereal (laced with spices, fruit, whiskey, honey, and cream). The meal is served in an intimate dining room, among family antiques, paintings, and candelabras. Lunch and dinner are available by request 24 hours in advance. ⊹ *8 km (5 mi) east of Belfast on A2* ⊠ *60 Demesne Rd., Holywood, Co. Down BT18 9EX* 🖷 *028/9042–5859* ⊕ *www.rayanne-house.activehotels.com* ⬎ *9 suites* ◊ *Dining room, meeting rooms* ⊟ *MC, V* ⦿ *BP, MAP.*

University Area

$$$ ⊞ **Wellington Park Hotel.** Formerly a private residence and currently run by the Mooney family, this modern establishment is among the best in the university area. The quiet contemporary bedrooms are well designed, with built-in wood furniture; some have sleeping lofts. You get traditional European food in both the bar and restaurant—though the menu in the restaurant is slightly more expansive and expensive than in the bar. There's live music at the bar Friday and Saturday nights (soul, jazz, and Irish). ⊠ *21 Malone Rd., University Area BT9 6RU* ☎ *028/9038–1111* 🖷 *028/9066–5410* ⊕ *www.mooneyhotelgroup.com* ⬎ *75 rooms with bath* ◊ *Restaurant, bar, laundry service, meeting rooms* ⊟ *DC, MC, V* ⦿ *BP.*

$–$$ ⊞ **Ash-Rowan Guest House.** Thomas Andrews, designer of the ill-fated *Titanic*, brought his bride to live here in this spacious Victorian home after their wedding, then went off to work 14-hour days at the Harland and Wolff shipyard. Former restaurateurs Sam and Evelyn Hazlett now own, run, and cook for this outstanding B&B on a tranquil residential avenue. Every bedroom has its own style, all with Victorian overtones. Feel free to take advantage of the reading lounge, as well as the books

Fodor's Choice
★

around the house, and the conservatory. Breakfasts and dinners are first-rate. ✉ *12 Windsor Ave., University Area BT9 6EE* ☎ *028/9066–1758* 🖷 *028/9066–3227* ⊕ *www.a1tourism.com/uk/ashrowan.html* ⇝ *5 rooms with bath* ♿ *Dining room, lounge; no smoking* ▭ *MC, V* ⑩ *BP, MAP* ☯ *Closed Christmas wk.*

$ ▦ **Dukes Hotel.** Although this distinguished redbrick Victorian building has only 20 rooms, it has big-hotel amenities, including a spacious lobby, extensive exercise facilities, and a restaurant that serves healthy, local cuisine (traditionalists won't be disappointed, however, as fried food can be had). The hotel's color scheme is a distinguished, executive-style gray, enlivened with plenty of greenery, and a waterfall splashes down parallel to the stairs. Although not exceptional, the rooms are modern and comfortable, decorated in neutral shades. The lively bar is popular with staff and students from nearby Queen's University. ✉ *65–67 University St., University Area BT7 1HL* ☎ *028/9023–6666* 🖷 *028/9023–7177* ⊕ *www.dukeshotelbelfast.com* ⇝ *20 rooms with bath* ♿ *Restaurant, sauna, bar, gym, meeting rooms* ▭ *AE, DC, MC, V* ⑩ *BP.*

$ ▦ **Madison's.** Another gracious hotel run by the Mooney family, this one is in one of Belfast's liveliest spots—surrounded by shops and cafés on the lovely, tree-lined Botanic Avenue. The facade and public areas are decorated in a modish Barcelona-inspired take on art nouveau. Modern rooms—in primary yellows, reds, and rich blues—are stylish if sparsely furnished. The downstairs houses a restaurant that serves tasty contemporary cuisine at reasonable prices, and hip Club 33 fills the basement. Staying here you have discounted access to the extensive fitness facilities of Queen's University, including a pool. ✉ *59 Botanic Ave., University Area BT7 1JL* ☎ *028/9050–9800* 🖷 *028/9050–9808* ⊕ *www.madisonshotel.com* ⇝ *35 rooms with bath* ♿ *Restaurant, bar, business services* ▭ *AE, MC, V* ⑩ *BP.*

$ ▦ **Old Rectory.** Mary and Jerry Callan's well-appointed house was built in 1896 as a rectory. Rooms are decorated in pastels and have good views of the mountains. Enjoy complimentary whiskey each evening in the parlor. Breakfast is hearty but healthy, a rarity in Ulster B&Bs: smoked salmon, scrambled eggs, fresh fruit salad, vegetarian sausages, homemade low-sugar jams, wheat bread, and freshly squeezed blended juices. ✉ *148 Malone Rd., University Area BT9 5LH* ☎ *028/9066–7882* 🖷 *028/9068–3759* ✍ *info@anoldrectory.co.uk* ⇝ *6 rooms with bath* ▭ *No credit cards* ⑩ *BP, MAP.*

Nightlife & the Arts

Nightlife

Belfast has dozens of pubs packed with relics of the Victorian and Edwardian periods. Although pubs typically close around 11:30 PM, many city-center/Golden Mile nightclubs stay open until 1 AM.

CENTRAL DISTRICT The **Apartment** (✉ 2 Donegall Sq. W, Central District ☎ 028/9050–9777), beside City Hall, is the city center's trendiest bar, serving drinks and brasserie-style pub grub to Belfast's cool young things. **Bittles Bar** (✉ 70 Upper Church La., Central District ☎ 028/9031–1088), on Victoria Square, serves pub grub. **Kelly's Cellars** (✉ 30–32 Bank St., Central District), open since 1720, has blues bands on Saturday night. **Madden's Bar** (✉ Berry St., behind Castle Court, Central District ☎ 028/9024–4114) is a popular pub with traditional tunes.

McHugh's (✉ 29–30 Queen's Sq., Central District ☎ 028/9050–9990), in Belfast's oldest building, dating from 1711, has three floors of bars and restaurants, and live music on weekends. **Pat's Bar** (✉ 19–22 Prince's Dock St., Central District ☎ 028/9074–4524) has first-rate sessions of traditional music on Saturday nights. The **Rotterdam** (✉ 54 Pilot St., Central District ☎ 028/9074–6021), which housed convicts bound for Australia until it became a pub in 1820, is filled with fascinating old junk. It hosts traditional Irish music on Mondays and Thursdays, jazz on Tuesdays, and rock on Fridays and Saturdays.

GOLDEN MILE AREA
The glorious Crown Liquor Saloon is far from being the only old pub in the Golden Mile area—most of Belfast's evening life takes place in bars and restaurants here. There are a number of replicated Victorian bars with more locals and fewer visitors.

The **Beaten Docket** (✉ 48 Great Victoria St., Golden Mile ☎ 028/9024–2986), named after a losing betting slip, is a noisy, modern pub that attracts a young crowd. Here they play up-to-the-minute music. **Benedict's** (✉ 7–21 Bradbury Pl., Golden Mile ☎ 028/9059–1999) is a bar, music venue, disco, 150-seat restaurant, and hotel. Straying from the Victorian-style public house, the **Limelight** (✉ 17 Ormeau Ave., Golden Mile ☎ 028/9032–5968) is a disco-nightclub with cabaret on Tuesday, Friday, and Saturday, and recorded music on other nights.

The **M-Club** (✉ 23 Bradbury Pl., University Area ☎ 028/9023–3131) is Belfast's hottest place for dedicated clubbers, with TV soap-opera celebrities flown in weekly to mix with the local nighthawks. **Morrisons** (✉ 21 Bedford St., Golden Mile ☎ 028/9032–0030) is a haunt of media types. It has a music lounge upstairs, and hosts discussions for film buffs arranged by local directors in conjunction with the Northern Ireland Film Council. **Robinson's** (✉ 38–40 Great Victoria St., Golden Mile ☎ 028/9024–7447), two doors from the Crown, is a popular pub that appeals to a young crowd with folk music in its Fibber Magee's bar on Sunday and funk in the trendy BT1 wine and cocktail bar on weekends.

UNIVERSITY AREA
The stylish and modern **Bar Twelve** (✉ Crescent Town House, 13 Lower Crescent, University Area ☎ 028/9032–3349) is an excellent venue for some fashionable wine sipping. The **Botanic Inn** (✉ 23–27 Malone Rd., University Area ☎ 028/9050–9740), known as "the Bot" to its student clientele, is a big popular disco-pub. The **Chelsea Wine Bar** (✉ 346 Lisburn Rd., University Area ☎ 028/9068–7177) is packed with affluent professionals determined to prove that 30 is where life begins. The contemporary cuisine is reasonably priced. **Cutter's Wharf** (✉ 4 Lockview Rd., University Area ☎ 028/9066–3388), down by the river south of the university, is at its best on summer evenings and during live music performances on Sundays after 6.

The **Eglantine Inn** (✉ 32–40 Malone Rd., University Area ☎ 028/9038–1994), known as "the Egg," faces the Bot across Malone Road. The **Empire Music Hall** (✉ 42 Botanic Ave., University Area ☎ 028/9032–8110), a deconsecrated church, is the city's leading music venue. Stand-up comedy nights are usually on Tuesday. The **Fly Bar** (✉ 5–6 Lower Crescent, University Area ☎ 028/9050–9750), with its over-the-top interior playing on the fly theme, is a lively spot for a cocktail in the evening.

Lavery's Gin Palace (✉ 12 Bradbury Pl., University Area ☎ 028/9087–1106) mixes old-fashioned beer-drinking downstairs with dancing upstairs. On the increasingly fashionable Lisburn Road, **TaTu** (✉ 701 Lisburn Rd., University Area ☎ 028/9038–0818) is a spacious emporium to industrial chic filled with a cool, under-30 crowd. It serves good casual food.

The Arts

The **Northern Ireland Arts Council** (☎ 028/9038–5200 ⊕ www.artscouncil-ni.org) produces the bimonthly *Artslink* poster-brochure listing happenings throughout Belfast and the North. It's widely available throughout the city. The **Belfast Festival at Queen's University** (Festival office ✉ 25 College Gardens, University Area ☎ 028/9066–6321 ⊕ www.belfastfestival. com), which lasts three weeks each November, is the city's major arts festival. The **Promenade Concerts** (☎ 028/9066–8798 ⊕ www.ulster-orchestra.or.uk) are special concerts in June performed by the Ulster Orchestra in conjunction with the BBC.

ART GALLERIES **Bell Gallery.** This gallery in Nelson Bell's Victorian home shows many of Ireland's more traditional and representational painters from the 18th to the 21st century. ✉ *13 Adelaide Park, at Malone Rd., South University* ☎ *028/9066–2998* ⊕ *www.bellgallery.com* ☉ *Mon.–Thurs. 9–5, Fri. 9–3.*

Fenderesky Gallery. Under the same roof as the Crescent Arts Centre, Iranian philosopher Jamshid Mirfenderesky's gallery is one of the few in Ireland with a staple of modern Irish artists known throughout Europe. ✉ *Crescent Arts Centre, 2 University Rd., University Area* ☎ *028/ 9023–5245* ☉ *Tues.–Sat. 11:30–5.*

Ormeau Baths Gallery. Work of major contemporary international and Irish artists now hang in the white airy spaces of this former municipal bathhouse. ✉ *18A Ormeau Ave., Golden Mile* ☎ *028/9032–1402* ☉ *Tues.–Sat. 10–6.*

FILM **Queen's Film Theatre** (✉ 20 University Sq., University Area ☎ 028/ 9024–4857), Belfast's main art cinema, shows domestic and foreign movies on its two screens. **UGC Cinemas** (✉ 14 Dublin Rd., Golden Mile ☎ 028/ 9024–5700) has 10 screens of major British and American box-office favorites.

MAJOR VENUES **Crescent Arts Centre.** Watch experimental dance and theater, witness provocative art in the Fenderesky Gallery, and listen to lively jazz concerts: it's all part of the Crescent. You can also take classes in this huge, rambling stone building, a former girls' high school off the campus end of Bradbury Place. ✉ *2–4 University Rd., University Area* ☎ *028/ 9024–2338* ⊕ *www.crescentarts.org.*

Grand Opera House. Shows from all over the British Isle—and sometimes farther afield—play at this beautifully restored Victorian theater. Though it has no company of its own, there's a constant stream of West End musicals and plays of widely differing kinds, plus occasional operas and ballets. It's worth going to a show if only to enjoy the opera house itself. ✉ *2 Great Victoria St., Golden Mile* ☎ *028/9024–1919* ⊕ *www.goh.co.uk.*

King's Hall. Pop and rock concerts take center stage at this venue that also serves as a conference center. ✉ *484 Lisburn Rd., South University* ☎ *028/9066–5225* ⊕ *www.kingshall.co.uk.*

Lyric Theatre. Traditional and contemporary Irish culture inspires the thoughtful dramas staged here. In the south of Belfast, it's at King's Bridge on the banks of the Lagan. ✉ *55 Ridgeway St., South University* ☎ *028/ 9038–1081.*

The Odyssey. This multipurpose megacomplex was built as a millennium project. On-site is a 10,000-seat arena, an IMAX cinema, an interactive science center, bistros, bars, and theme restaurants. In addition to major concerts, it also hosts Belfast's first professional ice hockey team, the Giants. ✉ *Queen's Quay, East Belfast* ☎ *028/9045–1055* ⊕ *www. theodyssey.co.uk.*

Old Museum Arts Centre (OMAC). A powerhouse of challenging, avant-garde theater and modern dance, OMAC also has a risk-taking art gallery. ⊠ *7 College Sq. N, Central District* ☎ *028/9023–3332* ⊕ *www. oldmuseumartscentre.org.*

Ulster Hall. This, the main home to the Ulster Orchestra, has excellent acoustics and a splendid Victorian organ. The classical music season runs from September through March; most concerts are on Friday. ⊠ *Bedford St., Golden Mile* ☎ *028/9032–3900* ⊕ *www.ulster-orcestra.org.uk.*

Waterfront Hall. Everyone in Belfast sings the praises of this striking civic structure. From the looks of it, the hall is an odd marriage of *Close Encounters* modern and Castel Sant'Angelo antique. It houses a major 2,235-seat concert hall (for ballet, and for classical, rock, and Irish music) and a 500-seat studio space (for modern dance, jazz, and experimental theater). The river-view Terrace Café restaurant and two bars make the hall a convenient place to eat, have a pint, and enjoy the river views before or after your culture fix. ⊠ *Lanyon Pl., Central District* ☎ *028/ 9033–4455* ⊕ *www.waterfront.co.uk.*

Shopping

Belfast's main shopping streets include High Street, Royal Avenue, and several of the smaller streets connecting them. The area is mostly traffic-free (except for buses and delivery vehicles). The long thoroughfare of Donegall Pass, running from Shaftesbury Square at the point of the Golden Mile east to Ormeau Road, is a unique mix of biker shops and antiques arcades.

Market & Mall

Castle Court (⊠ 10 Royal Ave. Central District ☎ 028/9023–4591) is the city's largest, most varied upscale shopping mall. If you've an interest in bric-a-brac, visit the enormous, renovated **St. George's Market** (⊠ May St. ☎ 028/9024–6609), an indoor flea market Friday and Saturday morning.

Specialty Shops

Clark and Dawe (⊠ 485 Lisburn Rd., University Area ☎ 028/9066–8228) makes and sells men's and women's suits and shirts. **Craftworks** (⊠ Bedford House, 16–22 Bedford St., Golden Mile ☎ 028/9024–4465) stocks crafts by local designers. **Natural Interior** (⊠ 51 Dublin Rd., Golden Mile ☎ 028/9024–2656) has Irish linen throws, trimmed in velvet, by the designer Larissa Watson-Regan. It also stocks her vividly colored wall panels and cushions.

Buy 12-inch-high puppets of Northern Ireland politicians at **Open Window Productions** (⊠ 1–3 Exchange Pl., Central District ☎ 028/9032–9669). For £175, you can have a puppet made to order of a favorite celebrity, or even of yourself. **Smyth and Gibson** (⊠ Bedford House, Bedford St., Golden Mile ☎ 028/9023–0388) makes and sells beautiful, luxurious linen and cotton shirts and accessories. Looking for linen souvenirs? **Smyth's Irish Linens** (⊠ 65 Royal Ave., Central District ☎ 028/9024–2232) carries a large selection of handkerchiefs, tablecloths, napkins, and other traditional goods. It's opposite Castle Court Mall. **The Steensons** (⊠ Bedford House, Bedford St., Golden Mile ☎ 028/9024–8269) sells superb, locally designed jewelry.

Side Trips

The three sights below are closer to Belfast than others covered in this chapter. However, none of the sites along the Ards Peninsula and the north coast are more than a few hours' drive from Belfast—perfect for day trips.

Belfast Castle

16 In 1934 the castle, originally built for the Marquis of Donegall in 1865, was passed to Belfast Corporation. Although the castle functions primarily as a restaurant, it also houses the Cave Hill Heritage Centre, which provides information about the castle's history and its natural surroundings in Cave Hill Country Park. The best reason to visit is to take a stroll in the lovely ornamental gardens and then make the ascent to McArt's Fort. This promontory, at the top of sheer cliffs 1,200 feet above the city, affords an excellent view across Belfast. Take the path uphill from the parking lot, turn right at the next intersection of pathways, and then keep left as you journey up the sometimes steep hill to the fort. ⊠ *4 km (2½ mi) north of Belfast on Antrim Rd.* ☎ 028/9077–6925 ✆ *Free* ⊙ *Visitor center daily 9–6.*

Belfast Zoo. The zoo has underwater views of the resident penguins and sea lions and a children's farm. It's near Belfast castle and city buses 45 and 51 will bring you to both. ⊠ *Antrim Rd.* ☎ 028/9077–6277 ✆ *£6* ⊙ *Apr.–Sept., daily 10–5; Oct.–Mar., daily 10–2:30.*

Irish Linen Centre & Lisburn Museum

17 In the 18th, 19th, and early 20th centuries, linen, a natural fabric woven from the fibers of the flax plant, was the basis of Ulster's most important industry—and thus of much of its folk history and song. A century ago, 240,000 acres were given over to flax, whose pretty blue flowers sparkle for just a week in early July. Four hundred acres were designated as "bleach greens," where the woven fabric whitened in the summer sun. Eventually, American cotton and Egyptian flax killed off the mass-production linen trade, which had been centered on Lisburn, in mills powered by the River Lagan. What now survives of the linen industry does so by producing high-quality designer fabrics, plus traditional expensive damask. Today at the Irish Linen Centre and Lisburn Museum, a series of rooms trace this history. Weaving is demonstrated on a turn-of-the-20th-century hand loom (although the attached shop has a disappointing choice of linen goods). ⊠ *12 km (8 mi) southwest of Belfast, Market Sq., Lisburn* ☎ 028/9266–3377 ✆ *Free* ⊙ *Mon.–Sat. 9:30–5.*

Ulster Folk & Transport Museum

18 Devoted to the province's social history, the excellent Ulster Folk and Transport Museum vividly brings Northern Ireland's past to life with a score of reconstructed buildings moved here from around the region. These structures represent different facets of northern life—a traditional weaver's dwelling, terraces of Victorian town houses, an 18th-century country church, a village flax mill, a farmhouse, and a rural school. Inside an appropriately dressed attendant explains what it was like actually to live in and use them. You start your visit with the Folk Gallery, which explains the background of each building. Across the main road (by footbridge) is the beautifully designed Transport Museum, where exhibits include locally built airplanes and motorcycles; the iconoclastic car produced by former General Motors whiz kid John De Lorean in his Belfast factory in 1982; and a moving section on the *Titanic*, the Belfast-built luxury liner that sank on her first voyage, in 1912, killing 1,500 of the passengers and crew. A miniature railway runs on Saturday in July and August. The museum is on the 70 acres of Cultra Manor, encircled by a larger park and recreation area. ⊠ *16 km (10 mi) northeast of Belfast on A2, Cultra* ☎ 028/9042–8428 ⊕ *www.nidex.com/uftm* ✆ *£5* ⊙ *Mar.–June, weekdays 10–5, Sat. 10–6, Sun. 11–6; July–Sept., Mon.–Sat. 10–6, Sun. 11–6; Oct.–Feb., weekdays 10–4, Sat. 10–5, Sun. 11–5.*

FodorsChoice ★

AROUND COUNTIES ANTRIM & DERRY

Starting in Belfast, the coastal route takes you through some fair-size towns, as well as driving in open country through splendid natural scenery. Mid-coast, the natural wonder of the Giant's Causeway and the man-made brilliance of the castle at Dunluce shine. The old walled city of Derry is enjoying a revitalization.

Carrickfergus

⑲ *16 km (10 mi) northeast of Belfast on A2.*

Carrickfergus, on the shore of Belfast Lough, grew up around its ancient castle. When the town was enclosed by ramparts at the start of the 17th century, it was the only English-speaking town in Northern Ireland. Not surprisingly, this was the loyal port where William of Orange chose to land on his way to fight the Catholic forces at the Battle of the Boyne in 1690. However, the English did have one or two small setbacks, including the improbable victory in 1778 of John Paul Jones, the American naval hero, over the British warship *HMS Drake*. (This, by the way, was America's first naval victory during the Revolutionary War.) After the sea battle, the inhabitants of Carrickfergus stood on the waterfront and cheered Jones because they supported the American Revolution.

Carrickfergus Castle, one of the first and one of the largest of Irish castles, is still in good shape. It was built atop a rock ledge in 1180 by John de Courcy, provincial Ulster's first Anglo-Norman invader. Apart from being captured briefly by the French in 1760, the castle stood as a bastion of British rule right up until 1928, at which time it still functioned as an English garrison.

Walk through the castle's 13th-century gatehouse into the Outer Ward. Continue into the Inner Ward, the heart of the fortress, where the five-story keep stands, a massive, sturdy building with walls almost 8 feet thick. Inside the keep is the Cavalry Regimental Museum with historic weapons and the vaulted Great Hall. These days Carrickfergus Castle hosts entertaining medieval banquets (inquire at Carrickfergus tourist information office or the Northern Ireland Tourist Board Information Centre). If you're here at the beginning of August, you can enjoy the annual Lughnasa festival, a lively medieval-costume entertainment. ⊠ *Off A2* ☎ *028/9335–1273* ⊕ *www.ehsni.gov.uk* ✑ *£3* ☉ *May–Sept., Mon.–Sat. 10–6, Sun. 2–6; Oct.–Apr., Mon.–Sat. 10–4, Sun. 2–4.*

Old buildings that remain from Carrickfergus's past include St. Nicholas's Church, built by John de Courcy in 1205 (remodeled in 1614) and the handsomely restored North Gate in the town's medieval walls. Dobbins Inn on High Street, which has been a hotel for more than three centuries, is a popular watering hole with locals.

The **Andrew Jackson Centre** tells the tale of U.S. president Andrew Jackson, whose parents emigrated from here in 1765. This thatched cottage just outside of town was not their actual home but a reconstruction of an 18th-century thatched cottage thought to resemble it. ⊠ *2 km (1 mi) northeast of Carrickfergus, Larne Rd., Boneybefore* ☎ *028/9336–6455* ⊕ *www.carrickfergus.org* ✑ *£1* ☉ *Apr., May, and Oct., weekdays 10–1 and 2–4, weekends 2–4; June–Sept., weekdays 10–1 and 2–6, weekends 2–6.*

en route
Signposted on the left, 2½ km (1½ mi) off A2, heading away from Carrickfergus, is **Dalway's Bawn.** Built in 1609, it's the best surviving example of an early bawn, or fortified farmhouse, occupied by a Protestant Planter.

Glens of Antrim

★ ⑳ *Beginning 24 km (15 mi) north of Carrickfergus at Larne.*

Soon after Larne, the coast of County Antrim becomes spectacular—wave upon wave of high green hills curve down to the hazy sea, dotted with lush and gently curved glens, or valleys, first carved out by glaciers at the end of the last ice age. Nine wooded river valleys occupy the 86 km (54 mi) between Larne and Ballycastle. A narrow, winding, two-lane road (A2, which splits from the coastal at Cushendall) hugs the slim strip of land between the hills and the sea, bringing you to the magnificent Glens of Antrim running down from the escarpment of the Antrim Plateau to the eastern shore. Until the building of this road in 1834, the glens were home to isolated farming communities—people who adhered to the romantic, mystical Celtic legends and the everyday use of the Irish language. The Glens are worth several days of serious exploration. Even narrower B-roads curl west off A2, up each of the beautiful glens where trails await hikers.

A little resort made of white limestone, **Carnlough** overlooks a charming harbor that's surrounded by stone walls. The harbor can be reached by crossing over the limestone bridge from Main Street, built especially for the Marquis of Londonderry. The small harbor, once a port of call for fishermen, now shelters pleasure yachts. Carnlough is surrounded on three sides by hills that rise 1,000 feet from the sea. There's a small tourist office inside the post office, which is useful if you need information on exploring the scenic Glens of Antrim and the coast road. ✉ *24 km (15 mi) north of Larne on A2.*

In **Glenariff Forest Park** you can explore the largest and most accessible of Antrim's glens. The valley opens onto Red Bay at the village of Glenariff (also known as Waterfoot). Inside the park are picnic facilities and dozens of good hikes. The 5½-km (3½-mi) Waterfall Trail, marked with blue arrows, passes outstanding views of Glenariff River, its waterfalls, and small but swimmable loughs. Pick up a detailed trail map at the park visitor center, which also has a small cafeteria. ⊕ *7 km (5 mi) north of Carnlough off A2* ✉ *98 Glenariff Rd., Glenariff* ☎ *028/2175–8232* 🎟 *Vehicles £3, pedestrians £2* ◷ *Daily 10–dusk.*

Turnley's Tower—a curious, fortified square tower of red stone, built in 1820 as a curfew tower and jail for "idlers and rioters"—stands in **Cushendall,** at a crossroads in the middle of the village. ✉ *3 km (2 mi) north of Glenariff on A2.*

The tiny jewel of a village **Cushendun** was designed by Clough Williams-Ellis, who also designed the famous Italianate village of Portmeirion in Wales. From this part of the coast you can see the Mull of Kintyre on the Scottish mainland. ✉ *2 km (1½ mi) north of Cushendall on Coast Rd.*

en route
A narrow and precipitous coastal road heads north from Cushendun past dramatically beautiful Murlough Bay to Fair Head and on to Ballycastle. An alternative to Antrim Coast Road is to rejoin A2 at Cushendun via B92 (a left turn). After a few miles the road descends—passing ruins of the Franciscans' 16th-century Bonamargy Friary—into Ballycastle.

Where to Stay & Eat

$$$ ✕◩ **Galgorm Manor.** The manor house itself is photogenic, and the estate grounds—where you may go riding, practice archery, and shoot clay pigeons—cinematic. Full privileges at an 18-hole, par-72 golf course five minutes from the hotel is an added treat. The River Maine (good for brown trout) flows within view of many of the large rooms, which have wood beams hanging on the ceilings above substantial dark wood beds. Gillies bar is decidedly Irish; the restaurant serves hearty portions of traditional Irish food ($–$$). Galgorm is off A42, 3 km (2 mi) west of Ballymena, 32 km (20 mi) inland of Larne, 40 km (25 mi) north of Belfast. ✛ *40 km (25 mi) east of Larne on A36* ✉ *136 Fenaghy Rd., Ballymena, Co. Antrim BT42 1EA* ☎ *028/2588–1001* 🖨 *028/2588–0080* ⊕ *www. galgorm.com* 🛏 *24 rooms with bath* ⚘ *Restaurant, golf privileges, fishing, archery, horseback riding, bar, meeting rooms* ▭ *AE, MC, V* ❘○❘ *BP, MAP.*

★ **$$** ✕◩ **Londonderry Arms Hotel.** What awaits at Londonderry Arms are lovely seaside gardens, ivy-clad walls, gorgeous antiques, regional paintings and maps, and lots of fresh flowers. This ivy-covered traditional inn on Carnlough Harbor was built as a coach stop in 1848. In 1921 Sir Winston Churchill inherited it; since 1947 it has been owned and run by the hospitable O'Neill family. Both the original and the newer rooms have Georgian furnishings and luxurious fabrics, and are immaculately kept. The restaurant serves substantial, traditional Irish meals that emphasize fresh, local seafood, simply prepared ($–$$). The hotel has an elevator and is wheelchair accessible. ✉ *20 Harbour Rd., Carnlough, Co. Antrim BT44 0EU* ☎ *028/2888–5255* 🖨 *028/2888–5263* ⊕ *www.glensofantrim. com* 🛏 *35 rooms with bath* ⚘ *Restaurant, bar, meeting rooms* ▭ *AE, DC, MC, V* ❘○❘ *BP, MAP.*

$$ ◩ **Ballygally Castle.** A baronial castle, built by a Scottish lord in 1625, rises dramatically beside Ballygally Bay. Attached to it is a modern extension that provides room for facilities but clashes a bit with the original. Bedrooms in the castle have retained beamed ceilings despite comfortable-if-bland furnishings throughout. Ask for a room in a turret—one comes complete with milady's ghost. On Saturday in the dining room, a decent table d'hôte evening meal is served to musical accompaniment; a Sunday bistro meal is available. ✉ *274 Coast Rd., Ballygally, Co. Antrim BT40 2QZ* ☎ *028/2858–1066* 🖨 *028/2858–3681* ⊕ *www.hastingshotels.com* 🛏 *44 rooms with bath* ⚘ *Dining room, bar, baby-sitting* ▭ *AE, DC, MC, V* ❘○❘ *BP.*

Ballycastle

㉑ *86 km (54 mi) northeast of Larne, 37½ km (23 mi) north of Carnlough.*

Ballycastle is the main resort at the northern end of the Glens of Antrim. People from the province flock here in the summer. The town is shaped like an hourglass—with its strand and dock on one end, its pubs and chippers on the other, and the 1-km (½-mi) Quay Road in between. Beautifully aged shops and pubs line its Castle, Diamond, and Main streets.

Every year since 1606, on the last Monday and Tuesday in August, Ballycastle has hosted the **Oul' Lammas Fair,** a modern version of the ancient Celtic harvest festival of Lughnasa (Irish for "August"). Ireland's oldest fair, this is a very popular two-day event at which sheep and wool are still sold alongside the wares of more modern shopping stalls. Treat yourself to the fair's traditional snacks, "dulse" (sun-dried seaweed), and "yellow man" (rock-hard yellow toffee).

From Ballycastle town you have a view of L-shape **Rathlin Island,** where in 1306 the Scottish king Robert the Bruce took shelter in a cave (under the east lighthouse) and, according to the popular legend, was inspired to continue his armed struggle against the English by watching a spider patiently spinning its web. It was on Rathlin in 1898 that Guglielmo Marconi set up the world's first cross-water radio link, from the island's lighthouse to Ballycastle. Bird-watching and hiking are the island's main activities. Unless the sea is extremely rough, a ferryboat makes twice daily journeys for £9. The trip can take up to 45 minutes; be mindful of the weather to ensure that you can return the same day. ⊠ *9½ km (6 mi) from Ballycastle.*

Off the Ballycastle coast you can see the **Carrick-a-Rede** rope bridge, which spans a 60-foot gap between the mainland and Carrick-a-Rede Island. The island's name means "rock in the road" and refers to how it stands in the path of the salmon who follow the coast as they migrate to their home rivers to spawn. For the past 150 years salmon fishermen have set up the rope bridge in spring, taking it down again after the salmon season ends. The bridge is open to the public and has some heart-stopping views of the crashing waves below. If you summon up the nerve to cross it once, of course you then have to do it again to get back to the mainland. ⊠ *8 km (5 mi) west of Ballycastle on B15* ✉ *Free* ◷ *Mid-Mar.–June and Sept., daily 10–6; July and Aug., daily 9:30–7:30.*

Where to Eat

★ ¢–$$ ✕ **Wysner's.** Head chef Jackie Wysner has won several awards for both this small family restaurant and the eponymous butcher shop next door. Menus vary daily, though the cooking emphasizes fresh local ingredients—from the hills and the sea. Specialties of the upstairs restaurant include North Atlantic salmon (caught nearby at Carrick-a-Rede), fillet of halibut with langoustine, and filet of beef with mustard-seed cream sauce. A daytime menu is served downstairs in the informal café. ⊠ *16–18 Ann St.* ☎ *028/2076–2372* ▭ *MC, V* ◷ *Closed Sun.*

Giant's Causeway

22 *19⅓ km (12 mi) west of Ballycastle.*

Fodor's Choice
★

Imagine a mass of 37,000 mostly hexagonal pillars of volcanic basalt, clustered like a giant honeycomb and extending hundreds of yards into the sea. This, the Giant's Causeway, is Northern Ireland's premier tourist draw. Legend has it the causeway was created 60 million years ago, when boiling lava, erupting from an underground fissure that stretched from Northern Ireland to the Scottish coast, crystallized as it burst into the sea, and formed according to the same natural principle that structures a honeycomb. As all Ulster folk know, though, the scientific truth is that the columns were created as stepping-stones by the giant Finn McCool in a bid to reach a giantess he'd fallen in love with on the Scottish island of Staffa (where the causeway resurfaces). Unfortunately, the giantess's boyfriend found out, and in the ensuing battle Finn pulled out a huge chunk of earth and flung it toward Scotland. The resulting hole became Lough Neagh, and the sod landed to create the Isle of Man.

To reach the causeway, you can either walk 1½ km (1 mi) down a long, scenic hill or take a minibus from the visitor center. West of the causeway, Port-na-Spania is the spot where the 16th-century Spanish Armada galleon *Girona* went down on the rocks. The ship was carrying an astonishing cargo of gold and jewelry, some of which was recovered in 1967 and is now on display in the Ulster Museum in Belfast. Beyond this, Chimney Point is the name given to one of the causeway structures on which the Spanish fired, thinking that it was Dunluce Castle, which is 8 km (5 mi) west.

Arriving by car at the Giant's Causeway, you first reach a cliff-top parking lot beside the visitor center, which houses displays about the area and an audiovisual exhibition explaining the formation of the causeway coast. ✉ *44 Causeway Rd., Bushmills* ☎ *028/2073–1855* ⊕ *www. nationaltrust.org.uk.* 🎞 *Visitor center movie £1, guided tours £2, parking £5* ⊙ *Visitor center Mar.–May, daily 10–5; June, daily 10–6; July and Aug., daily 10–7; Sept. and Oct., daily 10–5; Nov.–Feb., daily 10–3.*

Bushmills

㉓ *3 km (2 mi) west of Giant's Causeway.*

The oldest licensed distillery in the world, Bushmills was first granted a charter by King James I in 1608, though historical records refer to a distillery here as early as 1276. Bushmills produces the most famous of Irish whiskeys—its namesake—and what is widely regarded as the best, the rarer black-label version known to aficionados as Black Bush. One-hour tours begin in the mashing and fermentation room, proceed to the maturing and bottling warehouse, and end with a complimentary shot of *uisce beatha,* the "water of life," in the visitor center gift shop. ✉ *Off A2* ☎ *028/2073–1521* ⊕ *www.whiskeytours.ie* 🎞 *£4* ⊙ *Continuous tours Apr.–Oct., Mon.–Sat. 9:30–5:30, Sun. noon–5:30; Nov.–Mar., 5 tours a day weekdays 10:30–3:30, 3 tours weekends 1:30–3:30.*

Where to Stay

$$$–$$$$ 🏨 **Bushmills Inn.** Owner Roy Bolton oversees this cozy old coach inn. Stripped pine, peat fires, and gas lights warm the public rooms. Some of the bedrooms are quite small, so look before you decide. The livery stables now house the informal restaurant, which serves fresh and hearty food, and the bar. The staff can provide a baby listening service—you leave the tot in the room with a phone that records any noise, and they alert you to cries. The distillery is a stroll away from the main square and the inn, as is the salmon-filled River Bush. ✉ *9 Dunluce Rd., Bushmills, Co. Antrim BT57 8QG* ☎ *028/2073–2339* 📠 *028/2073–2048* ⊕ *www.bushmills-inn.com* 🛏 *32 rooms with bath* ⚭ *Restaurant, bar, Internet, meeting rooms* ▭ *AE, MC, V* ⑩ *BP.*

Dunluce Castle

★ **㉔** *3 km (2 mi) west of Bushmills.*

Halfway between Portrush and the Giant's Causeway, dramatically perched on a cliff at land's end, Dunluce Castle is one of the North's most evocative ruins. Originally a 13th-century Norman fortress, it was captured in the 16th century by the local MacDonnell clan chiefs—the so-called "Lords of the Isles." They enlarged the castle, paying for some of the work with their profits from salvaging the Spanish galleon *Girona,* and made it an important base for ruling northeastern Ulster. Perhaps they expanded the castle a little too much, for in 1639 faulty construction caused the kitchens (with the cooks) to plummet into the sea during a storm. ✉ *Coastal Rd., Portrush* ☎ *028/2073–1938* ⊕ *www. northantrim.com/dunlucecastle.htm* 🎞 *£2* ⊙ *Apr.–Sept., Mon.–Sat. 10–6, Sun. 2–6; July and Aug., Mon.–Sat. 10–6, Sun. 12–6; Oct.–Mar., Tues.–Sat. 10–4, Sun. 2–4.*

Dunluce Center is an entertainment complex with three floors of interactive play zones, shops, and a café near Dunluce Castle. ✉ *10 Sandhill Dr., Portrush* ☎ *028/7082–4444* ⊕ *www.dunlucecentre.co.uk* 🎞 *£5 plus rides* ⊙ *Easter week, daily 10:30–7; Apr. and May, weekends 12–7; June, weekdays 10–5, weekends 12–7; July and Aug., daily 10:30–7; Sept.–Mar., weekends 12–5.*

Where to Eat

★ ¢–$$ ✕ **Ramore Wine Bar.** On Portrush's picturesque harbor, this spot has panoramic views, with daily offerings posted on a blackboard. ⊠ *The Harbor, Portrush* ☎ *028/7082–4313* 🖨 *028/7082–3194* ▭ *MC, V.*

Sports & the Outdoors

The **Royal Portrush Golf Club** (⊠ Dunluce Rd., Portrush ☎ 028/7082–2311 ⊕ www.royalportrushgolfclub.com) has more than one course. The championship Dunluce is sea of sand hills and curving fairways (£85). The valley course is a less-exposed, tamer track (£30). Both are open to visitors on weekdays. **Portstewart Strand** (⊠ Coastal Rd., Portrush) has some of Ireland's best surfing. It's signposted as "The Strand" on all major junctions in town.

Coleraine

㉕ *13 km (8 mi) southwest of Dunluce Castle*

The 5th century BC town of Coleraine became the home of the University of Ulster in 1968. The River Bann flows through the town, dividing the county of Antrim from that of Derry. As well as being a fishing town, Coleraine has an important linen industry.

Some of Ireland's oldest remaining relics, dating from the very first inhabitants of this island (about 7000 BC), were found on Mountsandel, just south of Coleraine. One of the many dolmens in this region is called Slaghtaverty—after an evil dwarf who used his magical harp to mesmerize women. He was buried alive and upside down by the great Finn McCool (maker of the Giant's Causeway), so the sounds of his harp would not escape from the ground.

Where to Stay

$ 🏠 **Greenhill House.** This charming Georgian country house is a peaceful retreat run by Elizabeth and James Hegarty. Floral fabrics and antique, carved furnishings decorate pleasant rooms. Breakfasts are substantial. The excellent dinners—of locally caught fish, Ulster beef, and homemade bread and cakes—must be booked by noon. ⊹ *13 km (8 mi) south of Coleraine on A29* ⊠ *24 Greenhill Rd., Aghadowey, Co. Derry BT51 4EU* ☎ *028/7086–8241* 🖨 *028/7086–8365* ⊕ *www. greenhill.house.btinternet.co.uk* ➳ *6 rooms with bath* ⚹ *Dining room, Internet* ▭ *MC, V* ⑩| *BP, MAP* ⊙ *Closed Nov.–Feb.*

Upperlands

㉖ *32 km (20 mi) south of Coleraine, 56 km (35 mi) northwest of Belfast.*

The River Bann—rich in eels for roasting and smoking and in salmon for poaching—flows out of Lough Neagh. On its left bank are the towns and fortifications of the 17th-century Planters, built by London's Livery Companies, whose descendants developed the linen industry. Today, virtually all of that rural industrial heritage is gone, with the notable exception of the village of Upperlands. Make sure you tour **William Clark and Sons,** a working linen mill where age-old wooden machinery still beetles (polishes by pounding with hammers) threads for the linen linings of suits for England's Royals. There's also a small linen museum here. ⊠ *A29, Upperlands* ☎ *028/7954–7200* 🎫 *Free* ⊙ *By appointment Mon.–Thurs. 10–4.*

Where to Stay & Eat

$$$ ✕🏠 **Ardtara House.** A 19th-century Victorian home, Ardtara was built

*Fodor's*Choice by a descendant of the founder of the town's first linen mill. Eight large

★ bedrooms are furnished with antiques, and each has a fireplace—as do some of the marble bathrooms. The terra-cotta and pink drawing room, with plaster moldings and a marble fireplace, looks out on the wide front lawn and tennis court. The hotel's restaurant ($$) is in the former snooker room, with dark panels and a wallpapered hunting scene. The terrine of duck appetizer is popular, as is the stellar poached fillet of lamb with buttered Savoy cabbage entrée. ⊠ *8 Gorteade Rd., Co. Derry BT46 5SA* ☎ *028/7964–4490* 🖷 *028/7964–5080* 🛏 *8 rooms with bath* ♿ *Restaurant, tennis court, meeting room* 🖃 *AE, MC, V* ⍾◉⍾ *BP.*

Limavady

㉗ *21 km (13 mi) west of Coleraine, 27 km (17 mi) east of Derry.*

In 1851, at No. 51 on Limavady's Georgian main street, Jane Ross wrote down the tune played by a traveling fiddler and called it "Londonderry Air," better known now as "Danny Boy." While staying at an inn on Ballyclose Street, William Thackeray (1811–63) wrote his rather lustful poem "Peg of Limavaddy" about a barmaid. Among the many Americans descended from Ulster emigrants was President James Monroe, whose relatives came from the Limavady area.

Where to Stay & Eat

$$$ ✕▦ **Radisson Roe Park Hotel & Golf Resort.** A country estate serves as the model for the deluxe modern resort amid 155 acres on the banks of the River Roe. Regular guest rooms have simple, clean-line beds in woods and rich earth tones. Suite furnishings move a bit up the ornate scale: canopy beds and velvet armchairs. Green's restaurant is formal and international ($–$$$); the Coach House brasserie is a relaxed place where golfers congregate; and O'Cahan's bar takes its name from a local chieftain besieged on a riverside promontory, whose Irish wolfhound leaped an impossible chasm to bring relief—doubtless an inspiration to golfers flagging at the ninth. ⊠ *Roe Park, Co. Derry BT49 9LB* ☎ *028/ 7772–2222* 🖷 *028/7772–2313* ⊕ *www.radissonroepark.com* 🛏 *118 rooms with bath, 6 suites* ♿ *2 restaurants, 18-hole golf course, indoor pool, aerobics, gym, hair salon, massage, sauna, steam room, fishing, horseback riding, 2 bars, baby-sitting, Internet, meeting rooms* 🖃 *AE, DC, MC, V* ⍾◉⍾ *BP, MAP.*

Derry

27 km (17 mi) southwest of Limavady on A2, 109 km (68 mi) north of Belfast, 53 km (33 mi) north of Omagh.

Derry's name is a shadow of its history. Those in favor of British rule call the city Londonderry, its old Plantation-period name: the "London" part was tacked on in 1613 after the Flight of the Earls, and the city and county were handed over to the Corporation of London, which represented London's merchants. The corporation brought in a large population of English and Scottish Protestant settlers, built towns for them, and reconstructed Derry within the city walls, which survive almost unchanged to this day. Both before then and after, Derry's sturdy ramparts have withstood many fierce attacks and have never been breached, which explains the city's coy sobriquet, "The Maiden City." The most famous attack was the historic siege of 1688–89, after 13 apprentice boys slammed the city gates in the face of the Catholic king, James II. Inhabitants, who held out for 105 days and were reduced to eating dogs, cats, and laundry starch, nevertheless helped to secure the British throne for the Protestant king, William III.

Whatever you choose to call it, Derry is one of Northern Ireland's most underrated towns. If Belfast was the Beethoven of Northern Ireland, Derry would be the Mozart—fey, witty, and a touch surreal. Every Halloween, for example, the entire populace turns out decked in wild homemade costumes, and pubs have been known to refuse a drink to anyone who hasn't made the effort to dress up. Despite the derelict factories along the banks of the River Foyle and a reputation marred by Troubles-related violence, the city has worked hard to move forward. Such efforts show in the quaint, bustling town center, encircled by 20-foot-tall 17th-century walls. The city's winding streets slope down to the Foyle, radiating from the Diamond—Derry's historic center where St. Columba founded his first monastery in 546. Fine Georgian and Victorian buildings sit side by side with gaily painted Victorian-front shops, cafés, and pubs.

Derry, incidentally, has links to Boston that date as far back as the 17th and 18th centuries, when many Derry residents escaped their hardships at home by emigrating to that U.S. city and beyond. Aviation fans, take note: Derry was where Amelia Earhart touched down on May 21, 1932, after her historic solo flight across the Atlantic. Local lore has it that the first man to reach her airplane greeted her in typically unfazed Derry fashion: "Aye, and what do you want, then?"

28 To really experience Derry's history, stroll along the parapet walkway atop the ramparts of the **city walls,** built between 1614 and 1618 and one of the few intact sets of city walls in Europe. Pierced by eight gates (originally four) and as much as 30 feet thick, the gray-stone ramparts are only 1½ km (1 mi) all around. Today most of the life of the town actually takes place outside of them. You can join one of the guided tours given by information center, or follow the sites below in a counterclockwise direction.

Walking tours of the city walls leave from the **Tourist Information Centre** and last just under two hours departing at 2:30 weekdays year-round, as well as at 11:15 and 3:15 in July and August. ✉ *44 Foyle St., West Bank* ☎ *028/7126–7284 or 028/7137–7577* 🖷 *028/7137–7992* ⊕ *www. derryvisitor.com* ✒ *Center free, tour £4* ⊙ *Mar. 15–June and Oct., weekdays 9–5, Sat. 10–5; July–Sept., weekdays 9–7, Sat. 10–6, Sun. 10–5; Nov.–Mar. 15, weekdays 9–5.*

29 Derry city council meets monthly at **Guildhall,** an ornate Victorian stone and sandstone building dating from 1890. Large stained-glass windows that were shattered by two IRA bombs in June 1977 and rebuilt by the Campbell's firm in Belfast, which had installed the original windows in 1890 and still had the plans (now that's a filing system). The Guildhall also hosts occasional musical recitals. ✉ *Guildhall Sq., West Bank* ☎ *028/7137–7335* ✒ *Free* ⊙ *Weekdays 8:30–5.*

30 A reconstructed O'Dohertys Tower contains the **Tower Museum,** which chronicles the history of Derry. The building was originally constructed in 1615 by the O'Dohertys for their overlords, the O'Donnells, in lieu of tax payments. Highlights of the museum include a small section on the eccentric Bishop Frederick Augustus Hervey (1763–1803), who conducted a lifelong affair with the mistress of Frederick William II of Prussia, built the now derelict Downhill Castle above the cliffs outside the city, and allegedly had his curates stage naked sprints along the beach while he horsewhipped them. The winners were awarded with the most lucrative parishes in the district. There's excellent information celebrating the life and legacy of St. Columba. The vivid "Story of Derry" exhibition covers the city's history, from its origins as a monastic set-

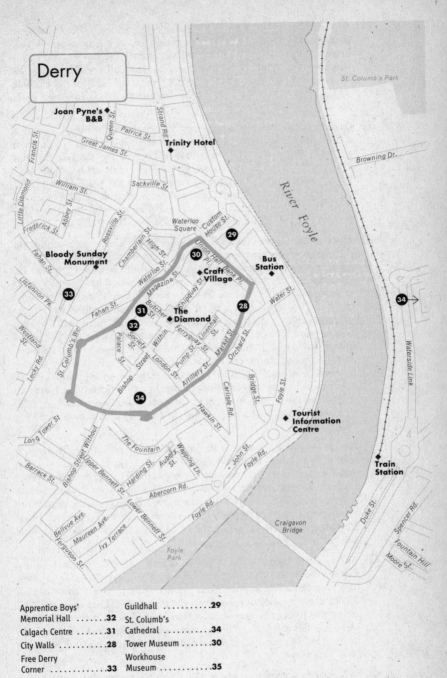

Derry

Joan Pyne's B&B
Trinity Hotel
Bloody Sunday Monument
Craft Village
The Diamond
Bus Station
Tourist Information Centre
Train Station

St. Columb's Park
River Foyle
Browning Dr.
Waterside Link
Craigavon Bridge
Foyle Park

Streets: Queen St., Strand Rd., Patrick St., Great James St., Francis St., William St., Sackville St., Little Diamond, Frederick St., Abbey St., Rossville St., Waterloo Square, Custom House St., Union Hall Pl., Bank Pl., Fahan St., Chamberlain St., High St., Waterloo St., Magazine St., Butcher St., Shipquay St., Water St., St. Columb's Well, Fahan St., Society St., Within, Palace St., Bishop Street, London St., Ferryquay St., Linenhall St., Pump St., Market St., Orchard St., Artillery St., Carlisle Rd., Bridge St., Foyle St., Lecky Rd., Westland St., Listennon Pk., Long Tower St., Barrack St., Bishop Street Without, Upper Bennett St., The Fountain, Harding St., Auberly St., Wapping Ln., Hawkin St., John St., Foyle Rd., Abercorn Rd., Bellvue Ave., Maureen Ave., Ivy Terrace, Ferguson St., Lower Bennett St., Duke St., Spencer Rd., Fountain Hill, Moore St.

tlement in an oak grove up to the Troubles, beginning in 1969 after years of institutionalized discrimination in jobs and public housing. (A well-known Derry innuendo is that the skeleton in the city's coat of arms was actually a Catholic waiting for a house.) Call ahead if you would like to visit the museum on a Sunday. ⊠ *Union Hall Pl., West Bank* ☎*028/ 7137–2411* 🖼 *£4* ⊘ *Sept.–June, Tues.–Sat. 10–5; July and Aug., Mon.–Sat. 10–5, Sun. 2–5.*

㉛ **Calgach Centre** provides a high-tech tour of the city's history, including its importance in creating the Irish diaspora of 17 million people. Sit in a comfortable armchair for a virtual-reality time trip through the coming of the Vikings and the Normans, the flight of the Irish nobility from English persecution in 1601, and the famine of 1845–49, when 1½ million emigrated to the United States and a million more died of starvation. At this writing the center was under repair with reopening date uncertain. ⊠ *4–22 Butcher St., West Bank* ☎ *028/7137–3177.*

㉜ The baronial **Apprentice Boys' Memorial Hall** is a meeting place for the exclusively Protestant organization set up in 1715 to honor 13 apprentice boys who slammed the city gate in the face of the Catholic King James in 1688 and began the Siege of Derry, which has been a symbol of Protestant stubbornness ever since. Inside, there's an initiation room in which 20,000 have pledged to uphold Protestant values, and a magnificently chaotic museum filled to the brim with furniture, firearms, books, bombs, swords, and sculpture. It's a fascinating glimpse into a mostly closed world. An upstairs bar and dance hall—now used for meetings, initiations, and social events, organized by the Apprentice Boys—has walls lined with 12 banners representing the lost tribes of Israel. (Some Protestants believe the lost tribes of Israel finally ended up in Northern Ireland and are their forebears.) ⊠ *Society St., West Bank* ☎ *028/ 7134–6677* 🖼 *Donations accepted* ⊘ *Tours by appointment; open to public second week of Aug.*

Walker Memorial, a statue of the governor of Derry during the siege, is a symbol of Derry's divided nature. It was blown up by the IRA in 1973, and the story goes that the statue's head rolled down the hill into the Catholic Bogside, where it was captured by a local youth. He ransomed it back to the Protestants for a small fortune, and today it sits on the shoulders of a replica of the original statue beside the Apprentice Boys' Memorial Hall. ⊠ *Apprentice Boys' Memorial Hall, Society St., West Bank.*

㉝ At **Free Derry Corner** is the white gable wall where Catholics defiantly painted the slogan "You are now entering Free Derry" as a declaration of a zone from which police and the British Army were banned until 1972, when the army broke down the barricades. That same year, 13 civil rights marchers were shot by British soldiers in an event that rankles Catholics to this day. "Bloody Sunday," as it became known, is commemorated by the mural of a civil rights march. ⊠ *Fahan and Rossville Sts., West Bank.*

㉞ **St. Columb's Cathedral** was the first Protestant cathedral built in the United Kingdom after the Reformation, and contains the oldest and largest bells in Ireland (dating from the 1620s). It's a treasure house of Derry Protestant emblems, memorials, and relics from the siege of 1688–89. The church was built in 1633 in simple Planter's Gothic style, and with an intricate corbeled roof and austere spire. In the vestibule is the 270-pound mortar ball that during the siege was fired over the wall with an invitation to surrender sent by King James. Legend has it that when they read it, every man, woman, and child in the city rushed to the walls and

A POLITICAL ABC

DUP. Right-wing Democratic Unionist Party, founded by firebrand preacher Reverend Ian Paisley in 1971. Now increasingly sidelined.

IRA. Irish Republican Army. Largest group of Republican paramilitaries, responsible for thousands of murders and bombings.

Loyalist. Extreme Unionist.

Nationalist. Anyone supporting a united Ireland.

Northern Ireland Assembly. Regional government, sitting at Stormont.

Orange Order. Protestant organization whose annual 12th of July marches celebrate the 1690 victory of Protestant King William of Orange over Catholic King James.

Police Service of Northern Ireland. Formerly Royal Ulster Constabulary, whose name was changed in 2001 as part of a package of reforms to attract more Catholics.

Republican. Extreme Nationalist.

SDLP. Social, Democratic, and Labour Party. Largest and most moderate Nationalist party.

Sinn Féin. Literally "Ourselves Alone," political counterpart of IRA, although now firmly installed in democratic Northern Ireland Assembly.

Troubles. The 1969–97 campaign by Republican and Loyalist terrorists in which 3,636 people were killed.

UDA. Ulster Defence Association. Largest Loyalist paramilitary group, involved in hundreds of murders.

UFF and UVF. Ulster Freedom Fighters and Ulster Volunteer Force, breakaway Loyalist paramilitary groups.

Ulster. Historic name for northern province of Ireland. Now generally used, especially by Protestants, to describe Northern Ireland.

Ulster Unionist Party. Largest and most moderate Unionist party.

Unionist. Anyone supporting continuing union with Great Britain.

shouted, "No surrender!"—a Protestant battle cry to this day. The attached Chapter House Museum has the oldest surviving map of Derry (from 1600) and the Bible owned by Governor George Walker during the siege. Knowledgeable tour guides are on hand. ✉ *London St., off Bishop St., West Bank* ☎ *028/7126–7313* ⊕ *www.stcolumbscathedral.org* ✑ *£1* ☉ *Apr.–Oct., daily 9–5; Nov.–Mar., daily 9–4.*

need a break? Derry is packed with agreeable pubs, but **Badgers** (✉ 16 Orchard St., West Bank ☎ 028/7136–0763) has the best choice of wholesome food. It's also the watering hole for local media types, artists, writers, and musicians.

35 Across the River Foyle from the city walls, the **Workhouse Museum** was built in 1832 to alleviate poverty but became the end of the road for people who had tried in vain to make their lives better. During the famine years (1845–49), the city was the main emigration port for Northern Ireland, and many families came to Derry hoping to get on a boat. Instead, unable to afford the trip, they ended up applying for aid at the workhouse where hard labor earned a bed and food. Many families were separated once inside, and this was often the last time children saw their parents alive. From the beginning to the end of the famine, 1½ million people left Ireland and 1 million died. The museum details life in the workhouse and has some thoughtful exhibits about famine in general.

Many of the descendants of those who left came back during the Second World War: thousands of U.S. servicemen arrived in the city in 1942 to turn it into a base for the Battle of the Atlantic. Exhibits on the top two floors of the Workhouse chronicle the story of that battle, from the

Yanks' arrival in the January rain (which prompted one of them to ask if the city's barrage balloons were actually there to stop the place from sinking) through the end of the war when 64 U-boats lined up in the harbor to surrender. By 1946 the city's biggest export was G.I. brides. There is a space for traveling exhibitions that change regularly; call for details. ✉ *23 Glendermott Rd., East Bank* ☎ *028/7131–8328* ✍ *Free* ⊙ *Sept.–June, Mon.–Thurs. and Sat. 10–4:30; July and Aug., Mon.–Sat. 10:30–4:30.*

en route For a delightfully rustic alternative to driving back to Belfast on A6, drive along the minor road B48, which skirts the foot of the Sperrin Mountains and reaches all the way to Omagh. Or, you may want to head north from Derry to explore the Inishowen Peninsula, the northernmost point of Ireland.

Where to Stay & Eat

$ ✕ **Spice.** It's worth the walk up the hill from town to this cozy restaurant with food that draws heavily on Pan-Asian influences. Main course highlights include crab claws and red Thai curry, served with plain or fried rice or noodles. ✉ *162–164 Spencer Rd., East Bank* ☎ *028/7134–4875* ⊟ *MC, V.*

$$ ▦ **Beech Hill.** Journey past a fairy-tale gatehouse among clumps of beech trees, past streams and a duck pond on the grounds at Beech Hill. This grand 1729 country home is very much attuned to the present with enough extras to satisfy the most demanding traveler (a trouser press, and tea and coffeemakers in room). The vast honeymoon suite, with a four-poster bed, overlooks the gardens. Rooms in the old building are decorated in Georgian style; 10 rooms in a modern extension are larger and contemporary. A small museum celebrates the fact that Beech Hill housed a contingent of U.S. Marines during World War II. ✛ *3 km (2 mi) southeast of town off A6* ✉ *32 Ardmore Rd., Beech Hill, Co. Derry BT47 3QP* ☎ *028/7134–9279* ▤ *028/7134–5366* ⊕ *www.beech-hill.com* ⇝ *28 rooms with bath, 5 suites* ⚹ *Restaurant, gym, massage, sauna, hot tub, tennis, bar, Internet, meeting rooms* ⊟ *AE, MC, V* ⦿ *BP, MAP.*

★ ¢ ▦ **The Merchant's House.** No. 16 Queen Street was originally a Victorian merchant's family town home built to Georgian proportions, then a rectory and bank, before Joan Pyne turned it into the city's grandest B&B. Garnet-color walls, elaborate plasterwork, and a fireplace make the parlor warm and welcoming. Previous guests have included the late Hurd Hatfield, star of the movie *The Picture of Dorian Gray.* Joan also owns a similar but smaller house three minutes' walk away, which serves as an annex. Many architecturally interesting homes occupy the neighborhood. ✉ *16 Queen St., West Bank, Co. Derry BT48 7EQ* ☎ *028/7126–4223* ▤ *028/7126–6913* ⊕ *www.thesaddlershouse.com* ⇝ *6 rooms without bath* ⊟ *MC, V* ⦿ *BP.*

Nightlife & the Arts

ART GALLERIES The **Context Gallery** (✉ *5–7 Artillery St., West Bank* ☎ 028/7137–3538) shows works by up-and-coming Irish and international artists. The **McGilloway Gallery** (✉ *6 Shipquay St., West Bank* ☎ 028/7136–6011) stocks a broad selection of representational modern Irish art. Owner Ken McGilloway serves wine on Friday evenings until 9 PM during selected exhibitions. The **Orchard Gallery** (✉ *Orchard St., West Bank* ☎ 028/7126–9675) is known across Europe for its political and conceptual art.

PUBS & CLUBS The **Gweedore Bar** (✉ 59–63 Waterloo St., West Bank ☎ 028/7126–3513) is a favorite for hip-hop and house music. Listen to traditional Irish music at **Peadar O'Donnell's** (✉ 63 Waterloo St., West Bank ☎ 028/7137–2318).

Sugar Nightclub (✉ 33 Shipquay St., West Bank ☎ 028/7126–6017) is the place for disco.

THEATER &
OPERA The **Playhouse** (✉ 5–7 Artillery St., West Bank ☎ 028/7126–8027) stages traditional and contemporary plays and also holds contemporary music concerts. The newest edition to the theater scene is the catch-all **Millennium Forum Theatre and Conference Centre** (✉ Newmarket St., West Bank ☎ 028/7126–4455 ⊕ www.millenniumforum.co.uk), where everything and anything—from comedians to musicians to plays—goes on stage. The **Verbal Arts Centre** (✉ Bishop St., Stable La. and Mall Wall, West Bank ☎ 028/7126–6946 ⊕ www.verbalartscentre.co.uk) celebrates literature through performances and classes. It re-creates the great old Irish tradition of fireside tales at regular storytelling events.

Shopping

Shopping in town is generally low-key and unpretentious, but there are some upscale gems of Irish craftsmanship. Stroll up Shipquay Street to find small arts and crafts stores and an indoor shopping center. **Bookworm** (✉ 18–20 Bishop St., West Bank ☎ 028/7128–2727) is the best bookshop in Ireland, according to writer Nuala O'Faoláin. **Occasions** (✉ 48 Spencer Rd., East Bank ☎ 028/7132–9595) sells Irish crafts and gifts.

Stop at the gift shop, **Pauline's Patch** (✉ 32 Shipquay St., West Bank ☎ 028/7127–9794), for knickknacks. Off Shipquay Street, the **Trip** (✉ 29 Ferryquay St., West Bank ☎ 028/7137–2382) is a teenage clothing shop that specializes in knitwear.

Thomas the Goldsmith (✉ 7 Pump St., West Bank ☎ 028/7137–4549) stocks exquisite work by international jewelry designers.

THE BORDER COUNTIES

During the worst of the Troubles, counties Tyrone, Fermanagh, Armagh, and Down, which border the Republic, were known as bandit country. But now you can enjoy a worry-free trip through the calm countryside and stop in at some very "Ulster" towns, distinct from the rest of Ireland. The area includes the great houses of Castle Coole and Florence Court; the ancient, ecclesiastical city of Armagh; and the wild Sperrin Mountains.

Omagh

55 km (34 mi) south of Derry on A5.

Omagh, the county town of Tyrone, lies close to the Sperrin Mountains, with the River Strule to the north. Playwright Brian Friel was born here. Sadly, it is more recently known as the scene of the worst atrocity of the Troubles, when an IRA bomb killed 29 people in August 1998. The town has two places of worship—a Church of Ireland church and a Catholic double-spire church. North of Omagh the country is pretty and rustic, with small farm villages.

❸❻ The excellent **Ulster-American Folk Park** re-creates a Tyrone village of two centuries ago, a log-built American settlement of the same period, and the docks and ships that the emigrants to America would have used. The centerpiece of the park is an old whitewashed cottage, now a museum, which is the ancestral home of Thomas Mellon (1855–1937), the U.S. millionaire banker and philanthropist. Another thatched cottage is a reconstruction of the boyhood home of Archbishop John Hughes, founder of New York's St. Patrick's Cathedral. Exhibitions trace the contribution of the Northern Irish people to American history. The park also has a crafts shop and café. Last admission is 1½ hours before closing. ⊠ *10 km (6 mi) north of town on A5,* ⊠ *Castletown, Omagh, Co. Tyrone* ☎ *028/8224–3292* ⊕ *www.folkpark.com* ⊡ *£4* ⊙ *Apr.–Sept., Mon.–Sat. 10:30–6, Sun. 11–6:30; Oct.–Mar., weekdays 10:30–5.*

③⑦ The **Ulster History Park** documents Irish history from the first known settlers to the 17th-century arrival of the Plantation settlers. The open-air displays include lath and rawhide huts, primitive farms and stockades, a round tower, and an oratory. Last admission is one hour before closing. ⊠ *11 km (7 mi) northeast of Omagh on B48, Gortin, Co. Tyrone* ☎ *028/8164–8188* ⊕ *www.omagh.gov.uk/historypark.htm* ⊡ *£4* ⊙ *Apr.–June and Sept., daily 10–5:30; July, Aug., and Oct.–Mar., weekdays 10–5.*

Take A5 north to **Strabane,** the birthplace of the surrealist novelist Brian O'Nolan, alias Flann O'Brien. James Wilson, grandfather of U.S. President Woodrow Wilson, emigrated from here. **Grays Printers Museum** (⊠ *49 Main St., Strabane* ☎ *028/7188–4094*) is in an 18th-century print shop with original 19th-century presses. John Dunlap (1746–1812), who apprenticed here before emigrating to Philadelphia, founded America's first daily newspaper, the *Philadelphia Packet,* in 1771 and was also the man who printed and distributed the American Declaration of Independence. ⊠ *31 km (19 mi) north of Omagh on A5.*

 en route Head east on A505 from Omagh into the pensive landscape of moist heath and peat bog. Left of A505, a few kilometers before Cookstown, Beaghmore is a strange Bronze Age ceremonial site preserved for millennia beneath a blanket of peat. It has seven stone circles and 12 cairns. A little beyond Wellbrook you come to Cookstown, an odd Plantation village with a broad main street. From here, head down the back lanes to Lough Neagh, at 396 square km the largest lake in the British Isles, noted for an abundance of eels. On its shore at Ardboe stands a remarkable 10th-century high cross more than 18 feet tall and richly carved with biblical scenes.

Wellbrook Beetling Mill is where locally made linen was first "beetled"—pounded with noisy, water-driven hammers to give it a smooth finish. The National Trust keeps the mill in working order. ⊠ *20 Wellbrook Rd., Cookstown, Co. Tyrone* ☎ *028/8674–8210* ⊕ *www.nationaltrust.org.uk* ⊡ *£3* ⊙ *Mar.–June and Sept., weekends noon–6; July and Aug., daily noon–6.*

Lower Lough Erne

③⑧ *38 km (23 mi) southwest of Omagh off A32.*

If you're driving in the vicinity of Lough Erne, don't rush—take your time and enjoy the panoramas of green wooded hills stretching down to the still waters.

Castle Archdale Country Park, on the northeast side of Lough Erne, has a lakeside marina and a museum containing a World War II exhibition on the Battle of the Atlantic. ⊕ *Down a narrow road about 6½ km (4 mi) from Kesh* ⊠ *Off B82, Co. Fermanagh* ☎ *028/6862–1588* ⊡ *Free* ⊙ *Daily 9–dusk.*

From Castle Archdale, a ferry (£3) runs from June through September, Tuesday through Sunday, taking passengers to see the carved Celtic figures on **White Island.** After you drive 13 km (8 mi) south from Castle Archdale Park to where the B82 joins the A32, a small sign shows the way to catch the little boat that goes to Devenish Island. The boat runs weekends-only April through September; you can also make a reservation with at least 24 hours' notice. On **Devenish Island** you can see Ireland's best example of a round tower, which stands 82 feet tall, and the extensive but ruined 12th-century monastery with a richly carved high cross.

Sports & the Outdoors

Inland cruising on the Erne waterway—777 square km (300 square mi) of lakes and rivers—is a major treat. Upper and Lower Lough Erne are enclosed by some of Ireland's finest scenery and are studded with more than 100 little islands. Out on the lakes and the River Erne, which links them, you have all the solitude you want, but you can find company at waterside hostelries. To hire a boat, contact **Erne Charter Boat Association** (✉ Belleek Charter Cruising, Erne Gateway Centre, Corry, Co. Fermanagh ☎ 028/6865–8027). Expect to pay at least £400 to hire a four-berth cruiser for two or three nights, available May to September.

Belleek

39 *3 km (2 mi) west of Lower Lough Erne on A47.*

World-famous Belleek Pottery is made in the old town of Belleek on the northwestern edge of Lower Lough Erne, at the border with northwest Ireland. Other porcelainware makers are a few kilometers across the border. On the riverbank stands the visitor center of **Belleek Pottery Ltd.**, producers of Parian china, a fine, eggshell thin, ivory porcelain shaped into dishes, figurines, vases, and baskets. There's a factory, showroom, exhibition, museum, and café. On tours of the factory you can get up close and talk to craftsman; there's hardly any noise coming from machinery in the workshops—everything here is made by hand in the same method used in 1857. The showroom is filled with beautiful but pricey gifts: a cup-and-saucer set costs about £16, and a bowl in a basket-weave style (very typical of Belleek) runs £69 and up. ☎ 028/6865–8501 ⊕ *www.belleek.ie* ✉ £4 ☉ *Apr.–June, Sept., and Oct., weekdays 9–5:30, Sat. 10–5:30, Sun. 2–6; July and Aug., weekdays 9–8, Sat. 10–6, Sun. 11–6; Nov.–Mar., weekdays 10–5:30.*

Enniskillen

40 *5 km (3 mi) south of Devenish Island, Lower Lough Erne, on A32.*

Enniskillen is the pleasant, smart-looking capital of County Fermanagh and the only place of any size in the county. The town center is, strikingly, on an island in the River Erne between Lower and Upper Lough Erne. The principal thoroughfares, Townhall and High Streets, are crowded with old-style pubs and rows of redbrick Georgian flats. The tall, dark spires of the 19th-century St. Michael's and St. MacArtin's cathedrals, both on Church Street, tower over the leafy town center.

The waterfront **Enniskillen Castle** is one of the best-preserved monuments in the North. Built by the Maguire clan in 1670, this stronghold houses the local history collection of the Fermanagh County Museum and the polished paraphernalia of the Royal Inniskilling Fusiliers Regimental Museum. A Heritage Centre also stands within the curtilage of the castle. ✉ *Castlebarracks, Co. Fermanagh* ☎ 028/6632–5000 ⊕ *www.enniskillencastle.co.uk* ✉ £2 ☉ *Jan.–Apr. and Oct.–late Dec., Mon. 2–5, Tues.–Fri. 10–5; May, June, and Sept., Mon. and Sat. 2–5, Tues.–Fri. 10–5; July and Aug., Mon. and weekends 2–5, Tues.–Fri. 10–5.*

At the Erne riverside, the 16th-century **Water Gate,** between two handsome turrets, protected the town from invading armies.

Beyond the West Bridge is **Portora Royal School,** established in 1608 by King James I. On the grounds are some ruins of Portora Castle. Among writers educated here are Samuel Beckett and Oscar Wilde, the pride of the school (until his trial for homosexuality).

Among the several relaxed and welcoming old pubs in Enniskillen's town center, the one with the most appeal is **Blake's of the Hollow** on the main street, a place hardly altered since it opened in 1887. Its name derives from the fact that the heart of the town lies in a slight hollow and the pub's landlord is named William Blake (don't ask, he's not related to the English poet, painter, and engraver). ⊠ *6 Church St., Co. Fermanagh* ☎ *028/6632–2143.*

off the
beaten
path

FLORENCE COURT – Legend has it you can hear the "song of the little people" here. It's an example of the north's grand Anglo-Irish mansions—and better, it's smack in an enchanting park. Built around 1730 for John Cole, father of the first earl of Enniskillen, the three-story Palladian Florence Court was damaged by fire in the 1950s. But thanks to a fine restoration, you can see abundant rococo plasterwork in the dining room, Venetian room, and the famous staircase—all are ascribed to Robert West, one of Dublin's most famous stuccadores (plaster workers). ⊠ *11 km (7 mi) south of Enniskillen on A4 and A32, Co. Fermanagh* ☎ *028/6634–8249* ⊕ *www.nationaltrust.org. uk* ⊠ *£4* ☉ *Grounds Oct.–Apr., daily 10–4; May–Sept., daily 10–8; mansion Mar.–May and Sept., weekends 12–6; June, weekdays 1–6, weekends 12–6; July and Aug., daily 12–6.*

Sports & the Outdoors

If you're over in the Enniskillen–Lough Erne area, guides at the **Ulster Lakeland Equestrian Park** can teach you to ride or take you on a pony trek through the 200 rolling acres of this Gothic-looking castle's grounds. Rates begin at £8 for 30 minutes. There are rooms to stay in, a bar, and a restaurant. ✛ *15 km (10 mi) north of Enniskillen on A32* ⊠ *Necarne Castle, Irvinestown, Co. Fermanagh* ☎ *028/6862–1919.*

Castle Coole

★ ㊶ *3 km (2 mi) east of Enniskillen on A4.*

In the 18th century and through most of the 19th, the Loughs of Erne and their environs were remote places—far from Ireland's bustling cities. But it was just this isolated green and watery countryside that attracted the Anglo-Irish gentry to build grand houses. This "uncommonly perfect" mansion (to quote the eminent architectural historian Desmond Guinness) is on its own landscaped oak woods and gardens at the end of a long tree-lined driveway. Although the Irish architect Richard Johnston made the original drawings in the 1790s, and was responsible for the foundation, the castle was, for all intents and purposes, the work of James Wyatt, commissioned by the first Earl of Belmore. One of the best-known architects of his time, Wyatt was based in London and did much work in Ireland, but he only visited the country once, and he never came here. Alexander Stewart was the resident builder-architect who oversaw much of the construction. The designer wasn't the only imported element; in fact, much of Castle Coole came from England, including the main facade, which is clad in Portland stone shipped from Dorset to Ballyshannon and then hauled over land by horse and cart. And what a facade it is—in perfect symmetry, white colonnaded wings extend from either side of the mansion's three-story, nine-bay center block, with a central portico and pediment. It is perhaps the apotheosis of the 18th century's reverence for the Greeks, and it bears a touch of Palladian sensibility.

Inside, the house is remarkably preserved; most of the lavish plasterwork and original furnishings are in place. On its completion in September 1798, the construction had cost £70,000 and the furnishings another £22,000, compared to the £6 million cost of a restoration in 1995–96, during which anything not in keeping with the original design was removed. The saloon is one of the finest rooms in the house, with a vast expanse of oak flooring, gilded Regency furniture, and gray scagliola pilasters with Corinthian capitals. The present earl of Belmore still lives on the estate and uses one wing of the house. ⊠ *Dublin Rd. (A4), Co. Fermanagh* ☎ *028/6632–2690* ⊕ *www.nationaltrust.org.uk* ✍ *Grounds free, mansion £4* ⊙ *Grounds Oct.–Apr., daily 10–4; May–Sept. daily 10–8; mansion Mar.–May and Sept., weekends 12–6; June, Wed.–Mon. 12–6; July–Aug., daily 12–6.*

Armagh

㊷ *74 km (42 mi) east of Castle Coole.*

The small but ancient ecclesiastical city of Armagh, despite the pleasing Georgian terraces around the elegant Mall east of the town center, can seem drab. Having suffered as a trouble spot in the sectarian conflict, though, it's now the scene of some spirited and sympathetic renovation. Here St. Patrick founded a church, and the town has remained a religious center to the present day; in fact, *two* Armagh cathedrals are dedicated to Ireland's patron saint. Despite the 1921 partition of Ireland into two parts, the seat of the Catholic archbishop of Ireland remains here, as does the seat of the archbishop of the Anglican Church of Ireland.

The **Astronomy Centre and Planetarium** is currently undergoing a major 1- to 3-year refurbishment. It contains models of spacecraft, video shows of the sky, and hands-on computer displays. The Earthorium explores the world from three levels—its interior, surface, and atmosphere. The outdoor 30-acre AstroPark has a model solar system. At press time, the 16-inch telescope as well as the Robinson Dome, also known as "the 10-inch dome" for the 1875 Grub telescope it houses, were both closed until further notice. ⊠ *College Hill, Co. Armagh* ☎ *028/3752–3689* ⊕ *www.armaghplanet.com* ✍ *AstroPark and Robinson Dome free; Earthorium £1; special shows and other exhibitions £3* ⊙ *Weekdays 2–4:45; closed first 2 wks of July.*

The pale limestone, Gothic **St. Patrick's Roman Catholic Cathedral,** the seat of a Roman Catholic Archdiocese, rises above a hill to dominate the north end of Armagh. Inside, the rather gloomy interior is enlivened by a magnificent organ whose potential is fully realized at services by Theodore Saunders. ⊠ *Hilltop, Co. Armagh* ☎ *028/3752–3142* ⊕ *www. armagharchdiocese.org.*

Near the town center, a squat, battlement tower identifies **St. Patrick's Anglican Cathedral,** in simple, early-19th-century, low-Gothic style. It stands on the site of much older churches and contains several relics of Armagh's long history, including sculpted, pre-Christian idols. Brian Boru, the great High King (king of all Ireland) who visited Armagh in 1004—and was received with great ceremony—is buried here. In 1014, at the Battle of

Clontarf, he drove the Vikings out of Ireland—but was killed after the battle was won. ⊠ *Abbey St., Co. Armagh* ⊕ *www.stpatricks-cathedral. org* ☜ *Free* ⊙ *Tours June–Aug., Mon.–Sat. 11:30 and 2:30.*

Past the 13th-century Franciscan friary ruins, in the stables of the former archbishop's demesne, the **Palace Stables Heritage Centre** presents a diorama of everyday life—upstairs and downstairs—in the 18th-century days of the extremely wealthy Baron Rokeby, Church of Ireland archbishop Richard Robinson. He commissioned local architect Francis Johnston, who had designed much of Georgian Dublin, to create a new Armagh out of the slums into which it had degenerated. The archbishop gave the city a clean water supply and a sewer system, then turned the city's racecourse into an elegant mall. He paved and lit the streets; financed improvements to the Bishop's Palace and the Protestant cathedral; and endowed the public library, the observatory, the Royal School, and the county infirmary. ⊠ *Palace Demesne, Friary Rd., Co. Armagh* ☎ *028/3752–9629* ☜ *£4* ⊙ *Apr.–Aug., Mon.–Sat. 10–5, Sun. 1–6; Sept.–Mar., Mon.–Sat. 10–5, Sun. 2–5.*

Just outside Armagh, **Navan Fort** is Ulster's Camelot—the region's ancient capital. Excavations date evidence of activity going back to 700 BC. The fort has strong associations with figures of Irish history and legend. Thousands of years ago it is said to have been the site of the palace of Queen Macha; subsequent legends call it the barracks of the legendary Ulster warrior Cuchulainn and his Red Branch Knights. Remains dating from 94 BC are particularly intriguing: a great conical structure, 120 feet in diameter, was formed from five concentric circles made of 275 wooden posts, with a 276th, about 12 yards high, situated in the center. In a ritual whose meaning is not known, it was filled with brushwood and set on fire. At press time the Navan Centre was closed for renovation, but the fort was freely accessible. ⊠ *3 km (2 mi) west of Armagh on A28, Co. Armagh* ☜ *Free.*

off the beaten path	**LINEN GREEN** – Looking for a bargain? Venture north to Linen Green, an outlet mall where you can purchase clothing, lingerie, shoes, gifts, and furniture. You can buy woven items from well-known producers—such as Paul Costelloe, Ulster Weavers, Foxford, and Anne Storey—at a discount. ⊠ *20 km (12 mi) north of Armagh off A29, Moygashel, Co. Armagh* ☎ *028/8775–3761* ⊕ *www. linengreen.com* ⊙ *Mon.–Sat. 10–5.*

The Mountains of Mourne

43 *52½ km (32½ mi) southeast of Armagh on A28, 51 km (32 mi) south of Belfast.*

In the words of the popular song by Percy French, the Mountains of Mourne "sweep down to the sea"—from 2,000-foot summits. East of the unprepossessing border town of Newry, this area was long considered ungovernable, its hardy inhabitants living from smuggling contraband into the numerous rocky coves on the seashore. Much of the Mourne range is still inaccessible except on foot. The countryside is gorgeous: high, windswept pasture and moorland threaded with bright streams, bound by a tracery of drystone walls, and dotted with sheep and whitewashed farmhouses snuggled in stands of sycamore. It's the perfect landscape for away-from-it-all walkers, cyclists, and serious climbers. Climbers should inform their hotel when and where they're going before setting off.

en route Driving from Armagh to the Mountains of Mourne, take a detour off A2 and follow B133, on the right, south of Markethill. This will lead you through a rustic, drumlin landscape of vivid green pastures. The appearance of villages changes as you return toward the River Bann; houses and farms begin to resemble those of Britain rather than those in the Republic.

The road to the **Silent Valley** reservoir park leads to mountain views and excellent photo-ops. ⊠ *6 km (4 mi) north of Kilkeel off B27, right turn, Co. Down* ☎ *028/9074–6581* 🖅 *Vehicles £3, pedestrians £2* ☉ *June–Aug., daily 10–6:30; Sept.–May, daily 10–4.*

Newcastle, a bracing Victorian cold-water bathing station, is the main center for visitors to the hills. Looming above Newcastle is **Slieve Donard,** its panoramic, 2,805-foot summit grandly claiming views into England, Wales, and Scotland "when it's clear enough"—in other words, rarely, say the pessimists. Covering 1,200 acres and entered through picturesque Gothic gateways, **Tollymore Forest Park** extends up the valley of the River Shimna. Many pretty stone bridges cross over the sparkling waters here. ⊠ *Tullybrannigan Rd., Newcastle, Co. Down* ☎ *028/4372–2428* ⊕ *www.forestserviceni.gov.uk* 🖅 *Vehicles £4, pedestrians £2* ☉ *Daily 10–dusk.*

A huge maze, grown to symbolize the convoluted path to peace, is the latest addition to **Castlewellan Forest Park,** which comprises 1,150 acres of forested hills running between the Mourne Mountains and Slieve Croob. With the maze, lake, secluded arbors, and arboretum, the park makes an excellent introduction to the area. ⊠ *Castlewellan, Co. Down* ☎ *028/4377–8664* ⊕ *www.forestserviceni.gov.uk* 🖅 *Vehicles £4, pedestrians £2* ☉ *Daily 10–dusk.*

Where to Stay

$$$$ 🏨 **Slieve Donard Hotel.** A lavish redbrick monument to Victoriana, this turreted hotel stands like a palace on green lawns at one end of Newcastle's 6½-km (4-mi) sandy beach. The traditional furnishings may make you feel as if you're stepping back to the town's turn-of-the-20th-century heyday as an elegant seaside resort (though the rooms have modern comforts). Ask for a room overlooking the water. At the entrance to the grounds, the Percy French gatehouse restaurant serves adequate seafood dishes; there's music Friday and Saturday night. The Royal County Down Golf Club is next door. The hotel has two exercise rooms. ⊠ *Downs Rd., Newcastle, Co. Down BT33 0AH* ☎ *028/4372–1066* 🖷 *028/4372–1166* ⊕ *www.hastingshotels.com* ⇔ *124 rooms with bath* ⚘ *2 restaurants, indoor pool, gym, beauty salon, hot tub, spa, steam room, bar, helipad* ▭ *AE, DC, MC, V* ❙❍❙ *BP, MAP.*

$$–$$$ 🏨 **Burrendale Hotel & Country Club.** Thanks to owner Sean Small, this low-slung modern building, shaded by clumps of beech, is one of the most relaxing establishments on the north's east coast. Staff members are cheery, and bedrooms are decorated in quiet tones. Chefs at the Cottage Kitchen and Vine restaurants are competent (the former is casual, the latter more formal) and clearly aim to please the locals, who like their plates overflowing. ⊠ *51 Castlewellan Rd., Newcastle, Co. Down BT33 0JY* ☎ *028/4372–2599* 🖷 *028/4372–2328* ⊕ *www.burrendale. com* ⇔ *69 rooms with bath* ⚘ *2 restaurants, indoor pool, gym, hot tub, sauna, steam room, 2 bars, Internet, meeting rooms* ▭ *AE, DC, MC, V* ❙❍❙ *BP, MAP.*

$$–$$$ 🏨 **Glassdrumman Lodge.** For those who wish to be pampered as well as immersed in the ancient Kingdom of Mourne, Graeme and Joan Hall's eclectically simple and stylish lodge is the place. The outside of the house is less than spectacular, but those at the busy estate grow their own crops, raise their own farm animals, churn their own butter, and bake their own bread. Rooms are decorated in bright colors and have large windows with glorious views. The Halls focus on service, providing overnight laundering and complimentary car washing. ⊠ *Mill Rd., Annalong, Co. Down BT34 4RH* ☎ *028/4376–8451* 🖷 *028/4376–7041* ➷ *10 rooms with bath, 2 suites* ⅃ *Restaurant, laundry service, business services, meeting rooms* ⊟ *AE, DC, MC, V* ⓞ *BP.*

Sports & the Outdoors

Northern Ireland Centre for Outdoor Activities (⊠ Bryansford, Newcastle, Co. Down ☎ 028/4372–2158) provides advice on mountain climbing and trails. The **Royal County Down** (⊠ Off A2, Newcastle, Co. Down ☎ 028/4372–3314 ⊕ www.royalcountydown.org) is considered by many golfers to be one of the finest courses in the world. Between April and October, a game on the Championship Links can run up to £105; the Annesley Links top at £28.

Downpatrick

❹❹ *21 km (18 mi) east of Newcastle on A2 and A25.*

Downpatrick once was called "Plain and Simple Down" but had its name changed by John de Courcy, a Norman knight who moved to the town in 1176. De Courcy set about promoting St. Patrick, the 5th-century Briton who was captured by the Irish and served as a slave in the Down area before he escaped to France, where he learned about Christianity and bravely returned to try to convert the local chiefs. Although it is not true that Patrick brought a new faith to Ireland—there was already a bishop of Ireland before Patrick got here—he must have been a better missionary than most because he did indeed win influential converts. The clan chief of the Down area gave him land at the village of Saul, near Downpatrick, to build a monastery.

Down Cathedral is one of the disputed burial places of St. Patrick. In the churchyard, a somber slab inscribed "Patric" is supposedly the saint's tomb, but no one knows where he is actually buried. It might be here, at Saul, or, some scholars argue, more likely at Armagh. The church, which lay ruined from 1538 to 1790 (it reopened in 1818), preserves parts of some of the earlier churches and monasteries that have stood on this site since the 6th century. Even before that time, the cathedral site had long been an important fortified settlement. Down takes its name from the Celtic word "dun," or fort. ⊠ *Hilltop, Co. Down* ⊕ *www. cathedraldown.anglican.org* ▦ *Free.*

For some hard facts concerning the patron saint of Ireland, visit the interactive exhibits of **St. Patrick Centre** next to the cathedral; It's housed, together with the Down Museum, inside a former 18th-century jail. ⊠ *The Mall, Co. Down* ☎ *028/4461–9000* ⊕ *www.saintpatrickcentre.com* ▦ *£5* ⊙ *Oct.–Mar., Mon.–Sat. 10–5; Apr., May, and Sept., Mon.–Sat. 9:30–5:30, Sun. 1–5:30; June–Aug., Mon.–Sat. 9:30–7, Sun. 10–6.*

Where to Stay & Eat

★ $ ╳▦ **Dufferin Arms Coaching Inn.** Stewart and Morris Crawford preside over this 1803 inn next to Killyleagh Castle. Rooms in the bright-red Georgian building are luxurious, with four-poster beds. Downstairs the original stables have been converted into the Kitchen Restaurant ($–$$), which sometimes hosts medieval feasts. It specializes in Irish cooking— poached salmon and roast duck in cherry sauce. One of the bars has snugs, another an open fire. Diversions such as pub quizzes and Cajun and jazz music keep things lively. ✛ *10 km (6 mi) north of Downpatrick*

✉ *31–33 High St., Killyleagh, Co. Down BT30 9QF* ☎ *028/4482–8229* 🖷 *028/4482–8755* 🌐 *www.dufferincoachinginn.co.uk* 🛏 *6 rooms with bath* ⚐ *Restaurant, 3 bars, Internet, meeting rooms* ▭ *AE, MC, V* ❙⊙❙ *BP.*

Portaferry

㊺ *13 km (8 mi) northeast of Downpatrick on A25.*

You have to cross Strangford Lough by ferry to reach Portaferry, another quiet fishing village with old fortifications to guard this once-strategic channel, which joins the lough to the sea. The **28-vehicle ferry** crosses between Strangford to Portaferry in 10 minutes or less, leaving every half hour. Departures from Strangford are on the half hour and hour, and from Portaferry on the three-quarter hour and the quarter hour. ✉ *Off A25, Strangford and Portaferry, Co. Down* 🖙 *Vehicles £5, pedestrians £1* ⊙ *Weekdays 7:30 AM–10:30 PM, Sat. 8 AM–11 PM, Sun. 9:30 AM–10:30 PM.*

☙ **Exploris,** Portaferry's unusual aquarium, has models of the underwater environment in Strangford Lough and examples of 70 species that call the lough their home. Some of these creatures may not be what you expect: seals, found regularly by the aquarium staff and rescued from death on nearby shores (and, in one mysterious episode, in the middle of an inland field), as well as several large, long-lived species of fish that still inhabit the lake. ✉ *Ropewalk, Castle St., Co. Down* ☎ *028/4272–8062* 🌐 *www.exploris.org.uk* 🖙 *£6* ⊙ *Apr.–Aug., weekdays 10–6, Sat. 11–6, Sun. 12–6; Sept.–Mar., weekdays 10–5, Sat. 11–5, Sun. 1–5.*

Where to Stay & Eat

★ **$$** ✕▥ **Portaferry Hotel.** A centuries-old whitewashed inn, Portaferry has well-kept, simply furnished double rooms. Book one of the sought-after rooms at the front, or head to the bar to watch the sun set across the water. The hotel is on the quayside overlooking the narrow channel that connects Strangford Lough to the sea. In the popular restaurant ($$) you can get huge breakfasts, country lunches, and evening meals such as grilled salmon, seabass with chive crème fraîche, and scallops with bacon and garlic. Dishes are served briskly to the many Belfast regulars who come for frill-and-fad-free seafood. ✉ *10 The Strand, Co. Down BT22 1PE* ☎ *028/4272–8231* 🖷 *028/4272–8999* 🌐 *www. portaferryhotel.com* 🛏 *14 rooms with bath* ⚐ *Restaurant, bar, meeting rooms* ▭ *AE, DC, MC, V* ❙⊙❙ *BP, MAP.*

Mount Stewart

㊻ *21 km (13 mi) north of Portaferry on A20.*

Mount Stewart is the grand 19th-century family home of the Marquesses of Londonderry, who also built one of London's most sumptuous residences on Park Lane. It was constructed in two stages where an earlier house stood: George Dance designed the west facade (1804–05), and William Vitruvius Morrison designed the neoclassic main part of the building (1845–49). The landscaped gardens are populated with surprising stone carvings of rare and extinct creatures. The house contains one of George Stubbs's most famous portraits, that of the celebrated racehorse Hambletonian, after he won one of the most prominent contests of the 18th century. The octagonal Temple of the Winds is a copy of a similar structure in Athens, and there's a remarkable bathhouse and pool at the end of the wooded peninsula just before the entrance to the grounds. ✉ *Portaferry Rd., Newtownards, Co. Down* ☎ *028/4278–8387* 🌐 *www.nationaltrust.org.uk* 🖙 *£5* ⊙ *Gardens Apr., daily 10–6;*

May–Sept., daily 10–8; Oct., daily 10–6; Nov.–Mar., daily 10–4; house by guided tour Mar. and Apr., weekends 12–6; May and June, Mon., Wed.–Fri. 1–6, weekends 12–6; July and Aug., daily 12–6; Sept., Wed.–Mon. 12–6; Oct., weekends 12–6.

Where to Eat

★ **$–$$** ✕ **Grace Neill's.** Reputed to be the oldest pub in Ireland, Grace Neill's served its first pint in 1611 and has hosted such luminaries as Peter the Great, Franz Liszt, and John Keats. Behind the original pub, a cubby under the stairs with bar stools, is a larger bar where you can try a simple peppered beef sandwich with a pint of Guinness. Saturday sees jazz, and on Sunday afternoons, there's music. ✣ *22 km (13 mi) from Mt. Stewart* ✉ *33 High St., Donaghadee, Co. Down BT21 0AH* ☎ *028/9188–4595* ☒ *028/9188–2553* ▭ *AE, MC, V* ◷ *Closed Mon.*

NORTHERN IRELAND A TO Z

To research prices, get advice from other travelers, and book travel arrangements, visit www.fodors.com.

AIR TRAVEL

Scheduled services from the United States and Canada are mostly routed through Dublin, Glasgow, London, or Manchester.

Frequent services to Belfast's two airports are scheduled throughout the day from London Heathrow, London Gatwick, and Luton (all of which have fast coordinated subway or rail connections to central London) and from 17 other U.K. airports. Flights take about one hour from London. Aer Arann flies twice daily from Dublin to Belfast on weekdays. British Airways flies to Belfast and Derry from Manchester, Glasgow, and Dublin. British Midland Airways flies from Belfast International and Belfast City to London Heathrow. British European Airways flies from Belfast City to Gatwick and London City Airport. EasyJet flies from Belfast International to Amsterdam, Bristol, Edinburgh, Glasgow, Liverpool, Luton, and Stansted.

🛈 Carriers **Aer Arann** ☎ 081/821-0210 or 0800/587-2324 ⊕ www.aerarann.ie. **Aer Lingus** ☎ 0845/084-4444 ⊕ www.aerlingus.com. **British Airways** ☎ 0845/773-3377 ⊕ www.britishairways.com. **British European Airways** ☎ 0870/567-6676 or 089/092-5532 ⊕ www.flybe.com. **British Midland Airways** ☎ 0870/607-0555 ⊕ www.flybmi. com. **EasyJet** ☎ 0870/600-0000 ⊕ www.easyjet.com.

AIRPORTS

Belfast International Airport at Aldergove is the north's principal air arrival point, 30½ km (19 mi) north of town. Belfast City Airport is the second airport, 6½ km (4 mi) east of the city. It receives flights from U.K. provincial airports, from London's Gatwick and Heathrow, and from Stanstead and Luton (both near London). City of Derry Airport is 8 km (5 mi) from Derry and receives flights from Dublin, Glasgow, and Manchester.

🛈 Airport Information **Belfast City Airport** ☎ 028/9093-9093 ⊕ www.belfastcityairport. com. **Belfast International Airport at Aldergove** ☎ 028/9448-4848 ⊕ www.bial.co. uk. **City of Derry Airport** ☎ 028/7181-0784 ⊕ www.cityofderryairport.com.

TRANSFERS Ulsterbus operates a bus every half hour (one-way £6, round-trip £9) between the Belfast International Airport and Belfast city center, as well as between Belfast City Airport and the city center (one-way £2). Contact Translink for information on all buses. From Belfast City Airport, you can also travel into Belfast by train from Sydenham Halt to Central Station or catch a taxi from the airport to your hotel. If you arrive at the City of Derry Airport, you may need to call a taxi to get to your destination.

📱 **Eglinton Taxis** ☎ 028/7181-1231. **Foyle Taxis** ☎ 028/7126-3905. **Translink** ☎ 028/9066-6630 ⊕ www.translink.co.uk.

BOAT & FERRY TRAVEL

Norse Merchant Ferries has 11-hour daytime or overnight car ferries that connect Belfast with the English west-coast port of Liverpool every day. P&O European Ferries has a one-hour sailing to Larne from Cairnryan, Scotland; infrequent trains take passengers on to Belfast. The *Sea-Cat* high-speed catamaran sails between Belfast and Troon in Scotland, between Belfast and Glasgow, and between the Isle of Man and Belfast. The *StenaLine HSS* fast catamaran sails between Belfast and Stranraer, Scotland. The catamaran sailing time is 1½ hours.

📱 Boat & Ferry Information **Norse Merchant Ferries** ✉ Victoria Terminal 2, West Bank Rd., Belfast ☎ 028/9077-9090 ⊕ www.norsemerchant.com. **P&O European Ferries** ☎ 0870/242-4777 ⊕ www.poirishsea.com. **SeaCat and Steam Packet Company Services** ☎ 0870/552-3523 ⊕ www.seacat.co.uk. **StenaLine HSS** ☎ 028/9074-7747 ⊕ www.stenaline.com.

BUS TRAVEL

Northern Ireland's main bus company, Ulsterbus, runs direct service between Dublin and Belfast. Queries about Ulsterbus service, or any other bus and rail transportation in Northern Ireland, can be answered by the national central reservation center, Translink. The Republic's Bus Éireann runs direct services to Belfast from Dublin. Buses arrive at and depart from Belfast's Europa Buscentre; the ride takes three hours. Buses to Belfast also run from London and from Birmingham, making the Stranraer ferry crossing.

You can take advantage of frequent and inexpensive Ulsterbus links between all Northern Ireland towns. The Europa Buscentre is just behind the Europa Hotel. The Laganside Buscentre is around the corner from the Albert Clock and about 1 km (½ mi) from Central Station. Within Belfast the city bus service is comprehensive. All routes start from Donegall Square, where there's a kiosk with timetables.

📱 Bus Depot **Europa Central Buscentre** ✉ Great Victoria St., Golden Mile, Belfast ☎ 028/9066-6630.

📱 Bus Lines **Bus Éireann** ☎ 01/836-6111 in Dublin ⊕ www.buseireann.ie. **Translink** ☎ 028/9066-6630 ⊕ www.translink.co.uk.

FARES If you want to tour the north by bus, contact Translink: a Freedom of Northern Ireland Ticket allows unlimited travel on bus or train (£12 per day, £30 for three days, and £45 per week). An Irish Rover bus ticket from Ulsterbus covers Ireland, north and south, and costs £42 for three days, £93 for eight, and £145 for fifteen. An Emerald Card (bus and rail) costs £124 for 8 days and £214 for 15 days.

CAR RENTAL

You can choose among several rental companies, but renting a car won't be cheap. A compact car costs £150–£250 per week (including taxes, insurance, and unlimited mileage). If you're planning to take a rental car across the border into the Republic, inform the company and check its insurance procedures. Main rental offices include Avis, Dan Dooley, Europcar, Ford, and Hertz. A £300 security deposit is required at the Ford agency in Derry, and a £500 to £750 security deposit is required by Hertz.

📱 Agencies **Avis** ✉ Belfast International Airport, Belfast ☎ 028/9442-2333 or 0870/606-0100 ✉ Belfast City Airport, Belfast ☎ 0870/606-0100 ✉ Great Victoria St.,

Belfast ☎ 028/9024-0404. **Dan Dooley** ✉ Belfast International Airport, Belfast ☎ 028/9445-2522 ⊕ www.dandooley.com. **Europcar** ✉ Belfast International Airport, Belfast ☎ 028/9442-3444 or 0800/068-0303 ✉ Belfast City Airport, Belfast ☎ 028/9045-0904 or 0800/068-0303 ⊕ www.europcar.ie. **Ford** ✉ Desmond Motors, City of Derry Airport, Derry ☎ 028/7181-2222. **Hertz** ✉ Belfast International Airport, Belfast ☎ 028/9442-2533 ✉ Belfast City Airport, Belfast ☎ 020/9073-2451.

CAR TRAVEL

Many roads from the Irish Republic into Northern Ireland were once closed for security reasons, but all are now reinstated, leaving you with a choice of legitimate crossing points. Army checkpoints at all approved frontier posts are rare, and few customs formalities are observed. The fast N1/A1 road connects Belfast to Dublin in 160 km (100 mi) with an average driving time of just over two hours.

In general, roads here are in much better shape and signposted more clearly than in the Irish Republic.

PARKING Belfast has many parking garages, as well as street meter-ticket parking. Before parking on the street, check the posted regulations: during rush hours many spots become no-parking.

TRAFFIC Bad rush-hour delays can occur on the West Link in Belfast joining M1 (heading south or west) and M2 (heading east or north). But on the whole, driving is quicker and easier in the north than in areas south of the border.

CONSULATES

🛈 Canada ✉ 35 The Hill, Groomsport Co. Down BT19 6JS ☎ 028/9127-2060.

🛈 New Zealand ✉ New Balance House, 118A Lisburn Rd., Glenavy, Co. Antrim BT29 4NY ☎ 028/9264-8098.

🛈 United States ✉ Queen's House, 14 Queen St., Golden Mile, Belfast BT1 6EQ ☎ 028/9032-8239.

EMERGENCIES

The general emergency number is 999. Belfast City Hospital is one of two main hospitals in Belfast with an emergency room; the Royal Victoria Hospital is the other. Altnagelvin Hospital in Derry has an emergency room.

🛈 **Altnagelvin Hospital** ✉ Glenshana Rd., Derry ☎ 028/7134-5171. **Ambulance, coast guard, fire, police** ☎ 999. **Belfast City Hospital** ✉ Lisburn Rd., Belfast, University Area ☎ 028/9032-9241. **Belfast's main police station** ✉ 6-10 N. Queen St., Belfast ☎ 028/9065-0222. **Royal Victoria Hospital** ✉ Grosvenor Rd., Belfast ☎ 028/9024-0503.

MONEY MATTERS

The north uses British currency. Euros are rarely accepted. You may sometimes be given bank notes, drawn on Ulster banks. Be sure not to get stuck with a lot of these when you leave, because they are accepted with reluctance, if at all, in the rest of the United Kingdom and will be difficult to change at banks back home.

Main banks are open weekdays 9:30–4:30, smaller branches weekdays 10:30–3:30. Changing money outside banking hours is possible at Thomas Cook branches. The branch at Belfast Airport is open daily 6:45 AM–8 PM; the branch at Donegall Place is open from Monday through Wednesday, Friday, and Saturday 9–5:30, Thursday 10–5:30. You can also change bills at Travelex Worldwide Money.

🛈 Currency Exchange **Thomas Cook** ✉ 11 Donegall Pl., Central District, Belfast ☎ 028/9088-3900 ⊕ www.thomascook.com. **Travelex Worldwide Money** ✉ Belfast International Airport, Belfast ☎ 028/9073-1703 ⊕ www.travelex.co.uk.

SPORTS & THE OUTDOORS

Bike rentals cost about £10 a day, £40 a week; local Tourist Information Offices can provide suggestions for good cycling routes. In Belfast rent from McConrey Cycles.

About 3 km (2 mi) south of center-city Belfast, the Lagan Valley Equestrian Centre runs horseback trail rides and lessons—both group and private. Group lessons and rides cost £10 hourly, private lessons are £15. The center is open weekdays 9 AM–10 PM, weekends 9–6.

🚲 Biking **McConvey Cycles** ✉ 183 Ormeau Rd., University Area, Belfast ☎ 028/9033-0322.

🚲 Horseback Riding **Lagan Valley Equestrian Centre** ✉ 170 Upper Malone Rd. Belfast ☎ 028/9061-4265.

TOURS

BIKE TOURS Irish Cycle Tours gives tours of Belfast (£12 singles, £20 couples) Saturday to Thursday at 6:30 PM and Sunday at 10 AM. They also organize 4- and 8-day tours of the Mournes, Glens of Antrim, and Causeway Coasts, and the Sperrin Mountains and Donegal.

🚲 Bike Touring **Irish Cycle Tours** ☎ 028/9064-2222 🌐 www.irishcycletours.com.

BIRD-WATCHING TOURS Murphy's Wildlife Tours leads tours in all seasons, though if you're an advanced birder, you may want to concentrate on wintering wildfowl and waders that have migrated all the way from North America to the shores of Loughs Foyle, Neagh, and Strangford. Northern Ireland Tourist Information Offices and the Royal Society for the Protection of Birds can provide birding information.

🦜 **Murphy's Wildlife Tours** ✉ Belvoir Park, 12 Belvoir Close, Belfast ☎ 028/9069-3232. **Royal Society for the Protection of Birds** ✉ Belvoir Park Forest, Belfast ☎ 028/9049-1547.

BOAT TOURS On the Lower Lough Erne, Erne Tours operates an approximately 2-hour-long trip (£7) aboard the *Kestrel*, a 63-seat water bus, which leaves Round O Pier at Enniskillen daily: May and June at 2:30, and July and August at 10:30, 2:15, and 4:15. Weekdays the boat stops for a half hour at Devenish Island. In September, tours leave Tuesday, Saturday, and Sunday at 2:30. Mid-May to mid-September it also has a Saturday evening dinner cruise departing at 6:30.

🚤 **Erne Tours** ✉ Round O Pier, Enniskillen ☎ 028/6632-2882; 028/6632-4822 for dinner cruise.

BUS TOURS Citybus in Belfast has three tours. The Belfast City Tour (£9) covers the Harland and Wolff shipyard, City Hall, Queen's University, the Ulster Museum, Botanic Gardens, and the Grand Opera House. Tours leave Castle Place, Monday and Friday at 11 AM and take 1½ hours. The Living History Tour (£5) passes Loyalist and Nationalist political wall murals, City Hall, the Odyssey complex, and the Waterfront Hall. It leaves Castle Place, Monday to Saturday at 2:30. The Titanic Tour (£5) is both a walking and bus tour that leaves Wednesday at 11 AM and Sundays at 2:30, also from Castle Place.

Ulsterbus operates half-day or full-day trips June through September from Belfast to the Glens of Antrim, the Giant's Causeway, the Fermanagh lakes, Lough Neagh, the Mountains of Mourne, and the Ards Peninsula. Ulsterbus has also teamed up with the Old Bushmills Distillery to run the Bushmills Bus: an open-top tour bus running from Coleraine (via Bushmills to observe whiskey making) to the Giant's Causeway and the coastal resorts. Contact Citybus and Ulsterbus through Translink.

MiniCoach operates day tours of Belfast (£8–£12), and to the Giant's Causeway, Bushmills Distillery, and Carrickfergus.

🚌 **MiniCoach** ✉ 22 Donegall Rd., Central District, Belfast ☎ 028/9032-4733 ⊕ www. minicoachni.co.uk. **Translink** ☎ 028/9066-6630 ⊕ www.translink.co.uk.

TAXI TOURS Belfast Cab Tours does 90-minute tours in a London-style black taxi of either Loyalist or Nationalist sights. The cost is £7 each for four or more, or £25 per taxi if three or less. Black Taxi Tours provide a similar itinerary at £8 per person for three or more; £20 per taxi for one or two people. The Loyalist tours leave from North Street or Bridge Street; the Nationalist tours pick you up at your hotel.

🚌 **Belfast Cab Tours** ☎ 078/1018-5884 ⊕ www.belfastcabtours.com. **Black Taxi Tours** ☎078/6012-7207 ⊕www.belfasttours.com. **Loyalist Tours** ☎028/9032-8775. **Nationalist Tours** ☎ 028/9059-0800.

WALKING TOURS Historical Pub Tours of Belfast walking tours of the city's pubs leave on Tuesday at 7 PM and Saturday at 4 PM. The cost is £5. In Derry, walking tours (£4) are organized through the city's Tourist Information Centre.

🚌 **Derry Tourist Information Centre** ✉ 44 Foyle St., West Bank ☎ 028/7126-7284 or 028/7137-7577 ⊕ www.derryvisitor.com. **Historical Pub Tours of Belfast** ☎ 028/ 9268-3665.

TRAIN TRAVEL

The Dublin–Belfast Express train, run jointly by Northern Ireland Railways and Iarnród Éireann, travels between the two cities in about two hours. Eight trains (check timetables, as some trains are much slower) run daily in both directions (three on Sunday) between Dublin and Belfast's misnamed Central Station—it's not in fact, that central. A free shuttle bus service from Belfast Central Station will drop you off at City Hall or Ulsterbus's city-center Europa Buscentre. You can change trains at Central Station for the city-center Great Victoria Street Station, which is adjacent both to the Europa Buscentre and the Europa Hotel.

Northern Ireland Railways runs only four rail routes from Belfast's Central Station: northwest to Derry via Coleraine and the Causeway Coast; east to Bangor along the shore of Belfast Lough; northeast to Larne (for the P&O European ferry to Scotland); and south to Dublin. There are frequent connections to Central Station from the city-center Great Victoria Street Station and from Botanic Station in the university area. A Freedom of Northern Ireland Ticket allows unlimited travel on trains (£12 per day, £30 for three days, and £45 per week). An Irish Rover train ticket provides five days of rail travel for £90.

🚌 **Train Lines Iarnród Éireann** ☎ 850/366222 for timetables ⊕ www.irishrail.ie. **Northern Ireland Railways** ✉ 28 Wellington Pl., Belfast ☎ Translink 028/9066-6630 ⊕ www.translink.co.uk.

🚌 **Train Stations Botanic Station** ✉ Botanic Ave., University Area, Belfast ☎ 028/ 9089-9411. **Central Station** ✉ E. Bridge St., Golden Mile, Belfast ☎ 028/9089-9411.

VISITOR INFORMATION

The Northern Ireland Tourist Board (NTIB) Information Centre in Belfast is the main tourist information center for the whole of the north. The office incorporates the plush, comprehensive Belfast Welcome Centre—the main tourist office for Belfast city, run by the Belfast Visitor and Convention Bureau. It's open October to May, Monday 9:30–5:30, Tuesday to Saturday 9–5:30; and June to September, Monday 9:30–5:30, Tuesday to Saturday 9–5:30, Sunday noon–5. Year-round Tourist Information Offices (TIOs) are listed below by town. June to August many more towns and villages open TIOs.

🚌 **NTIB Northern Ireland Tourist Board Information Centre** ✉ 47 Donegall Pl., Central District, Belfast BT1 5AU ☎ 028/9024-6609 ⊕ www.discovernorthernireland.com.

🏠 Regional Tourist Information **Armagh** ✉ 40 English St., Co. Armagh BT6 17BA ☎ 028/3752-1800. **Ballycastle** ✉ 7 Mary St., Co. Antrim BT54 6QH ☎ 028/2076-2024. **Bangor** ✉ Quay St., Co. Down BT20 5ED ☎ 028/9127-0069. **Carrickfergus** ✉ Heritage Plaza, Co. Antrim, BT38 7DG ☎ 028/9336-6455. **Coleraine** ✉ Railway Rd., Co. Derry BT52 IPE ☎ 028/7034-4723. **Derry** ✉ Foyle St., Co. Derry BT48 6AT ☎ 028/7126-7284 or 028/7137-7577. **Downpatrick** ✉ 53A Market St., Co. Down BT30 6L2 ☎ 028/4461-2233. **Enniskillen** ✉ Lakeland Visitor Centre, Shore Rd., Co. Fermanagh BT74 7EF ☎ 028/6632-3110. **Giant's Causeway** ✉ Visitor Centre, Co. Antrim BT57 8SU ☎ 028/2073-1855. **Killymaddy** ✉ Ballygally Rd., Co. Derry BT70 ITF ☎ 028/8776-7259. **Larne** ✉ Narrow Gauge Rd., Co. Antrim BT40 1XB ☎ 028/2826-0088. **Limavady** ✉ Connell St., Co. Derry BT49 OHA ☎ 028/7772-2226. **Lisburn** ✉ 53 Lisburn Sq., Co. Antrim BT28 IAG ☎ 028/9266-0038. **Newcastle** ✉ Central Promenade, Co. Down BT33 OAA ☎ 028/4372-2222. **Newtownards** ✉ Regent St., Co. Down BT23 4AD ☎ 028/9182-6846. **Newry** ✉ Town Hall, Bank Parade, Co. Armagh BT35 6HR ☎ 028/3026-8877.

IRISH GREENS

9

FODOR'S CHOICE

Ballybunion Golf Club, *Ballybunion*

The K Club, *Straffan*

Mount Juliet Golf Course, *Thomastown*

Portmarnock Golf Club, *Portmarnock*

Royal County Down, *Newcastle*

Royal Portrush, *Portrush*

By Muriel
Bolger
Updated by
Muriel Bolger
and Naomi
Coleman

ASK MOST GOLFERS WHERE TO FIND the golf vacation of a lifetime—breathtaking and diverse courses, lovely settings, history seeping into every shot—and they'll probably say Scotland. Unless, of course, they've been to Ireland. The nation's oldest course dates from 1881, and the Golfing Union of Ireland is the oldest such establishment in the world. It started in 1891: all of the nine original clubs were in Ulster. Now the number of affiliated golf clubs is 4,002, with over 200,000 members, and there are still more clubs that haven't joined.

Ireland is one of those remarkable places where mountains and sea often meet. Scraggly coastline and rolling hills of heather dominate the courses here, not the other way around. Real golfers are challenged, rather than deterred, by the vagaries of the elements—the wind, rain, and mist—and the lack of golf carts on courses in rougher terrain. Ireland's ever-beguiling (and often frustrating) courses attract players from around the globe. Tom Watson, winner of five British Opens, lists Ballybunion as his favorite course; so does the legendary writer Herbert Warren Wind—who, from an American viewpoint, put Irish golf on the map when he wrote, "To put it simply, Ballybunion revealed itself to be nothing less than the finest seaside course I have ever seen." And although Ballybunion is generally considered the Emerald Isle's prize jewel, many courses now rival it—from such classics as Portmarnock and Waterville to newer courses such as Mount Juliet, the K Club, and the Old Head of Kinsale.

There's more to Irish golf than its great links courses, though. Druids Glen features prominently alongside the likes of the K Club, Mount Juliet, Carlow, and Fota Island in every debate on the great inland golf courses. And although it's purely a matter of opinion—and, perhaps, your last score card—as to which is best, Druids Glen hosted the Irish Open Golf Championship for three years and was voted European Golf Course of the year at the prestigious Hertz International Travel Awards.

The wonderful, challenging natural terrain is one the things that makes Irish golf so remarkable. Of the estimated 150 top-quality links courses in the world, 39 of them are in Ireland. Most of their leading courses were designed by celebrated golf architects, such as Tom Morris, James Braid, Harry Colt, and Alister MacKenzie, who capitalized on spectacular landscapes. Others—such as Severiano Ballesteros, with his new course at Killenard in County Laois—will continue in their steps.

- **The Weather Factor.** You see all different kinds of weather in Ireland—driving winds, rain, sleet, and sunshine—and you may see it all in one round. There are no rain checks here. You play unless there's lightning, so pack your sweaters and rain gear, especially if you're planning your trip between fall and spring.

- **The Sunday Bag Factor.** If you don't have a golf bag that's light enough for you to carry for 18 holes, invest in one before your trip. Electric carts are generally available only at the leading venues, so you usually have the option of using a caddy or caddy car (pull cart) or of carrying your own bag. Many courses have caddies but don't guarantee their availability because they're not employed by the course directly—so you may have to tote your bag yourself. Be prepared with a carryall or a Sunday bag.

- **The Private Club Factor.** Unlike those in America, most private golf clubs in Ireland are happy to let visitors play their course and use their facilities. It's important to remember, however, that such clubs are there for their members first; guests come second. In some, you'll need a letter of introduction from your club in America to secure your playing privilege. There are often preferred days for visitors; call in advance to be sure that a club can make time for you.

- **The Northern Ireland Factor.** Some of the best and most beautiful courses are in Northern Ireland, where the leading venues—like Royal County Down and Royal Portrush—are less remote than in the republic. Remember that this part of the island is under British rule, so all currency is in U.K. pounds, although many clubs and business will accept the euro. There are no restrictions when traveling from one part of the country to the other.

North of Dublin

County Louth Golf Club. Like many other Irish courses, County Louth is better known as its hometown, Baltray, a village sandwiched by the Boyne Estuary to the west and the Irish Sea to the east. Long hitters will love the atypical layout, a par-73 that features five par-5s, but beware the well-protected, undulating greens. ⊠ *Baltray, Drogheda, Co. Louth* ☎ *041/982–2329* ⊕ *www.countylouthgolfclub.com* ⅃ *18 holes. Yardage: 6,783. Par 73. Practice area, caddies (reserve in advance), caddy carts, club rental, catering* ☒ *Fees: weekdays, €80; weekends, €110* ☉ *Visitors: Mon. and Wed.–Sun.*

Island Golf Club. Talk about exclusive—until 1960, the only way to reach this club was by boat. It was about as remote as you could get and still be only 24 km (15 mi) from Dublin. But things have changed. The Island has opened its doors to reveal a fine links course that rolls in and around sand hills, with small, challenging greens. ⊠ *Corballis, Donabate, Co. Dublin* ☎ *01/843–6205* ⊕ *www.theislandgolfclub.com* ⅃ *18 holes. Yardage: 6,800. Par 71. Practice area, caddies, caddy carts, catering* ☒ *Fees: €110* ☉ *Visitors: call ahead for times.*

Portmarnock Golf Club. Across an estuary from Ireland's easternmost point, Portmarnock is perhaps the most famous of Ireland's "Big Four" (Ballybunion, Royal County Down, and Royal Portrush are the others). Largely because of its proximity to Dublin, this links course has hosted numerous major championships. Known for its flat fairways and greens, it provides a fair test for any golfer who can keep it out of the heavy rough. ⊠ *Portmarnock, Co. Dublin* ☎ *01/846–2968* ⊕ *www.portmarnockgolfclub.com* ⅃ *27 holes. Yardage: 7,300, 3,449. Par 72, 37. Practice area, driving range, caddies (reserve in advance), caddy carts, catering* ☒ *Fees: weekdays, €165; weekends, €190* ☉ *Visitors: Mon., Tues., and Thurs.–Sun.*

Royal Dublin Golf Club. Links courses are usually in remote, even desolate areas, but this captivating one is only 6 km (4 mi) from the center of Dublin. On Bull Island, a bird sanctuary, Royal Dublin is Ireland's third-oldest club and is routed in the old tradition of seaside links— the front 9 goes out in a line (wind helping), and the back 9 comes back in a line (wind against). Don't expect to make a comeback on the way home if you've struggled going out. ⊠ *Dollymount, Dublin 3* ☎ *01/833–6346* ⊕ *www.theroyaldublingolfclub.com* ⅃ *18 holes. Yardage: 6,963. Par 72. Practice area, caddies, caddy carts, club rental, catering* ☒ *Fees: Mon., Tues., Thurs. €100; Fri. €115* ☉ *Visitors: Mon., Tues., Thurs., and Fri.*

St. Margaret's Golf and Country Club. Not all of the worthwhile golf in Ireland is played on century-old links courses. St. Margaret's, a parkland (inland) course, receives high praise from Ireland's golfing inner circle. If, after getting blown around on the seaside links, you long for a taste of Western golf, this is your haven. ⊠ *St. Margaret's, Co.*

Dublin ☏ *01/864–0400* ⊕ *www.stmargaretsgolf.com* 🏌 *18 holes. Yardage: 6,929. Par 73. Practice area, driving range, caddy carts, club rental, shoe rental, catering* 🖻 *Fees: weekdays €65; weekends €80* ⊗ *Visitors: daily.*

South of Dublin

Druids Glen Golf Club. Owner Hugo Flinn presented designers Pat Ruddy and Tom Craddock with the brief "Build me the finest parkland course in Ireland, whatever the cost." After an outlay of more than $16 million their handiwork was opened to the public. It has been chosen four times as the venue for the Murphy's Irish Open. Ruddy unashamedly admits to having copied some key elements of Augusta National—particularly the extensive use of water—in the layout. The course, about 40 km (25 mi) south of Dublin in County Wicklow, is beautiful, particularly around the glen from which its name derives. It's essentially an American-style target course incorporating some delightful changes in elevation, and its forbidding, par-3 17th has an island green, like the corresponding hole at TPC Sawgrass. ⊠ *Newtownmountkennedy, Co. Wicklow* ☏ *01/287–3600* ⊕ *www.druidsglen.ie* 🏌 *18 holes. Yardage: 7,026. Par 71. Practice area, caddies, caddy carts, buggies, catering* 🖻 *Fees: €140* ⊗ *Visitors: daily.*

FodorsChoice
★
The K Club. At just 27 km (17 mi) west of Dublin, this 18-hole, Arnold Palmer–designed parkland course offers a round of golf in lush, wooded surroundings bordered by the River Liffey. The generous fairways and immaculate greens are offset by formidable length, which makes it one of the most demanding courses in the Dublin vicinity. Additional stress is presented by negotiating the numerous doglegs, water obstacles, and sand bunkers. The on-site facilities are terrific and include a 95-room resort with three restaurants, a health club, tennis and squash courts, a pool, and massage and other spa treatments. ⊠ *Kildare Country Club, Straffan, Co. Kildare* ☏ *01/627–3333* ⊕ *www.kclub.ie* 🏌 *18 holes. Yardage: 6,244. Par 72. Practice area, driving range, caddies, caddy carts, club rental, shoe rental, catering* 🖻 *Fees: €185–€265* ⊗ *Visitors: daily.*

FodorsChoice
★
Mount Juliet Golf Course. The Jack Nicklaus–designed championship parkland course, 19 km (11 mi) from Kilkenny Town, includes practice greens, a driving range, and, for those who feel a little rusty, a David Leadbetter golf academy. The heavily forested course has 8 holes that play over water, including the three signature par-3s. The back 9 presents a series of difficult bunker shots. A sporting day out comes to a welcome end in the Hunter's Yard or Rose Garden lodge, which cater to both the thirsty and the hungry. Greens fees are above average, and although visitors are always welcome, a weekday round is better than a weekend one, as tees can be crowded with members flocking to the course at week's end. ⊠ *Mount Juliet Estate, Thomastown, Co. Kilkenny* ☏ *056/24455* 🏌 *18 holes. Yardage: 7,112. Par 72. Practice area, driving range, caddies, caddy carts, club rental, lessons, catering* 🖻 *Fees: weekdays, €135; weekends, €150* ⊗ *Visitors: daily.*

Tulfarris Golf Club. Less than a year after being officially opened, the $20 million development at Tulfarris was chosen as the venue for the Irish Senior Professional Open. Designed by Patrick Merrigan, it spans a 200-acre site beside Poulaphouca Lake, 50 km (31 mi) from Dublin, in an area of outstanding natural beauty. It's classic parkland and has the potential to be among the country's leading venues. ⊠ *Blessington, Co. Wicklow* ☏ *045/867–555* ⊕ *www.tulfarris.com* 🏌 *18 holes. Yardage: 7,116. Par 72. Practice area, caddies, caddy carts, catering* 🖻 *Fees: weekdays, €65; weekends, €80.*

Southwest

Adare Manor Golf Course. This parkland stretch is on the ancestral estate of the Earl of Dunraven. Its immediate success was virtually guaranteed by the international profile of its designer, Robert Trent Jones, Sr. The "grand old man" of golf-course architects seemed far more comfortable with the wooded terrain than he was when designing the second links at Ballybunion. As a result, he delivered a course with the potential to play host to events of the highest caliber. The front 9 is dominated by an artificial 14-acre lake with a $500,000 polyethylene base. It is in play at the 3rd, 5th, 6th, and 7th holes. The dominant hazards on the homeward journey are the River Mague and the majestic trees. Both combine to make the par-5 18th one of the most testing finishing holes imaginable. ⊠ *Adare, Co. Limerick* ☎ *061/395–044* ⊕ *www.adaremanor.com* 🏌 *18 holes. Yardage: 7,138. Par 72. Practice area, caddies, caddy carts, catering* ▨ *Fees: €115* ☉ *Visitors: daily.*

★ **Ballybunion Golf Club.** The Old Course was a virtual unknown until Herbert Warren Wind sang its praises in 1968, and today Ballybunion is universally regarded as one of golf's holiest grounds. On the shore of the Atlantic next to the southern entrance of the Shannon, it has the huge dunes of Lahinch without the blind shots. No pushover, but every hole is pleasurable. Watch out for "Mrs. Simpson," a double fairway bunker on the 1st hole, named after the wife of Tom Simpson, the architect who remodeled the course in 1937 (Tom Watson did the same in 1995). The Cashen Course, which opened in 1985, was designed by Robert Trent Jones, Sr. ⊠ *Sandhill Rd., Ballybunion, Co. Kerry* ☎ *068/27611* ⊕ *www.ballybuniongolfclub.ie* 🏌 *36 holes. Yardage: 6,593 (Old), 6,216 (New). Par 71, 72. Practice area, driving range, caddies, catering* ▨ *Fees: €110 (Old), €75 (Cashen), €135 (both on same day)* ☉ *Visitors: weekdays.*

Cork Golf Club. If you know golf-course architecture, you're familiar with the name Alister MacKenzie, who designed Cypress Point in California and Augusta National in Georgia. One of his few designs in Ireland is Cork, better known as Little Island. There's water on this parkland course, but it's not the temperamental ocean; instead, Little Island is in Cork Harbor, a gentle bay of the Irish Sea. The course is little known, but is one of the Emerald Isle's best. ⊠ *Little Island, Co. Cork* ☎ *021/435–3451* ⊕ *www.corkgolfclub.ie* 🏌 *18 holes. Yardage: 6,119. Par 72. Practice area, caddies, caddy carts, club rental, catering* ▨ *Fees: weekdays, €75; weekends, €85* ☉ *Visitors: daily.*

Dooks Golf Club. On the second tier of courses in Ireland's southwest, Dooks doesn't quite measure up to the world-class tracks. It is, nonetheless, a completely worthwhile day of golf if you're touring the area. Built in the old tradition of seaside links, it's shorter and a bit gentler, although the greens are small and tricky. It's an excellent way to take a breath. ⊠ *Dooks, Glenbeigh, Co. Kerry* ☎ *066/976–8205* ⊕ *www.dooks.com* 🏌 *18 holes. Yardage: 6,071. Par 70. Caddy carts, catering* ▨ *Fees: €40* ☉ *Visitors: weekdays.*

Heritage Golf and Country Club. The newest of Ireland's clubs is an 18-hole championship course, the only one in the country designed by Seve Ballesteros. The layout is suitably challenging, featuring four par-5s and splendid water obstacles in the form of five lakes. The result is a truly world-class parkland course. ⊠ *Killenard, Co. Loais* ☎ *0502/45040* 🏌 *18 holes. Yardage: 7,345. Par 70. Caddy carts, driving range, practice area, catering* ▨ *Fees: weekdays, €80; weekends, €100* ☉ *Visitors: daily.*

Killarney Golf and Fishing Club. Freshwater fishing is the sport here, for this club is among a stunning mixture of mountains, lakes, and forests.

There are three golf courses: the Killeen Course; Mahony's Point, set along the shores of Lough Leane; and the Lackabane, on the far side of the road from the main entrance. Killeen and Lackabane are longer; Mahony's places a premium on accuracy. Despite the abundance of seaside links, many well-traveled golfers name Killarney their favorite place to play in Ireland. ⊠ *Mahony's Point, Killarney, Co. Kerry* ☎ 064/31034 ⊕ *www.killarney-golf.com* ⅄ *54 holes. Yardage: 6,474 (Killeen), 6,164 (Mahony's), 6,410 (Lackabane). All 3 courses: par 72. Practice area, caddies, caddy carts, catering* ☒ *Fees: €75 on Killeen and Mahony's Point, €50 on Lackabane* ☺ *Visitors: Mon.–Sat.*

Old Head Golf Links. On a celebrated 215-acre County Cork peninsula, which juts out into the wild Atlantic nearly 300 feet below, you'll find an awe-inspiring spectacle that defies comparison. The only golfing stretches that could be likened to it are the 16th and 17th holes at Cypress Point and small, Pacific sections of Pebble Beach, from the 7th to the 10th and the long 18th. Even if your golf is moderate, expect your pulse to race at the stunning views and wildlife. ⊠ *Kinsale, Co. Cork* ☎ 021/477–8444 ⊕ *www.oldheadgolflinks.com* ⅄ *18 holes. Yardage: 7,215. Par 72. Practice area, caddies (reserve in advance), caddy carts, catering* ☒ *Fees: €250* ☺ *Visitors: daily.*

Tralee Golf Club. Tralee is what all modern-golf-course architects *wish* they could do in the States: find unspoiled, seaside links and route a course on it that's designed for the modern game. This is an Arnold Palmer–Ed Seay design that opened in 1984, and the location is fantastic—cliffs, craters, dunes, and the gale-blowing ocean. Don't let the flat front 9 lull you to sleep—the back 9 can be a ferocious wake-up call. ⊠ *West Barrow, Ardfert, Co. Kerry* ☎ 066/713–6379 ⊕ *www.traleegolfclub.com* ⅄ *18 holes. Yardage: 6,738. Par 71. Practice area, caddies, catering* ☒ *Fees: €130* ☺ *Visitors: Mon., Tues., and Thurs.–Sat.*

Waterville Golf Links. Here's what you should know about Waterville before you play: the 1st hole of this course is aptly named "Last Easy." At 7,184 yards from the tips, Waterville is the longest course in Ireland or Britain, and it's generally regarded as their toughest test. Now the good news—the scenery is so majestic you may not care that your score is approaching the yardage. Six holes run along the cliffs by the sea, surrounding the other 12, which have a tranquil, if not soft, feel to them. ⊠ *Waterville, Co. Kerry* ☎ 066/947–4545 ⅄ *18 holes. Yardage: 7,225. Par 72. Practice area, caddies, caddy carts, buggies, catering* ☒ *Fees: €125* ☺ *Visitors: daily.*

West

Carne Golf Links. This Eddie Hackett–designed links course takes advantage of its location, far to the west on the shores of Blacksod Bay. From the elevated tees and greens you can see a string of Atlantic islands: Inishkea, Inishglora, and Achill. ⊠ *Carn, Belmullet, Co. Mayo* ☎ 097/82292 ⊕ *www.carnegolflinks.com* ⅄ *18 holes. Yardage: 6,608. Par 72. Practice area, caddies, caddy carts, catering* ☒ *Fees: weekdays, €45; weekends, €50* ☺ *Visitors: daily.*

Connemara Golf Club. The local club for the town of Clifden, Connemara is a links course where you can get carried away not only by the golf but by the scenery. Immediately to the west you'll see the Atlantic and Ballyconneely Bay, and to the east you'll see the Twelve Bens Mountains. The course starts flat, then rises into the hills for the final, challenging 6 holes. ⊠ *Ballyconneely, Clifden, Co. Galway* ☎ 095/23502 ⅄ *27 holes. Yardage: 7,229. Par 72. Practice area, caddies, caddy carts, catering* ☒ *Fees: weekdays, €45; weekends, €50* ☺ *Visitors: daily.*

Lahinch Golf Club. The original course at Lahinch was designed by old Tom Morris, who, upon the unveiling in 1892, called it "as fine a natural course as it has ever been my good fortune to play over." That was when blind shots (those taken when you can't see your target) were in vogue; there are many here, as towering sand hills dominate every hole. Only a course with as much charm as this one could get away with that in today's modern game. The Castle Course is no less challenging, but conforms with today's standards. ⊠ *Lahinch, Co. Clare* ☎ *065/708–1003* ⊕ *www.lahinchgolf.com* ⅃ *36 holes. Yardage: 6,220 (Old Course), 5,594 (Castle Course). Par 71, 70. Practice area, caddies, caddy carts, catering* ⊠ *Fees: €110 (Old Course), €50 (Castle)* ⊙ *Visitors: daily.*

Westport Golf Club. Twice this inland course hosted the Irish Amateur Championship. It also lies in the shadows of religious history: rising 2,500 feet above Clew Bay, with its hundreds of islands, is Croagh Patrick, a mountain that legend connects with St. Patrick. The mountain is considered sacred, and it attracts multitudes of worshipers to its summit every year. All the prayers might pay off at the 15th, where your drive has to carry the ball over 200 yards of ocean. ⊠ *Westport, Co. Mayo* ☎ *098/28262* ⊕ *www.golfwestport.com* ⅃ *18 holes. Yardage: 6,667. Par 73. Practice area, caddies, caddy carts, catering* ⊠ *Fees: €40* ⊙ *Visitors: Sun.–Fri.*

Northwest

County Sligo Golf Club. More than a century old, the course at Sligo is one of the grand old venues of Ireland, having hosted most of the country's major championships. At 6,565 yards, this links course isn't particularly long; however, it still manages to have seven par-4s of 400 yards or more. Typical of Ireland's hidden jewels, Rosses Point clings to cliffs above the Atlantic. The third tee offers views of the ocean, the hills, and the unusual mountain Ben Bulben. ⊠ *Rosses Point, Co. Sligo* ☎ *071/77186* ⊕ *www.countysligogolfclub.com* ⅃ *27 holes. Yardage: 6,043. Par 71. Practice area, caddies (summer only), caddy carts, club rental, catering* ⊠ *Fees: weekdays, €60; weekends, €75* ⊙ *Visitors: Mon., Tues., Thurs., and Fri.*

Donegal Golf Club. On the shores of Donegal Bay and approached through a forest, the windswept links are shadowed by the Blue Stack Mountains, with the Atlantic as a backdrop. The greens are large, but the rough is deep and penal, and there's a constant battle against erosion by the sea. Legendary golf writer Peter Dobereiner called it "hauntingly beautiful," perhaps recalling his experience on the par-3 5th, fittingly called "The Valley of Tears." ⊠ *Murvagh, Laghey, Co. Donegal* ☎ *073/34054* ⊕ *www.donegalgolfclub.com* ⅃ *18 holes. Yardage: 7,153. Par 73. Practice area, caddies, caddy carts, catering* ⊠ *Fees: weekdays, €40; weekends, €55* ⊙ *Visitors: daily.*

Enniscrone Golf Club. Enniscrone's setting is a natural for good golf—it's a combination of flatlands, foothills, and the Atlantic. It's not overly long on the scorecard, but the persistent winds can add yards to almost every hole (an extra 18 holes are being added). It's among the small number of clubs in Ireland with electric carts ("buggies"). ⊠ *Enniscrone, Co. Sligo* ☎ *096/36297* ⅃ *27 holes. Yardage: 6,682. Par 73. Practice area, caddies (weekends and holidays), caddy carts, buggies, club rental* ⊠ *Fees: weekdays, €48; weekends, €60* ⊙ *Visitors: weekdays; weekends by appointment.*

Northern Ireland

Ballycastle Golf Club. Pleasure comes first here, with challenge as an afterthought. It's beautiful (5 holes wind around the remains of a 13th-century friary), short (less than 6,000 yards), and right next to Bushmills, the world's oldest distillery—at nearly 400 years. ✉ *2 Cushendall Rd., Ballycastle BT54 6QP, Co. Antrim* ☎ *048/2076–2536* ⛳ *18 holes. Yardage: 5,927. Par 71. Practice area, caddy cars, catering* 🍴 *Fees: weekdays, £20; weekends, £30* ☉ *Visitors: daily.*

Castlerock Golf Club. Where else in the world can you play a hole called "Leg o' Mutton"? It's a 200-yard par-3 with railway tracks to the right and a burn to the left—just one of several unusual holes at this course, which claims, year-round, to have the best greens in Ireland. The finish is spectacular: from the elevated 17th tee, where you can see the shores of Scotland, to the majestic 18th, which plays uphill to a plateau green. ✉ *65 Circular Rd., Castlerock, Co. Derry* ☎ *048/7084–8314* ⛳ *27 holes. Yardage: 6,499, 2,678. Par 73, 35. Practice area, caddies (reserve in advance), caddy cars, catering* 🍴 *Fees: weekdays, £35 weekends, £55* ☉ *Visitors: Mon.–Thurs.*

Malone Golf Club. Fisherfolk may find the 22-acre lake at the center of this parkland layout distracting because it's filled with trout. The golf, however, is just as well stocked—with large trees and well-manicured, undulating greens, this is one of the most challenging inland tests in Ireland. Bring your power game—there are only three par-5s, but they're all more than 520 yards. ✉ *240 Upper Malone Rd., Dunmurry, Belfast* ☎ *048/9061–2695* 🌐 *www.malonegolfclub.co.uk* ⛳ *27 holes. Yardage: 6,599, 3,138. Par 71, 36. Practice area, catering* 🍴 *Fees: weekdays, £40; weekends, £45* ☉ *Visitors: Mon., Thurs., and Fri.*

Portstewart Golf Club. Over a century old, Portstewart may scare you with its opening hole, generally regarded as the toughest starter in Ireland. Picture a 425-yard par-4 that descends from an elevated tee to a small green tucked between the dunes. The greens are known for uniformity and speed, and seven of the holes have been redesigned to toughen the course. Also, if you want a break from the grand scale of championship links, there's the Old Course 18 and the Riverside 9, 27 holes of downsize, executive-style golf. ✉ *117 Strand Rd., Portstewart, Co. Derry* ☎ *048/7083–2015* 🌐 *www.portstewartgc.co.uk* ⛳ *45 holes. Yardage: 6,779 (Championship), 4,730 (Old Course), 2,662 (Riverside). Par 72, 64, 32. Practice area, caddies, caddy cars, buggies, catering* 🍴 *Fees: weekdays, £60 (Championship), £10 (Old Course), £12 (Riverside); weekends, £80 (Championship), £14 (Old Course), £17 (Riverside)* ☉ *Visitors: Mon., Tues., and Fri.*

Fodor'sChoice ★ Royal County Down. Catch it on the right day at the right time and you may think you're on the moon; Royal County Down is a links course with a sea of craterlike bunkers and small dunes. And for better players, every day is the right one. Harry Vardon labeled it the toughest course on the Emerald Isle, and if you can't hit your driver long and straight, you might find it the toughest course in the world. ✉ *Golf Links Rd., Newcastle, Co. Down* ☎ *048/4372–2419* 🌐 *www.royalcountydown. org* ⛳ *36 holes. Yardage: 7,037 (Championship), 4,708 (Annesley). Par 71, 65. Practice area, caddies, caddy cars, catering* 🍴 *Fees: weekdays, £95 (Championship), £18 (Annesley); weekends, £105 (Championship), £28 (Annesley)* ☉ *Visitors: Sun.–Tues., Thurs., and Fri.*

Fodor'sChoice ★ Royal Portrush. The only club outside Scotland and England to have hosted a British Open, Portrush is perhaps the most understated of Ireland's "Big Four." The championship Dunluce course is named for the ruins of a nearby castle and is a sea of sand hills and curving fairways. The Valley course is a less-exposed, tamer track. Both are conspicuous for their lack of bunkers. The Dunluce, in a poll of Irish golf legends, was voted the best in Ireland. ⊠ *Dunluce Rd., Portrush, Co. Antrim* ☎ *048/ 7082–2311* ⊕ *www.royalportrushgolfclub.com* ⅃. *36 holes. Yardage: 6,845 (Dunluce), 6,304 (Valley). Par 72, 70. Practice area, caddies, caddy carts, buggies, catering* ⊠ *Fees: weekdays, £85 (Dunluce), £30 (Valley); weekends, £95 (Dunluce), £35 (Valley)* ⊙ *Visitors: weekdays.*

UNDERSTANDING
IRELAND

EIRE APPARENT

IF YOU FLY INTO IRELAND your descent will probably be shrouded by gray clouds. As your plane breaks through the mists, you'll see the land for which the famed Emerald Isle was named: a lovely patchwork of rolling green fields speckled with farmhouses, cows, and sheep. Shimmering lakes, meandering rivers, narrow roads, and stone walls add to the impression that rolled out before you is a luxurious welcome carpet, one knit of the legendary "forty shades of green." (If you're lucky you may even see a rainbow—something you'll see again and again if you travel the countryside.) This age-old view of misty Ireland may be exactly what you imagined. Travelers still arrive expecting Eire to be the land of leprechauns, shillelaghs, shamrocks, and mist. Be warned, however—the only known specimens of leprechauns or shillelaghs are those in souvenir shop windows; shamrock only blooms on St. Patrick's Day or around the borders of Irish linen handkerchiefs and table cloths; and the mists, in reality a soft, apologetic rain, can envelop the entire country, cities and towns included, in a matter of minutes.

The Celtic Tiger

The real Ireland is two-faced, like the Janus-stones and sheela-na-gigs of its pre-Christian past. It's a complex place where the mystic lyricism of Yeats, the hard Rabelaisian passions of Joyce, and the spare, aloof dissections of Beckett grew not only from a rich and ancient culture but also from 20th-century upheavals, few of which have been as dramatic as the transformation that has been changing Ireland for the past decade. Consider the evidence: more than 150 years since the apocalyptic Great Famine, Ireland's economy—christened the "Celtic Tiger"—is now one of the fastest-growing in the industrialized world. The country is the second-largest exporter of computer software in the world, after the United States. Unemployment, which was 11.5% in 1996, fell to 4.2% in 2003, and 41% of Ireland's populace are under the age of 25, with 24% under 15, making it one of Europe's youngest nation. Not to mention a 98% literacy rate. Most telling, however, is the fact that, in a profound demographic shift, Ireland's net emigration has reversed. There has been major *immigration* in each of the last three years—beginning in 2001 with 15,000—and that trend shows every sign of continuing. The young who once left for London and New York are now staying, more college graduates are returning than are leaving, and thousands of immigrants are arriving from other countries.

The foreign capital that has flowed into the country since it joined the Common Market (now the European Union) in 1973 has been crucial to this regeneration. But money alone doesn't guarantee culture, and Irish culture is thriving. Take just a few examples from literature: In 2003, after winning Ireland's fourth Nobel Prize for literature (in 1995), Seamus Heaney won the prominent Truman Capote Award for his *Selected Prose. Angela's Ashes* and *'Tis*, Frank McCourt's memoirs of his early life in Limerick, found millions of readers and won every major American literary prize. Dublin-born hell-raiser Colin Farrell, star of *Tigerland* and *Minority Report*, is Hollywood's new chosen one. You name it—food, music, movies, literature, poetry, theater, art, fashion—and something innovative is afoot among the Irish at home and abroad. If you've been moved by seeing *Riverdance* or *Lord of the Dance* or hearing the Corrs, Enya, Van Morrison, U2, The Irish Tenors, or any of the hundreds of other prominent Irish musicians, you're likely to feel the spirit that touched you more palpably in Ireland itself as you meet its people and witness them imagining—and creating—the Irish spirit anew.

A Friendly People

Liam Neeson, Kenneth Branagh, Daniel Day-Lewis, Neil Jordan, and the Cranberries are just a few of the envoys extraordinaire for Irish culture around the world. To find the real Ireland, however, you must venture down its back roads. You'll quickly discover that hospitality is counted among the greatest of Irish virtues, a legacy from Celtic times when anyone not offering the traveler food and drink was shamed. "You are welcome," people say in greeting the moment you cross the threshold of the smallest cottage, while total strangers will take you home for tea or supper and strike up conversations with ease and curiosity, entertaining you perhaps with an account of their second cousin's memorable fortnight in America (a fortnight's worth of stories if you have the time).

Time, in fact, is one of the greatest luxuries in Ireland—outside fast-forward Dublin, that is. On a fine day, along a lushly green country lane, you may pass a bicycle abandoned against a tree; looking for its owner, you'll find him reclining in the feathery hedgerows or on the long grass, contemplating fast-moving clouds like some philosopher-king. "Oh the dreaming, the dreaming, the heart-scalding bitter, maddening dreaming," cried the playwright George Bernard Shaw, but to knowing travelers in the stressed and industrialized world, this haven of dreamers is a pearl of great price, sought after and kept secret. Forget America's car culture—Ireland has cow culture. You'll find the moo-cows own the country lanes, staring haughtily and curiously at interloping motorists, lazily drooping timothy from their soft maws. In the end, with persuasion from harried livery, equipped with frisky dogs and long-knobbed sticks, they'll share the road—but on *their* schedule.

This may explain why Ireland is what some anthropologists call a "lived" culture, one that doesn't put all its stock in the outward monuments of achievement; where the most potent history is oral, where storytelling is an art, and where people will travel for miles for the *craic*, the Irish term for a rousing good time. Ireland teaches you patience, reminds you of the rhythms of the natural world, and convinces you, reassuringly, of the essential well-being of humanity.

This is nowhere more the case than in the local pub, the center of social life in Ireland. Even a small town such as Dingle in County Kerry (population 1,400) has 52 watering holes, open day and night. Protocol dictates that you enter and greet everyone, taking a seat alone until invited (as you inevitably are) to join a table. Then the ancient custom of rounds begins, with the newcomer offering to buy the first set of drinks, and when the pints are barely half full, another imbiber stands the round, and so on, in turn. Dark village pubs, with their scratched wooden counters, dusty tiled floors, and yeasty smell of Guinness, exude a feeling of sanctity and remove from worldly cares. Sit awhile and enjoy your stout, but know that wit also flows untapped. Nuance and irony are the law—anything less would be considered flat-footed. Irish expertise in double-think and the witty tongue makes for a universally acknowledged aptitude for legal affairs, a gift for words of imagination and persuasiveness that you can find in the crossroads shebeen (pub) much as in Dublin's Leinster House, where the Irish Dáil (legislature) sits.

DESPITE IRELAND'S ACCESSIBILITY, you may feel a sense of otherness, attributable not only to the evergreen climate and leisurely pace but also to the layering of history and legend dug deep under the country's rich grassy surface. Standing stones and court graves, mottes and dolmens, holy wells and mass stones, round towers and Celtic crosses, churches and country houses—the artifacts of Ireland's long, turbulent history are everywhere, from the barren limestone Burren in County Clare to the Neolithic tombs and defenses of Newgrange in County Meath. Even an island off the main island—Inishmore, one of the Aran Islands far out in Galway Bay—claims its antiquity: Dún Aengus, which is 5,000 years older than the pyramids of Giza. Given how tempestuous the fortunes of this small island have been, you may be surprised by just how many of these sights remain.

Iron Age Celts from Central Europe settled in Ireland in the 4th century BC and left a legacy of an agrarian society based on a democratic kingship, a justice system known as the Brehon laws, and an artisan caste proficient in working gold and precious metals. (The National Museum in Dublin displays heaps of this Bronze Age gold jewelry.) Christianity arrived in Ireland in 432 with St. Patrick (or, perhaps, as some scholars suggest, two and possibly more missionaries whose work became conflated into the Patrician story). By the 8th century, Ireland was in its golden age. In general, the country's proliferating religious orders received protection from God-fearing Irish kings. Monks labored for decades to produce the *Book of Kells* (now on display at Trinity College in Dublin). Having set up monasteries throughout Ireland, Irish monks set out for Europe, where they continued their expansion of monastic communities from England to northern Italy. According to the Thomas Cahill best-seller *How the Irish Saved Civilization*, the medieval Irish monks who copied and standardized the masterpieces of Virgil and Horace helped to prevent the loss of classical Latin, the written language of Rome, to the vernacular Romance tongues of Italy, Spain, and France.

About 800, Viking longboats scourged the island's coasts. The Norsemen established settlements in Wexford, Cork, and Dublin (and left the mark of bright-red hair behind on their Irish descendants). Brian Boru, last of the High Kings to sit at Tara, won the Battle of Clontarf, defeating a troop of Viking raiders off the coast near Dublin in 1014. But Boru's subsequent murder marked the end of an era. Without his leadership, the power of the Irish kings dissipated, and in 1155, English-born pope Adrian IV boldly granted dominion over Ireland to his fellow Englishman King Henry II. Fourteen years later Norman Strongbow arrived in Ireland, opening the door to more than 800 years of strife between the English and the Irish.

By 1609, the last of the Irish chieftains had lost their land to the British and sailed for exile, making way for the Plantation period. During this era 200,000 Scottish Lowlanders were "planted" on native Irish lands. Oliver Cromwell, "the Avenger," arrived with his troops in 1649, intent on making Ireland a Protestant country. He conducted a ruthless campaign of persecution against the already bitter Irish Catholics—a campaign that included beheading thousands of men, women, and children.

The Famine & Its Aftermath

Throughout the early 19th century, poverty was endemic and disease was a simple fact of life. Irish peasants worked for absentee British landlords and either paid exorbitant rents for land that had probably belonged to their parents or grandparents, or simply starved. The system was unjust, but somehow the bulk of Ireland survived the lean years prior to 1845. Within a year, however, potato blight ruined crops throughout the country. In a decade, the population was decimated, reduced from 8 to 6 million inhabitants. Starvation was largely to blame for the decline, but this period also marks the beginning of the large-scale emigration—to America, Canada, and Australia—that continued, albeit at a slower pace, until the mid-1990s. More than 70 million of Ireland's descendants are scattered abroad in the Irish diaspora—including 44 million in the United States.

The mid-19th century also saw the rise of an Irish Nationalist movement. Various groups, including the Fenians and the Irish Republican Brotherhood, agitated for equal rights for Catholics, land reform, the revival of Ireland's Gaelic heritage, and the expulsion of the British from Ireland. The movement exploded—literally—on Easter Sunday 1916, when Nationalists proclaimed a republic. England's merciless vengeance on the patriots—it shot 15 of the uprising's leaders—galvanized the country to the bitter War of Independence, which ended in 1920 with the partitioning of Ireland into 26 counties in the south, constituting the Irish Free State, and 6 in the north, making up the British-ruled province of Northern Ireland. The defining event of modern Irish history, the severing of north from south eventually spawned more than 30 years of Troubles in the north (though the roots of the Troubles date back 800 years) and cast a dark shadow over the country.

The Irish Ascendant

There's a place in an ancient Irish myth called Tír na nóg ("the land of the ever young"). Ancient though it may be, it's a surprisingly relevant image for Ireland today. The fact that the country is, for the first time in more than 150 years, holding on to many of its young, speaks volumes—it is the era of the ascendant Irish. While past history is still treasured, there's a growing feeling among the young to look ahead, not back. "Get over it!" was the headline cover about Boston's young Irish population and their increasing focus on the years ahead, not on time-stained sto-

ries ___ gro ___ f ___ b ___

ing ca ___ to take the n ___ republic's 3.6 m ___ capital. Dublin is the C ___ ing heart, a far cry from Joyce ___ dirty Dublin." Dozens of cranes ___ over new office buildings and hotels, and Georgian terrace houses are being brought back to glorious life. Visitors—especially weekenders from the Continent—fill Dublin's buzzing cafés, pubs, restaurants, and hotels and pour out onto busy Grafton Street and the narrow cobblestone alleys of Temple Bar. Outside Dublin, the country's quickening pulse is also palpable. New golf courses, housing developments, and blue-signed divided highways indicate the changes afoot.

Less conspicuously, in villages throughout the country, heritage and genealogical centers have sprung up to accommodate the surge of interest among the Irish diaspora for information about their roots. This relationship between the past and the present, between those who left and those who stayed, is an elemental part of Ireland's identity. Today, throughout the Irish diaspora, there's a boundless yearning for all that Ireland embodies: indomitable strength against all odds, the romance of an ancient place, the longing for a lost world, the solace and transcendent possibility of art. It's likely that a trip to Ireland will put you in touch with the sources—historical and concrete, ineffable and mysterious—of this longing.

YOU ORDER only a bally-
... , the Irish Evian, a visit to an
... pub (or two or three) is a
... ust. The Irish love to talk and
... no better forum than the pub for
... sort of activity. Conversation will
... m from the local GAA games (Gaelic
... thletic Association football and hurling
games) to the Ryder Cup, the state of the
nation, the latest political scandal—even
the price of the pint. Any one of life's
events provides reasons to head for the shebeen. It's not so much the drink that's the
attraction, but the craic.

The Pub

The Irish public house is an institution—
down to the spectacle, at some establishments, of patrons standing at closing time
to the playing of the national anthem.
Samuel Beckett would often repair to a
pub, believing a glass of Guinness stout was
the best way to ward off depression. Indeed, Dublin is for the stout of heart—the
city has one pub for every 450 of its
500,000 adults. There are actor's pubs,
sports pubs, even pubs for "less famous
literary types" (Grogan's on South William
Street). And any occasion—be it "ordi-
nations, liquidations, cremations," as one
storefront puts it—is the right occasion.

Although Irish pubs are being exported at
an unprecedented rate all around the
world, in Dublin it's a different story altogether. Surprisingly, modern, European-
style café-bars are fast replacing the
traditional drinking spots. The extraordinary prices being offered for the old
pubs by new entrepreneurs have proven
hard to resist for the longtime owners. In
the city center you'll now find high-con-
cept designer pubs with bright, arty facades
and a pervasive scent of affluence. To be
sure, in the City of 1,000 Pubs, there are
still plenty of good, old-fashioned watering holes. And if you do find yourself in
a new spot, surrounded by the trappings
of European chic, you'll still find the pint
of plain—the black stuff, the pint of Guinness—as well as good craic in the friendly,
irony-laced chatter that is quintessentially
Irish.

The Pint

There's a ritual involved with every pint
that's pulled. The barman first fills the
glass three-quarters of the way, lets the
brew settle, then tops the glass off and
brings it over to the bar. You should then
wait again until the top-up has settled, at
which point the brew turns a deep black.
The mark of a perfect pint? As you drink
the glass down, the brew will leave thin
rings to mark each mouthful.

It's said that of the 10 million pints of
Guinness produced daily, some 6 million
are consumed in Ireland alone—not bad
for a country whose population is 5 million. You'd start to believe infants must
be drinking it in their bottles. When it was
first concocted by Arthur Guinness in
1759, it wasn't known as a "stout" but
rather as a "porter," a name derived from
a heavy, cheaply made drink popular
with working-class porters in London.
Over the years, the name "stout" has
stuck, and it aptly describes the
formidable heartiness of this thick black
brew (and its effects on the human
physique). But if you ask for a "stout,"
you'll get the more bitter bottled brew,
so request "Guinness" if you want the
smoother draught. Every Dublin drinker
has heard the myths about exactly what
goes on at night in the Guinness brewery, and God only knows what they cast
into the huge turning vats to make the
stuff taste so damned good.

The Etiquette

Even if you're a veteran barfly who's been
booted out of gin mills and clip joints
from Bombay to Baton Rouge, there may
still be aspects of Irish public house be-
havior that will perplex you. Many of
these complexities come down to language
and the way the locals use it. The word
"whore," for instance, has many inter-
pretations—in much the same way that the
Eskimos have 84 different words for snow.
For starters, it's gender-flexible but is usually applied by males to other males. Go
figure. For instance, "He's a cute whore"
signifies that the so-described person is a
canny man to seal a business deal and is

a phrase much heard in towns where cattle are being bought and sold. Likewise, all the other swear words that are little heard in other developed countries find liberal employ here. The Irish have always been experts at giving a sentence even greater poetry with the inclusion of one of these epithets—they have no intention of giving offense, it's simply another tool used to spin a good yarn.

Clear a path for the locals when the clock strikes half-past 12 and the owner flicks the lights to signify last call. Were Marilyn Monroe herself to offer all her charms to a sheep farmer from the Connemara highlands, at 12:30 he'd put her on hold to get up there for that last pint. Maybe Ireland's pubs close too early, or maybe that final pint sipped amidst the publican's plaintive cry, "Have ye no homes to go to?," is the sweetest of them all.

The round system is also, unfortunately, a mystery to many visitors. If you get into conversation with them, locals will automatically include you in the round—it's good manners as far as they're concerned, and the strongest means they have of saying, "Good to meet you." Having accepted, woe betide you if the compliment isn't returned. The Irish won't care who you are or where you came from, but an absence of the required etiquette will not go down well.

Finally, a word to the ladies—know that most Irishmen under the age of 85 flirt outrageously with strangers. You'll hear poetry (Yeats continues to be the best aphrodisiac known on the island) and sonnets, and, as once witnessed at midnight on a rain-drenched street in Corofin, a man of 70 might just perform his version of a Fred Astaire tap dance for you. Don't be astonished. Consider it a form of theater, and take it as good fun. After all, that's what Irish women have been doing for generations.

BOOKS & MOVIES

Autobiography

Angela's Ashes (1996), Frank McCourt's enormously affecting memoir of growing up desperately poor in Limerick, has garnered every major American literary accolade, including the National Book Critics Circle Award. The memoir and its sequel, *'Tis* (1999), should definitely be on your must-read list. In *An Only Child* and *My Father's Son* (1969), Frank O'Connor, known primarily for his fiction and short stories, recounts his years as an Irish revolutionary and later as an intellectual in Dublin during the 1920s. Christy Brown's *My Left Foot* is the autobiographical account of a Dublin artist stricken with cerebral palsy. *On Another Man's Wound: A Personal History of Ireland's War of Independence* was republished in 2002. Originally published more than 60 years ago, it's the classic account of the years 1916–1921. Author Ernie O'Malley was only 23 years old when he joined the IRA and reported directly to Michael Collins. His memoirs are fascinating. Irish journalist Nuala O'Faolain's unsentimental and wrenching memoir, *Are You Somebody? The Accidental Memoir of a Dublin Woman* (1999), is an account of her Dublin childhood and the plight of Irish women. When published in Ireland, it stayed on the best-seller list for 20 weeks.

Travel Literature

Exploring Ireland, published by Fodor's, is a full-color guide packed with photographs; it is an excellent companion guide to this edition.

Peter Somerville-Large's *Dublin* is filled with anecdotes relating to the famed Irish city. *Georgian Dublin*, by Desmond Guinness, the founder of the Irish Georgian Society, explores the city's architecture, with photographs and plans of Dublin's most admirable buildings. An excellent work on the Aran Islands is Tim Robinson's award-winning *The Stones of Aran: Pilgrimage*. Robinson has also written a long introduction to the Penguin edition of J. M. Synge's 1907 classic, *The Aran Islands*. Tomas Ó Crohán's *The Islandman* provides a good background on Dingle and the Blasket Islands.

In *Round Ireland in Low Gear* (1988), famed British travel writer Eric Newby breezily pens the story of his bicycle journey with his wife around the wet Emerald Isle. Fifty years older but no less fresh is H. V. Morton's *In Search of Ireland* (1938). Rebecca Solnit uses Ireland as a sounding board for her meditations on travel in *A Book of Migrations: Some Passages in Ireland* (1997).

History & Current Affairs

For two intriguing studies of Irish culture and history, consult Constantine FitzGibbon's *The Irish in Ireland* and Sean O'Faolain's *The Irish: A Character Study*, which traces the history of Ireland from Celtic times. J. C. Beckett's *The Making of Modern Ireland*, a concise introduction to Irish history, covers the years between 1603 and 1923. *Modern Ireland*, by R. F. Foster, spans the years between 1600 and 1972. Thomas Cahill's *How the Irish Saved Civilization* is a lively look at how Irish scholars kept the written word and culture alive in the so-called Dark Ages. Cecil Woodham-Smith's *The Great Hunger* (1962) details the history of the Irish potato famine of the 1840s. For an acclaimed history of Irish nationalism, try Robert Kee's *The Green Flag*. Peter De Rosa's *Rebels: The Irish Rising of 1916* is a popular, novelistic take on the defining event of modern Irish history. John Ardagh's *Ireland and the Irish: Portrait of a Changing Society* (1997) is one of the best sociological and economic analyses of modern Ireland. *"We Wrecked the Place": Contemplating an End to the Northern Irish Troubles* (1996) by Belfast-based journalist Jonathan Stevenson gives an insightful take on the subject. John Conroy's *Belfast Diary: War as a Way of Life* (1995) was reissued with a new afterword on the cease-fire. *The Lost Lives* (1999) is a heart-wrenching collection of biographies about many who have died during the Troubles. Paddy Logue's *The Border: Personal Reflections from Ireland—North and South* (2000) presents impressions of activists, artists, athletes, and community workers on national ramifications and the significance of the border between north and south on their lives. Marie de Paor's book *Patrick: The*

Pilgrim Apostle of Ireland (2002) is a very modern interpretation of St. Patrick and his role as the patron saint of Ireland. Senan Molony's book *The Irish Aboard the Titanic* (2002) explores class structure and ethnic racism amongst the Irish and against them from the building of the *Titanic* in Belfast to the moment the last Irish citizens boarded the lifeboats that fateful day. Every aspect of Irish involvement with the vessel is investigated here.

Literature

Ulysses (1922) is the linguistically innovative masterpiece by James Joyce, one of the titans of 20th-century literature. Emulating the structure of *The Odyssey,* and using an unprecedented stream-of-consciousness technique, Joyce follows Leopold and Molly Bloom and Stephen Daedalus through the course of a single day—June 16, 1904—around Dublin. More accessible introductions to Joyce's writing include *A Portrait of the Artist as a Young Man* (1916) and *Dubliners* (1914), a collection of short stories. (Its most accomplished story, "The Dead," was made into a movie starring Angelica Huston in 1988.) Joyce aficionados may want to tackle his final, gigantic work, *Finnegan's Wake* (1939), which takes the linguistic experimentation of *Ulysses* to an almost incomprehensible level. Arguably the greatest literary challenge of the 20th century, its pages include word plays and phonetic metaphors in more than 100 languages. To prepare you for reading Joyce, you might seek out audio recordings in which he reads in his inimitable lilting tenor voice.

Samuel Beckett fills his story collection *More Pricks than Kicks* (1934) with Dublin characters; if you enjoy literary gamesmanship, you may also want to try Beckett's 1950s trilogy—*Molloy, Malone Dies,* and *The Unnameable.*

If you're drawn to tales of unrequited love, turn to Elizabeth Bowen's stories and her novel *The Last September* (1929), set in Ireland during the Irish Civil War. If you prefer reading more magical novels, take a look at James Stephens's *A Crock of Gold* (1912), a charming and wise fairy tale written for adults, and Flann O'Brien's *At Swim-Two-Birds* (1939), a surrealistic tale full of Irish folklore.

One of Ireland's foremost fiction writers working today, Edna O'Brien began her career with the comic novel *The Country Girls* (1960) and continues today with *House of Splendid Isolation* (1994) and *Down by the River* (1997). She is a superb short-story writer; her collection *A Fanatic Heart* (1985) is one of her best.

Thomas Flanagan's *The Year of the French* (1979) is a historical novel about the people of County Mayo, who revolted in 1798 with the help of French revolutionaries. *A Nest of Simple Folk,* by Sean O'Faolain, follows three generations of an Irish family between 1854 and 1916. Leon Uris's *Trinity* covers the years 1840–1916, as seen through the eyes of British, Irish Catholic, and Ulster Protestant families. In *No Country for Young Men,* Julia O'Faolain writes of two Irish families struggling to overcome the effects of the Irish Civil War. In John McGahern's prizewinning novel *Amongst Women,* modern-day Ireland attempts to reconcile itself to the upheavals of the early years of this century. For a more contemporary look at life in urban Ireland, try the phenomenally successful Roddy Doyle. All three works from his "Barrytown Trilogy"—*The Snapper, The Commitments,* and *The Van*—have been made into films; *Paddy Clarke Ha Ha Ha* has followed suit as another success. John Banville's *The Book of Evidence* and *Ghosts* deal with contemporary Ireland's ruling classes with great insight and seriousness.

Movies

A plethora of movies has been made in or about Ireland, and the number of Irish characters on screen is legion (the most numerous being priests, drunks, New York cops, and Old Mother Riley). *Juno and the Paycock* (known in the United States as *The Shame of Mary Boyle*) and *The Plough and the Stars* (1936), about the months leading up to the Easter Uprising, are early screen adaptations of Sean O'Casey's theatrical masterpieces. John Ford's superb *The Informer* (1935) is a full-blooded and highly stylized tale of an IRA leader's betrayal during the struggle for independence by a simpleminded hanger-on who wants to emigrate to the United States. Ford's boisterous comedy *The Quiet Man* (1952) is an Irish-village version of *The Taming of the Shrew,* with John Wayne playing a boxer who returns to his ancestor's village in the west of Ireland to claim local beauty Maureen O'Hara, and Barry Fitzgerald. David Lean's epic *Ryan's Daughter* (1970) is a four-hour pastoral melodrama of a village schoolmaster's wife falling for a British officer in the troubled Ireland of 1916; the film was a critical and commercial disaster for Lean, who didn't make another film for 14 years.

Daniel Day-Lewis and Brenda Fricker give Oscar-winning performances in Jim Sheridan's *My Left Foot* (1989), a biography of Christy Brown, the Irish writer and painter crippled from birth by cerebral palsy. *The Field* (1990), Ireland's first Oscar-nominated film, is a marker of just how far things have progressed in the Irish film business. Richard Harris and John Hurt played out the drama by John B. Keane around the village of Leenane in Connemara. Alan Parker's *The Commitments* (1991), from Roddy Doyle's best-seller, humorously recounts the efforts of a group of young, working-class northside Dubliners trying to make it as a soul band. *Into the West* (1992) has been embraced by movie-goers worldwide because of its fairy-tale plot. It follows two Irish traveler boys (gypsies) from Dublin projects to the west of Ireland in search of their beautiful horse Tír na nóg ("Land of Eternal Youth"), which was confiscated by an evil police officer. The film stars Gabriel Byrne.

In *A Man of No Importance* (1994), Albert Finney plays a sexually repressed bus conductor whose passion for poetry leads him to stage Wilde's *Salomé*. John Sayles hooked up with acclaimed cinematographer Haskell Wexler to make *The Secret of Roan Inish* (1996), a magical realist fable about a Selkie—a creature from Celtic folklore who is a seal in the water and a woman on land—and the fisherman's family whose lives she changes. *Waking Ned Devine* (1998) is a sidesplitting comedy about a small Irish village thrown into turmoil by a dead man's lottery winnings. *The Butcher Boy* is a dark comedy about a young boy who goes insane as his family splits up. Interestingly, it stars musician Sinead O'Connor as the Virgin Mary. *This is the Sea,* a contemporary love story set in Northern Ireland after the 1994 cease-fire, was directed by

Mary McGuickian. The film version of Frank McCourt's memoir *Angela's Ashes* (1999) has left an impact on some as strong as the book itself. Gerry Stembridge's *About Adam* (2002), starring Kate Hudson, is one of the first movies to take a close, humorous look at modern, urban Irish life.

Some of the best movies made in Ireland deal with the Troubles that have afflicted Northern Ireland. *Four Days in July* (1984), directed by Mike Leigh in classic cinema verité style, is a poignant and compelling portrayal of the sectarian divide in working-class Belfast. Helen Mirren stars as the widow of an executed Protestant policeman in *Cal* (1984), based on Bernard MacLaverty's masterful novel about the Troubles. Daniel Day-Lewis was nominated for an Academy Award for his portrayal of Gerry Conlon, the wrongfully imprisoned Irish youth, in Jim Sheridan's *In the Name of the Father* (1993). Neil Jordan's *Michael Collins* (1996), with Liam Neeson and Julia Roberts, depicts the turbulent life of the heroic commander in chief of the Irish Republican Army from the Easter Uprising in 1916, when Collins was 25, until his assassination in West Cork six years later. Day-Lewis appears once again in *The Boxer* (1997), the story of an ex-boxer and former IRA man who tries to put his life back together in contemporary, sectarian Belfast.

Poetry

The poems of William Butler Yeats, Ireland's most celebrated poet, often describe the Irish landscape, including the Sligo and Coole countryside. Go for the formidably large but marvelous *Collected Poems: 1909 to 1962* (1996 2nd rev. ed.), edited by Richard J. Finneran. A favorite poet among the Irish is Patrick Kavanagh, who wrote soberly—and exceptionally—about landscape, poverty, and rural farming life. His best-known and most controversial (long) poem, *The Great Hunger* (1942), caused some uproar when it was published, and won him a bit of notoriety. But now, finally, Kavanagh is seen as a tremendously important Irish poet. Born in Belfast in 1907 (his parents were from Connemara), Louis MacNeice is something of an anomaly. He is considered to be an Irish poet, though he spent much of his life in England. He worked as a writer and producer for BBC, for which he wrote some of his radio dramas. But MacNeice was mainly a poet, known for his long and marvelous poem *Autumn Journal*, which beautifully explores politics, history, and personal drama in alternating rhyming couplets. His poems are intimate, clever, and lyrical. MacNeice died in 1963.

For contemporary poetry, read Derek Mahon—the *Selected Poems* (1992) is a good start. Northern Ireland serves as the setting for many of Nobel Laureate Seamus Heaney's poems. *Opened Ground: Selected Poems 1966–1996* (1999) is a good overview of his lyrical, highly crafted style—like Yeats, Heaney is an intensely aural poet, a master of rhythm and sound. (He is also, thanks to his farmer father, obsessed with soil.) Diehard fans prefer his earlier, more rustic work. Take a look at his debut collection, *Death of a Naturalist* (1995 reprint), *The Haw Lantern* (1989), or *The Spirit Level* (1996) if you want options for smaller—and in some ways more worthwhile—collections. Paul Muldoon, from Belfast, is another major Irish poet. His *Selected Poems: 1968–1986* (1987) and *The Annals of Chile* (1994) are both good selections. Eavan Boland is widely regarded as among the top tier of Irish poets and the finest woman writing poetry in Ireland today. Two of her popular books are *Object Lessons: The Life of the Woman and the Poet in Our Time* (1995) and *An Origin Like Water: Collected Poems 1957–1987* (1996). One of Ireland's leading poets, Brendan Kennelly, selects and introduces his choices of the best Irish poetry in his book *Between Innocence and Peace: Favorite Poems of Ireland* (2002). He chooses from the works of Seamus Heaney, Eavan Boland, Michael Longley, Paul Durcan, and the grand masters—Yeats, Synge, and MacNeice.

Theater

Ireland's playwrights are as distinguished as its novelists and short-story writers. Samuel Beckett, who moved from Ireland to Paris and began writing in French, is the author of the comic modernist masterpiece *Waiting for Godot* (1952), among many other plays. Oscar Wilde's finest plays, *The Importance of Being Earnest* and *An Ideal Husband* (both 1895), were playing to packed audiences in London when he was charged by his lover's father as a sodomite, setting in motion the trials that led to his downfall. Among the many plays of George Bernard Shaw, who grew up in Dublin, are *Arms and the Man* (1894), *Major Barbara* (1905), *Pygmalion* (1913), and *Saint Joan* (1923).

The history of Irish theater includes a number of controversial plays, such as J. M. Synge's *The Playboy of the Western World*, which was considered morally outrageous at the time of its opening in 1907 ("Playboy riots" took place in Dublin when the play was produced at the Abbey Theatre) but is appreciated today for its poetic language. Sean O'Casey wrote passionately about social injustice and working-class characters around the time of the Irish Civil War in such plays as *The Plough and the Stars* (1926) and *Juno and the Paycock* (1924). *The Quare Fellow* (1956), by Brendan Behan, challenged accepted mores in the 1950s and at the time could only be produced in London. Behan is also well known for his play *The Hostage* (1958) and for *Borstal Boy* (1958), his memoirs. Hugh Leonard (*Da* [1974] and *A Life* [1980]) and Brian Friel (*Philadelphia, Here I Come!* [1964], *The Faith Healer* [1979], and *Dancing at Lughnasa* [1990]), write works that often illuminate Irish small-town life. A group of young, brash Irish playwrights have taken London and Broadway by storm. Martin McDonagh's *The Beauty Queen of Linnane* (1996) and Conor McPherson's *The Weir* (1997) have won awards on both sides of the Atlantic.

CHRONOLOGY

ca. 3500 BC Neolithic (new Stone Age) settlers (origins uncertain) bring agriculture, pottery, and weaving. They also build massive megaliths—stone monuments with counterparts in England (Stonehenge), Brittany (Carnac), and elsewhere in Europe.

ca. 700 BC Celtic tribes begin to arrive via Britain and France; they divide Ireland into "fifths," or provinces, including Ulster, Leinster, Connaught, Meath, and Munster.

ca. AD 100 Ireland becomes the center of Celtic culture and trade without being settled by the Romans.

432 Traditional date for the arrival of St. Patrick and Christianity; in fact, Irish conversion to Christianity began at least a century earlier.

ca. 500–800 Golden age of Irish monasticism; as many as 3,000 study at Clonard (Meath). Irish missionaries carry the faith to barbarian Europe; art (exemplified by the *Book of Kells,* ca. 8th or 9th century) and Gaelic poetry flourish.

795 First Scandinavian Viking invasion; raids continue for the next 200 years. Viking towns founded include Dublin, Waterford, Wexford, Cork, and Limerick.

1014 Vikings decisively defeated at Clontarf by Irish troops under King Brian Boru of Munster. His murder cuts short hopes of a unified Ireland.

1172 Pope Alexander III confirms Henry II, king of England, as feudal lord of Ireland. Over the next two centuries, Anglo-Norman nobles establish estates, intermarry with the native population, and act in a manner similar to that of the neighboring Celtic chieftains. Actual control by the English crown is confined to a small area known as "the land of peace," or "the Pale," around Dublin.

1366 Statutes of Kilkenny attempt belatedly to enforce ethnic divisions by prohibiting the expression of Irish language and culture and intermarriage between the Irish and English, but Gaelic culture prevails and the Pale continues to contract. Constant warfare among the great landowners keeps Ireland poor, divided, and isolated from the rest of Europe.

1534–40 Henry VIII's break with the Catholic Church leads to insurrection in Ireland, led by Garret Mor's grandson Lord Offaly ("Silken Thomas"). He is executed with five of his brothers.

1558–1603 Reign of Queen Elizabeth I; her fear of Irish intrigue with Catholic enemies of England leads to expansion of English power.

1580–88 Edmund Spenser, an administrator for the Crown in Ireland, writes *The Faerie Queene.*

1591 Trinity College, Dublin, is founded.

1607 The Flight of the Earls and the beginning of the end of Gaelic Ireland. The earl of Tyrone and his ally Tyrconnell flee to Rome; their lands in Ulster are confiscated and opened to Protestant settlers, mostly Scots.

1641 Charles I's policies provoke insurrection in Ulster and, soon after, civil war in England.

1649 August: British leader Oliver Cromwell, having defeated Charles and witnessed his execution, invades Ireland, determined to crush Catholic opposition. Massacres at Drogheda and Wexford.

1652 Act of Settlement—lands of Cromwell's opponents are confiscated, and owners are forced across the Shannon to Connaught. Never fully carried out, this policy nonetheless establishes Protestant ascendancy.

1690 Battle of the Boyne—William of Orange lands in England and Catholic James II flees to Ireland to rally opposition. William pursues him with a large army and defeats him on the banks of the River Boyne in County Meath.

1775 American War of Independence begins, precipitating Irish unrest. Henry Grattan (1746–1820), a Protestant barrister, enters the Irish Parliament.

1782 Grattan's Parliament—Grattan asserts independence of Irish Parliament from Britain. Britain agrees, but independence is easier to declare than to sustain.

1823 Daniel O'Connell (1775–1847), "the Liberator," founds the Catholic Association to campaign for Catholic Emancipation.

1828 O'Connell's election to Parliament (illegal, because he was a Catholic) leads to passage of Catholic Emancipation Act in 1829; later, he works unsuccessfully for repeal of the Union.

1845–49 Failure of potato crop leads to famine; more than 1 million die, others migrate.

1856 Birth of George Bernard Shaw, playwright (d. 1950).

1858 Fenian Brotherhood founded in New York by Irish immigrants with the aim of overthrowing British rule. A revolt in 1867 fails, but it compels Gladstone, the British prime minister, to disestablish the Anglican Church (1869) and reform landholding (1870) in Ireland.

1865 Birth of William Butler Yeats, the great Irish poet (d. 1939).

1871 Isaac Butts founds parliamentary Home Rule Party, soon dominated by Charles Stewart Parnell (1846–91), descendant of English Protestants, who tries to force the issue by obstructing parliamentary business.

1890 Parnell is named corespondent in the divorce case of Kitty O'Shea; his career is ruined.

1893 Second Home Rule Bill passes Commons but is defeated by Lords. Subsequent policy is to "kill Home Rule with kindness" with land reform, but cultural nationalism revives with founding of Gaelic League to promote Irish language. Yeats, John Synge (1871–1909), and other writers find inspiration in Gaelic past.

1898 On the anniversary of Wolfe Tone's rebellion, Arthur Griffith (1872–1922) founds the Dublin newspaper the *United Irishman,* preaching *sinn féin* ("we ourselves")—secession from Britain; Sinn Féin party founded 1905. Socialist James Connolly (executed 1916) founds the *Workers' Republic.*

1904 William Butler Yeats and Lady Gregory found the Abbey Theatre in Dublin.

1914 Despite fierce opposition the Third Home Rule Bill passes the Commons and the Lords but is suspended due to the outbreak of World War I.

1916   Easter Uprising—Irish Republican Brotherhood (IRB) stages insurrection in Dublin and declares independence; the uprising fails, but the execution of 15 leaders by the British turns public opinion in favor of the insurgents. Yeats writes "a terrible beauty is born."

1919   January: Irish Parliamentarians meet as the Dáil Éireann (Irish Assembly) and declare independence. September: Dáil suppressed; Sinn Féin made illegal.

1920–21   War breaks out between Britain and Ireland: the "Black and Tans" versus the Irish Republican Army (IRA). Government of Ireland Act declares separate parliaments for north and south and continued ties to Britain. Elections follow, but the Sinn Féin majority in the south again declare themselves the Dáil Éireann under Eamon de Valera (1882–1975), rejecting British authority. December 1921: Anglo-Irish Treaty grants the south dominion status as the Irish Free State, allowing the north to remain under Britain.

1922   De Valera and his Republican followers reject the treaty; civil war results. The Irish Free State adopts a constitution; William T. Cosgrave becomes president. Michael Collins, chairman of the Irish Free State and commander in chief of the army, is shot dead in County Cork, not far from where he was born. In Paris, James Joyce's *Ulysses* is published.

1923   De Valera is arrested and the civil war ends, but Republican agitation and terrorism continue. William Butler Yeats is the first Irish writer to be awarded the Nobel Prize in Literature; he also takes a seat in the first Irish Parliament.

1938   New constitution creates Republic of Ireland with no ties to Britain.

1939–45   Despite strong pressure from Britain and the United States, Ireland remains neutral throughout World War II.

1959   Eamon de Valera resigns as Taoiseach (prime minister) and is later elected president.

1963   John F. Kennedy, the first Irish-Catholic President of the United States, visits Ireland.

1972   Republic of Ireland admitted to European Economic Community. Troubles continue in the north. In Derry on January 30, British troops shoot 13 unarmed demonstrators on "Bloody Sunday." Stormont (the Northern Parliament) is suspended and direct rule from London is imposed. Acts of terrorism on both sides lead to draconian law enforcement by the British. "The Troubles," as the conflict is dubbed, will last 26 years and claim more than 3,000 lives.

1991   Mary Robinson becomes the first female President of the Republic of Ireland. Peace talks begin between the British and Irish governments and the main political parties of the north, excepting Sinn Féin.

1992   Ireland approves European Union. Sixty-two percent of the Irish vote "yes" in a referendum on whether to allow pregnant women to seek an abortion abroad.

1994   The IRA, in response to advances made by the Irish, British, and U.S. governments, announces a complete cessation of activities. Protestant paramilitary groups follow suit one month later. Gerry Adams, the leader of Sinn Féin, speaks on British TV and radio.

1996   Frustrated by the slow progress of the peace talks, the IRA explodes bombs on the British mainland, throwing the whole peace process into doubt. But violence has not returned to the province, and all parties say they are committed to peace.

1997   The Republic of Ireland legalizes divorce. Newly elected British prime minister Tony Blair apologizes for the British government's policies during Ireland's Great Famine, acknowledging that his predecessors' policies prolonged "a massive human tragedy." The IRA reestablishes its cease-fire.

1998   On Good Friday 1998, all sides in the conflict agree on an agreement for sharing power that guarantees the rights of the Catholic minority. Referenda in the north and the Republic show overwhelming support. A splinter IRA group opposed to the agreement explodes a bomb in Omagh, killing more than 20 people. Catholic leader John Hume and Protestant David Trimble share the Nobel Peace Prize.

1999   Despite sporadic violence by splinter loyalist groups, an executive branch of government, the Northern Ireland Assembly, is formed at Stormont in Belfast on November 27. Northern Ireland is no longer governed directly from Westminster.

2000   Proposals are made to reform the RUC (Royal Ulster Constabulary) by making it half Catholic and half Protestant and renaming it the "Northern Irish Police Force." Tensions remain high over the decommissioning of weapons.

2001   President Bill Clinton visits Dundalk and Belfast during the final weeks of his presidency to encourage continued implementation of the Good Friday Agreement. Due to a rise in pipe-bomb attacks, British troops are put back on patrol in certain neighborhoods in Belfast and Derry.

2002   The IRA begins to decommission weapons in the wake of the September 11 attacks on the United States. The euro is phased in as the Republic of Ireland's national currency.

2003   Direct rule in the north reintroduced as power-sharing talks come to a halt. New efforts to resolve the impasse undertaken by governments in Dublin and London. Irish economy starts to slow, but growth remains well above the European average.

IRISH FAMILY NAMES

Doherty

O'Hara
Quinn

Friel

Mooney McLaughlin DERRY McDonnell
Gallagher McNeill ANTRIM
O'Donnell Gormley
Boyle Quinn Cahan Hegarty O'Neill
McSweeney DONEGAL Kelly O'Neil

McGrath Donnelly Hagan
Clery Murphy TYRONE McCann Lynch White
Flanagan Cassidy DOWN
Clancy Corrigan McKenna
O'Rourke FERMANAGH Maguire ARMAGH
O'Dowd Rafferty McManus McMahon McGuinness
Boland O'Hara McCabe McGovern Connolly Hanlon
SLIGO McDonagh LEITRIM Boylan McMahon Hanratty
Dugan Higgins Molloy CAVAN McNally LOUTH
O'Malley Jordan Lynch McGowan O'Carroll
MAYO McDermot Sheridan Plunkett
Burke Castello McManus O'Reilly MEATH Dillon
Madden Flanagan Hanley Cusack Hennessey
Kelly Horan ROSCOMMON Murphy LONGFORD Hayes O'Casey
Gormley Kirwan O'Farrell Connolly Plunkett Plunkett
Joyce Jennings Moran Quinn WESTMEATH Quinlan
O'Flaherty Kelly Dillon Dalton Coffey
GALWAY Madden McKeogh Sheridan Daly O'Byrne DUBLIN
French Lynch Fallon White KILDARE O'Toole
Blake Burke Kenny Malone OFFALY Fitzgerald Kelly
Daly O'Halloran Coghlan Molloy Doran Cullen WICKLOW
O'Loughlin Fah(e)y Dempsey O'Byrne
Clancy Boland Clery O'Carroll Dunn(e) Kelly Nolan McKeogh
O'Dea Molon(e)y Meagher Moore CARLOW Doyle
CLARE O'Halloran Kennedy (Maher) LAOISE Fitzpatrick O'Neill
McMahon McInerney Purcell Kinsella Redmond
O'Brien McGrath Ryan O'Meara Butler KILKENNY Doran
McNamara Aherne Lynch Fogarty WEXFORD
Lynch O'Grady McKeogh O'Dwyer Hartley
Fitzgerald Woulfe O'Brien Tobin Kavanagh
Connor Fitzgibbon O'Carroll Walsh Keating
KERRY LIMERICK TIPPERARY
O'Cullane O'Brien
O'Shea Moriarty (Collins) O'Casey McGrath Power
Galvin O'Leary Roche Phelan Keane
O'Donoghue McCarthy Barry WATERFORD
Fitzgerald O'Keefe Callaghan Sheridan
O'Sullivan Flynn Nugent
McSweeney Scanlon
O'Connell O'Riordan Murphy
Lynch CORK
O'Mahony Donovan Cullinane
Hogan Hennessey
Driscoll

Antrim
Lynch
McDonnell
McNeill
O'Hara
O'Neill
Quinn

Armagh
Hanlon
McCann

Carlow
Kinsella
Nolan
O'Neill

Cavan
Boylan
Lynch
McCabe
McGovern
McGowan
McNally
O'Reilly
Sheridan

Clare
Aherne
Boland
Clancy
Daly
Lynch
McGrath
McInerney
McMahon
McNamara
Molon(e)y
O'Brien
O'Dea
O'Grady
O'Halloran
O'Loughlin

Cork
Barry
Callaghan
Cullinane
Donovan
Driscoll
Flynn
Hennessey
Hogan
Lynch
McCarthy
McSweeney
Murphy
Nugent
O'Casey
O'Cullane
(Collins)

O'Keefe
O'Leary
O'Mahony
O'Riordan
Roche
Scanlon
Sheridan

Derry
Cahan
Hegarty
Kelly
McLaughlin

Donegal
Boyle
Clery
Doherty
Friel
Gallagher
Gormley
McGrath
McLoughlin
McSweeney
Mooney
O'Donnell

Down
Lynch
McGuinness
O'Neil
White

Dublin
Hennessey
O'Casey
Plunkett

Fermanagh
Cassidy
Connolly
Corrigan
Flanagan
Maguire
McManus

Galway
Blake
Burke
Clery
Fah(e)y
French
Jennings
Joyce
Kelly
Kenny
Kirwan
Lynch
Madden
Moran
O'Flaherty
O'Halloran

Kerry
Connor
Fitzgerald
Galvin
McCarthy
Moriarty
O'Connell
O'Donoghue
O'Shea
O'Sullivan

Kildare
Cullen
Fitzgerald
O'Byrne
White

Kilkenny
Butler
Fitzpatrick
O'Carroll
Tobin

Laois
Dempsey
Doran
Dunn(e)
Kelly
Moore

Leitrim
Clancy
O'Rourke

Limerick
Fitzgerald
Fitzgibbon
McKeough
O'Brien
O'Cullane
(Collins)
O'Grady
Woulfe

Longford
O'Farrell
Quinn

Louth
O'Carroll
Plunkett

Mayo
Burke
Costello
Dugan
Gormley
Horan
Jennings
Jordan
Kelly
Madden
O'Malley

Meath
Coffey
Connolly
Cusack
Dillon
Hayes
Hennessey
Plunkett
Quinlan

Monaghan
Boylan
Connolly
Hanratty
McKenna
McMahon
McNally

Offaly
Coghlan
Dempsey
Fallon
(Maher)
Malone
Meagher
Molloy
O'Carroll
Sheridan

Roscommon
Fallon
Flanagan
Flynn
Hanley
McDermot
McKeogh
McManus
Molloy
Murphy

Sligo
Boland
Higgins
McDonagh
O'Dowd
O'Hara
Rafferty

Tipperary
Butler
Fogarty
Kennedy
Lynch
Meagher
(Maher)
O'Carroll
O'Dwyer
O'Meara
Purcell
Ryan

Tyrone
Cahan
Donnelly
Gormley
Hagan
Murphy
O'Neill
Quinn

Waterford
Keane
McGrath
O'Brien
Phelan
Power

Westmeath
Coffey
Dalton
Daly
Dillon
Sheridan

Wexford
Doran
Doyle
Hartley
Kavanagh
Keating
Kinsella
McKeogh
Redmond
Walsh

Wicklow
Cullen
Kelly
McKeogh
O'Byrne
O'Toole

INDEX

NOTES

NOTES

NOTES

NOTES

NOTES

NOTES

NOTES

NOTES